NUTRITION IN PUBLIC HEALTH

A Handbook for Developing Programs and Services

Mildred Kaufman, MS, RD
Professor and Chair
Department of Nutrition
School of Public Health
University of North Carolina
Chapel Hill, North Carolina

AN ASPEN PUBLICATION®
Aspen Publishers, Inc.
Rockville, Maryland
1990

Library of Congress Cataloging-in-Publication Data

Nutrition in public health : a handbook for developing programs and
services / edited by Mildred Kaufman.
p. cm.
"An Aspen publication."
Includes bibliographical references.
ISBN: 0-8342-0144-5
1. Nutrition. 2. Public health. 3. Medical policy. I. Kaufman, Mildred.
[DNLM: 1. Health Policy—handbooks. 2. Health Services—handbooks.
3. Nutrition—handbooks. 4. Public Health—handbooks.
QU 39 N976]
RA601.N84   1990
362.1'76—dc20
DNLM/DLC
for Library of Congress
90-51
CIP

Editorial Services: Ruth Bloom

Library of Congress Catalog Card Number: 90-51
ISBN: 0-8342-0144-5

Printed in the United States of America

1 2 3 4   5

To my many teachers, mentors, administrators, colleagues, and professional friends who enriched my philosophy and knowledge of public health and public health nutrition.

To colleagues, students, and alumni at the School of Public Health, University of North Carolina–Chapel Hill who inspired, encouraged, and assisted me with this book.

And to those who ask the recurring question, "What is it that public health nutritionists really do?"

Table of Contents

Contributors xv

Foreword xvii

Preface xix

Acknowledgments xxi

PART I—THINKING PUBLIC HEALTH 1

Chapter 1—Understanding Public Health 3
    Mildred Kaufman

      Reader Objectives 3
      Defining Public Health 3
      Dynamics of Public Health 6
      Governmental Responsibilities for Public Health 7
      Nutrition in Public Health 8
      Knowledge and Skills of Public Health Nutritionists 11
      Issues To Debate 12

Chapter 2—Applying Nutrition Science to the Public's Health 14
    Sara M. Hunt and Mildred Kaufman

      Reader Objectives 14
      Nutrition Expertise in Public Health 14
      Interpreting Research As the Base for Practice 16
      Evolution of Recommended Dietary Allowances 19

Limitations on the Use of Recommended Dietary
Allowances 20
Nutrition Science versus Nutrition Policy 23
Risk/Benefit Analysis and Professional Judgment 24
Concept of Nutrient Density 26
Dietary Recommendations to the Public 27
National Objectives 36
Monitoring Nutrition Research Literature for
Public Health Applications 38
Issues To Debate 38

PART II—ASSESSING THE COMMUNITY'S NEEDS 43

Chapter 3—Assessing the Community's Needs for Nutrition
Services 45
Mildred Kaufman

Reader Objectives 45
Many Different People, Many Different Needs 45
Subjective Data: Perceived Needs of Stakeholders 47
Objective Data: Statistical Indicators That Point
to Needs 53
Assessing the Capacity of Existing Community
Resources 58
Developing the Community's Nutrition Problem List 59
Issues To Debate 61

Chapter 4—Reaching Out to Those at Highest Risk 63
Catherine Boisvert-Walsh and Jan Kallio

Reader Objectives 63
Defining Vulnerability Factors 63
Poverty 64
Underemployment and Unemployment 66
Lack of Education and Illiteracy 66
Cultural Barriers 67
Housing and Homelessness 68
Hunger 69
Social Support 79
Access to Health Care 80
Empowering Vulnerable Families 80
Issues To Debate 83

**PART III—SHAPING POLICIES THAT AFFECT THE
PUBLIC'S HEALTH** 85

**Chapter 5—Developing Agency, Community, and State Nutrition
Policies** 87
Nancy Chapman

Reader Objectives 87
Defining Policy 87
Importance of Policies 88
Agency Policy 89
Local Policy 89
State Policy 90
Policy-Making Strategies 91
Leadership Roles for Nutritionists 96
Learning by Example 97
Issues To Debate 98

Chapter 6—Advocating for National Health and Nutrition Policies .. 100
Nancy Chapman

Reader Objectives 100
Private versus Public Sector Policies 100
Making National Policy 102
Evolution of the Nation's Nutrition Policy 104
Future Directions for National Nutrition Policy 113
Issues To Debate 114

**Chapter 7—Influencing Federal Health and Nutrition Legislation
and Regulations** 117
Robert Earl

Reader Objectives 117
The Public Health Professional As an Advocate 117
Understanding How the Federal Government Works 118
Federal Agencies and Programs Involved with Food,
Nutrition, and Health 126
The Judicial Branch 129
Promoting Health and Nutrition Issues 130
Legislative Activity for Public Employees 131
Taking Leadership 132
Issues To Debate 136

**PART IV—PROMOTING AND PROTECTING THE
PUBLIC'S HEALTH** 137

Chapter 8—Serving Women, Infants, and Children 139
MaryAnn C. Farthing and Mildred Kaufman

Reader Objectives 139
Issues in Maternal and Child Health 139
Women's Health, Family Planning, and
Preconceptional Health 140
Prenatal Care.. 143
Lactation and Infant Feeding 147
Preschool Child Health 149
Schoolchild Health 154
Adolescent Health 157
Dental Health 159
Children with Special Health Care Needs 159
Special Supplemental Food Program for Women,
Infants, and Children 164
Medicaid and Maternal and Child Health 166
Unmet Needs in Nutrition Services for Women and
Children 167
Issues To Debate 167

Chpater 9—Promoting the Health of Adults 172
Alice R. Thomson

Reader Objectives 172
Promoting Health, Preventing Disease 172
Prevention Strategies 174
Dietary Guidelines for Disease Prevention...................... 177
Nutrition Strategies To Prevent and Manage Risk
Factors 179
Roles for Nutritionists in Adult Health 194
Issues To Debate 195

Chapter 10—Assuring Nutrition Services for Older Adults 200
Mildred Kaufman

Reader Objectives.. 200
Aging of Americans... 200

Nutritional Status of Older Americans 202
Dietary Recommendations for Healthy Older Adults .. 203
Goals of Nutrition Programs in the Community 205
Nutrition Services That Promote Independent Living .. 207
Care for the Frail Elderly 216
Networking and Advocacy for Older Americans 218
Issues To Debate 219

Chapter 11—Providing Nutrition Services in Primary Care 221
Mildred Kaufman

Reader Objectives 221
Needs for Primary Care 221
Nutrition Services in Primary Health Care 223
State Primary Health Care Initiatives 224
Federally Funded Primary Health Care 226
Issues To Debate 240

Chapter 12—Maintaining Nutrition and Food Service Standards in Group Care 243
Nancy L. Johnson

Reader Objectives 243
Group Care Facilities in the Community 243
Licensure, Regulation, Certification, and
    Accreditation 244
Educating Administrators and Food Service
    Personnel 246
Counseling Clients and Their Families 250
Registered Dietitians in Group Care Facilities 251
Public Health Nutritionists As Consultants 251
Issues To Debate 252

Chapter 13—Safeguarding the Food Supply 254
Laura T. Harrill

Reader Objectives 254
Food Safety As a Public Health Nutrition Issue 254
Food Safety Issues 255
Protecting the Food Supply 266
Educating Consumers 269
Issues To Debate 274

PART V—MANAGING THE SYSTEM **277**

**Chapter 14—Planning and Evaluating Nutrition Services for the
          Community** **279**
          Mildred Kaufman

          Reader Objectives 279
          Defining Planning 279
          Using a Planning Group 281
          The Planning Process 282
          Implementing the Plan 291
          Monitoring and Evaluating Achievement 292
          Reporting Program Success 294
          Obtaining Review and Comment 294
          Issues To Debate 296

Chapter 15—Marketing Nutrition Programs and Services **297**
          Diane R. Kerwin

          Reader Objectives 297
          Defining Marketing 297
          Business Marketing versus Social Marketing 298
          Market Research 299
          The Social Marketing Mix 302
          Marketing Ethics 310
          Issues To Debate 310

Chapter 16—Managing Data **312**
          Deborah A. Spicer and Mildred Kaufman

          Reader Objectives 312
          Data Needs 312
          Community Assessment Data 314
          Program Management Data 321
          Collecting New Data 328
          Issues To Debate 340

Chapter 17—Managing Money **342**
          Katherine Cairns

          Reader Objectives 342
          Financing Public Health Nutrition Programs and
             Services 342

Preparing Budgets and Determining Program Costs 349
Developing Skills in Grantwriting 357
Issues To Debate 359

Chapter 18—Intervening To Change the Public's Eating Behavior ... 361
Alice R. Thomson and MaryAnn C. Farthing

Reader Objectives 361
Changing Eating Behavior 361
Levels of Intervention 365
Population-Based Interventions 365
Extending the Nutrition Message through Health
    Care Professionals 374
Direct Nutrition Care Services 375
Issues To Debate 378

PART VI—MOBILIZING PERSONNEL 381

**Chapter 19—Staffing Public Health Nutrition Programs and
    Services 383**
Mildred Kaufman

Reader Objectives 383
Employing Public Health Nutrition Personnel 383
Public Health Nutritionists 385
Direct Care Nutritionists 389
Nutrition Technicians 389
Nutrition Aides 390
Support Staff 391
Administrative Placement of Nutrition Personnel 391
Staffing Recommendations for Public Health
    Nutrition Personnel 393
Salaries for Public Health Nutrition Personnel 397
Issues To Debate 400

Chapter 20—Managing Public Health Nutrition Personnel 402
Nancy L. Johnson

Reader Objectives 402
Responsibilities of the Program Manager 402
Policies and Procedures 411
Staff Meetings 412
Performance Appraisal 413

Recognizing and Rewarding Staff 414
Building Careers 415
Mentoring in Public Health Nutrition 416
Taking Disciplinary Action 417
Issues To Debate 418

**Chapter 21—Leveraging Nutrition Education through the Public
Health Team** **420**
Gaye Joyner and Mildred Kaufman

Reader Objectives 420
Nutrition Care through the Public Health Team............ 420
Consulting on Client Care 422
Educating Health Care Professionals 424
Teams Functioning in the Health Agency 426
Teamwork 428
Benefits of Teamwork 435
Issues To Debate 435

Chapter 22—Networking for Nutrition **437**
Mildred Kaufman

Reader Objectives 437
Defining Networking 437
Networking To Promote and Protect the Public's
Health 438
Casting a Longer Shadow 439
Improving the Nutrition of the Public 441
Creating a State Network 445
Professional Networking 448
Networking Tips 450
Issues To Debate 451

PART VII—SURVIVING IN A COMPETITIVE WORLD **453**

Chapter 23—Earning Administrative Support **455**
Elaine B. Culberson

Reader Objectives 455
Where Is the Administrator Coming From? 455
Looking at the "Big Picture" 456
Sharing the Agency Vision 457
Developing Assertiveness 459

Winning with the Policy Board 460
Mobilizing Colleagues 461
Persuasion, Persistence, Negotiation 462
Empowerment 463
Issues To Debate 465

Chapter 24—Striving for Excellence **466**
Harriet H. Cloud

Reader Objectives 466
Motivation for Excellence 466
Agency and Legal Obligations 467
Quality Assurance 470
Professional Stature 472
Registration and Licensure 474
Malpractice and Liability 475
Ethical Issues in Public Health Nutrition 475
Issues To Debate 476

Chapter 25—Envisioning the Future **478**
Meg Binney Molloy

Reader Objectives 478
What Is? What Might Be? 478
Taking a Proactive Stand 479
The Public Health Nutritionist As an Investigator 481
New Approaches for Spreading the Nutrition
    Message 483
Partnerships and Networks 485
Harnessing New Technologies 486
Challenging and Changing the Cultural Norm 487
Issues To Debate 488

**Appendix A—Self-Assessment Tool for Public Health
        Nutritionists** **491**

Appendix B—Adequate Food for All **500**

Appendix C—Model State Nutrition Objectives **503**

**Appendix D—State and Territorial Public Health Nutrition
        Directors** **506**

**Appendix E—Congressional Committees and Government Agencies
Responsible for Nutrition Education, Labeling
Activities, Food Assistance Activities, Food Safety
and Quality Activities, and Nutrition Research and
Monitoring Activities and Issues** **509**

**Appendix F—Sources of Information on Federal Legislation and
Regulations** **514**

Appendix G—Federal Resources and Consultants **515**

Appendix H—Sources for National Data **521**

Appendix I—Prospecting for Grants **522**

**Appendix J—Schools of Public Health and Graduate Public Health
Programs Accredited for 1989 by the Council on
Education for Public Health (CEPH)** **523**

Appendix K—Graduate Programs in Public Health Nutrition **525**

**Appendix L—Organizations for Networking for Nutrition and
Health** **527**

**Appendix M—Nutrition and Public Health Information
Resources** **534**

Appendix N—The Public Health Nutrition Library **535**

Index **553**

Contributors

Catherine Boisvert-Walsh, MPH, RD
Assistant Director for Parent, Child, and Adolescent Nutrition
Massachusetts Department of Public Health
Boston, MA

Katherine Cairns, MPH, MBA, RD
Health Administration Manager
Ramsey County Health Department
St. Paul, MN

Nancy Chapman, MPH, RD
President
N. Chapman Associates, Inc.
Washington, DC

Harriet H. Cloud, MS, RD
Associate Professor
School of Health Related Professions
Director
Nutrition Division
Sparks Center for Development and Learning Disorders
University of Alabama
Birmingham, AL

Elaine B. Culberson, MBA, RD
Administrative Officer
Buncombe County Health Department
Asheville, NC

Robert Earl, MPH, RD
Administrator
Division of Government Affairs
The American Dietetic Association
Washington, DC

MaryAnn C. Farthing, PhD, RD
Clinical Associate Professor
Department of Nutrition
School of Public Health
University of North Carolina
Chapel Hill, NC

Laura T. Harrill, MS
Wellness Director
Blount Memorial Hospital
Maryville, TN

Sara M. Hunt, PhD, RD
Professor Emeritus, now residing in Knoxville, TN
Georgia State University
Atlanta, GA

Nancy L. Johnson, MPH, RD
Public Health Dietitian
Division of Maternal and Child Health
  Services
North Carolina Department of Environ-
  ment, Health, and Natural Resources
Raleigh, NC

Gaye Joyner, MS, RD
Director
Bureau of Nutrition
Jefferson County Health Department
Birmingham, AL

Jan Kallio, MS, RD
Assistant Director for Adult and Elderly
  Nutrition
Massachusetts Department of Public Health
Boston, MA

Mildred Kaufman, MS, RD
Professor and Chair
Department of Nutrition
School of Public Health
University of North Carolina
Chapel Hill, NC

Diane R. Kerwin, MPH, RD
Manager
Government Operations
Ross Laboratories
Columbus, OH

Meg Binney Molloy, MPH, RD
Nutrition Coordinator
Duke University Preventive Approach
  to Cardiology
Durham, NC

Deborah A. Spicer, MPH, RD
Nutritionist
Bureau of Nutrition
New York State Department of Health
Albany, NY

Alice R. Thomson, MPH, MS, RD
Former Nutrition Program Consultant
Adult Health Services
Division of Health Services
North Carolina Department of
  Human Resources
Raleigh, NC

Foreword

With perhaps the exception of safe, adequate water supplies, nothing is more important to the health of a nation than the general availability of nutritious foods in sufficient quantities. Indeed, the increase in longevity in the United States from age 47 in 1900 to the 70s in the 1990s is in part due to high technology, but it is largely due to public health measures applied on a communitywide basis. Improved nutrition for the majority of Americans is one of the most important of these communitywide measures.

Our understanding of the role of nutrition in health continues to expand dramatically, but we still have much to learn. Chapter 1 provides a long list of undesirable human conditions related to undernutrition, overnutrition, and/or an improper balance of food consumed.

The challenges are several and difficult: First, we must assure that adequate food is available to all our citizens—government food programs and private initiatives have contributed greatly, but much is still to be done for some segments of society. Second, nutrition education and behavioral changes in dietary habits are and will remain a constant challenge for nutritionists and health program administrators alike.

As the executive director of a local public health department serving 750,000 people, I appreciate how difficult that task is. Variations in economic resources, educational levels, cultural backgrounds, and ethnic food preferences make it impossible to construct nutrition programs where "one size fits all." The task is made even more difficult by the poor understanding on the part of elected officials and the public at large of the necessity of funding nutrition programs where the results are often not seen until the next generation.

The authors of this handbook have made a valuable contribution to helping us in public health go where we want to be. The keys to understanding and administering public health nutrition programs are contained herein.

I first had the pleasure of working with the principal author, Mildred Kaufman, several years ago on a national nutrition project. Since that time, our agency has had the opportunity to work with the real product of a teacher—her students. While not having her experience, her students reflect her good judgment, enthusiasm, and knowledge of current trends in nutrition.

Ms. Kaufman has done a masterful job of choosing appropriate subjects and selecting contributing authors. This handbook should be studied by nutritionists new to the field and by those experienced in public health. It will be especially valuable to nutritionists who practice public health nutrition but have not had traditional training in public health. Lastly, it is an excellent guide to contemporary nutrition practice; it should be in the reference library of every public health administrator.

Hugh Rohrer, MD, MPH
Director
Tri-County Health Department
Englewood, Colorado

Preface

The relationship of nutrition and diet to the public's health is now being discussed by people in their homes and at their work sites, by legislators in state houses and on Capitol Hill, by those in the media, and by executives managing the food industry, as well as by nutrition scientists and health professionals. Nutrition is one of the key areas in the nation's health promotion, disease prevention objectives for 1990 and the year 2000. *The Surgeon General's Report on Nutrition and Health* and the National Academy of Sciences' publication *Diet and Health* summarize the current research and set the agenda for public health workers, led by nutritionists with expertise in the science and practice of both public health and nutrition. A 1989 survey for the Association of State and Territorial Public Health Nutrition Directors identified about 4,500 public health and direct care nutritionists working in state and local official and voluntary public health agencies. This small number of workers bear large responsibilities. They need to leverage their efforts if the public's health is to be improved through better eating.

This handbook has been written for nutritionists employed to manage public health nutrition programs, whether they are single workers in their agencies, supervisors or directors of staff, or administrators who employ or contemplate employing nutritionists. The purpose of this handbook is to define and describe the scope of public health nutrition and the potential opportunities for nutrition services in health agency programs. It describes the roles, responsibilities, and qualifications of the various levels of nutrition personnel who should be employed to staff these programs.

The handbook provides a broad overview of key concepts in many areas important to the successful practice of public health nutrition. It is not a textbook, although it might be useful to students preparing for careers in public health nutrition or those who would like to know more about nutrition and health in their communities. It defines and gives a broad brush overview of many aspects involved in nutrition program management. To develop deeper understanding and gain proficiency in any of these areas, the reader is referred to appropriate resources including educational institutions, state or federal agency consultants, professional organizations, and public interest and voluntary health associations, as well as to the increasing volumes of useful books, journals, and newsletters.

Contributing authors were selected for their knowledge and experience in managing successful public health nutrition programs. They were asked to share practical tips along with more factual content. Each chapter begins with reader objectives to highlight and organize content. Each chapter concludes with a series of debatable issues to which there are no necessarily right or wrong answers. These issues are intended to challenge the reader to think about alternatives and to debate and discuss with colleagues. Some of the questions may suggest opportunities for applied research in the field.

The chapters are organized into seven parts:

    I.   Thinking Public Health
   II.   Assessing the Community Needs
  III.   Shaping Policies That Affect the Public's Health
  IV.   Promoting and Protecting the Public's Health
   V.   Managing the System
  VI.   Mobilizing Personnel
 VII.   Surviving in a Competitive World

This handbook encourages nutrition program managers to be proactive. It suggests the philosophy and approaches that will guide nutrition managers to reach out boldly in their communities so that people of all ages and socioeconomic levels will reap the benefits of optimal nutrition through enhanced well-being, productivity, and longevity.

Mildred Kaufman
April 1990

Acknowledgments

My deepest gratitude to all those who generously devoted time to writing this book. I wish to thank Margaret Mauney and Linda Tally who spent many hours at their word processors, typing and revising the text and preparing some of the tables, figures, and exhibits. Thanks, too, to JoAnn Roth for her typing and to Cynthia Deak, Virginia Ruarck, and Turner B. McCollom of the Learning Resources Center at the School of Public Health for many of the graphics. I appreciated the help of JuliSu Dimucci-Ward and Martha Burdick who diligently worked on the notes and references and Laurie Quint-Adler who assisted in preparing Chapter 13. Many thanks are due to my many professional colleagues who contributed their expertise by reading and commenting on the content through its several drafts—Connie Auran, Elizabeth Brannon, Dan Carroll, Janice Dodds, Lois Earl, Mary Egan, Sharon Ernst, Pamela Haines, William Herzog, Frances Hoffman, Ruth Kocher, Rebecca Lankenau, Laureen Lopez, Kay Lovelace, Melinda Maryniuk, Meg Molloy, Miriam Peterson, Hugh Rohrer, Carolyn Sharbaugh, Rachel Stevens, Boyd Switzer, Ellen Thompson, Nadine Tope, Mary Nelle Traylor, Margie Washbon, and Colette Zyrkowski—as well as to the students who read and commented on preliminary drafts of selected chapters used as assigned class readings. Most importantly, I thank the contributing authors who wrote the various chapters and those who assisted them, particularly Ruth Palombo, Carole Grandon, Diana Seder, and Jean Wiecha who helped with Chapter 4; Catherine Boisvert-Walsh and Jan Kallio who wrote sections for Chapter 11; Nadine Tope and Dan Carroll who advised on Chapter 13; Pamela Haines who prepared the cost-benefit and cost-effectiveness content in Chapter 14; and Rebecca Lankenau who provided information on new American Heart Association activities for Chapter 18.

part I

Thinking Public Health

chapter 1

Understanding Public Health

Mildred Kaufman

READER OBJECTIVES

- Define public health and public health nutrition.
- Differentiate between the community and the clinical approaches to health.
- Explain primary, secondary, and tertiary prevention.
- List some trends that affect public health work.
- List current nutrition- and diet-related public health problems.
- Conduct self-assessment of competencies as a public health nutritionist.

DEFINING PUBLIC HEALTH

Public health has been defined as "the science and art of preventing disease, prolonging life, and promoting health and efficiency through organized community effort, so organizing these benefits as to enable every citizen to realize his birthright of health and longevity."[1] Public health is dedicated to the common attainment of the highest level of physical, mental, and social well-being and longevity consistent with available knowledge and resources at a given time and place. It holds this goal as its contribution to the most effective total development of the life of the individual and the community.[2]

The recent Institute of Medicine report, *The Future of Public Health*, defines the mission of public health as fulfilling society's interest in assuring conditions in which people can be healthy. This report suggests that the mission of public health is addressed by private organizations and individuals, as well as by public agencies. But the governmental public health agency

3

has a unique function: to see to it that vital elements are in place and that the mission is adequately addressed.[3]

Public health has been envisioned as the scientific diagnosis and treatment of the community, defined as a geopolitical entity or "body politic."[4] In this vision the community, rather than the individual, is seen as the "patient." Each community has its own unique environment, personality, characteristics, power structure, and state of physical, mental, and social health or ill health. Health and well-being in the community encompass factors that go far beyond traditional definitions of physical or mental health. They include adequate food, housing, income, employment, education, and safety for all the people who live in that community.

An interdisciplinary team of public health workers participates in the diagnosis and treatment of the community. When each discipline contributes different expertise, the combined efforts are synergistic: They exceed the sum of the individual efforts. Thus, the team accomplishes more for the "body politic" than any one discipline could if working alone.

The public health, population based or epidemiological approach is distinguished from the clinical or one-on-one patient care approach. The public health approach

- uses interventions that promote health and prevent communicable or chronic diseases by managing or controlling the community's environment
- promotes a healthy life style as a shared value for all people
- directs money and energy to the problems that affect the lives of the largest numbers of the community's people
- targets the unserved or underserved populations who by virtue of income, age, ethnicity, heredity, or life style are particularly vulnerable to disease, hunger, or malnutrition
- requires the collaboration of the public, consumers, community leaders, legislators, policy makers, administrators, and health and human service professionals in assessing and responding to community needs and consumer demands
- continuously monitors the health of the people in the community to assure that the public health system achieves its objectives and responds to current and anticipated needs

Services that contribute to the public's health may be provided through organized collaboration of the official public health agency with non-profit and for-profit private health agencies, institutions, and practitioners. The role of the official or tax-supported state, county, or city health department is to assure that services are available, not necessarily to deliver all the services themselves. Figure 1-1 provides a matrix for thinking about community and individual health and health services throughout the various stages of life in the context of three levels of prevention: primary, secondary, and tertiary.

Primary prevention or health promotion efforts work to change the environment and the community, as well as family and individual life styles and behaviors, to enhance and maintain a state of wellness. Primary prevention should be part of all efforts directed to the whole population through the food distribution system, the media, schools, houses of worship, work sites, recreation centers, clubs, or social groups. Health promotion should be part of national, state, and local health policy and a cooperative responsibility of the public and private sectors. While important throughout the stages of life, obviously health promotion programs directed at the young have the greatest potential impact for "adding years to life" and "life to years."

Secondary prevention means risk appraisal and reduction. Interventions are designed to reduce risk among those who may be more susceptible to a health problem because of their family history, life style, environment, or

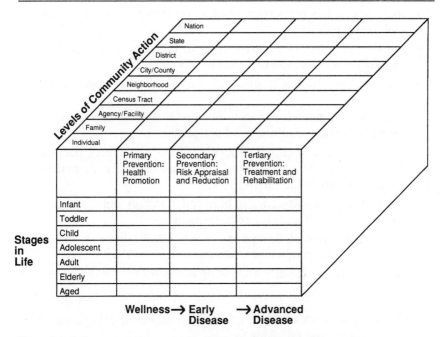

Figure 1-1 A Conceptual Framework for Public Health: Levels of Prevention

age. Secondary prevention interventions include screening, detection, early diagnosis, treatment, and followup before disease has had the opportunity to develop clear-cut symptoms. These interventions can be offered by public health agencies or private health care practitioners.

Tertiary prevention is directed at treating and rehabilitating persons with diagnosed health conditions in order to prevent or delay their disability, pain, suffering, and premature death. Tertiary prevention is part of the medical care for those already ill or disabled. These interventions are provided more commonly by ambulatory health care centers, hospital inpatient and outpatient facilities, and private practitioners and are disproportionately utilized by older persons.

DYNAMICS OF PUBLIC HEALTH

The trends in health status vary in each community. However, there are some projected societal changes that influence community patterns of health and disease and the nutritional status of populations. Public health workers must collect and analyze data to monitor the health trends in their communities and to assure that there are programs and services to respond to

- increases in the proportion of the population who are dependent children or elderly
- growing numbers of children living in homes with a single parent, usually the mother, and often in poverty
- increased numbers of mothers of young children employed outside the home
- families with children, as well as individuals, who are homeless or living in shelters or substandard housing
- the greater mix of ethnic minorities in the population, particularly Hispanics and Asians, many of whom speak only their native languages and desire their native foods
- the increased obsolescence of blue-collar worker skills, contributing to unemployment and underemployment
- changing patterns of chronic and communicable diseases, with growing numbers of men, women, and children with AIDS
- larger numbers of youths and young adults who are addicted to alcohol or illegal drugs

Meanwhile, the work of public health professionals is being made more efficient, effective, and satisfying by

- greater access to personal computers to quickly, completely, and accurately record, compile, analyze, and transmit volumes of population health statistics and program and client management data
- the new communications and media technologies available to reach larger populations with health and nutrition education messages
- advances in medical, biological, genetic, food, and nutrition research that more clearly define the roles and interactions of nutrients, dietary factors, and drugs in human metabolism, reproduction, growth, aging, and disease
- the availability of many new food products and food services designed to respond to the health, nutritional, and convenience needs of the population
- a more educated public that is motivated to take greater responsibility for managing personal and family health
- the greater receptivity of employers and employees to health promotion programs as a means of controlling health care costs and increasing worker morale and productivity.

GOVERNMENTAL RESPONSIBILITIES FOR PUBLIC HEALTH

State, city, and county governments became actively involved in public health during the 1800s when it became necessary to organize community effort against epidemics of communicable diseases and to assure safe water and food supplies and sewage disposal. The application of the sciences of bacteriology and epidemiology in the late nineteenth and early twentieth centuries brought the devastating fatal communicable diseases under control through vaccines developed for their prevention. When these successes were achieved, governmental public health agencies moved forward to promote the health of high-risk populations beginning with the reduction of maternal and child mortality (death) and morbidity (illness) in the 1920s and 1930s; moving to chronic disease prevention and control in the 1950s, 1960s, and 1970s; and currently focusing on health promotion and disease prevention for people of all age groups in the 1980s and 1990s. State and local public health agencies provide the framework for service delivery in varying degrees. The federal government has taken leadership by providing grants-in-aid; setting standards and guidelines; offering consultation, technical assistance, and training; developing data systems; and supporting research. The common core of the federal, state, and local governments' roles in public health is shown in Figure 1-2. These include assessment or community diagnosis, discussed in Chapters 3 and 4, policy development,

Figure 1-2 The Government Role in Health. *Source*: Reprinted with permission from *The Future of Public Health*, © 1989, by the National Academy Press, National Academy of Sciences, Washington, D.C.

---

discussed in Chapters 5, 6, and 7; and assurance through program development and evaluation, discussed in Chapter 14.

NUTRITION IN PUBLIC HEALTH

While early public health efforts focused on control of single-nutrient deficiency diseases and contributions of nutrition to maternal and child health, today compelling scientific evidence documents the relationship of multiple, often interacting, diet components to some of today's most serious and costly crippling and killing conditions. Those conditions most clearly associated with nutritional status are

- obesity
- iron deficiency anemia
- undernutrition
- growth retardation or stunting
- dental caries

Those health conditions in which diet is one of the several contributing risk factors include

- infant low birth weight
- birth defects and inborn metabolic errors such as phenylketonuria
- heart disease
- hypertension
- cancer (some types)

- osteoporosis
- stroke

Conditions in which diet contributes to treatment and control of a diagnosed health condition include

- acquired immune deficiency syndrome (AIDS)
- diabetes
- gastrointestinal diseases
- kidney disease

Solutions to the complex public health problems require cost-effective, community-based interventions that address their multiple causes. Since food, nutrition, and diet are woven into the economic, social, and emotional fabric, as well as the health fabric, of the community, the public health nutritionist is a key player on the team in the health agency that diagnoses and treats the "body politic." In diagnosing and preparing a "care plan" for the community, the SOAP (Subjective, Objective, Assessment, Plan) format used by clinicians in traditional patient care can be applied. For the public health team, however, the patient is the community in its most holistic sense. Figure 1-3 applies SOAP noting to the community as the patient.

With policy makers, legislators, administrators, community leaders, consumers, and their public health agency team colleagues, nutritionists participate in establishing policy (Chapters 5, 6, and 7). They identify and diagnose the food and nutrition needs and problems in their communities (Chapters 3 and 4). They design, implement, and evaluate programs that address the most urgent food-, nutrition-, and diet-related health needs detected in the community (Chapter 14). Public health nutritionists collaborate with health and human service colleagues to assure that everyone has access to a safe, affordable food supply (Chapter 13) and to change the nutrition knowledge, attitudes, and practices of the people in their community to instill more healthful eating and exercise habits (Chapter 18). Nutritionists advocate passage of federal, state, and local laws, regulations, and ordinances to assure both the safety of food distributed to the public in markets and public eating establishments and the accuracy of food labels and advertising. They encourage the media to produce educational nutrition messages that will reach the whole community through television, radio, newspapers, and magazines. Nutritionists work with schools, libraries, houses of worship, day care centers, grocery stores, restaurants, and civic and social clubs to establish contact with larger groups of people. And

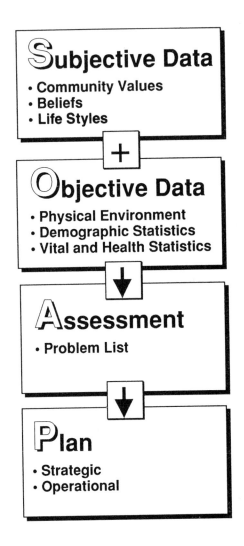

Figure 1-3 "SOAPing" the Body Politic

as they participate in assuring primary care to those who are unserved or underserved, they deliver nutrition care to selected populations (Chapter 11). Figure 1-4 puts in perspective the nutrition services in the public health system, including both population- and client directed programs and services.

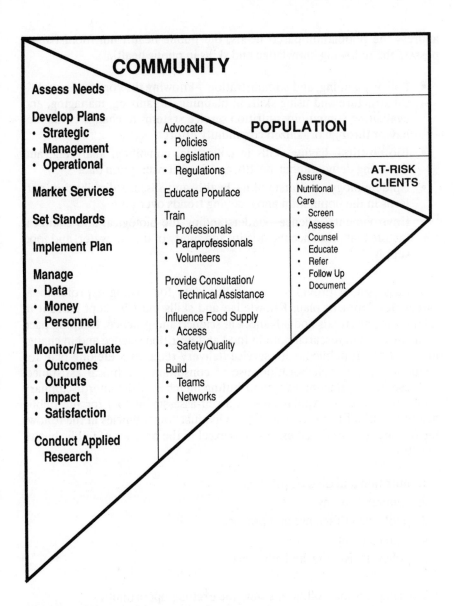

Figure 1-4 Nutrition Services To Reach the Public

KNOWLEDGE AND SKILLS OF PUBLIC HEALTH NUTRITIONISTS

All nutritionists must be experts in normal and clinical nutrition and be competent in bringing about changes in eating behavior. In addition, to address the population-based needs, the public health nutritionist must possess the following knowledge and skills in public health:

- Policy, planning, and administration—knowing the community political structure and using skills in planning, organizing, managing, and evaluating community nutrition service systems to change eating behavior through organized community effort
- Biostatistics—having skills in collecting, compiling, analyzing, and reporting demographic, health, and food consumption data
- Epidemiology—understanding health and disease distribution patterns in the population and studying trends over time
- Environmental science—understanding the biological and chemical factors that influence the quality and safety of the air, water, and food supply

Self-assessment provides the baseline data for writing a professional career development plan. Knowledge and skills must be kept current in relation to the trends and advances in science and practice. Keeping pace with advances in research both in food and nutrition science and in changing practices in public health service delivery requires a lifelong plan for continuing study, collaboration, use of consultants, technical assistance, and research to function as a contributing member of the interdisciplinary public health team. Appendix A is a self-assessment tool for the public health nutritionist to use to analyze individual competencies in the following five areas, considered essential to excel in the practice of public health nutrition:

1. nutrition and dietetic practice
2. communications
3. public health science and practice
4. management
5. policy, legislation, and advocacy

The chapters that follow examine the exciting opportunities.

ISSUES TO DEBATE

- How should health care dollars be distributed
  —between primary, secondary, and tertiary prevention?

—for care directed to the high-risk groups at the various stages in the life span?

- How should the public health nutritionist distribute time and energy between population-based dietary interventions, such as making changes in the food system, using the media, offering nutrition education to larger groups, or providing one-on-one nutrition care to high-risk clients served in clinics?
- What competencies are most important for the public health nutritionist to cultivate?

NOTES

1. C.E.A. Winslow, "The Untilled Field of Public Health," *Modern Medicine* 2 (March 1920): 183.

2. John J. Hanlon and George E. Pickett, *Public Health Administration and Practice* (St. Louis: Times Mirror/Mosby College Publishing, 1984), 4–5.

3. Institute of Medicine, *The Future of Public Health* (Washington, D.C.: National Academy Press, 1988), 138–59.

4. Edward G. McGavran, "What Is Public Health?" in *Edward G. McGavran: Guardian of the Body Politic*, ed. H.H. Barr and F.H. Barrie (Chapel Hill: University of North Carolina, 1979), 47–61.

BIBLIOGRAPHY

Congressional Research Service, CRS Review. *Public Health Policy and the Congress.* Washington, D.C.: Library of Congress, March 1989.

Rose, Geoffrey. "Sick Individuals and Sick Populations." *International Journal of Epidemiology* 14, no. 1 (1985):32–38.

chapter 2

Applying Nutrition Science to the Public's Health

Sara M. Hunt and *Mildred Kaufman*

READER OBJECTIVES

- List the values and constraints of the various approaches to nutrition investigation cited in the literature.
- Describe the basis and the uses and misuses of the Recommended Dietary Allowances in community nutrition programs.
- Identify some issues that create debate between nutrition scientists and nutrition policy makers.
- Discuss the use of benefit/risk analysis in selecting public health nutrition interventions from current nutrition research findings.
- Assess the usefulness and limitations of the several versions of dietary guidelines for nutrition education of the public.
- List some resources the public health nutritionist might use to keep pace with current research.

NUTRITION EXPERTISE IN PUBLIC HEALTH

The public health nutritionist advises the agency administrator, policy makers, and staff on current nutrition research findings that can contribute to the public's health and to the organization's mission, policies, and programs. Knowledge of current scientific findings in nutrition is the basis for

- planning nutrition interventions as part of community health programs
- providing technical assistance and in-service education to public health professionals and paraprofessionals, human service agency personnel, and educators

* serving as a resource to the public, the media, food marketers, restaurateurs, and food service directors
* assuring that nutrition messages to the public and clients are based on the current significant research
* advocating for needed agency, local, state, and national nutrition policy

To be a credible nutrition resource, the nutritionist must understand the fundamentals of nutrition science, food science, and dietetics, along with their underlying base in human physiology, chemistry, biochemistry, and the behavioral sciences. This includes in-depth knowledge of nutrition and diet applied to primary, secondary, and tertiary disease prevention at each stage in the life span. For the people in the community to reap the benefits of nutrition research findings requires that the science be translated into practical dietary guidance that makes sense to them in terms of appealing foods that they can find and afford in their markets. As the public becomes more science literate and as nutrient labeling appears on more food products, nutrition education for the public must include more scientific concepts and terminology.

Nutrition research in the twentieth century has made great strides since the identification of the individual vitamins and trace minerals which, when lacking in diets, caused deficiency diseases such as scurvy, pellagra, beriberi, and rickets. These were major public health problems before vitamins were identified in the early 1900s. Treating these diseases with the single missing nutrient produced dramatic cures.

Researchers investigating today's public health problems deal with multiple interrelated dietary, environmental, and life style factors with more subtle, long-term effects. Today's list of major public health problems includes low birth weight, birth defects, obesity, heart disease, stroke, cancer, osteoporosis, diabetes, and AIDS. While a body of knowledge relating dietary factors to these problems is accumulating in the published literature, there are many unanswered questions and continuing controversies. In this arena the scientist is the pessimist whose cup of knowledge is half empty. The researcher sees many unresolved problems that must be investigated before questions can be answered with certainty, a certainty that is continuously elusive. However, as practitioners, nutritionists must be optimists whose cup is half full of information to disseminate to benefit the health and quality of life of people in their communities.

The public health nutritionist must possess the knowledge and self-confidence to speak out and take a common-sense, but informed stand on the controversial issues which bewilder a public bombarded with conflicting nutrition information from the media, bookstores, health professionals, family, and friends. The public must be provided with guidelines to evaluate the evidence and be helped to realize that today's scientific understanding may change tomorrow as investigation advances knowledge.

INTERPRETING RESEARCH AS THE BASE FOR PRACTICE

The body of information on which nutrition practice is based has been established by researchers in biochemistry, physiology, nutrition, medicine, and related sciences. After scientists identified and described the major nutrients, their next steps were to quantify the human requirements for these nutrients. Methods ranged from dietary studies to determine the kind and amount of nutrients in foods eaten by healthy population groups to a variety of studies on how the human body digests, absorbs, stores, and metabolizes the various nutrients. Balance studies were used to determine protein and mineral needs, while vitamin requirements were estimated first by growth studies and then by "saturation" tests and cure and/or prevention of discrete disease symptoms.[1]

Researchers relating nutrition and diet to health utilize a number of different investigative designs. Practitioners need to understand the values and constraints of the various research designs in order to critically evaluate the findings and consider the potential applications. Several different research designs will be noted in the literature.

Epidemiological research is extensively reported in the nutrition literature. Epidemiologists observe naturally occurring health and disease patterns in free-living population groups and report their observations. Populations considered to have common dietary characteristics and observable patterns of health and disease are compared and contrasted. By observing symptoms seen in large numbers in a population and by observing the common characteristics of their diet, Goldberger identified pellagra in the southeastern United States and was able to attribute it to the lack of niacin and tryptophan in the region's corn-based diet. Recent observations of the lower heart disease rates among Eskimos, compared to other ethnic groups, led to the observations of the beneficial effects of omega-3 fatty acids.

Epidemiological studies observe and record data on free-living community populations, comparing and contrasting observations in different locations or trends in the same population over time. In evaluating epidemiological research, the concerns are whether the investigators have asked the right questions of the right population groups and whether the dietary factors they are studying are actually the attributable causes.

In free-living populations, ecological studies are usually simpler and cheaper to conduct than experimental studies are. Ecological associations are made after collecting statistical data on disease rates in different countries or regions. Associations between disease and exposure parameters can be demonstrated by a variety of data analysis methods.

Surveys are designed to describe and measure selected characteristics in a defined population. Survey data provide a statistical profile. Periodic surveys can provide baseline data and then measure progress over time. The National Health and Nutrition Examination Survey (NHANES), the National Food Consumption Survey (NFCS), and the Continuing Survey of Food Intakes by Individuals (CSFII) are examples of nationwide surveys conducted by federal agencies that contribute to the national nutrition monitoring system. These surveys, based on national probability (representative) samples, are major sources of the data used to measure the nation's progress toward meeting the health promotion/disease prevention objectives for the years 1990 and 2000.

In critiquing survey findings, it is necessary to understand the sample selection. For example, the probability sample used for NHANES is designed to characterize the U.S. population as a whole and the country by four regions. It cannot be generalized for state or local areas without adjusting the data for age, gender, ethnic, and economic distribution in the particular area (see Chapter 16). Surveys based on samples of convenience describe only the specific population surveyed. Surveillance may be considered a set of surveys repeated at periodic intervals on the same population. For example, the Centers for Disease Control's Pregnancy and Pediatric Surveillance data are specific to the clinic populations from which the data are collected. The quality of survey data depends on training of personnel on correct techniques and the validity and reliability of the tests and data collection instruments they use, as well as on the response of the subjects. In interpreting survey data the response rate must be known because poor response introduces bias; those who respond may have different characteristics than nonrespondents.

Experimental designs may be classified as either nonrandomized or randomized studies. Nonrandomized experimental designs would include the observational cohort study and the retrospective case-control study. In the observational cohort study, a relatively large population is chosen and followed forward in time to record subsequent occurrences of disease. For example, cancers resulting from exposure to environmental factors have long incubation times, so that observations are needed for many years or decades.

In the retrospective case-control study, investigators choose a group of people in whom the disease is already present and match a comparable control group for such characteristics as age, gender, race, smoking practices, etc. Although case-control may be smaller and less expensive than cohort design, problems can occur due to the selection of appropriate cases and controls, the control of socioeconomic factors or diet intake, and unknown early baseline conditions of the subjects.

The above designs can generate hypotheses which need to be further investigated in a randomized study. The gold standard of cause-effect research includes animal or metabolic studies or clinical trials.

Animal studies are a standby in experimental nutrition research because all aspects of the animal's life can be observed under carefully controlled laboratory conditions. The genetic background and living conditions of the animals and the nutrient composition of their rations are all known. In nutrition or diet studies in animals, the genetic background, living conditions, and reproductive activities of the animals are kept constant, while the specific nutrient, combination of nutrients, or dietary factors can be manipulated over the life span of the experimental group of animals. All factors are maintained constant for the controls. The life span of small animals is short, so that they can be observed over several generations in a relatively brief time period. Experimental and control groups can easily be kept separate. Live animals can be observed and their organs and tissues examined after death. Animals commonly used in nutrition research are various strains of rats or mice, rabbits, guinea pigs, dogs, sheep, and monkeys. Animals are selected for a particular study for those characteristics that are known to be most similar to humans in terms of digestion, absorption, and metabolism of the nutrient being studied. However, because of many obvious differences, questions still can be raised about generalizing findings from animals to human populations.

Metabolic diet studies are conducted with small numbers of human subjects in clinical research units where experimental subjects can be fed specifically formulated diets for relatively short periods of time and compared with a control group fed a "normal" diet. These studies may determine the nutrient levels in diets required to achieve specified physiological effects. Balance studies are used to determine the levels of nutrient intake needed to achieve an equilibrium between intake and output. Studies of calorie intake in relation to energy expenditure under various conditions are another example. Because it is difficult to obtain very many normal healthy subjects who are available to live and eat under laboratory-controlled conditions, such studies are usually done with small numbers of subjects for relatively short periods of time. College or health professional students or prisoners are often used as subjects, but may not be representative of the total population in terms of age, ethnicity, or socioeconomic status.

Randomized clinical trials are commonly used to determine the effectiveness and efficacy of drugs. They also have been used for dietary studies in which experimental and control groups are randomly assigned to test dietary interventions by consuming standardized diets with controlled kinds and amounts of foods, formula diets, or formulated food products. A blind study in which subjects do not know whether they are in the experimental or control group is desirable. The size of these studies is limited by cost and ability to maintain dietary control in a free-living population. Questions always can be raised about compliance with the controlled diet over the time of the study. Dropout rates are frequently a problem. In studies where the experimental group is counseled on a particular dietary regimen and the control group is not, there can be some crossover effects if the two populations are not widely separated geographically.

EVOLUTION OF RECOMMENDED DIETARY ALLOWANCES

Epidemiological, clinical, and laboratory research describing and quantifying human nutrient requirements culminated in the first Recommended Dietary Allowances (RDAs), published in 1943 by the National Research Council of the National Academy of Sciences.[2] Quantification of nutrient requirements became a critical issue in 1940 as the United States entered World War II. In the years immediately preceding the formulation of the first RDAs, the United States had experienced a severe economic depression; many people were without enough food, and nutrient deficiencies were common. Many of those selected for military service had to be rejected because of physical defects, many attributed to poor nutritional status.

At the request of the National Defense Advisory Committee, an expert group of nutrition scientists was appointed as the Food and Nutrition Board of the National Research Council to formulate the first RDAs. These allowances were formally adopted in May 1941 at a National Nutrition Conference convened by President Franklin D. Roosevelt. The allowances were designed for use in planning military rations and food supplies to stockpile for mass feeding for civilians. They also were used to plan food rationing allocations for the civilian population.

Recommendations were made for various age, sex, and physical activity groups at levels that would assure an adequate daily supply of specified nutrients needed by essentially healthy people in the population.[3] The narrative that went with the first RDA tables emphasized that most healthy people could obtain the recommended quantities of essential nutrients and calories by eating a suggested number of servings of a variety of nutritious foods. A "margin of safety" was added for all nutrients, but not for calories. The first edition of the RDAs specified intakes for energy, protein, iron, vitamin A, thiamin, riboflavin, niacin, ascorbic acid, and vitamin D.

To keep pace with new research between 1943 and 1980, the RDAs were updated every three to five years. The tenth edition of the RDAs, published in 1989, contains recommendations for kcalories plus 19 nutrients. Estimated safe and adequate daily intakes are suggested for another seven nutrients. The 1989 edition of the RDAs includes allowances for 17 age/sex groups with over 500 age/sex/nutrient-specific recommendations.

The tenth edition of the RDAs was postponed from its planned 1985 publication because of some controversial scientific and policy issues. The Food and Nutrition Board and the National Research Council Report Review Committee have now approved the tenth edition, satisfied that it reflects scientific concurrence and is appropriate for use in developing public health nutrition programs and policies.[4]

Major changes include increasing the previous age class from 19 to 22 years to 19 to 24 years, using median heights and weights for U.S. populations as reported in NHANES II for reference adults in each age/sex class, and tabulating absolute RDAs for women during pregnancy and lactation. RDAs for energy and protein are derived somewhat differently but remain similar to those in previous editions. RDAs are established for vitamin K and selenium for the first time. The allowances for vitamin C are unchanged, while those for vitamin B6, folate, and vitamin B12 have been lowered. The higher RDA for calcium has been extended through age 25. Lower allowances are suggested for magnesium for children, and the iron allowance for healthy adolescent and adult women has been lowered.[5]

Because of gaps in the research, several of these recommended allowances are based on extrapolated data. For example, allowances for persons over age 51 have been extrapolated from studies of the nutrient needs of younger adults, adjusting calories, thiamin, riboflavin, and niacin downward for known decreased metabolic rates and physical activity. Advances in research have led to the current complex set of nutrient recommendations. Establishment of national nutrition standards requires specifying different quantities of calories and essential nutrients needed by people of both sexes and of varying stages of growth, ages, and levels of activity. Of particular concern are those population groups considered to be at nutritional risk: rapidly growing infants and children; adolescents; women of childbearing age, especially those who are pregnant or lactating; and the elderly.

LIMITATIONS ON THE USE OF RECOMMENDED DIETARY ALLOWANCES

The RDAs are best estimates based on the professional judgment of the scientists appointed to the RDA Committee at any point in time. Estimates

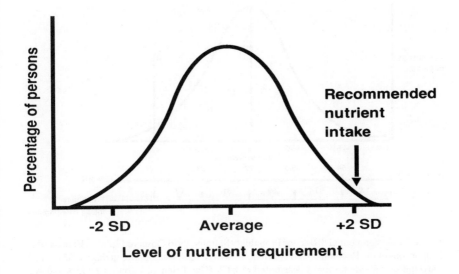

Figure 2-1 Distribution of Requirements for a Nutrient, Illustrating the Current Convention of Describing the Average + 2 SD for Nutrients. (This assumes normal distribution.) *Source*: Reprinted from *American Journal of Clinical Nutrition*, Vol. 41, No. 1, p. 156, with permission of American Society for Clinical Nutrition, © January 1985.

of adequacy vary with the criteria they select. The criteria for establishing a nutrient allowance are not constant.[6] For example, if the criterion for establishing the allowance for ascorbic acid is to prevent scurvy, the recommendation would be much lower than an RDA to achieve 90 percent tissue saturation. The human requirement for any nutrient is believed to fall on a normal distribution curve in a study population; therefore, once the criterion of adequacy is agreed on, the recommended intake is set at +2 standard deviations (SD) from the mean. At this level, few individuals are expected to have a higher requirement. Figure 2-1 identifies the point on the curve where the recommended intake falls.

The RDAs were developed to use to allocate ration allowances for people being fed in groups, as in the armed forces or in institutions. In recent years the RDAs have been used for developing standards for the amounts of foods to be allocated in the federally funded food programs, such as school and child day care food services and congregate meal programs for the elderly, and for costing out food stamp allowances.

The RDAs were never intended to be used as standards to assess the adequacy of any one individual's nutrient intake or risk of malnutrition.

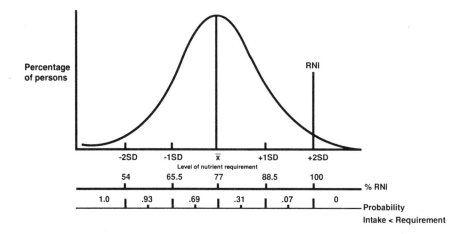

Figure 2-2 Assignment of "Risk" or Probability Statements to Observed Intakes Expressed as Proportions of the Recommended Nutrient Intake (RNI). [Assumptions in this model are that the requirements are normally distributed with CV (Coefficient of Variation) = 15% and that the recommended intake is set at the average requirement +2 SD.] *Source*: Reprinted from "Estimating Nutrient Deficiencies in a Population from Dietary Records: The Use of Probability Analyses" by G.H. Anderson, R.D. Peterson, and G.H. Beaton, *Nutrition Research*, Vol. 2, p. 409, with permission of Pergamon Press, Inc., © 1982.

However, the recommended dietary allowances are widely used to assess individual risk and to determine individual eligibility for nutrition services. If intake is equal to or greater than the recommended allowance, the risk of dietary inadequacy is very low. However, when an individual's intake falls below the recommended amount, the only observation that can be made about the degree of risk is that the farther the intake falls below the RDA, the greater the likelihood of dietary inadequacy is.

Quantitative statements are based on statistical measurement of probability of risk.[7] This measurement is shown in Figure 2-2. The probability of risk is identified within the given intervals below the distribution curve of requirements. As shown in this figure, when dietary intake is 77 percent of the recommended value, there is a 50 percent chance that it is inadequate. At one standard deviation below the mean, where intake is 65.5 percent of the recommended value, there is 81 percent probability that it is inadequate.[8] Risk of inadequacy so identified does not provide information about the individual's nutritional status; it only suggests the possibility of dietary inadequacy for the nutrient analyzed using the selected criterion. Assessment of an individual's nutritional status should not be based on nutrient analysis of food intake alone but requires careful anthropometric, clinical, and biochemical determinations.

NUTRITION SCIENCE VERSUS NUTRITION POLICY

As the country's affluence has increased in the last 40 years, so has the body girth of many of its citizens. Obesity now is recognized as an urgent public health problem in the United States. Meanwhile, hunger and/or undernutrition still remain problems among some of those who live on incomes at or below the poverty level. Rapidly growing infants and children, women of childbearing age, and the elderly are at the greatest nutritional risk. For families living on or below the poverty level, nutrition standards or guidelines are needed to establish the public assistance and food stamp allowances so that participants can purchase enough food to assure adequate intakes of kcalories and the essential nutrients. Some quantification of nutrients appears necessary, and the RDAs are now the only available scientifically recognized guidelines.

The RDAs have been used as nutrition standards on which public policy has been based. However, a single policy guide no longer can be applied unilaterally because the population is made up of people who are overnourished, people who are hungry or do not have access to enough food, and people who have unique nutritional needs as a result of a variety of disease conditions. One set of standards or allowances may need to be designed to protect people from excessive consumption of energy- and food-related factors that may be harmful to their health; another standard may be needed for those whose intake of protective nutrients is deficient, and still another for those who have special nutrient needs.

These considerations were brought into sharp focus when the Food and Nutrition Board did not accept the revision prepared by the RDA Committee for publication in 1985. The Board and the RDA Committee could not agree on the proposed RDAs for ascorbic acid (vitamin C) and vitamin A. In the establishment of nutrient standards, the criterion chosen to define adequacy of nutrient intake is pivotal. The 1985 RDA Committee chose the cutoff level of adequacy as the amount of each vitamin they judged to be necessary to maintain plasma levels for normal body functions. The nutritional biochemists recommended an allowance they believed would prevent any signs of deficiency in at least 97.5 percent of the population.[9] While this approach was logical, the results triggered many concerns. The recommended allowances for vitamin A and ascorbic acid would have been lowered at a time when epidemiological evidence was suggesting that more generous intakes of these vitamins might be factors in preventing some types of cancers. In a 1982 report entitled *Diet, Nutrition and Cancer,*[10] another committee of the National Academy of Sciences recommended that Americans eat more foods rich in vitamin A and ascorbic acid. Although there was no concrete evidence that these vitamins could prevent cancer, this committee was convinced by the suggestive evidence.

The advocates for the federal food programs further contributed to the debate about the suggested allowances. They saw the reduction of dietary allowances for vitamin A and ascorbic acid as providing a rationale for the administering agencies to reduce the number of recommended servings of fruits and vegetables, thus cutting the budgets for the Food Stamp Program; the school and preschool feeding programs; the Special Supplemental Food Program for Women, Infants, and Children (WIC); and the congregate meal programs for the elderly.

Rejection of the report stimulated discussion of the purposes and uses of the RDAs and the scientific and policy considerations for preparing these nutrient standards.[11] This discussion resulted in written guidelines for use by future RDA Committees. These guidelines were developed by the members of the Food and Nutrition Board with input from users of the RDAs, including both nutrition scientists and practicing nutritionists representing government agencies and industry.[12] Nutritionists should know that the RDAs are arbitrary judgments based on review of the currently available research and should always interpret them from that perspective.

RISK/BENEFIT ANALYSIS AND PROFESSIONAL JUDGMENT

Absolute proof of a beneficial outcome from a particular dietary recommendation would provide a firm basis for a nutrition intervention, but demanding such proof can impede action. Use of compelling suggestive evidence, on the other hand, can provide incentive for action, while stimulating further research. Deciding whether to develop new community interventions based on suggestive rather than concrete research evidence requires professional judgment. Implementing a program by taking relatively risk-free action has the potential of providing substantial benefits.

As illustrated in Figure 2-3, for every nutrient there is a distinct range of intake that confers optimal physiological function, while intakes above and below this range may impose risk.[13] In the case of ascorbic acid, exceeding the optimal physiological range by generous use of food sources appears to pose little risk.[14] Recommending intake of this vitamin only in the amount needed to perform its known physiological function might deprive the population of benefits not assured, but often suggested. This vitamin affects numerous bodily functions; it is needed literally to hold the body's cells together. Nonetheless, no unequivocal mechanisms of action have been established. The probable and proposed functions of ascorbic acid[15] are listed in Exhibit 2-1. The probable functions of the vitamin are those that apparently are possible at a level of intake commensurate with that needed to prevent scurvy. Additional suggested functions require a higher intake of the vitamin.[16] A nonspecific effect of ascorbic acid is its interaction with

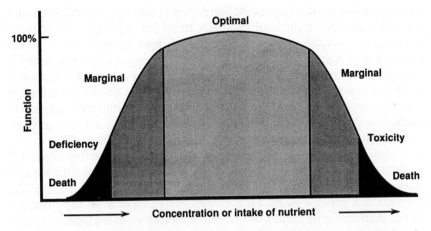

Figure 2-3 Dependence of Biological Function on Tissue Concentration or Intake of a Nutrient. (For nutrients and energy sources, there is a range of intake that confers optimal physiological function. Below this range, deficiencies can cause disease or death. Excessive intake also can lead to increasing symptoms of toxicity. The optimal range varies for each nutrient and is affected by many individual and environmental factors.) *Source*: Reprinted from *Science*, Vol. 213, p. 1333, with permission of the American Association for the Advancement of Science, © September 1981.

Exhibit 2-1 Proposed Biochemical Functions of Vitamin C

More Probable Functions

    Proline and lysine hydroxylation (necessary in synthesis of collagen)
    Carnitine synthesis (carnitine needed for transport of long chain fatty acids from cell cytoplast into mitochondria for oxidation)
    Dopamine hydroxylation (conversion of dopamine into norepinephrine)
    Peptide amidation (production of selected peptides which are active as hormones, hormone-releasing factors, or neurotransmitters)

Other Functions Which May Be Aided or Affected by Vitamin C at Higher Intake Levels

    Drug and cholesterol breakdown (drug and steroid metabolism in liver)
    Sulphation (proteoglycan synthesis)
    Lymphocyte and neutrophil function (increased immunity to infections)
    Folate reduction (maintenance of THF)
    Iron absorption, distribution, and storage (increased absorption of non-heme iron; effect on distribution and storage uncertain)

Source: Adapted with permission from *Vitamin C in Health and Disease* by T.K. Basu and C.J. Schorah, p. 59, Avi Publishing Company, © 1982.

nitrates and/or nitrites to prevent formation of carcinogenic nitrosamines and nitrosamides. Because of its ability to inhibit the formation of these carcinogens, ascorbic acid is believed to protect against cancer of the stomach and esophagus.[17] The American Cancer Society feels strongly enough about the protective effect of ascorbic acid against these types of cancer to include specific reference to the vitamin as one of the ten steps toward reduced cancer risk: "Add vitamin C to your diet by eating citrus fruits, cantaloupe, currants, strawberries, other fruits and cruciferous vegetables to protect against cancer of the stomach and esophagus."[18]

In contrast to ascorbic acid, acting on suggestive evidence that vitamin A might be a factor in carcinogenesis could prove risky because of the toxicity associated with an excessive intake or megadoses of vitamin A (Figure 2-3). Overzealous persons might take megadoses of vitamin A supplements, rather than confining themselves to eating foods high in the beta-carotenes and preformed vitamin A. In this case where benefit is not absolutely assured, the known risks suggest a more cautious approach.

CONCEPT OF NUTRIENT DENSITY

In the last 15 to 20 years the emphasis in nutrition education has shifted from recommending foods to overcome dietary deficiencies to suggesting foods to limit or avoid overconsumption of energy sources, while at the same time including generous amounts of certain "protective" nutrients or food-related substances. The concept of nutrient density relates nutrient allowances to 1,000 kcalories of intake. Nutrient density compares the quantity of the various nutrients in a food to its energy or caloric value. When nutrient density is used, foods can be examined and compared to determine how well each individually or in combination meets dietary allowances in relation to total calorie contribution.

The Index of Nutritional Quality (INQ) is one nutrient density approach.[19] It provides a quantitative measure for comparing the nutrient quality of a single food or a combination of foods relative to recommended dietary intakes.

$$INQ = \frac{\text{Amount of nutrient in 1,000 kcal of food (A)}}{\text{Human allowance of the nutrient per 1,000 kcal (B)}}$$

Table 2-1 provides single-value nutrient allowances per 1,000 kcal for heterogeneous populations one year of age and older. The INQ provides a unit of comparison of nutrient quality independent of age, gender, or activity of populations. Table 2-2 illustrates how nutrient density for one

Table 2-1 Single-Value Nutrient Allowances per 1,000 kcal for Heterogeneous Populations One Year of Age and Older

Nutrient	Allowance per 1,000 kcal	
protein	25	gm
fat	39	gm
carbohydrate	137.5	gm
sugar, added	25	gm
calcium	450	gm
iron	8	mg
magnesium	150	mg
zinc	8	mg
potassium	1,875	mg
sodium	1,100	mg
vitamin A	2,000	IU
thiamin	0.5	mg
riboflavin	0.6	mg
vitamin B-6	1	mg
vitamin B-12	1.5	mg
vitamin C	30	mg
folacin	200	mg
cholesterol	175	mg

Source: Reprinted from "Nutrition Intervention: Panacea or Pandora's Box?" by B.W. Wyse, C.T. Windham, and G.G. Hansen, *Journal of The American Dietetic Association*, Vol. 85, No. 9, p. 1088, with permission of The American Dietetic Association, © 1985.

food (skim milk) can be calculated. When the INQ (ratio A:B) is greater than 1, the food or group of foods can be considered a good source of the nutrient(s) under consideration.[20] Conversely, an INQ value of less than 1 suggests a food for which calorie intake would have to be excessive to meet the recommended allowances for the micronutrients.

DIETARY RECOMMENDATIONS TO THE PUBLIC

The first edition of the RDAs published in 1943 suggested a diet plan to meet the recommended nutrient levels, the Basic 7 Food Groups—(1) milk; (2) eggs, meat, fish, and fowl; (3) potato; (4) dark green and deep yellow vegetables; (5) vitamin C–rich fruits; (6) whole grain or enriched bread and cereals; and (7) butter or fortified margarine—the foods to provide for the recommended intake of the specified nutrients.[21] This plan classified foods

Table 2-2 Comparison of Composition of Skim Milk with Nutrient Allowances

Nutrient	(A) Composition of milk	(B) Allowances/ 1,000 kcal	Ratio A:B
energy (kcal)	1,000	1,000	1.0
calcium (mg)	3,514	450	7.8
zinc (mg)	11.4	8	1.4
riboflavin (mg)	4.0	0.6	6.7
vitamin B-6 (mg)	1.1	1	1.1
vitamin B-12 (mg)	10.9	1.5	7.2
protein (gm)	97	25	3.9
fat (gm)	5.7	39	0.1
cholesterol (mg)	57	175	0.3
sodium (mg)	1,486	1,100	1.3

Source: Reprinted from "Nutrition Intervention: Panacea or Pandora's Box?" by B.W. Wyse, C.T. Windham, and G.G. Hansen, Journal of The American Dietetic Association, Vol. 85, No. 9, p. 1088, with permission of The American Dietetic Association, © 1985.

by their common characteristics and recommended minimum numbers of servings of each food group to include in the daily diet. The only group without a recommended intake goal was cereals and breads, since these foods were being consumed in sufficient amounts. In 1957 the Four Food Group pattern was developed and published by the U.S. Department of Agriculture to translate the then current RDAs into suggested numbers of servings in four rather than seven categories of foods: (1) milk and milk products; (2) meat, fish, poultry, eggs, and legumes; (3) fruits and vege-tables; and (4) cereals and breads. Recommended intakes for various popu-lation groups were included along with comments about foods that did not fit into the four categories because they contributed primarily kcalories without significant amounts of any of the micronutrients.

The food group guides have limitations but continue to be used as tools in nutrition education for normal, healthy people.[22] Nutrients likely to be supplied in less than recommended amounts by the Four Food Group pattern include iron, vitamin B$_6$, magnesium, and zinc. Until 1979 the food group guides emphasized the foods needed to supply the recommended nutrients but did not mention the possibility of overconsumption of energy or fat. Table 2-3 compares the federal dietary recommendations for the general public from 1917 to 1988. The change in recommendations between 1958 and 1977 can be noted.

Table 2-3 Federal Dietary Recommendations for the General Public, 1917–1988

Year	Agency[b]	Publication	Variety	Maintain Ideal Body Weight	Include Starch and Fiber	Limit Sugar	Limit Fat	Limit Cholesterol	Limit Salt	Limit Alcohol
1917	USDA	What the Body Needs— Five Food Groups	•		•	+	+			
1942	USDA	Food for Freedom— Daily Eight	•		•		+			
1943	USDA	National Wartime Nutrition Guide—Basic Seven	•		•		+			
1946	USDA	National Food Guide— Basic Seven	•		•		+			
1958	USDA	Food for Fitness— Four Food Groups	•		•					
1977	US Senate	Dietary Goals for the US	•	•	•	•	•	•	•	•
1979	USDA	Building a Better Diet— Five Food Groups	•	•	•	•	•	•	•	
1979	DHEW	Healthy People: The Surgeon General's Report on Health Promotion & Disease Prevention	•	•	•	•	•	•	•	•
1979	DHEW/NCI	Statement on Diet, Nutrition, and Cancer—Prudent Interim Principles	•				•			•
1980	USDA/DHHS	Dietary Guidelines for Americans	•	•	•	•	•	•	•	•
1980	DHHS	National 1990 Nutrition Objectives	•	•	•	•	•	•	•	•
1984	DHHS/NHLBI	Recommendations for Control of High Blood Pressure		•			•		•	•
1985	USDA/DHHS	Dietary Guidelines for Americans, 2nd Edition	•	•	•	•	•	•	•	•

Recommendation[a]

Table 2-3 continued

Year	Agency[b]	Publication	Recommendation[+] Variety	Maintain Ideal Body Weight	Include Starch and Fiber	Limit Sugar	Limit Fat	Limit Cholesterol	Limit Salt	Limit Alcohol
1986	DHHS/NCI	Cancer Control Nutrition Objectives for the Nation: 1985-2000		•	•		•			•
1987	DHHS/NHLBI	National Cholesterol Education Program Guidelines	•	•	•		•	•		•
1988	DHHS/NCI	Dietary Guidelines for Cancer Prevention	•	•	•		•		•	•

+ Recommended for inclusion in the daily diet, as opposed to subsequent recommendations to limit intake.

* Other recommendations include: increased consumption of foods containing vitamins and minerals (USDA 1917-1958; NCI 1986), increased physical activity (USDA/DHHS 1980, 1985; DHHS 1980), and reduced intake of salt-cured or smoked foods (NCI 1988).

b USDA = US Department of Agriculture, US Senate = US Senate Select Committee on Nutrition and Human Needs, DHEW = Department of Health, Education, and Welfare, DHHS = Department of Health and Human Services, NCI = National Cancer Institute, NHLBI = National Heart, Lung, and Blood Institute.

Source: Reprinted from *Surgeon General's Report on Nutrition and Health*, pp. 43–44, U.S. Government Printing Office, Washington, D.C., 1988.

Dietary Guidance for Chronic Disease Prevention

In 1957 when the Four Food Groups were developed, the possible relationship between heart disease and dietary fat was just being proposed in the medical and scientific literature.[23] At that time the Bureau of Nutrition in the New York City Health Department began to test the "prudent" diet to determine the influence of a fat- and cholesterol-controlled diet in the prevention of coronary heart disease in groups of high-risk men.[24] In 1968, for the first time, the American Heart Association published eight dietary guidelines, advising the public to reduce the intake of foods containing animal fats. It based these recommendations on the judgment of investigators that epidemiological, animal, and clinical studies all suggested a relationship between diets containing animal fat with a high concentration of cholesterol and saturated fatty acids and the prevalence of coronary heart disease.

Concern about the relationship between the quality of food intake and several of the chronic diseases culminated in January 1977 in a staff report from the Senate Select Committee on Nutrition and Human Needs entitled *Dietary Goals for the United States*.[25] This report focused the attention of the American public on the prevention of chronic degenerative diseases in an affluent population. It principally cited ischemic heart disease; certain forms of cancer, particularly cancer of the colon and breast; diabetes; and obesity. The report used a public health promotion/primary prevention approach, recommending to the public that they reduce their intakes of fat, sugar, cholesterol, and salt and that they eat more complex carbohydrates (starches and fiber). The first report was criticized because it failed to emphasize the importance of maintaining ideal body weight and consuming a variety of foods, and the Dietary Goals were revised later in 1977 to include these admonitions.[26]

Many nutrition scientists and physicians questioned the scientific evidence that attributed a causal relationship between diet and several of the chronic diseases. Opponents of these Goals stressed that proof was lacking to relate specific foods or food components to the development of specific diseases. Since everyone was not equally at risk, they felt that recommending drastic changes in the usual eating habits of all Americans was not advisable. Supporters of the Goals contended that while the recommendations might be based on limited evidence, there was little risk, and the benefits might prove to be quite large.[27]

The principles in the Dietary Goals were supported in *Healthy People: The Surgeon General's Report on Health Promotion and Disease Prevention*.[28] Diet, one of the priority areas identified in this report, was used as the basis for developing national objectives to reduce health risks. *Healthy*

People cited the relationship between diet and disease, emphasized primary prevention, and urged Americans to change their eating habits.[29] The recommended changes were similar to the Dietary Goals, but were qualitative rather than quantitative.

Both *Dietary Goals for the United States* and *Healthy People* led to the 1980 publication *Nutrition and Your Health: Dietary Guidelines for Americans.*[30] This was the first joint publication of the Department of Agriculture and the Department of Health, Education, and Welfare (now the Department of Health and Human Services). These guidelines are a formal statement of U.S. public health nutrition policy. The Dietary Guidelines addressed the possible relationship between food patterns and prevention of an even larger number of diseases than was specified in the Dietary Goals. Excessive alcohol consumption was identified as a risk to health because of its threat to the maintenance of ideal body weight and its possible relationship to birth defects, accidents, certain types of cancer, and cirrhosis.

Some health professionals and food producer groups rejected the 1980 Dietary Guidelines. In March 1980 the Food and Nutrition Board of the National Academy of Sciences issued its version of dietary guidelines entitled *Toward Healthful Diets.*[31] This publication did not agree with the federal guideline recommending that the general public reduce cholesterol intake. The board noted that although decreases in cholesterol intake had been recommended since the early 1900s, no significant correlation between dietary cholesterol and serum cholesterol concentration had been demonstrated in free-living persons.[32] The Food and Nutrition Board recommended a clinical rather than a public health approach, suggesting that advice to reduce dietary cholesterol should be prescribed by a physician only for persons with elevated serum cholesterol tests. This report contended that dietary guidelines directed to the public would raise false hopes that some diseases could be prevented through diet.[33]

In 1985 the Dietary Guidelines were reviewed and slightly revised by the Departments of Agriculture and Health and Human Services. Major modifications were made in the supporting statement for each Guideline. These Guidelines failed to quantify the percentage of total kcalories to be provided by fat or the amount of sodium or fiber to include in the diet due to the belief that data were insufficient to warrant such specifics. However, the American Heart Association has made recommendations to the public that are consistent in concept with the federal agency Guidelines, but quantitative in nature.[34] Table 2-4 shows the similarities and differences among the various dietary recommendations published by official and voluntary health agencies from 1977 to 1989, indicating both the qualitative and the quantitative differences.

A nine-member Dietary Guidelines Advisory Committee was appointed in 1988 by the Departments of Agriculture and Health and Human Serv-

Table 2-4 Dietary Recommendations to the U.S. Public, 1977–1989

Type of Recommendation/ Reference	Maintain Appropriate Body Weight, Exercise	Limit or Reduce Total Fat (% kcal)	Reduce Saturated Fatty Acids (% kcal)	Increase Poly-unsaturated Fatty Acids (% kcal)	Limit Cholesterol (mg/day)	Limit Simple Sugars	Increase Complex Carbohydrates (% kcal from total carbohydrates)	Increase Fiber	Restrict Sodium Chloride (gm)	Moderate Alcohol Intake	Other Recommendations
General Health Maintenance											
U.S. Senate (1977)	Yes	27–33	Yes	Yes	250–350	Yes	Yes	Yes	8	Yes	Reduce additives and processed foods
Council on Scientific Affairs (AMA) (1979)	Yes	No	No	No	No	Yes	NC	NC	12	Yes	Consider high-risk groups
DHEW (1979)	Yes	Yes	Yes	NS	Yes	Yes	Yes	NS	Yes	Yes	More fish, poultry, legumes; less red meat
NRC (1980b)	Yes	For weight reduction only	No	No	No	For weight reduction only	No	No	3–8	For weight reduction only	Variety in diet; consider high-risk groups
USDA/DHHS (1980; 1985)	Yes	Yes	Yes	No	Yes	Yes	Eat adequate starch and fiber	Yes	Yes	Yes	Variety in diet; consider high-risk groups
DHHS (1988)	Yes	Yes	Yes	No	Yes	Yes	Yes	Yes	Yes	Yes	Fluoridation of water; adolescent girls and women increase intake of calcium-rich foods; children, adolescents, and women of childbearing age increase intake of iron-rich foods

Table 2-4 continued

Type of Recommendation/ Reference	Maintain Appropriate Body Weight, Exercise	Limit or Reduce Total Fat (% kcal)	Reduce Saturated Fatty Acids (% kcal)	Increase Polyunsaturated Fatty Acids (% kcal)	Limit Cholesterol (mg/day)	Limit Simple Sugars	Increase Complex Carbohydrates (% kcal from total carbohydrates)	Increase Fiber	Restrict Sodium Chloride (gm)	Moderate Alcohol Intake	Other Recommendations
Diet and Health (1989)	Balance energy intake and expenditure	≤30	<10 for individuals and 7–8 as population mean	Up to 10 for individuals and ~7 as population mean	<300	Yes	(At least 55); ≥ five daily servings of vegetables and fruits; ≥ six daily servings of cereals, breads, and legumes	Directly through vegetables, fruits, and cereals	≤6 gm/ day with a goal of 4.5 gm/ day	If you drink, limit to <1.0 oz. alcohol or <2 drinks/ day	Avoid dietary supplements, especially in excess of RDAs; drink fluoridated water; limit protein intake to moderate levels (less than twice the RDA)
Heart Disease											
Inter-Society Commission for Heart Disease Resources (1984)	Yes	<30	8	10	<250	NC	Increase to make up caloric deficit	NC	5	NC	NS
NIH (1985)	Yes	<30	<10	Up to 10	250–300			Endorsed recommendations of AHA (1982) and Inter-Society Commission for Heart Disease Resources (1984)	NC	NC	Specific recommendations for high-risk groups; also physicians, public, and food industry
AHA (1988)	Yes	<30	<10	Up to 10	<300	NS	(50 or more)	NS	≤3	1–2 oz. ethanol/ day	Protein to make up remainder of calories; wide variety of foods

Cancer

NRC (1982)	NC	~30	Yes	NC	NC	No	NC	NC	Through whole grains, fruits, and vegetables	NS	By limiting intake of salt-cured, pickled, smoked foods	Yes	Emphasize fruits and vegetables; avoid high doses of supplements; pay attention to cooking methods
ACS (1984)	Yes	30	Yes	NC	NC	No	NC	NC	Same as NRC (1982)	Yes	Same as NRC (1982)	Yes	Same as NRC (1982)
NCI (1987)	Yes	Yes	Yes	NC	NC	No	NC	NC	Yes, more whole grains, fruits, and vegetables	20–35 gm	NC	Yes	Variety in diet; avoid fiber supplements

Osteoporosis

NIH (1984)	Exercise	NC	NC	NC	NC	NC	NC	NC	NC		NC	NC	Raise calcium to 1,000 mg/day (premenopausal), 1,500 mg/day (postmenopausal); use calcium supplements if needed; use vitamin D for calcium absorption

Diabetes

American Diabetes Association (1987)	Yes	<30	Yes	No	Yes	<300	Yes	(55–60)	NC	Yes	Yes	Yes	Non-nutritive sweeteners permitted but not recommended; limit protein to RDA level; avoid supplements except in special cases.

Note: NC = No comment; NS = Not specified.
Source: Reprinted with permission from *Diet and Health: Implications for Reducing Chronic Disease Risk*, © 1989, by the National Academy of Sciences, National Academy Press, Washington, D.C.

ices. This committee is drafting recommendations for seven new guidelines which may be more behaviorally directive and may focus more on a positive approach to maintaining health.

The first *Surgeon General's Report on Nutrition and Health* was published in 1988.[35] This report attempts to summarize current scientific research evidence relating dietary excesses and imbalances to the prevalent chronic diseases and recommends dietary changes to improve the health of Americans. In Table 2-4 these qualitative recommendations from the *Surgeon General's Report* are compared and contrasted with the various available guidelines.

In 1989 the National Research Council published *Diet and Health: Implications for Reducing Chronic Disease Risk*,[36] their comprehensive research review. This report is population focused in contrast to their 1980 publication *Toward Healthful Diets*.[37] The 1989 report thoroughly reviews the research literature and provides an in-depth analysis of the dietary risk factors related to the entire spectrum of chronic diseases—atherosclerotic cardiovascular diseases, cancer, diabetes, obesity, osteoporosis, dental caries, and chronic liver and kidney diseases. The committee that prepared this report presents its criteria for assessing data and its rationale for evaluating the available evidence. In making recommendations, quantitative estimates of the potential benefits and possible adverse consequences of these dietary recommendations are suggested, with the caveat that these guidelines might change with future research. These quantitative guidelines are shown in Table 2-4, as are the recommendations from the *Surgeon General's Report*.

NATIONAL OBJECTIVES

Since 1977 several bodies within the National Institutes of Health have sponsored conferences dealing with a variety of timely medical and public health issues of interest to nutritionists. Recent conferences have dealt with obesity,[38] blood cholesterol and heart disease,[39] and non-insulin dependent diabetes.[40]

The 1990 nutrition objectives, an outgrowth of *Healthy People*,[41] were designed during a 1979 conference in which experts in nutrition and other public health fields participated.[42] Of the 226 objectives generated at this conference, 17 were ultimately included in a chapter devoted to nutrition. Of these objectives, three aimed to improve maternal and child nutritional health, and six focused on reducing diet-related risk factors for chronic diseases. One objective called for a national system to monitor both the progress of achievement toward the other 16 objectives and other indicators of nutritional status.[43]

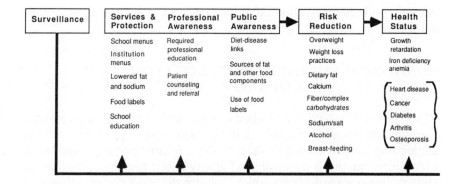

Figure 2-4 Priority Areas for Year 2000 Nutrition Objectives (Proposed). *Source*: Reprinted from *Promoting Health/Preventing Disease: Year 2000 Objectives for the Nation*, Draft for Public Review and Comment, US Department of Health and Human Services, Washington, D.C., 1989.

Promoting Health/Preventing Disease: Year 2000 Objectives for the Nation is being published in 1990. Chapter 1, "Nutrition," proposes 24 objectives of interest to nutritionists who are assessing their communities (Chapters 3 and 4) and setting objectives for planning programs and services (Chapter 14). Nutritionists should also study and use the nutrition-related objectives in the chapters on physical activity and fitness; maternal and infant health; immunization and infectious disease (foodborne illnesses), high blood cholesterol, and high blood pressure; cancer; other chronic diseases; oral health; health education and preventive services; and surveillance and data systems.

For each objective, baseline and data sources are suggested for use to monitor national progress. Figure 2-4 summarizes the priority areas in the nutrition chapter, organizing the objectives in categories that represent inputs or processes such as services and protection, professional awareness, and public awareness and outcomes in terms of levels of risk reduction and health status. To the extent possible, objectives are stated in quantitative or measurable terms. Surveillance is proposed through the components of the National Nutrition Monitoring System (see Chapter 16). These objectives, derived from the 1990 objectives for nutrition, draw on the recently published *Surgeon General's Report on Nutrition and Health*[44] and the National Academy of Sciences' report on *Diet and Health*.[45] Fundamental to achievement of the nutrition objectives are (1) a strong national program of basic and applied nutrition research, (2) enhancement of the scope and magnitude of the National Nutrition Monitoring System, (3) more and improved nutrition information and education for the public, and (4) more intensive and sustained efforts to implement and monitor achievement of the year 2000 objectives.[46]

MONITORING NUTRITION RESEARCH LITERATURE FOR PUBLIC HEALTH APPLICATIONS

Deciding how, whether, and when new research should be implemented in community programs requires that the nutritionist monitor the nutrition science literature to keep up to date. With the information explosion in the scientific world, this is no small task! Every public health nutrition office must maintain a mini-library which includes the most recent editions of several nutrition science textbooks. (See Appendix N.) These should include texts authored by respected nutrition researchers and one or more college-level nutrition textbooks that interpret the information in "user friendly" language. The 1988 *Surgeon General's Report on Nutrition and Health*[47] summarizes the state of the nutrition research for the various stages of the life cycle and the major public health problems. Each chapter has extensive bibliographies current at the time of publication. *Diet and Health: Implications for Reducing Chronic Disease Risk*[48] provides another summary of current research and a current bibliography. It is useful to note the similarities and differences in the interpretations of the scientific evidence and the recommendations made in these two reports.

Since the latest findings take time to get published in the textbooks, it is necessary to subscribe to current periodicals that report research. Recommended texts and periodicals are listed in the Public Health Nutrition Library in Appendix N. Several of the journals and newsletters contain abstracts of nutrition research for quick perusal, while the original research articles are identified for those desiring in-depth study.

Information obtained from reading, attending courses, or consulting with university faculty or nutrition consultants from federal or state agencies must be synthesized into concepts that can be defended. Regardless of how justifiable the research findings may appear, that they will be unanimously accepted and agreed to by all nutrition scientists and practitioners is unlikely. Skills in critical thinking, the ability to weigh the evidence, and confidence in one's professional judgment are important competencies for nutritionists to develop.

ISSUES TO DEBATE

- What compelling scientific evidence justifies the inclusion of nutrition and diet in the planning and implementing of a community risk-reduction program?

- Do professional judgment and common sense support acting on the scientific evidence available on such issues as salt and fiber when some controversy exists?
- Do the investigators who question the findings under debate have any known biases that might account for their divergent opinions?
- How should the public be educated about adequate intake of nutrients at a caloric level that maintains their desirable body weight?
- How can the nutritionist explain to the public the similarities and differences among the various versions of dietary guidelines being promoted by various official and voluntary health agencies?

NOTES

1. E. Niege Todhunter, "Historical Landmarks in Nutrition," in *Nutrition Reviews' Present Knowledge in Nutrition* (Washington, D.C.: Nutrition Foundation, 1984), 871–82.

2. National Research Council, *Recommended Dietary Allowances*, Reprint and Circular Series, no. 115 (Washington, D.C.: National Academy of Sciences, 1943).

3. Lydia J. Roberts, "Beginnings of the Recommended Dietary Allowances," *Journal of the American Dietetic Association* 34 (1958): 903.

4. National Research Council, *Recommended Dietary Allowances*, 10th ed. (Washington, D.C.: National Academy Press, 1989), vii.

5. Ibid., 2–8.

6. G.H. Beaton, "Uses and Limits of the Use of the Recommended Dietary Allowances for Evaluating Dietary Intake Data," *American Journal of Clinical Nutrition 41* (January 1985): 155–64.

7. G. Harvey Anderson, R. Dewey Peterson, and George H. Beaton, "Estimating Nutrient Deficiencies in a Population from Dietary Records: The Use of Probability Analyses," *Nutrition Research* 2 (1982): 409.

8. Alfred E. Harper, "Recommended Dietary Allowances in Perspective," *Food and Nutrition News* 58, no. 2 (March–April 1986): 7.

9. Harper, "Recommended Dietary Allowances."

10. Committee on Diet, Nutrition and Cancer, Assembly of Life Sciences, National Research Council, *Diet, Nutrition and Cancer* (Washington, D.C.: National Academy Press, 1982), 1–15.

11. Food and Nutrition Board, National Research Council, National Academy of Sciences, "Dietary Allowances: Scientific Issues and Process for the Future," *Journal of Nutrition Education* 18, no. 2 (1986): 82–87.

12. Ibid.

13. Walter Mertz, "The Essential Trace Elements," *Science* 213 (1981): 1332–38.

14. Maxine Briggs, "Vitamin C and Infectious Disease," in *Recent Vitamin Research*, ed. Michael H. Briggs (Boca Raton, Fla.: CRC Press, 1984), 39–81.

15. Ibid.

16. T.K. Basu and C.J. Schorah, *Vitamin C in Health and Disease* (Westport, Conn.: Avi Publishing Co., 1982), 38, 93, 104. Reginald Passmore, "How Vitamin C Deficiency Injures the

Body," *Nutrition Today* 12, no. 2 (1977): 6.

17. Basu and Schorah, *Vitamin C.*

18. American Cancer Society, *Nutrition and Cancer: Cause and Prevention.* American Cancer Society Special Report (New York: American Cancer Society, 1984).

19. Bonita W. Wyse, Carol T. Windham, and G. Gaurth Hansen, "Nutrition Intervention: Panacea or Pandora's Box?" *Journal of the American Dietetic Association* 85, no. 9 (September 1985): 1084–90.

20. Ibid.

21. National Research Council, *Recommended Dietary Allowances,* Reprint and Circular Series.

22. Kristen McNutt, "Dietary Advice to the Public: 1957 to 1980," *Nutrition Reviews* 38 (1980): 353–60. Doris Derelian, "The Four Food Groups: An Instructional Tool for Adults," *Nutrition News* 51, no. 1 (Spring 1988): 1.

23. Norman Jolliffe, Seymour H. Rinzler, and Morton Archer, "The Anti-Coronary Club: Including a Discussion of the Effects of a Prudent Diet on the Serum Cholesterol Level of Middle Aged Men," *American Journal of Clinical Nutrition* 7 (1959): 451.

24. Ibid.

25. Senate Select Committee on Nutrition and Human Needs, *Dietary Goals for the United States,* 2d ed. (Washington, D.C.: Government Printing Office, 1977).

26. Ibid.

27. D. Mark Hegsted, "Priorities in Nutrition in the United States," *Journal of the American Dietetic Association* 71 (1977): 9.

28. U.S. Department of Health and Human Services, *Healthy People: The Surgeon General's Report on Health Promotion and Disease Prevention* (Washington, D.C.: Government Printing Office, 1979), section 25.

29. McNutt, "Dietary Advice."

30. U.S. Department of Agriculture and U.S. Department of Health and Human Services, *Nutrition and Your Health: Dietary Guidelines for Americans* (Washington, D.C.: Government Printing Office, 1980).

31. Food and Nutrition Board, National Research Council, *Toward Healthful Diets* (Washington, D.C.: National Academy Press, 1980).

32. Ibid.

33. Ibid.

34. American Heart Association, "Dietary Guidelines for Healthy American Adults," *Circulation* 77 (March, 1988): 3.

35. U.S. Department of Health and Human Services, *Surgeon General's Report on Nutrition and Health* (Washington, D.C.: Government Printing Office, 1988).

36. National Academy of Sciences, *Diet and Health: Implications for Reducing Chronic Disease Risk* (Washington, D.C.: National Academy Press, 1989).

37. Food and Nutrition Board, *Toward Healthful Diets.*

38. National Institutes of Health, "National Institutes of Health Consensus Development Panel on Health Implications of Obesity, National Institutes of Health Consensus Development Conference Statement," *Annals of Internal Medicine* 103 (1985): 1073–77.

39. National Cholesterol Education Program, "Report of National Cholesterol Education Program Expert Panel on Detection and Evaluation and Treatment of High Blood Choles-

terol in Adults," *Archives of Internal Medicine* 148 (1988): 36-39.

40. National Institutes of Health, "Diet and Exercise in Non-Insulin Dependent Diabetes Mellitus," *Consensus Development Conference Statement* 6, no. 8 (December 19, 1986).

41. U.S. Department of Health and Human Services, *Healthy People.*

42. Marion Nestle, "Promoting Health and Preventing Disease: National Nutrition Objectives for 1990 and 2000," *Nutrition Today* 23 (1988): 26.

43. U.S. Department of Health and Human Services, *Promoting Health, Preventing Disease, Objectives for the Nation* (Washington, D.C.: Government Printing Office, 1980), 73–77.

44. U.S. Department of Health and Human Services, *Surgeon General's Report.*

45. National Academy of Sciences, *Diet and Health.*

46. Department of Health and Human Services, Public Health Service, *Promoting Health/ Preventing Disease: Year 2000 Objectives for the Nation* (Washington, D.C.: September 1989, Draft for public review and comment), 1–1 to 1–24.

47. U.S. Department of Health and Human Services, *Surgeon General's Report.*

48. National Academy of Sciences, *Diet and Health.*

BIBLIOGRAPHY

Monsen, E.R., and Cheney, C.L. "Research Methods in Nutrition and Dietetics: Design, Data Analysis and Presentation." *Journal of the American Dietetic Association* 88, no. 9 (September 1988): 1047–65.

National Research Council. *Diet and Health Implications for Reducing Chronic Disease Risk.* Washington, D.C.: National Academy Press, 1989.

U.S. Department of Health and Human Services. *The Surgeon General's Report on Nutrition and Health.* Washington, D.C.: Government Printing Office, 1988.

part II

Assessing the Community's Needs

chapter 3

Assessing the Community's Needs for Nutrition Services

Mildred Kaufman

READER OBJECTIVES

- Define community as it is used by the public health worker.
- List terms frequently used to describe community needs assessment.
- Describe the usefulness of subjective data to the public health nutrition planner.
- Specify readily available objective data that can be used for a community nutrition needs assessment.
- Discuss the process of determining community capacity for meeting nutrition needs of the population.
- Compare and contrast the assessed needs with the capacity of existing community agencies to meet these needs.

MANY DIFFERENT PEOPLE, MANY DIFFERENT NEEDS

Many contemporary public health problems are now being associated with dietary and nutritional inadequacies, excesses, or imbalances. To plan interventions to address the most urgent concerns in a specific community, the first step is to collect and analyze data in order to rank the issues in a priority order that can be justified. Major public health problems that particularly merit the attention of nutritionists are

- hunger and malnutrition
- teenage pregnancy
- low birth weight
- infant mortality
- birth defects

- developmental delays and disabilities
- failure to thrive
- obesity
- heart disease, hypertension, and stroke
- diabetes
- diet-related cancers
- high-risk life styles and diets

Nutritionists must also ask what community agencies are providing services to the populations at risk, how well they are serving those in need, and what the role of the public health agency is.

Funding and personnel are never adequate to address all of the needs observed. Community assessment or diagnosis is the key to setting priorities for the use of resources. Understanding and responding to community values, life styles, perceived needs, resources, and politics pave the way to winning support for selected intervention programs. Basing the plan on the community diagnosis assures that nutrition services respond to the most urgent needs and concerns of the people.

Communities are defined as groups of people who share common characteristics. The community of interest used in planning public health programs usually has geographic boundaries. It is frequently a politically designated jurisdiction such as a zip code, neighborhood, census tract, village, town, city, county, state, or nation. Within its boundaries the official or tax-supported health agency has mandated responsibilities for assuring services to protect and promote the health of the people who live, work, or visit within it.

A community may also be defined as a group of people who share common needs or interests. Many of the principles of community assessment may be applied to a clinic, catchment area, parish, school district, or target population with similar problems such as the same disease or disability.

The process of assembling and analyzing both subjective observations and objective statistics in order to present the profile of the community's needs and concerns is called by several names, all with similar intent.

- community assessment
- needs assessment
- community profile
- community diagnosis
- market research

Community assessment is used by many health and human service public and private agency planners, as well as by businesses (which call it market research). Community assessment looks at the community ecology using a systems approach to take in the "big picture." Because it uses statistics that are readily available and accessible, community assessment is the most cost-effective way to collect data. However, since much of the data may not be specific to nutrition and diet, the nutritionist must relate the available data to nutrition and diet issues. The nutritionist talks with many colleagues in the agency, as well as with key informants in other agencies, in colleges and universities, in local businesses, in community organizations, and in the legislative bodies to learn what pertinent, useful, and reliable information is available, both published and unpublished. It saves considerable time and energy to determine what information others might have and might be willing to share before embarking on an extensive, time-consuming search for data. The nutritionist focuses on data associated with conditions that relate to nutrition—for example, number of infants with low birth weight, number of people with income too low to buy adequate food.

It may appear logical to start by looking at statistical data sources for facts and figures. Recognizing that a mix of people makes up the community and that their individual and collective backgrounds, values, attitudes, life styles, and feelings and their ecology make the community "tick," a better understanding will probably be obtained by first gaining a more intuitive sense of the community.

"SOAPing the Body Politic," the concept introduced in Chapter 1, systemizes the collection of subjective and objective data and the analysis of this data to develop a prioritized problem list and plan. Comparing the food, nutrition, and health problems and the needs, concerns, and demands of the people with the capacity of existing agencies to respond places met, undermet, and unmet needs in focus. Listing the needs in a rank order problem list constitutes the diagnosis of the body politic.

SUBJECTIVE DATA: PERCEIVED NEEDS OF STAKEHOLDERS

A clinical SOAPing of a patient begins by observing and interviewing the individual to obtain a history and a current self-perception of health status, life style, values, feelings, and complaints. Similarly, in viewing the community as the patient, the public health worker tries to determine how the community feels about itself. However, when the community is the patient, there are many different perceptions, which may depend on how homogeneous or heterogeneous the population is.

The subjective assessment begins with a careful study of the mass media—reading the local newspapers, including those that serve the neighborhoods or ethnic groups; listening to the area radio stations, including those that target ethnic groups or special interests; and watching local television coverage. These media usually reflect local values, political views, interests, educational levels, and life styles.

By studying media coverage of meetings of local, state, and national governmental bodies, it is possible to determine the current "hot" issues and to identify the leaders and their opposing views. Public spending priorities show up in coverage of governmental budget hearings. The media present insights into the local economy and monitor employment and unemployment trends. They report the stresses and tensions among various ethnic, religious, or socioeconomic groups and social issues that arouse human interest. They often report sentinel events, such as stories about families who are hungry or homeless, adults and children with serious illnesses or disabilities, elderly persons coping with fixed incomes, or the plight of migrant farm workers. Food and health reporting reflects local food tastes, the latest diet fads, and the public's interest in fitness, diet, and exercise. Weekly supermarket ads provide information on plentiful foods and their prices. Reports and plans available from community agencies, civic groups, the Chamber of Commerce, or area planning agencies can be obtained to provide additional details on information covered by the media.

To get "in touch" with the community, it is useful to study the map of the jurisdiction with someone who knows the area well. This might be a professional who has had long experience in the agency, a geographer or an anthropologist from a local university, or a well-informed native of the area. This key informant can give history and background and point out the unique characteristics and idiosyncrasies of the geography and the people.

Collecting the subjective data requires all of the senses and sensitivities the public health worker can muster. Whether he or she is a newcomer to or a native of the area, it is timely to periodically travel around, listen to community people, and observe them in their environment. Much can be learned by walking or driving around the neighborhoods where people live, observing the type and quality of housing of rich, poor, and middle-income residents. Urban, suburban, and rural areas should be toured to look at the factories, businesses, farms, and other places of employment. The kinds and quality of shopping centers and stores may suggest the economy, tastes, life styles, prevailing age, and ethnic groups. The number, type, location, accessibility, and use of government buildings, senior citizen centers, schools, day care centers, places of worship, libraries, recreational and cultural facilities, health centers, hospitals, social services offices, and halfway houses reflect the values and quality of community life. The availability, routings, and cost of public transportation determine access to work places, shopping, and health and social services.

Visits to the various types of food markets and family-type cafeterias or restaurants inform the nutritionist about the price, quality, and choices of foods available, as well as the preferred regional or ethnic foods. Tasting the menu items featured in restaurants, schools, or group care facilities provides information on popular methods of food preparation and seasoning. Market or restaurant managers and food service directors can discuss what foods are preferred and any prevailing food beliefs or taboos. Conversing with many people provides insights into their perceptions of health and nutritional status and into their worries and aspirations for themselves and their children. These may be quite different from those reported by community leaders or health care providers. These explorations provide a sense of the flavor and color of community life, which is in constant flux.

More structured intelligence gathering might include soliciting community opinions through focus groups, a method used in social marketing. A focus group is a homogeneous group selected to be representative of a subpopulation in the community. A specific question or series of structured questions is posed to the group, soliciting their collective responses or recommendations. The leadership comes from within the group, while the professional sits outside the group as an observer and recorder.

Perceived problems and needs for nutrition services also can be solicited by interviews with professional colleagues in the health agency to ascertain their perspectives on the community.

- Health directors or administrators, public health physicians, and health planners will express their priorities and opinions regarding the role of nutrition services in the health agency's programs. They can share their knowledge of community health care services and facilities. They know the power structure, elected officials, and leaders. They may provide copies of special studies or surveys conducted in the area by federal, state, or local governmental agencies, legislative study groups, contract consultants, or universities. They can provide long- and short-term agency plans, grant proposals, and annual reports with informative statistics and descriptive information.
- Health educators are skilled in community organization and networks. They understand the political system and the power structure. They can identify knowledgeable contacts in state or local government, other health and human service agencies, schools, churches, businesses, and neighborhoods. They have insights into the interests

in fitness, nutrition, and health of the various subpopulations in the area. In their files they may have useful, up-to-date facts and figures.

- Public health nurses know the community through their close contacts with clients, families, schools, industries, clinics, and other health care facilities. Working within agency policies on confidentiality, their client and family health records may be reviewed to gather information on the health and nutritional status of the women they serve in family planning and prenatal clinics; the infants and children receiving well- or ill-child or special health care services; the adults seen for screening or primary care; the children enrolled in day care or schools; and the elderly or chronically ill patients visited for home health services. They can share their observations regarding prevalence of "failure to thrive" infants and families who are homeless or hungry, as well as local food habits, nutrition knowledge, and diet fads. Client and family records are confidential and must be treated carefully, using only aggregated data and not identifying any individuals.

- Environmentalists and sanitarians know the housing conditions in local neighborhoods, including whether kitchens have indoor plumbing, working ranges, and refrigerators. They know the safety of the public and private water supplies. They also can provide information on the safety, sanitation, and quality of the food services in the schools, child day care centers, hospitals, nursing homes, jails, and other group care facilities, and in public eating establishments and food markets.

Others in the community who can also provide useful assessment information

- Human service agency directors and social workers know the financial status, food and housing needs, and expenditures of individuals and families. They are aware of the prevalence of personal and family emotional and social stresses, including alcohol and drug use; child, spouse, and elder abuse; and special needs of single-parent families. They can describe the ethnic and religious mix and its influence on community relations. They can list and describe the public and private agencies and institutions that provide food and financial assistance; food stamps; emergency food and shelter; and mental health and family counseling to residents, immigrants, and migrants. They know or can advise on how to find out about eligibility and application procedures for the various services and their caseloads.

- Hospital administrators and their staff can provide access to data on hospital discharges and on any existing or anticipated community services. Clinical dietitians can discuss diagnostic categories of patients they serve and the distribution of therapeutic diets served in the hospital and among patients discharged to home health agencies.

- Health maintenance organization administrators often have extensive information on the health status and educational needs of the population they serve. Where dietitians are employed in HMOs, they can provide data on age groups and diagnoses of their clients.
- School superintendents and principals can approve access to school health records. They can introduce the nutritionist to teachers and school food service directors who observe the health and growth of children and know the children who come to school hungry. They can provide data on participation in school feeding programs and nutrition education and on the numbers of free and reduced-priced meals served. Special educators and school counselors and psychologists can describe the problems of children with developmental disabilities, social and emotional needs, eating disorders, or other nutrition-related health conditions.
- Cooperative extension specialists include agronomists who have information on local crops, growing conditions, and family gardens. Extension home economists know the practices and competencies of area homemakers in meal planning, food purchasing, food preparation, use of food stamps, and other areas of family life.
- Local television, radio, or newspaper medical or science reporters can share extensive community profiles with useful statistics and human interest stories.
- The clergy of local churches and synagogues may share information on the food needs and health status of the people in their congregations. Some of the families in their congregations may need and use soup kitchens, shelters, and food pantries.

Exhibit 3-1 suggests a format for recording, organizing, and scaling the subjective assessment data from these various community informants. The subjective data deal largely with the individual and group opinions, beliefs, attitudes, life styles, and feelings of the people interviewed. This type of information is used to help understand and interpret community behavior and to identify barriers and facilitators that must be handled. In program planning it is used as a beginning for involving the stakeholders and as a basis for developing programs that respond to their perceived needs and that they will accept and claim as their own.

Exhibit 3-1 Subjective Data: Community Nutrition Assessment

	Perceived Nutrition Needs in the Community	Attitude toward Nutrition Services			Knowledge of Nutrition		
	List	+	0	−	+	0	−
Clients/Patients							
Public							
Media							
Government Officials							
Agency Administrators							
Physicians/ Dentists							
Hospital Administrators							
Nurses							
Health Educators							
Nutritionists/ Dietitians							
Agency Board Members							
Principals/ Teachers							
Social Workers							
Clergy							

Code + = positive, supportive attitude toward nutrition and health services
      0 = neutral or apathetic attitude toward nutrition
      − = negative attitude toward nutrition

OBJECTIVE DATA: STATISTICAL INDICATORS THAT POINT TO NEEDS

In SOAPing the body politic, objective facts and figures are collected to determine what is known about the community's population in the aggregate as compared with what is known about individuals. Readily available demographic statistics may not be specific for nutrition, but can point the planner to populations who may be at risk for nutrition-related or diet-related health problems because of age, income, education, or diagnosis. Demographic statistics are obtained from publications reporting the national decennial census. As the decade progresses, estimates are projected by the state demographer.

For much of the assessment, the statistic that is the reference point or denominator for comparisons with the other data is the total population or the number of residents living in the jurisdiction. In areas where the population is seasonally enlarged by an influx of students, summer or winter residents, tourists, or migrant workers who use health and nutrition services, their numbers must be known and factored in. The population figure can be distributed according to the following demographic characteristics:

- age—infants, preschool children, school age children, adolescents, adults in the middle years, women of childbearing age, elderly, aged
- gender or sex—female, male
- ethnic groups—white, nonwhite; with additional breakdowns for black, Hispanic, Asian, and American Indian
- education—number of years of school completed by adults over age 18
- income—numbers or percentages of individuals who live on incomes at various levels above and below the current poverty index (see Chapter 4)
- employed and unemployed—number or percentage of the work force (see Chapter 4).

Exhibit 3-2 provides a format to organize these data.

Vital statistics on births and deaths that are reported to the state health agency are also used in the community assessment. All births and deaths are recorded through a local registrar or clerk, usually in the city or county health department. Because these registrations are mandated by law, data obtained from birth and death certificates cover virtually the entire population and are a reliable statistical basis for community assessment. Newborn birth weights aggregated from birth certificates make it possible to deter-

Exhibit 3-2 Objective Data: Demographic Data

1. Age distribution

Age	Male %	Female %	Ethnic/Racial Composition	%	Completed Years of School	%
1–5 years			White		< 8 years	
6–18 years			Black		9–12 years	
19–64 years			Hispanic		> 13 years	
65–74 years			Asian			
75–84 years			American Indian			
> 85 years			Other			
Total population						

2. Family characteristics
    a. Average family size _____
    b. Families headed by female _____%
3. Socioeconomic data
    a. Area which is rural _____%, urban _____%, suburban _____%
    b. Major industries or sources of employment:

    _____

    _____

    _____

    _____

    c. Employment
        Population employed _____%, unemployed _____%
4. Annual median income for family of four $_____, per capita income $_____

	%
Families living on incomes below the poverty index	
Female-headed households living on incomes below the poverty index	
Elderly (over 65) living on incomes below the poverty index	
Households on Aid to Families with Dependent Children (AFDC)	
Households on Supplemental Security Income (SSI) (elderly, blind, disabled)	
Medicaid eligible	

5. Housing characteristics

	# or %
Total housing units (number)	
Homes without indoor water (percentage)	
Homes without electricity (percentage)	
Homes without cooking facilities (percentage)	
Homeless (estimated number)	

mine numbers and percentages of infants born at a weight below 2,500 grams (considered low birth weight—LBW) or 1,500 grams (very low birth weight—VLBW) and to categorize the infants by gestational age and age and race of the mother. Death certificates document neonatal, postneonatal, and infant death rates. Infant birth and death certificates can be linked for such factors as low or very low birth weights, ages of the infants, and ethnicity of the mothers. To compare vital statistics from one geographic area to those of another (i.e., a city or county to the state and nation) or one population to another, various rates are calculated (see Exhibit 3-3).

Death certificates provide information on primary and secondary causes of death (mortality). Dietary factors are now linked with five of the ten leading causes of death in the United States. These are hypertension, heart disease, cancer, cirrhosis, and non-insulin-dependent diabetes mellitus. In the community assessment the rates of deaths from these diseases indicate the size of the local problem. Community death rates can be compared with other localities, the state, and the nation. Trends in rates observed in the local area over time may be used to monitor communitywide interventions.

Each state health agency has a state center or bureau of health statistics that publishes its data for the state as a whole. Many states publish their data for each county. These publications are available on request, usually at no cost. Some state statistical offices publish pocket guides and county data books, making the data needed for community assessment readily available

Exhibit 3-3　Calculating Rates To Compare Vital Statistics from One Area or Population to Another

$$\text{Birth rate} = \frac{\text{\# of live births}}{\text{population of area}} \times 1000$$

$$\text{Fetal mortality rate} = \frac{\text{\# of fetal deaths}}{\text{\# of live births} + \text{\# of fetal deaths in area}} \times 1000$$

$$\text{Infant mortality rate} = \frac{\text{\# of infant deaths}}{\text{\# of live births in area}} \times 1000$$

$$\text{Death rate} = \frac{\text{\# of deaths}}{\text{population of area}} \times 1000$$

in a user-friendly format. Statisticians and epidemiologists in state and local health agencies are usually available as consultants to help in the appropriate use and interpretation of data. They may assist in sorting the data into more usable formats. Health statistics should be obtained for the most recent year available, but there may be a two- to three-year lag time between collection and publication. If data for the local area, state, and nation are to be compared, it is necessary to obtain and compare data for the same year, recognizing that to get all the data needed for comparison it may be necessary to go back several years.

Public health nutritionists looking for specific nutrition and dietary status data may use available secondary data sources, collected by national and state organizations or by universities experienced in statistical sampling methodology. The National Health and Nutrition Examination Survey (NHANES) directed by the National Center for Health Statistics meticulously collects data by administering a battery of nutritional and health status measures to a national probability sample of the population. Synthetic estimates for states and local areas with large populations can be calculated by adjusting the data for age, gender, ethnicity, and income, as discussed in Chapter 16 and Table 16-1. These estimates make it possible to project the prevalence of obesity, impaired growth status, hypertension, high-risk serum cholesterol, diabetes, stunted growth, low serum vitamins A and C, and use of vitamin and mineral supplements.

Disease prevalence (numbers of people in the population living with a communicable or chronic disease) and disease incidence (new cases of a disease) would be very useful community assessment data to have for planning. Since the nutrition-related chronic diseases are not required to be reported to the official health agency, prevalence or incidence data are not easily available. Hospital discharge data provide useful indicators or clues. If resources permit, special surveys can be conducted on random population samples or samples of convenience, as discussed in Chapter 16. Exhibit 3-4 provides a framework to display the available data.

The clinician assesses a client's nutritional status, collecting observable data using the following generally accepted parameters, which are described in more detail in Simko, Cowell, and Gilbride's *Nutrition Assessment: A Comprehensive Guide to Planning Intervention*[1]:

- Anthropometric or body measurements such as height, weight, skinfolds, and infant head circumference. These measures indicate normal or abnormal growth patterns, undernutrition, overweight, or obesity.
- Biochemical tests done in the laboratory using standardized procedures to measure levels of nutrients in body fluids. Most common procedures used in public health programs are hemoglobin and hema-

Exhibit 3-4 Objective Data: Nutrition- and Diet-Related Health Problems

Health statistical indicators for the last year reported: _____								
Pregnancy outcome		Total	W	NW	Perinatal/infant mortality rates			
						Total	W	NW
Live births, number					Fetal			
% low birth weight (under 2500 grams)					Neonatal			
					Postneonatal			
% mothers under 17 years					Infant			

Leading causes of deaths	Number			Rates			Prevalence rates for leading nutrition-related health problems-- synthetic estimate from NHANES data		
	Total	W	NW	Total	W	NW			
1.								Estimated Rates	
2.								Total	W	NW
3							1. Obesity			
4							2. Cardiovascular disease			
5							3. Hypertension			
6							4. Cancer			
7							5. Stroke			
8							6. Diabetes			
9							7. Cirrhosis			
10							8. Iron deficiency anemia			

Other pertinent nutrition-related health problems:

W = White   NW = Nonwhite

tocrit to measure iron nutriture, serum cholesterol or triglycerides to assess cardiovascular disease risk, or blood glucose to screen for diabetes risk or to measure its control.

- Clinical or physical examination for signs and symptoms of severe malnutrition that may be particularly observable as abnormalities of the skin, hair, mouth, eyes, or face.

- Dietary intake obtained by interview, self-administered written questionnaire, or computer-assisted program for a food record, 24-hour or usual day's intake, or quantified food frequency. These records may be quickly assessed by use of a food group guide or by computer to determine the calories, carbohydrate, protein, fat, and alcohol consumed and the relative adequacy of essential vitamins and minerals. Nutrient density and distribution of foods in the usual diet may also be of interest.

- Economic, social, and environmental factors that influence the client's access to food and resources for food storage and preparation are also obtained by interview. (See Chapters 4 and 16.)

Ideally for the community assessment, individual nutritional assessment data collected from all clients from one or more clinics, health centers, hospitals, health care facilities, schools, day care centers, work sites, or congregate meal sites should be aggregated. If systematically recorded, tabulated, analyzed by demographic characteristics, and interpreted, such data could be useful in describing the nutritional status of the specific populations from whom they are collected. Such a process is labor intensive and expensive, and it requires extensive training to collect such primary data in a way that represents an entire population and to collect it using standardized procedures and reporting methods. When these data are used, their limitations must be explained clearly.

The Centers for Disease Control (CDC) Pediatric and Pregnancy Nutrition Surveillance Systems are examples of systems that collect and compare anthropometric and iron nutriture data on selected health agency clients. (See Table 16-1.) State or local client data systems used for the Special Supplemental Food Program for Women, Infants, and Children (WIC) or statewide computerized maternal and child health or adult client health or health services information systems might collect and report nutritional data for specific populations served. (See Chapter 16.) Similarly, data might be collected to describe the nutritional status either of Medicaid-eligible children assessed in a local/state Early Periodic Screening, Diagnostic, and Treatment Program (EPSDT) or of schoolchildren, whether or not they are part of the CDC Nutrition Surveillance Systems.

ASSESSING THE CAPACITY OF EXISTING COMMUNITY RESOURCES

The assessment must also determine the capacity of existing agencies to provide food and nutrition services needed by the community's people. These include agencies that provide

- diet counseling, nutrition education, and health care
- health promotion with weight management, nutrition education, and exercise programs
- food stamps, financial aid, emergency food or meals, supplemental food
- housing and emergency shelter
- nutrition and consumer education and homemaking skill development
- mass media nutrition education

Many communities support a community coordinating council or an information and referral system with the responsibility of both monitoring community services and linking individuals and families to the services they need. Computerized data banks or printed directories are useful in learning about the capacity of agencies and in making an inventory of community resources.

Information needed for the community assessment includes

- brief descriptive information on the specific population and services provided and whether the services meet long- or short-term needs
- eligibility criteria for the service
- current caseloads and numbers on waiting lists for each specific food assistance or nutrition service

If a printed directory or computerized data bank is not available, detailed assessment information may be gained through a personal or telephone interview with the director or a responsible staff member of each agency or institution. Exhibit 3-4 is a useful format to organize and display data on the community's resources and to show to what degree services reach all those who need them.

DEVELOPING THE COMMUNITY'S NUTRITION PROBLEM LIST

Using the community data base created from the subjective and objective data displayed in formats such as those shown in Exhibits 3-1, 3-2, 3-4, and 3-5, the community nutrition problem list can be prepared. The nutrition problem list would compare and rank the needs identified by the subjective data on perceived or felt needs with those emerging from the objective data.

Exhibit 3-5 Community Food, Nutrition, and Health Resources

Food Assistance Programs			Health Care Facilities/Services		
Program	# Programs	# Participants		#	# beds
Food stamps			Hospitals		
Child day care food programs			Nursing homes		
School breakfast			Other (specify)		
School lunch			Group Care Facilities		
Special summer feeding				# Facilities	# Residents
			Residential facilities		
Congregate meals			Child care		
Home delivered meals			Elderly		
			Drug abuse		
Food pantries			Alcoholic rehabilitation		
Soup kitchens			Homeless shelters		
Other (specify)			Jails		
Supplemental feeding programs			Youth Offender		
WIC Women			Community Health Agencies		
Infants				#	# of registered patients
Children					
Commodity Supplemental Food Program (CSFP)			Community health centers		
Women			Home health agencies		
Infants			Hospices		
Children			Other, list		
Elderly					
Educational Facilities					
				#	Enrollment
Public Schools			Elementary		
			Secondary		
Private Schools			Elementary		
			Secondary		
Colleges/Universities			2-year		
			4-year		
Vocational Training/Adult Education					

Resources for Nutrition Education/Diet Counseling	# Available	# Served
City/County Health Department		
Community Health Center		
Health Maintenance Organizations (HMOs)		
Head Start		
Cooperative Extension		
Industry-Sponsored Worksite Wellness Programs		
Private Practice RDs		
Weight Management Programs		
Other (specify)		

	#	Competitive Prices		Variety of Nutritious Foods	Nutrition Information Available
		Yes	No		
Food Markets					
Supermarkets					
Small neighborhood stores					
Convenience stores					
Other (specify)					

In smaller jurisdictions the problem list may reflect a communitywide concern. In more densely populated or more geographically spread out jurisdictions, nutrition problems may be targeted to census tracts, neighborhoods, postal zip code areas, or ethnic or age groups where there are concentrated high-risk populations. As needs are quantified, they should be compared and contrasted with the capacity of existing agencies to meet the needs. The community problem list to be used for program planning would balance subjective and objective data with informed professional judgment and pragmatism. There is no universal formula or blueprint for ranking or selecting priorities. The assessment serves as a guide to make and justify rational choices. It should be used as a basis for discussion with all of the stakeholders who participate in developing the plan. Since the community assessment must be updated periodically, it is useful to maintain the data base on a computer. Then new statistics can be readily inserted on a regular schedule.

ISSUES TO DEBATE

- What is the relative value of conducting the periodic community assessment in relation to other demands on the nutritionist's time?
- When time and resources are limited, what are the most important and readily available data to use?
- How can nutritionists use generic data available about the socioeconomic status and health conditions in the community to infer the nutritional health status of the population?
- Having collected community assessment data, what criteria should be used to rank the problems to be addressed in the program plan?

NOTE

1. M.D. Simko, C. Cowell, and J.A. Gilbride, Nutrition Assessment: A Comprehensive Guide to Planning Intervention (Rockville, Md: Aspen Publishers, Inc., 1984).

BIBLIOGRAPHY

Chamberlin, R.W. *Beyond Individual Risk Assessment: Community Wide Approaches to Promoting the Health and Development of Families and Children*. Washington, D.C.: National Center for Education in Maternal and Child Health, 1988.

Christakis, G., ed. *Nutritional Assessment in Health Programs*. Washington, D.C.: American Public Health Association, 1973, 1–10.

Dignan, M.B., and Carr, P.A. *Program Planning for Health Education and Health Promotion.* Philadelphia: Lea and Febiger, 1987. Chapter 2, "Community Analysis," 17–50.

Food Research and Action Center. *How To Document Hunger in Your Community.* Washington, D.C.: FRAC, 1983.

Leavell, H.R., and Gurney, E.C. *Preventive Medicine for the Doctor in His Community,* 3d ed. New York: McGraw-Hill Book Co., 1965.

Paige, D.M., and Davis, L.R. "Nutritional Assessment: An Index to the Quality of Life." *Clinical Nutrition* 7 (March–April 1988): 77.

Robertson, G.C., ed. *Guide for a Community Health Diagnosis: A Special Report for Local Health Departments.* Raleigh: State Center for Health Statistics, North Carolina Department of Human Resources, undated.

Ross Laboratories. *Nutritional Screening and Assessment as Components of Hospital Admission, Report of the Eighth Ross Roundtable on Medical Issues.* Columbus, Ohio: Ross Laboratories, 1988.

Simko, M.D., Cowell, C., and Gilbride, J.A. *Nutrition Assessment: A Comprehensive Guide to Planning Intervention.* Rockville, Md.: Aspen Publishers, Inc., 1984. Chapter 4, "The Nutrition Profile as a Tool for Identifying Who Needs Nutritional Care," 37–55.

Simopoulos, A.P. "Assessment of Nutritional Status." *American Journal of Clinical Nutrition* 35 (Supplement) (May 1982): 5.

Yetley, E., and Johnson, C. "Nutritional Applications of the Health and Nutrition Examination Surveys (HANES)." *Annual Review of Nutrition* 7 (1987): 441.

Reaching Out to Those at Highest Risk

Catherine Boisvert-Walsh and *Jan Kallio*

READER OBJECTIVES

- List social and environmental factors that increase the risk of malnutrition in communities, families, and individuals.
- Compare and contrast these social and environmental factors, their causes, and their impact on nutritional status.
- Discuss the vulnerability factors to be investigated in assessing communities, families, and individuals.
- Suggest the knowledge and skills needed by the nutritionist to respond to these factors.
- Describe the community services that provide food, financial assistance, housing, education, and health care.

DEFINING VULNERABILITY FACTORS

A vulnerability factor is a biological, economic, environmental, or social insult that increases risk. Factors that place individuals, families, and communities at risk must be investigated and described in the community assessment. Social and environmental factors that contribute to nutritional risk include

- poverty
- unemployment and underemployment
- deficits in education and job skills
- illiteracy
- inability to speak English

- cultural barriers
- homelessness, substandard housing
- hunger
- geographic or social isolation

These complex societal issues require the concerted attention of all those who are concerned about the quality of community life. The immediate needs of families and individuals are a shared responsibility of the interdisciplinary teams and networks that provide health and human services. Many clients and their families are known to multiple caregivers and agencies. Collection of assessment data can be coordinated in a family record or computer data base that is shared with all the workers who have a legitimate reason to use it. Clients and families should be spared the hassle and embarrassment of responding to the same questions from each service provider. All who use the data must be committed to maintaining confidentiality.

POVERTY

Poverty income guidelines were first set in 1964, using an index developed by Mollie Orshansky of the Social Security Administration. Findings of the 1955 U.S. Department of Agriculture (USDA) National Food Consumption Study indicated that at that time the average American family spent approximately one-third of its net income for food. Therefore, the poverty line was established at three times the cost of the USDA's Low Cost Food Plan for a family of four. In 1974 the USDA established the Thrifty Food Plan, using even more economical food choices than for the Low Cost Food Plan. The Thrifty Food Plan (also used to calculate food stamp allowances) is now multiplied by three and adjusted for the size of the family unit and the current consumer price index in order to calculate the official poverty income guidelines each year. These guidelines are used by federal agencies as criteria for eligibility for various federal assistance programs and as a basis for compiling data on poverty.[1] Table 4-1 shows the 1989 poverty income guidelines established and used by federal government agencies.

In 1987 an estimated 32.5 million individuals in the United States lived in poverty, defined that year for a family of four as having an annual income of less than $11,200. One in three black Americans (33.1 percent) and one in four Hispanics (28.2 percent) lived in poverty.[2] The poverty rate for the

Table 4-1   1989 Poverty Income Guidelines for All States (Except Alaska and Hawaii) and the District of Columbia

Size of Family Unit*	Poverty Guideline
1	$ 5,980
2	8,020
3	10,060
4	12,100
5	14,140
6	16,180
7	18,220
8	20,260

* For family units with more than 8 members, add $2,040 for each additional member.

Source: Federal Register, Vol. 54, No. 31, p. 7098, February 16, 1989.

---

elderly was 12.2 percent, which included one in three older black Americans and one in four elderly Hispanics.[3] One in every five children lived in poverty, including nearly one of every two black children and two of every five Hispanic children.[4] Statistics on poverty in the United States also show that the poor are growing poorer; in 1987 two of every five poor people had incomes below half of the poverty level.[5] These are the poorest of the poor who live on incomes under $5,600 per year for a family of four. And 5.4 million children (8.6 percent) live in these families.[6]

The infant mortality rate is three times higher among poor families than it is among nonpoor families.[7] More children living in poverty suffer from iron deficiency anemia, poor growth, dental caries, and lead poisoning.[8] Poor children are sick more often and are more likely to be hospitalized.[9] Hypertension, diabetes, and cardiovascular disease impair health and contribute to higher rates of disability and death more often among the poor than among those with higher incomes.[10]

Housing and utility costs may use up the major portion of the poor family's take-home pay, leaving them little or no money for food and other essentials. To understand the choices low-income families must make, their total income should be compared to their fixed costs for housing and utilities (heat, gas, electricity, water, telephone), medical care, transportation to and from work, and child care. This calculation will prove their urgent needs for financial and food assistance, job training, health care, and social service programs.

UNDEREMPLOYMENT AND UNEMPLOYMENT

More than half of the 32.5 million people living in poverty in 1987 lived in a household in which at least one member worked during the year. Five million lived in households where one member worked full time year-round.[11] Two out of three poor children live in households in which a family member is working.[12] A wage earner working 40 hours a week, 52 weeks a year, at the 1990 minimum wage of $3.80 per hour will earn $7,904 annually, about two-thirds of the 1989 poverty level income of $12,100 for a family of four. Even at the April 1991 minimum wage of $4.25 per hour, one wage earner will earn $8,840 annually, still well below the 1989 poverty level for a family of four. Furthermore, earning a minimum wage at a job may jeopardize a family's eligibility for public assistance and Medicaid benefits, while incurring costs for child care and transportation.

With the recent technological changes in U.S. industry, many blue-collar workers who thought they had secure jobs have been laid off. Needs of the newly unemployed differ from the needs of those who have been unemployed for extended periods of time. For the newly unemployed it is important to know if their income prior to unemployment was moderate, low, or below the poverty level; if their previous work had been continuous or sporadic; and if there is another wage earner in the household.

Assessment of the food intake prior to unemployment may show consistent adequacy or episodes when the individual or family had little or no food and their nutrient intake was poor. Individuals who have been unemployed for some time may have run out of unemployment benefits, as well as savings, gifts, or loans from relatives.

Eligibility requirements for benefits vary depending on whether the unemployed worker was laid off, on strike, or on medical disability. Recently unemployed individuals and working families are less likely to know about the available food and financial assistance programs and services and may not be familiar with their eligibility and application processes.

LACK OF EDUCATION AND ILLITERACY

Among adults in the United States, 17 percent of whites, 28 percent of blacks, and 45 percent of Hispanics and Native Americans have not graduated from high school.[13] Poor people, regardless of race, are more likely to drop out of school.[14] Nearly 20 percent of adult Americans (one out of every five) lack the literacy to function effectively in today's society, with reading skills below the fifth grade level. Another 34 percent of the population are considered marginally competent.[15] These adults generally have sufficient skills to cope with their usual daily activities but are not eligible for jobs that require reading and writing proficiency. In today's economy, most jobs require basic skills in reading, writing, and mathematics. As the educational requirements of jobs increase, people with less education do not qualify. For families in the cycle of inadequate education, unemployment, and poverty, improving the education of one or more family members can be the key to breaking this cycle.

Refugees and immigrants may have limited literacy in their own language, making learning to communicate in a new language even more difficult. They may learn to understand some English and to meet basic needs for daily living before they learn to speak, read, and write this new language.

Nutrition education interventions and materials must consider the clients' ability to speak, read, write, and comprehend English. The simple SMOG Readability Formula or Fry Graph Reading Level Index can be utilized to evaluate written materials to determine the appropriateness of their reading level.[16] Programs designed for individuals with limited education or poor reading skills should use "show and tell," participation, and hands-on activities. In a small group, participants may enjoy exchanging experiences and traditional foods, observing nutritious foods being prepared, tasting new foods, or being guided on a supermarket tour.

Programs presented to non-English-speaking populations must build on their cultural food preferences and customs. Written materials should use many colored pictures of food to communicate nutrition messages. Pictures and text should be field tested with the target audience to assure that the materials are acceptable to them and easy for them to understand. Videos, audiotapes, films, slide shows, skits, and demonstrations in the audience's language improve the health worker's ability to communicate with these clients.

CULTURAL BARRIERS

During the past three decades, political, social, cultural, religious, and economic oppression in Central America, South America, the Caribbean Islands, Eastern Europe, and Southeast Asia has brought an influx of refugees into the United States. An estimated 6.2 percent of the U.S. population (approximately 14.5 million people) are now foreign-born.[17] Each year approximately 570,000 immigrants enter the United States legally, and at least 200,000 more enter illegally.[18] New immigrants need guidance and support as they resettle in an adopted land.

Within each cultural group, patterns and practices of families and individuals differ according to their socioeconomic status, religion, education, and age when they immigrated to the United States. Immigrants face an unfamiliar choice of foods in large and impersonal supermarkets, more "high tech" kitchen equipment, and high prices for their traditional foods. They frequently give up their more nutrient-dense traditional foods in favor of U.S. snack foods and "fast foods." Many choose to feed their babies formula instead of following traditions of breast-feeding.

Religion, tradition, beliefs, taboos, medical uses and philosophies, and the traditional roles of family members influence food habits. Nutrition education for any ethnic group should begin with a study of the core foods that are a regular part of their daily diets, and should consider the nutrient contributions and typical preparation of these foods. This knowledge should serve as the beginning point for nutrition education, suggesting more emphasis on familiar or similar foods before introducing new foods.

Citizenship status affects family members' employability, income, and eligibility for tax-supported services. Immigrants and refugees who are not naturalized citizens or legal residents may have difficulty finding jobs with adequate pay or even finding work at all. They may hesitate to follow through on referrals to government assistance programs, because they fear deportation or future problems in obtaining citizenship. When working with undocumented clients, their fears and concerns must be respected. Professionals must know about program eligibility, make referrals on a case-by-case basis, and maintain the family's confidentiality.

HOUSING AND HOMELESSNESS

In the 1980s the dramatic rise in rents and housing costs, the decreased availability of newly built government-subsidized housing, and condominium conversion of much of the rental property have made housing unavailable or unaffordable to families who must live on a fixed income, limited budget, or public assistance allowance.

As housing costs rise beyond the means of low-income families and as affordable rental units are more difficult to obtain, many move in with friends and extended family. Families who are guests in someone else's household have little or no control over the kinds or quality of foods purchased or how foods are prepared.

Although they may have a roof over their heads, many poor families live in substandard housing, lacking an adequate refrigerator, range, oven, or running water to prepare foods. Facilities to wash dishes, pots, and pans may be inadequate. There may be improper food storage or trash and garbage disposal with rampant rodent and insect infestation. Old housing may have lead-containing paint that is peeling, cracked, or chipped. Lead poisoning can result in impaired growth, learning disabilities, and even mental retardation for infants and young children.

For some families the housing crisis has resulted in homelessness, a growing problem among women, children, and young families. Many homeless families are housed temporarily in hotels, motels, or shelters, while some find themselves on the street. Many mothers who live in shelters or on the street feel guilty when they are not able to prepare adequate, nutritious meals for their children. Some shelters for the homeless serve meals or provide refrigerators and possibly hot plates. However, many of the hotels and motels do not provide refrigerators, hot plates, group kitchens, or any place to store food, and they may even prohibit the use of small appliances to cook food in the rooms. These hotel and shelter residents may need to choose between spending their few dollars on high-priced restaurant or ready-to-eat foods and not eating.

Nutrition assessment identifies many of the problems communities, families, or individuals experience with housing, which directly relate to access to food. A recent study identified a high prevalence of underweight, short stature, and overweight in homeless children.[19] Nutritionists must identify potentially malnourished children and adults in the homeless population. They must advocate and assist in improving the availability of nutritious food for the homeless who live on the streets and in hotels, motels, or shelters. (See Chapter 11.)

HUNGER

Hunger has usually been defined by nutritionists as insufficient food to provide the calories and nutrients needed for activity, body function, and growth. A definition of hunger that has been suggested recently is lack of food security—food security being a condition in which people have access at all times to nutritionally adequate food from the customary food distributors, such as markets, gardens, restaurants, or fast-food outlets.[20] Food security includes both purchasing power and food availability. Another definition relates hunger to the federal poverty guidelines. Because these guidelines are linked to a family's ability to purchase a nutritionally adequate diet, households living on incomes below the poverty level index risk hunger.[21] Families with incomes above the poverty level index may also risk hunger when high costs for housing or utilities or excessive medical bills reduce the amount of money they have left to buy food.

Hunger has a devastating effect on people at any age, but it especially compromises the health of pregnant women and their developing fetuses, the growth and emotional development of infants and children, and the health and functioning of the elderly. The effects of hunger may be measured in terms of low birth weight, infant mortality, impaired growth, iron deficiency anemia, and other indicators of malnutrition. Social consequences attributed to hunger include incurring debt to buy food, stealing food or money to buy food, skipping meals, and sending children to eat with friends or relatives.[22]

The community assessment should identify the percentage of the population living on incomes below the poverty index, the cost of housing in the community, the location and kinds of local markets, and the quality and prices of the foods they offer. To assess the extent of hunger in the community, data are needed on local food costs, household resources to obtain and prepare food, and barriers that constrain individuals or families in obtaining adequate food. In poor urban neighborhoods and isolated rural areas, access of families to supermarkets and small neighborhood markets needs to be explored. Neighborhood markets often charge higher prices for foods of limited variety and quality. Culturally preferred foods may be unavailable or costly.

Using food security as a definition for hunger enables policy makers to focus on food purchasing power and food availability to families in their community. This perspective makes it possible to detect and measure the extent of hunger, develop strategies to alleviate the problem, and monitor progress in its elimination.

The U.S. Department of Agriculture's Family Economics Research Group periodically determines the cost of food plans at four different levels that would meet the nutrient needs of individuals of various ages and genders and of families of various sizes. The thrifty food plan is designed to meet basic nutrient needs with least variety and lowest cost. The U.S. Department of Agriculture uses the cost of this very austere food plan as the basis for the Food Stamp Allowances. Table 4-2 displays the cost of food prepared at home estimated for the USDA's thrifty and low-cost levels in May 1989. It can be assumed that families who have less than these amounts of money and/or food stamps to spend for food will risk being hungry. The higher the food prices in the local food markets, the greater the risk.

Communities can work to achieve food security by assuring that all eligible families utilize the federally funded food stamp, child nutrition, WIC, and elderly meal programs in combination with local food banks, soup kitchens, and food pantries.[23] The federal food assistance programs are described in Table 4-3. The food stamp and child nutrition programs are federally funded entitlement programs available in every community to

Table 4-2 Cost of Food at Home. (Cost of food at home estimated for food plans at 2 low cost levels, May 1989, U.S. average[1])

	Cost for 1 Week		Cost for 1 Month	
Sex-Age Group	Thrifty Plan	Low-Cost Plan	Thrifty Plan	Low-Cost Plan
Families				
Family of 2:[2]				
20-50 years	$44.90	$56.60	$194.30	$245.20
51 years and over	42.30	54.30	183.80	235.70
Family of 4:				
Couple, 20-50 years and children				
1-2 and 3-5 years	65.20	81.30	282.10	352.00
6-8 and 9-11 years	74.70	95.50	323.80	413.70
Individuals[3]				
Child:				
1-2 years	11.70	14.30	50.70	61.80
3-5 years	12.70	15.50	54.80	67.30
6-8 years	15.50	20.60	67.30	89.30
9-11 years	18.40	23.40	79.90	101.50
Male:				
12-14 years	19.30	26.60	83.70	115.10
15-19 years	20.00	27.50	86.70	119.00
20-50 years	21.40	27.40	92.70	118.60
51 years and over	19.40	26.00	84.30	112.80
Female:				
12-19 years	19.10	23.00	82.90	99.70
20-50 years	19.40	24.10	83.90	104.30
51 years and over	19.10	23.40	82.80	101.50

1. Assumes that food for all meals and snacks is purchased at the store and prepared at home. Estimates for the thrifty food plan were computed from quantities of foods published in *Family Economics Review* 1984(1). Estimates for the other plans were computed from quantities of foods published in *Family Economics Review* 1983(2). The costs of the food plans are estimated by updating prices paid by households surveyed in 1977-78 in USDA's Nationwide Food Consumption Survey. USDA updates these survey prices using information from the Bureau of Labor Statistics, *CPI Detailed Report*, table 3, to estimate the costs for the food plans.

2. 10 percent added for family size adjustment. See footnote 3.

3. The costs given are for individuals in 4-person families. For individuals in other size families, the following adjustments are suggested: 1-person—add 20 percent; 2-person—add 10 percent; 3-person—add 5 percent; 5- or 6-person—subtract 5 percent; 7-or-more-person—subtract 10 percent.

Source: U.S. Department of Agriculture, *Family Economics Review*, Vol. 2, No. 3, p. 20, 1989.

serve all who meet the income eligibility criteria. The Summer Food Service Program for Children, School Breakfast, WIC, and Meal Programs for the Elderly are available when a service provider in a community takes the

Table 4-3 Federally Funded Food and Nutrition Programs

Food Assistance and Nutrition Programs	Service Provider	Who Qualifies	Services/Benefits	Funding	Administrative Agency
National School Lunch Program Provides nutritious low-cost lunch to children enrolled in school	All public schools; voluntary in private schools	All children attending school may participate: reduced-price meals to children from families with incomes between 130 and 185% of poverty level; free meals to children from families with incomes at or below 130% of poverty level	Nutritious low-cost lunch at full or reduced prices, or free	USDA	State departments of education; local school districts
School Breakfast Provides nutritious breakfast to children in participating schools or institutions	Voluntarily by public and private schools	All children attending schools where the breakfast program operates may partipate: reduced-price breakfast available to children from families with incomes between 130 and 185% of poverty level; free breakfast to children from families with incomes at or below 130% poverty level	Nutritious low-cost breakfast at full or reduced prices, or free	USDA	State departments of education; local school districts
Special Milk Program Provides milk to school-aged children, in child care centers, and in schools or institutions where there is no school lunch program	Schools, camps, and child care institutions not participating in other school nutrition programs	All children attending schools and institutions with special milk program	Milk at reasonable price or free	USDA	State departments of education; local school districts

Program				
Summer Food Service for Children Provides one nutritious meal to children as a substitute for the National School Lunch and School Breakfast programs during summer vacation	Public and nonprofit private schools; public or nonprofit private residential facilities of local, municipal, or county government	Children under 18 years and persons over 18 years who are handicapped and participate in a sponsored program of county government; no income requirements; eligibility is determined by location and sponsor	Nutritious meals (breakfast, lunch, and/or snacks)	USDA — State departments of education; local sponsors
Child Care Food Program Provides financial assistance for nutritious food in child care setting	Licensed child care centers or family day care homes; Head Start programs	Children 12 years and under; children of migrant workers 15 years and younger; physically/ mentally handicapped individuals provided care in a center where majority are age 18 or younger	Free or reduced-price meals to eligible children in centers and free meals to all children in family day care homes; reimbursements for up to two meals and one snack daily	USDA — State departments of education; local providers
Head Start Provides comprehensive health, educational, nutrition, social, and other services to low-income preschool children and their families	Local Head Start program	Children ages 3-5 years from low-income families receiving public assistance or total annual income not more than 100% of poverty level; at least 10% of total enrollment available for handicapped children	Educational, comprehensive medical, dental, nutrition, and social services through assessment, early intervention, and prevention; nutritious meals and snacks (through Child Care Food Program); nutrition education; family counseling and referrals for social services	DHHS — DHHS regional offices; local providers

Table 4-3 continued

Food Assistance and Nutrition Programs	Service Provider	Who Qualifies	Services/Benefits	Funding	Administrative Agency
Special Supplemental Food Program for Women, Infants, and Children (WIC) Provides supplemental food, nutrition education as an adjunct to health care to low-income pregnant, postpartum, and breast-feeding women; infants; and children at nutritional risk	Health agencies, social services, community action agencies	Pregnant women, postpartum women (6 months), breast-feeding women (up to 1 year), infants and children (up to 5 years); must be certified to be at nutritional risk; household income determined to be at or below 185% of poverty level	Monthly foods or coupons for milk, cheese, eggs, fruit juice, cereal, peanut butter or legumes, infant formula, and infant cereal; nutrition education	USDA	State health agencies; local agencies
Commodity Supplemental Food Program (CSFP) Provides commodity foods to low-income women (pregnant, breast-feeding, or postpartum), infants and children to 6 years of age, and the elderly in certain cases	Public and private nonprofit agencies (community health or social service agencies)	Pregnant women, postpartum women, breast-feeding women, infants and children (up to 6 years); household income determined to be at or below 185% of poverty level; low-income elderly may be served if it does not reduce benefits to eligible women, infants, and children	Monthly commodity canned or packaged foods including fruits, vegetables, meats, infant formula, farina, beans, other as available	USDA	State health agencies
Food Stamps Provides low-income households with coupons to increase food purchasing power	Local public assistance or social services offices	U.S. citizen; recognized refugee with visa status or legal alien; households with low income and with resources (aside from income) of $2,000 or less/$3,000 or less with at least one elderly person (age 60 or older); eligibility determined after formal application to local public assistance or social services	Food coupons to purchase foods at participating food markets	USDA	State welfare, social service, or human service agencies

Temporary Emergency Food Assistance Program (TEFAP)
Provides commodity foods to low-income households through local public or private nonprofit agencies; quarterly distributions by emergency providers

Public and private nonprofit agencies (community action agencies, councils on aging, local health or local school districts)

Household with income at or below 150% of poverty level

Quarterly distribution: cheese, butter, rice, occasionally flour, cornmeal, and dry milk; emergency food available once per month: dairy products, rice, flour, cornmeal

USDA

State; local

Nutrition Assistance Program (NAP) for Puerto Rico
Block grant program in which Puerto Rico receives the cost of food assistance benefits (provided to recipients in cash) and half of the Commonwealth's administrative costs, up to a legislatively set total

Commonwealth of Puerto Rico

Program operates under eligibility rules similar to the Food Stamp Program

Cash to be used by recipients to supplement their food budget

USDA

Puerto Rico Commonwealth government

Food Distribution Program on Indian Reservations (FDPIR)
Operates as a substitute for food stamps for eligible needy families living on or near Indian reservations

Local agency

Indian families living on or near reservations

Offers USDA commodities monthly

USDA

Indian tribal councils

Table 4-3 continued

Food Assistance and Nutrition Programs	Service Provider	Who Qualifies	Services/Benefits	Funding	Administrative Agency
Meal Program for the Elderly Provides older Americans with meals and nutrition education in congregate setting or delivered to their homes	Area agency on aging or other aging services provider	People age 60 or older with social or economic needs; spouses of eligible people; handicapped or disabled people under 60 who reside in housing occupied primarily by the elderly	Nutritious meal; nutrition education; access to social and rehabilitative services; transportation	DHHS; Administration on Aging; state; individual donations	State agencies on aging; area agencies on aging
Cooperative Extension— Expanded Food and Nutrition Education Program (EFNEP) Provides nutrition education to low-income families and individuals	Local cooperative extension office where program is available	Families with children under 19 years; income at or below 125% of federal poverty level; at nutritional risk	Education and training on food and nutrition for homemakers and youth	USDA	State land grant universities; cooperative extension

Table 4-4 Food and Nutrition Program Income Eligibility Guide

This table is a guide and does not guarantee a client's acceptance into any program. If a household is at or below the poverty level listed in the left column, it may be eligible for the assistance programs listed in the right column. In many programs, factors other than income are also considered to determine eligibility. The Child Care Food Program guidelines vary according to the sponsor and are not included.

Percentage of Federal Poverty Income Guideline* (%)	Food and Nutrition Assistance Programs
100	WIC, Free School Breakfast, Free School Lunch, Summer Food Service for Children, Food Stamps (net income), TEFAP, EFNEP, Head Start, CSFP
125	WIC, Free School Breakfast, Free School Lunch, Summer Food Service for Children, Food Stamps (gross income), TEFAP, EFNEP, CSFP
130	WIC, Free School Breakfast, Free School Lunch, Summer Food Service for Children, Food Stamps (gross income), TEFAP, CSFP
150	WIC, Reduced Price School Breakfast, Reduced Price School Lunch, Summer Food Service for Children, TEFAP, CSFP
185	WIC, Reduced Price School Breakfast, Reduced Price School Lunch, Summer Food Service for Children, CSFP
No income standard	Congregate and Home-Delivered Meal Programs for the Elderly

*Federal poverty income guidelines are published each year in the *Federal Register* by the Department of Health and Human Services. See Table 4-1.

Source: Adapted from *Community Food Resources for Families: An Eligibility Guide* by C. Grandon, Massachusetts Department of Public Health, Office of Nutrition, Boston, Massachusetts, January 1988.

initiative to establish, implement, and direct the programs. Household income is used to determine eligibility for all of the federally funded food assistance programs except Meal Programs for the Elderly. Table 4-4 shows the maximum allowable incomes for federal program eligibility. Unfortunately, the federal food assistance programs now serve only a small proportion of those who are eligible.

Participation in one or more food assistance programs extends the family's food purchasing power to better meet the nutritional needs of family members. In assessing family needs, each household member's participation in or eligibility for food assistance programs must be determined. When their household incomes are very low, families may not be able to meet their food needs even when they participate in one or more federal food assistance programs. In these cases families may turn to emergency food assistance programs such as food pantries and soup kitchens. Between 1984 and 1988 many cities reported significant increases in requests for emergency food by families with children.[24] During 1984, for example, Boston, Chicago, and Dallas reported increases of 200 percent, 182 percent, and 100 percent, respectively, in the number of meals served by emergency food programs.[25] While these emergency food assistance programs provide food to satisfy immediate needs, they are not designed to provide food for extended periods of time.

Over the long term, increased utilization of the federal food programs could decrease the growing burden on private relief agencies, while better meeting the food needs of communities, families, and individuals. Many families still do not know about these programs or have inaccurate or insufficient information regarding their eligibility requirements.[26] Complicated application forms and procedures, excessive eligibility documentation, and/or inconsistent administrators deter many families from applying for food assistance. Nutritionists must know eligibility requirements and application procedures so that they can assist potentially eligible clients in applying. Some families feel that there is a stigma attached to the use of government assistance programs. The negative perceptions and attitudes associated with these programs may foster shame and embarrassment, and prevent families in need from applying for food assistance. Nutritionists should be sensitive to these feelings so that they can support clients and break down negative stereotypes attributed to people using public assistance programs.

Additional barriers for clients applying for food assistance include busy telephone lines, inconvenient service hours, long waiting lines, complicated appointment procedures, and cultural and language barriers. Administrative and program barriers to participation should be documented in the community assessment. Specific recommendations for change can then be made to federal, state, and/or local food program administrators so that they can facilitate more effective, efficient management and develop services that are more responsive to client needs. Adequate Food for All (see Appendix B) is the position statement of the Association of State and Territorial Public Health Nutrition Directors with the endorsement of the Association of State and Territorial Health officials. It suggests the direction for public health agencies in addressing the problem of hunger in the U.S.

SOCIAL SUPPORT

Families who live in remote areas some distance from a settled community or in areas blocked from social support systems by deserts, mountains, waterways without bridges, poor roads, and no public transportation are geographically isolated. A family who does not have transportation or the money to pay for it may be unable to obtain adequate food at affordable prices or unable to use food assistance or health care programs. The geographically isolated include migrant and seasonal farm workers, mountain families, the rural poor, Native Americans on reservations, and homeless, displaced families without access to public transportation even in urban areas.

Social isolation occurs when individuals or families are unable to establish supportive relationships with others and is more subtle and difficult to recognize and to plan to overcome than geographic isolation is. When people have difficulty establishing or maintaining supportive interpersonal relationships, within either their community or their family, they become quite lonely. This may occur when people move to new communities or when their cultural or ethnic background or their primary language differs from that of the community. When they are homeless, are unemployed, experience a marriage breakup, or suffer mental illness or emotional breakdowns, people often distance themselves from their friends and family. Drug use, alcoholism, violence, and abuse dramatically change family dynamics and communication. Social isolation may prevent an individual from seeking health care, food, financial or housing assistance, or other services they need. An individual who lacks social support may find it difficult to continue health care or follow recommendations.

One family member or community decision maker, often referred to as the "gatekeeper," may control the use of health care, social services, and food assistance. When the health professional gains the approval and support of that gatekeeper, the individual's and the family's use of services and their ability to follow recommendations can be improved.

Single and/or teen parents are often overwhelmed by their parenting responsibilities, limited employment opportunities, low income, and lack of transportation, child care, and family support. They may be unable to cope with buying and preparing nutritious meals for themselves and their children.

Parents caring for a handicapped or chronically ill child or adults caring for a disabled or homebound spouse or parent are also stressed emotionally, physically, and often financially. Nutritionists should not expect to deal alone with the overwhelming social crises that may affect their clients. They must be sensitive, supportive, and responsive to client needs, but they must work with other members of the health and human service agency teams to address the multiple and often longstanding problems faced by many families.

ACCESS TO HEALTH CARE

Many pregnant women do not seek prenatal care, and ill or disabled children and adults go without needed treatment because they have no insurance and not enough money to pay physicians or hospitals. Physicians may be unwilling to provide free care or to accept Medicaid or Medicare payments that are less than their usual fees.

Nutritionists should know the medical care services in the community and the barriers low-income families face in trying to obtain services. They need to work with other health professionals and community members to foster medical care that is available and responsive to the needs of vulnerable families. When basic health care services are in place, nutrition intervention, referral, and follow-up should be integrated into the public and private health care delivery system in order to make these services available to all who need them. (See Chapter 11.)

EMPOWERING VULNERABLE FAMILIES

Having investigated the vulnerability factors in their community, family, and client assessments, public health nutritionists and other team members should speak out on the nature and extent of the problems that place their community and clients at risk. Table 4-5 presents key factors to include in the assessment. This information documents needs and suggests priorities for development of community services and family and individual care plans. These risk factors can be used in planning professional and in-service training and in speaking to concerned citizen groups.

Some innovations in the health care and nutrition service delivery system that might improve service to vulnerable families include the following:

- recruiting and training health or nutrition aides, lay health advisors, peer counselors, or volunteers from the community to interpret, reach out, and guide vulnerable families through the system
- arranging with the food stamp, public assistance, and social services agencies to send a staff member or trained volunteer to busy clinics or health centers to enroll eligible clients for health and social services at

Table 4-5 Assessing Nonmedical Vulnerability Factors in the Community, the Family, and the Individual

Vulnerability Factor	Community Assessment	Family/Household Assessment	Individual Assessment
Income	Median family income; per capita income; % of population below 100% of poverty level; % of population below 200% of poverty level; AFDC benefit levels	Family/household income; family size; # of wage earners; participation in federal/state nutrition programs; income supplement such as AFDC, unemployment benefits, general relief, fuel assistance, utility bills; moving costs, educational expenses, child care	Individual's monthly income; lives alone or with others; household expenses; child support; participates in federal/state food assistance; income supplement such as AFDC, unemployment benefits, general relief, fuel assistance; moving costs, educational expenses, child care; single parent; homebound, disabled, elderly
Employment opportunities	State or local unemployment rate; median wage; predominance of minimum-wage, service-sector jobs; layoff or strike in community; jobs available; seasonal jobs (e.g., agriculture, construction)	Household member laid off or on strike; children dropped out of school to help support the household	Individual unable to find work at a wage that meets basic needs; recently laid off or on strike; barriers that prevent individual from finding adequate employment (lack of child care, job opportunities)
Educational level, reading level, literacy	% of adults over age 18 with less than eighth grade education; % of adults over age 18 who are functionally illiterate; % of teen high school dropouts (by race)	Education level of head of household and mother; education obtained in country of origin	Education level; education obtained in country of origin; ability to read, speak, write English; if in school, age, grade level
Cultural or language barriers	Ethnic/cultural distribution in community; languages spoken, read, and/or written; availability of English as a Second Language classes; availability of services representing the ethnic community; signs and information in appropriate languages; availability of traditional foods; prevailing community attitudes	Ability of head of household to speak, read, write English; ability to read/write native language; use of traditional foods; use of traditional healers, folk medicine; power structure in family; degree of acculturation	Ability to speak, read, write English; ability to read/write native language; use of traditional foods; use of traditional healers, folk medicine
Housing	Rental unit vacancy rate; % of substandard housing (lacking indoor plumbing, electricity, kitchen facilities with working refrigerator, stove, oven); % of rental units built before 1950 (risk of lead paint); availability of subsidized housing and length of waiting list; average and range of rents for 1–2–3 bedroom units; median purchase price for a house; condo conversion in community; estimated number of homeless individuals and families	Family lives in substandard housing; problems with rodents, roaches, chipping or peeling paint or plaster; family living in a hotel, motel, shelter, car or on the street; recently moved in with friends or relatives due to the inability to obtain adequate housing; % of the family-household income spent on rent and utilities	Individual lives in substandard housing; living in hotel, motel, shelter, car or on the street; lives in room without cooking facilities or without working refrigerator or stove; % of income spent on rent/utilities; inability to pay rent; evicted for nonpayment of rent

Table 4-5 continued

Vulnerability Factor	Community Assessment	Family/Household Assessment	Individual Assessment
Food availability, food costs, accessibility of food markets	Supermarkets in the neighborhood offer a variety of nutritious, good-quality foods at competitive prices; culturally preferred foods at a reasonable price; accessible by public transportation or within walking distance; food delivery or shopping services available	Family access to transportation to available markets; cultural foods available at reasonable price	Individual's food needs met by himself/herself or other household members; elderly or disabled individual able to arrange for assistance with shopping for food
Geographic or social isolation	Public transportation available; dispersed rural community; geographic barriers; condition of roads; cultural, ethnic, rural hostilities; immigrant, refugee, or migrant community; highly transient community	Supportive relationships; transportation or money for transportation; cultural or language barrier; victim of cultural, ethnic, racial prejudice; immigrant, refugee, migrant family; mobile family; homeless family; family stress, unstable family, alcoholism, drug abuse, domestic abuse, violence	Single parent; teen parent; homebound living alone; physical or mental disability; lack of supportive relationships; lack of transportation or money for transportation; victim of cultural, ethnic, racial prejudice; immigrant, refugee, migrant; mobile; alcoholic, drug abuser
Access to health services	Public health, health centers, and medical practices available (e.g., obstetrics, pediatrics, family practice); sliding fee scale; number of persons receiving and eligible for Medicare and Medicaid; services near public transportation; % of no-shows in a clinic or health program; preventive programs offered at no cost or reasonable cost; Medicaid payments accepted	Satisfaction of family with health services available; family members go without needed care	Satisfaction of individual with health services available; perceived barriers to utilization of services; repeatedly misses scheduled appointments
Health insurance coverage	Health insurance coverage provided by employers includes maternity care; Medicaid available to low-income married couples; coverage for prenatal care for low-income teens living with parents; % of jobs with no health insurance benefits; sliding fee scale or free health care available. Medicaid payment accepted by community physicians	Household members covered by health insurance, HMO, or Medicaid coverage; uninsured families have access to sliding fee or free health care; father had to leave household in order for family to access Medicaid benefits; Medicaid unavailable because teen lives in parents' household; family's insurance covers preventive care, well-child care	Individual has health insurance, HMO, Medicaid coverage; types of services covered, amount of deductible; denial of health care due to lack of medical coverage or Medicaid

a one-stop location
- scheduling clinic hours so families do not need to take time off from their work and lose pay in order to obtain services
- enlisting volunteer church groups or women's clubs to adopt a service project to provide layettes, clothing, nutritious foods, or essential transportation to families who need them
- applying for a community service grant to provide innovative services to help high-risk families work toward self-sufficiency

Concerned health professionals can join political leaders and concerned citizens to propose long-term approaches to these complex economic and social issues. The community assessment data can be presented in public meetings, legislative hearings, or other forums. An ongoing surveillance system can be developed to monitor hunger, malnutrition, diet-related health problems, and utilization of food assistance programs. Grant funding can be sought to implement outreach and nutrition education and to improve access to and use of various food assistance programs. Community coalitions can recommend and work for state and federal legislation that will address universal food access, housing, job training, health care, and employment.

Adequate Food for All, a position statement of the Association of State and Territorial Public Health Nutrition Directors, is a guiding policy statement for public health nutritionists to use in developing strategies to alleviate hunger in their communities.[27] (See Appendix B.)

ISSUES TO DEBATE

- How might health professionals advocate on behalf of clients regarding social issues that affect health, such as housing, transportation, crime, and drug use in the community?
- How can useful data be collected on population groups that are new to the community, such as immigrants, migrants, and homeless families?
- How should vulnerable families be empowered to present their needs, participate in planning programs, and participate in developing policies for the agencies that serve them and their families?

NOTES

1. Ruth Sidell, "The Changing Maternal and Child Health Population: Sociological Parameters," in *Maternal and Child Health Practice*, 3d ed., ed. Helen M. Wallace, George Ryan, Jr., and Allen C. Oglesby (Oakland, Calif.: Third Party Publishing Co., 1988), 79–84.

2. *Analysis of Poverty in 1987* (Washington, D.C.: Center on Budget and Policy Priorities, September 1, 1988).

3. Ibid.

4. Ibid.

5. Ibid.

6. Ibid.

7. William S. Nersesian, "Infant Mortality in Socially Vulnerable Populations," *Annual Review of Public Health* 9 (1988): 361–77.

8. Ibid.

9. Ibid.

10. J. Larry Brown and Deborah Allen, "Hunger in America," *Annual Review of Public Health* 9 (1988): 503-26.

11. Isaac Shapiro and Robert Greenstein, *Making Work Pay: A New Agenda for Poverty Policies* (Washington, D.C.: Center on Budget and Policy Priorities, March 21, 1989).

12. Ibid.

13. Vincent N. Parrillo, John Stimson, and Ardyth Stimson, *Contemporary Social Problems* (New York: John Wiley & Sons, Inc., 1985), 251.

14. Children's Defense Fund, *A Children's Defense Budget, FY 1989—An Analysis of Our Nation's Investment in Children* (Washington, D.C.: Children's Defense Fund, 1988).

15. Cecilia Doak, Leonard G. Doak, and Jane H. Root, *Teaching Patients with Low Literacy Skills* (Philadelphia: J.B. Lippincott Co., 1985).

16. U.S. Department of Health and Human Services, National Institutes of Health, National Cancer Institute, *Pretesting in Health Communications Methods, Examples, and Resources for Improving Health Messages and Materials*, NIH Publication no. 83-1493 (Bethesda, Md.: NIH, December 1982).

17. "Where To Find the New Immigrants," *American Demographics* (September 1988).

18. Ibid.

19. Daniel S. Miller and Elizabeth H.B. Lin, "Children in Sheltered Homeless Families: Reported Health Statistics and Use of Health Services," *Pediatrics* 81, no. 5 (May 1988): 668–73.

20. Barbara E. Cohen, "Food Security Policy for the 1990s: Eliminating Hunger," Executive Summary (The Urban Institute, Washington D.C., 1989, unpublished).

21. Brown and Allen, "Hunger in America."

22. Cohen, "Food Security Policy."

23. Ibid.

24. Brown and Allen, "Hunger in America."

25. Ibid.

26. Jo-Ann Eccher, "How to: Food Stamp Outreach," *Seeds* (June 1986).

27. ASTPHND, *Adequate Food for All*, Position Statement (Boston: Massachusetts Department of Public Health, 1988).

part III

Shaping Policies That Affect the Public's Health

chapter 5

Developing Agency, Community, and State Nutrition Policies

Nancy Chapman

READER OBJECTIVES

- Define policy, and discuss its importance for public health nutrition.
- Describe the players, process, and intent of policy making at the agency, local, and state levels.
- List the steps to formulate successful policy.
- Identify leadership roles for the nutritionist in formulating, implementing, and evaluating policy.
- Give some examples of how nutritionists are influencing policy.

DEFINING POLICY

A policy is a statement of principle or intent that guides the selection of priorities and sets the direction of programs and actions of an individual, organization, or government. Values, convictions, and beliefs usually form the basis for a policy statement.

Carefully formulated policies assure consistent actions and prevent short-sighted or impulsive decisions. Mission statements, position papers, policy and procedure manuals, protocols, office rules, and written memorandums from administrators or program managers convey policies within an organization. Local ordinances and state and federal laws and regulations articulate formal policies of governments.

A policy is not a plan for action, nor is it an anticipated outcome of an action, although policy statements may include these elements. Without clear, comprehensive policies that are written and communicated to those who are affected by them, actions can be narrow, fragmented, inconsistent, and even contradictory. The absence of a well-articulated guiding statement impairs the assessment of programs or initiatives that are implemented.

The process of establishing policy differs according to the individual or group formulating it, the position of the policymaker in the power structure, and the number of people or the size of the population whose lives or work will be affected. Policies provide the framework to

* select priorities from competing options
* guide plans for programs, services, products, or campaigns
* set standards for measuring the quality of programs, services, or products
* specify eligibility criteria and benefit levels for target populations of programs
* allocate funds
* select and deploy personnel
* generate revenue for projects, programs, or organizational work
* set directions and priorities for research and development

IMPORTANCE OF POLICIES

Agency administrators, as well as local, state, and federal governments, generate policies to address specific concerns appropriate to or associated with the agency's mission. Since policies have far-reaching influence, nutritionists must understand policy, how policies have evolved, their current intent, and implications for the future. By working with other interested groups and broadening their networks or coalitions, nutritionists can be effective in promoting and protecting the public's health through public policy.

To initiate or change a policy requires knowing (1) its importance to the policymaker(s), (2) who benefits, and (3) why it was initiated and adopted. A historical review of nutrition services, education, food assistance, food safety, nutrition research, and monitoring offers insights for answering these questions. Scientific evidence, discussed in Chapter 2, should provide a foundation for nutrition and health policies. Policy making should balance scientific evidence with the values, priorities, needs, and concerns of stakeholders and constituents. Policymakers are always constrained by budget realities.

AGENCY POLICY

While authority and funding for many public health nutrition programs originate in Washington, D.C., agency administrators and local and state government officials can authorize additional funds and programs to address observed community needs. Many policies originate at the program level as the nutrition staff and agency administrators develop their strategic plans, operational plans, and protocols for delivering services and write grant proposals for innovative new programs.

Nutritionists participate in developing agency policy when they

- assess their community's food, nutrition, and health needs and present these findings to program directors, agency administrators, and boards
- recommend programs using results of assessments
- monitor and report their agency's progress in meeting nutritional objectives
- establish policies, procedures, and protocols for nutrition services for their agency
- adopt national model standards for their nutrition services[1]

To accomplish these tasks requires understanding of the formal and informal power structures and policy-making processes in the agency. It is important to know the values and priorities of administrators or officials who make the overall policies of which nutrition policies are a part. Nutrition programs and services are often affected by agency, local, state, and federal policies not specific to food or nutrition, such as personnel policies or policies on health professional training, health care financing, or public assistance.

LOCAL POLICY

With the diversity of local political structures in the United States, nutritionists must investigate the workings of their own local governments. Many states have strong county governments with elected boards of commissioners or supervisors who pass ordinances and approve the county budget. Where the county government is responsible for public health services, the county commissioners usually appoint the county manager and the county's board of health.

In large cities a city council promulgates local ordinances, budgets local revenues, and appoints the city board of health. An elected mayor or appointed city manager administers the daily activities of the city. The county or city board of health appoints the chief health official, who may or may not be a health professional. The agency health official is responsible for local public health policy. In these agencies the nutritionist should advise the health official and the board of health on nutrition policy. *Model Standards: Guidelines for Community Attainment of the Year 2000 Objectives* provides a framework of reference for organizing and implementing local health services. It includes a chapter on nutrition services.[2]

In states where there are no official local public health agencies, the state health agency may provide services through district or regional offices. Another model is for the state health agency to contract with local hospitals, health centers, or other institutions to provide health and nutrition services. When a locality lacks a public health official or when the local health agency does not employ a nutritionist, nutritionists in the state health agency or other community agencies must build coalitions to advance nutrition policies.

STATE POLICY

State government policy-making structures and processes closely parallel those of the federal government. (See Chapter 6.) At the state level government officials are usually accessible and, as a rule, look to the state health agency's public health nutrition staff as their experts on the nutritional status of their community.

State Legislature

Every state has two houses of elected legislators except Nebraska, which has a unicameral legislature. State senates and houses of representatives or general assemblies function through a committee and subcommittee system, much like the U.S. Congress. To influence nutrition policy it is essential to understand the state legislative process and to know the key committees and the legislators on those committees who are responsible for health, nutrition, food, professional licensure, budget, personnel, education, and consumer affairs. The nutritionist should consult the legislative liaison on the state health agency staff for guidance on how to participate in the process within agency policy. The legislative liaisons for the state public health or dietetic associations are other useful resource persons.

State Executive Branch

The governor is the state's chief executive officer who directs the state agencies responsible for administering programs and allocating resources. These include both state revenues and federal grants to states. To successfully compete for funds, it is necessary to understand the state budget process and how to prepare a competitive budget request.

State Health and Nutrition Policy

Of the 55 state agencies responsible for public health, 33 are free-standing health departments responsible directly to the governor and 22 are divisions of human service agencies with an appointed secretary. The secretary of the state human service department, the director of the state health agency, or the designated state health official is the chief public health advisor to the governor. It is usually the role of the state public health nutrition director or chief nutrition consultant to advise this state health official on nutrition policy. Other nutritionists working in the local and state health agencies can provide input into state nutrition policy through their state public health nutrition director or their lead public health nutritionist. (See Appendix D.)

Nutrition policy should reflect the food and nutrition needs of the public based on (1) results of formal and informal assessments and market research, (2) consensus recommendations of the public and of health and nutrition professionals throughout the state, and (3) national published nutrition objectives and model standards for nutrition services. Several recent documents are useful in developing state nutrition objectives: *Preventing Disease/Promoting Health, Year 2000 Objectives for the Nation*,[3] the American Public Health Association's *Model Standards: Guidelines for Community Attainment of the Year 2000 Objectives*,[4] and, from the Association of State and Territorial Public Health Nutrition Directors, *Model State Nutrition Objectives*.[5] (See Appendix C.) The supplement to *Public Health Reports* entitled "Nutrition Services in State and Local Public Health Agencies" is a basic reference, setting forth a comprehensive agenda for public health nutrition services in state and local health agencies.[6]

POLICY-MAKING STRATEGIES

In-depth knowledge of the community based on the subjective and statistical data base from the community assessment (Chapters 3 and 4) is essential to policy development. Studying the community considers political, social, economic, and geographic implications as well as health and scientific concerns.

Policymakers, whether they are state legislators, county commissioners or supervisors, members of boards of health, or state or local health officials, whether elected or appointed, are necessarily political. Even policy recommendations strongly buttressed by scientific rationale and evidence of program effectiveness yield to budgetary constraints and special interests.

In recent years there have been major cuts in the federal grants-in-aid to states for health and social programs. As a result, competition for available state and local revenues has intensified. State and local advocates who have identified needs close to home have generated public support for policies not tenable at a national level. Local initiatives can often succeed with less funding and more cooperative voluntary efforts.

Well documented community assessments, feasible recommendations, local community support, and persuasive presentations influence policymakers. For example, Texas nutritionists asked the state legislature to examine hunger and malnutrition. As a result of a well presented, extensive needs assessment, the state appropriated $12 million to supplement federal grants for food stamp, WIC, and elderly nutrition programs. Policies that respond to documented community needs and that affect the lives of a large constituency are more likely to gain support and be adopted. Success is more likely to come to those who advocate broad innovative programs than to those who plead for more money, staff, or resources to maintain the status quo.

Formulating Policy

At the agency, local, state, or national level the general steps to develop policy are as follows:

- Document needs through community assessments, direct observations, communications from consumers, scientific studies, and government reports.
- Draft a preliminary policy statement, using past and existing policies as models.
- Seek and gain support from key administrators and policymakers.
- Mobilize a broad grassroots constituency.
- Invite public and professional comments and refine the statement to reflect this input.
- Implement the policy and monitor its community application to ensure that programs operate according to their intent.

Framing a Policy To Win

The more simple, relevant, and immediate the issue, the more likely it is to succeed. Both the public and the policymakers must agree on the benefits. The many paradoxes and controversies in nutrition science need clarification. As policymakers confront questions regarding nutrition services, nutrition education, food labeling, food assistance, and nutrition research, the cost effectiveness and public benefits of each nutrition intervention must be clearly communicated.

A winning policy capitalizes on the policymakers' agenda. Most policymakers have several paramount concerns. They seek job advancement, either in an agency or in the legislature. They intend to be reappointed or re-elected. If an agency administrator seeks reappointment, then it is important to accentuate successful programs conducted by the agency to make the official "look good." If a legislator seeks a leadership position, then consensus building on a successful campaign issue counts. Issues they support must enjoy general popularity among a wide group of constituents. Policymakers like to be perceived as serving their constituents. Arguments that demonstrate the human and health benefits, as well as the cost benefits, of a nutrition program boost its chances of gaining support.

The specific purpose of a winning policy must be clear to the audience. For example, the specific purpose of state bills to license dietetic practitioners can be to control the quality of nutrition services available to the public. The consistency in quality of care achieved by licensed nurses and physicians attests to the fulfillment of their purpose. Improvement of the public's health is an expected consequence of licensing bills. Policymakers want tangible proof that harm to the public will be minimized when non-qualified individuals are prohibited from practicing and that good to the public will result when only qualified nutrition professionals serve the public.

Securing Approval of Policy

Successfully promoting policies does not depend on luck. It depends on choosing the right strategies.

Strategy 1: Prepare a scientific base

Begin with a comprehensive study of the issue, the target audience, and the environment, and prepare clear answers to these questions: Is there a need for this policy or legislation? What studies have been conducted on this issue? By whom? What were the findings? Does any similar policy exist? Who sponsored it? Who opposed it? What were the arguments for or against it? Nutritionists and health colleagues in key administrative or legislative positions or on university faculties can often answer these questions. Information might come from state or local nutritionists, the state dietetic or public health association, nutrition educators, or other professional organizations. Careful research provides data to buttress arguments and strategic assumptions.

Strategy 2: Develop broad support

Building broad organizational coalitions and grassroots support requires a far-reaching educational campaign. Forming active coalitions among diverse groups such as researchers, health professionals, educators, farmers, consumers, religious groups, women's groups, and environmentalists brings nutrition issues to public attention. Nutrition networks should include not only nutrition experts, but also influential citizens in the community; friends of decision makers; respected community groups with political power, including the League of Women Voters, Chamber of Commerce, Parent and Teachers Associations, and local affiliates of the voluntary health agencies, such as the American Heart Association, the American Diabetes Association, and the March of Dimes; and lead media personalities. Networking mobilizes multiple voices to move legislators to action. (See Chapter 22.) Policymakers need to understand that past reductions in funding for nutrition programs may indicate not a failure of programs to meet goals, but rather an unorganized constituency. They need to recognize that immediate savings may mean much larger costs for health care in the future. Finding that cuts in federal health expenditures reversed the previous decline in infant mortality rates has motivated legislators in several states to increase health care coverage for pregnant women and to provide state monies to supplement the federal WIC and Medicaid funds.

If uninformed or confused, colleagues, organization members, and agency staff who could be potential allies can engender skepticism and even launch an opposition campaign. Wide dissemination of concise and informative fact sheets and press releases on the policy should mobilize the greatest number of potential supporters in the widest geographical area.

Strategy 3: Analyze the opposition

A successful campaign responds constructively to the opposition's arguments and contributes to their defeat. Since policymakers must weigh all views, they need to hear strong factual arguments that refute the opponent's position.

Strategy 4: Anticipate problems, and develop alternative approaches or compromise positions

For example, the desire to decrease infant mortality might compel policymakers to increase state Medicaid benefits, thus creating a potential risk of high government costs and subsequent taxpayers' revolts. An alternative solution might be to provide tax advantages to private health care providers so that they can significantly reduce their fees to low-income women who need prenatal care. When no clear solution can be found, policymakers may elect to study several alternatives.

Strategy 5: Estimate needed resources and time

The resources and time that must be devoted to an issue differ depending on whether the issue can be resolved within agency policy or whether it requires legislation. Costs for carrying out a legislative campaign must be paid, and it takes time to identify resources or contributions in-kind. Before the campaign begins, significant resources must be in place. Media coverage must be arranged, key contributors identified, and individuals who will maintain contact with policymakers secured.

Strategy 6: Adopt successful strategies from others

Learning from the successful experiences and strategies of other professionals or other interest groups provides a competitive edge. The drive for dietetic licensure legislation illustrates how dietitians have learned from experiences in the states that initiated the movement.

Strategy 7: Set a clear direction before starting

Points for possible compromise must be decided and points for "bailout" established. Being readily accessible to policymakers during the process is essential to staying on track and being able to negotiate as necessary.

Communicating the Message

Charismatic messages are concise, consistent, creative, and sensitive to the community. Successful persuaders communicate precisely what they want their audience to remember. The persuasive message focuses on a single critical point and leaves the details to the fine print.

Effective communicators establish credibility over time by being consistent and by avoiding tangential statements that detract from their central message. When rallying support for their viewpoint, they rarely confront the opposition. Good communicators interpret the science simply and clearly. Popular nutrition issues must offer direct, positive solutions to public concerns, while representing the consensus of the scientific and professional community. Popularizing a nutrition issue requires skillful use of the media to assure clear community understanding.

The memorable message is creative. It must be heard and seen repeatedly. The central idea is personalized for the specific audience—whether they are health professionals, the public, consumers, administrators, or legislators. To trigger legislative or administrative action, catchy phrases have been launched in the media to capture public attention.

- "SMART—Stop Marketing Alcohol on Radio and TV"
- "Healthy Mothers, Healthy Babies"
- "Hunger Watch"
- "Best Start"

The message must focus policymakers on community needs, successful programs using public funds, and the negative impact of budget cuts on the lives of the people in their own communities. Elected officials are especially interested in the views of their constituents, including nutritionists, but more importantly those the nutritionists serve.

LEADERSHIP ROLES FOR NUTRITIONISTS

Policy development has often begun in the offices of professionals. The process of planting and nurturing the seed until it becomes policy utilizes a network of persons who serve in a variety of influential roles.

- advisors to state or local health officials
- staff of key boards or committees
- educators and researchers on university faculties
- members of key advisory committees, commissions, or expert panels
- members of one or more health and nutrition professional societies
- members of consumer, citizen, or service clubs
- constituents of legislators
- speakers or writers appearing in the media

In their capacity of advising officials on food and nutrition policy, nutritionists function as organizers, network builders, and resource persons. As staff to policymakers, they analyze and interpret findings of research, another possible channel to influence their administrators. Nutritionists are also often asked to write speeches for key health or elected officials, to communicate with the press, and to conduct public relations.

Another natural and most persuasive role is that of constituent of an elected official. From that perspective, too, a nutritionist may advise as an expert. Nutritionists have served in advisory positions to elected or appointed officials and as professional staff on boards or committees.

Officials and legislators often ask nutrition experts to provide relevant research or to evaluate a food program or an educational campaign. As part of an evaluation team, nutritionists have helped to answer policy questions directly or indirectly; for example: Was the intended target audience reached? What was accomplished? Were the costs justified? What other alternatives exist? At what cost?

Representatives of professional societies educate policymakers through written and oral communications that address current critical food and nutrition issues. A nutritionist may serve as an expert witness at the public hearing of an appointed or elected panel. When their own staff is limited, policymakers may use the expertise of interested and available professions to suggest witnesses for hearings or even to draft policy statements or legislation.

The most powerful and influential position in the policy process is that of decision maker. This may be a member of an advisory committee, commission, or expert panel or a person to be appointed as a health agency administrator.

LEARNING BY EXAMPLE

Two brief case studies illustrate how nutritionists have participated in state policy development by establishing a nutrition-monitoring system for those at highest nutritional risk in California and by securing state supplemental funding for federal nutrition programs in New York.

Nutrition-Monitoring Action in California

California's Nutrition Monitoring Act, passed in 1986, places the complementary responsibility for nutrition among several levels of government and demonstrates how nutrition monitoring fits into a contemporary redefinition of government's proper role in society.[7] Findings from hunger surveys and a surveillance system spurred nutritionists and other staff of the Northern California Anti-Hunger Coalition (NCAHC) to draft and seek passage of the Monitoring Act.[8] NCAHC included the California Dietetic Association, the California Church Council, and the California Legal Assistance Foundation. Analysis by the coalition showed that policymakers favored legislation that (1) links diet and disease, (2) demonstrates how electronic data systems can economically target existing resources, and (3) shows that nutrition interventions are cost effective.[9] Active participation of local public health nutrition groups and NCAHC's quick response to legislative and administrative requests for data brought success. The 1989 report to the governor and legislature on nutrition monitoring for California identifies the gaps in data collection and makes eight policy recommendations for the computer-based coordinated system of nutrition data management to improve program planning, management, and accountability.[10]

Hunger Watch and the Implications for Public Health Policies

New York state's governor authorized Hunger Watch to direct future public health policies and intervention programs. Program goals were to determine the scope and distribution of undernutrition among high-risk populations in order to evaluate contributing causes and to ascertain whether reduced socioeconomic status adversely affected the nutritional status of certain populations. Health professionals and medical students conducted two studies: a descriptive survey of populations at nutritional risk and a case-control study of observed differences in the growth of preschool children. Data from these studies prompted the New York State Assembly to establish the Supplemental Nutrition Assistance Program (SNAP), which adds state dollars to the federal funding for WIC, elderly meal programs, and emergency feeding. Out of the studies were developed methods to estimate the seriousness of hunger, determine reasons for hunger, identify undernourished children, and analyze associated risk factors.[11]

Policy development begins with identifying problems, collecting data, and establishing networks. After a policy is adopted and implemented, it must be monitored and evaluated. Opportunities to influence policy making are unlimited for those who are assertive, energetic, and creative.

ISSUES TO DEBATE

- As priorities for public health dollars shift to new concerns (e.g., AIDS and emergency care for the homeless), how can nutritionists link nutrition to quality of care, preventive interventions, or sustained independence for high-risk individuals?

- Which coalitions should public health nutritionists join that will allow them to anticipate legislative actions, shifts in funding, and revisions of health implementation plans?
- How can public health nutritionists make time in their overcrowded schedules to participate in formal and informal policy making in their agency, city, county, or state?

NOTES

1. American Public Health Association, *Model Standards: Guidelines for Community Attainment of the Year 2000 Objectives*, 3d ed. (Washington, D.C.: American Public Health Association, 1990), 1–9.
2. Ibid.
3. U.S. Department of Health and Human Services, *Promoting Health/Preventing Disease, Year 2000 Objectives for the Nation*, Draft for Public Review and Comment (Washington, D.C.: Government Printing Office, 1989), 1-1 to 1-24.
4. American Public Health Association, *Model Standards*.
5. Association of State and Territorial Public Health Nutrition Directors, "Model State Nutrition Objectives" (ASTPHND, McLean, Va., 1988, Unpublished).
6. ASTHO Foundation Nutrition Services Project Committee, "Nutrition Services in State and Local Public Health Agencies," *Public Health Reports* 98, no. 1 (Special Supplement) (1983): 9–20.
7. L. Neuhauser, "Northern California Hunger Surveys: 1984–85," *National Nutrition Monitor* 11, no. 8 (1985): 2–6.
8. Sally H. Cohenour, "Monitoring Legislation in California," *National Nutrition Monitor* 11, no. 9 (1985): 4–6.
9. Department of Health Services. *Report to the Governor and the Legislature on Nutrition Monitoring in California* (Sacramento: Department of Health Services, 1989).
10. Ibid.
11. Jo-Ann Lamphere, "Hunger Watch—New York State," *National Nutrition Monitor* 11, no. 4 (1984): 2–4.

chapter 6

Advocating for National Health and Nutrition Policies

Nancy Chapman

READER OBJECTIVES

- List the interacting private and public sector influences on national nutrition policy.
- Discuss the important roles of public health officials and nutritionists in shaping national nutrition policy.
- Know how federal nutrition policy evolves and the operational steps.
- Review the history of national nutrition policy as background for revising existing policies or formulating new policies.
- Examine the current climate in which nutrition emerges as a national focus.

PRIVATE VERSUS PUBLIC SECTOR POLICIES

At the national level, food and nutrition policies have evolved over the years from both private and public sector initiatives. Figure 6-1 shows the converging forces that influence food and nutrition policy development. These include scientific bodies, industry, health professional associations, voluntary health organizations, consumer interest groups, media, and government. The influence each entity exerts varies with the issue, the profile of that entity's leadership, and its stature.

All along the food system, which includes farmers, producers, food processors, food retailers, food services, and industry, policy decisions affect consumer food choices. Producer and distributor policies guide pricing, marketing, production, distribution, safety, sanitation, and product promotion decisions. In turn, what food consumers can obtain and at what price profoundly influences the public's health and nutritional status.

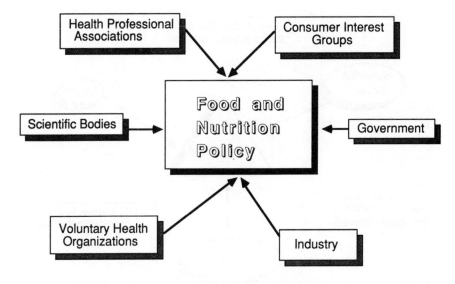

Figure 6-1 Influences on Food and Nutrition Policy Development

Nutrition professional associations, voluntary health organizations, and consumer interest groups also adopt policies that affect the public. These organizations' policy statements[1] guide their legislative initiatives, public awareness campaigns, standards of practice, continuing education requirements, and the content of their publications. Appendix L lists some of the influential health and nutrition organizations, food trade associations, and consumer advocacy groups.

Quasi-governmental scientific bodies such as the National Academy of Sciences (NAS) issue publications with important policy implications. Influential NAS reports include the *Recommended Dietary Allowances*,[2] *Diet, Nutrition, and Cancer*,[3] *Designing Foods*,[4] and *Diet and Health*.[5]

In government, federal food, nutrition, and health policy initiatives are implemented through laws enacted by the Congress and through regulations promulgated and enforced by the executive branch agencies. Figure 6-2 illustrates the three branches of the federal government—the legislative, executive, and judicial branches—that develop policy; these are discussed further in Chapter 7. The public is at the center as both the benefactor and the beneficiary of these policies. The media, special interests, and scientific evidence exert their influences.

In the legislative branch, food, nutrition, and health issues are under the jurisdiction of a number of committees of the House of Representatives and the Senate. In the executive branch, a number of agencies in the cabinet-

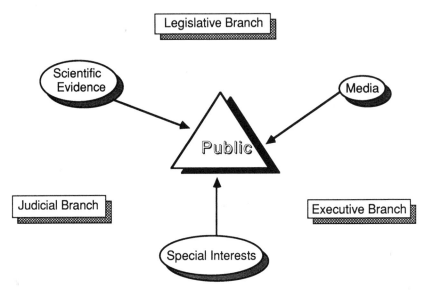

Figure 6-2 The Three Branches of the Federal Government Determine Food and Nutrition Policy

level departments take responsibility for various aspects of food, nutrition, and health. The Department of Health and Human Services (DHHS) and the Department of Agriculture (USDA), however, dominate federal nutrition activities. (Chapter 7 discusses some specific programs within these departments.)

Appendix E lists the key congressional committees and their counterpart executive agency offices responsible for nutrition education, food assistance, nutrition research and monitoring, and food safety. Most of the federal agencies have staff who offer consultation; administer grants, contracts, or cooperative agreements; sponsor continuing education; and prepare and distribute publications appropriate to their respective nutrition program areas. Federal agency resources are listed in Appendix G. These activities influence, implement, and disseminate policies. Evaluations of the federal food programs, for example, have been widely cited when new policies or changes in existing policies are being considered.

MAKING NATIONAL POLICY

Successes and failures in nutrition services, education, food assistance, and research reflect, among other things, the status of federal nutrition

Exhibit 6-1 Operational Steps of Policy Making

1. Identify needs
2. Draft preliminary policy statements
3. Generate strong support
4. Hear public testimony
5. Refine policy document
6. Reject or approve policy statement
7. Implement approved policy
8. Monitor implementation to ensure compliance

policy in the United States over time. Understanding the steps and identifying the participants in federal policy making prepare the nutritionist to contribute to the process. Sequencing the steps suggests that there is a logical progression, but, in reality, steps may be omitted or reversed.

The eight policy-making steps described below are summarized in Exhibit 6-1:

1. Policymakers (e.g., members of Congress or heads of federal agencies) identify needs from reported assessments or direct communications from constituents, scientific studies, or governmental reports. The media often amplify these needs by focusing broader and more dramatic attention on the problem. Legislative and administrative staffs also attempt to forecast future needs by studying trends. The Office of Technology Assessment of the U.S. Congress is charged with responsibility for generating reports based on its objective analyses of emerging issues.
2. Staff from Congress or the administration draft preliminary policy statements (e.g., legislation or regulations). In drafting statements, staff review past and current policies and actions, and address concerns related to the identified need.
3. Policymakers generate strong advocacy for a new policy or a policy change. Staff assess likely sources of support or opposition as they develop the purpose, scope, and rationale for the policy. Effective policy statements are worded to maximize support and minimize opposition. Support is sought from scientists, educators, professionals, concerned constituents, and other policymakers who will commit time and resources to an issue campaign.
4. Policymakers hear public testimony.
5. Staff refine the policy document to reflect public sentiment.

6. Policymakers approve (or reject) the policy statement and appropriations, if authorized.
7. Agency staff translate approved policy statements or legislation into programs to be implemented in communities across the nation. Regulations are written to guide program implementation.
8. Program staff and the public monitor implementation to ensure program compliance with the new policy.

Nutritionists need to understand each step in the development of food, nutrition, and health policies. They should be ready and willing to provide data from their needs assessments, recommend policies, participate in drafting statements, mobilize support, testify, and refine policy statements. They should also know how to translate policies into funding priorities, regulations, standards, and implemented programs.

EVOLUTION OF THE NATION'S NUTRITION POLICY

The broad concern of preventing disease as a step beyond curing it has traditionally guided public health legislation and administrative policies. Historically, nutrition policy emerged as a companion to some more central concern—public health, food safety, consumer protection, national security, antipoverty reforms, or international relations. Exhibit 6-2 lists selected federal domestic nutrition policy initiatives from 1862 to 1988.

Early Developments in National Nutrition Policy

In the early 1900s, concerns about food safety provided the impetus for strong legislation on pure food and drugs, milk inspection, and better sewage disposal. The federal Pure Food and Drug Act of 1906 prohibited interstate commerce in misbranded and adulterated food, beverages, and drugs.

Also during the early 1900s, researchers such as E.V. McCollum isolated vitamins A, B, and D and strongly advocated eating a proper diet to prevent deficiency diseases and perhaps to guard against the more or less constant, but unperceived causes that undermine health.[6] In 1917, the USDA published its first dietary guidance plan, *Five Food Groups*, to help consumers select nutritionally balanced diets.

Continuing the prevention movement in a different direction, the state of Michigan began the first iodine fortification campaign in 1924 to prevent the endemic problem of goiters caused by iodine deficiency.[7] George

Exhibit 6-2 Selected Federal Domestic Nutrition Policy Initiatives, 1862–1988

Year	Initiative
1862	US Department of Agriculture (USDA) created. Morrill Act establishes land grant colleges.
1867	Office of Education established with responsibilities for nutrition education within public schools.
1887	Hatch Act establishes agricultural experiment stations. Federal research laboratory established at Staten Island. (Name is changed to the National Institute of Health in 1930.)
1889	US Public Health Service Commissioned Corps authorized for duty on communicable, nutritional, and other diseases.
1893	USDA authorized by Congress to conduct research on agriculture and human nutrition.
1906	The Pure Food and Drug (Wiley) Act prohibits interstate commerce in misbranded and adulterated foods, drinks, and drugs. Federal Meat Inspection Act passed.
1914	Cooperative Extension Service created as part of USDA.
1916	USDA publishes *Food for Young Children*, first dietary guidance pamphlet.
1917	US Food Administration established to supervise World War I food supply. First dietary recommendations issued by USDA—*Five Food Groups*.
1921–29	Maternity and Infancy Act enabled state health departments to employ nutritionists.
1924	Addition of iodine to salt to prevent goiter is first US food fortification program.
1927	Food, Drug, and Insecticide Administration established. Name is changed to Food and Drug Administration (FDA) in 1932.
1930	USDA and Federal Emergency Relief Administration buy and distribute surplus agricultural commodities as food relief. Public Health Service Hygienic Laboratory designated as National Institute of Health (later changes to National Institutes of Health).
1933	Agricultural Act amendments permit purchase of surplus commodities for donation to child nutrition and school lunch programs.
1935	Food Distribution Program established. Social Security Act authorizes grants to states for nutrition services to mothers and children.
1936–37	USDA conducts first Nationwide Food Consumption Survey (NFCS).
1938	The Food, Drug, and Cosmetic (FD&C) Act includes provisions for food standards. FDA nutrition research program established. Social Security Act provides support for role of nutrition in health.
1939	Federal Surplus Commodities Corporation initiates experimental Food Stamp Program.
1940	National Defense Advisory Commission draws attention to malnutrition in the United States.
1941	President Roosevelt calls National Nutrition Conference, with announcement of first Recommended Dietary Allowances by the Food and Nutrition Board. FDA promulgates standards for enrichment of flour and bread with B-complex vitamins and iron.
1946	National School Lunch Program established.
1947	Laboratories of Nutrition, Chemistry, and Pathology of the National Institutes of Health incorporated into Experimental Biology and Medicine Institute.
1954	Special Milk Program established.
1955	Interdepartmental Committee on Nutrition for National Defense established (discontinued 1967).
1956	Title VII of the Public Health Service Act authorizes funds to support graduate training in public health nutrition.
1958	Food Additives Amendment to FD&C Act prohibits use of a food additive until safety established by manufacturer. Delaney Clause prohibits carcinogenic additives. GRAS (Generally Recognized as Safe) list established.
1961	President Kennedy expands the use of surplus food for needy people at home and abroad and announces a new pilot Food Stamp Program.
1963 & 1965	Maternal and Child Health and Mental Retardation Planning Amendments to the Social Security Act allow for an expanded number of nutritionists in health care programs.
1965	Food Stamp Act passed by Congress. Nationwide Food Consumption Survey collects first data on dietary intake of individuals.
1966	Child Nutrition Act passed. School Breakfast Program established.

Exhibit 6-2 continued

1966–70	President Johnson outlines Food for Freedom Program, the "war on hunger." Allied Health Professions Personnel Training Act includes support for training of dietitians. The Department of Health, Education, and Welfare (DHEW), which later becomes the Department of Health and Human Services (DHHS), sponsors a National Academy of Sciences study, Maternal Nutrition and the Course of Pregnancy, which makes major recommendations related to the role of nutrition in human reproduction.
1968	US Senate Select Committee on Nutrition and Human Needs established.
1968–70	DHEW sponsors Preschool and Ten-State Nutrition Surveys that report evidence of hunger and malnutrition in poverty groups in the United States.
1969	President Nixon calls White House Conference on Food, Nutrition, and Health. Secretary of Agriculture establishes the Food and Nutrition Service to administer federal food assistance programs.
1971–74	The National Center for Health Statistics conducts the first National Health and Nutrition Examination Survey (NHANES) to measure the nutritional status of the US population. This is followed by NHANES II in 1976–80, Hispanic HANES in 1982–84, and NHANES III in 1988.
1972	USDA establishes Special Supplemental Food Program for Women, Infants, and Children (WIC). Agriculture and Consumer Protection Act provides price supports to farmers.
1974	US Senate Select Committee on Nutrition and Human Needs issues Guidelines for a National Nutrition Policy, prepared by the National Nutrition Consortium. Safe Drinking Water Act passed. National Institutes of Health establish Nutrition Coordinating Committee.
1975	US Senate Select Committee on Nutrition and Human Needs issues two editions of Dietary Goals for the United States. Food and
1978	Agricultural Act and Child Nutrition and National School Lunch Amendments passed. Joint Subcommittee on Human Nutrition Research established in Office of Science and Technology Policy (in 1983 becomes Interagency Committee on Human Nutrition Research under joint direction of USDA and DHHS). DHEW and USDA submit proposal to Congress for National Nutrition Monitoring System.
1979	DHEW establishes departmentwide Nutrition Policy Board and issues Healthy People: The Surgeon General's Report on Health Promotion and Disease Prevention.
1980	USDA and DHHS jointly issue Nutrition and Your Health: Dietary Guidelines for Americans. A second edition follows in 1985. DHHS issues Promoting Health/Preventing Disease: Objectives for the Nation, which contains 17 nutrition objectives to be achieved by the year 1990. The Surgeon General's workshop on Maternal and Infant Health makes recommendations about improving nutrition for these vulnerable groups.
1981	DHHS and USDA issue Joint Implementation Plan for a Comprehensive National Nutrition Monitoring System, revised in 1987 as the Operational Plan for the National Nutrition Monitoring System. The Select Panel for the Promotion of Child Health, created by Public Law 95-626, submits to Congress and the Secretary of DHHS its report, which includes recommendations on nutrition.
1984	The Surgeon General's Workshop on Breastfeeding and Human Lactation develops strategies for promoting breast-feeding.
1985	USDA initiates Continuing Survey of Food Intakes by Individuals, repeated in 1986.
1986	DHHS and USDA issue Nutrition Monitoring in the United States, the report of the Joint Nutrition Monitoring Evaluation Committee.
1988	DHHS publishes the Surgeon General's Report on Nutrition and Health.

Source: Reprinted from *Surgeon General's Report on Nutrition and Health*, pp. 29–33, U.S. Government Printing Office, Washington, D.C., 1988.

Rosen, in his *History of Public Health*, described the attention to nutrition as an elixir in America: "By the third decade of this century, scientific nutrition had become in the United States not only an important medicine, but an important component of industry and commerce as well as a major instrument of social policy."[8]

The early pioneers in community nutrition—Lucy Gillet in New York, Frances Stern in Boston, and Lydia Roberts in Chicago—worked with pediatricians to advance nutrition as essential to child growth and development.[9] The high percentage of Selective Service rejectees in World War I suggested that poor nutrition delayed physical development of the nation's youth. To reverse this trend, several public policy initiatives were launched, among them (1) the 1918 Children's Year Campaign that included weighing and measuring infants and preschool children, (2) federal publications that stressed giving children priority milk allocations, and (3) volunteer community feeding programs that supplemented the food of the poor.[10]

Nutrition services as part of public health were first suggested at the White House Conference on Children in 1910. Services began about 1915 in the Children's Bureau, part of the Department of Labor, with efforts to educate health and welfare workers and teachers who worked with children and families.[11] During this time, a bureau survey found malnutrition to be prevalent in children of low-income families in the Appalachian area of Kentucky.

During the 1920s, federal funds provided under the Shepherd Towner Maternity and Infancy Act enabled nine states to employ the first nutritionists as consultants to other health workers. Passage of Title V in the Social Security Act of 1935 expanded public health nutrition services in state and local health agencies. With the 1963 and 1965 amendments to Title V of the Social Security Act, nutrition services were further expanded in direct health care programs such as the Maternal and Infant (M&I) and Children and Youth (C&Y) projects and in diagnostic and treatment programs for children who are mentally retarded or have developmental disabilities.

Federal food assistance programs began in 1930 when the USDA and the Federal Emergency Relief Administration bought and distributed surplus agricultural commodities as food relief. Distribution of surplus commodities marked the beginning of child nutrition, school lunch, and food stamp programs during the 1930s. The National School Lunch Program and the Special Milk Program were established in 1946 and 1954, respectively.

National Nutrition Policy from the 1960s to the Present

The 1969 White House Conference on Food, Nutrition, and Health positioned food and nutrition on the national agenda in its own right.[12]

Conference participants made recommendations to

- enhance nutrition in health services throughout the life span
- improve nutrition education in schools, in the training of health care providers, and for the public
- improve food assistance to low-income families
- expand and coordinate basic and applied nutrition research
- establish a nutrition monitoring and surveillance system for the entire population and for targeted high-risk groups
- strengthen food safety and inspection activities[13]

These concepts laid the groundwork for today's array of national nutrition policies.

Nutrition Services and Education

Policymakers in the 1970s continued to view nutrition as an integral part of many public health and food programs. The Special Supplemental Food Program for Women, Infants, and Children (WIC) passed in 1972 as part of child nutrition legislation. Though primarily designed as a food assistance program, it strengthened the food-nutrition-health connection.

State- and locally funded primary health care programs began requiring nutrition services. Nutrition became a component of community health education programs that reached persons with diabetes, hypertension, and other chronic diseases. More state and local nutritionists' positions were funded from such federal grants as WIC, maternal and child health, health promotion, home health services, congregate meals for the elderly, and the Head Start Program.

Nutrition policy shifted from defining nutrition problems as too little food to recognizing the risks of too much of certain dietary factors. This concept ushered in federal dietary guidance on health promotion and disease prevention. The Senate Select Committee on Nutrition and Human Needs examined the evidence linking diet and the major killing and crippling chronic diseases and, in 1977, issued the *Dietary Goals for the United States.*[14]

As discussed in Chapter 2, after much debate, in 1980, the USDA and DHHS jointly published nonquantitative recommendations in *Nutrition and Your Health: Dietary Guidelines for Americans.*[15] A 1985 revised version closely followed the earlier publication. In 1989, a third panel of nutrition experts was convened to consider revisions to the dietary guidelines.

As is evident in the 1988 *Surgeon General's Report on Nutrition and Health,*[16] the current nonquantitative recommendations remain the federal policy on dietary advice for Americans. The National Research Council's report *Diet and Health*[17] may signal a shift to quantifying dietary guidelines for the intake of fat, cholesterol, saturated fat, sodium, fruits, vegetables, and grain products. For adults at risk of chronic diseases, both the National Cancer Institute and the National Heart, Lung, and Blood Institute have launched their own national nutrition education campaigns.

The 1979 Surgeon General's report, Healthy People,[18] focused significant attention on nutrition, as did a follow-up DHHS publication, *Promoting Health/Preventing Disease: Objectives for the Nation.*[19] This latter report devoted one of the fifteen chapters to nutrition and identified seventeen objectives to reduce nutritional risk factors. Objectives proposed for the year 2000 include, in Chapter 1, twenty-four nutrition objectives.[20]

To monitor progress toward meeting the 1990 objectives, DHHS conducted a midcourse review in 1986.[21] This analysis found that the lack of baseline data and data collection systems hindered assessing progress. Some evidence suggested gains in the number of women breast-feeding and in the number of persons adopting weight control regimens; however, the prevalence of overweight and high blood cholesterol remains critical. To achieve national nutrition objectives, a more comprehensive approach to nutrition programming, more resources, and more extensive nutrition-monitoring systems are needed that include data for each state, as well as for the federal level.[22]

In the 1970s, use of the food label as a nutrition education tool added to the listing of ingredients information on the nutrient content of foods. The Food and Drug Administration (FDA) implemented the voluntary Nutritional Labeling Program, permitting food product labels to present the nutrient content based on U.S. Recommended Dietary Allowances (RDAs). The U.S. RDAs are the nutrient standards set for nutrition labeling and reflect the highest of the RDAs for all sex-age categories for most nutrients as published in 1968.

As nutrition policy embraced health promotion, the FDA issued regulations that extended voluntary nutrition labeling to include sodium.[23] Proposed regulations and legislation would extend labeling to cholesterol and several of the individual fatty acids.[24] Food companies view nutrient labeling as an opportunity to make claims about the potential health benefits associated with a product. This marketing approach has brought this nutrition policy issue to national attention, and the resolution of the health claims debate awaits the FDA's issuance of final regulations.

The 1980s have seen a policy climate of consolidation and fiscal constraint. In passing the Omnibus Budget Reconciliation Act of 1981, Congress combined a large number of categorical public health programs under several federal block grants and reduced levels of funding. With block grants, more responsibility for public health policy was delegated to state and local health agencies.

After three years of reduced health expenditures, studies by the National Academy of Sciences,[25] the National Commission To Prevent Infant Mortality,[26] and Congress documented negative effects on low-income populations and a leveling off in the infant mortality rate decline. In response, Congress began to reinstate modest increases in funds to the Maternal and Child Health block grant, Medicaid, and other public health programs.

Reduced government regulation has also been a policy thrust of the 1980s. For example, in 1987, the Health Care Financing Administration (HCFA) issued a proposed rule that, among other things, dropped the requirement for dietary services staffing and professional qualifications from Medicare and Medicaid regulations. Using its legislative network and joining a coalition, The American Dietetic Association successfully mobilized forces to stop this HCFA proposal and maintained the standards for dietary services.

Food Assistance

In the 1970s, congressional representatives responded to identified problems of poverty by improving food assistance programs to needy families. They expanded the Food Stamp Program and the National School Lunch Program. They created the National School Breakfast Program and the Special Supplemental Food Program for Women, Infants, and Children (WIC). Faced with rising budget deficits in the early 1980s, Congress reduced expenditures for food assistance programs by one-third. Tightened program eligibility criteria, coupled with reduced or frozen benefits, substantially decreased the number of recipients. Ironically, as program reductions were being enacted, evidence from several program evaluations confirmed the effectiveness of programs and recommended areas for program improvement.

By 1983, hunger emerged again as a powerful social and public health issue. Nutritionists and others reported expanding lists of eligible WIC applicants. Soup kitchens were serving increasing numbers of families with children, and there was heavy demand for emergency food packages. Staff of hospital emergency rooms reported observing children and adults suffering from malnutrition.[27]

Responding to the paradox of reports of increased hunger at the time that agricultural surpluses were swelling in warehouses, Congress enacted the Temporary Emergency Food Assistance Program (TEFAP) of 1984. TEFAP distributed surplus commodities to families at nutritional risk. In further response, Congress began to reverse earlier legislative actions that had reduced benefits and eligibility for the Food Stamp, National School Lunch, National School Breakfast, Commodity Food Distribution, and WIC programs.

By gathering relevant data and communicating their observations to policymakers, nutritionists have influenced the direction of legislation. Their findings provided part of the justification for strengthening food assistance programs. For example, based on the national evaluation,[28] lawmakers have secured additional appropriations for WIC from 1984 through 1989. This evaluation showed that infants participating in WIC had larger head circumferences, that fetal death rates were reduced, and that intakes of key nutrients were improved in the diets of women, infants, and children. The recommendation from a national evaluation of school breakfasts[29] that the meal include more iron and vitamins A and B$_6$ led to the authorization of increased reimbursements for breakfasts in the 1986 School Lunch and Child Nutrition Program amendments.

Nutrition Research

Several legislative and administrative actions served to expand and coordinate inter- and intra-agency nutrition research. The Food and Agriculture Act of 1977 designated the USDA as the lead agency for investigations in human nutrition. A structure to coordinate research and dietary guidance was then created under one director in the Department of Agriculture. The Department of Health and Human Services (DHHS) was authorized to study the causes, diagnosis, treatment, control, and prevention of physical and mental diseases of man. A nutrition coordinating office was set up to oversee research at the National Institutes of Health. The Office of Science and Technology Policy under the Executive Office of the President formed a Joint Subcommittee on Human Nutrition Research, raising nutrition to unprecedented status. The congressional Office of Technology Assessment reviewed federal nutrition research activities and published reports that contributed to enhanced coordination.

Although some of the formal organizational structures have disappeared, some efforts to coordinate federal nutrition research continue. The report *Human Nutrition Research: The Federal Five-Year Plan*[30] identifies current and proposed areas for governmentwide nutrition research. The *Surgeon General's Report on Nutrition and Health*[31] reviews current scientific literature and suggests future directions for nutrition research.

Nutrition Monitoring and Surveillance

Since policy development depends in part on scientific data, lack of quality data has often translated into inaction or inappropriate policy. The

USDA has surveyed household food consumption since 1936; however, the system has not tracked individual dietary intakes or nutritional status.

In 1968, Congress sought information on the nutritional health of the nation and mandated the Ten-State Nutrition Survey. Between 1968 and 1970, nutrition status indicators of populations in five low-income and five high-income states were surveyed and reported by DHHS. This survey spearheaded implementation of the DHHS National Health and Nutrition Examination Survey (NHANES) as a periodic survey, beginning in 1971. The USDA National Food Consumption Survey added an individual interview component in 1977–78 and the Continuing Survey of Intakes by Individuals in 1985. The Centers for Disease Control began tracking nutrition indicators for children and women through the Pediatric and Pregnancy Nutrition Surveillance Systems developed in collaboration with state public health agencies. These surveys are discussed in detail in Chapter 16.

Evidence from national nutrition surveys has often guided policy decisions on nutrition education initiatives, food assistance, health programs, and food fortification. At the request of Congress, joint reports of the national nutrition-monitoring activities conducted by the USDA and DHHS were published in 1986 and 1989, reporting the dietary and nutritional status of the U.S. population as shown by the available survey data. For the past ten years, Congress, lobbied by nutrition, health, and antihunger advocacy groups, has questioned the timeliness and completeness of the data it receives. In 1988, Congress passed the National Nutrition Monitoring and Related Research Act, calling for improvements in federal monitoring activities. This bill was vetoed by President Reagan, but was reintroduced in the Senate and House in 1989. A coalition of nutrition professional societies, private health organizations, commodity groups, and advocacy groups continues to lobby for the nutrition-monitoring bill.

Public health nutrition researchers have contributed to policy development by improving the quality of scientific data available. In the future, they can help (1) develop new systems to collect and analyze data, (2) create new methodology to gather data from hard-to-reach populations (e.g., the homeless, deaf, elderly, institutionalized, migrant, Native American, and non-English-speaking populations), and (3) document changes in nutrition knowledge, dietary behavior, and nutrition-related health outcomes in local programs or communities.

Food Safety and Quality

In the late 1970s and early 1980s, food safety debates expanded from concerns about food contamination because of poor sanitation and inspection practices to concerns about birth defects, cancers, and health problems associated with pesticides, drugs, and such additives as nitrates, saccharin, and cyclamates in foods. The 1958 Delaney Clause was enacted to prevent food processors from adding any substance to food that has been shown to induce cancer in humans or in laboratory animals. Subsequently, animal drugs were covered by this prohibition. Drugs found to be carcinogens could be used if no residues were found in the food analyzed by acceptable methods.

Exemptions to absolute prohibition under the anticancer clause have been created for numerous substances. In the absence of an acceptable substitute for the artificial sweetener saccharin or the curing agent nitrite, the public and hence policymakers found ways to place a moratorium on a ban of saccharin and to postpone action on nitrites.[32] The 1977 saccharin debate and the 1978 nitrite case tested the concept of absolute abolition and initiated an examination of food safety policy.[33]

In 1981, some scientists, regulators, consumers, and policymakers and the food industry attempted to reform food safety laws to redefine acceptable levels of risk associated with food additives. Current and more sensitive analytical techniques for risk assessment had rendered the legal definitions of "safe" (the zero standard of the Delaney Clause) obsolete. To correct the perceived problem, some members of Congress sought changes in the Food, Drug, and Cosmetic Act that would substitute risk/benefit appraisals for the hazard-free approach of the Delaney Clause. Strong opposition from consumer groups stalled the reform initiative in Congress, although administrative and congressional actions have permitted exceptions to the Delaney Clause to remain. This debate continues.

Reports of serious outbreaks of food-borne illnesses and media attention to pesticides in food have again raised questions about food safety and the need to examine meat and poultry inspection policies,[34] the cleanliness of water and fish products, the use of antibiotics in livestock, and pesticide residues on plants.[35] As biotechnology changes the methods of food production, preservation, and protection and manipulates the composition of the food supply, public health professionals must raise more questions and sharpen their understanding of the tradeoffs. (See Chapter 13.)

FUTURE DIRECTIONS FOR NATIONAL NUTRITION POLICY

To anticipate the future of national nutrition policy requires learning lessons from past and present policy priorities. It also requires attempting to forecast population dynamics, budget realities, technological capabilities, and the expansion of the science base through research. An advisory panel of scientists under the National Academy of Sciences has been convened to receive testimony from nutritionists and other public health professionals to shape nutrition policy for the year 2000. To protect the public's health at lower cost, policymakers will be looking at opportunities to combine the more traditional public sector approaches with private sector innovations.

ISSUES TO DEBATE

- Will today's advances in food technology, which are changing the food supply, extending shelf life, removing fat and sugar, and shortening preparation time, benefit or imperil the nation's long-term health? What safeguards, such as testing, monitoring, and/or regulating, should the federal government undertake to protect the public's health? What standards for food safety and nutritional adequacy are needed? How can nutritionists work with agribusiness and food processors to assure that corporate policies consider public health implications of biotechnological advances?

- What will be the effect on public health and public health nutrition services in the future if today's public health policy continues to focus on "putting out fires" by using most of the available funds to respond to the crisis of the moment?

- If universal health insurance becomes a reality in the next five years, what nutrition services and education programs should be covered? What steps should be implemented now to assure collection of data to justify the inclusion of nutrition services as promoting health and reducing health care costs?

- How can the food label be a credible source of health and nutrition information and be more informative and understandable?

NOTES

1. The American Dietetic Association, "Position Paper on National Nutrition Policy," *Journal of The American Dietetic Association* 76 (1980): 596–97. American Public Health Association, "Policy Statements Adopted by the Governing Council," *American Journal of Public Health* 78, no. 2 (1988): 187–216. National Nutrition Consortium, Inc., "A National Nutrition Policy," *Nutrition Today* 2 (1974): 33–35.

2. National Research Council, *Recommended Dietary Allowances*, 10th ed. (Washington, D.C.: National Academy Press, 1989).

3. National Research Council and National Academy of Sciences, *Diet, Nutrition, and Cancer* (Washington, D.C.: National Academy Press, 1982).

4. National Research Council and National Academy of Sciences, *Designing Foods, Animal Product Options in the Marketplace* (Washington, D.C.: National Academy Press, 1988).

5. National Research Council, *Diet and Health* (Washington, D.C.: National Academy Press, 1989).

6. Elmer V. McCollum, *The Newer Knowledge of Nutrition*, 2d ed. (New York: Macmillan, 1922), 269–383.

7. Howard Markel and David Murray Cowie, "'When It Rains It Pours': Endemic Goiter, Iodized Salt, and David Murray Cowie, MD," *American Journal of Public Health* 77, no. 2 (1987): 219–29.

8. George Rosen, *History of Public Health* (New York: M.D. Publications, 1958), 404–419.

9. Mary Egan, "Public Health Nutrition Services: Issues Today and Tomorrow," *Journal of the American Dietetic Association* 77, no. 4 (1980): 423–33.

10. Ibid.

11. Mary Egan, "Federal Nutrition Support Programs for Children," *Pediatric Clinics of North America* 24, no. 10 (1977): 229–39.

12. White House Conference on Food, Nutrition, and Health, *Summary of Actions on Food, Nutrition, and Health* (Washington, D.C.: Government Printing Office, 1970).

13. Ibid.

14. Senate Select Committee on Nutrition and Human Needs, *Eating in America: Dietary Goals for the United States* (Cambridge, Mass.: MIT Press, 1977), 12–51.

15. Ibid.

16. U.S. Department of Health and Human Services, *The Surgeon General's Report on Nutrition and Health* (Washington, D.C.: Government Printing Office, 1988).

17. National Research Council, *Diet and Health.*

18. U.S. Department of Health, Education, and Welfare, *Healthy People: The Surgeon General's Report on Health Promotion and Disease Prevention* (Washington, D.C.: Government Printing Office, 1979).

19. U.S. Department of Health and Human Services, *Promoting Health/Preventing Disease: Objectives for the Nation* (Washington, D.C.: Government Printing Office, 1980).

20. U. S. Department of Health and Human Services, *Promoting Health/Preventing Disease: Year 2000 Objectives for the Nation* (Washington, D.C.: Government Printing Office, 1989), 1–24.

21. U.S. Department of Health and Human Services, *The 1990 Health Objectives for the Nation: A Midcourse Review* (Washington, D.C.: Government Printing Office, 1986).

22. Mildred Kaufman, Jerianne Heimendinger, Susan Foerster, and MaryAnne Caroll, "Progress toward Meeting the 1990 Nutrition Objectives for the Nation: Nutrition Services and Data Collection in State/Territorial Health Agencies," *American Journal of Public Health* 77, no. 3 (1987): 299–303.

23. House Subcommittee on Investigations and Oversight, Committee on Science and Technology, *Sodium in Food and High Blood Pressure*, 97th Cong., 1981 .

24. Food and Drug Administration, Department of Health and Human Services, "Food Labelling: Declaration of Sodium Content of Foods and Label Claims for Foods on the Basis of Sodium Content: OMB Approval and Effective Date," *Federal Register* 49, no. 126 (1984).

25. Institute of Medicine, *Preventing Low Birth Weight* (Washington, D.C.: National Academy Press, 1985).

26. National Commission To Prevent Infant Mortality, *Death before Life* (Washington, D.C.: National Commission To Prevent Infant Mortality, 1988).

27. Institute of Medicine, *Preventing Low Birth Weight.* National Commission To Prevent Infant Mortality, *Death before Life.* Food Research and Action Center, *Hunger in the Eighties: A Primer* (Washington, D.C.: Food Research and Action Center, Inc., 1984). *Report of the President's Task Force on Food Assistance* (Washington, D.C.: President's Task Force on Food Assistance, January 10, 1984), i–xi. House Select Committee on Hunger, *Alleviating Hunger: Progress and Prospects*, 98th Cong., 1984, Serial No. 98-2. Subcommittee on Domestic Marketing, Consumer Relations, and Nutrition, Committee on Agriculture, *Hunger in the United States and Related Issues*, 98th Cong., 1984, Serial No. 98-63. Senate Subcommittee on Nutrition, Committee on Agriculture, Nutrition, and Forestry, *Oversight on Nutritional Status of Low-Income Americans in the 1980s*, 98th Cong., 1983.

28. David Rush, *The National WIC Evaluation* (Washington, D.C.: Office of Analysis and Evaluation, Food and Nutrition Service, U.S. Department of Agriculture, 1985).

29. Systems Development Corporation, *National Evaluation of School Nutrition Programs: Overview and Presentation of Findings*, vol. 1. Final report prepared for the U.S. Department of Agriculture (1983).

30. Interagency Committee on Human Nutrition Research, *Human Nutrition Research: The Federal Five-Year Plan* (Washington, D.C.: Government Printing Office, March 1986).

31. U.S. Department of Health and Human Services, *The Surgeon General's Report.*

32. Donna V. Porter, *The Delaney Clause: Current Application and Proposed Changes* (Washington, D.C.: Congressional Research Service, 1984).

33. Senate Committee on Agriculture, Nutrition, and Forestry, *Food Safety: Where Are We?* (Washington, D.C.: Government Printing Office, 1979).

34. National Research Council and National Academy of Sciences, *Meat and Poultry Inspection* (Washington, D.C.: National Academy Press, 1985).

35. Ibid. National Research Council and National Academy of Sciences, *Regulating Pesticides in Food* (Washington, D.C.: National Academy Press, 1987).

chapter **7**

Influencing Federal Health and Nutrition Legislation and Regulations

Robert Earl

READER OBJECTIVES

- Compare and contrast the functions of the legislative, executive, and judicial branches of the U.S. government.
- Describe the major federal agencies that administer programs relating to public health and nutrition.
- Discuss how the nutrition professional can influence federal legislation and regulations.
- List the strategies that can be used to advocate for public programs.
- Discuss the acceptable ways that public agency staff prohibited from legislative activity can work for public policies in which they believe.

THE PUBLIC HEALTH PROFESSIONAL AS AN ADVOCATE

Most public health personnel are employed in jobs that were established to carry out programs and services enabled by federal or state legislation or city or county ordinances. They are obligated to assure that their services meet the legislators' intent, that these services are cost effective, and that there is no waste, fraud, or abuse in their operation. When operational problems arise because of the red tape of the legislation or regulations, public health personnel should advocate for the changes needed. When the community assessment identifies unmet or undermet needs in the community, public health personnel are challenged to advocate for the creation of new programs and services.

In a democracy, laws are enacted by representatives elected by the people. Elected officials—whether they are city or county commissioners, state legislators, or federal representatives or senators—should represent

117

the prevailing values and the will of the majority of their constituents. Such officials should be approachable by their constituents and responsive to their concerns and their needs. However, nutritionists should be sophisticated enough to understand that in the political process there is an ongoing power play among conflicting values, vested interests, and ambitious personalities. Both the public and the elected officials constantly change their views as they are pressured by multiple conflicting interests. Negotiation and tradeoffs are the ground rules of politics.

To influence the governing process requires an understanding of how it works and where the power lies. The federal government of the United States has evolved over two hundred years, based on a Constitution which provides a system with checks and balances that distribute the decision making responsibilities and the power among the legislative, judicial, and executive branches.

UNDERSTANDING HOW THE FEDERAL GOVERNMENT WORKS

Legislative Branch Responsibilities

The United States Congress, comprised of the House of Representatives and the Senate, is the legislative branch. The legislative branch enacts laws that initiate, modify, authorize, and appropriate funds for all programs and services administered by the federal government. In Congress, most action occurs in the committees or subcommittees. Several types of committees consider food, nutrition, and health issues.

Standing committees are permanently established to create and approve legislation, to authorize programs, and to oversee program implementation. The following standing committees have jurisdiction over food-, nutrition-, and health-related programs:

Senate

- Committee on Agriculture, Nutrition, and Forestry (child nutrition and other food programs)
- Committee on Appropriations (program funding)
- Committee on Finance (Medicare and Medicaid programs)
- Committee on Foreign Relations (international hunger)
- Committee on Labor and Human Resources (Department of Health and Human Services programs: elderly nutrition, maternal and child health, food labeling)

House of Representatives

- Committee on Agriculture (food programs)
- Committee on Appropriations (program funding)
- Committee on Education and Labor (child and elderly nutrition programs)
- Committee on Energy and Commerce (food labeling)
- Committee on Ways and Means (Medicare and Medicaid)

See Appendix E for more information on these committees.

Select committees are established for a limited and a specific purpose. They do not have the authority to authorize or to appropriate funds for programs. Following are the currently active select committees working on food, nutrition, and health issues:

- Senate Special Committee on Aging
- House Select Committee on Children, Youth, and Families
- House Select Committee on Hunger

Differences between the versions of a bill passed by the House and the Senate are reconciled by a conference committee appointed from members of the relevant House and Senate committees. Thus, these joint committees have representation from both the House and the Senate.

The Legislative Process—How a Bill Becomes a Law

Congress enacts legislation through an intricate system of development, review, debate, negotiation, and approval. Ideas for new legislation may be conceived by members of Congress based on problems and concerns brought to their attention by their staff or their constituents, as well as on needs evidenced in the operation of federal programs. Nutritionists as individuals or through their professional organizations can propose new legislation to meet a demonstrated community need or program changes they identify as being needed. The National Nutrition Monitoring bill was conceived by a nutritionist who recommended it to a member of Congress.

Knowing the steps in the legislative process, the key decision makers at each step, and their responsibilities suggests the appropriate actions for the concerned professional to take. Knowing the times to contact the key decision makers is critical to success. By studying the sequence shown in Figure 7-1, the strategic contact points can be identified. This suggests when

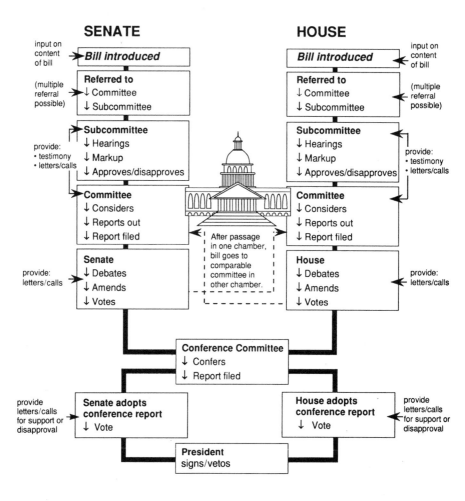

Figure 7-1 How a Bill Becomes Law—Typical Path to Passage of Legislation

---

to offer to testify or when to write or telephone during the time that a critical piece of health or nutrition legislation is being considered.

Federal Budget Development and Control

Through the federal budget system, funds for federal programs are allocated, balancing national needs with available resources. Each year the federal budget is developed simultaneously by the president and the Con-

Table 7-1 Federal Budget Timetable

Budget Action	Deadline
• President submits budget to Congress	First Monday after January 3
• Authorizing, joint, and appropriations committees submit reports to budget committees	February 25
• Congress adopts first budget resolution	April 15
• Authorizing committees report authorization bills, providing budget authority	May 15
• House committees complete action on appropriations bills	June 30
• Congress adopts 13 appropriations bills, providing spending authority	September
• President signs appropriations bills	October 1
• Fiscal year begins	October 1

gress. The nation's budget is shaped in three interfacing phases: executive branch development, congressional action, and budget execution (see Table 7-1).

When it passes legislation, Congress authorizes the maximum funding level for a program. Then each year it appropriates the actual amount to be spent, which may be less than it authorizes. Authorizing legislation can create programs or agencies for a specific time period or indefinitely.

Congressional Action on the Federal Budget

When Congress receives the president's budget request, it approves, modifies, or disapproves it by passing legislation. Congress can change the level of program funding, eliminate programs, or add programs not requested by the president. It can also enact legislation to raise or lower various types of federal taxes or generate other sources of revenue.

The Congressional Budget Act of 1974 requires that current services estimates be transmitted to Congress with the budget to provide a basis for reviewing the president's budget recommendations. The current services estimates of budget authority and outlays are estimates of the funds required to continue federal programs and activities at their existing level during the fiscal year in progress. Current services estimates have been very important in efforts to maintain funding for the Special Supplemental Food Program for Women, Infants, and Children (WIC).

Table 7-2 Maximum Federal Deficit Amounts under the Gramm-Rudman-Hollings Act

Fiscal Year	Deficit (billions)
1988	$144.0
1989	$136.0
1990	$100.0
1991	$ 64.0
1992	$ 28.0
1993	$ 0.0

The Balanced Budget and Emergency Deficit Control Act of 1985 (the Gramm-Rudman-Hollings Act) was passed because Congress had failed to establish budget targets for federal programs and to keep federal expenditures within available revenues. As amended in 1987, the Act requires the federal budget deficit to be reduced each year to achieve a zero deficit in FY 1993. The act requires the president to submit a budget that does not exceed the maximum deficit amount for the applicable fiscal year. Similarly, congressional budget resolutions must not exceed this maximum deficit amount. See Table 7-2 for a listing of the maximum federal deficit amounts under the Gramm-Rudman-Hollings Act, FY 1988-1993.

An automatic procedure, called a sequestration order, requires across-the-board cuts to achieve deficit reduction targets. It is important to know that Food Stamp, Child Nutrition, and the WIC programs are not subject to sequestration or limits on the level of sequestration. Members of Congress have made several unsuccessful attempts to remove the exemption status from some of these privileged programs. See Exhibit 7-1 for a listing of the major programs exempted from sequestration by the Gramm-Rudman-Hollings Act. Under the requirements of the Gramm-Rudman-Hollings Act, Congress considers the budget totals before acting on individual appropriations. This results in the adoption of a concurrent budget resolution developed by the House and Senate Committees on the Budget. This resolution guides the House and Senate Committees on Appropriations in setting spending levels for the several agencies and individual programs.

Appropriation legislation establishes the specific funding level to support federal programs and agencies for the fiscal year. It generally follows the enactment of authorization legislation. Congress does not vote directly on the level of outlays, but rather on budget authority to incur obligations for immediate or future outlays of federal funds. The appropriation cycle begins in the House of Representatives. Once appropriations have been passed by the House, the bills are considered by the Senate. Differences

Exhibit 7-1 Major Programs Exempted from Sequestration by the Gramm-Rudman-Hollings Act

---

- Aid to Families with Dependent Children (AFDC)
- Child Nutrition Programs
- Earned Income Tax Credits
- Family Support Payments
- Federal Military and Civilian Retirement Benefits
- Food Stamps
- Guaranteed Student Loans
- Interest on the National Debt
- Medicaid
- Medicare
- Outlays from Prior Year Appropriations
- Social Security
- Special Supplemental Food Program for Women, Infants, and Children (WIC)
- State Unemployment Benefits
- Supplemental Security Income
- Veterans' Compensation and Pensions

---

between the House and Senate decisions on program funding are reconciled through a House-Senate conference committee. After the differences are reconciled, the appropriations bills are sent to the president, who signs or vetoes them.

When action on appropriations has not been completed by the beginning of the federal fiscal year, Congress must enact a continuing resolution to authorize the affected federal agencies to continue paying their obligations up to a specified date or until the regular appropriations are enacted. In recent years, Congress has enacted continuing resolutions to keep the federal government operating. These bills, generally called omnibus budget reconciliation acts (OBRAs), allow operations to continue into the next fiscal year.

Executive Branch Budget Development and Control

Each September, one year in advance of the following fiscal year (October 1 to September 30), federal agencies submit budget requests to the Office of Management and Budget (OMB). These requests are reviewed, and budget decisions are made based on the president's fiscal policy, the resources needed to carry out programs, congressional budget authority, current receipts, and anticipated economic conditions.

During the formulation of the administration's budget, there is a continual exchange of information, proposals, evaluations, and policy decisions among the president, OMB, other executive office units, and the federal agencies. Budget decisions are based on and influenced by the results of previous budgets, including that currently in use by the federal agencies and the previous year's budget being considered by Congress. Final decisions on budget requests are greatly influenced by the requirements of the Congressional Budget Act of 1974 and the Balanced Budget and Emergency Deficit Control Act of 1985.

The president's proposed financial plan presents the administration's priorities for the federal government. This budget process operates as a multiyear plan to accomplish the programmatic and fiscal goals for the four years of the president's administration. Law in effect requires the president to submit the budget proposal to Congress on or before the Monday that follows January 3 of each year. However, in recent years, the budget has been transmitted later due to delays in congressional action on the previous year's budget.

Once the president signs the budget into law, it serves as the basis for financing federal agency operations. OMB apportions appropriations to each agency by time periods and activities (line items) to ensure the effective use of resources and to guard against the need for additional program funding. Under the Impoundment Control Act of 1974, the executive branch has the authority to regulate the amount of spending through deferrals or rescissions in budget authority. Such withholding of appropriated funds is executed to provide for contingencies or to achieve savings.[1]

Executive Branch Responsibilities

When a piece of legislation has passed both houses of Congress, it is sent to the president to sign into law. Writing to the president to urge him to sign desirable legislation or to veto opposed legislation is another important responsibility of advocates. When the president vetoes a piece of legislation, it is sent back to Congress. If Congress is in session, both the House and Senate can override the veto by passing the bill with a two-thirds majority vote.

Once the legislation is passed and signed by the president, or a veto overridden, implementation and enforcement of the law become the responsibility of the executive branch agency to which it is assigned. In the federal agencies, appointed and career service bureaucrats write detailed regulations or rules that define the requirements for implementing the law. These regulations are designed to carry out the intent of Congress, have the power of laws, and can be legally enforced with fines for noncompliance. How closely the regulations carry out the legislative intent may depend on whether the philosophy and policies of Congress and the administering agency officials coincide. When the president and the majority of the members of both houses of Congress are of the same political party, there is usually some degree of unanimity. When they are of opposing parties, some discrepancies may be noted between the legislation and the proposed rules and guidance materials.

The *Federal Register*

Regulations for federal programs are compiled in the *Code of Federal Regulations* (CFR), which is revised and published each year. The *Federal Register* is the principal document that disseminates federal regulations. Interim regulatory activity is published in the *Federal Register*. Copies of the CFR and the *Federal Register* are usually available at state health agency, university, or public libraries and at courthouses and federal office buildings. Individual issues of the *Federal Register* can be purchased from the Government Printing Office.

The *Federal Register* is published daily. Items in the *Federal Register* are categorized by the type of action to be taken. A notice generally announces meetings or other items under agency review. A notice of proposed rule-making (NPRM) announces an action that an agency is considering. Such notices precede the issuance of a proposed rule, and the response to an NPRM can affect the form and substance of a proposed rule. A proposed rule is a draft of a new regulation or a revision of an existing regulation. The public is invited to comment in response to both the NPRM and the proposed rules. Comment periods are set at 30, 60, or 90 days, at the discretion of the agency. Usually, the more complex the proposal, the longer the comment period.

After proposed program regulations are revised and approved by the agency and the administration, the final rule is published. The final rule carries an effective date which can range from immediately to several years in the future. Corrections are issued to rectify problems with the content of regulations; generally, these are technical corrections such as dates, rates, and program formulas.

Petitions are also published in the *Federal Register*. A petition is a formal request made to an agency by an individual, firm, or organization that a certain action be taken or not be taken or that a regulation or order be established, revoked, or revised. In the public health arena, most petitions are submitted to the Food and Drug Administration.[2]

Responding to Proposed Rules

Commenting on proposals or other items in the *Federal Register* is as important as communicating views to Congress about specific pieces of legislation. As much can happen in administrative agencies as in Congress. Nutritionists must continuously monitor the activities of administrative agencies related to food and nutrition programs. At the federal level, the primary agencies to watch are the Department of Health and Human Services and the Department of Agriculture. The quickest way to keep informed is to establish a network of federal agency contacts who will call or write to advise on current and upcoming administrative proposals.

When writing comments on a regulatory proposal, the comments should be accurately indexed to specific regulatory citations in the *Federal Register*. Comments should be stated concisely and, when necessary, reference the scientific literature. The identity and expertise of the respondent should also be included in the letter. Regulations may influence program plans and content, staff qualifications, required services provided, budget use, and reporting requirements. Therefore, proposed rules should be carefully studied and analyzed for cost effectiveness and potential agency and staff overload of red tape and paperwork.

FEDERAL AGENCIES AND PROGRAMS INVOLVED WITH FOOD, NUTRITION, AND HEALTH

Several federal agencies administer most of the food, nutrition, and health legislation. These agencies usually offer consultation, training, and guidance materials to interpret their laws and regulations. Getting to know key agency staff and contacting the federal consultants for their advice and guidance facilitate program implementation and help resolve any misunderstandings of the laws and regulations. See Appendix G for a listing of federal agencies employing nutrition consultants with their addresses and telephone numbers.

Department of Health and Human Services

The Department of Health and Human Services (DHHS) is the second largest federal agency in terms of dollars received from the federal budget for its programs. It administers the majority of public health and nutrition programs.

Public Health Service

The Office of Disease Prevention and Health Promotion (ODPHP) coordinates federal health promotion and disease prevention activities. It has published *Healthy People, Promoting Health/Preventing Disease: Objectives for the Nation*, and the *Surgeon General's Report on Nutrition and Health*. ODPHP is the agency coordinating the development and implementation of the National Health Objectives for the Year 2000.

The Food and Drug Administration (FDA) is responsible for the regulation of food, drugs, cosmetics, and other products. The FDA regulates nutrition labeling on food product packages and is considering proposals for fat and cholesterol labeling and health messages on food labels.

Several components of the National Institutes of Health (NIH) manage nutrition research and education programs. The National Cholesterol Education Program (NCEP) and the National High Blood Pressure Education Program (NHBPEP) are administered by the National Heart, Lung, and Blood Institute (NHLBI). The National Cancer Institute (NCI) is taking leadership in research on innovative nutrition education interventions for cancer prevention.

The Centers for Disease Control (CDC) administer nutrition monitoring and other nutrition surveillance activities of DHHS. (See Chapter 16.) In 1987, the National Center for Health Statistics (NCHS) became a center within CDC. NCHS administers the periodic National Health and Nutrition Examination Surveys (NHANES) and publishes and disseminates the data. The Division of Chronic Disease Control of the Center for Environmental Health and Injury Control and the Center for Health Promotion and Education have been combined to form a new Center for Chronic Disease Prevention and Health Promotion (CCDPHP). The preventive health services block grant, which covers screening and referral for many chronic diseases, is administered by CCDPHP. The Division of Nutrition in CCDPHP manages pediatric and pregnancy surveillance programs. The Center's Behavioral Risk Factor Survey (BRFS) includes some nutrition questions.

The Health Resources and Services Administration (HRSA) administers the maternal and child health block grant through the Division of Maternal and Child Health Resources Development (Title V, Social Security Act). Since 1935, this agency has fostered public health nutrition programs at the state and local levels by providing expert consultation through its central and regional offices, training materials, and funding for continuing education and graduate training of public health nutritionists. It administers grants for research and for innovative projects, Special Projects of Regional and National Significance (SPRANS). HRSA also administers funds for community health centers, migrant health, rural health, AIDS education, and allied health professions training.

Office of Human Development Services

The Office of Human Development Services (ODHS) includes the Administration on Aging (AoA) which administers meal programs for the elderly under Title III of the Older Americans Act (OAA). The act was reauthorized by Congress in 1987, and a new provision for preventive health services was added. Nutrition education and counseling for older Americans are among the six services allowed under this new program.

The Administration for Children, Youth, and Families (ACYF) administers the Head Start Program, which provides health, food, and nutrition education for children and their parents. The health component of Head Start, including nutrition, is administered through a cooperative agreement among HRSA, PHS, and ODHS.

Health Care Financing Administration

The Health Care Financing Administration (HCFA) administers the Medicare (Title XVIII, Social Security Act) and Medicaid (Title XIX, Social Security Act) programs. Medicare provides insurance coverage for health services for older Americans. Medicare regulations cover nutrition and dietetic services in hospitals, nursing homes, home health agencies, hospices, and other facilities that meet the Medicare conditions of participation. Medicaid, administered through state agencies, funds health services for economically disadvantaged individuals and the disabled. Among other services, Medicaid regulates the Early Periodic Screening, Diagnosis, and Treatment Program (EPSDT) for children through a state partnership.

Department of Agriculture

The Department of Agriculture (USDA) has responsibility for food and agriculture programs. USDA agencies that offer useful resources to public health nutrition programs are the Human Nutrition Information Service, the Food and Nutrition Service, the Food Safety Inspection Service, the Cooperative Extension Service, and the National Agricultural Library. (See Appendix G.)

The Human Nutrition Information Service (HNIS) administers the nutrition-monitoring activities of USDA, including the Nationwide Food Consumption Survey (NFCS), the Continuing Survey of Food Intakes by Individuals (CSFII), and the nutrient data bank. HNIS produces a variety of educational materials related to the U.S. Dietary Guidelines for Americans.

The Food and Nutrition Service (FNS) administers the National School Lunch Program; National School Breakfast Program; Summer Feeding Program; Child Care Food Program; Special Supplemental Food Program for Women, Infants, and Children (WIC); Commodity Supplemental Food Program; and Nutrition Education and Training Program (NETP).

The Food Safety and Inspection Service (FSIS) regulates the safety of meat and poultry products and some aspects of food labeling related to those products.

Department of Education

Consistent with its overall responsibilities for working with states in relation to public education, the Department of Education has responsibility for educational programs for handicapped children. Public Law 99-457, the Education of the Handicapped Amendments of 1986, integrates health services into early intervention programs for infants and children with special needs. Nutrition services are listed as one of the health services, with nutritionists designated as part of the early intervention team.

Department of the Treasury

The Bureau of Alcohol, Tobacco, and Firearms regulates the sale and labeling of alcoholic beverages (e.g., "lite" beer labeling and the surgeon general's health warnings).

Federal Trade Commission

The Federal Trade Commission (FTC) regulates the content of food advertisements and truth-in-labeling laws.

THE JUDICIAL BRANCH

Involvement with the judicial branch generally occurs only when there is evidence that legal authority has been violated and when legislative and executive branch (regulatory) options have been exhausted. The judicial system (courts) should never be approached without employing an attorney and thoroughly weighing the potential costs in terms of money and time against the possibility of winning the case. In 1973 and 1974, class action suits in the federal courts successfully forced the release of program funds for WIC which had been impounded by the president.

PROMOTING HEALTH AND NUTRITION ISSUES

Speaking As an Individual

As responsible citizens, nutritionists should study the qualifications of candidates running for their local, state, and federal public offices. They should vote in all primary and general elections to help put into office those whose platform supports public health. Once the candidate is in office, as concerned citizens they should take time to write, telephone, or visit with elected officials to present their expert views.

Informed professionals should study, discuss, and speak out on current issues related to the public's health and well-being, particularly those related to food and nutrition policy. As private citizens, nutritionists can join coalitions and attend legislative open houses, town meetings, field hearings, and other legislative and regulatory forums held in their city, county seat, or state capital. This is of particular importance when public health issues are being discussed and debated.

Organizing a Telephone Tree

A telephone tree is a particularly effective way to extend influence through national or state professional associations or coalitions. This method of quick response to legislative alerts targets key legislators for the purpose of influencing their vote on a critical issue.

The specialist model targets "experts" who speak with authority on an issue in their legislative district, statewide, or across the nation. The nutrition expert at the top of the tree contacts expert colleagues to respond to calls for action on legislative proposals where specific scientific or technical knowledge is required. An expert in each critical legislative district calls the second and third tiers of members of the tree who are responsible for telephoning an agreed-on number of peer experts at subsequent levels, each then contacting the offices of legislators who will cast a crucial vote.

With the district model, the purpose is to generate massive numbers of phone calls and letters to influence a vote on the floor of Congress or to respond to a regulatory proposal in the *Federal Register*. Advocates are contacted in a similar tiered structure. Congressional handbooks list zip codes within each congressional district. (See Appendix F.) Members of an alert tree are identified and partitioned by zip code through membership directories and rosters of local coalitions. Each member of a tier of the telephone tree is responsible for alerting a specific number of individuals at the next level (e.g., three, five, or seven persons).

The telephone tree should be carefully designed, disseminated in writing, and monitored. The written plan for the tree should list the names and correct daytime and evening telephone numbers for all callers. The tree is only as effective as the callers are responsible and effective, so the message must be specific, and all callers must be committed to making their calls both to the assigned persons on the next tier on the tree and to the legislative or regulatory office. Through these action alerts, specific information to use to respond to legislative and regulatory proposals can be provided for immediate use in telephone calls, FAX messages, or letters. Telephone trees mobilize a massive response quickly and effectively.

LEGISLATIVE ACTIVITY FOR PUBLIC EMPLOYEES

Many agencies encourage their professional staff in advocacy efforts on behalf of policies, legislation, and regulations that promote and protect the public health. Such activities should always be conducted in compliance with agency policy. They should conform to professional and ethical standards of conduct, be nonpartisan, and be without conflict of interest. The Hatch Act applies to employees of federal and state agencies and prohibits certain types of political activity, including running as a candidate for public office. Agency employees should seek the approval of their administrators before using work time, travel funds, or postage to engage in any legislative activity in behalf of public programs. They must always be sure that their stand is consistent with their agency's position and that they have administrative support.

Agency policy dictates whether any advocacy activities can be undertaken as an agency representative on official time or whether these activities must be done as an informed citizen on personal time, using a home address on any correspondence. If agency policy frowns on active advocacy, it is possible to work behind the scenes through the efforts of professional organizations, religious groups such as Bread for the World, and issue-oriented citizen lobbies such as the League of Women Voters and Common Cause.

With their administrator's approval, nutritionists who manage federal-or state-funded programs should invite their legislators or legislative staff to visit and observe nutrition programs in action. This provides legislators with the opportunity to see how the programs benefit their constituents. They can also be shown any problems in administering the legislation. Media coverage of the visit adds interest for the legislator and visibility for the program and the agency. Media coverage of service programs at any time showcases accomplishments and will usually be seen by legislators or staff who monitor media coverage.

TAKING LEADERSHIP

Lobbying

The process by which individuals or groups advocate actively to pass or to block passage of legislation is popularly called lobbying. In the democratic process, shaping policy decisions through lobbying is a privilege and a right. Many people think that one voice makes no difference in the legislative halls. In reality, it is the process or strategy by which that one voice presents an issue that can make the difference between success and failure.

Credible lobbying uses accurate and appropriate information and disseminates it to gain public support for an issue that has value to society. Each issue must be approached differently, and no one strategy always works. The effectiveness of lobbying depends as much on the method of communication as it does on the content.

To be effective with busy officials, communication must be concise, convincing, consistent, and cordial.[3] Communication can be by personal contact, letter, FAX message, telephone, or telegram. Communication can express a viewpoint on an issue or seek information about the legislator's stand on an issue or his or her voting record.

Visiting an elected official's office benefits both the official and the constituent. In Washington, visits are generally scheduled with a congressional staff member expert in health, nutrition, or human service legislation, but it may be with the member of Congress. During congressional recesses, visits can be scheduled when representatives are in their home district. (See Exhibit 7-2.) Because of busy schedules, these meetings are usually brief. An appointment should always be made in advance by phone or in writing and confirmed shortly before the scheduled date. The meeting should begin with the nutritionist introducing him/herself and stating his/her profession and professional affiliation. Conversation should clearly and concisely identify the legislative bill of concern by number, title, and key issues. It is wise to speak from notes that highlight the pertinent points. Supporting written material can be given to the member or staff. A follow-

Exhibit 7-2 Usual Schedule for Congressional Recesses

Congress usually recesses for one week around selected holidays during the following months:	
February	Lincoln's Birthday (February 12)
March/April	Easter
May	Memorial Day
July	Independence Day (July 4)
August	Nonelection, odd-numbered years: Congress in recess; election, even-numbered years: Congress works in August to adjourn earlier to run for re-election
September	Labor Day
October	Rosh Hashana/Yom Kippur/Columbus Day
November	Thanksgiving
December	Christmas

up letter should summarize the discussion and thank the member or staff person for taking the time to discuss the issue.

Writing to members of Congress and other elected officials establishes ongoing dialogue. In congressional offices, letters and postcards are recorded on a tracking system by issue. Frequent letters related to legislative proposals provide a record of the opinions of constituents. Letters should begin with the correct address and salutation. The recommended salutation is The Honorable [__name__], Dear Senator, or Dear Representative. The zip code for senators is Washington, D.C. 20510, and for representatives it is Washington, D.C. 20515. Letters should be limited to one page. Each letter should begin by identifying the correct bill number and title and the writer's professional affiliation. The body of the letter should identify the writer's position on the issue and include brief statements in support or opposition. When in opposition, an alternative proposal should be suggested. The letter should close with an offer to provide additional information. Letters that contain an individual, professional, and personal viewpoint are given more attention than are form letters or preprinted postcards.

Telephone calls, FAX messages, and telegrams are essential when an immediate vote is expected on a piece of legislation. Phone calls can be made to the legislator's Washington or district office. Congressional district office telephone numbers and addresses can be found in one's local telephone book in the U.S. Government listings. Phone numbers of congressional offices in Washington can be obtained by calling the Capitol Switchboard at (202) 224-3121. Opening a line of communication through a variety of channels establishes the nutritionist as an interested constituent and a nutrition expert in public health issues.

Testifying at Hearings

Getting to know legislators and other elected officials can result in invitations to testify at hearings. Testifying at hearings before congressional committees or regulatory bodies provides the opportunity for expert input that can influence the outcome as well as the authorization or appropriations level of legislation. Congressional hearings are generally conducted in Washington, but they may be held at field sites where a specific problem concerns a particular member of Congress.

Testifying means presenting oral and written information. While both become part of a hearing report, oral remarks should highlight the written testimony. Testimony on legislation is generally conceptual in nature. Each individual testifying has a five-minute time limit. Five pages of double-spaced typewritten text can usually be delivered in the five minutes.

Testimony must be well researched and adhere to the rules of communication with elected officials. Content and style of presentation are equally important. Testimony should include

- an introduction identifying the speaker, group represented, and proposal under consideration
- a position on the issue as a clear statement supporting the proposal, supporting it with modifications, or opposing it
- an explanation of the position which elaborates on the position and issues within the proposal in nontechnical language; references to written testimony or supporting documents are appropriate
- a summary restating the position and recommendations; if testimony partially supports or opposes a proposal, an alternative should be suggested

In conclusion, the official conducting the hearing should be thanked and an offer made to answer any questions and provide additional information.

The record for congressional hearings is open for ten working days so that additional supporting documents can be provided to the committee conducting the hearing. Following the hearing, the person testifying will be provided with a copy of his/her transcribed remarks to edit for accuracy since the testimony will be published.

Professional organizations or health agencies may be invited to testify on a specific subject. To handle questions with ease, the most knowledgeable person should be selected, and this may not be the organization's president or agency director. The public health nutritionist should maintain a file of experts on specific current topics to suggest if asked to recommend persons to testify at legislative hearings.

Cultivating Public Officials

As a private citizen or as a member of a civic or professional organization (never as an agency representative), becoming involved in political campaigns is an effective way to influence policy decisions. Involvement in campaigns provides an informal opportunity to meet and talk with the candidates and elected officials, easing the way for approaching them and being recognized by them once they are elected.

Working with political action committees (PACs) provides another way to become involved in political campaigns. PACs represent a group of volunteers who join together to support the candidates of their choice.[4] After collecting funds from individuals and pooling them, PACs contribute directly to candidates or political fund raisers. They sponsor events or finance printing and/or mailing of campaign materials. Although PACs are frequently criticized for buying votes or promoting single issues, those devoted to health and nutrition can play an important role in the political process by generating interest in food, nutrition, and health issues.

Building Coalitions To Promote Food and Nutrition Issues

Coalitions supplement involvement in the legislative and regulatory processes. When building a coalition to achieve a public policy goal, it is critical to work not only with those who wholeheartedly support the same issues but also with those who have differing views. In conferring with colleagues interested in the public policy proposal, the following questions might be asked:

- Who are the key players?
- What groups are allied with similar views?
- What groups are expressing opposing views?

A coalition can be established temporarily to address a single issue or permanently to address multiple issues over time. Coalitions are effective because advocacy work can be shared among several members of the coalition according to expertise, contacts, and time commitment. In coalitions, an impressive number of diverse constituents can join together to demonstrate strength and unity to policymakers.

Competency as an advocate requires understanding the legislative and regulatory processes and cultivating skill in communicating, persuading, and negotiating. Nutritionists cannot work in a vacuum, but they can function as coordinators, either behind the scenes or out in front, to facilitate continuation, improvement, or expansion of existing public health and nutrition programs, as well as establishment of new programs. By understanding political power, governmental operations, and the mechanics of advocacy, they can positively influence the nutrition and health status of the American public.

ISSUES TO DEBATE

*   When faced with drastic budget cuts in a public program, what rationales and explanations could be proposed to influence congressional budget assumptions and program appropriations?
*   When there are agency restraints on advocacy activity, what types of coalitions could be joined to promote public health and nutrition programs?
*   How can clients who benefit from a tax-supported program be mobilized as advocates for its continuation or expansion?

NOTES

1. *The Budget of the United States Government, FY 1989* (Washington, D.C.: Government Printing Office, 1988).

2. R. Thompson, "Speaking Up about FDA Regulations," *FDA Consumer* 19, no. 6 (July–August 1985): 23–25.

3. Ibid.

4. *The American Dietetic Association: ADA Political Action Committee* (Chicago: The American Dietetic Association, 1985).

BIBLIOGRAPHY

Society for Nutrition Education. *Influencing Food and Nutrition Policy: A Public Policy Handbook*. Oakland, Calif.: Society for Nutrition Education, 1987.

part IV

Promoting and Protecting the Public's Health

chapter 8

Serving Women, Infants, and Children

MaryAnn C. Farthing and Mildred Kaufman

READER OBJECTIVES

- State the case for including nutrition services in women's health, preconceptional health, and family planning programs.
- Discuss nutritional care for pregnant women.
- Describe ways to promote and support breast-feeding.
- Discuss anticipatory guidance for parents in feeding their infants and children.
- List and describe services to meet the unique nutrition needs of adolescents.
- Describe nutrition services for children requiring special health care.
- List and describe the roles of public health nutrition personnel in maternal and child health services.

ISSUES IN MATERNAL AND CHILD HEALTH

In response to congressional concerns about maternal and infant mortality and morbidity, the Maternity and Infancy Act was passed and was in effect from 1920 to 1929. In 1935, Title V of the Social Security Act provided formula grants to the states for maternal and child health and crippled children's services. This legislation was first administered by the Children's Bureau of the Department of Labor; since the 1960s, it has been administered by the Public Health Service Department of Health and Human Services. It has facilitated a federal-state partnership to develop the network of maternal and child health services delivered by state and county and/or city health departments. In 1981 changes in the legislation created the current Maternal and Child Health Block Grant program to replace the

139

formula grant program. Since 1935 Title V has provided not only funding for delivery of maternal and child health and disabled children's services but also guidance materials, technical assistance, and support for special projects, professional training, and research.

Promoting health and preventing disease during the periods of rapid growth and development—gestation, infancy, childhood, and adolescence—impact on people's health, productivity, and well-being for the rest of their lives. Maternal and child health services cover the populations in early stages of life, including women during their childbearing years, infants, children, and youths up to age 21. Issues specific to the health of women and children to be investigated in assessing the community and to be addressed in the program plan include

- infant mortality rates and the incidence of low birth weight and very low birth weight infants
- households in the community headed by single parents
- children who are in out-of-home or day care
- prevalence of teen pregnancy
- prevalence of developmental disabilities and handicapping conditions among children in the community according to their diagnostic categories and ages

WOMEN'S HEALTH, FAMILY PLANNING, AND PRECONCEPTIONAL HEALTH

Promoting the health and nutritional status of women throughout their childbearing years can reduce the number of infant deaths, low birth weight infants, and infants who have developmental disabilities. Many women do not seek prenatal care until after their first eight weeks of pregnancy. Inadequate nutrient intake, smoking, and alcohol and drug use prior to and during these eight weeks may endanger early fetal organ development.

Before a woman becomes pregnant is the most opportune time to assess whether she has any medical, nutritional, or psychosocial risks that would contribute to poor pregnancy outcome. Any identified health or behavioral problems can then be diagnosed and treated, and the woman can be educated about healthful life styles. Since most women seek their preventive health care at women's health and family planning clinics, these settings provide special opportunities for health promotion and disease prevention. Educating women attending these clinics can guide them to sound eating

Exhibit 8-1   Nutrition Guidance To Promote Women's Health during the Years of Childbearing

---

Achieve and maintain desirable weight for height through a nutritionally adequate diet and regular exercise.

Choose a variety of nutritious foods with emphasis on fruits and vegetables; whole grain breads and cereals; low-fat dairy products; and chicken, fish, dried beans, and lean meats (based on the Dietary Guidelines for Americans).

Prevent or correct iron deficiency anemia through a diet rich in iron, vitamin C, and adequate protein.

Promote bone health with an adequate intake of calcium-rich foods and vitamin D.

Refrain from smoking, and if alcohol is used, use it in moderation.

Maintain a moderate approach to eating, abstaining from self-induced vomiting and abuse of laxatives.

Manage any diagnosed medical conditions by complying with physician-prescribed diets for such conditions as hypertension, diabetes, renal disease, and phenylketonuria.

---

practices that may also reduce their risks for cardiovascular disease, cancer, and osteoporosis later in their lives.

A woman's nutritional status prior to pregnancy is actually more important to successful reproduction than is her diet during the nine months of pregnancy. Therefore, nutrition education and diet counseling should be part of all women's health care. The nutritionist should increase the awareness and knowledge of physicians and nurses who work with young women, emphasizing the preconceptional period as the time for them to achieve their desirable weight and to build up nutrient stores. Recommended nutritional guidance is summarized in Exhibit 8-1.

Nutrition risk assessment using anthropometric, biochemical, and dietary measures identifies women with nutrition-related health problems that can significantly influence the outcome of pregnancy.

- Prepregnancy weight. Women who weigh less than 90 percent of their desirable weight for height more often give birth to preterm or low birth weight infants. Women who weigh more than 20 percent above their desirable weight for height are more subject to gestational diabetes or hypertension. Women who develop gestational diabetes during pregnancy and who do not control their weight often develop non-insulin-dependent diabetes later in life.

- Insulin-dependent diabetes. When their blood glucose levels are poorly controlled, women with diabetes are three to four times more likely than nondiabetic women are to give birth to infants with congenital anomalies such as heart defects and skeletal abnormalities.[1]
- Iron deficiency anemia. Women who are anemic more often give birth to infants with reduced iron stores and/or low birth weight. Women should correct anemia with a prescribed iron supplement and foods rich in iron, protein, and vitamin C.
- Phenylketonuria (PKU). Women who have PKU risk reproductive failure or may give birth to a mentally retarded infant. Blood levels of phenylalanine should be managed by diet prior to conception and throughout pregnancy.
- Oral contraceptive agents (OCAs). OCAs interfere with the metabolism of such nutrients as vitamin B_6, folacin, and vitamin C. Women who use OCAs frequently gain excessive weight and show a rise in their serum cholesterol. They need to be advised to control their weight and the type and amount of fat in their diets.
- Nutrient deficiencies. Eating disorders such as anorexia nervosa and bulimia may cause severe nutrient depletion, frequently making it difficult for a woman to become pregnant. Fad weight-reduction diets, bizarre eating practices, and alcohol or other substance abuse can lead to nutrient deficiencies which may affect growth and development of the fetus. These nutrient deficiencies should be corrected before a woman becomes pregnant.
- Nutrient excesses. Self-prescribed megadoses of nutrient supplements such as vitamins A and D may be toxic and possibly teratogenic. Women should be encouraged to obtain their vitamins and minerals from a well-balanced diet and to avoid the use of supplements that provide amounts of nutrients in excess of the current Recommended Dietary Allowances (RDAs).

Nutritionists can research and respond to questions raised about the safety of artificial sweeteners such as aspartame or of drugs containing high concentrations of a nutrient such as acutane which has excessive vitamin A. It is also necessary to monitor drug-nutrient interactions. For example, the anticonvulsant Dilantin produces a folic acid deficiency that may increase a woman's risk of bearing an infant with neural tube defects.

Nutrition services in women's health primary care or family planning clinics include

- Consultation to physicians, nurses, social workers, and health educators on current research relating nutrition to medical and psychosocial

risks. Informed health professionals who provide routine family planning services can counsel low risk clients about the impact of their
contraceptive method on nutritional status and the need to increase
foods rich in any nutrients adversely affected.

- Screening and assessment of all women clients, using a health appraisal such as the one developed by Moos and Cefalo[2] to identify diet/
  nutrient-related problems. This questionnaire can be self-administered by the client and reviewed by a nurse. The nutritionist in
  collaboration with the physicians and nurses can develop protocols or
  guidelines for clinic personnel to use to make referrals to the nutritionist.
- Nutrition counseling. Low-risk clients can be counseled by the nurses.
  Clients who are underweight or overweight might be counseled by the
  nutritionist in groups. Those who have high-risk conditions require
  individual counseling by the nutritionist. Nutrition counseling visits
  should be scheduled at the time of the client's regular appointments.
- Nutrition education materials for clients and professionals. Client
  counseling should be reinforced by relevant, reliable take-home nutrition education materials.
- Referral for health or community services. Clients who smoke, abuse
  alcohol, or have eating disorders (anorexia nervosa or bulimia) may
  need to be referred for psychological counseling. Those who need
  food assistance can be referred for food stamps or to food pantries or
  social services.

PRENATAL CARE

Infant mortality rates (IMRs), essential data elements in the community
assessment, are used to monitor pregnancy outcome in the population. The
national IMR has been slowly declining, reaching 10.0 per 1,000 live births
in 1987.[3] The infant mortality rate increases as birth weights decrease. In
1987, almost 6.9 percent of all live newborns weighed less than 2,500 grams
(5 1/2 pounds) and were classified as low birth weight (LBW). Over 1.2
percent of live infants weighed less than 1,500 grams (3 1/3 pounds) and
were classifed as very low birth weight (VLBW).[4] Twice as many black as
white infants were LBW. Women most likely to have a low birth weight
infant

- are adolescents
- are unmarried

Table 8-1 Risk Assessment Schedule in Prenatal Care

WEEKS	Preconception Visit	6-8 (First visit)	14-16	24-28	32	36	38	39	40	41
History										
Medical and psychosocial	●									
Update medical/psychosocial		●	●	●	●	●	●	●	●	●
Physical Examination										
General	●									
Blood pressure/pulse	●	●	●	●	●	●	●	●	●	●
Height, weight, ht/wt profile	●	●	●	●	●	●	●	●	●	●
Pelvic examination/pelvimetry	●	●								
Breast examination	●	●								
Fundal height			●	●	●	●	●	●	●	●
Fetal position/heart rate			●	●	●	●	●	●	●	●
Laboratory Tests										
Hemoglobin or hematocrit	●	●		●						
Rh factor, PAP smear	●									
Diabetic screen				●						
MSAFP			●							
Urine dipstick, protein, sugar	●									

Source: Adapted from *Caring for Our Future: The Content of Prenatal Care*, pp. 48-49, Public Health Service, Department of Health and Human Services, Washington, D.C., 1989.

- are less educated
- have eating disorders
- are late to enter prenatal care
- are underweight prior to pregnancy
- gain less than 24 pounds during their pregnancy
- have a history of infant death and low birth weight infants
- are high parity[5]

While many factors contribute to infant mortality and low birth weight, diet and adequate maternal weight gain are controllable environmental factors that can contribute to more favorable pregnancy outcomes. Guidelines such as *Nutrition Services in Perinatal Care*,[6] *Guidelines for Perinatal Care*,[7] *Guide to Quality Assurance in Ambulatory Nutrition Care*,[8] and *Caring for Our Future: The Content of Prenatal Care*[9] are useful references

Exhibit 8-2 Nutrition Guidance To Women to Promote Healthy Pregnancy and Lactation

---

Choose a variety of nutritious foods with emphasis on fruits and vegetables; whole grain breads and and cereals; milk and dairy products; and meat, eggs, fish, poultry, dried beans, and peanut butter.

Consume approximately 36 to 45 kcalories/kilogram of current maternal weight daily during the second and third trimesters.

Monitor weight gain on a prenatal weight grid to show a gain of 24 to 30 pounds during the course of pregnancy (if normal prepregnancy weight).

Supplement diet with 30 to 60 milligrams of elemental iron and 300 to 800 micrograms of folic acid daily.

Develop a daily routine of appropriate exercise.

Avoid the use of alcohol, and give up smoking.

Learn about the values of breast-feeding for both mother and baby.

During lactation, increase food consumed to about 500 kcalories above the prepregnancy needs.

Maintain adequate intake of fluids.

---

in planning and implementing prenatal nutrition services. The National Academy of Sciences publication *Nutrition during Pregnancy: Weight Gain and Nutrient Supplements* provides the latest guidance for prenatal nutritional care.[10]

Table 8-1 suggests a risk assessment schedule in prenatal care. Risk assessment is a continuing process during pregnancy. Those who are at high risk require more frequent prenatal visits. Successful interventions can change risk status.

In health agency clinics, pregnant women who are at low nutritional risk should receive their dietary advice as part of their routine prenatal care with their physician, nurse-midwife, or nurse-practitioner. (See Exhibit 8-2.) Nutritionists should educate these health professionals on the nutrition requirements in pregnancy; dietary interviewing and counseling techniques; and community food assistance resources to keep their professional colleagues on the health care team up to date. The March of Dimes teaching package *Maternal Nutrition: Contemporary Approaches to Interdisciplinary Care* provides ten modules on the various aspects of prenatal nutrition useful for in-service training.[11] Clinic policies should be established for the use of a weight gain grid in all prenatal records, the monitoring of weight gain, and the selection and use of vitamin-mineral supplements. Clients screened and found to be at nutritional risk can be referred to the nutritionist and to the Special Supplemental Food Program for Women, Infants, and Children (WIC); the Commodity Supplemental Food Program; the Food Stamp Program; Aid to Families with Dependent Children; or other emergency food or financial assistance.

Nutritional care should begin with assessing the client's nutritional status prior to conception or at the first prenatal visit. Women who gain less than 2.2 pounds or 1 kilogram a month during their last two trimesters risk having a low birth weight baby. Obese women who gain an excessive amount of weight during their pregnancy tend to produce large infants, which may also result in higher rates of perinatal mortality. Pregnant women who have anemia or poorly controlled diabetes mellitus risk poor pregnancy outcomes. The low-income teenage mother having her first child may develop preeclampsia (toxemia), characterized by hypertension, proteinuria, and generalized edema for the mother and by growth retardation for the infant.[12] Protocols should be in place to establish screening criteria that identify clients whose nutritional needs warrant referral to the nutritionist for evaluation and in-depth counseling.

Counseling pregnant women either one-on-one or in groups should include the following:

- Reviewing and charting data on the prenatal weight gain grid at each visit and checking iron nutriture at the first visit and at 24 to 28 weeks into the pregnancy.[13]
- Obtaining food intake information, using a 24-hour dietary recall plus food frequency, a food record, or an eating habits questionnaire at each visit to evaluate the intake of foods and fluids (both kinds and amounts) against a recommended food guide for pregnancy. When a woman is not gaining enough weight or gaining too much weight, it may be useful to estimate nutrient intake with a hand-calculated or computerized diet assessment to determine her usual caloric intake in relation to her activity and the distribution of carbohydrate, protein, and fat.
- Determining socioeconomic factors that influence eating practices, such as income, ethnic food traditions, taboos, cravings, educational achievement, housing, and family situation.
- Considering other factors affecting food choices, such as appetite, food preferences, access to food and food markets, transportation, cooking and storage facilities in the home, and cooking skills; use of

alcohol or drugs or smoking; practice of pica.

- Analyzing the collected information to respond to key concerns from both the client's and the counselor's points of view.
—Which nutritional needs are being met?
—What food practices should be continued, and which need to be changed?
—What assistance is necessary to help overcome problems (inadequate weight gain or low hemoglobin)?
—How capable and interested is the woman in changing her food choices?
—What other help does the woman need to enable her to cope?

The assessment information is used to counsel the client and help her set goals and objectives based on her perceived needs and resources. References on counseling suggest skills to help the professional communicate successfully with clients.[14]

For pregnant women who do not usually use public health clinical services, the health agency can offer classes for those who are referred by their private physicians. In these classes the nutritionist or nurse can discuss the connection between nutrition and food intake and the birth of a healthy full-term infant. Interactive informal discussion can be used to recommend foods that meet nutrient and energy needs and that contribute to optimal weight gain during pregnancy. Women may share their solutions to anemia, nausea, constipation, and heartburn which several may be experiencing. All pregnant women should be cautioned to avoid alcohol, smoking, drugs, and other hazardous substances. By exchanging experiences, the women learn from one another and enjoy peer support. Classes should be conducted in or translated into the language common to the members of the group. Foods recommended should be those preferred by the women in the community.

LACTATION AND INFANT FEEDING

In 1988, an estimated 54.3 percent of newborns were breast-fed at hospital discharge; only 21.1 percent of infants were breast-fed at five to six months of age.[15] Breast-feeding rates are much lower among low-income black, teenage, and less educated mothers.[16] During prenatal care, prospective parents should be introduced to breast-feeding and be encouraged to consider it. They should also be given the opportunity to ask questions so that they can make an informed choice. Discussing the diet during pregnancy as preparation for breast-feeding is a comfortable way to approach the discussion while the mother is deciding how she will feed her infant.

Experienced breast-feeding mothers are successful peer counselors in classes promoting breast-feeding. Peer counselors trained to work with their own ethnic or population group help women who contemplate breast-feeding to overcome their fears and resolve some of their apprehensions. They can also help new mothers learn the techniques of proper breast-feeding.[17]

When physicians and nurses in delivery and after-care are convinced that breast-feeding is preferred for most infants, they will give the support and encouragement mothers need as they start to nurse their newborns. Nutritionists can consult with staff in hospitals and work places as they develop policies to make it easier and more comfortable for mothers to breast-feed their infants. Obstetricians, pediatricians, and family practice physicians can be offered policy statements and references to design protocols that promote breast-feeding of newborns in the hospital. The American College of Obstetricians and Gynecologists and the American Academy of Pediatrics have published guidelines on breast-feeding and lactation[18];The American Dietetic Association has published a statement in support of breast-feeding.[19] In-service education programs for hospital and public health professionals can disseminate research documenting the benefits of breast-feeding for mothers, their infants, and society as a whole. These professionals need to be oriented to practical skills that support women and help them manage and maintain their breast-feeding.

Trained peer counselors, nutritionists, or nurses should telephone or visit new mothers to answer their questions and encourage them as they get started. Many new mothers discontinue breast-feeding if their nipples become sore when their baby is not properly positioned during feeding, if they become fatigued, or if they receive misinformation or negative advice from well-meaning relatives and friends.

Organized community groups, such as La Leche League and Nursing Mothers, and classes for new parents support and encourage mothers to continue to breast-feed. Key professionals and lay groups in the community that support breast-feeding can join forces to advocate for needed policies and community supports.[20]

For the mother choosing not to breast-feed her infant, proprietary formulas provide a suitable alternative. The infant formula industry has followed standards set by the American Academy of Pediatrics to develop formulas with a nutrient composition similar to that of human milk.[21] However, the immunologic factors present in human milk cannot be duplicated in the proprietary formulas. The kind of formula may be recommended by a pediatrician, nutritionist, or nurse. The mother should be taught how to follow the manufacturer's directions for correctly reconstituting dry or diluting concentrated formula. Anticipatory guidance should inform new parents about

- safe, sanitary, correct methods of preparing formula
- variation of intakes among normal infants
- normal stool patterns
- spitting up versus vomiting
- satiety cues from the infant to avoid overfeeding
- importance of holding the infant while giving the bottle

Table 8-2 gives recommendations for preventive child health care from birth to age four. Anticipatory nutritional guidance should be given to parents attending well-baby clinics that provide health screening and supervision. The nutritionist who advises physicians and nurses in the infant-screening and well-child clinics extends nutritional care to a large number of babies. Protocols or guidelines for infant feeding should be written for the clinic based on expert recommendations.[22] These protocols or guidelines for infant feeding should be kept current as new research is done, technologies change, and new formulas are developed. The gradual addition of cereals, solid foods, and chopped table foods throughout the year should help the infant progress toward a regular meal and snack pattern by the first birthday. Anticipatory guidance helps parents identify the developmental cues that indicate when their infant is ready for solid foods and ready to be weaned from breast or bottle to cup. Parents are counseled to hold the bottle-fed infant until the infant falls asleep to provide the infant with needed bonding and to reduce the risk of nursing bottle caries.

Growth charts developed by the National Center for Health Statistics (NCHS) are used to monitor the infant's linear growth and weight gain. Parents may need nutrition counseling when the infant's rate of growth deviates from the reference percentiles, as indicated by periodic assessments of weight in relation to length and age. Parents may be advised about the kinds and amounts of food the infant needs to grow and develop. (See Exhibit 8-3.)

PRESCHOOL CHILD HEALTH

Children grow at a slower, but steady rate from infancy up until they reach adolescence. Most American preschool and school-age children are

Table 8-2 Recommendations for Preventive Child Health Care—Birth to Age 4

	INFANCY						EARLY CHILDHOOD				
AGE [1]	By 1 mo.	2 mos.	4 mos.	6 mos.	9 mos.	12 mos.	15 mos.	18 mos.	24 mos.	3 yrs.	4 yrs.
(N) HISTORY											
Initial/Interval	●	●	●	●	●	●	●	●	●	●	●
(N) MEASUREMENTS											
Height and Weight	●	●	●	●	●	●	●	●	●	●	●
Head Circumference	●	●	●	●	●	●					
(N) Blood Pressure										●	●
SENSORY SCREENING											
Vision/Hearing	S	S	S	S	S	S	S	S	S	S	o
(N) DEVEL./BEHAV. ASSESSMENT [2]	●	●	●	●	●	●	●	●	●	●	●
PHYSICAL EXAMINATION [3]	●	●	●	●	●	●	●	●	●	●	●
PROCEDURES											
(N) Hered./Metabolic Screening [4]	●										
Immunization		●	●	●			●	●			
Tuberculin Test [5]	◄———————————— ●◄——————► ●◄————————►										
(N) Hematocrit or Hemoglobin [6]	◄——————————— ● ——————► ●◄————————►										
(N) Urinalysis [7]	◄——————— ● —————————► ●◄————————►										
(N) ANTICIPATORY GUIDANCE [8]	●	●	●	●	●	●	●	●	●	●	●
Breast-feeding (or formula feeding)	●	●	●	●	●	●	●	●			
Addition of nutrient-dense solid foods				●	●	●					
Meal pattern and healthful snacks						●	●	●	●	●	●
DENTAL CARE											
Prevention of baby bottle caries				●	●	●	●				
Initial dental visit										●	

1. If any items are not accomplished at the suggested age, the schedule should be brought up to date at the earliest possible time.

2. By history and appropriate physical examination; if suspicious, by objective developmental testing.

3. At each visit, a complete physical examination is essential, with infant unclothed, older child undressed and suitably draped.

4. Metabolic screening (e.g., thyroid, PKU, galactosemia) according to state law.

5. For high-risk groups, annual TB skin testing recommended.

6. Medical evidence suggests re-evaluation of the frequency and timing of hemoglobin or hematocrit tests. One determination is suggested during each time period. Additional tests are left to the individual experience.

7. Medical evidence suggests re-evaluation of the frequency and timing of urinalysis. One determination is suggested during each time period. Performance of additional tests is left to the individual experience.

8. Counseling should be part of each visit for care.

Key: ● = to be performed; S = subjective, by history; (N) = nutrition related;
o = objective, by a standard testing method.

Source: Adapted from Guidelines for Health Supervision II, pp. 156-157, with permission of American Academy of Pediatrics, © 1988.

Exhibit 8-3 Nutrition Guidance To Promote Infant Health

Birth to six months:

Breast-feed for the first four to six months. Supplement with iron, vitamin D, and fluoride if the infant is breast-fed or if these nutrients are deficient in the formula.

If not feasible to breast-feed, feed the infant an iron-fortified formula that approximates the composition of breast milk. Prepare formula correctly, using safe water and handling and storing formula under sanitary conditions. Formula-fed infants should be given supplemental fluoride if the water supply is not fluoridated.

At four to six months, begin introduction of solid foods as the infant gives cues of being developmentally ready.

Monitor the infant's length and weight on the appropriate NCHS growth chart.

Six months to one year:

Continue breast-feeding, or feed iron-fortified formula.

Introduce solid foods in gradual steps as the infant shows readiness.

Gradually wean the infant to a meal pattern and family foods.

Prepare foods to help the infant self-feed, and take the time to encourage self-feeding.

Monitor the infant's length and weight on the appropriate NCHS growth chart.

---

considered to be relatively healthy and well nourished. Parents must be helped to understand that as the pace of growth slows down, children have smaller appetites and need nutrient-dense foods.

Children living in families with incomes below the poverty level, particularly those who are homeless, suffer more iron deficiency anemia and growth retardation. In 1986, 22 percent of all children under six years old lived in families with incomes under the poverty level, including 46 percent of black children and 41 percent of Hispanic children.[23]

On the other hand, obesity and extreme obesity are considered to be increasing in children, with estimates ranging from 10 to 30 percent of children.[24] Obesity is defined as an excess deposition of fat as evidenced in children who are above the 90th percentile of weight for height, confirmed by a measure of triceps skinfold. Obesity in children, as in adults, may result from lack of exercise as much as from excessive calorie intake.

The use of cholesterol-lowering diets is proposed by some physicians for children over two years of age to prevent the onset of cardiovascular disease

Exhibit 8-4 Nutrition Guidance To Promote Child Health, Ages One to Five

Offer a selection of nutritious foods including fruits, vegetables, whole grain cereals, milk, cheese, lean meat, fish, poultry, or eggs in forms suitable for the child's stage of development. Use whole milk at least until the child's second birthday.

Offer the child the opportunity to try small tastes of a variety of nutritious new foods.

Do not use food as a reward or punishment.

Select licensed day care homes or centers that meet standards for providing nutritious meals and snacks.

Monitor growth on the appropriate NCHS growth chart.

Encourage daily exercise through active play.

Teach the child to clean his or her teeth properly and to avoid sticky, sugary snacks.

Manage any diagnosed health conditions with a physician-prescribed diet for obesity, familial hyperlipidemia, allergies, diabetes, inborn metabolic errors, etc.

in later life. They suggest that dietary fat be reduced to 30 percent of total calories, saturated fat to less than 10 percent of total calories, and cholesterol intake to between 250 to 300 milligrams or less. These recommendations are still debated except for children with a family history of elevated blood lipids.[25]

The kinds and amounts of food children consume during their periods of growth and development determine the extent to which physical and mental growth potentials are reached. Many inexperienced parents need nutrition guidance to deal with such childhood problems as food jags, overweight, underweight, or growth retardation. They may want to know about recommended foods for meals and snacks and about regular exercise to prevent obesity. (See Exhibit 8-4.) Public service messages disseminated through the media and the interventions discussed in Chapter 18 can provide information about normal child nutrition to young families that may or may not be health agency clients.

Out-of-Home Child Care

In 1985, 20 million women, or 65 percent of mothers with children under age 18, worked outside the home. By 1995, over 34 million schoolchildren and almost 15 million preschool children are projected to have mothers who work.[26] As more women are employed, more infants and preschool children require care away from their homes. Many children eat breakfast, lunch, and snacks in a child care facility.

Some children are placed in licensed day care centers that meet established standards of care. Others are in unlicensed facilities or family day care homes where staff may have limited knowledge about children's food needs. Many state licensing regulations include nutrition and food service standards. These can be useful models for states still developing licensure programs.[27] The Child Care Food Program (CCFP) administered by the U.S. Department of Agriculture (USDA) provides standards, technical assistance, and financial assistance for food served in public child day care centers and family day care homes serving low-income children. Programs are sponsored by schools, local departments of social services, and nonprofit organizations. All eligible day care providers should be encouraged to take advantage of the CCFP. Nutritionists in the public health agency can train center administrators and cooks, provide food guides and recipes, and consult with program directors to assure that they plan menus and prepare meals and snacks that meet children's nutrient needs. (See Chapter 12 on food service in group care facilities.) Centers caring for infants need guidance on feeding them and advice on handling bottled breast milk or formulas. Centers should be encouraged to provide comfortable facilities for the mothers who come to the center to breast-feed their infants.

A model child day care program has evolved from Project Head Start, which was initiated as an eight-week summer program by the Office of Economic Opportunity in 1965.[28] It was established to provide low-income preschool children with a comprehensive program based on their special educational, psychological, emotional, health, and nutritional needs. Head Start programs provide nutrition education for children and their parents, using the meals to set a good example. Head Start has now become a full-year program administered by the Administration for Children, Youth, and Families of the Department of Health and Human Services (DHHS).

In 1975, performance standards were adopted to ensure that every Head Start project provides services that meet the goals of the four major components: (1) education; (2) health, including medical and dental, nutrition, and mental health services; (3) parent involvement; and (4) social services. A nutritionist supervises the nutrition activities of the Head Start program, helps staff assess the needs of the children, provides guidance for the food service funded by the CCFP, and plans educational programs for parents and nutrition education, food preparation, and tasting parties for children.[29] Programs too small to employ a full-time nutritionist must arrange for regularly scheduled consultation from a qualified nutritionist as defined in the Head Start guidance material.[30]

Nutritionists should be prepared to take leadership to implement the much more comprehensive national standards for out-of-home child care currently being developed through a three-year (1988–1991) joint project of the American Academy of Pediatrics and the American Public Health Association. Nutrition is one of the ten content areas. When available, these performance standards will serve as the reference code for writing state and local licensure regulations. Performance standards will be written so as to be measurable and achievable at two levels: (1) minimum acceptable and (2) ideal or desirable. Model standards will differentiate family day care (FDC), child care centers (CTR), and group homes (GH) and will cover programs that serve infants from eight weeks through school-age children, including those who are well, ill, and handicapped. Nutrition standards will discuss child nutrition assessment; food to meet nutritional requirements of children, as well as the appropriate Dietary Guidelines; food safety, sanitation, and equipment; nutrition learning activities for children; and nutrition education for care providers and parents. Staffing qualifications and ratios will be specified for nutrition personnel employed in state and local licensing agencies, as well as for child care food service managers and food service assistants employed at the child care facility. These standards are being developed to coordinate with the federal Act for Better Child Care. This legislation should be the impetus for nutritionists to seek much more active involvement in the licensure of out-of-home care for children.

SCHOOLCHILD HEALTH

While school-age children are generally considered to be at low nutritional risk, as they begin to make more of their own food choices and are influenced by peers and television advertising, some children develop poor eating habits. Lack of exercise, as well as excessive high-calorie snacking, can contribute to obesity. Table 8-3 provides recommendations for preventive child health care for children ages 5 to 20 as outlined by the American Academy of Pediatrics. The nutritionist can advise school nurses, teachers, and guidance counselors regarding the assessment and follow-up of children who may have diet-related health problems. (See Exhibit 8-5.) The nutritionist can conduct or help teachers or school nurses conduct weight-control programs for students who are obese, are underweight, or have eating disorders. The nutritionist can also provide or arrange for nutrition counseling for parents of children who are referred to the health agency.

School breakfast and lunch programs administered by the USDA through state departments of education contribute significantly to the

Table 8-3 Recommendations for Preventive Child Health Care—Age 5 to 20

	LATE CHILDHOOD					ADOLESCENCE[1]			
AGE [2]	5 yrs.	6 yrs.	8 yrs.	10 yrs.	12 yrs.	14 yrs.	16 yrs.	18 yrs.	20+ yrs.
HISTORY									
Initial/Interval	●	●	●	●	●	●	●	●	●
MEASUREMENTS									
Ⓝ Height and Weight	●	●	●	●	●	●	●	●	●
Ⓝ Blood Pressure	●	●	●	●	●	●	●	●	●
SENSORY SCREENING									
Vision	O	O	O	S	O	O	S	O	O
Hearing	O	S[3]	S[3]	S[3]	O	S	S	O	S
Ⓝ DEVEL./BEHAV. ASSESSMENT [3]	●	●	●	●	●	●	●	●	●
PHYSICAL EXAMINATION [4]	●	●	●	●	●	●	●	●	●
PROCEDURES									
Immunization	●					●			
Tuberculin Test	←————————→					←————————●————————→			
Ⓝ Hematocrit or Hemoglobin[5]	←————————●————————→					←————————●————————→			
Ⓝ Urinalysis [6]	←————————●————————→					←————————●————————→			
Ⓝ ANTICIPATORY GUIDANCE [7]	●	●	●	●	●	●	●	●	●
Appropriate meals and snacks	●	●	●	●	●	●	●	●	●
Control of fat, cholesterol									
Selection of exercise program and balance of calorie intake and expenditure	●	●	●	●	●	●	●	●	●
DENTAL HEALTH									
Regular tooth brushing and dental visits	●	●	●	●	●	●	●	●	●
Fluoride supplement									

1. Adolescent-related issues (e.g., psychosocial, emotional, substance usage, and reproductive health) may necessitate more frequent health supervision.
2. If a child comes under care for the first time at any point on the schedule, or if any items are not accomplished at the suggested age, the schedule should be brought up to date at the earliest possible time.
3. By history and appropriate physical examination: if suspicious, by specific objective developmental testing.
4. At each visit, a complete physical examination is essential, with child undressed and suitably draped.
5. Evidence suggests the need for re-evaluation of the frequency and timing of hemoglobin or hematocrit tests. One determination is suggested during each time period. Performance of additional tests is left to the individual practice experience.
6. One determination is suggested during each time period. Additional tests are left to individual practice experience.
7. Counseling should be an integral part of each visit.

Key: ● = to be performed; S = subjective, by history; Ⓝ = Nutrition related; O = objective, by a standard testing method.

Source: Adapted from *Guidelines for Health Supervision II*, pp. 158–159, with permission of American Academy of Pediatrics, © 1938.

Exhibit 8-5 Nutrition Guidance To Promote Child Health, Ages Six to Ten

---

Offer and encourage selection of nutritious foods including fruits and vegetables; whole grain breads and cereals; low-fat milk and dairy products; and lean meat, fish, poultry, peanut butter, dried beans, and eggs.

Learn about moderation in dietary fat, salt, and sugar and increased use of fruits, vegetables, cereals, and beans that are high in fiber.

Develop a daily exercise routine through play activities and sports.

Make a habit of eating regular meals and choosing nutritious snacks.

Support a model school lunch program in the local schools by regular participation.

Monitor growth on the appropriate NCHS growth chart.

Manage any diagnosed medical condition with a physician-prescribed diet for obesity, allergies, diabetes, familial hyperlipidemia, inborn metabolic errors, etc.

---

nutritional status of all participating children. These include those who pay as well as those from low-income families who receive free or reduced price meals. Nutritionists can explain the values of these meals to school boards and parent-teacher associations. School food service personnel may invite the nutritionist to speak at their continuing education programs or consult with them to help assure that school meals meet the federal guidelines and the Dietary Guidelines for Americans, adapted to the food likes and dislikes of local children.

The nutritionist advises on and recommends nutrition education components to be incorporated into the curricula in health, sciences, and home economics. Funding to support nutrition education in the schools was provided in 1977 when Congress passed Public Law 95-166 as part of the National School Lunch Act and the Child Nutrition Amendments.[31] This Nutrition Education and Training (NET) Program is usually administered through state departments of education to local school systems. NET Program funds support projects that

- teach children about the relationship of food to health
- train school food service personnel in the principles and practices of child nutrition and food service systems management
- instruct teachers to teach nutrition in their classrooms
- develop and use innovative classroom materials and curricula.[32]

Innovative materials and programs developed under the NET Program are designed to increase the nutrition education content in school curricula and make it more relevant to the interests of the children. Nutritionists serving on advisory committees have stimulated the use of nutrition education materials for weight control and have motivated the use of the Dietary Guidelines for Americans.

Middle- and upper-income parents concerned about their children's fitness may appreciate guidance to help them set realistic goals for weight, food intake, and exercise. Nutritionists can reach these parents by appearing on the media, consulting with teachers, and speaking to parent groups.

ADOLESCENT HEALTH

During adolescence, children move toward adulthood with an accelerated growth spurt. Sexual maturity is evidenced by differentiated patterns of linear growth, weight gain, and body composition between the male and the female. The adolescent growth spurt usually occurs at a younger age for females, but the timing of sexual development varies by individual. Once adolescents achieve sexual maturity, their increase in stature and weight gain slows down and then ceases. It is normal for the female to build body fat stores from about 15 to 19 percent in childhood to about 23 percent in adolescence. Males gain more muscle mass and bone, with about 12 percent of body fat being their norm. These differences result in very different nutrient needs for girls and boys.

As adolescents struggle with their changed bodies, they must also mature emotionally, socially, and intellectually—as they strive for independence. They experiment in many areas as they seek an adult identity. Nutritionists working with adolescents must study the complex physiological and psychological changes they are undergoing and help them understand how these changes influence their nutrient requirements, food habits, and behavior.[33]

Recommendations for preventive health care for well adolescents are shown in Table 8-3. Exhibit 8-6 briefly summarizes nutrition guidance to promote adolescent health.

Hectic schedules with meals on the go, excessive snacking, and irregular choices of foods are common to the teenage life style. Adolescent girls often follow extreme diet regimens to lose weight. Both male and female athletes may use unneeded and risky dietary supplements or bizarre diets to try to achieve their ideal body image or to prepare for athletic competition. Adolescents are particularly receptive to food and nutrition misinformation. The nutritionist can advise them on alternatives to this nutrition

Exhibit 8-6 Nutrition Guidance To Promote Adolescent Health

Choose nutritious foods including fruits and vegetables; whole grain breads and cereals; low-fat milk and dairy products; and lean meat, fish, and poultry.

Maintain moderation in the choice of foods high in fat, salt, and sugar, such as fried foods, pastries, and rich ice cream, and increase the use of fruits, vegetables, breads, and cereals high in fiber.

Develop a regular pattern of eating meals and nutritious snacks to meet needs for growth and energy.

Develop a realistic perception of body image and appropriate weight for height.

Develop a daily exercise routine through walking, swimming, bicycling, or participating in team sports.

Monitor growth on the appropriate height/weight chart.

Investigate any special dietary interest or need, and research facts (e.g., vegetarian diet, athletic performance, weight control).

Manage any diagnosed medical condition that requires a physician-prescribed diet such as obesity, allergy, or hyperlipidemia.

---

misinformation. Documenting the type and extent of health problems prevalent among teenagers, the nutritionist and other public health workers can advocate for nutrition information in health and fitness or family living courses in the schools. Nutritionists with expertise in adolescent nutrition educate and counsel in school-based clinics, special projects, and community health centers where health care is designed to meet the unique needs of adolescents. Some adolescent medicine programs located in university medical centers employ nutritionists on their interdisciplinary team, with physicians, nurses, psychologists, and social workers. School-based clinics for adolescents may be staffed by local health agencies and include a nutritionist to offer nutrition counseling and education. These clinics serve adolescents with health problems, including weight management.

Because they are neither gynecologically nor emotionally mature, young teenage girls who become pregnant are at particularly high risk for bearing a low birth weight infant which may or may not survive. An estimated one million teenage girls become pregnant each year, and about two-thirds of these give birth. Some school districts in collaboration with the public health agency or community health center offer special programs that combine academic education, prenatal and infant health services, and parenting and homemaking education for teenage parents.[34] Nutritionists from the public health agency may teach classes, consult with teachers and school nurses, and counsel individual students.

DENTAL HEALTH

Recent surveys show a marked decline in dental caries in 5- to 17-year-old children, attributed to fluoridated water supplies and topical fluoride application.[35] However, most children have mild or moderate gingival conditions, a precursor to the very prevalent adult periodontal disease. Dental health promotion for children includes prevention of nursing bottle caries in bottle-fed infants. Parents should be advised not to prop the bottle and not to use fruit juices in a bottle as a pacifier. They should not put a child to sleep with a bottle containing anything but water.

Dental health services are offered through cooperative arrangements between many public health agencies and school systems. Providing information on promoting healthy foods and on reducing the amount of sugar and the number of exposures to refined carbohydrates in the diets of children is part of dental health education. Nutritionists advise dentists, dental health educators, dental hygienists, school teachers, and nurses about nutrition assessment and diet counseling techniques. Since clients often ask dental care providers questions about diet, dental professionals can screen for nutrition problems as part of their routine assessment.

About 56 percent of the U.S. population now has access to public water systems with natural or adjusted fluoridation.[36] The nutritionist should join dentists and other health professionals in advocating for fluoridation of all community water supplies.

CHILDREN WITH SPECIAL HEALTH CARE NEEDS

The phrase "children with special health care needs" describes infants, children, and adolescents who have a variety of disabilities, handicaps, and chronic illnesses. Estimates of the number of children with chronic illnesses or disabling conditions range from 10 to 20 percent of U.S. children, depending on the definition and the degree of the disability. Increases in prevalence rates noted in recent years may be due to better detection and diagnosis, as well as to the increased survival of high-risk infants through neonatal intensive care.[37] Table 8-4 summarizes the estimated prevalence of selected handicapping conditions and the associated problems and factors contributing to high nutritional risk.

Table 8-4 Prevalence of Certain Handicapping Conditions with Associated Nutrition-Related Problems

| | | Examples of nutrition problems and factors contributing to high nutritional risk | | | | | | | | | | | | | |
| | | Child-related | | | | | | | | | | Care-giver-related | | | |
Disorder	Prevalence Estimates per 1000 (and range)	Altered Nutrient Needs	Altered Energy Needs/Intake	Problems with Oral Cavity	Nutrient Deficiencies	Constipation/Diarrhea	Poor Appetite	Delayed Feeding Skills	Malabsorption	Nutrient/Drug Interactions	Maladaptive Behaviors	Lack of Knowledge	Difficulty Understanding Diet	Does Not Limit Intake	Inappropriate Feeding Practices
Asthma Moderate to Severe	38 (20-53) 10 (8-15)	●	●		●		●			●	●				
Visual Impairment Impaired Visual Activity Blind	30 (20-35) 20 0.6 (0.5-1)						●				●				
Mental Retardation	25 (20-30)	●	●	●	●	●	●	●			●				
Hearing Impairment Deafness	16 0.1 (0.6-1.5)														
Congenital Heart Disease Severe Congenital Disease	7 (2-7) 0.5	●	●		●		●			●	●				
Seizure Disorder	3.5 (2.6-4.6)	●								●					
Cerebral Palsy	2.5 (1.4-5.1)	●	●	●	●	●	●	●	●		●	●	●	●	●
Arthritis	2.2 (1-3)	●	●				●				●	●		●	
Paralysis	2.1 (2-2.3)	●	●		●		●				●	●		●	
Diabetes Mellitus	1.8 (1.2-2.0)	●	●		●					●		●	●	●	●
Cleft Lip/Palate	1.5 (1.3-2.0)	●	●	●	●		●	●							
Down's Syndrome	1.1		●	●		●		●			●	●		●	●
Sickle Cell Disease	< 1.0														
Neural Tube Defect	<1.0	●	●												
Autism	<1.0														
Cystic Fibrosis	<1.0	●	●		●				●	●		●	●	●	●
Hemophilia	<1.0														
Acute Lymphocytic Leukemia	<1.0	●	●		●	●	●			●					
Phenylketonuria	<1.0	●	●				●	●				●	●	●	●
Chronic Renal Failure	<1.0	●	●		●		●			●	●	●			

Source: Reprinted from *Maternal and Child Health Practices*, 3rd ed., by H.M. Wallace, G.E. Ryan, and A.C. Oglesby, p. 274, with permission of Third Party Publishing Company, © 1988.

Services for children with special health care needs, formerly called crippled children's services in Title V of the Social Security Act, cover early identification, evaluation, treatment, and follow-up for children with developmental disabilities or chronic handicapping conditions and chronic illnesses. Most children who receive this care have chronic organic diseases, physical or mental defects, learning disabilities, or other conditions that prevent them from growing and developing normally. An extensive system of regional clinics operated by or contracted by state health agencies to major medical centers assesses, diagnoses, and treats eligible children. In many states regional developmental and evaluation centers (DECs) are staffed by interdisciplinary teams of health professionals who provide clinical evaluation, treatment, and case management for children who have or are at risk of having mental or physical disabilities or delays. Priority is given to infants, preschoolers, and school-aged children with multiple problems whose families cannot afford private medical care.

Health professionals and educators now recognize that devoted families, rather than professionals, should manage their children's care. The family can be stable and constant, while professionals "come and go." Parents who choose to take charge of their children's care draw on the professionals they need for expertise, recommendations, and support. Families working with the professionals can formulate a realistic care plan based on their strengths, priorities, and abilities to cope. This partnership requires that both families and professionals learn and understand each other's language in order to share information and exchange ideas openly. Professionals must listen to parents, grandparents, brothers, and sisters so that they can provide information in manageable doses as the family is ready to act on it.[38] Since food and mealtimes are pivotal in family life, nutritionists participating in family-centered care assess the unique nutritional status and needs of the child in the context of total family mealtime activities.

In comprehensive, community-based, family-centered care, the nutritionist from the health agency should participate on the team of health care professionals that includes physicians; nurses; social workers; physical, occupational, and speech therapists; audiologists; psychologists; and special educators. Continuing education, consultation, and technical assistance extend nutrition information to the members of the care team and through them to the families.

Depending on their child's developmental evaluation, parents may require intensive nutrition counseling from the nutritionist. Expert advice is required to help families manage complicated diets for phenylketonuria (PKU) or other inborn metabolic errors, cystic fibrosis, cerebral palsy, juvenile diabetes, and renal disease. When severely handicapped children require enteral or parenteral feedings at home, the nutritionist must serve as a liaison between the dietitians and pharmacists in developmental evaluation centers or tertiary care hospitals and the health professionals in their own community who provide the continuing care and follow-up. Nutritionists involved with nutrition services for handicapped children are referred to the publication *Nutrition Services for Children with Handicaps: A Manual for State Title V Programs.*[39]

The network of university-affiliated programs (UAPs) grew out of recommendations from the 1962 President's Panel on Mental Retardation designed to reduce the societal impact of mental retardation and developmental disabilities. Federal funds were made available in 1963 for the construction of facilities to house services affiliated with universities or hospitals.[40] Since that time, the scope of services of the UAPs has expanded. Specialists in nutritional care of children with special needs are on the core teams of these programs. The UAPs provide practicing nutritionists and other health professionals with an expert resource for

- interdisciplinary training in work with children and adults who are mentally retarded or developmentally disabled, or at risk of developing such conditions
- demonstration of the full range of services that should be available
- consultation, technical assistance, and dissemination of information to state, regional, and community service programs through training, education, publications, and training materials
- applied research into related disorders and the efficacy of prevention, treatment, and remedial strategies[41]

Public Law 99-457, the Education of the Handicapped Act Amendments of 1986, provides new impetus for reaching children with handicaps and their families through a better coordination of health and educational services. Part H of this legislation establishes a new early intervention program for infants and toddlers with handicaps. (Infants and toddlers are those from birth up to their third birthday.) Early intervention services are defined in the legislation as developmental services to meet a handicapped infant's or toddler's developmental needs in any one of the following areas: (1) physical development, (2) cognitive development, (3) language and speech development, (4) psychosocial development, or (5) self-help skills. The range of services includes health services necessary to enable the infant or toddler to benefit from the other early intervention services. Nutritionists are named in the legislation among the qualified personnel to provide services. Services are to be provided in conformity with an individualized family service plan (IFSP) prepared for each child and family. Key elements are the case management and the community base.[42]

Home-Based Care

Advances in medical technology now make it possible to save the lives of children who require external life support systems. The technology that supports children in the hospital is becoming more available, less costly, and portable so that it can sustain these children in their homes, where they can be with their families in familiar and nurturing surroundings. The Office of Technology Assessment (OTA) defines the technology-dependent child "as one who needs both a medical device to compensate for loss of a vital body function and substantial and ongoing nursing care to avert death or further disability."[43] OTA identifies four groups of these children:

1. ventilator users
2. children who require intravenous substances or drugs over a prolonged period of time
3. children who use other devices for respiratory or nutritional support, such as tracheostomies or tube feedings
4. children with prolonged dependence on other medical devices such as apnea monitors or urinary catheters[44]

OTA estimates that there are from 2,300 to 17,000 children in the first three groups and 81,000 or more in the fourth group.[45]

To be cared for at home, each of these children needs

- a competent, willing family, able to take on their child's medical, nutritional, developmental, emotional, and educational care
- access to a tertiary children's health care facility with a team of specialists who will train the child, family, and community agency counterparts and back them up when acute or emergency care is required
- case management to arrange, coordinate, and monitor the comprehensive range of services the child requires
- a home with the space, equipment, and resources to provide a suitable environment for the child's medical care and education
- stable financial support[46]

As more community or public health agencies provide home health services to severely ill or handicapped children, nutritionists will need in-depth knowledge and skills in clinical nutritional care to work with them. Families will need counseling on normal nutrition and physician prescribed diets.

When children require enteral or parenteral feeding, collaboration with the hospital nutrition support team will be important in order to learn about the use and care of the equipment and the formulation of the feedings. As with all children, the goal is to meet the child's nutritional needs for growth, which vary with age and stage of development. Children who may benefit from home nutrition support are those who have disorders that require continuous feeding, those who have conditions that impair their ability to take food by mouth, and those who may be severely malnourished. Chapter 10, "Pediatric Nutrition in the Home," in the book *Nutrition Support in Home Health* provides guidelines for counseling families and members of the nutrition support team.[47]

Children receiving home- or community-based health care who would otherwise require more expensive institutional care are eligible for Medicaid benefits under waivers or state Medicaid plan amendments covering children under age 19 who live at home. Nutritionists working with home health services for special health care children should investigate Medicaid coverage for nutrition services through their state health or Medicaid agency.[48]

SPECIAL SUPPLEMENTAL FOOD PROGRAM FOR WOMEN, INFANTS, AND CHILDREN

Recognizing the needs of many poor women and children for assistance to purchase nutrient-dense foods, federal maternal and child health nutrition consultants advocated for a program of targeted supplemental food assistance. This effort culminated in the amendment to the Child Nutrition Act in 1972, establishing the Special Supplemental Food Program for Women, Infants, and Children (WIC) as a two-year pilot program. WIC programs began to serve clients in 1974.[49] Administered at the federal level by the Food and Nutrition Service of the USDA, WIC distributes cash grants to state health agencies and Indian agencies (recognized by the Bureau of Indian Affairs) which in turn allocate funds to city or county health departments or to other local nonprofit agencies in their jurisdictions. Authorized as a $20-million-a-year pilot program for FY 1974, the WIC program was authorized at $2.1 billion in FY 1990. It is currently estimated to serve 4.4 million women, infants, and children, about half of those estimated to be eligible.[50]

As an adjunct to health care, the WIC program provides food to participating pregnant, postpartum, and lactating women and to infants and children up to their fifth birthday. It funds the purchase of supplemental foods and the administrative costs incurred by health agencies in conducting nutrition education and carrying out other program services. Federal WIC regulations require that income and nutritional-risk eligibility criteria be used to certify program participants. State and local WIC agencies establish family income guidelines between 100 and 185 percent of the federal poverty guidelines, usually consistent with the guidelines they use for other reduced-price health and food service programs. While nutritional-risk criteria are established by each state agency, the federal regulations recommend the following indicators of poor nutritional status:

- detrimental or abnormal nutritional conditions detectable by anthropometric or biochemical measurements
- documented nutrition-related medical conditions
- dietary deficiencies that impair or endanger health
- conditions that predispose persons to inadequate nutritional patterns or nutritionally related medical conditions[51]

Professionals in the health agencies certify clients using the risk criteria and prescribe the appropriate food package. The WIC food package is limited to USDA-authorized foods that are rich in protein, iron, calcium, and vitamins A and C. The WIC packages are intended to supplement the foods that participants would ordinarily purchase or receive through other food assistance programs. While a few agencies distribute foods directly to clients, most issue vouchers or checks redeemable for the WIC food package at participating retail food stores.[52]

Two nutrition education contacts within each six-month certification period are mandated for WIC participants. The purpose of the education contacts is to guide participants to use the WIC food package to the best advantage and to reduce nutrition-related health problems. The nutritionist designs, develops, and conducts or supervises the nutrition education activities. Self-instructional computer-assisted instruction, video or audio cassettes, and nutrition games used with clients by trained peer educators and volunteers can impart routine nutrition information and feeding recommendations. Nutrition professionals then may counsel clients with more complex nutritional problems.

Integrating the WIC services into existing maternal, infant, and child health care clinics in the community requires joint planning by the WIC staff and other maternal and child health program managers. Integrated services mean that clients receive WIC services as a part of their regularly scheduled prenatal, infant, or child health visits. Assessment, counseling, and education are combined into a consistent message, saving time for both clients and staff. In a coordinated approach, the WIC program offers services at the same or a nearby site, but may have separate staff. A study of coordination between MCH and WIC conducted and reported in 1986 describes "best practices" for different administrative structures.[53]

MEDICAID AND MATERNAL AND CHILD HEALTH

Medicaid was enacted by Congress in 1965 as Title XIX of the Social Security Act. It establishes cooperative federal and state funding of health care for low-income populations. Each state legislature sets its own state's eligibility standards and policies within broad federal guidelines. Federal guidelines require mandatory eligibility for families receiving Aid for Families with Dependent Children (AFDC). To qualify for AFDC in most of the states, a family's annual income must be 48 percent of the federal poverty level or less. States vary from 14 percent in Alabama to 79 percent in California.[54] States have the option to cover persons who are medically needy if their incomes are not more than 133% of the maximum cash payment provided to families receiving AFDC.[55]

The Early Periodic Screening, Diagnosis, and Treatment Program

The Early Periodic Screening, Diagnosis, and Treatment Program (EPSDT) was established in 1969 by an amendment to Title XIX of the Social Security Act (Medicaid), which funded screening, diagnosis, treatment, and surveillance for low-income children under 21 years of age. EPSDT was designed to monitor needy children for existing health problems or risks of health problems and to see that those problems were diagnosed and treated in their early stages. The program requires outreach and primary and secondary preventive services on a periodic basis. States vary in the extent to which guidelines for the program are implemented.[56]

In 1984, new federal regulations incorporated recommendations for comprehensive child health services, including physical examination and physician-prescribed treatment and referral to ameliorate any chronic conditions found through EPSDT.[57] Children can be referred for nutrition intervention for growth retardation, iron deficiency anemia, and obesity. Nutrition counseling for these problems is reimbursable. Brochures from the state agency promote EPSDT services and inform clients on how to obtain health and nutrition information and services for children who need them.[58] The nutritionist should plan with health agency pediatricians and nurses to conduct this nutritional assessment, counseling, and follow-up for low-income children eligible for services.

Provisions of the Omnibus Budget Reconciliation Acts

The Omnibus Budget Reconciliation Acts (OBRAs) of 1986 (Public Law 99-509) and 1987 (Public Law 100-203) permitted states the option to expand Medicaid coverage and to determine the income eligibility to provide health services to medically indigent pregnant women, infants, and children up to age five whose family incomes are above the AFDC qualifying level. Under these laws, states are able to pay to meet the health care needs of medically indigent women, infants, and children, now providing them with access to health care. Married women and pregnant adolescents living with their families are eligible. These new provisions of Medicaid now provide funding for nutrition assessment, counseling, and education. Forty-four states have implemented Medicaid expansion options. In 16 states, Medicaid and Title V Block Grant–funded maternal and child health services are developing and monitoring standards that pay for more nutrition services.[59]

UNMET NEEDS IN NUTRITION SERVICES FOR WOMEN AND CHILDREN

Even with most of the nutritionist positions in state and local public health agencies supported by funds designated for maternal and child health program areas (WIC and Title V Block Grants), several groups among this population are not receiving nutrition services. These include pregnant women not participating in health agency prenatal care services or WIC programs, women before or between pregnancies who do not use family planning services, school-aged children among whom obesity is a growing problem, many children with special health needs, and many adolescents. Nutritionists must continuously monitor new legislation that expands or enhances maternal and child health benefits. For example, the OBRAs of 1986 and 1989 allow states to raise income eligibility for services funded by Medicaid for pregnant women and their young children. To assure that nutrition services are integrated into the continuum of health care, the nutrition component must be planned when new programs are initiated and funds are allocated.

ISSUES TO DEBATE

- How can public health nutritionists obtain a share of available resources to develop the nutrition services needed by mothers, infants, and children?
- How can physicians, nurses, dentists, health educators, and other health professionals be educated so that the nutrition information they give in their client health care contacts is credible and realistic?

- What are the minimum knowledge and skills in maternal and child nutrition that should be recommended to colleges and universities preparing nutritionists and other health professionals for entry-level positions in maternal and child health?
- How can public health nutritionists facilitate ongoing intervention and coordination between
  —Title V–funded maternal and child health services and WIC?
  — children's special health services and education for handicapped children?
  —public health and school health services?
- What possibilities exist for monitoring the nutritional status of women during their childbearing years, infants, and children who are not reached by public health agency programs?

NOTES

1. K. Fuhrmann, H. Reiher, K. Semmler, F. Fischer, M. Fischer, and E. Glockner, "Prevention of Congenital Malformations in Infants of Insulin-Dependent Diabetic Mothers," *Diabetes Care* 6, no. 3 (May–June 1983): 219.

2. Merry K. Moos and Robert C. Cefalo, *Preconceptional Health Appraisal*, revised ed. (Chapel Hill: University of North Carolina, Department of Obstetrics and Gynecology, 1987).

3. National Center for Health Statistics, "Births, Marriages, Divorces, and Deaths for 1988" (provisional data), *National Center for Health Statistics Monthly Vital Statistics Report* 37, no. 12 (28 March 1989): 1.

4. National Center for Health Statistics, "Advance Report of Final Natality Statistics, 1987" (final data), *National Center for Health Statistics Monthly Vital Statistics Report* 38, no. 3 (29 June 1989): 28–29.

5. Sarah Buchanan Ducey, *Poor Infants, Poor Chances* (Washington, D.C.: Food Research and Action Center, 1981), 10–11.

6. Committee on Nutrition of the Mother and Preschool Child, Food and Nutrition Board, National Research Council, *Nutrition Services in Perinatal Care* (Washington, D.C.: National Academy Press, 1981).

7. American Academy of Pediatrics and American College of Obstetricians and Gynecologists, *Guidelines for Perinatal Care*, 2d ed. (Elk Grove Village, Ill.: American Academy of Pediatrics, 1988).

8. M. Kaufman, ed., *Guide to Quality Assurance in Ambulatory Nutrition Care* (Chicago: The American Dietetic Association, 1983).

9. Public Health Services Expert Panel on the Content of Prenatal Care, *Caring for Our Future: The Content of Prenatal Care* (Washington, D.C.: U.S. Department of Health and Human Services, 1989).

10. National Academy of Sciences, *Nutrition during Pregnancy: Weight Gain and Nutrient Supplements* (Washington, D.C.: National Academy Press, 1990).

11. M. Kaufman, J. Kotch, W. Herbert, B. Rumer, C. Sharbaugh, and C. France, *Maternal*

Nutrition: Contemporary Approaches to Interdisciplinary Care (White Plains, N.Y.: March of Dimes, Birth Defects Foundation, 1988).

12. B.S. Worthington-Roberts, J. Vermeersch, and S.R. Williams, *Nutrition in Pregnancy and Lactation*, 4th ed. (St. Louis: Times Mirror/Mosby, 1989).

13. Public Health Services Expert Panel, *Caring for Our Future*, 48–49.

14. L.G. Snetselaar, *Nutrition Counseling Skills: Assessment, Treatment, and Evaluation* (Rockville, Md.: Aspen Publishers, Inc., 1983), 23–62.

15. Rebecca B. Catey, *Breastfeeding of All Infants, Columbus, Ohio, Ross Mothers Surveys*, Ross Laboratories, 1988, personal communication.

16. Food and Nutrition Services, *Promoting Breastfeeding in WIC: A Compendium of Practical Approaches* (Arlington, Va.: U.S. Department of Agriculture, 1988), 1.

17. Ibid.

18. American Academy of Pediatrics, Committee on Nutrition, *Pediatric Nutrition Handbook*, 2d ed., ed. Gilbert B. Forbes and Calvin W. Woodruff (Elk Grove Village, Ill.: American Academy of Pediatrics, 1985), 2–15. American Academy of Pediatrics and American College of Obstetricians and Gynecologists, *Guidelines for Perinatal Care*, 2d ed. (Elk Grove Village, Ill.: American Academy of Pediatrics, 1988), 196–198.

19. ADA Reports, "Position of The American Dietetic Association: Promotion of Breastfeeding," *Journal of the American Dietetic Association* 86, no. 11 (1986): 1580.

20. U.S. Department of Health and Human Services, Division of Maternal and Child Health, *Report of the Surgeon General's Workshop on Breastfeeding and Human Lactation*, DHHS Pub. no. HRS-D-MC-84-2 (Washington, D.C., 1984), 67–68.

21. American Academy of Pediatrics, Committee on Nutrition, *Pediatric Nutrition Handbook*, 16, 17, 369.

22. American Academy of Pediatrics, Committee on Nutrition, *Pediatric Nutrition Handbook*, 12–36.

23. Robert Pear, "Poverty Rate Dips as the Median Family Income Rises," *New York Times*, 31 July 1987.

24. American Academy of Pediatrics, Committee on Nutrition, *Pediatric Nutrition Handbook*, 247.

25. American Academy of Pediatrics, Committee on Nutrition, "Prudent Life Style for Children: Dietary Fat and Cholesterol," *Pediatrics* 78 (1986): 21.

26. U.S. Department of Labor, Women's Bureau, *Facts on Women Workers*, Fact Sheet no. 86-1 (Washington, D.C.: March 1985).

27. ADA Reports, "Position of the American Dietetic Assocation: Nutrition Standards in Day-Care Programs for Children," *Journal of the American Dietetic Association* 87, no. 4 (1987): 503. M.A.C. Farthing and M.G. Phillips, "Nutrition Standards in Day-Care Programs for Children: Technical Support Paper," *Journal of the American Dietetic Association* 87, no. 4 (1987): 504.

28. U.S. Department of Health and Human Services, Office of Human Development Services, Head Start Bureau, *Head Start: A Child Development Program* (Washington, D.C.: Government Printing Office, 1983), 1–13.

29. Ibid.

30. U.S. Department of Health and Human Services, Office of Human Development Services, Administration for Children, Youth, and Families, Head Start Bureau, *Head Start Program Performance Standards*, 45-CFR 1304 (Washington, D.C.: 1984), 49.

31. National School Lunch Act and Child Nutrition Amendments of 1977, Public Law 95-166, 95th Congress, 1st Session, *U.S. Code Congressional and Administrative News* (91 Stat.), 1325–46.

32. Ibid.

33. Jane M. Rees and M. Kathleen Mahan, "Nutrition in Adolescence," in *Nutrition throughout the Life Cycle*, ed. Sue Rodwell Williams and Bonnie Worthington-Roberts (St. Louis: Times Mirror/Mosby, 1988), 297–302.

34. Jane M. Rees, Jeanette Endres, and Bonnie Worthington-Roberts, "Nutrition Management of Adolescent Pregnancy: Technical Support Paper," *Journal of the American Dietetic Association* 89, no. 1 (1989): 105.

35. Kenneth C. Troutman, "Preventive Dental Health for Women and Children," in *Maternal and Child Health Practices*, 3d ed., ed. H.M. Wallace, G.M. Ryan, and A.C. Oglesby (Oakland, Calif.: Third Party Publishing Co., 1988), 228.

36. Ibid., 234.

37. Henry T. Ireys, "Description of the Population," in *Maternal and Child Health Practices*, 3d ed., ed. H.M. Wallace, G.M. Ryan, and A.C. Oglesby (Oakland, Calif.: Third Party Publishing Co., 1988), 601–603. S. Gortmaker and W. Sappenfield, "Chronic Childhood Disorders: Prevalence and Impact," *Pediatric Clinics of North America* 31, no. 1 (February 1984): 3–18.

38. Terri L. Shelton, Elizabeth S. Jeppson, and Beverly H. Johnson, *Family Centered Care for Children with Special Health Care Needs*, 2d ed. (Washington, D.C.: Association for Care of Children's Health, 1987), 4–5, 7–10, 15–18.

39. M.T. Baer, *Nutrition Services for Children with Handicaps: A Manual for State Title V Programs* (Los Angeles: Children's Hospital of Los Angeles, 1982).

40. E.M. Eklund, "University Affiliated Facilities Program," in *The Right to Grow: Putting Nutrition Services for Children with Special Long-Term Developmental and Health Needs into Action*, ed. J. Dwyer and M.C. Egan (Boston: Frances Stern Nutrition Center, New England Medical Center Hospital, 1986), 78–89.

41. Ibid.

42. National Center for Clinical Infant Programs, *National Center for Clinical Infant Programs: The Intent and Spirit of P.L. 99-457, A Sourcebook* (Washington, D.C.: 1989): A-2, A-3, 90.

43. U.S. Congress, Office of Technology Assessment, *Technology Dependent Children: Hospital vs. Home Care—A Technical Memorandum* (Washington, D.C.: Government Printing Office, 1987), 3–4.

44. Ibid., 3–4.

45. Ibid.

46. Shelton, Jeppson, and Johnson, *Family Centered Care*, 22, 23.

47. Karen Yowell-Warner and Patricia Queen, "Pediatric Nutrition in the Home," in *Nutrition Support in Home Health*, ed. Mindy Hermann-Zaidens and Riva Touger-Decker (Rockville, Md.: Aspen Publishers, Inc., 1989), 142–44.

48. Shelton, Jeppson, and Johnson, *Family Centered Care*.

49. Mary C. Egan, "Development of Maternal/Perinatal Nutrition Services: A Lesson in Interdependence," *Currents* 3, no. 1 (1987): 23.

50. Stefan Harvey, Center for Budget and Policy Priorities, Washington, D.C. Personal Communication, January 11, 1990.

51. U.S. General Accounting Office, *Need To Foster Optimal Use of Resources in the Special Supplemental Food Program for Women, Infants, and Children (WIC)* (Washington: GAO, 1985), 3, 4.

52. Ibid.

53. Professional Management Associates, Inc., *Improving MCH/WIC Coordination: Final Report and Guide to Good Practices* (Washington, D.C.: 1986), 49–74.

54. U.S. General Accounting Office, *MEDICAID, States Expand Coverage for Pregnant Women, Infants, and Children* (Gaithersburg, Md.: GAO, 1989),

55. Stephen E. Saunders, "Medicaid and Maternal and Child Health and Programs for Children with Special Needs," in *Maternal and Child Health Practices*, 3d ed., ed. H.M. Wallace, G.M. Ryan, and A.C. Oglesby (Oakland, Calif.: Third Party Publishing Co., 1988), 123–33.

56. American Academy of Pediatrics, Committee on Child Health Financing, *Medicaid's EPSDT Program: A Pediatrician's Handbook for Action* (Elk Grove Village, Ill.: American Academy of Pediatrics, 1987), 1, 4–6.

57. Saunders, "Medicaid."

58. North Carolina Department of Human Resources, *The Healthy Children and Teens Program (Formerly EPSDT)*, DMA 4078 (Raleigh, N.C.: Division of Medical Assistance, 1987).

59. National Governors' Association, Medicaid Enhanced Prenatal Care Services, *National Governors' Association Survey of Medicaid Enhanced Prenatal Care Programs* (Washington, D.C., National Governors' Association, 1989).

BIBLIOGRAPHY

Wallace, Helen M.; Ryan, George M.; and Oglesby, Allan C., eds. *Maternal and Child Health Practices*. 3d ed. Oakland, Calif.: Third Party Publishing Co., 1988.

chapter 9

Promoting the Health of Adults

Alice R. Thomson

READER OBJECTIVES

- Identify the leading causes of death and disability in adults.
- Understand the concepts of primary, secondary, and tertiary prevention in relation to nutrition programming in adult health promotion.
- Identify risk factors and their implications for chronic disease prevention.
- Describe the dietary risk factors associated with the leading causes of death and disability.
- Compare and contrast the types of dietary interventions the public health nutritionist addresses to the community, the family, or the individual at risk.

PROMOTING HEALTH, PREVENTING DISEASE

Mounting scientific evidence indicates that changes in dietary intake by adults could produce measurable gains in the health and longevity of the population. The human life span can exceed 100 years, though few people live to that age. Adult health programs strive to "add life to years as well as years to life." Escalating costs of crisis medical care add an economic incentive for both individuals and the nation to prevent chronic diseases. Nutrition interventions are essential components of programs to promote adult health and prevent the leading chronic diseases.

The Leading Causes of Death and Disability

Programs to promote health and longevity begin with examining the leading causes of death and disability. Statistics exist to document the

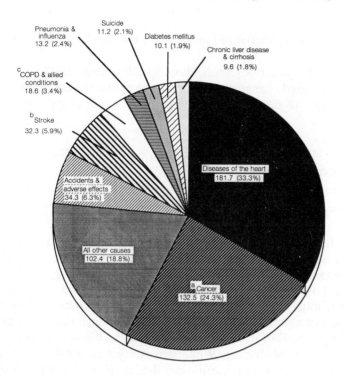

a
Cancer = malignant neoplasms, including neoplasms of lymphatic and hematopoietic tissues
b
Stroke = cerebrovascular diseases and allied conditions
c
COPD = chronic obstructive pulmonary diseases

Notes: (Provisional estimated data.) This chart displays death rates per 100,000 population, age adjusted to the 1940 U.S. population. Numbers in parentheses indicate percentages of total age-adjusted death rate. The sum of data for the ten leading causes may not equal the total because of rounding.

Figure 9-1 Age-Adjusted Rates for Leading Causes of Death in 1985 (Total: 546/100,000). *Source*: Reprinted from *Prevention '86–'87*, Federal Programs and Projects, U.S. Department of Health and Human Services. (Data obtained from National Center for Health Statistics.)

leading causes of death. The vital statistics system requires death certificates to record every death and its causes. The leading causes of death are cancer and cardiovascular diseases, including stroke and heart attacks (Figure 9-1). In contrast, with the exception of certain communicable diseases, illnesses and disabilities are not systematically recorded. Evidence suggests that the same diseases that are the leading causes of death are also the leading causes of illness, disability, and health care costs. Supporting data include Social Security disability insurance awards,[1] disability awards made by private insurance companies,[2] the National Health Interview Surveys,[3] and hospital discharge data.[4]

Risk Factors—A Focus for Public Health Programs for Chronic Diseases

Research is identifying risk factors, those specific characteristics associated with an increased chance of developing the chronic diseases that are the leading causes of death and disability. There are four types of risk factors.

1. biological factors such as inherited traits, gender, and age
2. environmental hazards
3. deficits in coverage and accessibility to the health care system
4. unhealthy life styles or behavioral factors[5]

Biological factors cannot now be changed. The other factors can be changed and are therefore controllable. In 1976, an assessment of the relative importance of these various factors to U.S. mortality suggested that only 20 percent of mortality was due to biological factors. (See Figure 9-2.) Fifty percent of mortality was attributed to life style, which society, families, and individuals can control.[6] People can and do influence the length and quality of their lives. Diet is a major and controllable life style factor that influences the onset of disease. While it is not yet possible to specify precisely the proportion of chronic diseases that can be reduced by dietary changes, it is speculated in *The Surgeon General's Report on Nutrition and Health* that "for the two out of three adult Americans who do not smoke and do not drink excessively, one personal choice seems to influence long-term health prospects more than any other: what we eat."[7]

PREVENTION STRATEGIES

As discussed in Chapter 1, disease prevention strategies are divided into three levels according to the point in the disease development when the strategy intervenes.

Primary Prevention

Primary prevention targets generally healthy individuals to decrease the probability that they will develop a disease or disability.[8] A classic example of a primary prevention strategy is fluoridation of public water supplies to prevent dental caries. For chronic diseases, primary prevention strategies are those that influence the entire population to adopt healthier life styles.

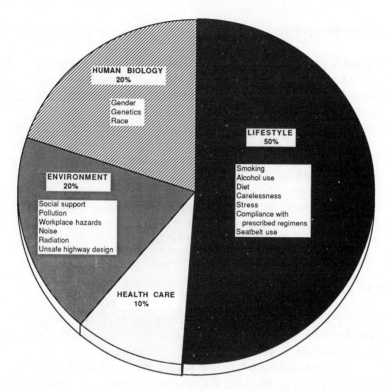

Figure 9-2 Risk Factors That Influence Health. *Source*: Adapted from *Healthy People: The Surgeon General's Report on Health Promotion and Disease Prevention* by Ad Hoc Advisory Group on Preventive Services, Institute of Medicine, U.S. Government Printing Office, Washington, D.C., 1979.

Health promotion/disease prevention objectives relating to nutrition for the adult population will largely be achieved by primary prevention strategies. Information must be widely disseminated to encourage consumers to follow the Dietary Guidelines for Americans.[9] Food markets, schools, houses of worship, libraries, and the media reach consumers in their daily activities. Exercise, fitness, and smoking cessation programs must be more broadly accessible. Incentives for food processors, restaurant chefs, and school and work site cafeteria managers should encourage them to prepare and serve foods lower in fat, calories, and sodium. Legislation and regulations can be enacted to ensure more complete nutrition labeling. (See Chapter 18.)

Secondary Prevention

Secondary prevention is detection, diagnosis, and intervention early in the disease process to minimize detrimental and disabling effects.[10] Strategies include screening with follow-up education, counseling, and referral. For screening to be useful, positive findings must be followed by prompt diagnosis and treatment. It is only of value for individuals to "know their cholesterol number" if they do something to reverse an elevated finding. For those with elevated blood cholesterol levels, this includes eating less total fat, saturated fat, and cholesterol and, if this is not effective, adding drug treatment. Secondary prevention strategies also include education on self-care for persons with chronic disease. An example is an education program that teaches persons having non-insulin-dependent diabetes how to control their weight through diet and exercise.

Tertiary Prevention

"Tertiary prevention or medical treatment comes into play when a defect or disability is fixed, stabilized, or irreversible. Rehabilitation, the goal of tertiary prevention, is more than halting the disease process; it is restoring the individual to optimum function within the constraints of the disability."[11] These strategies promote the individual's recovery from the disease by learning to live as fully as possible within the constraints of any lasting debilitating effects. Examples include cardiac rehabilitation through diet, exercise, and stress management and home health services.

Implications of the Prevention Levels

The prevention-level concept is useful in setting the objectives for public health programs concerned with adult health. Public health efforts focus on primary or secondary prevention. When planning a program, it is important to select the appropriate prevention level. To reduce the prevalence of high blood pressure and elevated blood cholesterol, both risk factors for cardiovascular disease, two different approaches are suggested. Ninety-nine percent of Americans have had their blood pressure measured at least once in their lives,[12] and 73 percent have had their blood pressure measured within the past year. Ninety-two percent of Americans are aware that high blood pressure increases the risk of heart disease, and 75 percent know that high blood pressure increases the risk of stroke.[13] Three-quarters of all hypertensives know about their condition, but only 34 percent take their medication and maintain their blood pressure at a level under 160/95.[14] These data suggest that to reduce mortality due to the effects of hypertension in the population as a whole, secondary prevention strategies to promote control among diagnosed hypertensives would be more effective than primary prevention strategies to increase public awareness. An exception would be the use of both primary and secondary prevention strategies to increase awareness and identify undiagnosed hypertensives in subpopulations known to be less aware of this risk factor, but also known to have a higher prevalence of hypertension.

In contrast, many Americans are just beginning to recognize the significance of an elevated blood cholesterol level and to understand the feasibility of lowering this risk factor.[15] There is considerable evidence that populationwide dietary changes could shift the distribution of cholesterol levels in the entire population to a lower range. Given the high prevalence of the risk factor (an estimated 50 percent of all American adults), populationwide efforts could be more cost effective than efforts to identify those having the risk factor would be. One such primary prevention effort is Project LEAN,[16] a nutrition education campaign to lower the fat consumption of Americans by informing the public and health professionals about the significance of this risk factor. It publicizes dietary changes to lower fat intake and strives to increase the availability of low-fat foods in supermarkets, restaurants, and work site and school cafeterias.

With new technology for detecting disease early, much public health programming has shifted toward secondary prevention strategies such as screening. Screening must be linked to education, counseling, referral, and follow-up. Education and counseling include providing information about the availability and costs of needed health care, along with encouraging changes in behavior that would lower the risk factors identified. Follow-up assures that those who have positive screening tests obtain the medical care they need.

For most of the leading causes of death and disability, nutrition strategies can focus on all levels of prevention. For some diseases, the nutrition strategy may be similar at each level of prevention. For example, weight reduction may prevent the onset of hypertension or be an element in the treatment of hypertension or congestive heart failure. For other diseases, the dietary strategies may vary with the prevention level, as with cancer.

DIETARY GUIDELINES FOR DISEASE PREVENTION

The popular concept that different diets are recommended to lose weight, to perform well athletically, to prevent cancer, to prevent heart disease, or to prevent osteoporosis may be reinforced by the publication of separate dietary guidelines by several different official and voluntary health organizations. (See Table 2-4.) In 1982, the National Research Council issued provisional dietary guidelines to minimize the risk of cancer.[17] These guidelines were also promoted by the American Cancer Society. In the fall of 1986, the American Heart Association updated its dietary guidelines for healthy American adults.[18] In December 1986, the American Dietetic Association issued nutrition recommendations for women.[19] In January 1987, the American Diabetes Association issued nutrition recommendations and principles for individuals with diabetes,[20] the latter being directed at individuals with diabetes. In 1989, the National Research Council re-

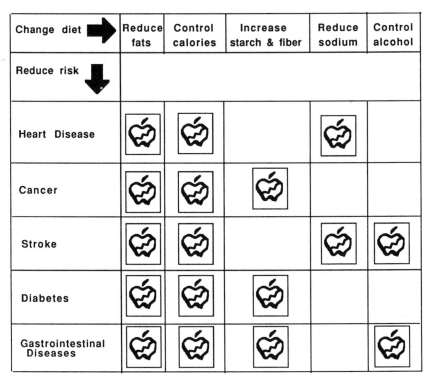

Starch refers to complex carbohydrates provided by fruits, vegetables, and whole-grain products. Gastrointestinal diseases affected by dietary factors are primarily gallbladder disease (fat and energy), diverticular disease (fiber), and cirrhosis of the liver (alcohol).

Figure 9-3 Consistency of Dietary Recommendations To Reduce the Risk of Selected Chronic Diseases. *Source:* Reprinted from *American Journal of Clinical Nutrition*, Vol. 49, pp. 23–28, with permission of American Society for Clinical Nutrition, © 1989.

leased a report entitled *Diet and Health: Implications for Reducing Chronic Disease Risk*, a review of the evidence regarding all major chronic conditions that diet is believed to influence.[21] Despite their varying origins and distinct purposes, all of these guidelines are compatible.

As discussed in Chapter 2, all of these guidelines recommend eating less fat; consuming more complex carbohydrates and fiber by eating more fruits, vegetables, and whole grain cereal products; using less sodium; and drinking alcohol in moderation. The 1988 *Surgeon General's Report on Nutrition and Health* sought to achieve "a scientific consensus on the role of diet in health as the basis for nutrition policy decisions."[22] This report concluded that "similar dietary recommendations apply to virtually all diet-related chronic diseases."[23] This consistency of dietary recommendations is summarized in Figure 9-3. All guidelines are compatible with and encompassed in *Dietary Guidelines for Americans*.[24] Simplifying the nutrition message to the public by consistently encouraging the use of these guidelines makes the message more easily understood and remembered.

NUTRITION STRATEGIES TO PREVENT AND MANAGE RISK FACTORS

Nutrition strategies are fundamental to prevent or manage several of the chronic diseases and their risk factors. For the most prevalent diseases, community-based nutrition services are essential components in the public health programs being developed. (See Chapter 18.)

Preventive health services for adults include nutrition assessment and counseling. Exhibits 9-1 and 9-2 display preventive health services recommended for adults aged 19 to 39 and 40 to 64, respectively.

Selecting Risk Factors To Address in Chronic Disease Programs

Given the limited resources allocated for public health programs, risk factors to be addressed must be prioritized. Four criteria can be used. The risk factor

1. has an established association with one of the leading causes of death
2. is prevalent, affecting a significant number of people
3. is modifiable so that it can be reduced or overcome through community or individual action
4. has a modification that is effective in decreasing mortality due to the associated disease

Exhibit 9-1 Preventive Health Services, Ages 19–39 (Schedule: Every 1–3 Years*)

Leading Causes of Death:
Motor vehicle crashes
Homicide
Suicide
Injuries (non-motor-vehicle)
Heart disease

SCREENING

History
Dietary intake
Physical activity
Tobacco/alcohol/drug use
Sexual practices

Physical Exam
Height and weight
Blood pressure
HIGH-RISK GROUPS
Complete oral cavity exam
Palpation for thyroid
nodules
Clinical breast exam
Clinical testicular exam
Complete skin exam

**Laboratory/Diagnostic
Procedures**
Nonfasting total blood
cholesterol
Papanicolaou smear[1]
HIGH-RISK GROUPS
Fasting plasma glucose
Rubella antibodies
VDRL/RPR
Urinalysis for bacteriuria
Chlamydial testing
Gonorrhea culture
Counseling and testing for
HIV
Hearing
Tuberculin skin test (PPD)
Electrocardiogram
Mammogram
Colonoscopy

COUNSELING

Diet and Exercise
Fat (especially saturated fat),
cholesterol, complex carbohydrates,
fiber, sodium, iron,[2] calcium[2]
Caloric balance
Selection of exercise program

Substance Use
Tobacco: cessation/primary prevention
Alcohol and other drugs:
Limiting alcohol consumption
Driving/other dangerous activities
while under the influence
Treatment for abuse
HIGH-RISK GROUPS
Sharing/using unsterilized needles
and syringes

Sexual Practices
Sexually transmitted diseases: partner
selection, condoms, anal intercourse
Unintended pregnancy and contraceptive options

Injury Prevention
Safety belts
Safety helmets
Violent behavior[5]
Firearms[3]
Smoke detector
Smoking near bedding or upholstery
HIGH-RISK GROUPS
Back-conditioning exercises

Dental Health
Regular tooth brushing, flossing, dental
visits

Other Primary Preventive Measures
HIGH-RISK GROUPS
Discussion of hemoglobin testing
Skin protection from ultraviolet light

IMMUNIZATIONS

Tetanus-diphtheria (TD)
booster[4]
HIGH-RISK GROUPS
Hepatitis B vaccine
Pneumococcal vaccine
Influenza vaccine[5]
Measles-mumps-rubella
vaccine

**This list of preventive serv-
ices is not exhaustive.**
It reflects only those topics
reviewed by the U.S. Pre-
ventive Services Task
Force. Clinicians may wish
to add other preventive
services on a routine basis
and after considering the
patient's medical history
and other individual circumstances. Examples of target
conditions not specifically
examined by the Task Force
include:
Chronic obstructive pul-
monary disease
Hepatobiliary disease
Bladder cancer
Endometrial disease
Travel-related illness
Prescription drug abuse
Occupational illness and
injuries

Remain Alert For:
Depressive symptoms
Suicide risk factors
Abnormal bereavement
Malignant skin lesions
Tooth decay, gingivitis
Signs of physical abuse

*The recommended schedule applies only to the periodic visit itself. The frequency of the individual preventive services listed in this table is left to clinical discretion, except as indicated in other footnotes.

1. Every 1-3 years.   2. For women.   3. Especially for young males.   4. Every 10 years.   5. Annually.

Source: Reprinted from *Promoting Health/Preventing Disease: Year 2000 Objectives for the Nation, Draft for Public Review and Comment,* p. 22-12, U.S. Department of Health and Human Services, Washington, D.C., 1989.

Exhibit 9-2 Preventive Health Services, Ages 40–64 (Schedule: Every 1–3 Years*)

Leading Causes of Death:
Heart disease
Lung cancer
Cerebrovascular disease
Breast cancer
Colorectal cancer
Obstructive lung disease

SCREENING

History
Dietary intake
Physical activity
Tobacco/alcohol/drug use
Sexual practices

Physical Exam
Height and weight
Blood pressure
Clinical breast exam[1]
HIGH-RISK GROUPS
Complete skin exam
Complete oral cavity exam
Palpation for thyroid
nodules
Auscultation for carotid
bruits

**Laboratory/Diagnostic
Procedures**
Nonfasting total blood
cholesterol
Papanicolaou smear[2]
Mammogram[3]
HIGH-RISK GROUPS
Fasting plasma glucose
VDRL/RPR
Urinalysis for bacteriuria
Chlamydial testing
Gonorrhea culture
Counseling and testing for
HIV
Tuberculin skin test (PPD)
Hearing
Electrocardiogram
Fecal occult blood/colon-
oscopy
Bone mineral content

COUNSELING

Diet and Exercise
Fat (especially saturated fat), cholesterol,
complex carbohydrates, fiber, sodium,
calcium[4]
Caloric balance
Selection of exercise program

Substance Use
Tobacco cessation
Alcohol and other drugs:
Limiting alcohol consumption
Driving/other dangerous activities
while under the influence
Treatment for abuse
HIGH-RISK GROUPS
Sharing/using unsterilized needles
and syringes

Sexual Practices
Sexually transmitted diseases: partner
selection, condoms, anal intercourse
Unintended pregnancy and contraceptive
options

Injury Prevention
Safety belts
Safety helmets
Smoke detector
Smoking near bedding or upholstery
HIGH-RISK GROUPS
Back-conditioning exercises

Dental Health
Regular tooth brushing, flossing, and
dental visits

Other Primary Preventive Measures
HIGH-RISK GROUPS
Skin protection from ultraviolet light
Discussion of aspirin therapy
Discussion of estrogen replacement
therapy

IMMUNIZATIONS

Tetanus-diphtheria (TD)
booster[5]
HIGH-RISK GROUPS
Hepatitis B vaccine
Pneumococcal vaccine
Influenza vaccine[6]

**This list of preventive serv-
ices is not exhaustive.**
It reflects only those topics
reviewed by the U.S. Pre-
ventive Services Task
Force. Clinicians may wish
to add other preventive services on a routine basis
and after considering the
patient's medical history and
other individual circum-
stances. Examples of target
conditions not specifically
examined by the Task Force
include:
Chronic obstructive pul-
monary disease
Hepatobiliary disease
Bladder cancer
Endometrial disease
Travel-related illness
Prescription drug abuse
Occupational illness and
injuries

Remain Alert For:
Depressive symptoms
Suicide risk factors
Abnormal bereavement
Signs of physical abuse or
neglect
Malignant skin lesions
Peripheral arterial disease
Tooth decay, gingivitis,
loose teeth

*Applies only to the periodic visit itself. The frequency of the individual preventive services listed in this table is left
to clinical discretion, except as indicated in other footnotes.

1. Annually for women.   2. Every 1-3 years for women.   3. Every 1-2 years for women beginning at age 50.
4. For women.   5. Every 10 years.   6. Annually.

Source: Reprinted from *Promoting Health/Preventing Disease: Year 2000 Objectives for the Nation, Draft for
Public Review and Comment,* p. 22-14, U.S. Department of Health and Human Services, Washington, D.C., 1989.

Obesity

Obesity, an excess accumulation of fat in the body, increases the risk of high blood pressure, elevated blood cholesterol, and diabetes mellitus and, in turn, cardiovascular disease. It also increases the risk of certain types of cancers. Obesity has an *established* relationship to the leading causes of disability and death.[25] Although survey methods and definitions of obesity vary, it is prevalent because it is estimated that between 15 and 49 percent of Americans are obese. Rates are higher for minorities, the poor, and older adults than is the rate for the population as a whole.[26] A number of hypotheses are proposed to explain obesity. Obesity probably has different contributing behavioral or metabolic causes in different individuals. Obese individuals do consume food energy in excess of their particular requirements and need to adopt new habits of eating and physical activity consistent with their requirements for energy and other nutrients.

The goal of weight-management programs should be to reduce the proportion of body fat and maintain that reduction. Of the Americans who lose weight each year via "quick fix" weight loss programs, it is estimated that only 5 to 20 percent maintain the weight-loss for any significant period of time. Research indicates that persons who repeatedly lose weight and gain it again may seriously distort their body's weight-regulation system. Indications are that this "yo-yo" dieting may (1) increase the proportion of fat to lean body mass; (2) redistribute body fat, shifting it from the thighs and hips to the abdomen in a way that is deleterious to health; (3) increase the desire for fatty foods; and (4) raise the risk of coronary heart disease.[27] Therefore, maintaining long-term changes both in eating habits and in physical activity is essential to controlling weight successfully. Despite the many difficulties, the risk factor of obesity can be successfully addressed, thereby lowering its many health risks. The risk factor of obesity can be modified to decrease the risks of mortality and morbidity.

Weight-management programs require special dedication and sensitivity from staff of the sponsoring health agency. Programs should be staffed by persons with a variety of skills in nutrition, behavior modification, and exercise physiology and with time to offer services of the intensity needed to be effective. Programs should

- enroll participants by informing them that their continuing commitment is necessary for their success, assisting them to assess their readiness to lose weight and identifying any special health needs that must be accommodated in the program
- advise participants on the elements of a nutritionally adequate diet and provide practice in selecting and preparing food lower in calories,

fat, and sodium

- offer participants guidance in selecting from alternative enjoyable ways to increase and continue a program of regular physical activity
- work with participants to examine their eating behaviors, factors that influence those behaviors (eating styles, attitudes, self-concept, relationships, emotions, environmental influences, etc.), and ways to build skills to change undesirable eating behaviors
- encourage self-monitoring through record keeping to assess and understand eating behavior
- reward successful behavior change rather than pounds lost
- offer ongoing follow-up, encouragement, and support.

In evaluating the success of the weight-management program, the following outcome and client satisfaction questions should be asked:

- Were the needs and expectations of the clients met?
- What percentage of participants who started the program completed it?
- What continuing support and help did the clients need and use?
- What behavior changes were the participants able to achieve? Are they eating and exercising differently?
- Did the participants achieve any changes in their health status? Did they change their body weight, blood lipids, blood pressure, medication use, etc.?
- Was weight loss maintained? If so, for how long?

Weight management is a means of primary prevention for a number of chronic diseases. It is the cornerstone of secondary and tertiary prevention of diagnosed hypertension, elevated blood cholesterol, diabetes, and arthritis. When persons with known chronic diseases enroll in a public health agency weight-management program, arrangements must be made to coordinate the regimen with their physicians. The coordinator should determine whether the client can safely increase the level of physical activity, who should monitor prescribed dosages of medicines as weight is lost, and how to accommodate any prescribed diet the client might be following. Persons who have their own physicians should have a written prescription documenting each of these issues. If the agency sponsoring the weight-management program also offers primary care or chronic disease care, these services might be coordinated with the client's prescription in the weight-management program.

Cardiovascular Disease

Cardiovascular disease is the leading cause of death in the United States, causing almost one million deaths per year.[28] It causes more deaths than cancer and accidents combined.[29] Cardiovascular diseases include coronary heart disease, stroke, and peripheral vascular disease. These conditions are all characterized by inadequate blood circulation at various sites throughout the body, often due to atherosclerosis, the build-up of plaque in the arteries. Reduction in the prevalence of cardiovascular disease can be anticipated when populations at risk reduce hypertension, reduce blood cholesterol levels, lose weight, give up smoking, and increase their exercise. These risk factors are responsive to public health interventions.

Hypertension

Uncontrolled high blood pressure can lead to both heart disease and kidney disease. The relationship of this risk factor to cardiovascular disease is established. With almost one in three adult Americans having high blood pressure, defined as greater than or equal to 140/90 mm Hg or controlled by antihypertensive medication,[30] this risk factor is prevalent. In the Hypertension Detection and Follow-up Program, aggressive treatment of high blood pressure resulted in a 36 percent reduction in strokes and a 20 percent reduction in total mortality for patients with levels of 90–99 mm Hg diastolic.[31] This risk factor is modifiable, and its modification is effective in decreasing cardiovascular disease mortality.

The latest guidelines for the treatment of hypertension are found in *The 1988 Report of the Joint National Committee on Detection, Evaluation, and Treatment of High Blood Pressure.*[32] This report advocates nonpharmacologic therapy for all hypertensive patients, either as the sole form of therapy or as an adjunct to drug therapy. Nonpharmacologic therapy includes reducing weight to within 15 percent of ideal body weight, limiting alcohol intake to less than one ounce daily, and restricting sodium intake to between 1.5 to 2.5 grams per day. Some evidence suggests increased potassium and calcium intakes may lower blood pressure. Additional steps that may help control high blood pressure and reduce the risk of cardiovascular disease include biofeedback and relaxation, exercise, and reduced amounts of fat in the diet.

Cholesterol

Animal, epidemiologic, and metabolic research that associate elevated blood cholesterol with increased risk of atherosclerosis and heart attack establishes the relationship of elevated blood cholesterol to cardiovascular disease. More than one in four American adults have a blood cholesterol level of over 240 mg/dl.[33] An estimated half of American adults have a blood cholesterol level of over 200 mg/dl. This risk factor is prevalent. Epidemiologic studies and clinical trials have consistently suggested that for individuals with blood cholesterol levels between 250 and 300 mg/dl, each 1 percent reduction in blood cholesterol level yields approximately a 2 percent reduction in coronary heart disease rates. The risk factor is modifiable, and its modification is effective in decreasing cardiovascular disease mortality.

In 1987, the National Cholesterol Education Program released the report of its Expert Panel on Detection, Evaluation, and Treatment of High Blood Cholesterol in Adults, referred to as the Adult Treatment Panel.[34] The report states criteria for blood cholesterol levels that require medical intervention and guidelines for detecting elevated blood cholesterol levels, setting goals, and treating and monitoring patients with such elevated levels. The report recommends diet as the treatment of choice for the 50 percent of Americans who have total blood cholesterol levels of 200 mg/dl or above.[35]

For persons at "borderline risk" whose blood cholesterol falls between 200 and 239 mg/dl, and who have no other cardiovascular disease risk factors and no history of cardiovascular disease, the panel advocates its Step One Diet, in which less than 30 percent of the calories come from fat, less than 10 percent of the calories come from saturated fat, and the intake of cholesterol is less than 300 mg per day.[36]

Persons having a blood cholesterol level of 240 mg/dl or above, or over 200 mg/dl with a history of cardiovascular disease or with two or more cardiovascular disease risk factors, are advised to have their blood lipoprotein levels determined and, if abnormal, to begin dietary treatment.[37] Their goal is to lower their low-density lipoprotein (LDL) cholesterol levels through a three-month trial of the Step One Diet. LDL is the cholesterol fraction most closely identified with cardiovascular disease risk. If the Step One Diet is not effective, the person is usually moved to the Step Two Diet, in which saturated fatty acids are limited to 7 percent or less of the total caloric intake and dietary cholesterol intake is limited to 200 mg or less per day. If after six months dietary treatment is unsuccessful, drug treatment is recommended to be added.[38]

As people learn more about this risk factor, they will demand more nutrition services to help them reduce their blood cholesterol levels. This challenges nutritionists to get the information to all those who would benefit by long-term changes in their eating habits. Environmental supports to individuals in the community who are trying to lower their fat and cholesterol intakes can be enhanced by decreasing the fat in the food supply and by improving community education.

Nutritionists who understand the science and practice of the Step One and Step Two diets can adapt them to their prevailing regional and ethnic eating habits. To reach a larger population, nutritionists can train and consult with physicians and nurses so that they can assess clients' dietary intake, counsel them on the principles of these cholesterol-lowering diets, and monitor their long-term adherence. Protocols, policies, and procedures should be established for use by all health care providers who treat hypercholesterolemia. These can be adapted from national, state, and community guidelines developed by official and voluntary health agencies to demonstrate how nutrition care for the Step One and Step Two diets can be provided.

Smoking and Diet

Public health professionals concerned about risk factors for cardiovascular disease must discuss smoking since it is a leading risk factor. Smoking is associated with 30 percent of coronary heart disease deaths and 21 percent of deaths from other cardiovascular diseases.[39] The relationship of smoking to cardiovascular disease is well established. One in three Americans smokes, so this risk factor is prevalent.[40] Smoking cessation is effective in preventing heart disease.[41] A reduction in the incidence of heart attacks is seen even for older, lifelong heavy smokers one to five years after they quit.[42] The risk factor is modifiable, and its modification is effective in decreasing cardiovascular disease mortality. Smoking cessation is especially important for those with risk factors such as hypertension and elevated blood cholesterol since these factors appear to work synergistically. Smoking is also a significant risk factor for other leading causes of death and disability, including cancer and lung diseases.

A fear of gaining weight discourages many people from quitting smoking. However, the health advantages of quitting smoking far outweigh the disadvantages of the ten-pound weight gain which typically accompanies smoking cessation. To eliminate weight gain as a disincentive, participants in smoking cessation programs may need and want help with weight management. Smoking cessation programs should include discussion of weight management and refer participants who need or request it to safe, effective community weight-management programs. For the many persons who can change only one behavior at a time, weight reduction might be deferred until smoking cessation has been mastered.

Lack of Exercise

The National Health and Nutrition Examination Survey has shown that only 40 percent of Americans of all ages exercise or participate regularly in sports.[43] Thus the sedentary life style is a prevalent risk. A number of studies have demonstrated that men who were physically active throughout their adult life had up to half the risk of coronary heart disease that men who were sedentary had, independent of the other major risk factors for cardiovascular disease.[44] Exercise seems to increase the efficiency of the circulatory, skeletal, and respiratory systems, as well as to manage weight. It appears to lower blood pressure and LDL cholesterol levels, while raising high-density lipoprotein (HDL) cholesterol levels, the cholesterol fraction that appears to have a protective effect. While the nature and magnitude of these effects remain to be clarified, the relationship of exercise to cardiovascular disease is well established.[45] This risk factor is modifiable, and its modification is effective in decreasing cardiovascular disease mortality. Nutritionists should learn about the types of physical activity recommended for each individual. This is particularly important when exercise is used in secondary or tertiary prevention programs in which the participants may have impaired circulation due to cardiovascular disease.

Trends

Between 1964 and 1984, coronary heart disease deaths in the United States declined 40 percent, while deaths due to stroke declined 55 percent.[46] Much of this decline has been attributed to risk factor modification. More people than ever are being treated for hypertension,[47] while serum cholesterol levels are declining,[48] as is the number of smokers.[49] Those studying changing trends in food intake note lowered consumption of red meat and eggs and increased consumption of poultry, low-fat milk, and vegetables.[50] However, the rate of decline of cardiovascular disease mortality is leveling off, particularly among white females and blacks of both sexes.[51]

Cancer

Cancer is the term used for a large group of diseases characterized by the uncontrolled growth and spread of abnormal cells which, when not checked, cause death. Each year almost one million Americans are diagnosed as having cancer, and about one-half million Americans die from cancer. About four out of ten persons diagnosed with cancer will be alive five years after their diagnosis. Each year the number of deaths increases. The major increase is in cancer of the lung. Age-adjusted cancer death rates for the other major sites are leveling off, and in some cases declining.[52] This is due in large part to more effective detection and treatment. The potential for even more effective prevention strategies remains.

Although susceptibility may be inherited, most cancers have external causes. Dietary factors and smoking are two of the leading external causes. Respiratory tract cancers are caused primarily by smoking. Smoking accounts for 30 percent of all cancer deaths.[53] Diet may play a role in cancers of the gastrointestinal tract, the breast, and tissues subject to hormonal influence such as the reproductive organs.[54] Doll and Peto estimate that dietary factors could be responsible for approximately 35 percent of all cancer mortality.[55] Dietary factors probably exert their effect as promoters or inhibitors of the process by which cells carrying mutations proliferate into tumors. These dietary factors may also act indirectly by modulating the secretion of hormones, prostaglandins, bile acids, or other metabolic substances.[56]

No definitive clinical trials have linked diet and cancer, as with blood cholesterol and coronary heart disease. Highly suggestive evidence indicates that the intake of fat and/or calories and pickled, salted, and smoked foods may promote carcinogenesis. There is evidence that dietary fiber, selenium, and vitamins A, C, and E, and a constituent of cruciferous vegetables may inhibit carcinogenesis. This evidence is epidemiological and from the laboratory. The strength of the demonstrated relationship varies among the nutrients listed and for various cancer sites.

Several factors make obtaining definitive evidence difficult.[57] Cancer may develop over the course of 10 to 30 years. There are no early clinical markers now known to identify incipient cancer. Dietary assessment methods are inadequate to estimate exposure accurately and precisely over long time periods. Retrospective examinations of dietary intake may be biased, and comparisons in levels of nutrient intakes between free-living subjects in the same culture may not be sufficient to reveal the diet-cancer relationship.[58] While dietary recommendations to lower cancer risk are controversial, the possibility of a diet-cancer link requires that they be included in cancer risk reduction programs.

A diet to lower cancer risk limits calorie and fat intake and increases fiber intake. Dietary recommendations include using more fresh fruits and vegetables, whole-grain breads and cereals, lean meats, poultry and fish, and low-fat dairy foods.[59]

In contrast, nutrition support during cancer treatment increases the intake of protein and calories to address cachexia, the common syndrome associated with diagnosed cancer. Cachexia is characterized by progressive weight loss stemming from loss of appetite and from poor absorption and utilization of nutrients. While cachexia is associated with terminal cancer, it can also appear early. It is exacerbated by surgery, chemotherapy, and radiation, currently the standard cancer treatments. Cachexia can reduce the effectiveness of these treatments and make them harder for the client to tolerate. The weakness and progressive tissue loss due to cachexia precipitate as many as two-thirds of all cancer deaths.[60] The greater the degree of the client's weight loss, the poorer the prognosis.[61] The challenge to those providing nutrition care and education is to entice these cancer patients to eat despite their poor appetite, loss of taste, diarrhea, constipation, dry or sore mouth, and nausea and vomiting.[62] By counseling cancer patients about ways to maintain their food intake from the time of diagnosis and onset of treatment, weight loss may be minimized and their prognosis improved. Improving nutritional status helps the patient withstand the disease and survive until treatment is successful.

It is becoming more and more common for cancer treatments, particularly chemotherapy and radiation, to be offered on an outpatient basis. Hospital stays for surgery are growing shorter as health care costs rise. Nutritionists encounter very sick cancer patients in the caseloads of home health agencies. Even if patients with cancer do not appear as participants in established public health programs, they may represent a significant unmet need for nutrition services in the community.

Some cancer patients may require home enteral nutrition support. This support may be needed not only by cancer patients, but also by others with impaired ability to ingest, digest, or absorb nutrients. Patients who receive nutrition support need ongoing nutritional status monitoring, including weight, hydration, and biochemical parameters.[63] The interdisciplinary team that plans and provides home nutrition support should include a nutritionist. The American Society for Parenteral and Enteral Nutrition has developed standards to guide the planning of home nutrition support services.[64] Hermann-Zaidens and Touger-Decker's *Nutrition Support in Home Health* is included in the listing for the Public Health Nutritionist's Library (Appendix N).

Diabetes

Only about half of the estimated 11 million Americans who have diabetes know of their condition. Ninety percent of these have non-insulin-dependent diabetes mellitus (NIDDM), which generally begins in adulthood. Each year one-half million new cases of diabetes are diagnosed.[65] In 1984, diabetes was the primary cause of death for 35,000 Americans and a contributing cause of death for more than twice as many more (95,000). Diabetes is the leading cause of new blindness, nearly 6,000 cases each year. Thirty percent of all end-stage renal disease is caused by diabetes. Approximately 50 percent of all nontraumatic amputations in the United States occur in people with diabetes. Heart disease is twice as common and more often fatal in people with diabetes than it is in the population as a whole. Women with diabetes have a risk of atherosclerotic disease five times greater than that of the population as a whole. Hypertension is two and one-half times more common among persons with diabetes.[66]

Risk factors for NIDDM are (1) age; (2) race, with the relative risk of diabetes among Native Americans being 10.8 times that of whites; for Hispanics, 3.1 times that of whites[67]; and for blacks, 1.4 times that of whites[68]; (3) family history; (4) history of gestational diabetes in females; and (5) obesity. Women are more likely to develop diabetes than are men, due in part to their greater longevity. Obesity is the single risk factor for diabetes that is preventable and modifiable. To prevent NIDDM, weight-reduction and/or weight-management strategies should be directed to persons who have a family history of NIDDM and to women who have a history of gestational diabetes. The 1986 National Institutes of Health Consensus Development Conference on "Diet and Exercise in Noninsulin-Dependent Diabetes Mellitus"[69] agreed that weight management is the most urgent issue in the management of NIDDM. Of the 90 percent of diabetics who have NIDDM, 80 percent are 15 percent or more overweight at the time they are diagnosed. Weight loss reverses two manifestations of the disease, fasting hyperglycemia and glucose intolerance. When they lose weight, 75 percent of persons with an elevated blood sugar level have their glucose tolerance return to normal.[70]

Objectives for the nutrition management of diabetes include

- providing optimal nutrition through a balanced diet that meets the Dietary Guidelines for Americans and the Recommended Dietary Allowances
- supporting normal growth during pregnancy or childhood
- minimizing glycosuria and normalizing plasma glucose
- minimizing hyperlipidemia
- preventing or delaying the onset of complications

Within the health agency's primary care services, a nutrition care plan individualized for each person's educational level, life style, budget, and personal, ethnic, or regional food preferences is critical in order to manage diabetes.

Group classes provided for clinic clients or offered by the health agency for the community can reach more persons, foster an exchange of information, and develop a support network. Within the group, each individual's needs must be met. Most persons with diabetes need diet counseling and encouragement indefinitely. Planning with clients for a program of continuing dietary guidance contrasts with the all-too-frequent diet instruction at diagnosis and/or at times of medical crisis. Ongoing individual and group education enables and supports the client in managing self-care to meet life's changes and prevent medical emergencies.

Several recent steps have been taken to assure the quality of diabetes education. National Standards for Diabetes Patient Education Programs were established by the National Diabetes Advisory Board as criteria against which the quality of patient education programs can be evaluated. These are published in Powers' *Handbook of Diabetes Nutritional Management.*[71]

The American Diabetes Association has developed a Recognition Program whereby diabetes education programs that meet the National Standards can apply for review to be formally "recognized" for their performance and quality. As of March 1989, 61 programs, including some in public health agencies, had been recognized.

A health professional can become a member of the American Association of Diabetes Educators and a certified diabetes educator (CDE) after completing a minimum of 2,000 hours of direct diabetes patient education experience and successfully passing a certification examination. Approximately 20 percent of the CDEs are registered dietitians, with registered nurses making up the largest percentage.

The American Dietetic Association (ADA) offers numerous resources, such as cookbooks, patient teaching materials, annotated bibliographies in current research topics, a series on ethnic food habits and diabetes, and a resource manual for dietitians to use when developing meal plans. In the American Dietetic Association nutritionists can join the Diabetes Care and Education Practice Group, a network of over 2,000 registered dietitians sharing a common interest in diabetes. For addresses of these organizations, see Appendix L.

Arthritis

Arthritis is a group of diseases affecting joints and connective tissue. It is painful and often disabling. While not a cause of death, arthritis and related diseases are a leading cause of disability, affecting some 37 million Americans.[72] Arthritis is quite heterogeneous in its pathophysiology. It includes

- osteoarthritis or degenerative joint disease—a wearing out of articular cartilage, especially in weight-bearing joints
- rheumatoid arthritis—thought to be an autoimmune response characterized by tissue inflammation and damage to articular cartilage, ligaments, tendons, and bones ˙
- gout—associated with elevated blood levels of uric acid, resulting in urate crystal deposits in and around the joints

Although some different nutritional issues relate to each of these diseases, weight management to reduce the stress on diseased or weakened joints and bones is common to all. Another compelling concern is the pervasiveness of nutrition quackery. Persons who live in constant pain are particularly responsive to the hope that some particular dietary constituent, whether added to or restricted from their diets, will cure them. Unfortunately, no such dietary constituent is now known. Persons with arthritis benefit from education in basic nutrition to assure that they eat a balanced and adequate diet, do not gain excessive weight, and avoid wasting money on quackery. Clients who may eat less when pain affects their appetite and/ or their ability to prepare food and/or their ability to feed themselves may need dietary guidance for these problems. Persons disabled with arthritis may appreciate advice on devices that make it easier for them to feed themselves or prepare their food.

Osteoporosis

The skeleton grows, increases in mass, and becomes stronger throughout childhood and adolescence and into early adulthood. Between the ages of 20 and 40, men and women begin to lose bone mass, a process that continues as they age. Osteoporosis results when the bone loss is so extensive that fractures occur easily, sometimes spontaneously.

Osteoporosis affects 15 to 20 million Americans, including half of all women over the age of 45 and 90 percent of all women over the age of 75.[73] Osteoporosis, a significant cause of disability with important economic consequences, is estimated to contribute to 1.3 million or 70 percent of all bone fractures occurring among persons over age 45.[74] It has been estimated that one in four women over the age of 65 will suffer a fracture related to osteoporosis.[75] Of the 200,000 annual hip fractures, 12 percent result in death due to complications. The disease is not readily diagnosed by conventional X-ray until damage to the skeleton is quite extensive. New techniques to measure bone density and detect early bone loss are not yet widely available.

Caucasian women beyond menopause are at higher risk for osteoporosis. Risk increases as the years beyond menopause increase. Those who have an inadequate dietary intake of calcium over a long period of time, who are physically inactive, or who are underweight and have a family history of osteoporosis are at increased risk.[76] Women may have a higher risk of osteoporosis than men do because men between the ages of 15 and 50 tend to consume twice as much calcium as women. Male intake of calcium is consistently above the Recommended Dietary Allowance, while that of females is consistently below.[77] More women than men follow calcium-deficient weight-loss diets. Women also have less bone mass and therefore are at greater risk when bone mass decreases.[78] Loss of bone mass is accelerated by menopause. Because women tend to live longer than men, they lose bone mass over a longer period of time.

Risk factors for osteoporosis that can be modified are an inadequate dietary intake of calcium, lack of exercise, and being underweight. The hormonal changes associated with menopause can be modified through estrogen therapy, the only risk factor change for which there is evidence of effectiveness in the prevention of fractures from osteoporosis.[79] Many experts feel that because of its effects on osteoporosis, the benefits of estrogen replacement outweigh its other associated health risks.[80] The most effective dietary strategy to prevent osteoporosis is assuring adequate calcium intake throughout life, particularly during growth, pregnancy, and lactation. It is not clear whether or not dietary calcium stops bone loss once it begins, particularly in postmenopausal women. There is evidence that an increase in dietary calcium can retard bone loss. However, the effects vary according to the baseline intake and how much the intake of calcium is increased.[81] The NIH Consensus Development Conference on Osteoporosis[82] recommended that premenopausal and older women who take estrogen need about 1,000 mg of calcium daily to prevent bone loss, while other postmenopausal women need 1,500 mg per day. Adequate intake of other nutrients, particularly fluoride and vitamin D, along with moderate weight-bearing exercise throughout life, appears to be important in preventing osteoporosis.

Given the serious problem of osteoporosis, both females and males need to be advised to incorporate sources of calcium into their daily food intake, starting in the early years. The use of low-fat and nonfat dairy foods from which calcium is readily absorbable should be emphasized. Females, particularly adolescents and those of childbearing age, may particularly benefit by increasing their calcium intake.

Acquired Immune Deficiency Syndrome

Acquired immune deficiency syndrome (AIDS) was first identified among Americans in 1981. AIDS is a deadly communicable disease which suppresses the body's defenses against disease. It is spread by sexual contact and by the exchange of blood from infected to uninfected individuals when unsterilized needles are shared among drug users or from mother to fetus. Between 1981 and mid-1988 over 66,000 cases were reported to the Centers for Disease Control in Atlanta.[83] The incidence of the disease is climbing. Although it is a communicable disease, many tertiary prevention nutrition approaches demonstrated for debilitating diseases are appropriate for AIDS.

Complications of AIDS include progressive weight loss and malabsorption, which place its victims at high nutritional risk. As with cancer, poor nutritional status may be exacerbated by the treatment.[84] Adequate nutrition can optimize immunological status and minimize body wasting. Diet counseling and home-delivered meal services can assist the client in maintaining nutrition status in the presence of diarrhea, sore mouth and throat, fatigue, and fever.[85] Counseling may be most effective if begun soon after diagnosis and before weight loss begins, or when HIV positive status is first identified. As AIDS becomes more common among the population, the role of nutrition will become more clear, and more program examples will appear in the literature.

ROLES FOR NUTRITIONISTS IN ADULT HEALTH

The national health promotion, disease prevention objectives for the year 2000[86] and *Model Standards: Guidelines for Community Attainment of the Year 2000 Objectives*[87] both include chapters on nutrition and provide useful guidelines for nutrition services in adult health promotion and chronic disease prevention, as do such federal initiatives as the National Cholesterol Education Program, the National High Blood Pressure Program, and publications from the National Cancer Institute. Project LEAN, spearheaded by the Kaiser Family Foundation, coordinates a coalition of health professional and trade associations that are developing guiding strategies to reduce the excessive fat in the American diet. Campaigns and programs sponsored by voluntary health organizations include the American Heart Association's "Food Festival," "Eating Away from Home," work site and school site programs, and the consumer health information program, Heart Guide. (See Chapter 18.) Packaged guidelines include press releases, public service announcements, and published materials for public and professional education. Other voluntary health associations that support and collaborate in community adult health promotion are the American Cancer Society and the American Diabetes Association. The voluntary health associations also provide access to dedicated volunteers who are available to work in community programs.

As diet and fitness spas, weight-loss centers, and health food stores spring up in their communities, nutritionists can assess their validity and quality and guide the public in making choices between those that base their products and services on sound nutrition science and those that are fraudulent and exploitive. Licensure of nutrition care providers, which can protect the public's health, is becoming more common.

Public health nutritionists contribute to health agency screening programs by arranging or directing weight screening, dietary assessment, nutrition education, counseling, referral, and follow-up. Prior to conducting screening programs, arrangements for referrals and follow-up must be in place for those identified as being overweight, having high blood pressure or cholesterol, or having dietary excesses or inadequacies.

Federal funds for adult health promotion are available primarily from the Preventive Health Services Block Grant. These funds can be used to employ nutrition personnel. Some state and local health agencies are budgeting for health promotion and nutrition services. Nutrition services for adult health can also be funded through contracts with industry for work site wellness programs, fees for services, or foundation grants. Nutrition consultation to home health staff is chargeable to Medicare as an administrative cost. In some states, direct services to clients may be supported through special state and federal agency grants. Nutrition counseling to clients and their caretakers in hospice programs is directly billable to Medicare. (See Chapter 10.)

Nutrition services can and should include a broad range of strategies, including services offered by health professionals other than nutritionists. For discussion of intervention strategies, see Chapter 18.

ISSUES TO DEBATE

- Which nutrition strategies should be incorporated into public health programs to prevent premature death and disability in the community?
- How much responsibility should society expect individuals to take for reducing their controllable risk factors like smoking and obesity to decrease the burden on society in terms of medical care costs?

• How should public funds be allocated for primary, secondary, and tertiary prevention versus crisis medical care? What share of these funds should be allocated for nutrition services?
• What are the implications of for-profit weight-loss centers for public health program planning?

NOTES

1. M.E. Burdette and M. Mohr, *Characteristics of Social Security Disability Insurance Beneficiaries, 1975,* SSA Pub. no. 13-11947 (Washington, D.C.: U.S. Department of Health, Education, and Welfare, 1979).

2. Society of Actuaries, *Transactions: 1977 Reports of Mortality and Morbidity Experience.* (Chicago: University of Chicago, 1978).

3. O.T. Thornberry, R.W. Wilson, and P. Golden. "Health Promotion and Disease Prevention Provisional Data from the National Health Interview Survey, United States, January–June 1985," *Advance Data from Vital Statistics* (Public Health Service, Hyattsville, Md.) 126 (September 19, 1986): 1–16.

4. D.A.K. Black and J.D. Pole, "Priorities in Biomedical Research. Indices of Burden," *British Journal of Preventive Medicine* 29 (1975): 222–27. B.S. Cooper and D.P. Rice, "The Economic Cost of Illness Revisited, *Social Security Bulletin* 39 (1976): 21–36. D.P. Rice, "Estimating the Cost of Illness," *American Journal of Public Health* 57 (1967): 424–40.

5. *Healthy People: The Surgeon General's Report on Health Promotion and Disease Prevention,* DHEW (PHS) Pub. no. 79-55078 (Washington, D.C.: 1979), 8–9.

6. Ibid.

7. U.S. Department of Health and Human Services, *The Surgeon General's Report on Nutrition and Health Summary and Recommendations,* DHHS (PHS) Pub. no. 88-50211 (Washington, D.C.: Government Printing Office, 1988), 1.

8. Sherry L. Shamansky and Cherie L. Clausen, "Levels of Prevention: Examination of the Concept," *Nursing Outlook* 28 (1980): 104–108.

9. U.S. Department of Agriculture and U.S. Department of Health and Human Services, *Dietary Guidelines for Americans* (Washington, D.C.: Government Printing Office, 1985).

10. Sherry L. Shamansky and Cherie Clausen, *Levels of Prevention..*

11. Ibid.

12. *With Every Beat of Your Heart* (Bethesda, Md.: U.S. Department of Health and Human Services, 1987), 7.

13. Ibid., 5.

14. Ibid.

15. Beth Schucker et al., "Change in Physician Perspective on Cholesterol and Heart Disease: Results from Two National Surveys," *Journal of the American Medical Association* 258 (25 December 1987): 3521, 3527.

16. Project LEAN, *Idea Kit for State and Community Programs to Reduce Dietary Fat* (Menlo Park, Calif.: Kaiser Family Foundation, 1989).

17. Committee on Diet, Nutrition, and Cancer, National Research Council, *Diet, Nutrition, and Cancer* (Washington, D.C.: National Academy Press, 1982), I-14–I-15.

18. American Heart Association, *Dietary Guidelines for Healthy American Adults,* 71-003-C

(Dallas: American Heart Association, 1986).

19. The American Dietetic Association, "The American Dietetic Association's Nutrition Recommendations for Women," *Journal of the American Dietetic Association* 86 (1986): 1663–64.

20. American Diabetes Association, "Nutritional Recommendations and Principles for Individuals with Diabetes Mellitus: 1986," *Diabetes Care* 10 (1987): 126–32.

21. National Research Council, *Diet and Health: Implications for Reducing Chronic Disease Risk* (Washington, D.C.: National Academy Press, 1989).

22. J. Michael McGinnis and Marion Nestle, "The Surgeon General's Report on Nutrition and Health: Policy Implications and Implementation Strategies," *American Journal of Clinical Nutrition* 49 (1989): 23–28.

23. Ibid.

24. U.S. Department of Agriculture and U.S. Department of Health and Human Services, *Dietary Guidelines.*

25. National Institutes of Health, "Health Implications of Obesity," *NIH Consensus Development Conference Statement* 5, no. 9 (February 1985).

26. Ibid.

27. Kelly Brownell, "The Yo-Yo Trap," *American Health* 7 (1988): 78.

28. *With Every Beat of Your Heart*, 4.

29. Ibid.

30. Hypertension Detection and Follow-Up Program Cooperative Group, "Five-Year Findings of the Hypertension Detection and Follow-Up Program: I. Reduction in Mortality of Persons with High Blood Pressure, Including Mild Hypertension," *Journal of the American Medical Association* 242 (1979): 2562–72.

31. Ibid.

32. "The 1988 Report of the Joint National Committee on Detection, Evaluation, and Treatment of High Blood Pressure," *Archives of Internal Medicine* 148 (1988): 1023–38.

33. Schucker et al., "Change in Physician Perspective."

34. National Cholesterol Education Program, *Report of the Expert Panel on Detection, Evaluation, and Treatment of High Blood Cholesterol in Adults*, NIH Pub. no. 88-2925 (National Heart, Lung, and Blood Institute, U.S. Department of Health and Human Services, January 1988).

35. Ibid.

36. Ibid.

37. Ibid.

38. Ibid.

39. *With Every Beat of Your Heart*, 4.

40. Burdette and Mohr, *Characteristics. With Every Beat of Your Heart*, 5.

41. *With Every Beat of Your Heart*, 5.

42. Ibid.

43. Thornberry, Wilson, and Golden, "Health Promotion."

44. Peter Wood, "The Exercise Explosion—Is It Healthy?" in *The Role of Nutrition and Exercise in Health* (Seattle: University of Washington, 1984), 60.

45. National Cholesterol Education Program, *Report of the Expert Panel.*

46. National Heart, Lung, and Blood Institute. *Fact Book, Fiscal Year 1985* (Bethesda, Md.:

National Institutes of Health, 1985), 23.

47. National Center for Health Statistics, *Health, United States, 1985*, DHHS (PHS) Pub. no. 866-1232 (Washington, D.C.: Government Printing Office, December 1985).

48. S. Abraham et al, "Decline in Serum Cholesterol Levels among Adults in the United States," *Circulation* 68 (1983): 111–179.

49. P.L. Remington et al, "Current Smoking Trends in the United States: The 1981 to 1983 Behavioral Risk Factor Surveys," *Journal of the American Medical Association* 253 (1985): 2875–78.

50. Mary Winston and Anita Owen, "Measurement and Patterns of Food Consumption in the United States," *Cholesterol and Coronary Disease . . . Reducing the Risk* 1, no. 4 (February 1987): 5–9.

51. Christopher Sempos, Richard Cooper, Mary Grace Kovar, and Marilyn McMillen, "Divergence of the Recent Trends in Coronary Mortality for the Four Major Race-Sex Groups in the United States," *American Journal of Public Health* 78 (1988): 1422–27.

52. American Cancer Society, *Cancer Facts and Figures—1987* (New York: American Cancer Society, 1987), 3.

53. Ibid., 10.

54. Committee on Diet, Nutrition, and Cancer, National Research Council, *Diet, Nutrition, and Cancer* (Washington, D.C.: National Academy Press, 1982), I-14.

55. R. Doll and R. Peto, "Avoidable Risks of Cancer in the United States," *Journal of the National Cancer Institute* 66 (1981): 1191–1208.

56. Leonard A. Cohen, "Diet and Cancer," *Scientific American* 257, no. 5 (1987): 42–48.

57. Ibid. James P. Herbert and Donald R. Miller, "Methodological Considerations for Investigating the Diet-Cancer Link," *American Journal of Clinical Nutrition* 47 (1988): 1068–77.

58. Herbert and Miller, "Methodological Considerations," 1068–77.

59. National Cancer Institute, *Diet, Nutrition and Cancer Prevention: The Good News* (Bethesda, Md.: National Cancer Institute, December 1986) NIH Pub. no. 87-2878.

60. K.A. Kern and J.A. Norton, "Cancer Cachexia," *Journal of Parenteral and Enteral Nutrition* 12 (1988): 286–98.

61. Ibid. J. Van Eys, "Effect of Nutritional Status on Response to Therapy," *Cancer Research* 42 (supp.) (1982): 747s–753s.

62. C.L. Buss, "Nutritional Support of Cancer Patients," *Primary Care* 14 (1987): 317–35.

63. Jo Ann Davey and Nancy Hall, "Current Practices for Home Enteral Nutrition," *Journal of The American Dietetic Association* 89 (1989): 233–240.

64. American Society for Parenteral and Enteral Nutrition, "Standards for Home Nutrition Support," *Nutrition in Clinical Practice* 3, no. 5 (1988): 202–205.

65. National Diabetes Advisory Board, *The National Long Range Plan to Combat Diabetes*, NIH Pub. no. 87-1587 (Washington, D.C.: U.S. Department of Health and Human Services, 1987).

66. Ibid.

67. Carter Center of Emory University, "Closing the Gap: The Problem of Diabetes Mellitus in the United States," *Diabetes Care* 8, no. 4 (1985): 391.

68. M.I. Harris, National Diabetes Data Group, ed., *Diabetes in America*, NIH Pub. no. 85-1468 (Bethesda, Md.: National Institutes of Health, 1985).

69. National Institutes of Health, "Diet and Exercise in Noninsulin-Dependent Diabetes

Mellitus," *NIH Consensus Development Conference Statement* 6, no. 8 (December 1986): 51–7.

70. Ibid.

71. Margaret Powers, *Handbook of Diabetes Nutritional Management* (Rockville, Md.: Aspen Publishers, Inc., 1987).

72. National Institute of Arthritis, Diabetes, and Digestive Diseases, *Arthritis, Rheumatic Diseases, and Related Disorders*, DHHS (NIH) Pub. no. 85-1983 (Bethesda, Md.: National Institutes of Health, 1985).

73. National Institutes of Health, *Osteoporosis: Cause, Treatment, Prevention*, NIH Pub. No. 86-2226 (Bethesda, Md.: National Institutes of Health, May 1986).

74. Ibid.

75. National Dairy Council, *Calcium, A Summary of Current Research for the Health Professional*, Pub. no. 0147N (Rosemont, Ill.: National Dairy Council).

76. National Institutes of Health, *Osteoporosis*. Robert E. Olson, ed., "Calcium Intake and Bone Loss," *Nutrition Reviews* 46, no. 3 (1988): 123–25.

77. National Dairy Council, "The Role of Calcium in Health," *Dairy Council Digest* 55, no. 1 (January–February 1984).

78. Ibid. *The Surgeon General's Report on Nutrition and Health* (Washington, D.C.: U.S. Department of Health and Human Services), DHHS (PHS) Pub. no. 88-50210, p. 314.

79. National Institutes of Health, *Osteoporosis*.

80. Ibid.

81. Olson, "Calcium Intake."

82. National Institutes of Health, "Osteoporosis," *NIH Consensus Development Conference Statement* 5, no. 3 (April 1984).

83. Centers for Disease Control, *Acquired Immunodeficiency Syndrome (AIDS) Weekly Surveillance Report—United States*, 4 July 1988.

84. M.E. Garcia, C.L. Collins, and P.W.A. Mansell, "The Acquired Immune Deficiency Syndrome: Nutritional Complications and Assessment of Body Weight Status," *Nutrition in Clinical Practice* 2 (1987): 108–10.

85. C.L. Collins, "Nutrition Care in AIDS, *Dietetic Currents* 15 (1988): 11–16.

86. Public Health Service, *Promoting Health/Preventing Disease: Year 2000 Objectives for the Nation* (Washington, D.C.: U.S. Department of Health and Human Services, 1990).

87. American Public Health Administration, *Model Standards: Guidelines for Community Attainment of the Year 2000 Objectives* (Washington, D.C.: American Public Health Administration, 1990).

BIBLIOGRAPHY

Halpern, S.L., ed. *Quick Reference to Clinical Nutrition*. Philadelphia: J.B. Lippincott Co., 1979.

National Dairy Council. *Lifesteps: Weight Management: A Summary of Current Theory and Practice*. Rosemont, Ill.: National Dairy Council, 1985.

The Surgeon General's Report on Nutrition and Health, Summary and Recommendations. DHHS (PHS) Pub. no. 88-50211. Washington, D.C.: U.S. Department of Health and Human Services, 1988.

chapter 10

Assuring Nutrition Services for Older Adults

Mildred Kaufman

READER OBJECTIVES

- Differentiate between chronological aging and physiological aging.
- Discuss the problems in using available nutritional assessment methodologies for older adults.
- Specify dietary recommendations for healthy older adults.
- Compare and contrast community nutrition services for older adults in relation to their degree of dependency.
- Suggest the roles of the nutritionist in serving the older population in the community.

AGING OF AMERICANS

The proportion of the American population living to old age is rapidly escalating, causing major shifts in demands for services, including various types of nutrition and food services. Eligibility for social security and retirement benefits establishes the age of 65 as the commonly used cutoff point to classify individuals as older adults, senior citizens, or elderly. In 1900, persons over 65 years of age made up less than 5 percent of the population. In 1980, over 12 percent of the population were over 65 years old, with a ratio of three women to every two men. In the year 2040, this age group is projected to reach over 21 percent of the population, as the "baby boomers" age.[1] (See Figure 10-1.)

To more clearly differentiate the population of older adults by age, the U.S. Census Bureau defines people between the ages of 65 and 74 as "elderly," people between 75 and 84 as "aged," and people who live beyond age 85 as "very old." Those in the growing group of the "very old" are more

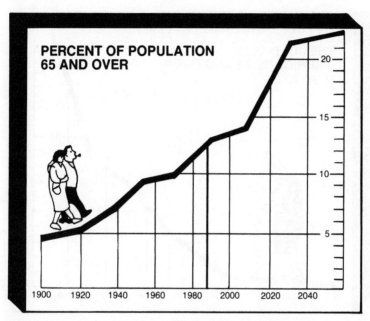

Figure 10-1 Percentage of Population 65 and Older, 1900–2040. *Source*: Adapted with permission from "Growing Old in America," *The Washington Post*, © 1987.

likely to be frail and dependent. The "very old" or "old old" are projected to increase from about 2 million in 1980 to about 12 million in 2040.[2] (See Figure 10-2.)

Past life experiences and present circumstances take their toll on the health and nutritional status of people as they age. As digestive, circulatory, metabolic, and excretory systems age, the body gradually loses its efficiency in absorbing, transporting, and metabolizing nutrients. Biological changes often attributed to the aging process vary in their degree of impact on individuals. With differences in severity and pace, as years advance most persons experience changes such as loss of teeth, decreasing acuity of taste and smell, impaired hearing and vision, and lessened neuromuscular coordination,[3] all of which affect the ability to eat, to prepare food, and to enjoy mealtimes.

The chronic diseases more prevalent with aging—heart disease, cancer, stroke, arthritis, and diabetes—contribute to disabilities, decrease mobility, and cause difficulties with activities of daily living.

Environmental, life style, and socioeconomic influences interrelate with these biological changes. Loneliness and grief as spouse, relatives, and

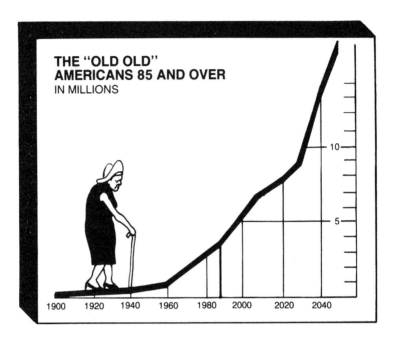

Figure 10-2 "Old Old" Americans (85 and Over), 1900–2040. *Source*: Adapted with permission from "Growing Old in America," *The Washington Post*, ©1987.

friends pass away; fear of illness and disability; or moving out of the home of a lifetime can cause many people to lose their appetites and interest in eating. Declining income, substandard housing, lack of transportation, and limited education all contribute to poor food choices.

NUTRITIONAL STATUS OF OLDER AMERICANS

The NHANES II sample of people from 60 to 74 years of age classified 50 percent of the women and 18 percent of the men as obese.[4] Dietary studies suggest low intakes of calories, calcium, iron, and vitamins A and C. More specific nutritional assessment data on the elderly population, particularly for people older than age 74, are very much needed for those living both at home and in institutions. Especially lacking are the longitudinal data gathered on the same individuals over time needed to more clearly understand changing nutritional status with advancing age. Interpretation of nutrition assessment data in the elderly needs to distinguish the findings related to normal aging from those that should be attributed to the prevalent degenerative diseases. The accuracy of food and nutrient intake data gathered using the usual interview methods may be limited by memory lapses and impaired hearing or vision. Changes in body composition and stature may influence anthropometric measurements. Thus, methods and standards for anthropometric, biochemical, clinical, and dietary assessment need to be developed specifically for older populations.[5]

Much of the research on aging is carried out or supported by the National Institute on Aging (NIA). Created by Congress in 1974, it conducts and supports biomedical, social, and behavioral research and training related to the aging process and degenerative diseases and to other special problems and needs of older people. Through its Gerontology Research Center in Baltimore, NIA conducts longitudinal studies to understand the aging processes and to differentiate changes due to aging from those due to disease processes. The U.S. Department of Agriculture (USDA) Human Nutrition Research Center on Aging at Tufts University investigates nutrition questions.

Unique characteristics to consider when assessing nutritional status for older adults are

- decreasing physical activity and metabolic rate
- poor dentition
- decreasing organ function which adversely affects absorption, transport, metabolism, and/or excretion of essential nutrients
- increasing prevalence of chronic diseases, such as cardiovascular disease, atherosclerosis, hypertension, stroke, osteoporosis, diabetes, arthritis, and cancer
- increasing use of prescription and over-the-counter medications which may contribute to adverse drug-nutrient interactions
- alterations in psychological and social well-being and financial status, often causing diminished ability to shop and prepare adequate meals.[6]

Preventive health services recommended for adults 65 years and over include annual nutrition assessment and diet and exercise counseling. (See Exhibit 10-1.)

DIETARY RECOMMENDATIONS FOR HEALTHY OLDER ADULTS

The Recommended Dietary Allowances (RDAs) of the Food and Nutrition Board of the National Research Council are usually cited as the

Exhibit 10-1 Preventive Health Services, Ages 65 and Over (Schedule: Every Year*)

		Leading Causes of Death: Heart disease Cerebrovascular disease Obstructive lung disease Pneumonia/influenza Lung cancer Colorectal cancer
SCREENING	**COUNSELING**	**IMMUNIZATIONS**

History
Prior symptoms of transient
  ischemic attack
Dietary intake
Physical activity
Tobacco/alcohol/drug use
Functional status at home
	Diet and Exercise
	Fat (especially saturated fat), cholesterol,
	  complex carbohydrates, fiber, sodium,
	  calcium
	Caloric balance
	Selection of exercise program
		Tetanus-diphtheria (TD)
		  booster⁵
		Influenza vaccine¹
		Pneumococcal vaccine
		HIGH-RISK GROUPS
		Hepatitis B vaccine

Physical Exam
Height and weight
Blood pressure
Visual acuity
Hearing and hearing aids
Clinical breast exam¹
HIGH-RISK GROUPS
Auscultation for carotid bruits
Complete skin exam
Complete oral cavity exam
Palpation of thyroid
  nodules
	Substance Use
	Tobacco cessation
	Alcohol and other drugs:
	  Limiting alcohol consumption
	  Driving/other dangerous activities
	    while under the influence
	  Treatment for abuse
	
	Injury Prevention
	Prevention of falls
	Safety belts
	Smoke detector
	Smoking near bedding or upholstery
	Hot water heater temperature
		This list of preventive serv-
		ices is not exhaustive.
		It reflects only those topics
		reviewed by the U.S. Pre-
		ventive Services Task
		Force. Clinicians may wish
		to add other preventive serv-
		ices on a routine basis,
		and after considering the
		patient's medical history and
		other individual circum-
		stances. Examples of target
		conditions not specifically
		examined by the Task Force
		include:

Laboratory/Diagnostic
Procedures
Nonfasting total blood
  cholesterol
Dipstick urinalysis
Mammogram²
Thyroid function tests³
HIGH-RISK GROUPS
Fasting plasma glucose
Tuberculin skin test (PPD)
Electrocardiogram
Papanicolaou smear⁴
Fecal occult blood/sigmoid-
  oscopy
Fecal occult blood/colon-
  oscopy
	Dental Health
	Regular dental visits, tooth brushing, and
	  flossing
	
	Other Primary Preventive Measures
	Glaucoma testing by eye specialist
	HIGH-RISK GROUP
	Discussion of estrogen replacement
	  therapy
	Discussion of aspirin therapy
	Skin protection from ultraviolet light
		Chronic obstructive pul-
		  monary disease
		Hepatobiliary disease
		Bladder cancer
		Endometrial disease
		Travel-related illness
		Prescription drug abuse
		Occupational illness and
		  injuries

		Remain Alert For:
		Depressive symptoms
		Suicide risk factors
		Abnormal bereavement
		Changes in cognitive function
		Medications that increase risk
		  of falls
		Signs of physical abuse or
		  neglect
		Malignant skin lesions
		Peripheral arterial disease
		Tooth decay, gingivitis,
		  loose teeth

*Applies only to the periodic visit itself. The frequency of the individual preventive services listed in this table is left to clinical discretion, except as indicated in other footnotes.

1. Annually.   2. Every 1–2 years for women until age 75, unless pathology detected.   3. For women.
4. Every 1-3 years.   5. Every 10 years.

Source: Reprinted from *Promoting Health/Preventing Disease: Year 2000 Objectives for the Nation, Draft for Public Review and Comment,* p. 22-16, U.S. Department of Health and Human Services, Washington, D.C., 1989.

reference for energy, protein, mineral, and vitamin needs for groups of healthy older adults. However, there has been little research on the specific nutrient requirements of the older human adult. The published RDAs treat all adults over age 51 as one group.[7] As in previous editions, the 1989 RDAs do not differentiate age groupings for adults over age 51. The committee concluded that the data are not sufficient to establish separate RDAs for people 70 years of age and older.[8] The major recommendation with aging is to decrease calories because of lower metabolic rate and less physical activity. Controlling calories while maintaining levels of protein and essential vitamins and minerals requires a nutrient-dense diet.

The USDA and U.S. Department of Health and Human Services (DHHS) Dietary Guidelines for Americans, which emphasize a variety of foods, are particularly appropriate for healthy older persons. The recommended increases in dietary fiber from fruits, vegetables, and whole grains, in addition to other health benefits, can be useful in alleviating constipation, a common complaint. Controlling calories to combat obesity; decreasing fat, saturated fat, and cholesterol to reduce blood lipids and prevent digestive distress; and reducing sodium intake to manage high blood pressure are consistent with common dietary recommendations for older adults.

About one-third to one-half of older adults take vitamin and mineral supplements. Many consider them a panacea. Use of a variety of nutrient-dense foods should meet the vitamin and mineral needs of healthy older adults. Those with poor appetites, those following modified diet plans, and those having special dietary needs may require professional guidance in selecting the appropriate kinds and amounts of supplements. Older people are heavy users of both self-selected over-the-counter and physician-prescribed drugs. Many drugs interact with nutrients and reduce their absorption. Other drugs affect appetite or cause gastrointestinal disturbances. Conversely, food components may interfere with the action of some drugs. Nutritionists who work with older adults need to understand specific drug-nutrient interactions.

GOALS OF NUTRITION PROGRAMS IN THE COMMUNITY

Currently, the 12 percent of the population that is over age 65 use over 30 percent of the nation's health care budget. While the taxpayers bear the heavy burden of these expenditures, many older adults are not receiving the kind and amount of preventive services, medical care, and supportive services they need to promote maximum independence and quality of life. Community services are generally fragmented, insufficient, and uncoordinated.[9]

Health professionals who work with groups planning community services must assess the wide variations in competencies of older adults and observe the continuum of physical and mental function between the well and the ill, the vigorous and the frail, the alert and the confused, the affluent and the poor, and the involved and the isolated. While there are many dependent older persons who need care services, there are many others who plan independently to meet their own needs. Among the older population there is a vast potential pool of retired professional, technical, and business people with energy and expertise to tap as volunteers in planning and delivering services to their peers.

Goals of community nutrition services for older adults are to

- promote maximum health and independent function through nutritionally adequate meals that consider the variations in individual physical, social, and emotional needs
- protect consumers in relation to safety, cost, quality, packaging, and labeling of those foods that are nutritious
- provide older persons or their caregivers with current, scientifically sound, understandable nutrition education and diet counseling
- advocate for supportive community food and nutrition services for those older adults with health needs, physical disabilities, need for social contacts, or inadequate income.
- assure standards of nutritional care and quality of food services for all community and group care/health care programs serving the older population
- provide education, training, and technical assistance in nutrition, dietetics, and food service management to personnel caring for older persons in community programs, in their homes, or in institutions
- conduct research to advance knowledge regarding the unique nutritional requirements of the aging and test cost-effective interventions to meet these needs.[10]

Some nutrition education and health promotion programs may serve older adults along with younger adults. However, there are needs to develop programs around the unique concerns and life styles of the elderly.[11] Dependent older adults require special supportive nutrition services to remain in the community. Different programs need to be specifically designed for older adults who are[12]

- vigorous, independent, and able to care for themselves
- semidependent, needing services to enable them to live at home with assistance

- dependent or frail, requiring skilled nursing care at home or in a long-term care facility

The range of needs among the aging population suggests a comprehensive continuum of care that includes medical, nutrition, and supportive services based on individual health needs and degrees of dependency. The availability of a spectrum of services for continuity of care prolongs independent living and supports the quality of life with dignity.[13] The continuum of need applied to nutrition programs and services is illustrated in Figure 10-3. The nutritionist using the concept of continuity of care advocates for integration of nutrition education and counseling at each level in the continuum. Assessing the needs and participating in the early stages of planning for community programs assure that appropriate nutrition services are integrated into the system, with arrangements for nutrition consultation and continuing education to all care providers.

NUTRITION SERVICES THAT PROMOTE INDEPENDENT LIVING

Health Promotion for the Elderly

"The aim of public health, with regard to the aging population is not merely to extend life further, nor to cure or prevent diseases and disorders which increase with age. Its primary goal is the improvement of the quality of life, both for the elderly and the future elderly."[14] Public health workers are challenged to test health promotion/disease prevention programs for older adults and monitor their effect throughout the lengthening life span.

A health promotion initiative directed specifically to the elderly is the national public education program called Healthy Older People, developed by the Office of Disease Prevention and Health Promotion of the U.S. Public Health Service and the Administration on Aging to foster state interagency coalitions for health promotion.[15] It provides funding for health and nutrition education along with federally funded meal programs. Another initiative is the Health Promotion and Wellness National Resource Center, started under the auspices of the American Association of Retired Persons.[16] These programs offer resources and linkages that the nutritionist can use in planning with community agencies.

Many older adults are interested in measures they perceive will help them remain healthy or manage any chronic or crippling conditions they may have. This receptivity motivates them to adopt more health-promoting behaviors. Many older people are avid readers and know about the current

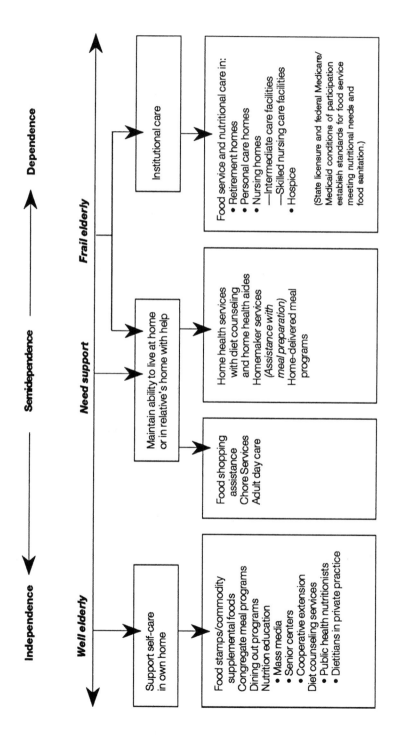

Figure 10-3 Overview of Community Food/Nutrition Programs for Older Adults. *Source:* Adapted from *Aging and Public Health* by H.T. Phillips and S.H. Gaylord (Eds.), p. 89, Springer Publishing Company, Inc., New York 10012, © 1985. Used by permission.

nutrition issues covered in the popular media. Health-conscious senior citizens welcome nutrition education offered through the radio, television, local newspapers, or a hotline that they can call for answers to their nutrition questions.

Health departments, senior centers, university elderhostel programs, community colleges, adult education programs, peer or shared learning groups, homemaker clubs of the Cooperative Extension Program, voluntary health agencies, chapters of the American Association of Retired Persons, libraries, and congregate meal programs can offer regularly scheduled nutrition education. To be useful, the content should be responsive to the health concerns, interests, income and education levels, ethnic backgrounds, and life styles of the participants. Food preparation demonstrations with tasting parties, supermarket tours, group discussions, contests, book reviews at the local library, debates, and nutrition games make sessions lively.

Lacking scientific knowledge, elderly health seekers easily fall prey to those who would sell them nutrient supplements, megadose vitamin and mineral supplements, diet cures, or "quick fix" books. Credible nutrition education programs compete with the slick promoters of diet fads and frauds. Using the marketing strategies discussed in Chapter 15 can help the nutritionist design nutrition education programs that meet the needs and interests of the older audience. The use of focus groups representing the older consumers in the community can assist the nutritionist to respond to their demands. Successful nutrition education programs for older audiences respect their lifetime of knowledge and experiences. Nutritionists can train and supervise peer educators or counselors to conduct nutrition education programs for their own age group.

Diet Counseling Services

Older adults are often advised by their physicians to "cut down on salt," "eat less saturated fat and cholesterol," "stay away from sugar," "lose some weight," "follow a low-fat diet," or "eat more fiber." Many are bewildered by such advice. They are either afraid to eat many foods they enjoy or ignore the vague instructions. They need specific guidance to plan meals, purchase foods, read package labels, and prepare suitable meals and snacks, particularly for diets prescribed to reduce body weight, manage non-insulin-dependent diabetes, control elevated blood pressure, control cholesterol, or overcome digestive problems. Assisting older clients to manage and maintain their physician-prescribed diets helps them to function at home or in the home of a relative. This can contribute to their independence and self-esteem and possibly reduce the need for costly medical, hospital, or long-term care.

Diet counseling may be provided by nutritionists in public health agencies at no cost or based on a sliding fee scale. If the public health agency does not provide direct services, the nutritionist can encourage registered dietitians at the community hospital or in private practice to provide counseling services with fees based on realistic cost determinations. (See Chapter 17.) When a physician prescribes a diet as part of medical treatment, a number of health insurance companies will reimburse registered dietitians for diet counseling. Most clients who need help in designing a modified meal plan will require a series of counseling sessions to be sure that they understand and can apply the principles of the diet. The diet counselor provides the support and encouragement the client and family often need to continue the modified meal pattern and make it a way of life. Supervised practice and return demonstrations test the degree of understanding the client has of the kinds and amounts of foods to choose.

Food Stamps

The Food Stamp Program provides bonus food purchasing power to senior citizens as well as to persons of all ages who live on incomes at or below the poverty index. This program is federally funded and directed by the USDA through state and local welfare or social service agencies. As an entitlement program, all applicants who meet the income criteria are served. Applicants must document that they meet the income guidelines through a detailed eligibility application. In 1987, over 2 million eligible low-income older Americans were reported to receive food stamps.[17] Older adults can use food stamps to buy food at participating food markets, at congregate meal sites, and at some "dining out" programs. Since the food stamp allowance is based on the USDA Thrifty Food Plan, it provides the recipient with minimal food needs. No additional food stamp allowances are provided for foods required for prescribed diets or extra nutritional needs.

Nutritionists in public health agencies who are knowledgeable about their local food stamp programs can refer clients they consider eligible, help them complete the lengthy application, and advise them about the documents they need to take to the food stamp office with their completed application. Nutritionists can work with the Cooperative Extension agent, staff of area agencies on aging or congregate meal programs, or other community agencies to educate elderly food stamp participants on how to get the most benefit from the food stamps and to purchase foods that promote health. Advocates for the elderly can identify barriers to senior citizens' participation in the Food Stamp Program and work cooperatively with other agencies to facilitate older clients' entry into the process.

Federal commodity foods are distributed through community action organizations to older persons who receive public assistance or whose incomes do not exceed 150 percent of the federal poverty guidelines. Types and amounts of food vary with agriculture reserves and funding. Recently some states have transferred these commodities to food banks which then distribute them to clients through local food pantries. Whatever the method of distribution, the elderly may need special arrangements to take advantage of these foods.

Congregate Meal Programs

The Older Americans Act implemented by the Administration on Aging in the DHHS provides a nationwide network of social services for older adults. Each state has an agency on aging; some state and area agencies employ qualified nutritionists to work with their area agencies on aging to supervise the meal services in local communities. In 1972, Congress authorized funds to provide nutritious meals to senior citizens. Title VII (now Title III) of the Older Americans Act was passed in response to recommendations of the 1969 White House Conference on Nutrition and Health and the 1971 White House Conference on Aging to meet the unique nutritional needs of older Americans. Earlier demonstration programs had shown that congregate meals served to elderly people foster social interaction, facilitate the delivery of supportive services, meet emotional needs, and improve nutrition. Title III supports nutrition projects that serve at least one hot meal per day, five or more days per week.

Nationally, the Congregate Meal Program served about two million individuals in 1988.[18] Meals are required to meet one-third of the RDAs established for older adults. State agencies usually suggest a menu pattern to achieve these nutrient levels; some attempt to limit calories from fat to 30 percent and suggest that caterers use a minimum amount of salt.

The majority of congregate meal participants live on low incomes and are served the meals at no cost or pay with food stamps. Diners who can afford it are encouraged to contribute according to their ability up to the full cost of the meal. However, Congress has prohibited the use of any means test in admitting individuals to Title III–funded programs. Many sites transport isolated older participants to join in the activities of the senior "diners' club."

Meals are usually served in senior centers, club rooms in senior citizen housing, churches or synagogues, schools, or community centers. The objective of the meal program is to serve a nutritious meal and offer companionship to low-income or socially isolated persons who are 60 years of age or older and their spouses. The area agency on aging in cooperation with other health, education, and human service agencies can use the meal program to attract participants for health screening, education, and recreational and social activities. Nutritionists working with congregate meal programs may arrange with health agencies to conduct health risk appraisals or chronic disease screenings at meal sites and then follow up the screenings with nutrition and health education.

Nutrition education at congregate meal sites encourages participants to make healthful food choices, promoting economical buying of food and proper preparation of meals at home. Nutritionists can consult and train staff of agencies on aging, peer counselors, students, and volunteers to develop interactive, lively nutrition education programs tailored to the needs, values, and interests of the participants.

The District of Columbia Office on Aging has demonstrated particularly innovative outreach and nutrition education. Contests stimulate competition among participants and sites. A senior cookbook contest invited participants to enter favorite recipes modified to meet the Dietary Guidelines. A cookbook featuring the recipes was widely distributed and used by the caterer in the meal program's cycle menus. Salad bars at the meal sites introduced diners to raw vegetables to increase their dietary fiber intake, contribute to sociability, and provide some physical activity during the mealtime.[19] Peer nutrition education leaders were trained through the American Red Cross's Better Eating for Better Health Program.[20] Nutritionists conducted health fairs and provided diet counseling and nutrition education at the sites. Positive results of nutrition education have been documented in a health needs assessment telephone survey in which the majority of the elderly respondents stated that they regularly ate more fruits, vegetables, and whole-grain cereals in meals at home.[21]

Dining Out Programs

In some communities, nutritionists and the area agencies on aging have encouraged cafeterias and family restaurants in residential areas to serve low-priced nutritious meals to older customers. Small portions of a selection of foods, including a protein-rich food, vegetable or salad, bread, and beverage, are offered. To obtain the reduced price, seniors are invited to be "early bird" diners, avoiding lunch or dinner rush hours. Some restaurants accept food stamps for these meals. Nutritionists can encourage and educate restaurant chefs to plan menus and use recipes that follow the Dietary Guidelines for Americans.

Many independent and middle-income senior citizens prefer restaurant dining to the congregate meal site. Community-minded restaurant or cafeteria managers may welcome nutritionists as consultants in planning menus and preparing food to reduce calories, fat, cholesterol, and sodium. Notes on the menu, table tents, or attractive brochures can be used to disseminate nutrition messages or publicize a nutrition hotline or a series of nutrition education classes in the community.

Food Shopping Assistance

Many older persons do not have transportation to competitively priced supermarkets; others live in high-crime neighborhoods where they are afraid to venture out alone on the streets. For them, food shopping assistance would be a bus, taxi, or volunteer driver who transports them to the store and helps them carry their grocery bags into their kitchens. In some communities, a food market hires a bus or van driver who picks up older shoppers at their homes or apartments. A bus or taxi company may offer the service for a small charge. Food markets catering to older clientele may take orders over the telephone and offer home delivery.

Personal assistance is needed by those with impaired vision or those who use a cane, walker, or wheelchair. They need a volunteer food shopper to assist them in the store. Volunteers who help older persons shop at the supermarket should be aware of their most frequent dietary modifications and be able to advise them on how to get the most nutritious food for the money they spend or the food stamps they use. At the store, elderly shoppers appreciate help in selecting nutritious food, locating needed food items and "best buys," reading labels and prices, and getting through the checkout line. When reaching home, older persons appreciate assistance in carrying heavy food packages into the kitchen and storing food properly. A volunteer personal food shopper also might assist the older person to prepare a shopping list and then go to the store and buy and deliver the food.

Food shopping services are often organized by area agencies on aging, social service agencies, and nutrition service providers or as a volunteer service of civic clubs, churches or synagogues, or women's groups. Funding for transportation and food shopping is authorized under the Older Americans Act.

Nutritionists who know the needs of the elderly in the community can advocate for a food shopping service, find an appropriate sponsor, apply for funding, and train the volunteers about the nutrition and dietary needs of the clients.

Chore Services

Area agencies on aging and social service agencies may sponsor chore workers to help elderly persons in their homes. Chores include planning meals and snacks, shopping for food, preparing simple foods or meals, and cleaning up the kitchen. Chore workers may be paid workers or volunteers. Agencies employing chore workers may use the nutritionist to train the workers on nutritional needs of their clients, economical food buying, and suitable methods of food preparation and storage. Chore workers are usually trained on the job to perform very simple homemaking tasks. They do not give personal or nursing care or supervise physician-prescribed diets.

Homemaker/Home Health Aide Services

Homemaker services are usually sponsored by social service agencies and assist clients with light housekeeping, shopping for food, and preparation of simple, nutritious meals. Home health aides sponsored by home health or nursing agencies are trained to provide personal care as well as homemaking services. Home health aides' training should cover geriatric nutrition, food preparation methods and adjustments for the most frequently prescribed therapeutic diets, assisting the ill or handicapped in eating, and recording their food and fluid intake.

Homemaker/home health aide services may be reimbursed under Medicare, Medicaid, and some private insurers or by direct payment by the client or family. Nutritionists or dietitians can be reimbursed by Medicare or Medicaid to train the home health aides, as well as to provide continuing education and consultation for the nurses and therapists who supervise them.

Home-Delivered Meals and Meals on Wheels

Home-delivered meals can be provided to short- or long-term homebound elderly as a component of the Congregate Meal Program funded by

Title III of the Older Americans Act. In 1988 about half a million people were served.[22] These meals usually follow the menus for meals served at the congregate sites and meet the same nutritional standards.

Meals on wheels programs are nonprofit services sponsored by volunteers under the auspices of hospitals, community or women's service groups, churches or synagogues, or interfaith councils or as a commercial enterprise by local caterers or restaurants. Community-sponsored meals on wheels programs generally charge for meals on a sliding scale and serve a limited geographic area.

Most programs deliver one meal a day, five days a week. However, communities are beginning to recognize the need for weekend service as more elderly are without family support. Some programs add a light snack. The meal and snack may be delivered ready to eat, or they may be frozen or canned, requiring the client to heat the food. Meal programs that are federally funded must serve one-third to one-half of the RDAs. All must conform to the local health department's food service sanitation requirements. Some provide modified diets prescribed by a physician. Meals are delivered to the home by a friendly visitor whose cheerful greeting may be as welcome to the homebound as the nutritious food is. Home-delivered meals are valuable to older persons who are confined to their home during a temporary illness or convalescence or by bad weather, as well as to older persons receiving long-term home health care. Nutritionists in the community should know the home-delivered meal services available, advocate for programs to serve all of those who need them, and assist programs to meet clients' nutritional requirements by serving quality, tasty food and to comply with sanitation standards.

Home-delivered meal programs should be coordinated with home health agencies or agencies on aging since persons who need meals delivered to them at home usually have other health and social problems. Many communities provide an initial assessment by a public health nurse, social worker, or nutritionist to determine if the client can be safely served at home and to assist with planning for meals not provided by the service. This assessment assures that where the number of clients who can be served is limited, those most needing home-delivered meals are served. Often families seek home-delivered meals when a happier solution might be to encourage more eating out, assistance with shopping for food, and/or adaptation of the kitchen for handicapping conditions. A professional assessment can provide families with information about other resources. When delivered meals are appropriate, the assessment can identify other problems, such as the need for food stamps, medical assistance, home nursing care, or nutritional counseling, and make the appropriate referrals.

Adult Day Care

Adult day care, like child day care, is supervised care provided in a center for older persons who have physical or mental disabilities. Adult day care makes it possible for the older person to be at home with the family at night and on weekends but at the center while the responsible relative works during the weekdays. Adult day care centers are usually sponsored by agencies on aging or social agencies or as an auxiliary service of a home for the aged. Businesses, aware of the needs of workers to care for aging parents, are beginning to explore sponsoring adult as well as child day care. Day care centers serve one or more nutritious meals and snacks. They should employ a full-time or consultant dietitian with the expertise to serve clients who need modified diets. They may offer nutrition education. Nutritionists might consult in menu planning, food preparation, and nutrition education. Beginning in 1989, adult day care centers were eligible to receive cash and commodity food assistance through USDA's Child Care Food Program.

CARE FOR THE FRAIL ELDERLY

Home Health Care

Home health agencies provide a coordinated spectrum of services including skilled nursing, home health aides, social work, and physical, occupational, and speech therapy to homebound clients requiring convalescent or long-term care. While coordinated home care programs designed to provide in-home services were piloted in the late 1940s, these programs got major impetus in the mid 1960s when Title XVIII of the Social Security Act (Medicare) stipulated conditions of participation and reimbursement for home health services. Agencies certified to provide home health services include public health departments, not-for-profit visiting nurse and home health agencies, community and for-profit hospitals, and proprietary home health agencies.

A second major impetus in the 1980s has been the changes in Medicare reimbursement to hospitals based on diagnosis related groups (DRGs), resulting in patients being sent home "quicker and sicker." While skilled nursing care and the various therapies are reimbursed by Medicare, home visits for diet counseling by a registered dietitian are not reimbursable. However, a home health agency can cover the costs of services by a registered dietitian in its administrative overhead. The nutritionist can function as a case consultant and in-service educator to nurses, therapists, and home health aides. Some state Medicaid programs and a recent federal demonstration program allow reimbursement of any care provider, including the nutritionist, who offers the skilled medical or related health services required to maintain the client at home. Many home health clients require nutrition counseling to enhance their nutritional status or to manage a physician-prescribed diet.

With the recent trend of sending sicker patients home, many patients are sent home on enteral or parenteral feedings. This has increased the awareness of home health agency administrators and staff that they need to employ a registered dietitian who understands these complex feeding systems. It has also heightened the need for careful discharge planning and open communication between the hospital and the home health agency. The nutritionist in the public health agency can work with area hospitals to assure that assessments of patients' nutritional needs are included in referral information.

Hospice

Hospice, a more recent service in the United States, is humane care of the terminally ill at home or in a homelike group care facility. The hospice provides comfort and support to the patient and family and allows the patient to die with dignity. Many home health agencies offer hospice care as well as the traditional home health services. Legislation providing for hospice care does allow reimbursement for registered dietitians who provide diet counseling directly to clients and their caretakers. In the spirit of comfort and respect for the patient, this diet counseling should be particularly sensitive to the client's appetite, food preferences, and ability to eat. It should also respect the family's need to use food to demonstrate their caring. Nutritionists working with hospice programs benefit from training in death and dying which will better prepare them to support client and family needs and to cope with their own feelings as they work with terminally ill clients.

Respite and Support Services for Care Providers

Many agencies serving the elderly are becoming aware of the need to support families or care providers who carry a tremendous burden when they keep a dependent person at home. Thus, communities have developed respite services and support groups to help care providers deal with emotional and physical fatigue. Respite services provide for the temporary admission of a client to a nursing home or the assignment of around-the-clock aides in the home to allow the family time for a vacation or to deal with family business. Support groups provide education and allow care providers to exchange concerns. Nutritionists can discuss food and nutrition concerns with these dedicated care providers. Support groups are organized by gerontology centers, home health agencies, and agencies on aging.

Institutional Care

An estimated 5 percent of the elderly, most often the "very old," live in long-term care facilities.[23] With greater geographic separation of families and more women working, more frail elderly are placed in institutional care. Since 1965, federal funds have become available for nursing home care through Medicare and Medicaid. State licensure laws and regulations and federal conditions of participation for intermediate and skilled nursing care facilities reimbursed under Medicare and Medicaid assure minimum standards of personal, health, nursing, and nutritional care, as well as safety and sanitation. Conditions of participation require that the facility employ a registered dietitian as a consultant for the food service and for nutritional assessment and care. The nutritionist in the public health agency may be asked to consult with group care facilities on their food and nutrition services or to help them recruit a qualified consultant or educate staff. Specific initiatives may be required to assure that nutrition services are included in the discharge planning process as clients move from the institution to the home and possibly back to the institution. Chapter 12 discusses food service and nutritional care in group care facilities.

NETWORKING AND ADVOCACY FOR OLDER AMERICANS

Nutritionists assess their community and their agency's mission and programs to assure an appropriate emphasis on care for the older population. They then seek ways to strengthen the nutrition component of the community network of health and social services in cooperation with the area agency on aging. The nutritionist may facilitate and participate in Title III–funded health promotion activities and collaborate in planning in-home services to foster continuity of care and appropriate utilization of services.

Nutritionists can network with area agencies on aging, home health and social service agencies, senior housing officials, ombudsmen programs, and university gerontology centers to advocate for federal, state, and local funding for nutrition education and diet counseling services to meet the unique needs of the older population. In collaboration, the various agencies and volunteer groups should determine the need for expanding services that will support older persons in their homes, including congregate meal and dining out programs, diet counseling, shopping assistance, chore services, homemaker/home health services, and home-delivered meals. Community programs need to develop the capacity to serve all who need them.[24] Nutritionists should provide or arrange for appropriate nutrition consultation and training for the staff and volunteers for the various in-home services. To provide data to support program development, nutrition monitoring and surveillance systems for the frail older population should be designed and integrated into the service programs, as has been piloted by New York State Health Department.

The elderly themselves are powerful advocates who will assist in seeking funds if they understand and support the service being promoted. They should be involved early in data gathering and planning.

ISSUES TO DEBATE

- How can the public health nutritionist's time be justified to work with older adults when most funding is available for work with maternal and child health and when the time spent on the younger population has more long-term benefits?

- Considering the questions regarding the usefulness of available nutrition assessment measures for older adults, what methods should be recommended for a health screening program at a congregate meal site? In a nursing home?

- How much compliance should be expected in counseling "old old" patients on restrictive diets prescribed by physicians for treatment of diagnosed chronic diseases?

NOTES

1. *Growing Old in America* (Washington, D.C.: Washington Post Co., 1987), 1–10.

2. Ibid.

3. Susan H. Gaylord, "Biological Aging: Public Health Implications," in *Aging and Public Health*, ed. Harry T. Phillips and Susan H. Gaylord (New York: Springer Publishing Co., Inc., 1985), 81.

4. Barbara B. Bowman and Irwin H. Rosenberg, "Assessment of the Nutritional Status of the Elderly," *American Journal of Clinical Nutrition* 35 (supp.), no. 3 (May 1982): 1142–49.

5. Ibid.

6. Gaylord, "Biological Aging," 81.

7. National Research Council, *Recommended Dietary Allowances*, 10th ed. (Washington, D.C.: National Academy Press, 1989), 19.

8. Ibid.

9. Harry T. Phillips, "Organizing Community Health Services for the Elderly," in *Aging and Public Health*, ed. Harry T. Phillips and Susan H. Gaylord (New York: Springer Publishing Co., Inc., 1985), 251–266.

10. Marie T. Fanelli and Mildred Kaufman, "Nutrition and Older Adults," in *Aging and Public Health*, ed. Harry T. Phillips and Susan H. Gaylord (New York: Springer Publishing Co., Inc., 1985), 88.

11. Department of Health and Human Services, *Surgeon General's Workshop on Health Promotion and Aging Proceedings* (Washington, D.C.: Department of Health and Human Services, 1988), 35–40.

12. Fanelli and Kaufman, "Nutrition," 88.

13. The American Dietetic Association, "Position of The American Dietetic Assocation: Nutrition, Aging and Continuum of Health Care," *Journal of The American Dietetic Association* 87, no. 3 (March 1987): 344.

14. American Association of Retired Persons, "Announcement of Establishment of Health Promotion and Wellness National Resource Center," 1988.

15. U.S. Department of Health and Human Services, *Surgeon General's Workshop*, 35–40.

16. American Association of Retired Persons, "Announcement."

17. U.S. Department of Health and Human Services, *The Surgeon General's Report on Nutrition and Health* (Washington, D.C.: Government Printing Office, 1988), 598.

18. Ibid., 598.

19. Lois Earl, "Meal Programs for Older Adults," in *Building Support for Population-Based Dietary Change*, ed. Mildred Kaufman (Chapel Hill: University of North Carolina, 1987), 117–118.

20. American Red Cross, *Better Eating for Better Health* (Washington, D.C.: American Red Cross, 1983).

21. Earl, "Meal Programs," 117–118.

22. U.S. Department of Health and Human Services, *Surgeon General's Report*, 598.

23. "Growing Old in America," 3.

24. U.S. Department of Health and Human Services, *Surgeon General's Workshop*, 80–83.

BIBLIOGRAPHY

Phillips, Harry T., and Gaylord, Susan H., eds. *Aging and Public Health*. New York: Springer Publishing Co., Inc., 1985.

U.S. Department of Health and Human Services. *The Surgeon General's Report on Nutrition and Health*. Washington, D.C.: Government Printing Office, 1988. Chapter 16, "Aging," 595–617.

chapter 11

Providing Nutrition Services in Primary Care

Mildred Kaufman

READER OBJECTIVES

• List the needs for primary care in the community.
• Define primary care.
• Discuss nutrition services in primary care.
• Compare and contrast the focus of state- and federal-funded initiatives.
• Identify and describe populations with high-risk needs for primary care.

NEEDS FOR PRIMARY CARE

Some 45.3 million Americans under age 65 are estimated to be at risk for medical indigency. The medically disadvantaged cannot afford a regular source of medical care; many need care, but are unable to obtain it. The medically indigent are largely poor, unemployed or underemployed, young, black, Hispanic.[1] They live in the inner cities and in the country, in migrant camps and on Indian reservations. *Health United States, 1988* confirms that minorities and those with low incomes suffer from poor health much more than does the population as a whole. Black women give birth to over twice as many low birth weight infants as white women do. More than twice as many enter prenatal care in their third trimester or not at all. Death rates for all causes are substantially higher for blacks than for whites for both men and women. Years of potential life lost before age 65 for black men and women are double those lost for whites. About 24 percent of persons with incomes under $10,000 per year report some limitation of activity, compared to about 9 percent of those with incomes over $35,000 per year.

221

About 21 percent of persons living on less than $10,000 per year consider their health "fair" or "poor," contrasted to about 5 percent of those with incomes over $35,000 per year. Hospital discharges for those whose incomes are under $10,000 are almost double what they are for those with annual incomes over $35,000, and their days of hospital care are also more than twice as many.[2]

Many poor people delay going to the doctor until they are too sick to work because they do not have the money to pay the doctor, have no transportation to the clinic, have no child care, or lose wages if they take time off from their hourly paying jobs. Then they go to the emergency room or the hospital. Many poor and homeless families use hospital emergency rooms as their customary source of primary care. Because of the extraordinary costs to society in terms of tax dollars and days of work lost, as well as human suffering, health care for the indigent is being acknowledged as a public health responsibility. The Institute of Medicine Committee that studied the future of public health recommends that ultimate responsibility for assuring equitable access to health care for all be borne by a partnership involving the public and the private sectors. Until adequate federal action is forthcoming, public health agencies must continue to serve with quality and respect and to the best of their ability the priority personal care needs of uninsured, underserved, and Medicaid clients.[3]

Defining Primary Care

Primary care is first contact care or the basic level of medical care to ambulatory patients who usually walk into the medical office or clinic. It spans the levels of primary, secondary, and tertiary prevention defined in Chapters 1 and 9. Primary care should range from preventive services and anticipatory guidance to care for acute symptoms and management of chronic conditions and diseases. Patients receive primary care in physicians' offices; community, neighbornood, or migrant health centers; hospital outpatient or ambulatory health care clinics; health maintenance organizations; or public health departments. Primary care has traditionally been provided by physicians, including family practitioners, general practitioners, pediatricians, obstetricians, gynecologists, and internists. Now, in many settings, primary care is being provided by physician's assistants and nurse practitioners who have the back-up of a physician as a consultant and resource. The complex and multiple pressing problems of patients living under the stresses of poverty require additional services from dentists, nutritionists, social workers, health educators, and pharmacists.[4]

NUTRITION SERVICES IN PRIMARY HEALTH CARE

Users of indigent health care are at particularly high risk for hunger, malnutrition (see Chapter 4), and diet-related chronic diseases (see Chapter 9). Unfavorable effects of poor nutrition and diet are seen in the increased risk of negative outcomes of pregnancy in inadequately nourished women; low birth weights of infants with accompanying risks of retarded physical and mental development; high prevalence of overweight and underweight in school-age children and adults; debilitated, malnourished elderly; widespread dental disease; and high prevalence of chronic illnesses, many of which are nutrition related and require dietary treatment, monitoring, and follow-up.[5]

As part of primary care, nutrition services should be included in screening and diagnosis, health maintenance, health supervision, and health promotion. Integration of nutrition services in primary health care requires administrative support within the agency and linkages between nutrition personnel in the federal and state official health agencies and the various free-standing primary health care programs. Health planners, program administrators, physicians, nurses, and the other health disciplines involved in health care delivery all have a role in planning and providing nutrition services. They can make a significant contribution to the nutrition care provided in the primary health care program.[6]

A primary health care nutrition program should include the following essential components:

- Patient care:
  - —individual screening by the primary health care physician, physician's assistant, or nurse practitioner to identify patients with nutritional risks who need referrals made according to established criteria
  - —nutrition assessment using dietary, biochemical, clinical, and anthropometric measures utilizing currently accepted methodology and equipment
  - —nutrition care plans developed routinely and monitored periodically in cooperation with an interdisciplinary staff
  - —individual counseling documented in the medical record with follow-up as needed and with the assistance of interpreters when the patient does not speak English and the health care professional does not speak the patient's language
  - —appropriate referrals through linkages with food assistance resources (e.g., food stamps, WIC, child day care feeding programs,

food pantries, soup kitchens, congregate meal programs)
- Program level:
  - —coordination with related food and nutrition programs at the local, state, and national levels
  - —nutrition program plans based on needs assessment for specific target areas and populations; the plan must specify who will provide each of the essential nutrition services and arrange for periodic evaluation
  - —quality assurance systems including nutrition standards and a system for peer review
  - —written protocols, policies, and procedures for nutrition care provided by nutrition personnel and the other health care providers
  - —plans for periodic, planned in-service continuing education, technical assistance, and case consultation
  - —plans for community education in nutrition and outreach to promote nutrition education in the community and in the schools, work sites, churches, and recreation centers[7]

STATE PRIMARY HEALTH CARE INITIATIVES

Several state governors, legislators, and health officials have become disenchanted with Medicaid as its costs soar while many poor people who need care are not eligible. Many eligible patients are unable to find physicians who will accept the fees that Medicare and Medicaid pay. Public health agencies recognize that their role is to take responsibility as "residual guarantor," or provider of services when the private sector cannot respond to the needs.[8] Several states are taking the leadership to test systems to provide primary care. Their target populations are persons who have no regular source of care, who are ineligible for Medicaid, or who cannot find a physician who accepts it.

Primary care offered through participating county health departments in Florida was enabled as a part of the Omnibus Health Care Access Act passed by the state's legislature in 1984.[9] In this program, primary care can be offered by health departments alone, contracted to existing community health centers or hospitals, or provided as a cooperative endeavor between the county health unit and private providers.[10] Florida's primary care program is state funded and operates through selected county health units. Key components include

- medical direction
- emphasis on provision of a "medical home"
- provision of acute care
- provision of preventive services
- eligibility based on federal poverty standards
- eligibility for all family members
- 24-hour call system
- weekend and evening hours
- coordination with existing primary care providers
- consultation and referral agreements with specialists and hospitals
- cost and productivity standards
- quality assurance requirements

State funding was provided to county health units that responded to a request for proposal. "Funds were to be used to recruit the personnel and obtain the equipment to perform new medical and patient management and administrative tasks."[11] In 1987, primary care projects were operating in 18 of Florida's 67 county health units. Based on the data, this state-funded program is reducing health care costs and diverting emergency room use. It also appears to be enlisting more providers to serve indigent patients.[12]

North Carolina implemented primary care in 21 of its local health departments in 1978. Its standards and guidelines called for

- provision of medical care by "at least a nurse practitioner or physician's assistant with physician back-up"
- financial eligibility criteria that would not exclude anyone because of inability to pay
- interagency provider agreements for services not provided directly
- program evaluation procedures to provide quality assurance
- fiscal reporting/accounting procedures approved by the Department of Human Resources
- written clinical policies and procedures[13]

Programs in North Carolina vary from serving the total population in the more rural counties that do not have sufficient numbers of physicians to serving only the medically indigent, the elderly or children.[14]

Model standards for primary care in community preventive health services include nutrition as a personal preventive service and nutritionists as a support service.[15] In public health agencies involved in primary care projects, nutritionists should assess the needs and write nutrition into the program plan. Primary care grants can be used as a source of funding to employ or contract for nutritionist services.

Nutritionists seeking a reference that clearly documents the objectives, activities, monitoring/evaluation, and funding mechanisms for a comprehensive range of conditions that patients might present in ambulatory care are referred to *Guidelines for Nutrition Services in Local Health Jurisdictions*, 2d ed., published in 1987 by the California Conference of Local Health Department Nutritionists, San Bernardino, California.[16]

FEDERALLY FUNDED PRIMARY HEALTH CARE

The federal government directly funds primary care for the medically unserved and underserved through

- community health centers
- migrant health centers
- health care for the homeless
- the Indian Health Service[17]

Community and migrant health care centers and health care for the homeless are funded directly by the U.S. Department of Health and Human Services (DHHS), Public Health Service, Bureau of Health Care Delivery and Assistance. Recent revisions in the legislation and regulations encourage linkages, technical assistance, resource sharing with state health agency–administered programs, and maximum use of Medicaid funding. While nutrition services can be funded by the health center grants, budget cuts in the 1980s reduced many centers to the minimum core staff of physicians, nurses, and perhaps a social worker. Nutritionists are funded in many health centers that are the local providers of the WIC program. However, this focuses the center's nutrition services on pregnant, postpartum, and breast-feeding women, infants, and children and excludes many patients who need nutrition services. In the community health centers, almost all of these women, infants, and children up to age five are eligible for WIC because of their low incomes.

Indian health services are directly managed by the Public Health Service or contracted with the tribes. Nutrition and dietetic services have been a component of these programs since 1954.

Community or Neighborhood Health Centers

Neighborhood health centers were funded by the federal government through the Economic Opportunity Act of 1964 and expanded by an amendment to the act in 1966. The Comprehensive Health Amendments of 1967 funded additional centers. The Special Revenue Sharing Act of 1975 expanded authorized funding for community health centers and provided separate legislative authority under the Public Health Service. Under the 1981 Budget Reconciliation Act, health centers were to be funded with a Primary Care Block Grant to be administered by the states. However, in 1986 Congress passed Public Law 99-280 which repealed the Primary Care Block Grant and again authorized funding for community and migrant health centers as categorical grant programs directly administered by the Public Health Service.

Memorandums of understanding with state agencies outline the states' roles in assessing primary care needs, planning and evaluating health centers, and providing them with technical assistance. Although legislation from 1981 to 1986 increased funding for health centers by 20 percent, medical care costs increased by 50 percent. The Consolidated Omnibus Budget Reconciliation Act of 1986 facilitates contract arrangements between health centers and state Medicaid agencies. For financial survival, community health centers are currently trying to attract nongrant dollars by competing for middle-class insured patients enrolled in prepaid medical plans, enrolling Medicare and Medicaid patients in prepaid plans, opening up services in new geographic areas, and containing costs. The future of health centers depends on their ability to compete and at the same time to fulfill their promise to deliver comprehensive, responsive care to the low-income populations who need it so desperately.[18]

Community or neighborhood health centers are free-standing health clinics (i.e., they are not connected to a hospital or medical center). They are located in both rural and inner city medically underserved communities throughout the United States. These centers provide medical care and preventive health education to minority groups, low-income families, the uninsured, and others who are medically underserved in the community. Consumers of the services participate in policy development, planning, and decision-making for the community health center by holding positions on its board of directors. Membership on the board by health care consumers helps to assure that the health needs they perceive and the quality of care they desire are addressed through the health center's programs and policies and carried out by the staff. Services usually include well-child care, adult physical examinations, prenatal care, and chronic disease treatment and follow-up. The health center arranges specialty and inpatient care, coordinates health care services for the clients, and provides follow-up within the health center and the community. Comprehensive care should include medical care, nursing, social work, mental health, nutrition, health education, and dental health at the health center or by referral to providers in the community. Health centers generally have strong links to health, social service, and financial assistance programs, including Medicaid. Many operate the Special Supplemental Food Program for Women, Infants, and Children (WIC). Otherwise, they refer clients to their local WIC program.

Some community health centers receive supplemental infant mortality funds to expand their maternal and infant care services through outreach, case management, nutrition counseling, and other family and community support activities. Because of insufficient federal funding, only about one-third of the existing health centers receive the infant mortality reduction supplemental funds.[19]

Many centers fund additional services by applying for other federal, state, or private grants. Grant funds allow health centers to strengthen their services or to provide additional services in an area of high need (such as outreach, diabetes education, hypertension control, pediatric AIDS, etc.). More than half of the grant recipients under the new federal Health Care for the Homeless program are community health centers.[20] These grants make it possible for centers to serve homeless individuals through shelter-based health clinics, provide outreach, and offer drug abuse treatment and mental health services.

Staffing

The staffing of community health centers varies depending on the size and mix of their funding sources. Employment of physicians and nurses is the first priority. Physician care is often complemented by physician's assistants, nurse practitioners, and/or nurse midwives. Social workers and family service workers may be employed to assist families with their multiple needs, including coping with mental health problems, meeting financial needs, finding housing they can afford, and working on family problems: child, spouse, or elder abuse; alcoholism; drug use; or other issues affecting family function. Health educators may provide preventive health education in the clinic and in the community. Health centers prefer to employ staff from the cultural groups in the community who speak the language of the clients. In addition to health professionals, many health centers employ community health workers to extend services and health education into the neighborhoods and homes of clients from the community.

Nutrition Services

Many community health centers employ nutritionists to work with clients on their many nutrition-related health problems. The nutritionist may be assigned to manage a specific program (e.g., WIC), a specific population group (e.g., mothers and children, the elderly), or a specialty area (e.g., chronic disease, developmental disabilities, health promotion). Whatever the assigned responsibilities, the nutritionist should develop a written plan for nutrition services based on the identified needs of the health center clients and the community. (See Chapter 14.) Nutritionists with specific program responsibilities such as WIC can develop a nutrition plan that identifies the specific nutrition needs and problems of their target population, looking at these problems in relation to the strengths, resources, and nutrition-related health problems of the community as a whole.

The nutritionist works with the health center administrator and other health team members to define appropriate standards, policies, and criteria for nutrition services; advocates for adequate nutrition staffing; recruits and trains nutrition personnel; and mobilizes and coordinates community resources.[21] In the current cost containment climate, the nutritionist also should take responsibility for managing a budget and seeking new funding sources through grants, contracts, and possibly sliding scale fees.

Nutrition assistants from the community may be trained to extend nutrition services. They can provide nutrition information in the clients' primary languages and based on their food preferences and life styles. Paraprofessionals must be oriented to health center policies and procedures and trained in the foods needed for health and growth. Trained, supervised paraprofessionals can be very effective in transmitting nutrition information to improve the nutrition knowledge and skills of health center clients and the community.

Migrant Health Services

In 1984, there were an estimated 700,000 migratory farm workers and family members. Since the target population for migrant health centers includes other seasonal farm workers and their families, the total of migrant and nonmigrant farm workers was estimated as 3.5 million.[22]

Migrant and seasonal farm workers follow the nation's growing season to plant, cultivate, and harvest vegetables, flowers, and fruit. Many travel 1,000 miles or more each year in search of work. Much of the work is backbreaking stoop labor. Farm work depends on the weather. It is unpredictable and erratic work, and it pays poorly. Those who choose farm work are generally educational dropouts with no vocational skills. Most workers are rural blacks and Hispanics from Texas, Mexico, or Central America, including both legal immigrants and undocumented aliens. There are also some Puerto Ricans, Caribbean islanders, and Haitians. Many do not speak English.

The migrant seasonal work force tends to take one of three routes when following the growing season going north in April or May: from Florida up the East Coast; from Texas, fanning out through the upper Midwest; and from the Southwest up the West Coast to Washington, Idaho, and Oregon. They return to the states with a warm winter growing season in about October. Florida, Texas, Arizona, and California are considered the home-base states with the largest concentrations of both migrant and seasonal farm workers. Usually black male farm workers leave their families in their home-base states as they follow the crops up north during the summer. Hispanic farm workers usually travel with their families.[23]

Seasonal farm workers are usually employed through a crew leader who negotiates with the farmer for wages, working conditions, and housing. This crew leader role, while necessary, has also been abused. Workers are paid hourly or daily wages or at a piece rate for harvesting by the bushel or box. On a good day, working long hours, a worker may earn what sounds like "good pay." However, workers are not paid when they do not work, and there are no benefits or workman's compensation.

Housing in camps is usually supplied by the growers. While some grower-supplied or public housing is adequate, much of the housing is dilapidated, unsafe, overcrowded, and infested with rats and roaches. Cooking may be done on a hot plate, and the refrigerator may not work. The water supply may be out of doors and may be unsafe. Toilets and showers are usually shared.[24]

Poverty, the migratory life style, inadequate housing, and stress contribute to health and nutrition problems. Adults suffer from respiratory, digestive, and infectious diseases and children from parasites, diarrhea, ear infections, and skin infections.[25] A nutrition survey in Florida identified some growth retardation in Hispanic children, iron deficiency anemia, obesity among black women, and rampant dental caries and periodontal disease.[26]

In response to the plight of migrant farm workers and their lack of access to primary health care, Public Law 87-692, the Migrant Health Act, was passed by Congress as a section of the Public Health Service Act in 1962. This legislation provided for family health service clinics for migrant farm workers and their families. It has essentially continued since that time, adding the requirement for consumer governing boards in the early 1970s.

Migrant health centers provide primary health services very similar to those offered by community health centers. Because of acute problems with safety and sanitary conditions in migrant farm worker housing, they may also provide environmental health services; infection and parasitic disease screening and control; accident prevention; and prevention of excessive pesticide exposure.[27]

As with the community health centers, primary health services are defined to include services by physicians and also by physician's assistants and nurse clinicians; laboratory and radiologic services; preventive services including perinatal care, well-child care, and family planning; emergency medical services; transportation; preventive dental services; and pharmaceutical services. Supplemental services permitted to support primary care include hospital services; home health services; extended care facility services; rehabilitative services; mental health services; dental services; vision services; allied health services; therapeutic radiologic services; public health services (social and other nonmedical needs that affect health status); counseling, referral for assistance, and follow-up services; ambulatory services; and health education (including nutrition education).[28] In January 1984, there were 108 migrant health grant–supported projects in 35 states and Puerto Rico, delivering services to migrants and seasonal farm workers at 300 sites.[29]

A key issue in migrant health services is to provide continuity of care from one location to the next for highly mobile clients. Referral systems must include a personal health record designed for migrants to carry with them. Referral and continuity of care are particularly important for high-risk pregnant women and adults with chronic diseases who need life-sustaining medication for diabetes, hypertension, epilepsy, or cancer.[30]

Nutrition Care

Basic nutrition services in primary care in migrant health centers are the same as those discussed for community health centers. However, some adaptations must be made when counseling migrants and seasonal farm workers. Because of their brief time in the area, and because of their limited food storage and preparation facilities, any dietary advice must be simple to follow and limited to foods that the families can buy in local food markets. When clients do not speak or read English, use of food, food models, or colored pictures is helpful. Show-and-tell food preparation demonstrations and tasting parties may be useful for group nutrition education, but many migrant clients are not comfortable in groups. Small flip charts with pictures and a few Spanish or Creole words may be helpful teaching aids. Familiarity with ethnic preferred foods and food taboos makes counseling and education more acceptable to the migrants. Counseling and nutrition education must be based on foods that clients will eat, can afford to buy, and have the facilities to prepare. When their clients are largely Hispanic, nutritionists should learn to speak Spanish so that they do not need to depend on interpreters.

Knowing the policies, procedures, and eligibility codes of the WIC programs in the states from which clients come or to which they will be referred will facilitate the clients' transition between programs. While the verification of certification (VOC) documents their WIC eligibility, clients also need help to understand how food delivery systems and clinic practices may differ.

When migrants arrive in a new area, many need help in obtaining emergency food from food pantries or soup kitchens and help in applying for food stamps or food distribution programs. Having the eligibility worker come to the health center to accept referrals smoothes the application process. Because they are poor, uneducated transients who work hard and live in substandard housing, migrant farm worker families need sensitive guidance and respect for their needs in order to build the supportive relationship that might help them improve their food choices.

Health Services for the Homeless

The Homeless Assistance Act was enacted in July 1987 as Public Law 100-77. It defines as homeless an individual or family who (1) lacks a fixed, regular, and adequate nighttime residence; or (2) has a primary nighttime residence that is (a) a supervised or publicly operated shelter designed to provide temporary living accommodations; (b) an institution that provides temporary residence for individuals intended to be institutionalized; or (c) a public or private place not designed for or ordinarily used as a regular sleeping accommodation for human beings.[31]

The National Alliance To End Homelessness speculated that, in 1988, on any given night 735,000 people were homeless in the United States, and that during the course of the year, 1.3 million to 2.0 million were homeless for one night or more. They estimated that another six million were at extreme risk of homelessness because of disproportionately high housing costs.[32]

The stereotype of the homeless person as a white, middle-aged, male, chronic alcoholic living on skid row has changed during the last two decades. The homeless of the 1970s were younger men and women suffering from mental illness, but no longer institutionalized. During the 1980s there was a significant rise in homeless families, particularly single women with children who are usually under five, and primarily minority.[33] The homeless are usually long-term residents of their city.[34] Social and economic situations that contribute to homelessness include inflation, unemployment, reduced funding for public services, gentrification of inner cities, lack of affordable housing, and decreases in available rent subsidies. Other causes include eviction, estrangement of family members, divorce or domestic violence, criminal victimization, illness, loss of employment, disaster (fire, flood), and substance abuse.

As for other poor individuals and families, the most significant barrier to health care for the homeless is lack of money to pay for it. With no money or insurance, they are often refused services. While eligibility for Aid to Families with Dependent Children (AFDC) or Supplemental Security Income (SSI) automatically qualifies eligibility for Medicaid, persons on SSI who reside for more than three months of a year in a shelter lose their SSI and consequently their Medicaid benefits. For the homeless, the availability of Medicaid is erratic. Single parent families on AFDC are generally eligible. Single individuals without children or certified disabilities are not. States have considerable latitude to define services that are covered as well as payment levels. These payment restrictions are barriers to obtaining services, especially in the traditional, private practice, fee-for-service system.

Limited, costly, and complicated public transportation; clinic hours that conflict with times when it is necessary to secure a shelter space for the night or to obtain meals during the day; and child care difficulties also interfere with the homeless person's ability to obtain health care. Theft, loss, or damage of personal identification papers; lack of a permanent mailing address; a limited ability to keep an appointment schedule (caused by lack of a watch or clock, mental disorders, substance abuse); unpleasant confrontations; hostile providers; and cultural differences add barriers.

Over the years, some health services for the homeless have been provided by missions or shelters sponsored by religious groups or nonprofit agencies. The homeless have used emergency rooms and outpatient clinics in public or teaching hospitals and community or migrant health centers.

In some communities, as many as 40 percent of the homeless adult men are veterans, many from the Vietnam war.[35] Veterans with honorable discharge status are automatically eligible for free Veterans Administration (VA) health care for treatment of service-connected illnesses or disabilities. Those living in poverty or the elderly can also receive care. The VA has undertaken initiatives to expand services to homeless veterans. However, the location of these services and the system that determines eligibility may make it difficult for homeless veterans to use this health care.

The Health Care for the Homeless project, funded by the Robert Wood Johnson Foundation and Pew Memorial Trust, is considered to be the most effective network of health care services developed for the homeless in the 1980s. Nineteen projects funded across the country, through community coalitions, target the needs of the homeless, improve access to supportive services and entitlements, and develop strategies to continue projects after the grant funding period.

Since 1987, the Homeless Assistance Act administered by the Public Health Service has awarded funds to grantees to provide primary health care, outreach, substance abuse and mental health treatment, and case management to homeless individuals.[36] Services for the homeless must go beyond traditional health care and meet the survival needs of their clients for food, shelter, clothing, and employment.

A model health care program for the homeless in Baltimore provides services at a downtown clinic located near several soup kitchens and shelters. At the clinic, clients can receive medical evaluation and treatment, mental health and social work services, referrals, and educational programs. The clinic also offers clients shower and laundry facilities. Outpost clinics are located at five soup kitchens and five shelters. Off-site dental, podiatry, ophthalmology, laboratory, X-ray, and other specialty services are provided, as are a pharmacy, transportation, and inpatient care. Social services staff provide information and referral. Emergency services and crisis intervention include food or clothing and emergency responses when homeless persons are in danger. Caseworkers link clients to case management, locate shelter or housing, and advocate for the clients' needs. This project has developed a comprehensive health education program for clients and for staff in shelters and soup kitchens. Shelter-based outpost units, a joint venture with three community health centers, provide health screening, education, and referral.[37]

In New York City and St. Petersburg, Florida, mobile clinics move around the city and locate near homeless shelters and soup kitchens. Medical care is free to the homeless and is sponsored by the local government. These mobile medical teams provide acute care and plug their patients into established clinics when they have more complex problems needing long-term care. They arrange for food, financial assistance, or job training.[38]

Basic components of primary care for the homeless are

- outreach to homeless people wherever they are, including the streets
- linkage with immediate resources for food, clothing, shelter, transportation, and crisis care
- general medical assessment, treatment, and follow-up for acute and chronic illness and related problems such as hypertension and diabetes

- maternal and child health services, including well-child, prenatal and women's health care
- ancillary services, including dental, podiatry, eye care, and nutrition services
- mental health, psychiatric care, and substance abuse services
- arrangements for hospital, convalescent, and long-term care
- health education, including prevention of sexually transmitted diseases[39]

Staff and volunteers who work with the homeless must have very special sensitivity along with their professional expertise. They must be willing to work against all kinds of odds and be able to break away from protected settings to go where the people are. They must be innovative and flexible in approaching people and situations, recognizing that some homeless people are distrustful, rejecting, or hostile as they have developed ways to cope with living in the street. Staff must be willing to work as members of an interdisciplinary team.[40]

Nutrition Services for the Homeless

Most people who are homeless are too poor to purchase food to meet their nutritional needs, and even when they can purchase food, they usually have no place to store or prepare it. Emergency food programs such as food pantries and soup kitchens do not provide nutritionally balanced meals and find that the lack of food and/or poor nutrition is a serious problem for homeless individuals and their families.[41] Feeding infants is particularly difficult because mothers lack refrigeration for formula or milk and are unable to sanitize bottles and nipples.[42]

Children of homeless families have been observed to have a higher prevalence of abnormal growth patterns, overweight, underweight, and short stature.[43] Other problems include anemia, infestational ailments, gastrointestinal disorders, dental problems, heart and circulatory problems, and neurologic disorders.[44] A Massachusetts study noted that 50 percent of homeless children have psychosocial problems demonstrated by developmental delays, severe regression and anxiety, and learning disabilities.[45] Overall, homeless children are at higher risk for all common illnesses associated with childhood, such as upper respiratory and ear infections, gastrointestinal infections, and lice infestation. Most ailments are a result of unsanitary living conditions and environmental exposure.[46] Studies have found that children who are homeless suffer twice the rate of illness that children in the general population do.[47]

Major federal food programs are available to contribute to meeting the nutrition needs of the homeless. These include Food Stamp, WIC, Commodity Distribution, Child Day Care Food, School Breakfast and Lunch, Summer Feeding, and Congregate Meals for the Elderly programs. Eligibility requirements, complex application procedures, and bureaucratic hassles may make these programs less accessible to the homeless unless they have an advocate.

Through the collection of subjective and objective data in their community assessment, nutritionists will quickly identify the urgent needs of the homeless for food and nutrition services. The needs of this vulnerable group demand attention in the program plan for services, whether through a public health agency or a community health center (see Chapter 14). Strategies depend on the funding base for nutrition services. Existing services can be redesigned to be more sensitive and responsive to the needs of the homeless. Examples include the following:

- Study the unique needs of the homeless individuals and families in the community and work with networks within and outside the agency to redesign maternal and child health, WIC, or adult health promotion programs within existing resources to be more responsive (e.g., possibly change the hours and locations of services).

- Locate WIC clinics at shelters, hotels, or health centers that serve homeless women, infants, and children.

- Offer nutrition education, food service management, and food handling training to the staff and volunteers of the soup kitchens, shelters that serve meals, and food pantries.

- Enlist volunteers to provide transportation and child care to assist homeless individuals and families in using all of the health and nutrition services for which they qualify.

- Collaborate with professionals and administrators working with school food services, child day care, food stamps, and congregate meals to review the regulations and reduce the barriers preventing access to these programs.

- Seek grant or contract funds to provide food and nutrition services as a component of all health services for the homeless in the community. Build in a monitoring or surveillance system to provide for program evaluation.

- Network and join community coalitions that seek long-term solutions to problems of hunger and homelessness in the community, the state, the nation, and the world.

Responding to the needs of homeless individuals and families takes the nutritionist out of the traditional clinical model. Flexible, innovative, targeted approaches must encourage homeless individuals and families to enter the health care setting to obtain needed diagnosis, treatment, and ongoing care.

Indian and Alaska Native Services

In 1987, the estimated count of American Indians, Eskimos and Aleuts residing in or near reservations in the 32 reservation states (Alabama, Alaska, Arizona, California, Colorado, Connecticut, Florida, Idaho, Iowa, Kansas, Louisiana, Maine, Michigan, Minnesota, Mississippi, Montana, Nebraska, Nevada, New Mexico, New York, North Carolina, North Dakota, Oklahoma, Oregon, Pennsylvania, Rhode Island, South Dakota, Texas, Utah, Washington, Wisconsin, and Wyoming) was 1,017,000 with about a 2.8 percent increase per year. The median age of 22.6 years compares to 30.0 years for the United States as a whole. The percentage of all persons below the poverty level is 28.2 percent, compared with 12.4 percent for the U.S. population. The birth rate was 28.4. The infant mortality rate of 9.7 in 1983-85 was slightly lower than the corresponding rate for the United States, and in that time period, the percentage of low birth weight infants was 6.1, compared to 6.7 percent for the whole U.S. population. Considering age-adjusted mortality rates in 1985, the death rates from cardiovascular disease, cancer, and chronic obstructive pulmonary disease were lower for Indians and Alaska natives, while their rates were more than double for accidents, chronic liver disease and cirrhosis, and diabetes mellitus, and triple for tuberculosis. In 1980, life expectancy at birth was 71.1 years for Indians/Alaska natives, compared to 74.4 years for the U.S. white population.[48]

Health services to Indians and Alaska natives became the responsibility of the Public Health Service in 1954 under the Transfer Act (Public Law 83-568). The intent was to improve the health of American Indians and Alaska natives and to provide them with access to comprehensive health care that involved the consumers in defining their own needs and managing their own health care system. The Indian people were to be made aware and to be encouraged to use all of the federal, state, and local health programs to which they were entitled as American citizens. Public Law 93-638, the Indian Self-Determination Act, passed in 1975, gave tribes the option of managing their own health programs and contracting for health services.

The Indian Health Care Improvement Act (Public Law 94-437), passed in 1976 and amended by Public Law 96-537 in 1977, intended to bring the health status of American Indians and Alaska natives up to the level of that of the U.S. population as a whole by increasing the Indian Health Service (IHS) budget and increasing the number of Indian health professionals. It also, for the first time, provided health care access to 650,000 Indians living in urban areas.[49]

The Indian Health Service is directly administered by the Public Health Service through 12 administrative units called area offices, under which there are 127 service delivery units, considered equivalent to a city or county health department. Of these, 49 service units are operated by the tribes. Tribes also operate 6 hospitals, 70 health centers, 1 school health center, 231 health stations and Alaska village clinics, and 31 other treatment sites. In addition, the Indian Health Service operates 45 hospitals, 65 health centers, 6 school health centers, 66 health stations, and 201 other treatment sites. Of 33 urban projects, 28 are health clinics and 5 are facilities providing community services.[50] Through its system, the Indian Health Service

- provides
  —primary medical care
  —emergency medical services
  —preventive health services
  —environmental health services
  —professional training
- emphasizes
  —maternal and child health
  —accidents and injuries
  —aging
  —alcoholism
  —mental health
  —diabetes
  —otitis media
- and includes
  —dental health
  —community health nursing
  —nutrition
  —health education
  —medical social work[51]

Nutrition Services

Both in hospitals and in the community, nutritional care and nutrition education are incorporated into every health, social, and education service and food assistance program. The nutrition and dietetics program includes patient care; operation of hospital dietetics departments; and in-service education, training, and career development for Indians engaged in food services and community nutrition.[52] In 1986, the Indian Health Service was staffed with 49 public health nutritionist positions, 28 full-time hospital dietitians, and 20 nutritionists employed by the tribes. Consulting dietitians were employed for hospitals not having a full-time dietitian.[53]

In FY 1987, there were 232,173 nutrition and dietetics patient/client contacts, with over one-third in the hospitals, one-third in the communities, and less than one-third in the ambulatory clinics. About one-half were for clinical nutrition counseling, about one-third for health promotion/nutrition education, and the remainder for consultation/technical assistance and training for staff. The leading clinical nutrition client contacts were for (in descending order) diabetes, maternal and child health, general nutrition, and weight control.[54]

Several studies suggest that obesity is epidemic among Indian and Alaska native populations and contributes to their increased prevalence of diabetes, hypertension, and cardiovascular disease. Rates of obesity in several of the tribes studied in recent years range between 30 and 65 percent of the adults. One study reported 75 percent of those studied as obese, with an average of 145 percent of ideal body weight.[55]

Because of their high rates of poverty, American Indians and Alaska natives depend heavily on the federal food assistance programs even though not all programs operate in all communities and some communities have no programs. In September 1988, 127,699 households participated in the USDA Family Food Distribution Program, and an additional 107,198 households participated in the Food Stamp Program. It was estimated that 40 to 50 percent of the intakes of most nutrients in Navajo diets were contributed by commodity foods. [56]

Nutrition and dietetic services are well integrated into Indian health services. Indians and Alaska natives make maximum use of the available federal food assistance programs.[57] However, while Indians and Alaska natives receive nutrition services and food assistance integrated throughout their health delivery system, their needs will persist as long as they continue to suffer from poverty, unemployment, substandard housing, educational deficits, and social stress.[58] The excessively high prevalence of obesity and obesity-related diseases merit continuing research to determine interventions for both prevention and treatment. Considering the availability of programs and services, there would now appear to be the need for a comprehensive system to establish baseline data on health and nutritional status so that there can be some ways to measure progress and document where programs need to be strengthened to be more responsive to the needs of the native Americans.[59]

ISSUES TO DEBATE

- What are the alternative approaches to serving the medically unserved and underserved?
- What are the cost-benefit and cost-effectiveness justifications for employing nutritionists on the primary health care team?
- What data can be collected to monitor outcomes of nutrition services in primary care?
- What coalitions can most successfully advocate for food, clothing, and shelter for the homeless and the hungry?
- What nutrition training should be provided for paraprofessionals and volunteers who serve vulnerable populations?

NOTES

1. Gloria J. Bazzoli, "Health Care for the Indigent: Overview of Critical Issues," *Health Services Research* 21, no. 3 (August 1986): 353–69.

2. U.S. Department of Health and Human Services, *Health United States, 1988* (Washington, D.C.: Government Printing Office, 1989), 47, 53, 93, 95, 111.

3. Institute of Medicine, *The Future of Public Health* (Washington, D.C.: National Academy Press, 1988), 13, 21–23, 109–10.

4. Gary J. Clarke, "Primary Care and Public Policy: The Florida Experience," *Journal of Florida Medical Association* (April 1987): 269–78. William H. Hicks, *Community-Oriented Primary Care, The Health Center Experience* (Washington, D.C.: National Association of Community Health Centers, 1985), Introduction, Glossary.

5. Mildred Kaufman and Elizabeth Watkins, *Promoting Comprehensive Health Care with Emphasis on Nutrition and Social Work Services* (Chapel Hill: School of Public Health, University of North Carolina, 1981), 5–7.

6. Ibid.

7. Ibid. *Guide for Developing Services in Community Health Programs* (Rockville, Md.: U.S. Department of Health, Education, and Welfare, 1978), 12–18.

8. Hugh H. Tilson and Paul Jellinek, "Primary Health Care and the Local Health Department: The North Carolina Experience," *American Journal of Public Health* 71 (supp.) (January 1981): 35–45. American Public Health Association, Association of State and Territorial Health Officials, National Association of County Health Officials, United States Conference of Local Health Officers, Department of Health and Human Services, Public Health Service,

and Centers for Disease Control, *Model Standards: A Guide for Community Preventive Health Services*, 2d ed. (Washington, D.C.: American Public Health Association, 1985), 125.

9. Clarke, "Primary Care," 260–278.

10. Ibid.

11. Ibid.

12. Ibid.

13. Tilson and Jellinek, "Primary Health Care," 33–45.

14. Ibid.

15. American Public Health Association, *Model Standards*, 125.

16. Carla Bouchard and Martha Bureau, eds., *Guidelines for Nutrition Services in Local Health Jurisdictions*, 2d ed. (San Bernardino: California Conference of Local Health Department Nutritionists, San Bernardino County Department of Health, 1987).

17. Division of Special Populations Program Development, *Fact Sheet, Program Overview* (Washington, D.C.: U.S. Department of Health and Human Services, 1988).

18. Alice Sandel, *The U.S. Experiment in Social Medicine: The Community Health Center Program, 1985–86* (Pittsburgh: University of Pittsburgh Press, 1989), 20–199.

19. Children's Defense Fund, "Community and Migrant Health Centers," *Fact Sheet* (Washington, D.C., January 1989).

20. Ibid.

21. *Guide for Developing Nutrition Services in Community Health Programs* (Washington, D.C.: U.S. Department of Health, Education, and Welfare, 1978).

22. Helen L. Johnston, *Health for the Nation's Harvesters* (Farmington Hills, Mich.: National Migrant Workers Council, 1985).

23. Ibid.

24. Ibid.

25. Ibid.

26. Mildred Kaufman, Eugene Lewis, Albert Hardy, and Joanne Proulx, *Families of the Fields, Their Food and Their Health* (Jacksonville: Florida Department of Health and Rehabilitative Services, 1973).

27. Johnston, *Health for the Nation's Harvesters.*

28. Ibid.

29. Ibid.

30. Ibid.

31. Committee on Health Care for Homeless People, *Homelessness, Health and Human Needs* (Washington, D.C.: National Academy Press, Institute of Medicine, 1988).

32. Ibid.

33. American Academy of Pediatrics, Committee on Community Health Services, "Health Needs of Homeless Children," *Pediatrics* 82, no. 6 (December 1988): 938–39; Andrea L. Solarz, *Homelessness: Implications for Children and Youth*, Social Policy Report III, no. 5 (Washington, D.C.: Washington Liaison Office and the Committee on Child Development and Social Policy of the Society for Research in Child Development, Winter 1988).

34. Committee on Health Care for Homeless People, *Homelessness.*

35. Ibid.

36. Division of Special Populations Program Development, *Fact Sheet.*

37. Bureau of Health Care Delivery and Assistance, *Focus, Responding to Special Health Care Needs* (Rockville, Md.: U.S. Department of Health and Human Services, Winter 1988), 2.

38. Pat Leisner, "Medical Unit Serves Street People," *The Chapel Hill Newspaper*, 11 July 1989.

39. Committee on Health Care for Homeless People, *Homelessness*.

40. Ibid.

41. Solarz, *Homelessness*.

42. Ibid.

43. Daniel S. Miller and Elizabeth H.B. Lin, "Children in Sheltered Homeless Families: Reported Health Status and Use of Health Services," *Pediatrics* 81, no. 5 (May 1988): 668–73.

44. Ibid.

45. Ellen L. Bassuk, Lenore Rubin, and Alison Lauriat, "Characteristics of Sheltered Homeless Families," *American Journal of Public Health* 76, no. 9 (September 1986): 1097–1101.

46. Solarz, *Homelessness*.

47. Ibid.

48. U.S. Department of Health and Human Services, *Indian Health Service Chart Series Book* (Washington, D.C.: Government Printing Office, 1988), 1, 2, 4, 16, 18, 35, 53.

49. Indian Health Service, *A Comprehensive Health Care Program for American Indians and Alaska Natives* (Rockville, Md.: U.S. Department of Health and Human Services, undated), 2.

50. U.S. Department of Health and Human Services, *Indian Health Service*.

51. Indian Health Service, *A Comprehensive Health Care Program*.

52. M. Yvonne Jackson, "Nutrition in American Indian Health: Past, Present and Future," *Journal of the American Dietetic Association* 86, no. 11 (November 1986): 1561–65.

53. Ibid.

54. U.S. Department of Health and Human Services, *Indian Health Service*.

55. E.T. Lee, P.S. Anerson, J. Bryan, C. Buher, T. Conegilone, and M. Cleves, "Diabetes, Parental Diabetes, and Obesity in Oklahoma Indians," *Diabetes Care* 8, no. 2 (March–April 1985): 107–13.

56. David Shanklin and Connie Brooks, "Evaluation of the Food Distribution Program on Indian Reservations: A Selected Review of the Literature: Food Intake and Nutritional Status among Native Americans" (University of North Carolina, Chapel Hill, 1989).

57. Jackson, "Nutrition in American Indian Health."

58. Shanklin and Brooks, "Evaluation."

59. Ibid. Jackson, "Nutrition in American Indian Health."

chapter 12

Maintaining Nutrition and Food Service Standards in Group Care

Nancy L. Johnson

READER OBJECTIVES

- Identify the aspects of food service and nutritional care in group care facilities that should be addressed by licensing regulations.
- List activities the nutritionist can undertake to assure safe, adequate nutrition services in group care facilities.
- Discuss the impact that nutrition consultation to group care facilities can have on the public's health.
- Discuss the nutrition care and food service management information needed by administrators and food service staff in group care facilities.

GROUP CARE FACILITIES IN THE COMMUNITY

Most communities have a variety of care facilities that feed people in groups. Sponsorship may be proprietary, denominational, private non-profit, or public (governmental). Some of these facilities provide housing; others do not. Most people who eat their meals in a group care facility do so because they have a physical or mental disability or need health, educational, or rehabilitative services or emergency food assistance.

Nonresidential facilities that serve clients one or more meals, five to seven days a week, include

- child and adult day care centers
- congregate meal and home-delivered meal programs
- day camps
- schools
- soup kitchens

243

Facilities that serve residents three or more meals a day, five to seven days a week, include

- adult congregate living facilities (retirement homes)
- children's homes
- colleges, universities, and boarding schools
- halfway houses for the mentally ill, mentally retarded, and those undergoing alcohol or drug rehabilitation
- mental retardation centers
- overnight children's camps
- personal care or boarding homes
- prisons, jails, and juvenile detention facilities
- shelters for the homeless or for battered or abused women and children

Health care facilities serving three or more meals a day, seven days a week, to their patients along with providing health and nutritional care include

- hospices
- hospitals for acute, long-term, or mental health care
- nursing homes providing intermediate or skilled nursing care
- rehabilitation centers

LICENSURE, REGULATION, CERTIFICATION, AND ACCREDITATION

Most state and some city or county health or human service agencies license child and adult day care, group care, and health care facilities to protect the health and safety of the public they serve. The licensing agency usually is the state health agency, but it may be a social service agency, a human service agency, or an agency specifically established to license group or health care facilities. Licensure laws and regulations cover sanitation and safety of facilities; staffing; quality of care; and clients' rights. Regulations cover the safety and sanitation of the food services and the nutritional adequacy of the menus. In health care facilities, regulations cover not only the quality of the food service but also the individualized nutrition care, such as providing client nutrition assessment, serving therapeutic diets as prescribed by the patient's physician, and counseling the individual and family about nutrition and dietary needs. To obtain and maintain the license, all standards and regulations must be met. The complexity and specificity of the standards and regulations vary by state and type of facility.

Standards for voluntary accreditation by a national commission also cover food service and nutrition care requirements. Two examples are the American Hospital Association's Joint Commission on Accreditation of Healthcare Organizations and the American Correctional Association's Commission on Accreditation for Correctional Institutions.

Facilities certified to provide services paid for by Medicare and Medicaid must meet conditions for participation that include dietetic services. These conditions are established by the Health Care Financing Administration (HCFA) of the U.S. Department of Health and Human Services (DHHS).

Food service regulations for all types of facilities usually require that complete menus be written in advance for a specified time period; posted where they can be read by clients, families, and staff; and filed for later review. These written menus should stipulate the kinds and quantities of foods to be served to meet nutrient needs as stated in the current Recommended Dietary Allowances of the National Research Council and as adjusted for the age, activity, and health status of the clients receiving care in the facility. The menus should describe the kinds, amounts, and methods of preparation of all foods to be served at each day's meals and snacks. The meals should be scheduled at customary meal hours depending on the number of meals the clients are served. When required, therapeutic menus should be served as prescribed by physicians, and the menu for each type of diet or individual requiring a therapeutic diet should be written or approved by a registered dietitian. Regulations address the need for adequate dining room space and suitable furnishings to serve comfortably the number and type of residents who will use them. In child care, health care, or facilities for the elderly, help must be provided to feed those clients who need it.

Because of the diversity of group care facilities and the bodies promulgating regulations, the nutritionist must be familiar with all of the applicable regulations for the various types of group care facilities in the community. The content of the food service regulations should be monitored to advise the licensing bodies of new scientific evidence and changes in dietetic practice. For example, existing regulations regarding nutritional quality of menus and food served do not generally refer to the Dietary Guidelines for Americans. As licensure regulations are revised, this reference should be used to require health-promoting menus containing foods that reduce the risk of various chronic diseases, as well as meeting nutrient requirements.

To assure the public that food services in group care settings are safe and adequate, nutritionists should

- participate in writing or recommending standards for quality of food service and for client nutritional assessment and care to be promulgated into licensing laws and regulations, conditions of participation for third party reimbursement, and/or criteria for accreditation by private nonprofit standard setters
- participate on the agency team that inspects and recommends licensing, certification, or accreditation of facilities
- recommend staffing patterns to require employment of full-time, part-time, or consulting registered dietitians, qualified food service supervisors, and trained personnel; recommendations for staffing should be based on the number and type of clients served and the complexity of their nutritional care
- review and approve the layout and equipment for new or renovated food service facilities; consult on-site to assist the facility with food service layout and design, food service equipment specifications, and organization of dietetic services
- collaborate with environmental and other health care providers to plan and conduct training for administrators and food service staff to enable them to meet the regulations
- network with public health and dietetic professionals and consumers to assure quality nutrition services to meet the needs of clients in all group care facilities

EDUCATING ADMINISTRATORS AND FOOD SERVICE PERSONNEL

Maintaining licensure standards for any aspect of food service or nutritional care requires in-service education and training of the facility administrators and personnel so that they can meet the requirements. Nutritionists can collaborate with environmental health specialists or sanitarians to plan and conduct training courses for food service workers on a quarterly, semiannual, or annual schedule. To reach the largest number of administrators and food service workers from group care facilities in the community, planned continuing education programs may be conducted through the local vocational technical or community college or by the public health agency. Courses might focus on the specific needs of each type of group care facility, such as child day care or nursing homes, or on the more generic needs of all types of group care facilities.

Important generic topics for continuing education include basic principles of nutrition, dietary guidelines, food purchasing, food cost and inventory control, menu planning, use of standardized recipes and methods of food preparation, attractive food presentation, food safety and sanitation, and development of an internal quality assurance system.

In-service education can be reinforced and extended by selecting, preparing, and mailing out guidelines, manuals, newsletters, and other educational materials to improve and promote quality food services and nutritional care in the facilities. Announcements can be mailed to the qualifying public and nonprofit facilities so that they can apply for any of the federally subsidized food assistance programs and available donated commodity foods.

Menu Planning

Group care providers are obligated to meet their population's nutritional needs based on the best current scientific recommendations. Children and adults who eat in group care are captive populations who can exercise limited control over their food choices. Consideration must be given to their individual food preferences or customs. Each group care facility has its unique clientele whose nutritional requirements are influenced by their age, mental and physical conditions, physical activity levels, and medications.

Frequently administrators and staff need and want guidance to assist them in planning menus. In addition to basic information on the types and amounts of food to be included, they may desire guidance on how to plan menus in a systematic fashion. Although menu writing may be seen as a weekly activity, it can be done more efficiently on a seasonal basis using a set of cycle menus in rotation. Regulations usually require that these cycle menus be planned or approved by a registered dietitian employed full time, part time, or as a consultant. The cycle should be long enough so that the clients do not recognize the day of the week by the menu items served. In long-term care facilities, clients should be given an opportunity to suggest menu items they would like and to contribute favorite or family recipes.

To promote the health of their clients, all group care facilities should plan and serve menus that provide

- calories appropriate to meet each resident's activity needs and maintain desirable weight
- a desirable distribution of complex carbohydrates and protein, and

limited fat, saturated fat, and cholesterol
- recommended levels of vitamins and minerals
- adequate fluids and fiber
- foods consistent with the Dietary Guidelines
- foods appropriate to each individual's age, ability to eat, and medical and physical conditions
- foods that the clients will eat and enjoy

Food Preparation

Food service workers employed by group care facilities may have experience in family, school, or restaurant food preparation, but have little formal training. They may need to learn to use new food preparation techniques that will reduce the use of total fats, saturated fats, cholesterol, salt, and sugar and to prepare appropriate foods for clients who require physician-prescribed diets or who have chewing, swallowing, or eating problems. They need information and guidance in using alternate seasoning agents to win acceptance of health-promoting meals or prescribed fat-controlled or sodium-restricted diets.

Requiring the use of standardized recipes that stipulate measured amounts of ingredients, such as fat, salt, and sugar, rather than "the dump or pour" method, can reduce significantly the wasteful use of these items in many kitchens, thereby controlling food costs. Untrained personnel may not be accustomed to using recipes when they prepare food. They need to be convinced of the value of recipes and trained to use them. Facilities may need to purchase cookbooks with quantity recipes suitable for the number and type of clients and staff they usually serve. Nutritionists can recommend cookbooks with tasty recipes based on the Dietary Guidelines for Americans. Several suitable cookbooks are listed in the Public Health Nutrition Library (see Appendix N).

Meal Service

Persons eating in group care look forward to mealtimes as highlights of their days. Every effort should be made to make the food appealing and the surroundings attractive and comfortable. For children and adults, mealtimes should be emotionally as well as nutritionally satisfying and should provide for sociability. Food should be served in forms that promote maximum independence and a positive self-image for those dining together. For example, ground or chopped food for adults with chewing problems is more attractive when served in a mixed casserole than when served in separate dishes. When possible, self-service items and a choice of foods should be made available.

Colorful, tasty meals stimulate interest and appetite and promote a positive image for the facility. The attractive presentation of meals tells clients and their families that the staff care for them and take pride in their work.

Special attention must be given to individuals who require assistance with eating. Most children and adults prefer to feed themselves. Serving cut-up foods, finger foods, and foods that are easy to eat; providing special adaptive feeding devices for the handicapped; positioning the individual for comfort in eating; and providing tables and chairs of appropriate height promote independence. Administrators should be encouraged to consult with physical or occupational therapists to train their staff on ways to assist handicapped clients with eating disabilities. Adequate staff or volunteers must be available to feed infants, disabled, or elderly persons who cannot feed themselves. It takes time, patience, and skill to ensure that the patient who needs to be fed consumes enough food to meet nutritional needs.

Nutritional Care

Staff must be available during meals to provide needed assistance and to monitor client food and fluid intake. In all types of group care, staff should observe and record each client's food choices and the kinds and amounts of food eaten and rejected. Weight status should be assessed periodically. When sudden weight gains or losses are noted, administrators should consult with a physician and a registered dietitian. In licensed health care facilities, regulations mandate that the nutritional assessment of each client be documented in the health record.

Beginning in 1989, the New York State Health Department's surveys of long-term care facilities focused on outcomes of resident care. Semiannually facilities submit information about the health status of their residents, including their physical condition, ability to perform activities of daily living, and level of care required. These data are analyzed by a central bureau to determine the prevalence of conditions with high care needs and to identify over time those patients whose condition is deteriorating. A multidisciplinary survey team from the state agency then visits the facility to review the complete care provided to a sample of these residents. Examples of nutrition conditions that are considered in reviewing resident outcomes are parenteral and enteral feedings, dehydration, deteriorating eating ability, and continuing weight loss. This changes emphasis from "paper" to patient.[1]

New federal conditions of participation for intermediate and skilled nursing care facilities require use of patient care outcomes for facilities to qualify for Medicare and Medicaid reimbursement. Participating facilities must maintain a quality assurance committee that will identify issues in resident care for which quality assessment and assurance are needed and develop and implement plans of action to correct deficiencies. Through demonstration projects and cooperative arrangements, the Health Care Financing Administration is attempting to develop reliable and valid measures of quality of care for different payment systems and treatment settings.[2] Objective measurable criteria must be developed from published standards of practice. A monitoring system must be established to collect data on a periodic schedule. The quality assurance committee must annually review preventive measures; promotion of behavioral, cognitive, and social functioning of each client; and their quality of life—as well as the facility's patient care planning and resolution of client grievances. These new approaches underscore the need for a responsible professional to maintain complete and descriptive nutritional care data in each client's medical record.[3]

COUNSELING CLIENTS AND THEIR FAMILIES

Both young and older group diners learn about nutritious food choices through the meals that are served to them each day. An education program can teach the principles of basic nutrition through foods served in daily meals that demonstrate excellence in meal planning and food preparation. Children eating in Head Start programs, day care centers, or residential facilities can be introduced to a wide variety of healthful foods through the menus and food preparation activities planned into their daily educational activities.

Family members should be involved in nutrition education so that they can encourage their child or adult relative to consume an adequate and appropriate food intake. Frequently family members need guidance to understand the reasons why certain foods are selected, prepared, and served in the facility. They especially need to understand the underlying principles for any physician-prescribed therapeutic diet so that they can serve appropriate meals and snacks at home or bring appropriate food gifts when visiting their relative in the health care or residential facility.

Those adults who eat only one meal a day in group care or who will be discharged from a group care facility can learn some basic nutrition principles and gain skill in selecting, purchasing, and preparing health-promoting food at home. Residents who will continue to live in group care facilities need to understand the objectives of the food service, the rationale for the menus, and, when applicable, the importance of their physician-prescribed diet. A resident food service and nutrition committee can improve client satisfaction and contribute helpful ideas to the food service staff.

REGISTERED DIETITIANS IN GROUP CARE FACILITIES

Many large facilities, particularly those providing child care or health care, employ full-time registered dietitians, dietetic technicians, and certified dietetic managers or trained food service supervisors. These qualified nutrition personnel assume the responsibility for maintaining a safe, sanitary food service that meets their clients' nutritional needs and is responsive to their appetites and tastes. These trained personnel are responsible for maintaining a program of nutrition assessment and care that addresses individual clients' dietary and nutrition education needs. They are accountable to the administrator for quality assurance and control of food costs, supervision and training of the food service staff, and compliance with state and local licensing laws and regulations, as well as pertinent conditions of participation for third party reimbursement. Several smaller facilities may share in employing a registered dietitian or contract with a registered dietitian in private practice for regularly scheduled consultation and staff training.

In facilities where residents will be returning to their own homes or be transferred to other types of group care, registered dietitians should participate in discharge planning, provide appropriate nutrition education and diet counseling, and make referrals for follow-up at home or in the community. By coordinating counseling and referral, registered dietitians in health care facilities and nutritionists in community agencies collaborate to assure continuity of nutritional care for clients.

PUBLIC HEALTH NUTRITIONISTS AS CONSULTANTS

Many smaller facilities or non-health-care facilities do not employ staff with the training and education necessary to meet the nutritional needs of their clients. Frequently administrators of small facilities, as well as administrators of government-sponsored group care, will turn to the local public health agency, expecting that nutrition consultation will be provided to help them meet licensure requirements. Some local health agencies are prepared to provide expert nutrition consultation to group care food services, particularly those that are nonprofit or public. In the state health agency, specialized nutrition consultants—titled institution nutrition consultants, consulting dietitians, or public health dietitians—may assume these functions. Education and experience requirements for these positions usually specify training in food service systems management as well as advanced nutrition and dietetics.

If the public health agency does not currently employ staff or have funding to serve these group care facilities, they might charge a cost recovery or sliding scale fee in order to employ registered dietitians to provide the requested food service consultation. In some communities, registered dietitians in private practice may contract to provide the needed services.

Whenever possible, group care facilities should be encouraged to employ their own consulting registered dietitians. Food service administrators, supervisory staff, and food service workers should have the education and training to develop a quality food service program that meets the needs of the residents for whom they take responsibility, including those requiring therapeutic diets.

When nutritionists from the public health agency work with group care food service operations, they need to clearly define their role. Sufficient public health nutrition personnel are not usually available to provide in-depth consultation to all group care food services in the community that need such service. The appropriate role should be that of a consultant or educator. Educational strategies that reach out to groups of administrators and their food service staff need to be developed. Depending on the nature of the relationship with the facility, it may be appropriate to provide services in cooperation with the monitoring or licensing agency which has the ability to follow up to see that recommendations have been implemented.

Nutritionists can have an important impact on the health of the community by assisting group care facilities in developing quality food service and nutrition education. Appropriate funding mechanisms need to be developed to enable the public health agency nutrition staff to provide expert consultation to these community programs.

ISSUES TO DEBATE

- How can public health professionals balance responsibilities that include regulatory or licensing (policing) functions and consultative or educational functions?

- When working on food service regulations for group care facilities, how can the nutritionist obtain the support of administrators, licensing agency staff, and client advocates to strengthen requirements for health-promoting diets, nutrition care, and nutrition education?
- What should be the health agency criteria for determining which group care facilities might receive on-site consultation from the public health nutritionist and which should be encouraged to employ a consultant registered dietitian?

NOTES

1. Bureau of Long-Term Care, *New York Quality Assurance System (NYQAS) Implementation Manual* (Albany, N.Y.: New York State Department of Health, October 1988), 1–7, 10–20.

2. Health Care Financing Administration, "Medicare and Medicaid Requirements for Long-Term Care Facilities," *Federal Register* 54, no. 21 (2 February 1989).

3. Karen Herbelin, "Quality Assessment and Assurance in a Long-Term Care Facility: Meeting Current Federal Requirements," *Journal of The American Dietetic Association* 89, no. 10 (October 1989): 1499–1500.

chapter *13*

Safeguarding the Food Supply

Laura T. Harrill

READER OBJECTIVES

- List and describe current food safety issues for consumers.
- Discuss the role of federal, state, and local agencies responsible for safeguarding the U.S. food supply.
- Describe the several ways in which the nutritionist can incorporate food safety education into the public health nutrition program.
- List some food safety rules for consumers.
- Identify resources that the public health nutritionist can use to keep informed about food safety.

FOOD SAFETY AS A PUBLIC HEALTH NUTRITION ISSUE

In the 1988 Food Marketing Institute annual survey of consumer attitudes, respondents rated food safety second only to taste as a reason for selecting foods.[1] News headlines put before the public the real or perceived dangers of microbial contamination, pesticides, hormones, antibiotics, chemical additives, and carcinogens in the food supply. While most cases of foodborne illness are not reported, each year an estimated 24 to 80 million Americans are struck by "food poisoning."[2] Infants, pregnant women, the elderly, and people with chronic illnesses are particularly susceptible to serious complications from illness due to bacterial or viral contamination of food.[3] Improper food handling in the home, as well as in public food services, causes most of the problems. The nutritionist must understand the issues surrounding the safety of the food supply and use the most authoritative and up-to-date scientific references to keep consumers informed. Since this is a very dynamic field, it is necessary to monitor information about the rapidly changing food technologies and the evolving regulations that affect food safety. The weight of evidence of possible risks of environmental contaminants must be carefully weighed in relation to the benefits of the foods recommended in the Dietary Guidelines for Americans. Consumers must understand that no food supply can be 100 percent free of risk. The nutritionist can collaborate with environmental health specialists, health educators, and other public health colleagues to educate consumers about proper food handling and their responsibility for storing, preparing, and handling food to keep it safe.

FOOD SAFETY ISSUES

The first federal food safety law was the Pure Food and Drug Act of 1906. It was passed by Congress after several decades of public concern about adulteration of their food supply.[4] Consumers continue to have questions about food quality and safety today, as evidenced by over 55,000 calls to the Food and Drug Administration (FDA) in 1987.[5]

Microbial Contamination

Microbial contamination remains by far the greatest threat to food safety. The Centers for Disease Control (CDC) have estimated that 99 million acute cases of intestinal infectious diseases, 250,000 of which require hospitalization, occur in the United States each year. Hospitalizations incur millions of dollars in medical costs as well as in lost productivity. Nonhospitalized cases incur even more millions in medical costs and in lost productivity.[6] The awareness of the problem has increased due to better methods of detecting the disease-causing microbes, as well as more centralized food processing as more meals are eaten outside the home. Mishandling of food at home and in restaurants is the major cause of contamination. The most common bacteria associated with foodborne illness are described in Table 13-1. Two of these, *Salmonella* and *Listeria monocytogenes*, are of particular concern. Also listed are several foodborne pathogens considered to be emerging in terms of public health significance.[7]

Salmonella, a large, ubiquitous group of bacteria, has received increased public attention during the last several years. Poultry and other animals carry *Salmonella* in their intestines; during processing the bacteria can contaminate the carcass. When people eat *Salmonella*-contaminated meat, poultry, or eggs that are not thoroughly cooked, they develop a gastroenteritis characterized by cramps, diarrhea, vomiting, headache, and fever.

Table 13-1 Common Bacterial Contaminants

Bacteria	Where It's Found/How It Works	Symptoms	How To Prevent It
Campylobacter Jejuni	From intestinal tract of animals. Found in untreated water, raw milk, and raw or undercooked meat, poultry, and shellfish. Spread by consumption of contaminated food or water.	Severe (possibly bloody) diarrhea; cramping, fever, and headache; duration is generally 2 to 7 days.	Do not drink untreated water or unpasteurized milk. Wash hands, utensils, and surfaces that touch raw meat, poultry, or shellfish. Thoroughly cook meat, poultry, and fish.
Clostridium Botulinum	Found in improperly underprocessed canned foods; warning signs are usually clear liquids turning milky, loose lids, and swollen lids. Contents may not appear spoiled. Also occurs in cooked low-acid foods which remain at room temperature. Spread by consumption of contaminated food that is not sufficiently reheated.	Symptoms are indicative of mostly central nervous system impairment: double vision, droopy eyelids, difficulty with speech and swallowing, and difficulty in breathing. Can be fatal.	Home canning should always be done in a pressure cooker that reaches high enough temperatures to destroy bacterial spores. Follow reliable directions for canning low-acid vegetables, meat, fish, and poultry. Toxin is destroyed by boiling food for 10 to 20 minutes. Call physician immediately if symptoms are observed.
Clostridium Perfringens	In intestinal tract. Can develop in foods kept warm at temperatures below 140° F and in foods that cool slowly.	Gas pains/diarrhea 8 to 24 hours after exposure; duration is generally less than a day.	Keep food hot (over 140° F) or cold (under 40° F). Cook meat, meat dishes, poultry, and gravies thoroughly.
Escherichia Coli (hemorrhagic)	Raw or undercooked meat, particularly ground beef or unpasteurized milk. Carried in the gut and feces of animals and humans.	Abdominal cramps, nausea, vomiting, bloody diarrhea. Can damage blood vessels in the kidney, causing kidney failure in children and nervous system problems such as strokes and seizures due to blood clots in the brain in older adults.	Thoroughly cook meat, particularly ground beef and poultry. Do not use unpasteurized milk. Wash hands, utensils, and surfaces that come in contact with raw meat or poultry.
Listeria Monocytogenes	Found in improperly pasteurized cheese and raw milk products, raw and processed meats, shellfish, and raw vegetables. Spread by direct consumption of a contaminated food or by cross-contamination from a contaminated food to other raw or cooked foods.	Fever, followed by headache, nausea, and vomiting 7 to 30 days after exposure. Symptoms have been reported as early as 2 to 3 days after consumption of heavily contaminated foods. Spontaneous abortion in pregnant woman, death in persons with compromised immune systems.	Always use pasteurized milk and dairy products. Wash hands and work surfaces to prevent cross-contamination.

Organism	Source	Symptoms	Prevention
Salmonella	Carried in intestinal tracts of animals, birds, and humans. Found in raw or undercooked eggs, poultry, meat, and fish. Spread by direct consumption of a raw or undercooked contaminated food or by cross-contamination from a contaminated food to other raw or cooked foods. Spread by poor hygiene of food handler.	Fever, vomiting/diarrhea 12 to 36 hours after exposure; duration is generally 2 to 7 days.	Keep raw food away from cooked food. Thoroughly cook meat, poultry, and fish. Heat food to 140° F for 10 minutes or to 144° F for a few seconds. Wash hands and work surfaces after handling raw meat or poultry. Chill foods at 40° F, in small quantities.
Shigella	Found in milk, dairy products, poultry, and potato salad. Food becomes contaminated when a human carrier handles moist food that is not properly cooked. Organisms multiply in food stored above room temperatures.	Abdominal pain, cramps, diarrhea, fever, sometimes vomiting, and blood, pus, or mucus in stools. Serious in infants, the elderly, and persons who are debilitated.	Wash hands thoroughly before handling food. Wash hands, utensils, and surfaces before preparing food. Refrigerate food at below 40° F.
Staphylococcus Aureus	Found on the skin, in nasal passages, and in boils, pimples, and throat infections. Spread by an infected person handling food; problem if it multiplies in food at warm temperatures.	Vomiting/diarrhea 2 to 8 hours after exposure; duration is generally 1 to 2 days.	Check bacteria that produce the toxin by keeping hot foods at 140° F and cold foods at or below 40° F. Chill food rapidly in small quantities. Once the toxin is formed, it is not easily destroyed by heating. Wash hands and utensils before preparing food. Do not leave foods out of the refrigerator. Susceptible foods are meat, poultry, meat and poultry salads, salads with mayonnaise, custards, and cream-filled desserts.
Vibrio Cholera	Found in fish and shellfish from waters contaminated by human sewage. Chief food sources are raw shellfish—crabs, shrimp, oysters.	Ranges from mild uncomplicated diarrhea to intense diarrhea with dehydration.	Cook all shellfish thoroughly. Do not eat raw. Wash hands, utensils, and surfaces that have been in contact with raw shellfish.
Yersinia Enterocolitica	Found in raw milk, chocolate milk, pork, and other raw meats; contaminated raw or leftover foods.	Enterocolitis may mimic acute appendicitis; abdominal pain, fever, headache, diarrhea, vomiting, chills, pharyngitis.	Cook foods thoroughly. Wash hands thoroughly, and protect from contamination. Control rodents.

Sources: Food News for Consumers, Vol. 5, No. 2, p. 14, U.S. Department of Agriculture, Summer 1989; *Food News for Consumers*, Vol. 6, No. 2, pp. 11–12, U.S. Department of Agriculture, Summer 1989; *Diseases Transmitted by Foods* by F.L. Bryan, Centers for Disease Control, 1982; and *Journal of The American Dietetic Association*, Vol. 89, No. 7, p. 949, The American Dietetic Association, © July 1989.

Many cases go unreported because the illness is frequently confused with flu, but there is evidence that cases of *Salmonella* infections have increased 50 percent over the past ten years.[8] Recent evidence indicates that even uncracked eggs may carry the bacteria, suggesting that the public must be advised not to eat raw or undercooked eggs.[9]

Listeria monocytogenes has long been recognized as causing a bacterial illness called listeriosis. Only in the past several years, however, have scientists and epidemiologists recognized that the bacterium may be carried by food. The *Listeria* organism has been found in cheese, milk products, and even lettuce. It is extremely common in the environment and therefore in foods. It survives and grows at refrigerated temperatures. Generalized *Listeria* infections are serious and may lead to bacteremia, encephalitis, and/or meningitis. *Listeria* infections can cause spontaneous abortion during the latter half of pregnancy. Public health workers should be especially concerned about three populations who are at particularly high risk of developing listeriosis: newborns, pregnant women, and immuno-compromised individuals, such as those with HIV virus (AIDS).[10] Fetal and newborn deaths from *Listeria* were reported following maternal consumption of contaminated soft cheese in a recent outbreak in California. Even though *Listeria* can grow at cold temperatures, refrigeration helps prevent its rapid multiplication. The food safety principles outlined in Table 13-1 apply in preventing *Listeria* infection.[11]

Norwalk viruses cause infections that lead to vomiting, diarrhea, abdominal pain, nausea, fever, and loss of appetite. Drinking water and foods such as shellfish and salads are media that transfer this virus from an ill person to the next victim. Cooking kills this virus.

Hepatitis A virus may be transmitted through food with a resulting two- to six-week incubation period before symptoms of nausea, loss of appetite, vomiting, and jaundice appear. Raw or undercooked shellfish, as well as unsanitary food handling, are the culprits that cause this infection. Careful hand washing before touching or preparing food prevents transfer of hepatitis A virus.[12]

Naturally Occurring Toxicants in Food

Many foods contain natural toxicants that may be undesirable when consumed in large quantities. One of several such toxicants is aflatoxin, which is produced by a mold.

The *Aspergillus flavus* mold produces four aflatoxins that are highly toxic.[13] Aflatoxins are produced by molds on animal feeds, corn, and peanuts. Milk may be contaminated by a less toxic form of aflatoxin when dairy herds consume contaminated feed. Aflatoxin produces liver cancer in every animal species tested; most of the evidence for human cancers from aflatoxins comes from developing countries where aflatoxin-laden foods are often eaten.[14]

In the United States, the FDA sets limits for the amount of aflatoxin allowed in animal feeds and foods typically contaminated, such as peanuts and peanut butter, corn, milk, and vegetable oils. The U.S. Department of Agriculture (USDA) inspects these foods to monitor compliance. There is no formal FDA tolerance level for aflatoxins, but informal action levels are usually 0.5 parts per billion (PPB) for milk and 20 PPB in other foods (although levels as low as 1 to 3 PPB may be detected).[15]

Cooking and freezing do not eliminate aflatoxins already formed. The public should be advised to throw out mold-contaminated peanuts, peanut butter, and corn products such as grits and cornmeal. Most large producers of peanut and corn products have quality assurance measures to control aflatoxin.

Toxins that cause paralytic shellfish poisoning (PSP) are not inherent in the shellfish; they are produced by microscopic algae, dinoflagellates, otherwise known as *red tide*. The Interstate Sanitation Conference promotes cooperative monitoring of shellfish by the FDA, state agencies, and industry.[16]

It is important to put food choices into perspective, remembering that toxicity is dose related. The first dietary guideline that states "Eat a variety of foods" provides the public with a margin of safety.

Chemical Additives

Throughout recorded history, chemicals have been added to foods—salt for curing and herbs for flavoring are examples. Policy decisions governing which chemical additives go into the food supply are increasingly made not by home cooks, but by corporate food processors. Consumers are often confused by the purposes of food additives and the meanings of the chemical names they read on food ingredient labels. Adding to the confusion are some popular authors who denounce the use of any chemical additives, while food-industry-sponsored publications offer complacent reassurances. Nutritionists can guide consumers to study alternative arguments in the food additives debates so they can weigh the evidence and make informed choices.

The FDA regulates chemicals added to foods primarily under the 1958 Food Additives Amendment to the 1938 Food, Drug, and Cosmetic Act.

The 1958 amendment stipulates that a new food additive must be proved safe before a manufacturer will be allowed to use it.[17]

Food additives in use before 1958 were given "prior sanctioned" status on the basis of their accepted use over time. The 1958 Amendment also established the Generally Recognized as Safe (GRAS) list, which allows substances to be added to foods after an established scientific testing or safe history. A review of GRAS list substances has been completed.[18]

The most controversial part of the Food Additives Amendment is the Delaney Clause. It prohibits chemicals that have been found to be carcinogenic in either animals or humans. In 1960, the Delaney Clause was applied to food colorings by passage of the Color Additives Amendment. Debate continues about the limits of this law as advances in technology allow for detection of carcinogenic substances at increasingly lower levels.[19]

Chemical additives serve a variety of purposes. They may increase a food's nutritional quality, as in the case of vitamin and mineral enrichment and fortification; they may help in food processing, as with emulsifiers, stabilizers, and thickeners; they may enhance or add color, flavor, or sweetness to food; they may inhibit microbial growth; or they may help preserve the quality and stability of the food. For each of these functions there are a variety of alternative processes or substances that might exert the same effect, leading to debates about the necessity, safety, and expense of some additives in preference to others. These debates affect the approval of new additives.[20]

Enrichment and Fortification

The FDA makes no legal distinction between enrichment and fortification of food with vitamins and minerals. However, the terms are generally used to represent differing amounts.

The term *enrichment* is usually used for white flour and cereal products in which the nutrients removed or destroyed in processing are replaced. Enrichment of flour and grain products with iron and B vitamins began in the 1940s to decrease nutrient deficiencies then prevalent because of the diets of the U.S. population.

The term *fortification* is used when nutrients considered to be deficient in most diets are added to a commonly used food or product. The addition of iodine to salt to prevent goiter was the first U.S. food fortification program. Skim milk and nonfat dry milk are presently fortified with vitamins A and D.[21] The fortification of foods with nutrients not naturally present in them is increasing. For example, calcium is being added to orange juice to increase calcium consumption by persons who do not drink milk, and vitamin C is being added to sweetened fruit-flavored drinks. This type of fortification is controversial because diets then lack other nutrients that would have been consumed if the natural source of the nutrient had been eaten. It is important to monitor new products and weigh their usefulness against their tradeoffs and costs.

Emulsifiers and Other Texturizers

Food processing aids include emulsifiers, stabilizers or texturizers, and thickeners. Emulsifiers such as lecithin and monoglycerides keep food mixtures homogeneous. Gums, gelatin, cellulose, starch, and carrageenan may serve as stabilizers, texturizers, and thickeners, keeping food product consistency even and smooth. Product taste and texture may be manipulated by the addition of acids and alkalis which control acid-base balance. These additives have a long history of use.

Colors

Food color may be enhanced by either natural or synthetic sources. Yellow dye no. 5 is the only artificial color required to be named on food labels since allergic reactions to this color have been reported by people sensitive to aspirin or aspirin derivatives.[22]

Flavors

The FDA allows flavors to be listed on the label using general terms such as "flavorings," "artificial flavor," and "spices." Some people are sensitive to the flavor enhancer monosodium glutamate (MSG) and report reactions including headaches, dizziness, and a burning sensation in their chest. However, since 1985, reactions to MSG accounted for less than 5 percent of the reactions due to additives reported to the FDA.[23]

Sweeteners

Sweeteners may be nutritive or noncaloric. Nutritionists should help consumers recognize the various forms of naturally occurring sugars that appear on food labels, including sucrose, fructose, dextrose, corn syrup, high fructose corn syrup, honey, and invert sugar. Many consumers purchase low calorie or noncaloric artificially sweetened foods because they are concerned about weight reduction, dental caries, or diabetes management. Products using low calorie sweeteners will undoubtedly continue to appear in food markets in larger numbers.

Sodium saccharin is an artificial sweetener that has been sold since the turn of the century. It was banned by the FDA in 1977 after debates over evidence that it caused bladder cancer in laboratory animals. Under public pressure, Congress temporarily lifted the ban and has extended it ever since. However, since 1983, saccharin has gradually been replaced by a new artificial sweetener, aspartame.

Aspartame, composed of the amino acids phenylalanine and aspartic acid, is also known by the trade names NutraSweet® and Equal®. It is a nutritive sweetener, supplying four calories per gram. Because aspartame tastes about 200 times sweeter than sugar, much less is needed to achieve the same sweet taste; thus, the caloric contribution to foods is lowered considerably. Foods processed with aspartame must display warning labels that caution people with phenylketonuria (PKU) to avoid this product because it contains phenylalanine, which they cannot tolerate. Aspartame was tested for safety prior to approval by the FDA. While there has been some debate regarding the relationship of aspartame to tumor development, it has been concluded that it is not associated with any harmful effects in the general population.[24] Both the American Medical Association and the American Diabetes Association endorse the safety of aspartame, now approved for use in over 15 product categories.[25]

Acesulfame (ay-see-sul-fame) K is marketed as Sunette® and is the newest artificial sweetener approved by the FDA. Like aspartame, acesulfame K (K is for potassium) also tastes 200 times sweeter than sugar. It is noncaloric because it is not metabolized by the body. Acesulfame K's original approval is for use in packets or tablets and as an ingredient in chewing gum, dry drink mixes, gelatins, puddings, and nondairy creamers.[26] As products sweetened with acesulfame K reach the market, it will be important to keep informed about the use of this ingredient.

Preservatives

Preservatives maintain food quality by retarding chemical or microbial spoilage, thus allowing an extensive food supply regardless of the season and the locale.

Nitrites are used in processed meats to retain their pinkish color, add flavor, and control bacterial growth. Nitrites themselves are harmless, but may be converted to carcinogenic nitrosamines by high cooking temperatures (as when frying bacon) and during normal digestion. Nitrates occur naturally in such vegetables as beets, celery, lettuce, spinach, and radishes. Like nitrites, they may ultimately be converted to produce nitrosamines. Citric acid, ascorbic acid, and sodium erythrobate can inhibit the conversion of nitrites and nitrates to nitrosamines. For this reason, they are now added to processed meat products, reducing the amount of sodium nitrite needed and reducing potential nitrosamine formation. Some producers of processed meat have recently eliminated nitrites from their products.[27]

Sulfites are a source of sulfur dioxide (SO_2), which is an antioxidant and a microbial inhibitor. Sulfites are used to delay browning in dried or cut fruits and vegetables and to stabilize wine. Sensitive individuals, including many persons with asthma, experience adverse reactions to sulfites, with several deaths reported. Sulfite use in restaurant and supermarket salad bars was banned in 1986. Despite the ban, sulfites may still appear in salad bars because the regulations do not cover pre-prepared salads which restaurants may use.

Sulfite-sensitive persons should be advised to read the labels of processed foods found in the supermarket. Sulfites are listed on ingredient labels as sodium sulfite, sodium bisulfite, sulfur dioxide, and sodium metabisulfite. Products that may contain sulfites include instant dehydrated potatoes, some frozen potatoes, wine, dried fruits, gravy, and soup mixes.

Butylated hydroxyanisole and butylated hydroxytoluene, better known as BHA and BHT, are antioxidants. They are normally used to prevent rancidity in fat-containing foods. BHA and BHT are directly added to a product, as in potato chips, or applied to product packaging, as in breakfast cereals. The additive in the packaging migrates into the food. The use of BHA and BHT in the food supply may increase as products are reformulated to avoid the saturated fat from palm and coconut oils. The replacement of saturated fats with polyunsaturated oils may make products more susceptible to oxidation; therefore, antioxidants will be needed to assure shelf-life stability. BHA and BHT appear to be safe.[28] Vitamins C and E are also used for their antioxidant properties. The fact that these vitamins are not used more widely as antioxidants may reflect their higher cost to manufacturers, as well as their lack of the same effectiveness for all purposes.

Irradiation is used in foreign countries to prevent the sprouting of potatoes and onions, sterilize spices, control insect infestation of fruits and grains, and pasteurize poultry and seafood. Irradiation is considered to be a food additive by the FDA, although it is technically a process of food preservation. As such, it requires the agency's premarket approval as an alternative to preservatives. The FDA allows low-level irradiation of potatoes and onions to prevent sprouting, fresh fruits and vegetables, spices and seasonings, and fresh pork. Irradiated food does not become radioactive. Irradiation reduces the need for postharvest pesticides, as well as extending the shelf life of fresh foods.[29] Although much research has been done, the interactions among level of irradiation, processing conditions, and specific food components are not known for all foods. The labeling of irradiated foods is still controversial. Nutritionists need to be informed about the issues related to irradiation and to monitor progress in this debated area of food preservation.

Sodium

Sodium as an additive is of concern because of evidence of its relationship to hypertension in salt-sensitive individuals. As a food ingredient, sodium is used in many forms: sodium chloride, or table salt (flavor); sodium nitrite (preservative); sodium bicarbonate (leavening agent); and many others. Sodium labeling has been required as a part of nutrition labeling since 1986; it identifies the amount of sodium in a product in milligrams per serving.[30] Even when nutrition labeling is not used, sodium-containing compounds are listed in the ingredient list. One teaspoon of salt (40 percent sodium) is equivalent to 2,000 milligrams of sodium. The recommended daily intake ranges from 1,100 to 3,300 milligrams,[31] but most Americans consume about 4,000 to 6,000 milligrams daily.[32]

Fat Substitutes

New fat substitutes, known by the generic name olestra and the trade name Simplesse®, are being tested for FDA approval. Olestra is a chemical combination of sucrose and fatty acids called sucrose polyester. The product is noncaloric because it is neither digested nor absorbed by the body. Olestra may be liquid or solid and can be used in place of shortenings, frying oils, and cooking fats to lower fat intake and calories in a variety of fried foods and pastries. Vitamin E is added to olestra because it is found in vegetable oils that the substitute would replace. Olestra may lower blood cholesterol both by replacing dietary saturated fat and by increasing cholesterol excretion.[33] Simplesse® is a protein derived from either egg white or milk protein. Because of its processing, the protein is shaped into very small particles perceived as smooth and creamy on the tongue. This ingredient becomes a gel when heated so its use appears to be limited to frozen desserts, other dairy products, or oil-based products such as salad dressings. It contributes only one to two calories per gram versus nine calories per gram of fat.[34]

Unintentional Additives

Four times a year the FDA through its Total Diet Study analyzes a sample market basket of 234 foods to determine the level of unintentional additives, or contaminants, present in the U.S. diet. Animal drug residues, pesticide residues, and fish contaminants are of particular concern to consumers.[35]

Animal Drug Residues

Antibiotics and hormones are the two main types of drugs used in the production of animal foods. Both drugs promote animal growth rates, helping to lower meat prices. Antibiotics such as penicillin and tetracycline are used at subtherapeutic levels to prevent disease. One concern is that continued dietary intake of antibiotic residues in meat and poultry could inhibit people's responses to these drugs when they are prescribed to treat infection. In addition, antibiotic-resistant strains of bacteria develop in the food animals, increasing the risk of human illness from contaminated meat. In 1984, the CDC identified antibiotic-resistant strains of *Salmonella* bacteria in beef.[36]

Hormones, when used properly, are generally considered by scientists to leave acceptably safe levels of residues in meat. In 1985, the National Research Council of the National Academy of Sciences criticized the USDA Food Safety and Inspection Service (FSIS) for routinely inspecting only 1 percent of animal carcasses for chemical residues, a level that may not adequately protect consumers.[37]

Pesticides

Pesticides are regulated by the Environmental Protection Agency (EPA), with pesticide residues in foods monitored by the FDA. As the technology develops to more sensitively detect pesticide residues, there is growing concern among both scientists and consumers about the levels of pesticides in foods. Reports released in 1986 from the General Accounting Office (the investigative arm of Congress) criticized the FDA's monitoring of pesticide residues as insufficient.[38]

Pesticide use in food crops involves several additional public health issues, including adverse health effects to farm workers and pollution of the environment. Some consumers are concerned about eating more fruits and vegetables when such practices may cause increased ingestion of pesticides. Alar (daminozide), a chemical used to retain apple crispness, was voluntarily removed from the U.S. market by the Uniroyal Chemical Company in 1989. Even though a proposed ban by the EPA was not expected until 1990, consumer boycotts of apples and apple products forced this action. Suggestions to consumers to minimize risks are discussed under the heading "Educating Consumers."

Fish Contamination

Those who encourage consumers to eat more fish must be aware of the risks of contaminants such as dioxin, mercury, and other heavy metals that accumulate in fatty fish tissue and suggest that the fatty tissue be cut away.[39] The FDA sets allowable levels for fish contaminants, but monitoring is virtually nonexistent due to inadequate resources and staffing. In general, the least contaminated fish are the offshore, lower fat species, such as cod, haddock, pollock, yellowfin tuna, and perch, and the fish raised in the increasing number of "fish farms." Some state agencies recommend safe consumption levels of local game fish, particularly for pregnant women.[40] Currently there is public interest and interest in Congress in developing legislation for fish inspection.

Natural and Organic Foods

Consumer interest in "natural" and "organic" foods is increasing with news coverage of pesticide contamination. Consumers should be informed that the word "natural" has not been defined by the FDA and is therefore meaningless when displayed on a processed food label. In fact, some products labeled "natural" actually contain artificial colors and flavors. In contrast, the USDA does define "natural" for use on fresh meat labels, where it indicates that the product is minimally processed.

The term "organic" has not been defined by either the FDA or the USDA, but several independent organizations and states are working to make this term meaningful. Over 40 independent agencies certify that foods and food ingredients marked "organic" have been grown without chemical fertilizers and pesticides. Certification standards may vary from one agency to another. The Organic Foods Production Association, a trade organization composed of organic producers, retailers, and certifying agencies, is working on uniform national guidelines for organic certification. As of December 1988, 15 states had laws defining how food must be grown to be labeled "organic." Public interest in these foods is growing, and it is useful to investigate the types of foods labeled "organic" or "natural" that are sold locally in natural food stores, supermarkets, and farmers markets. These foods will be more expensive and possibly less uniform in color and shape. There also may be some concern about *Listeria* if organically grown leafy vegetables that are eaten raw are raised with animal manure.

PROTECTING THE FOOD SUPPLY

Federal Agencies

In the United States, a network of federal, state, and local governmental agencies is responsible for regulating and monitoring food safety. The principal federal agencies and their roles are as follows:

- The Food and Drug Administration (FDA) is a part of the Public Health Service (PHS) of the Department of Health and Human Services (DHHS). This agency oversees the safety of all foods sold in interstate commerce except meat, poultry, and eggs, which are handled by the Department of Agriculture (USDA). The FDA regulates food and color additives and inspects food processing plants, imported food products, and animal feeds. The FDA maintains monitoring programs to prevent food contamination and recalls unsafe food products as they are identified. The agency is also responsible for the accuracy of ingredient and nutrition labeling of foods.
- The Centers for Disease Control (CDC), also part of the PHS of DHHS, monitor and direct communicable disease programs investigating emergencies where foodborne illness is suspected.
- The Food Safety and Inspection Service (FSIS) of the USDA grades and inspects meat, poultry, and eggs produced in the United States and enforces quality and safety standards for these products. The FSIS also inspects grains, fruits, vegetables, and dairy products for quality.
- The National Marine Fisheries Service (NMFS) of the Department of Commerce sets standards and monitors seafood quality, using the FDA to enforce these standards.
- The Environmental Protection Agency (EPA) regulates pesticides and drinking water quality. The FDA monitors and enforces the food-related standards established by the EPA.
- The Bureau of Consumer Protection of the Federal Trade Commission (FTC) regulates food advertising claims.
- The Bureau of Alcohol, Tobacco, and Firearms (BATF), an agency of the Department of the Treasury, regulates alcoholic beverages and their labeling. Wines containing less than 7 percent alcohol are under the jurisdiction of the FDA.
- The Department of Justice seizes products and prosecutes violators of any of the federal food safety laws.[41]

State and Local Collaboration

State and local governmental agencies cooperate with federal agencies to protect the safety of the food supply within their jurisdictions. Public health departments and state agriculture departments are usually the delegated authorities; responsibility varies both by state and by jurisdiction within states. Environmental health specialists or sanitarians employed in state or local health agencies periodically inspect and certify restaurants, other

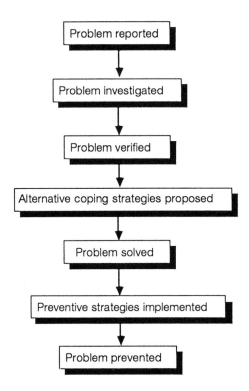

Figure 13-1 Plan of Action for Response to a Food Safety Problem

public food services, food markets, and food processing plants. State food sanitation codes usually meet or exceed model federal standards.

Public health nutritionists should know their jurisdiction's regulatory authorities for food sanitation and safety and work with them to protect the health of clients and the public. Nutritionists may assist environmental health specialists and epidemiologists who investigate outbreaks of illness attributed to unsafe or contaminated food. A timely response to outbreaks of foodborne illnesses requires all knowledgeable professionals to critically assess the situation and work together to resolve the problems and keep the public informed.

At the time when a concern regarding the safety of a particular food or food product is being investigated, the nutritionist can suggest alternative foods or methods of preparation. For example, when a batch of a popular commercial baby food was found to be contaminated with glass, mothers needed information on alternatives to ready-prepared baby food. A television news segment demonstrating sanitary techniques for home preparation and storage of baby food was quickly developed. The same type of response is appropriate whenever any foods are suspected of being unsafe. Figure 13-1 outlines a sequence of planned steps for responding to an outbreak of foodborne illness.

Within 24 to 48 hours after a problem is reported, it should be investigated and verified. Coping strategies should also be disseminated within this 24- to 48-hour period. The nutritionist can work with the investigative team and the press to put a coping strategy in place to avert public panic. The investigation can then proceed in orderly, careful steps.

Specific problems, such as allergic reactions attributed to food additives, should be reported to the nearest FDA field office. (See Exhibit 13-1 for a list of their addresses and telephone numbers.) Since 1985, the FDA's Adverse Reaction Monitoring System (ARMS) has been monitoring this type of complaint.[42]

In state and local health departments, environmental health specialists and sanitarians are usually designated as responsible for food safety programs. Nutritionists can work more closely with these specialists. One way to accomplish this is to discuss and exchange current information on food safety issues at periodic in-service training sessions for sanitarians and nutritionists.

EDUCATING CONSUMERS

In their communities, nutritionists and sanitarians can plan and conduct training programs for food service personnel. In a food handler's workshop, the nutritionist can demonstrate safe methods of preparing the foods that promote good nutrition. The program can be publicized to the variety of local food service establishments, including day care centers, schools, hospitals, nursing homes, and restaurants. Figure 13-2 can be used as a basis for food service training since it shows the cause-effect relationships of foodborne illnesses and how to prevent them.

A community food safety awareness campaign, sponsored jointly by nutritionists, environmental health specialists/sanitarians, and health educators, can inform consumers about the roles and responsibilities of these experts. News releases or public service announcements on the prevention of foodborne illness could track health-promoting foods from farm to dinner table. The story could focus on high-risk areas and prevention tips for foods that are commonly served at home or in food service establishments. A health agency hotline could answer callers' questions or mail them informative brochures.

Exhibit 13-1   The Food and Drug Administration's Consumer Affairs Offices around the United States

Atlanta, GA 30309
60 8th Street, NE
(404) 347-7355

Arlington, VA 22201
1000 N. Glebe Rd.
Room 743
(703) 285-2578

Baltimore, MD 21201
900 Madison Ave.
(301) 962-3731

Bothell, WA 98021-4421
22201 23rd Dr., SE
(206) 483-4953

Brooklyn, NY 11232
850 3rd Ave.
(718) 965-5043

Brunswick, OH 44212
3820 Center Rd.
(216) 273-1038

Buffalo, NY 14202
599 Delaware Ave.
(716) 846-4483

Chicago, IL 60607
433 West Van Buren St.
1222 Main Post Office
(312) 353-7126

Cincinnati, OH 45202
1141 Central Parkway
(513) 684-3501

Dallas, TX 75202
1200 Main Tower Bldg.
Room 2100
(214) 767-5433

Denver, CO 80225
Denver Federal Center
Bldg. 20, B-1121
6th & Kipling St.
P.O. Box 25087
(303) 236-3018

Detroit, MI 48207
1560 E. Jefferson Ave.
(313) 226-6260

Houston, TX 77008
Houston Resident Post
1445 North Loop West
Suite 420
(713) 220-2322

Indianapolis, IN 46204
575 N. Pennsylvania
Room 693
(317) 269-6500

Kansas City, MO 64106
1009 Cherry St.
(816) 374-6366

Los Angeles, CA 90015
1521 W. Pico Blvd.
(213) 252-7597

Miami, FL 33159-2256
6601 NW 25th St.
P.O. Box 59-2256
(305) 526-2545

Minneapolis, MN 55401
240 Hennepin Ave.
(612) 334-4103

Nashville, TN 37217
297 Plus Park Blvd.
(615) 736-2088

New Orleans, LA 70122
4928 Elysian Fields Ave.
(504) 589-2420

Orlando, FL 32809
7200 Lake Ellenor Dr.
(407) 855-0900

Philadelphia, PA 19106
Room 900
US Customhouse
2nd & Chestnut Sts.
(215) 597-0837

Rockville, MD 20857
Consumer Affairs Coord.
5600 Fishers Lane
(301) 443-4166

San Antonio, TX 78206
727 East Durango
Room B-406
(512) 229-6737

San Francisco, CA 94102
50 United Nations Plaza
Room 524
(415) 556-1364

San Juan, PR 00906-5719
P.O. Box 5719
Puerto De Tierra Station
(809) 729-6852

St. Louis, MO 63102
Laclede's Landing
808 North Collins
(314) 425-5021

Stoneham, MA 02180
1 Montvale Ave.
(617) 279-1479

West Orange, NJ 07052
61 Main St.
(201) 645-6365

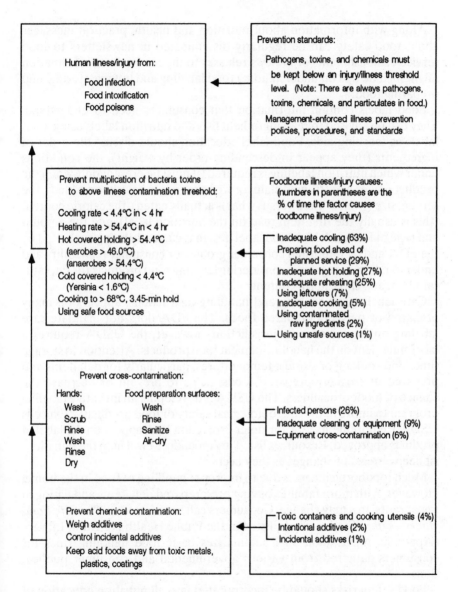

Figure 13-2 Causes/Prevention of a Foodborne Illness as a Basis for Community Education. *Source*: Adapted from *Food Technology*, Vol. 40, No. 7, p. 128, with permission of Institute of Food Technologists, © July 1986.

Along with information about nutrition and health, practical messages about food safety can be regularly disseminated in newsletters to food service establishments or in news releases to the media. Such information might include tips on understanding food labeling and buying, storing, and preparing food.

Food labels contain information that consumers need to understand. They can be advised to read ingredient lists and nutrition labels using food labels as teaching aids. Food label education should discuss the order of ingredients (they appear in descending order by weight), the conditions under which nutrition labeling is required (it must be present only when the product makes a nutritional claim or when nutrients have been added), the serving size (what is listed versus what is actually eaten), the calorie content (this is usually the first item read on the nutrition label), and the amount and type of fat listed. Nutrition label design is currently being evaluated by the FDA and by interested consumer groups for consumer readability and understanding. Congress is considering labeling food products for fat, saturated fat, and cholesterol content.

Care labeling, or cooking and handling instructions, appears on many prepared or partially prepared foods. The FDA does not mandate care labeling on foods under its jurisdiction; however, the USDA requires a label statement on the handling of meat food products. Attention to storage times and cooking or storage temperatures, particularly for deli items and prepared or partially prepared foods, helps to prevent or decrease the chance of foodborne illness. The USDA is developing an incentive labeling program to improve the microbiological safety of food products. "Exceeds USDA Requirements for Consumer Protection" will appear on the label of products approved. Resources listed in Appendix M will help the nutritionist keep abreast of changes as they occur.[43]

Much foodborne illness is due to improper handling of food in the home. However, with more families buying pre-prepared deli items and eating in restaurants, this may change. Consumers can be referred to *The Safe Food Book—Your Kitchen Guide*, listed in the Public Health Nutrition Library (Appendix N). Exhibit 13-2 summarizes basic food handling rules for consumers gathered from various governmental and consumer publications.

Food safety risks should be incorporated into all nutrition education of the general public and clients, particularly to pregnant women, and for infants, the elderly, and persons whose immune system is compromised.[44] Consumers must understand the tradeoffs of risks versus benefits, such as the important values of fruits and vegetables versus their concerns about pesticides.

Exhibit 13-2 Food Handling Rules for Consumers

To prevent foodborne illness from microbial contamination:

- Do not use unpasteurized dairy products or cracked eggs.
- Wash hands with warm soapy water before food preparation. Also wash the surfaces the food will touch before and after preparation, being careful to avoid any cross-contamination.
- Wash hands any time you have handled raw meat, poultry, fish, or eggs.
- Do not handle food when you have cuts, sores, or burns on your hands.
- Do not thaw food on kitchen counters and/or leave perishable food out for over two hours.
- Thoroughly cook all meat, poultry, fish, and eggs.
- Keep hot foods hot (above 140° F) and cold foods cold (below 40° F).
- Refrigerate or freeze leftovers promptly after preparation. Reheat to bubbling to reuse.
- Refrigerator temperatures should be 40° F or less.
- When in doubt about the safety of a food, throw it out.

To reduce exposure to unintentional additives such as pesticides:

- Buy domestically grown produce whenever possible. Imported produce may have pesticides not approved in the United State, since not all can be tested.
- Rinse and scrub fruits and vegetables thoroughly with a brush and water. Peel if appropriate.
- Remove and discard the outermost leaves of lettuce and cabbage.
- Trim the fat from meat and fish and remove the skin from poultry. Discard fat drippings as residues from pesticides concentrate in the animal's fat.
- Ask your food market to carry produce grown without pesticides. If enough people ask, they will begin to stock these products.

Source: Developed by L. Quint-Adler and M. Kaufman and adapted from *FDA Consumer*, Vol. 22, No. 8, p. 10, U.S. Food and Drug Administration, October 1988.

Risk assessment empowers consumers to make informed decisions about hazards over which they can have some degree of control. Consumers must be helped to understand that the food supply cannot be 100 percent safe; nor is the environment free of risks. In discussing risks with consumers, it is important to acknowledge the wide diversity of published risk estimates and the limitations of the available knowledge base. It is important for the professional to present expertise, give personal examples, be honest, and be sincere in trying to understand the consumer viewpoint. From their viewpoint, consumers may tend to be more overwhelmed by risks that appear to them to be new, unknown, uncontrollable, involuntary, and potentially catastrophic. Health professionals can help consumers separate the serious from the trivial risks and point out where and how as individuals they can take control.[45]

ISSUES TO DEBATE

- How can food safety risks be balanced with current dietary recommendations?
- How can the nutritionist effectively collaborate with other health agency staff on food safety issues? What special expertise can the nutritionist provide?
- In considering the risks versus the benefits of nonnutritive sweeteners, what specific recommendations should be made to clients concerned about weight management?
- How can the nutritionist advocate for a safer food supply at the community, state, and federal levels?
- What is the responsibility of the nutritionist in reducing the incidence of foodborne illness in the community?

NOTES

1. "Updates: Food Safety a Growing Concern," *FDA Consumer* 22, no. 7 (September 1988): 2.

2. Expert Panel on Food Safety and Nutrition, Institute of Food Technologists, "Bacteria Associated with Foodborne Illness," *Food Technology* 42, no. 4 (1988): 181.

3. Frank E. Young, "A Golden Anniversary of Consumer Protection," *FDA Consumer* 22, no. 5 (June 1988): 4.

4. Ibid.

5. Chris W. Lecos, "A Summertime Hotline for Food Safety Questions," *FDA Consumer* 22, no. 5 (June 1988): 11.

6. W.E. Garthright, D.L. Archer, and J.E. Kvenberg, "Estimates of Incidences and Costs of Intestinal Infectious Diseases in the United States," *Public Health Reports* 103, no. 2 (March–April 1988): 107–15.

7. Elliot T. Ryser and Elmer H. Marth, "New Food-Borne Pathogens of Public Health Significance," *Journal of the American Dietetic Association* 89, no. 7 (July 1989): 948–54.

8. R.B. Chalker and M.J. Blaser, "A Review of Human Salmonellosis: III. Magnitude of Salmonella Infection in the United States," *Reviews of Infectious Diseases* 10, no. 1 (January–February 1988): 111–24.

9. M.E. Laus, "The Emergence of Grade A Eggs as Major Source of Salmonella Enteritis Infections: New Implications for the Control of Salmonellosis," *Journal of the American Medical Association* 259, no. 14 (April 1988): 2103–07.

10. Ryser and Marth, "New Food-Borne Pathogens."

11. E.G. Steenbuigge, R. But Barly, and Michael B. Liewen, "Fate of Listeria Monocytogenes

in Ready to Serve Lettuce," *Journal of Food Protection* 55 (August 1988): 596. Elmer H. Marth, "Disease Characteristics of Listeria Monocytogenes," *Food Technology* 42, no. 4 (1988): 165. Bruce G. Gellin and Claire V. Broome, "Listeriosis," *Journal of the American Medical Association* 261, no. 9 (3 March 1989): 1313–20.

12. Mitchell Carl, Donald P. Francis, and James Maynard, "Food-Borne Hepatitis A: Recommendations for Control," *Journal of Infectious Diseases* 148, no. 6 (December 1983): 1133–35.

13. National Research Council, *Diet and Health, Implications for Reducing Chronic Disease Risk* (Washington, D.C.: National Academy Press, 1989), 12, 486–87, 662, 665.

14. S.J. Van Rensburg, "Primary Liver Cancer Rate and Aflatoxin Intake in a High Cancer Area," *South African Medical Journal* 48, no. 60 (1974): 2508a.

15. Leonard T. Flynn, *Does Nature Know Best? Natural Carcinogens in American Food* (American Council on Science and Health, July 1987).

16. Ibid.

17. "A Primer on Food Additives," *FDA Consumer* 22, no. 8 (October 1988): 13.

18. M.V. Smith and A.M. Rulis, "FDA's GRAS Review and Priority-Based Assessment of Food Additives," *Food Technology* 35, no. 12 (December 1981): 71–74.

19. Ken Flieger, "How Safe Is Safe?" *FDA Consumer* 22, no. 7 (September 1988): 16.

20. "A Primer on Food Additives."

21. "AMA/IFT Symposium on Safety of the Food Supply in the Twenty First Century: Concerns and Challenges," *Journal of Food Technology* 42, no. 5 (May 1988): 66.

22. "Food Additives," *University of California, Berkeley Wellness Letter* 4, no. 2 (November 1987): 4.

23. Judy Falkenberg, "Reporting Reactions to Additives," *FDA Consumer* 22, no. 8 (October 1988): 16.

24. National Research Council, *Diet and Health Implications for Reducing Chronic Disease Risk* (Washington, D.C.: National Academy Press, 1989), 473–74.

25. "Report Calls Aspartame Safe," *Science Digest* 93, no. 11 (November 1985): 24.

26. "Updates: New Sweetener Approved," *FDA Consumer* 22, no. 8 (October 1988): 4.

27. National Research Council, *Diet and Health Implications*, 474–76.

28. Ibid., 476–78.

29. "AMA/IFT Symposium."

30. Chris W. Lecos, "New Regulations to Help Sodium Conscious Consumers," *FDA Consumer* 20, no. 4 (May 1986): 17.

31. *The Surgeon General's Report on Nutrition and Health* (Washington, D.C.: Government Printing Office, 1988), 52, Table 1-7.

32. Ibid., 150.

33. National Research Council, *Diet and Health Implications*, 479.

34. Consumer Affairs Center, *Simpless, All Natural Fat Substitute, a Scientific Overview.* (Deerfield, Ill.: The NutraSweet Company, 1989), 1. International Food Council, "New Fat Substitutes: Health Boom or Bust?" *Food Insight* (Summer 1988): 4.

35. Dixie Farley, "Chemicals We'd Rather Dine Without," *FDA Consumer* 22, no. 7 (September 1988): 10.

36. S.D. Holmberg et al., "Resistant Salmonella from Animals Fed Subtherapeutic Antimicrobials," *New England Journal of Medicine* 311 (September 6, 1984): 617.

37. National Research Council, *Meat and Poultry Inspection—The Scientific Bases of the*

Nation's Program (Washington, D.C.: National Academy Press, 1985).

38. U.S. General Accounting Office, *Pesticides: Better Sampling and Enforcement Needed in Imported Food*, 1986.

39. Farley, "Chemicals."

40. Senate Committee on Agriculture, Nutrition, and Forestry, *Food Safety, Where Are We?* (Washington, D.C.: Government Printing Office, 1979), 106–21.

41. V. Modeland, "America's Food Safety Team: A Look at the Lineup," *FDA Consumer* 22, no. 6 (July–August 1988): 18.

42. Falkenberg, "Reporting Reactions."

43. Liz Lapping, "USDA Approves New Labelling Program," *Food News for Consumers* 5, no. 4 (Winter 1989): 13.

44. Mary Ann Parmley, "Rx for Food Safety, How Physicians, Nurses, Dietitians and Nutritionists Can Help in the Fight against Foodborne Illness," *Food News for Consumers* 6, no. 1 (Spring 1979): 10–11.

45. "Weighing the Odds: Risk Communications and Public Health Food Insight," *Current Topics in Food Safety and Nutrition* (Winter 1988): 1, 4, 5.

part *V*

Managing the System

chapter 14

Planning and Evaluating Nutrition Services for the Community

Mildred Kaufman

READER OBJECTIVES

- Discuss the values of planning.
- List factors that influence the plan for nutrition services.
- Discuss the use of a planning group, and suggest its membership.
- List and describe each step in the planning process.
- Discuss the use of cost-benefit analysis and cost-effectiveness analysis in selecting and prioritizing nutrition program objectives and interventions.
- Compare and contrast the several types of measures useful in internal program evaluation.

DEFINING PLANNING

The nutritionist must participate in the planning processes of the agency, study the agency or community health plans, know those who participate in the planning group, and get involved. Plans for nutrition services should be integrated, but visible in the overall agency health plan. There may be a single comprehensive agency health plan or separate plans for each categorical program, especially those using external funding. For example, the Maternal and Child Health Block Grant requires a plan called a Report of Intended Expenditures.

The public health nutritionist as a midlevel manager contributes to the agency's strategic plan, while taking specific responsibility for the management and operational plans for nutrition services delivery. Even if the agency does not use a formal planning system, there will be significant advantages in developing a written plan for the nutrition services. To be an

279

effective planner requires understanding the planning process, the terminology, and the methods of program development.

A plan is a careful, thoughtful course of action. Planners recognize the need to continuously critique and re-evaluate the services that are being offered. Monitoring and evaluating are integral to planning, often suggesting some changes or new directions—reaching out to larger audiences, focusing on new problems, serving different populations, evaluating innovative interventions, testing the use of "state of the art" technologies, reallocating resources, and activating different networks. The planner knows the need to maintain continuous feedback so that the selected courses of action can be fine tuned, expanded, redesigned, or overhauled. This can be uncomfortable and threatening to those who prefer "business as usual" or the status quo. However, in the current economy, the planner understands that resources are finite and that program survival requires keen competition and wise use of funds to demonstrate measurable results.

The written public health nutrition services plan, either as part of the health agency plan or as a separate document, specifies the nature and scope of the problems to be addressed and the services to be delivered by the agency's staff. This plan describes nutrition services. It justifies the budget request, guides the work of the nutrition personnel, and is the frame of reference for monitoring and evaluating achievement. In addition to the ranked community nutrition problem list generated by the community diagnosis discussed in Chapters 3 and 4, important factors to consider in writing the plan are

- the established and emerging scientific evidence from research findings in nutrition and food science with application to the public's health (Chapter 2)
- agency mission and philosophy mandating health protection and promotion
- federal and state legislation either requiring or permitting nutrition services in the community's health and human services system
- federal, national, state, local, public, or private sector funds that are earmarked or available to finance or reimburse for nutrition services
- opportunities to contract with other community health and human service agencies to provide nutrition services
- model nutrition objectives (see Appendix C) or standards published by expert groups that are pertinent to the community

The plan should be progressive; it should be designed to improve, strengthen, and expand services, leading the program to higher levels of achievement and recognition. Since the plan is a political as well as a professional document, consideration must be given to its potential for achieving visibility and support, and ultimately for achieving success.

Using today's best knowledge and vision, planning sets the direction toward the future. Since the future is unknown, plans must build in flexibility. Planning is a logical, orderly process toward change. Making changes can be painful, and it involves taking some risks. That makes planning exciting! The purpose of planning is to initiate immediate actions that will result in the greatest probability of reaching the desired objectives by a predicted time.

Planners must weigh and balance the variety of causes and effects, ask many "What ifs?" and deliberate about alternative scenarios. At each step of the planning cycle, priorities must be selected from among many often equally appealing alternative choices.

USING A PLANNING GROUP

Diets to promote health and fitness, prevent or cure disease, and control weight entice the public and the media, as well as policymakers, administrators, and health and human service professionals. Based on their education and orientation to nutrition, some people's perceptions of desirable dietary practices may differ from those of professional nutritionists, who may consider some of the popular notions to be misinformed or faddish. Involving recognized leaders in the community who have an interest in planning nutrition services can educate them and win their respect for the nutritionist as the expert in food, nutrition, diet, and public health. Mobilizing the diverse viewpoints of the stakeholders enhances creativity and may reveal some previously unknown resources, all while building support.

The public health nutrition planner can harness community energy by working with the agency administrator to appoint either an advisory or a working committee to be involved in developing the nutrition plan. An advisory committee is purely consultative. Such a committee might review and discuss the community nutrition problem list and other environmental factors, help select priorities, and make recommendations that a smaller staff working group would study, consider, and use judiciously. A working committee would not only study the community diagnosis and rank priorities, but also draft the plan that the staff would be obligated to use.

Persons selected for either type of committee should have some knowledge and convictions about the contributions nutrition can make to addressing the community's health problems. They should be willing to commit several hours throughout the year to committee activities, with more time being required for the working committee than for the advisory committee.

Committee members should have vision and see beyond their own interests. They must be good listeners and communicators. The committee members should be oriented to the planning process, the agency, and its current nutrition programs. Their orientation should include review of previous plans, budgets, reports, educational materials, policies, and procedures. The committee members might also observe nutritionists at work in the community, office, and clinics. The planning committee should seek suggestions and ideas from a wide variety of other interested persons within the community and the agency. Brainstorming and nominal group process are useful techniques for facilitating committee discussions.

While diversity is desirable, the committee should be small, probably no more than seven to nine people. Appointees to either type of committee would include representatives selected from the public, agency clients, agency board members, administrators, and health and human service professionals. A physician, public health nurse, health educator, and social worker, as well as one or two nutritionists who will be involved in implementing the plan, would be desirable committee members.

THE PLANNING PROCESS

The program development cycle in Figure 14-1 shows the interfaces in planning involving agency management responsible for overall strategy and policy formulation, the midlevel operational planning and program management, and the staff who delivers the services. This model demonstrates the concept of management by objective in which each level in the organization has interrelated planning functions. It can be used as a conceptual framework in preparing the nutrition content for the health agency plan and the nutrition program plan. It sequences a series of steps that progress as the plan is implemented, evaluated, and evolves over succeeding years. Each step is discussed in some detail.

Analyzing Subjective Data

This is the collection and analysis of data on the various stakeholder's perceived needs. This includes the clarification of community values, and the analysis of the community (external) and agency (internal) environments in which the nutrition program plan will operate, as discussed in Chapters 3 and 4.

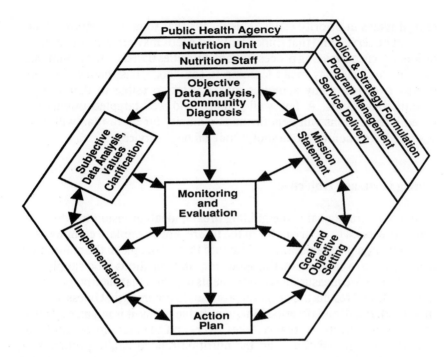

Figure 14-1 Program Development Cycle

Analyzing Objective Data

This is the collection and analysis of objective data, using available demographic and health statistics to prepare the community diagnosis and problem list. It is discussed in Chapters 3 and 4.

Writing a Mission Statement

The mission statement written for nutrition services must be in concert with that written for the agency. The mission statement tells what nutrition services can contribute to the health and well-being of the people in the community, what population groups will be served, and how they will benefit as a result of nutrition programs and services. This statement must be clear, concise, and realistic, yet inspirational. In writing the mission statement, as well as in the subsequent steps of writing the objectives and the action plan or activities, it is necessary to select and rank the most critical issues in priority order. This means that some population groups may not be served and that some identified needs may remain unmet. It is a rational decision-making process to rank priorities based on the community assessment. This may mean learning to say "no." Dissipating time and energy over too many activities makes it less possible to demonstrate quantifiable results. A few well-planned and well-targeted population-based interventions will benefit the community far more than will many scattered, fragmented, "one shot," "one on one" services.

Setting Goals and Objectives

As used here, a goal is the guiding dream, ideal, or vision to which the program aspires to or strives for in the future. For example, a common goal for a nutrition program is this: "To assure that all people in the community have access to a safe, adequate, appealing, and nutritious food supply."

Objectives are measurable commitments to action that clearly specify the magnitude and results the program promises to accomplish. Unless it can be measured, rated, and described in quantifiable terms, it is not an objective. In selecting objectives, reality takes over, and planners must select the population or populations and the nutrition-related health problems on which to focus energies and resources. In preparing local objectives, it is useful to study and assess the appropriateness of the published national health promotion, disease prevention objectives for the year 2000; the model state objectives (see Appendix C); and the standards for community preventive health services.

Cost-benefit analysis (CBA) is useful in selecting objectives from several possible alternatives. CBA is the appropriate analysis strategy to use when one is attempting to determine the economic worthiness of useful alternative projects. That is, will the dollars saved for the community by reductions in client use of health resources such as hospital or nursing home care—the benefits of the program—exceed the dollars required to operate the program—the costs? The nutritionist may ask the economic worthiness question from a number of perspectives (e.g., from that of the public at large, from that of the agency or institution, and from that of the nutrition program). CBA can be used to compare several programs that have different objectives and different outcomes, such as women's health, school health, and home health services, since both the costs and the benefits of providing the nutrition services must be defined in dollar terms. A cost-beneficial program is one in which the net dollars saved by providing the services are more than the dollars the public would spend if the services were not provided. That is, the benefits-to-costs ratio exceeds one.

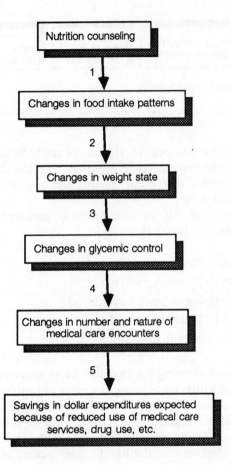

Figure 14-2 Potential Economic Benefits Associated with Nutrition Counseling in Diabetes Care

Determining program costs is discussed in Chapter 17. The more challenging aspect of CBA is the process of estimating the economic value of program benefits. To determine the economic benefits of a prenatal counseling program, linkages between the changes in pregnancy weight gain and infant birth weight and the differences in subsequent medical care utilization rates would need to be determined. Then representative estimates of the dollar savings resulting from the reduction in the use of crisis perinatal medical care would need to be made. In diabetes care, linkages might reflect intermediate changes which may then result in health care savings, as shown in Figure 14-2. The second challenging aspect of CBA requires

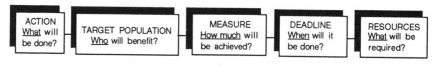

Figure 14-3 Structure of an Objective

definition of a time perspective. If benefits are to be achieved at a time in the future after the program costs are spent, as is the case with most health promotion programs, then program costs and benefits must be discounted to present dollar value.

The number of objectives selected must be manageable. Each objective should be written to specify the

- action to be taken—what will be done?
- target population—who will benefit?
- measure—how much will be achieved?
- deadline—by when will it be done?
- resources—what will be required?

See Figure 14-3 showing the structure of an objective and Exhibit 14-1 suggesting some action verbs to use in writing objectives. Objectives should be realistic or achievable with available or anticipated staff, money, and facilities. Objectives should be relevant to the agency and the nutrition program mission. They should be understandable and clearly stated so that every lay or professional reader has the same picture of what is to be done.

Objectives are stated as

- *Outcome*—benefits or changes in the attitude, knowledge, nutritional, or health status of the consumer, client, or public. For example, "By 6/30/2000, 50 percent of the full-term infants enrolled in the well-child clinic will be breast-fed for their first five months of life."
- *Process*—practices or procedures carried out by health and nutrition workers. These should be those standardized policies and procedures considered essential to achieve predictable outcomes under most conditions. These processes should be "state of the art," based on recent research findings and professional standards of practice. For example, "By 6/30/2000, 100 percent of the infant and child health records will include weight for age, height for age, weight for height, and head circumference plotted at each child health visit on a National

Exhibit 14-1 Action Verbs for Health and Nutrition Program Objectives

OUTCOME objectives—POPULATION, CONSUMER, OR CLIENT knowledge, health/nutrition status change

Achieve	Consume	Improve	Participate
Adapt	Decrease	Increase	Reach
Attain	Eliminate	Know	Reduce
Complete	Identify	Maintain	Select/Choose

PROCESS objectives—PROVIDER action to achieve desired outcomes

Advise	Counsel	Identify	Receive
Assess	Deliver	Implement	Refer
Attend	Demonstrate	Instruct	Screen
Calculate	Detect	Investigate	Serve
Collect	Develop	Maintain	Speak
Compile	Distribute	Measure	Survey
Complete	Educate	Monitor	Teach
Compute	Enroll	Participate	Train
Conduct	Establish	Prepare	Write
Consult	Evaluate	Promote	

Center for Health Statistics child health chart."

- *Structure*—number, qualification, and scheduling of staff; budget; space and equipment recommended by experts in the field as necessary to carry out the processes to achieve quality services and desired outcomes. For example, "By 6/30/2000, each health clinic providing well-child services will employ one full-time registered dietitian for each 500 clients who require nutrition counseling."

Clearly written explicit objectives organize and communicate a complex plan in a few descriptive statements. The more precise the statement of the objective is, the more clear the direction for the action plan is and the more easily a data system can be developed to monitor progress.

Activating the Objectives

The action plan is a concise statement of the methods, activities, or intervention strategies to be undertaken. Interventions must be sufficiently intensive or forceful to achieve the objectives by the target date. Cost-effectiveness analysis (CEA) can be used to select from the several alternative interventions discussed in Chapter 18. CEA is used to compare alternative programs or interventions. It assumes that the objectives are economically worthwhile. Cost-effectiveness ratios can be constructed to answer similar questions: "Which intervention provides the greatest units of outcome per dollar spent?" (benefits/costs) versus "Which program provides a unit of outcome at the lowest cost?" (costs/benefits).

In contrast to CBA, in which benefits must be valued in dollar terms, CEA allows many possible outcome candidates. Possibilities include outcomes related to actual behaviors or risk factors (dietary or weight changes), disease rates, service delivery outcomes, or other outcomes that reflect changes in morbidity such as number of sick days averted and mortality rates such as the years of life saved.

However, approaches to be compared by CEA must be measured in the same outcome. For example, one might wish to examine the relative cost effectiveness of a weight-loss program delivered through group sessions directed by a nutritionist versus use of self-help modules. The outcome measure of effectiveness of both approaches could be reflected in pounds lost or in changes in the body weight of program participants. The approach that achieved the greater number of pounds lost per dollar spent would be considered the more cost effective. (See Exhibit 14-2.)

Exhibit 14-2   Question: Which Alternative Provides the Greater Level of Benefits per Dollar Spent?

1. $$\frac{B_A}{C_A} = \frac{\text{Total Units of Outcome (O), Program A}}{\text{Total Costs, Program A}}$$

$$= \text{Units of Outcome (O) per Dollar Spent}$$

vs.

2. $$\frac{B_B}{C_B} = \frac{\text{Total Units of Outcome (O), Program B}}{\text{Total Costs, Program B}}$$

$$= \text{Units of Outcome (O) per Dollar Spent}$$

For CEA, compare 1 and 2.

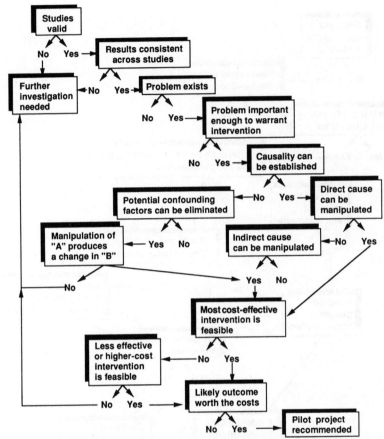

Figure 14-4 Evaluating the Evidence for Providing an Intervention. *Source*: Reprinted from "Evaluating the Evidence for Nutrition Interventions: Two Algorithms" by L. Lopez, *Journal of The American Dietetic Association*, Vol. 86, No. 8, pp. 1056–1057, with permission of The American Dietetic Association, © August 1986.

Other considerations in selecting interventions are the number and competencies of the staff and the acceptability of the interventions to the target population. Based on successful past experiences, the choice of some interventions may be clear. For others, a demonstration or pilot period might be designed into the plan. Before committing much money or staff time, it may be useful to test several different intervention approaches in different settings—or at different times in one setting—to determine the most acceptable, most cost effective, and most feasible. The two algorithms for evaluating the evidence with regard to providing a new nutrition intervention or continuing an existing intervention give practicing nutritionists useful analytical models. (See Figures 14-4 and 14-5). An algorithm is a

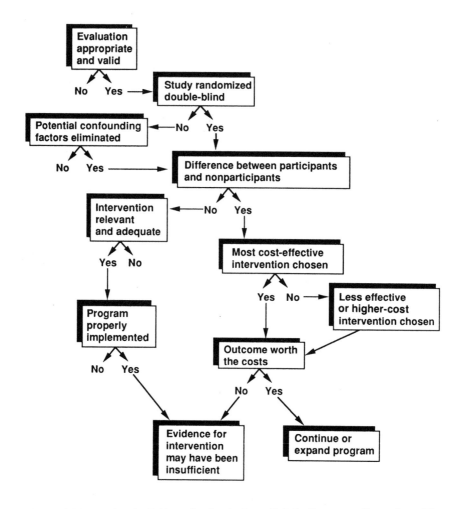

Figure 14-5 Evaluating the Evidence for Continuing an Existing Program or Expanding a Pilot Project. *Source*: Reprinted from "Evaluating the Evidence for Nutrition Interventions: Two Algorithms" by L. Lopez, *Journal of The American Dietetic Association*, Vol. 86, No. 8, pp. 1056–1057, with permission of The American Dietetic Association, © August 1986.

logical step-by-step process for solving a problem. Figure 14-4 goes through the steps to use in studying the literature to decide whether research supports selecting an intervention and whether it will be cost effective. Figure 14-5 suggests an experimental evaluation design to use to decide whether to continue an existing program or expand a pilot project.

The methods selected must be feasible given the agency's facilities and budget. If the needed facilities and personnel do not exist or cannot be obtained through the agency budget request process, it should be determined if they can be obtained through charging a fee for the service or writing a contract or grant application to obtain external funding. Writing the action plan offers the opportunity for planners to brainstorm and use their imaginations. The activity statements in the program plan should be descriptive, but concise. An expanded list of specific tasks may be detailed in the operational plan prepared by staff who will actually carry out the activities. Implementation requires that adequate resources be requested through a detailed and justified line item budget, as discussed in Chapter 17. Also required in the more detailed implementation plan is a time line showing the planning, implementation, and evaluation tasks that must be scheduled over the project period. A weekly or monthly calendar schedule assigns staff to routine and special project activities. This schedule can be used for planning, delegating work, and assessing productivity (Chapter 19).

IMPLEMENTING THE PLAN

Effective program implementation requires the following:

- Administrative support with a budget that provides realistic staff, space, and equipment resources. Staff must have a work schedule that assures that they can accomplish the required tasks within the time available. For new programs, extra time must be built in for training, field testing, trouble-shooting, and revising.
- Commitment of staff to the goals, objectives, and interventions. Staff must be completely oriented to their responsibilities and trained to assure their competency to perform the required tasks. They must feel confident that their work is valuable and that they can do the tasks required.
- Support and respect of the target population who are also convinced of the benefits of the program and willing to commit their time and effort to participate. Social marketing strategies (Chapter 15) and networking (Chapter 22) may be useful in obtaining community involvement. The community representative on the advisory or working committee may be a useful liaison with the participants.

Putting the plan into action is its "reality check." A well-designed plan should provide for dry runs, pilot testing, the trying out of alternative strategies, and contingencies. Murphy's law can be anticipated: "If anything can go wrong, it will." Unexpected situations should not come as a surprise. On-site changes may be required during implementation. The need to make changes does not necessarily mean that the plan was ill conceived. The keys to successful implementation are open communication and efficient program management. This includes fiscal management (Chapter 17) and personnel management (Chapter 20).

MONITORING AND EVALUATING ACHIEVEMENT

The program implementation must be systematically monitored, with the collection and analysis of appropriate data providing continuous feedback to use to assess performance. Evaluation is the systematic measurement of results by comparing the data collected with pre-established standards or controls. Programs that spend public money must be accountable and responsible for analyzing and reporting their results. Results of program evaluations should be used to decide whether to continue, expand, redesign, or terminate the program. Evaluation is part of every step in the plan. If each objective is stated in measurable terms, specifying the criterion and the performance level or standard, evaluation is built into the planning cycle.

In developing each activity, a data system must be designed to capture the information to be recorded at the beginning (base line), at specified intermediate points, and at the end point of the implementation phase. Data collection instruments must be validated to be sure that they are, in fact, measuring what they intend to measure and that they are reliable in yielding the same results on repeated use and when used by different workers. The data system must be quick and easy to use, preferably allowing entry of the information into readily accessible computers. During implementation, data must be systematically, meticulously, and objectively collected. (See Chapter 16 for a discussion of data management.)

Measures used in program evaluation are

- *Outcomes*—changes in consumers' nutrition and health knowledge measured by pre- and post-tests; changes in eating practices as measured by repeated dietary intake assessments, using standardized validated methods and forms; changes in health or nutritional status as measured by changes in standardized anthropometric measures or biochemical tests. At the clinic or service delivery level, changes can be monitored by periodic audits of agency medical or health records; by periodic studies of the reports from the Centers for Disease Control pediatric and pregnancy nutrition surveillance systems; by reviews of nutrition data in automated client information systems; or by special studies. Population outcomes can be monitored by observing trends over time in data aggregated from birth and death certificates, school and child day care (Head Start) health records, or hospital discharge reports. When data are collected and analyzed, outcome evaluations provide the response to the frequently asked question, "What has the nutrition program actually accomplished?"

- *Outputs*—statistical reports and logs of activities, services provided, or work performed: for example, numbers of encounters or unduplicated counts of clients served; numbers of classes held and rosters of attendees at each; numbers of copies of educational materials printed and distributed; numbers of speeches given and sizes of the audiences; numbers of media presentations; or numbers and types of telephone calls answered. Measures may also be recorded for the various process objectives. When the services provided can be measured against predetermined protocols or standards of practice, outputs measure achievement of process objectives. This type of evaluation measures work performed.

- *Inputs*—dollars budgeted and expended; numbers and qualifications of staff; sizes and equipment of facilities. Documentation for inputs are organization charts, job descriptions, schedules, personnel and expenditure reports, and inventories. Input documents relate to structure objectives.

- *Consumer satisfaction*—determination of public and client awareness of nutrition services and their opinion of the usefulness, quality, and convenience of the services and of the responsiveness and expertise of the staff. Satisfaction is assessed by clients and the public. This type of information is obtained by conducting surveys of a randomly selected group of consumers at periodic intervals, usually once a year, using special written questionnaires or personal or telephone interviews. Results from this type of evaluation are used to improve the quality, scheduling, or location of services. While this type of evaluation is subjective, clients and the public may consider this the most important evaluation. Satisfied consumers are good will ambassadors to the community.

Once output and outcome data are collected, some correlations can be made to show

- *Program efficiency*—relates output to each unit of input to determine the dollar value of resources used to accomplish each stated process objective

- *Program coverage or penetration*—compares output or services provided to the estimated number of people in the eligible target population who need the service, as determined in the community assessment
- *Program impact*—compares outcome data for a specified health or nutrition status measure with the estimated number of people in the target population who are at risk for the particular problem, as identified in the community assessment

In addition to these internal evaluations, some programs may arrange for a more rigorous unbiased evaluation, using an experimental or quasi-experimental design. For external evaluation, the agency contracts with a university research group or private consultant with expertise in evaluation methodology. Funding for an external evaluator can be included as a line item in grant applications and will strengthen the proposal.

REPORTING PROGRAM SUCCESS

Results and recommendations from the various program evaluations should be summarized, analyzed, and interpreted at regular intervals in statistical, graphic, and narrative reports written according to agency requirements and outlines. The reporting should be in the form of weekly or monthly informal feedback to the staff, quarterly or semiannual written and verbal program review with the staff and administrator, and annual written reports to the agency board, funding agencies, and the public. Most agencies publish annual reports which summarize their work during the year and disseminate these to the community. Nutrition services should be highlighted in these reports. Successful evaluations merit media coverage to showcase the program to the community.

OBTAINING REVIEW AND COMMENT

The draft of the written plan in a format such as the one shown in Exhibit 14-3 should be circulated to the administrator, peers, and coworkers for review and comment. Suggestions should be carefully considered and incorporated as appropriate. The completed plan should be widely distributed in the agency and community.

As a written document, the program plan shares a vision with the community, the agency administrator, other health professionals, and nutrition peers. It records the planning process, and it guides the staff as they implement and monitor their activities. The format may be dictated by

Exhibit 14-3 Format for a Nutrition Program Plan

I. INTRODUCTION (brief comprehensive paragraph)

II. PROBLEM STATEMENT (one paragraph for each problem area) (e.g., women of childbearing age, infants/children, adult health promotion, program management)

III. OBJECTIVES	IV. ACTION PLAN, METHODS, ACTIVITIES	V. EVALUATION (DATA SYSTEM)
Measurable objectives to be achieved within stated time period. Identify: • Outcome (O) • Process (P) • Structure (S)	Briefly describes each kind of service designed to achieve the objective, frequency, numbers to be reached, etc..	Briefly lists how achievement of the objective will be measured (e.g., record audit, client survey, activity log, pre-/post-test results).

Append
  Budget
  Schedules

VI. SUMMARY OF PROGRAM EVALUATION AND REPORTING SYSTEM (monthly, quarterly, annually)

regulations or guidelines from the funding agencies or from the agency administration. If no format is required, it may be developed by the planning group to suit its own style. The format is less important than the fact that there is a written plan. A format that includes the common elements of a program plan is displayed in Exhibit 14-3 and may suggest a starting point for the planner not provided with other guidelines. Most important is that the plan be sequenced in logical order and be brief, clear, and written in words that will be understood by the public and the media, as well as by nutrition, health, and planning professionals. Professional or scientific jargon, government gobbledygook, and acronyms that are not defined should be avoided.

The planning process focuses the thinking of influential stakeholders and administrators on the role of nutrition in addressing critical community health problems. It makes nutrition interventions tangible and visible. It justifies the funds allocated to nutrition services. The written plan provides a frame of reference for observable action and feedback of results. As a continuous, evolving process, the plan maintains a sense of direction against which progress can be measured. It must be continuously studied and revised, periodically going through the steps in the planning model.

ISSUES TO DEBATE

- Who are the most important stakeholders to involve in developing the nutrition service plan?
- How are priorities selected considering community nutrition needs versus offering services for which there are readily available funding sources?
- What approaches can be made to community agencies that had been getting services at no cost to suggest that they contract for services?
- What evaluation strategies can be designed to collect the most meaningful data without generating excessive paperwork?
- How can time for planning be justified when there are many pressures to provide services?

BIBLIOGRAPHY

American Public Health Association. *Nutrition Practices. A Guide for Public Health Administrators*. New York: American Public Health Association, 1955.

DeFriese, G.H., ed. "Goal-Oriented Evaluation as a Program Management Tool." *Baseline* 1 (May 1983): 4.

Gup, B.E. "Begin Strategic Planning by Asking Three Questions." *Managerial Planning* (November–December 1979): 28–31.

Herzog, W. Lecture notes. Department of Health Policy and Administration, School of Public Health, University of North Carolina, Chapel Hill.

Kasten, M.L. "Why and How of Planning." *Managerial Planning* (July–August 1979): 33–35.

Lopez, L. "Evaluating the Evidence for Nutrition Interventions: Two Algorithms." *Journal of The American Dietetic Association* 86, no. 8 (August 1986): 1055–58.

Spain, Carol; Eastman, Eileen; and Kizer, Kenneth W. "Model Standards Impact on Local Health Department Performance in California." *American Journal of Public Health* 79, no. 8 (August 1989): 969–74.

Speigel, A.D., and Hyman, H.H. *Basic Health Planning Methods*. Rockville, Md.: Aspen Publishers, Inc., 1978.

Steiner, G. *Strategic Planning: What Every Manager Must Know: A Step-by-Step Guide*. New York: The Free Press, 1979.

U.S. Department of Health, Education, and Welfare. *Guide for Developing Nutrition Services in Community Health Programs*. Rockville, Md.: Public Health Service, 1978.

chapter 15

Marketing Nutrition Programs and Services

Diane R. Kerwin

READER OBJECTIVES

- Compare and contrast social marketing with business marketing.
- Discuss types of market research and how these can be used in preparing a plan for a public health nutrition program.
- List and define the four Ps of marketing.
- Discuss the ethics of marketing.

DEFINING MARKETING

Marketing has come into vogue to describe many activities related to the field of communication. Slick television advertisements for carbonated beverages, glossy free-standing inserts (FSIs) in Sunday newspapers offering free merchandise in return for food product labels, highway billboards advertising weight-control products, and public speaking engagements by celebrities sponsored by food manufacturers are examples of marketing tactics. However, marketing consists of much more than these tactics. Health care professionals and organizations now realize the value of marketing to reach their desired objectives. The nutritionist must understand marketing and use its concepts to develop and implement an effective nutrition program plan.

Marketing is defined as satisfying the needs of the consumer through a product or service. It includes everything associated with creating, delivering, and finally consuming the product or service.[1] Marketing starts with the consumer's actual or perceived wants and needs, not with the product or service.

297

BUSINESS MARKETING VERSUS SOCIAL MARKETING

When people buy products or services, they are really purchasing satisfaction. Their definition of marketing applies to business marketing in which an exchange of goods or services occurs between a buyer and a seller. Business marketing is also known as commercial, conventional, or traditional marketing. Is there a role for business-type marketing in situations in which consumers are not satisfying their own needs, but in which society or a health or human service agency believes that behavioral changes are in the consumers' best interests? Many health professionals believe that there is an important role for so-called social marketing.[2]

In the early days of television, this question was asked: "Why can't you sell brotherhood and rational thinking like you sell soap?"[3] The nutritionist could ask: "Why can't we sell good nutrition like food manufacturers sell cereal?" These questions were answered in 1971 when the term *social marketing* was introduced.[4]

Social marketing is defined as "the design, implementation, and control of programs calculated to influence the acceptability of social ideas and involving considerations of product planning, pricing, communication, distribution, and marketing research."[5] This definition describes the activities of a nutritionist who designs, implements, and controls programs to change eating behavior. Business marketing focuses on fulfilling customers' needs and desires. Social marketing focuses on changing personal or social behaviors for the benefit of the public, even when the public neither recognizes their need nor desires the change.

Social marketing most often is used to accomplish three objectives.

1. disseminate new data and information on practices to individuals
2. offset the negative effects of a practice or promotional effort by another organization or group
3. motivate people to move from intention to action[6]

Some examples of ways nutritionists might use social marketing in a program plan are

- to inform the public about the role of dietary saturated fats and cholesterol in the prevention of heart disease
- to offset the promotion of megavitamin supplements
- to motivate clients to take control of their weight

Use of social marketing in the development of a nutrition program plan requires

- adequate resources
- strong support from the sponsoring agency's administrators and community leaders
- marketing skills
- clear authority to make the necessary marketing decisions and implement them in a timely fashion[7]

All of these conditions must be present if a program is to succeed.

The first step in developing a nutrition program plan is to identify the problem or opportunity. Chapters 3 and 4 review the steps in assessing community nutrition needs and setting priorities for satisfying these needs. This community assessment includes efforts to identify the target consumer group's values, attitudes, habits, or customs as they relate to the assessed need. This can be done through market research. Goals and objectives for the nutrition program are then determined (Chapter 14).

MARKET RESEARCH

Market research uses primary data and secondary data, both of which are also used in community assessment for the nutrition program plan (see Chapters 3, 4, and 16).

Primary Data

Information gathered, recorded, and used for the first time is primary data. Common techniques for gathering primary data include

- observations
- personal or telephone interviews
- focus groups
- client panels
- mail surveys
- questionnaires

Primary data are used more frequently than secondary data to develop strategies and tactics specific to the targeted population and, for this reason, are frequently used in social marketing. Techniques to collect primary data focus on local needs, trends, and behaviors. A client questionnaire can provide a tremendous amount of information useful in identifying clients' awareness and knowledge of a specific nutrition issue.

Secondary Data

Secondary data are secondhand bits of information gathered by other agencies, organizations, and individuals. Such data can be internal (found within one's own organization) or external (obtained from outside sources). Examples of internal data include medical records, clinic attendance records, correspondence, and the log of telephone requests for services. External sources of available data are federal, state, and local governmental or university publications and reports, professional journals, trade association publications, and the wealth of information found in agency, public, and university libraries.

Secondary data are generally the easiest and least expensive sources of information to use. They provide the program planner with an idea of directions and trends. However, they may not be relevant to assessing the local situation or to determining the targeted population's specific needs and behaviors. Secondary data are used as the basis for the community nutrition assessment discussed in Chapters 3, 4, and 16.

Market Segmentation

The objectives in the community nutrition plan will usually specify the overall audience or market for nutrition services—women of childbearing age, schoolchildren, adults with diabetes, athletes, or other population groups. Within the broad market, there are subgroups or segments with particular characteristics or consumer profiles that are similar and with needs that can be met through social marketing. Exhibit 15-1 reviews major market segmentation categories. Primary data within each category can be collected by marketing research techniques.

The specific data to collect depend on the objectives of the nutrition program and how narrowly or specifically targeted the audience needs to be. For example, a process objective of a program of prenatal nutrition education classes could be to increase awareness about this service among pregnant women in a city. Data on age, education, residence, employment, media use, and sources of prenatal care for pregnant women in the community may be helpful. Other data such as sources of prenatal nutrition information or willingness to use the service could also be collected. If the marketing objective is to increase awareness of nutrition classes for family planning patients attending a specific public health center, residence and employment data may not be needed because the women are already enrolled in the health center and the data are available.

Exhibit 15-1 Market Segmentation Categories

Demographic	Geographic	Psychographic	Consumer-Behavioral
Age	Country	Leader or follower	Rate of usage
Sex	Region	High or low achiever	Benefits sought:
Income	State	Extrovert or introvert	Economy
Occupation	Size of population	Compulsive or placid	Reliability
Religion	Climate	Independent or dependent	Comfort
Race	Density of population	Conservative or liberal	Health
Education		Dominant or submissive	Safety
Social class			Method of usage
			Frequency of usage

Source: The Basic Book of Business by J.R. Klug, p. 152, Van Nostrand Reinhold, © 1977.

The advantage of market segmentation is that social marketing strategies and tactics can be planned for the specific consumer profile. Targeting the group enhances program cost effectiveness and success.

THE SOCIAL MARKETING MIX

The components of a business marketing plan are known as the marketing mix, or the four Ps of marketing: (1) product, (2) place, (3) price, and (4) promotion.[8] These components are also used in the social marketing plan. The marketing mix can fit into the overall nutrition program plan. The framework for developing a marketing plan, as shown in Figure 15-1, is quite similar to that used in preparing a nutrition program plan.

Product

Unlike the product of most businesses, the product in public health nutrition programs is not always tangible. It can be a service such as nutrition information dissemination, diet counseling, food service consultation, or food preparation demonstrations. The product deals with awareness, knowledge, or motivation. Another difference between business and social marketing is product use. In social marketing, the product is often a service that is provided to the consumer on an involuntary basis and is not viewed by the client as a need. For example, all mothers attending a child health clinic may be referred to the nutritionist as a matter of clinic policy and not because they want the service. They may be aware of the nutritional needs of their children but may not see the personal benefit of seeking help. The product, child nutrition counseling services, must be defined in a way to bring about a change or action that is acceptable to the consumer. An example of a product that has gained consumer acceptance is an adolescent weight-control program using behavior modification techniques.

Designing the Product

Factors to consider in designing the nutrition program's product include

- branding or naming
- packaging
- differentiating the product from others in the market
- considering the life or length of usefulness

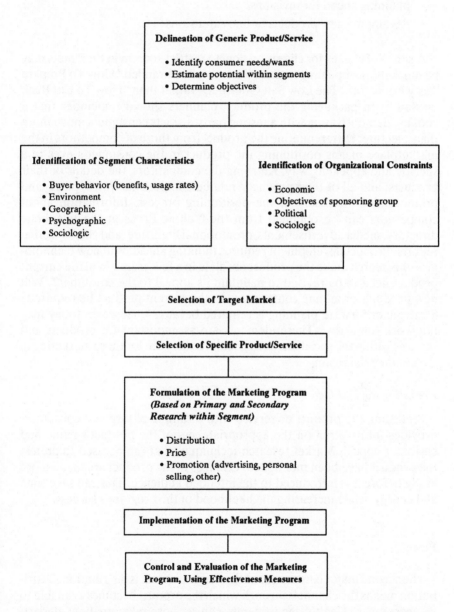

Figure 15-1 A Framework for Marketing Program Development. *Source*: Adapted with permission of the author from *Marketing Principles: The Marketing Process* by B.M. Enis, p. 261, Goodyear Publishing Company, © 1977.

- planning ahead for revisions
- developing new products or line extensions

A series of classes for clients on how to restrict sodium in their diets may be much more appealing to them if it is titled or branded "How To Prepare Tasty Foods" or "The Low Salt Gourmet," rather than "How To Cut Back on Salt." In packaging the product, planners should remember that a cooking demonstration with a tasting party attracts consumers much more than a lecture. Differentiating the product from those of competitors in the marketplace means positioning the product in the consumer's eyes in a specific and appealing way. Knowing the competitors, the details of their products, and all of their products' related components (price, place, and promotion) is necessary in the positioning process. Information about competitors can be obtained from the Yellow Pages in the telephone directory, media advertisements, promotional literature, and clients' verbal reports. Product development requires thinking ahead. Will new technologies or research make the product obsolete in a few years? Will the current product need to be revised to maintain its appeal to the consumer? Will new products or adding components to the current product be required? Strategic or forward planning is required because what works today may not work tomorrow. These elements are as important for products and services within the social marketing realm as they are for those marketing in the commercial realm.

Pretesting the Product

Pretesting the product or service with a sample of targeted consumers provides information on the appropriateness of the product's name and customer appeal. Market research techniques that can be used to pretest the product have been mentioned. Changes in the product are made more easily before it is introduced to the intended audience. This can save time and energy, while increasing the likelihood of the program's success.

Place

The second major component of the marketing mix is distribution. Distribution means the channels through which the product becomes available to the consumer. Health departments, clinics, hospital outpatient departments, child day care centers, congregate meal sites, and other similar facilities have traditionally served as distribution channels for nutrition programs and services. Because distribution and promotion are so closely related in the marketing plan, alternative channels might be investigated once promotional tactics are set. For example, if awareness of nutrition services for weight control is the objective of the nutrition plan, channels of distribution could include local broadcast media or public forums at community centers. Schools, libraries, recreation centers, places of worship, work sites, and meeting rooms at shopping malls might be explored as possible sites. Place should take into account the convenience of the product or service to the consumer and where the consumer can obtain it most readily. Access to parking, handicapped parking, and ancillary or related services should be considered. Selection of the most appropriate site is a part of the second P of marketing: place.

Price

Price is the third component in both business and social marketing, but its purposes differ in the two contexts. A business marketer will set a profitable price for a product that is acceptable to both consumers and the business. The business marketer must meet the needs of consumers, but must also satisfy the financial commitments to employees, management, and shareholders. The social marketer is not interested in financial gain. The emphasis is on the value to society in terms of safety, health, or other social issues, rather than cost.

Three different pricing strategies are used in social marketing: (1) cost recovery, (2) market incentives, and (3) market disincentives.[9]

Cost Recovery

Because many public health nutrition programs receive grants, foundation funds, or federal, state, or local government financial support, a price may not need to be set for the product. However, a sliding scale fee for service based on ability to pay may be desirable to recover a portion of the costs and to obtain funds to expand services. The solicitation of donations could also be considered a cost recovery strategy.

Market Incentive

Market incentives are used to stimulate the adoption of a product. Offering a product at a price below current costs, at a price lower than that of a competitor, or at no cost reflects this pricing strategy. If the objective of a sliding scale fee-for-service weight-control program is to increase the number of enrollees, the incentive could be $10 off the set price. The "buy-one-get-one-free" approach appeals to many consumers.

Market Disincentives

Pricing can sometimes be used to discourage consumers from using a product. High taxes on cigarettes and liquor are examples of attempts by the government to discourage their use. An example of a market disincentive for a nutrition program might be to price soft drinks higher than fruit juices in vending machines at meal program sites or work site cafeterias.

Promotion

The fourth P in the marketing mix, promotion, usually is the first that comes to mind when thinking of marketing. Promotion is the communications component of marketing. It identifies the specific tactics or activities needed to create awareness, provide knowledge, and motivate the consumer to action. Promotion includes advertising, personal selling, public relations, and consumer incentives. The combination of these various tactics promotes social as well as business marketing plans. The goal of promotion is to move the consumer through the stages from unawareness to action, as shown in Figure 15-2.

Advertising

Advertising is just one piece of a promotion. Advertising is any paid form of mass presentation and promotion of ideas, goods, or services by an identified sponsor.[10] Advertising is paid publicity. In social marketing, advertising differs from commercial or business advertising in the following ways: (1) the product is usually a social cause or service, (2) the advertiser is not a commercial enterprise, and (3) the advertiser's motivation is to benefit others, rather than commercial benefit to the advertiser.[11] These characteristics usually exist in a public health nutrition program.

Advertising is not a one-time activity. It must be ongoing in a planned series of activities known as an advertising campaign. To enhance the effectiveness of the promotion, the purpose of the campaign must be clear. The media used for advertising include

* television
* radio
* newspapers
* magazines
* brochures
* billboards

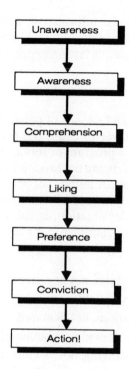

Figure 15-2 Consumer Stages in Product Promotion. *Source*: Reprinted from "A Model for Predictive Measurements of Advertising Effectiveness" by R.J. Lavidge and G.A. Steiner, *Journal of Marketing*, Vol. 25, p. 59, with permission of American Marketing Association, © October 1961.

- posters
- bumper stickers
- buttons
- tee shirts

The selection of advertising media depends on local time, money, and material resources. It should be based on how to achieve the greatest impact on the target audience in terms of

- number of people exposed to the advertisement
- frequency or number of times the message is seen or heard

Advertising must always be informative, accurate, tasteful, clear, and valid. It can be entertaining, amusing, or serious, but it must always be competitive and leave a pleasing lasting impression on the consumer.

Personal Selling

Salesmanship is the art and science of persuading another person to do something when direct power to cause the action does not exist.[12] Any direct contact to promote a program or service to a consumer or group of consumers is selling. Contacts can be through letters, telephone calls, client encounters, or group classes. A number of personal selling situations have been described as population-based interventions in Chapter 18. In any buyer-seller or user-provider situation, establishing and maintaining warm relationships are essential. Seller/provider actions that promote good relationships include

- initiating positive contacts, not negative situations
- being reliable, not unavailable
- making recommendations, not demands
- using candid, not accommodative language
- using "we" problem-solving, not "I want" language
- using easily understood terms or local jargon, not long, scientific explanations
- showing respect and concern, not disdain, hostility, or indifference
- being courteous, not abrupt
- being attentive, not interruptive

Public Relations

Public relations is free publicity and an image builder for a service, idea, or individual. It can stimulate the demand for a product. Public relations is a valuable promotional tool in social marketing because it is free; air time and print space are provided as a public or community service. Although public relations activities involve time and materials, these can be donated by local companies, the media, or individuals.

The paying advertiser controls the message and the time in which the message is received by the customer. Public service channels usually do not allow such controls. Press releases, media interviews, and articles can and usually are edited by the publisher or producer. Nevertheless, public relations can be effective in promotion. Planned activities could include sponsorship of a special community event such as a fun-run, cosponsorship of a health fair with another group such as the local diabetes association, press briefings or conferences on new nutrition research findings, public speaking engagements with community groups, and a visit to the office of a local legislator. Many of the population-based interventions addressed in Chapter 18 are public relations.

Public service announcements (PSAs) are commonly used in social marketing promotions. Because PSAs are often aired late at night or during the early morning hours, they have been referred to jokingly as "People Sound Asleep."[13] Good networking with local television and radio stations may help to obtain more prime viewing or listening times for PSAs and other public relations messages. Radio stations may be more willing than television stations to provide prime time.

The image-building aspect of public relations also deals with the environment in which services or products are delivered. Attractive and comfortable client waiting rooms, colorful and current educational materials, friendly and caring professional staff, and convenient locations project a powerful positive message to the consumer about the importance of the program or service.

Other Promotional Tools

In addition to advertising, personal selling, and public relations, sales promotional tools that can be included in a nutrition program plan include

- food demonstrations and tasting parties at schools, places of worship, work sites, service club meeting sites, congregate meal sites, supermarkets, and malls
- booths and exhibits at malls, libraries, recreation centers, and fairs
- cooking contests with prizes for recipes that demonstrate health-promoting foods
- public recognition programs in cooperation with the media for those who achieve weight-control successes
- nutrition poster contests for children through their schools
- health promotion and food fairs in parks, malls, or recreation centers
- promotion of National Nutrition Month with a multimedia campaign of community activities

The purpose of sales promotion is to support, supplement, reinforce, or complement the other promotional tactics. Sales promotion cannot exist in a vacuum, but must be integrated into the overall plan.

Integration of the Marketing Mix into the Nutrition Program Plan

"People change their food habits when two prerequisites are satisfied. First, the individual believes that such a change will help him toward some personally desired goal: weight loss, better health, more physical attractiveness, etc. Second, the mechanism of the change process must be uncomplicated and easily activated."[14]

Considering each of the four Ps of marketing helps develop an action-oriented and effective nutrition program plan. A quality product offered in a convenient place at an economical price and promoted with an appealing message will be successful.

MARKETING ETHICS

It has been said that "when judging social marketing from an ethical standpoint, it appears to be difficult to separate the ethics of applying marketing techniques to social ideas and programs from the ethics of the ideas themselves."[15] The Standards of Professional Responsibility of The American Dietetic Association,[16] as discussed in Chapter 24, should guide the conduct of the nutritionist.

Just as the business marketer can be accused of selling or promoting a product in an unethical way, so can the social marketer who misuses marketing tools to compound a social abuse or manipulate public opinion. Social marketing is meant to inform, educate, or bring about a change in behavior that will improve health or the quality of consumer and community life. It differs from business marketing, which responds to needs and wants of consumers who are pursuing their own self-interests. Regardless, any marketer must understand ethics and the social consequences of any marketing action.

Nutritionists can learn to think and plan like marketers. They must listen to and seek out the nutrition wants and needs of the public and then create, develop, or redesign services and programs to meet these wants and needs. The targeting of services to a specific population group is critical. The business marketer's approach to planning and using market research techniques, product concepts, distribution channels, pricing strategies, and promotional tactics can be successfully applied to the nutrition program planning process.

ISSUES TO DEBATE

- How can a nutritionist promote healthful eating practices in a community where these recommendations are contrary to well-entrenched regional or ethnic food habits?

- How can and should a tax-supported public health agency market a weight-management program that competes with for-profit weight-loss programs?
- What pricing strategies are appropriate for a public health agency offering a new nutrition service directed to middle- and upper-income taxpayers?
- How can a public health agency respond to the results of a satisfaction survey that indicate consumers' frustration with the excessive waiting time and hours lost from work required to obtain health and nutrition services?

NOTES

1. John R. Klug, *The Basic Book of Business* (Boston: Cahners Books International, Inc., 1977), 145.

2. G.D. Wiebe, "Merchandising Commodities of Citizenship on Television," *Public Opinion Quarterly* 15 (Winter 1951): 679.

3. Ibid.

4. Philip Kotler and Gerald Zaltman, "Social Marketing: An Approach to Planned Social Change," *Journal of Marketing* 35 (1971): 5.

5. Ibid.

6. Karen F.A. Fox and Philip Kotler, "The Marketing of Social Causes: The First 10 Years," *Journal of Marketing* 44 (1980): 26–27.

7. Population Information Program, "Social Marketing: Does It Work?" *Population Reports* Series J, no. 21 (January 1980): J394.

8. Edmund J. McCarthy, *Basic Marketing: A Managerial Approach* (Homewood, Ill.: Richard D. Irwin, 1968), 32.

9. M. Muskkat, Jr., "Implementing Public Plans: The Case for Social Marketing," *Long Range Planning* 13 (August 1980): 27.

10. Ralph S. Alexander and the Committee on Definitions of the American Marketing Association, *Marketing Definitions: A Glossary of Marketing Terms* (Chicago: American Marketing Association, 1963), 9.

11. Keith Crosier, "The Advertising Dimension of 'Social Marketing,'" *Advertising* (Autumn 1978): 33.

12. Fredrick A. Russell, Frank H. Beach, and Richard H. Buskirk, *Textbook of Salesmanship* (New York: McGraw-Hill Book Co., 1974), 3.

13. Richard K. Manoff, "Marketing Not Society's Enemy," *Advertising Age*, 15 July 1985, 18.

14. Ann W. Sorenson and R. Gaurth Hanson, "Index of Food Quality," *Journal of Nutrition Education* 7 (1972): 53.

15. Gene R. Laczniak, Robert F. Lusch, and Patrick E. Murphy, "Social Marketing: Its Ethical Dimensions," *Journal of Marketing* 43 (Spring 1979): 30.

16. The American Dietetic Association, *Standards of Professional Responsibility* (Chicago: The American Dietetic Association, 1985).

chapter **16**

Managing Data

Deborah A. Spicer and Mildred Kaufman

READER OBJECTIVES

- List purposes for which data are needed by nutrition program managers.
- Compare and contrast the uses of the local, state, and national data bases available for public health nutrition program management.
- Calculate local prevalence approximations for nutrition-related health problems using a synthetic estimate of national data.
- List the steps in developing a new data collection, analysis, and reporting system.

DATA NEEDS

Webster's *Ninth New Collegiate Dictionary* defines data as factual information, including statistics which are used as a basis for reasoning, discussion, or calculation. Statistics is the branch of mathematics that deals with the collection, analysis, interpretation, and presentation of numerical data. Using statistics makes it possible to measure the size of need, degree of achievement, and costs in relation to accomplishment. The comparative ease of collecting statistics in this computer age can lead to an overload of numbers which, to be useful, must be aggregated, analyzed, interpreted, and reported. Key data are needed for the effective management of a public health nutrition program in order to

- describe and measure the size of the populations at risk for nutrition-related and diet-related health problems

- compare and contrast the nutritional health status of the people in the jurisdiction with populations in similar jurisdictional areas and in the state, the region, and the nation
- plan programs and allocate resources to target at-risk populations in the community
- assess whether the resources invested in interventions are achieving the outcomes anticipated
- evaluate intervention results against published norms, standards, or objectives

In deciding what data to collect for the nutrition program, the critical questions are the following:

- For what purposes will quantitative data be more convincing than descriptive or anecdotal data are?
- What is the minimum set of data needed for each purpose?
- In what form will the information be most useful?
- Who else in the agency is or may be planning to collect the same or related information? Is it possible to piggyback or collaborate?
- What statistical expertise is available?
- What resources will be required to obtain the needed information? Consultants? Personnel? Computer or computer time?

Data are needed in several stages of program planning: in carrying out the community assessment (see Chapters 3 and 4), in setting objectives for the plan, and in evaluating the program (see Chapter 14). The community assessment involves collecting and analyzing data on the health and nutrition needs of the population. Using data to measure the size of need is important in order to select priorities from among competing nutrition concerns, identify high-risk areas or population groups for targeting services, and determine the budget needed to design an intervention for a particular nutrition problem. In evaluation, data are needed to determine the coverage of the program or services (the percentage of the need that is being met) and the success of the interventions and to find out whether the program is having the desired impact on the population.

Data are also required in the ongoing management of a program to track the delivery of services with the flow of dollars and personnel time. Management information systems (MIS) are developed for guidance in monitoring money and personnel. (See Chapter 17.)

COMMUNITY ASSESSMENT DATA

The different purposes for using statistics determine the potential sources and suggest the rigor needed in their collection and analysis. For example, community assessment is a "quick and dirty" measurement. It uses key indicators to broadly characterize the population. For community assessment, a large amount of readily available secondary data from published sources can be used to fill in the blanks in Exhibits 3-2 and 3-3 in Chapter 3. These data provide a "sense of the community," using approximate numbers which must be acknowledged in the written assessment as "best estimates."

Demographic Characteristics

For community assessment, it is important to profile the community's population, knowing its total numbers and how they break out by age, gender, income, education, and ethnicity. These numbers are readily available from U.S. census publications. Public and university libraries and state and local health agency and planning offices usually have these documents and staff who can assist in their use.

Census data are available for state, county, and subcounty areas (census tracts or minor civil divisions). A disadvantage is that census statistics are updated only every ten years. However, statisticians (in a county planning office, state demographer's office, or state data center) have methods for estimating characteristics of the population as the years progress through the decade. One of the most important risk factors for poor nutrition is poverty, and the census provides a wealth of information on the percentages of people with incomes at various percentages of the poverty index by age, ethnicity, gender, and household composition.

Another indicator for nutrition-related health problems is education, usually stated in terms of grades adults have completed in school and also enumerated in census data. Census data also describe the condition of local housing, including homes without indoor water supplies, electrification, and cooking equipment.

Health Indicators

Vital statistics data, as discussed in Chapter 3, are the most readily accessible local data. Information on births and deaths recorded at the county level are summarized, reported, and published annually by the city or county and state health departments and the National Center for Health

Statistics. Information on causes of all infant deaths, infant birth weights, and births by age of mothers certainly say something about the needs for nutrition services in maternal and child health. Numbers of deaths (mortality) due to heart disease, stroke, cancer, and diabetes provide information on the potential magnitude of diet-related diseases for adult health promotion.

Another source of data on diet-related diagnostic categories are hospital discharge data. Some states have comprehensive hospital reporting systems which collect data on every person admitted to and discharged from each hospital. Basic demographic information is often available on these individuals, along with their primary diagnoses (morbidity). Thus, one could determine the number of residents of a locality who were discharged from a hospital with various diagnoses such as coronary heart disease, diabetes, or osteoporosis. Local or state health department statisticians or statistical clerks can assist in obtaining such data.

National Nutrition Monitoring System

The most complete data on food intakes, nutrition, and health problems are from the national surveys conducted by federal agencies. The National Health and Nutrition Examination Survey (NHANES) and the National Food Consumption Survey (NFCS) contain specific nutrition data and are conducted on a periodic schedule. Other surveys such as the National Health Interview Survey (NHIS), the Survey of Income and Program Participation (SIPP), and the Consumer Expenditure Survey also collect and report information useful for background for the community assessment. (See Appendix H for sources of data from national studies.) *Nutrition Monitoring in the United States: The Directory of Federal Nutrition Monitoring Activities* briefly describes each of the federal surveys that contribute to the national nutrition monitoring data base. It also gives ordering and price information for those who would like to order print copies or computer data sets.[1] The descriptions and findings of the several national nutrition monitoring surveys are also presented in published reports of the U.S. Department of Health and Human Services (DHHS) and the U.S. Department of Agriculture (USDA).[2]

National Health and Nutrition Examination Survey

The NHANES surveys are conducted by DHHS. NHANES I was carried out in 1971–1974, NHANES II in 1976–1980, and NHANES III was begun in 1988. NHANES collects extensive health and nutrition information from a national probability (representative) sample of civilian, noninstitutionalized residents of the United States. Participants receive a complete physical exam, undergo a battery of biochemical tests and anthropometric measurements, respond to an extensive health interview, and report their dietary intake.

NHANES III, which began to collect data in late 1988, is being conducted over two three-year cycles. Data from the first cycle, information from 15,000 people in 44 locations throughout the country, will be completed by 1991. Information from this cycle will be available in 1992. The second similar-sized cycle will be conducted from 1992 to 1994. Data from each cycle will be able to stand alone, but combining data from both cycles will enable better estimates to be made of the health and nutritional status of minority groups.

Dietary data are collected through a 24-hour food intake recall and a food frequency. Follow-up 24-hour recalls by phone are planned for people over age 60 to obtain a better estimate of their usual dietary intake. Additional information will be collected on respondents' use of nutrient supplements and their use of special diets.

Reports are published periodically in *Vital and Health Statistics, Series 11*. Numerous articles using NHANES data are published in health and nutrition journals.

Synthetic Estimates from NHANES Data for State or Local Planning

The national monitoring surveys are designed using probability samples representative of the national population, but not representative of states or localities. However, data from NHANES can be used to make synthetic estimates of nutrition and health problems among smaller groups of people. Data are presented by age, gender, race, and income groups, the usual factors that significantly affect nutritional status or dietary habits. Assuming that people of similar age, gender, race, and income have common characteristics regardless of where they live, the national estimates can be applied to local population data to arrive at a reasonable estimate of the number of persons in the local jurisdiction who might be expected to have each specific nutritional problem. When no local data are available, Table 16-1 demonstrates how synthetic estimates are calculated, adjusting the national data for age, gender, and race to suggest the possible number of persons in a selected local population who might have the problem.

Hispanic HANES

Because NHANES I and II samples did not include a sufficient number of Hispanics to allow for estimates of their unique health and nutrition

Table 16-1 Use of NHANES Data To Produce a Synthetic Estimate; Sample Calculation of the Expected Number of Females Age 20–74 in a Local Area Who Might Be Overweight

	A National percentage overweight (Source: NHANES II)	B Population in area in this age/ sex/ethnic group (Source: U.S. census data)	C Estimated number overweight in this group in area (Source: [AxB]/100)
White Females			
Age			
20–24	9.6	1000	*96*
25–34	17.9	2000	*358*
35–44	24.8	2000	*496*
45–54	29.9	1500	*449*
55–64	34.8	1000	*348*
65–74	36.5	500	*183*
Black Females			
Age			
20–24	23.7	1000	*237*
25–34	33.5	2500	*838*
35–44	40.8	2000	*816*
45–54	61.2	1500	*918*
55–64	59.4	500	*297*
65–74	60.8	200	*122*
TOTALS	27.1%	15,700	*5,158*
Estimated percentage overweight in area (Total C/Total B)			*33*

characterisics, a separate Hispanic HANES (HHANES) was conducted from 1982 to 1984. The same data were collected from a probability sample of civilian, noninstitutionalized Hispanics in three areas of the United States: Puerto Ricans in New York City, Mexican-Americans in the Southwest, and Cuban-Americans in Dade County, Florida. Data from this survey are also available in published reports from DHHS and in journal articles. These data will be useful in geographic areas with growing Hispanic populations.

National Food Consumption Surveys

Since 1936–1937, this series of surveys has been conducted about every ten years by the USDA. The most recent survey was conducted in 1987–1988. Data are collected from a national probability sample of households throughout the 48 contiguous states. In addition to the basic sample, there is a separate low-income sample.

Detailed information about food purchases and methods of preparation is collected from the household member who usually prepares the food. A 24-hour recall is obtained, along with a two-day diet record for each household member. The survey also collects data on the amount, price, and form of food coming into the household and used during a one-week period. Published reports include information on the nutrient content of the diets of individual household members, as well as on the proportion of defined age-gender groups consuming items from designated food groups. Information is presented on the economic and nutritional value of foods eaten away from home. Reports are available from the National Technical Information Service. As with the NHANES data, researchers publish journal articles using data from the NFCS.

Continuing Survey of Food Intakes by Individuals

In 1965, the USDA began to conduct the Continuing Survey of Food Intakes by Individuals (CSFII), a smaller annual survey of individual food consumption intended to provide dietary data more frequently. In 1985 and 1986, information was collected from three separate representative samples: women 19 to 50 of all incomes and their children, low-income women 19 to 50 and their children, and men 19 to 50 at all income levels. Individuals contacted for the CSFII were asked to provide six separated days of dietary data over a one-year period. Reports have been published for each sample, providing information on food eaten and its nutrient composition by age, gender, race, and income level. After completion of the full NFCS in 1988, the CSFII continued in 1989. Beginning in 1989, the survey began collecting information from a sample population representing all ages of both men and women, along with a separate low-income sample.

National Health Interview Survey

This survey is conducted annually by the National Center for Health Statistics. Each year a core questionnaire is administered to a representative sample of the U.S. population, asking them questions about their health status, use of health services, and a variety of other health-related issues. Each year a different supplement is added to the core questionnaire. The most recent supplements are listed in Exhibit 16-1.

Exhibit 16-1 National Health Interview Survey Supplements, 1982–1989

1982	Preventive Care Health Insurance
1983	Alcohol and Health Practices Doctor Services Dental Care Health Insurance
1984	Health Insurance Aging
1985	Health Promotion and Disease Prevention
1986	Health Insurance Dental Health Functional Limitations Longest Job Vitamins and Minerals Longitudinal Study of Aging
1987	AIDS Cancer Control Adoption
1988	AIDS Medical Devices and Implants Child Health Alcohol Occupational Safety and Health
1989	Health Insurance Adult Immunization Mental Health Dental and Oral Facial Pain Diabetes Digestive Disorders

Consumer Expenditure Survey

This is an annual survey conducted by the Bureau of Labor Statistics to collect information on all household expenditures. Results of this survey can be used to estimate what portion of the household budget is spent on food, on eating away from home, etc. Reports are produced annually.

Survey of Income and Program Participation

This survey, conducted by the Census Bureau, follows a sample of people for 2 1/2 years and measures changes in their family incomes and their use of the various benefit programs. Special supplements collect information on such topics as pension coverage, disability, and child care arrangements. A catalog of reports can be obtained from the Census Bureau.

Local Program Reports

Data to use to complete Exhibit 3-4 in Chapter 3 are collected from the reported statistics of the various food, nutrition, and health programs serving the population. Public programs generally are required to account for their funds and report the numbers of participants on a regular schedule. Whether reports of local or state programs are published or unpublished, they are public information and should be available on request. It is important to determine whether data represent an unduplicated count of the number of individuals or households served or the number of encounters. When encounters are reported, each participant may be counted several times as he or she returns for repeat or continuing services.

Comparing the number of people participating in the program with the estimated number of people eligible or at risk in the community suggests the number or percentage of the population that has met, undermet, or unmet needs for services. For example:

How well is the WIC program reaching the low-income pregnant women in the community who need it?

Calculate:

| number of births in community in 1990 | × | % of women between 15 & 50 with income below 185% poverty | = | Estimated # of women eligible for WIC by virtue of income in 1990 |

$$\frac{\text{Number of pregnant women (unduplicated count) served by WIC in 1990}}{\text{Estimated \# of women eligible for WIC by virtue of income in 1990}} = \begin{array}{l}\text{\% of income-eligible}\\ \text{pregnant women served}\\ \text{by WIC program in the}\\ \text{community in 1990}\end{array}$$

This same method of estimating need can be applied to elderly meal, food stamp, Head Start, health screening, and other programs.

PROGRAM MANAGEMENT DATA

Program plans state measurable objectives. Note from Chapter 14, Figure 14-3, that the structure of an objective raises the questions for which data must be collected to determine if the objective is being met.

* Action to be taken—What will be done?
* Target population—Who will benefit?
* Measure—How much will be achieved?
* Deadline—By when will it be done?
* Resources—What will be required?

These questions specify the data needed to measure achievement of the program objectives. For example, assume that the following program objective has been established: "By 6/30/2000, 75 percent of new mothers served in health agency clinics will breast-feed their infants at hospital discharge, and 50 percent will continue to breast-feed their babies for five months." A breast-feeding initiative has been implemented in five of the agency's satellite clinics. The key questions are these.

* What percentage of mothers seen in each of the five health agency clinics are breast-feeding
  —at hospital discharge?
  —at three months?
  —at five months?

Through drafting dummy tables (Exhibit 16-2) the data needed are displayed, and the information to be collected is limited. By specifying the data elements required from which population and from what clinics at what times, it is possible to limit data collection to that which is needed and will be used to answer the questions.

As in this example, many program plan objectives are addressed to agency clientele, so the source information can be obtained from client health records. Many client information systems depend on client record audits or a computerized system for continually collecting and reporting client data through a client information or surveillance system.

Exhibit 16-2 Dummy Table—Mothers Breast-feeding in Public Health Agency Clinics at Hospital Discharge and at Three Months and Five Months Postpartum

Health Agency Clinics	Total Number of Mothers of Infants 0 to 5 Months	Mothers Breast-feeding					
		At Hospital Discharge		3 Months Postpartum		5 Months Postpartum	
		N	%	N	%	N	%
Clinic A							
Clinic B							
Clinic C							
Clinic D							
Clinic E							

State Health Services Client Information Systems

Several state health agencies have designed and implemented computerized health services information systems (HSIS) or client information systems (CIS) to routinely collect and report data on clients receiving state and local health agency services. These systems may collect information on all clients receiving agency services, or they may be limited to those participating in one or more categorical programs, such as primary care, women's health, family planning, prenatal, child health, or WIC clinics. Computerized programs are used to collect demographic data and health outcome information and to maintain a continuing record of encounters when care services are provided. Data routinely collected include height, weight, hemoglobin or hematocrit, and blood pressure. Exhibits 16-3 and 16-4 show the computer screens for entry of data on maternal health and pregnancy outcomes in North Carolina's HSIS. Note that this system can track maternal weight gain, infant birth weight and gestational age, WIC food received, and nutrition counseling given.

Nutritionists should participate in the design, field testing, and revision of these systems so that the key anthropometric, biochemical, clinical, dietary, and demographic data they need can be collected, analyzed, and reported as part of this master data system. As these systems develop in the states, the nation can move toward the achievement of a minimum core data set for public health services. In the absence of a uniform state health informa-

Exhibit 16-3 North Carolina HSIS Family Planning/Maternal Health History

```
                    NORTH CAROLINA HSIS
           FAMILY PLANNING/MATERNAL HEALTH HISTORY

   LAST NAME ............... FIRST NAME ............. MI . ID NUMBER 000000000H

                         MARITAL STATUS
   (1=MARRIED, 2=SEPARATED, 3=DIVORCED, 4=WIDOWED, 5=NEVER MARRIED)

   HIGHEST GRADE COMPLETED: ..          NO. LIVE BIRTHS: ..
   NO. OF LIVING CHILDREN: ..           NO. FETAL DEATHS: ..

                       MATERNAL HEALTH ONLY

   WEIGHT AT FIRST VISIT:   ... lbs .. oz   OR ...(.) .. kg
               HEIGHT:      ... ins .. /8in OR ... (.) .. cm

   REQUIRED FOR FAMILY PLANNING—OPTIONAL FOR MATERNAL HEALTH

      FAMILY SIZE: ...  ANNUAL FAMILY INCOME: $ .......(.)00
```

```
            NORTH CAROLINA HSIS—MATERNAL HEALTH

   LAST NAME ......................      FIRST NAME ................. MI.
      ID NUMBER ........H               SERVICE DATE: .. /../..
      SERVICE SITE: ........           MEDICAID ID: .................

                        SERVICE TYPE(S)
   CLINIC VISIT/COMPLETE:        . OR CLINIC VISIT/LIMITED:              .
   CARE COORD/INITIAL MONTH:     . OR CARE COORD/SUBSEQUENT MONTH:  .
      HOME VISIT: .   CHILD BIRTH CLASSES: .   PARENTING CLASSES: .

                          PROVIDER(S)

   NURSE       . LAB STAFF    . PHYSICIAN   . CHA/CHT    . NP/PA    .
   NUTRI STAFF . HEALTH EDUC  . SOC WORKER  . PHARMACIST . CNM      .

         COMPLETE THE FOLLOWING FOR CLINIC VISITS ONLY
   PATIENT TYPE: .              NON STRESS TEST: .      ULTRASOUND: .

                           OPTIONAL

      CPT CODE(S): ..... ..... ..... ..... ..... ..... ..... ..... .....
      LOCAL CODE(S): ... ... ... ... ... ...
              PRESS SPACE BAR TO CONTINUE:
```

Source. Reprinted from *North Carolina Health Services Information Systems Manual* with permission of North Carolina State Center for Health Statistics, North Carolina Division of Health

Exhibit 16-4 North Carolina HSIS Pregnancy Outcome

```
              NORTH CAROLINA HSIS—PREGNANCY OUTCOME—SCREEN 1

LAST NAME ......................       FIRST NAME ................  MI.
ID NUMBER ........H                    REPORT DATE: .. /../..
SERVICE SITE: .........                MEDICAID ID: ..................

MULTIPLE BIRTH/OUTCOME: .             MONTHS RECEIVED CARE COORDINATION: ..
REASON FOR CLOSURE: .                 PREGNANCY OUTCOME: .

ENTER INFANT DATA WHEN PREGNANCY OUTCOME IS LIVE BIRTH.
ENTER FETAL DEATH DATE WHEN PREGNANCY OUTCOME IS FETAL DEATH.


     BIRTH WEIGHT: ..lbs .. oz OR ... grams
     BIRTH DATE OR FETAL DEATH DATE: ../../..
     FIRST AND LAST NAME INITIALS: ..        SEX: .
     GESTATIONAL AGE AT BIRTH: .. (WEEKS)
     NEONATAL DEATH .  CONGENITAL ANOMALY .  C-SECTION .
     RECEIVING WELL CHILD CARE: .  RECEIVING WIC/SUPL. FOOD: .
```

```
              NORTH CAROLINA HSIS—PREGNANCY OUTCOME—SCREEN 2

LAST NAME ...................  FIRST NAME ................  MI.   ID NUMBER ........H

ENTER MATERNAL DATA WHEN PREGNANCY OUTCOME IS LIVE BIRTH.
     WEEKS GESTATION WHEN PRENATAL CARE BEGAN: ..
     NUMBER OF PRENATAL VISITS: ..
     WEIGHT PRIOR TO DELIVERY: .. lbs .. ozs OR ..(.).. kgms
     RECEIVED WIC/SUPPLEMENTAL FOOD: .
     RECEIVED POSTPARTUM OR FAMILY PLANNING EXAM: .
     MEDICALLY HIGH RISK: .

     HIGH RISK CODES(S):   ...(.).  ...(.).  ...(.).  ...(.).  ...(.).  ...(.).
                           ...(.).  ...(.).  ...(.).  ...(.).  ...(.).  ...(.).

     CLIENT NEEDS (Y = MET, N = NOT MET, . = NOT NEEDED)

CHILD CARE:        . NUTRITION COUNSELING:        . EMPLOYMENT:              .
FOOD ASSISTANCE: . PSYCHOLOGICAL COUNSELING:.   JOB TRAINING:              .
HOUSING:           . SOCIAL WORK COUNSELING:     . SCHOOL ENROLLMENT: .
TRANSPORTATION: .

LOCAL USE CODES: ... ... ... ... ... ... ... ...

              PRESS SPACE BAR TO CONTINUE:
```

Source: Reprinted from *North Carolina Health Services Information Systems Manual* with permission of North Carolina State Center for Health Statistics, North Carolina Division of Health

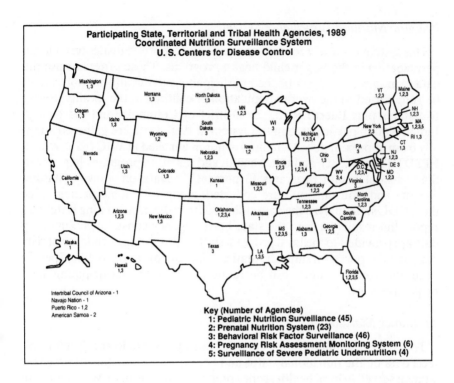

Figure 16-1 Participating State, Territorial, and Tribal Health Agencies, 1989 (Coordinated Nutrition Surveillance System, U.S. Centers for Disease Control). *Source*: Nutrition Monitoring Project, California Department of Health Services, Sacramento, California.

tion system, some state nutrition program units have developed nutrition or WIC automated data bases, used by all local agencies in the state to collect data of interest in managing public health nutrition and/or WIC programs.

Centers for Disease Control Surveillance Systems

The Centers for Disease Control (CDC) have taken the lead in assisting states in collecting and analyzing data on nutrition-related health problems among their populations. There are currently pediatric and pregnancy nutrition surveillance systems and an adult behavior risk factor surveillance system. The state agencies currently participating in each of these systems are shown on the U.S. map in Figure 16-1.

Pediatric Nutrition Surveillance System

This system routinely collects, analyzes, and reports statistics on children participating in the larger child health programs. These programs use the data to monitor and describe their participants, but the information cannot be generalized to the overall population of children in the locality. Forty-five states plus Puerto Rico, the District of Columbia, and the Navajo Indian Nation participated in the system in 1989. Data are gathered annually from approximately 3.2 million children enrolled in WIC (85 percent), EPSDT (12 percent), and other health and nutrition programs [e.g., Head Start, school health programs (3 percent)]. Data on growth (stature, weight) and iron nutriture are collected, along with some demographic data. CDC staff analyze the data collected from the participating states and report the results back to the state health agency consultants. Summary data are provided to the local program staff, with a listing of children at risk. An annual report with summary statistics is available to the public. Specific state and county reports can be requested from the participating state health agencies.

Pregnancy Nutrition Surveillance System

This system, similar to the Pediatric Nutrition Surveillance System, collects data on the nutritional status and behavioral risk factors of pregnant women served in local health agency prenatal clinics, usually WIC clinics. In 1989, 23 state agencies were participating. The data elements collected include pre-pregnant weight status, pregnancy weight gain, iron status, smoking behavior during pregnancy, alcohol intake during pregnancy, and information on pregnancy outcome. Demographic data are also collected. Participating state and local health agencies receive an annual summary of the data on their prenatal population, including behaviors and health outcomes. These data are available from the participating state health agencies. An annual report summarizing the data from all of the participating states is available from the Centers for Disease Control.

Behavioral Risk Factor Surveillance System

This system, also developed by the Centers for Disease Control, is population based rather than client based. Information is collected from a representative sample of the adults in each of the 46 participating states. The respondents are chosen by random digit dialing or randomly selected telephone numbers. Interviews are conducted over the phone. Data are collected on a range of health-related behaviors including seat belt use, smoking, alcohol consumption, physical activity, and presence of hypertension. Nutrition-related items include self-reported height and weight and weight-control practices. A module is being developed to collect dietary intake information. Data are available to the participating state health agencies, and national summaries of the data are published in CDC's *Morbidity and Mortality Weekly Report.*

Public Health Reporting System

The Public Health Reporting System is managed by the Public Health Foundation, an organization established by the Association of State and Territorial Health Officials. Data are voluntarily submitted each year by the 55 state health agencies. Since 1970, this reporting system has collected and published data on their services, programs, and expenditures. There are three standardized reporting forms: one for fiscal information; one for personal health, which can include nutrition services and the Special Supplemental Food Program for Women, Infants, and Children (WIC); and one for environmental health. On the Personal Health Program Inventory and Expenditure Summary, the agency lists its various programs, its funding sources, and individual program expenditures. The program report form requests information on the kinds of services provided and the counts for selected services or activities, with space for descriptions of program elements not covered by the form. The foundation defines a program as a "set of identifiable services organized to solve health related problems or to meet specific health or health related needs provided to or on behalf of the public by or under the direction of an organizational entity in a state health agency and for which reasonably accurate estimates of expenditures can be made."[3]

Nutrition services clearly meet the above definition. However, because of their diverse organizational structures, states may or may not report non-WIC nutrition services in their annual inventory of personal health programs. Because WIC has now become the largest single federal grant coming into the state health agencies, all state health agencies report it as a line item.

Each state health official appoints three primary contacts to collect the state's data: a project coordinator; a data manager, usually from the agency's statistical staff; and a fiscal coordinator familiar with the agency's financial management system.[4] Nutritionists interested in this data system should contact their state health agency data coordinator.

The annual summary report, *Public Health Agencies 19XX: An Inventory of Programs and Block Grant Expenditures,* can be obtained from the Public Health Foundation.[5]

COLLECTING NEW DATA

When no available data sources provide the information needed for program management, then a new method must be developed to collect and analyze data. Since new data collection is labor intensive and costly, the first step is always to consult a statistician in the agency, a center or bureau of health statistics, or a department of statistics in a local university. The statistician can advise on the feasibility of the proposed project, alternative methods, and required resources. When designing a data system, it is very tempting to gather a lot of information that might "come in handy" some day. It is more efficient to collect limited data for which there is a specific use and to recognize that not all the questions about the surveyed population can be answered in one survey. In the planning stage, it is useful to ask the statistician the following: "If we found this result, what would we do? What additional information would we need in order to do this?" The basic steps in conducting a survey are listed in Exhibit 16-5, with a checklist and time line. When planning a survey, adequate time and resources should be allocated for each step.

Data Collection Methods

There are basically five methods of collecting data about individuals: face-to-face interview, self-assessment, telephone interview, mailed questionnaire, and chart or record review. Face-to-face interviews are labor intensive and costly. Interviewers must be sensitive to the population being surveyed and carefully trained in general interview techniques as well as the specific questionnaire to be used. Assistance in training interviewers can often be obtained from local university faculties, particularly from departments of sociology, psychology, business (marketing), and social work.

Telephone and mail surveys are less expensive than face-to-face interviews and are easier to use for a population-based survey. Don Dillman's book on mail and telephone surveys discusses the advantages and disadvantages of each type and explains how to design questionnaires for easier response.[6] Not all people, particularly low-income people, have telephones. Information on the percentage of the population with telephones is available from the local telephone company. This problem may be overcome by including a larger number of low-income people in the sample to make up for the number who do not have phones or by conducting face-to-face interviews with a subsample of low-income people. Combining different data collection techniques in one survey must be done with caution because people may respond differently on the phone than they do face to face.

Exhibit 16-5 Checklist for Planning a Survey

Steps	Planned Completion Date	Completed
1. Decide upon exact data needs and characteristics of survey		
2. Develop questionnaire Wording Layout Precoding (if applicable)		
3. Pretest questionnaire		
4. Revise questions		
5. Print copies		
6. Select sample		
7. Train interviewers (face-to-face and/or telephone)		
8. Begin data collection		
9. Complete data collection		
10. Code questionnaire for computer entry		
11. Enter data into computer		
12. Clean data		
13. Analyze data		
14. Prepare report		

Both face-to-face and telephone interviewers must be carefully trained and monitored so that they collect consistent data.

Lists of addresses to use for mailed surveys can be obtained from a variety of sources, including the local department of motor vehicles. With mail surveys, the number of completed forms returned is often disappointing. When the response is low, those who return the forms may be different from those who do not. Results from a mail survey with a low response rate may not represent the entire population. The response rate can be improved by generating advance media publicity, sending out announcements ahead of the actual survey forms, using a cover letter on official stationery, and sending reminder postcards to those who have not returned the form. It may be desirable to offer an incentive such as a brochure, a coupon, a prize, or money to those who return the completed forms. Probably the most effective strategy is to keep the questionnaire very short, simple, and easy to fill out. The best example of an effective mail survey is the national census.

Chart or record reviews are an effective method of collecting data when clinic or program participants are the population of interest or are an appropriate convenience sample. However, the data elements of interest may not be consistently available in the charts, and because the data were probably collected and recorded by many different people, the quality may be inconsistent or questionable. One concern with this type of data collection is maintaining the confidentiality of the participant since the chart or health record contains information beyond the scope of the survey.

Dietary Data Collection

Nutritionists are keenly interested in information on the dietary intake of population groups. A number of methods for assessing dietary intake are used in research. Two commonly used survey methods are the 24-hour recall and the food frequency. Obtaining accurate 24-hour recall information requires a highly skilled interviewer who uses visual prompts such as measuring cups or spoons, food models, different sized cups, bowls, etc., to estimate portion sizes accurately. These requirements prohibit the use of 24-hour recalls in telephone or mail surveys.

Recent work on dietary intake methodology has led to the development of various quantified food frequency tools which estimate usual nutrient intake. Based on more extensive survey data such as NHANES and NFCS, lists of commonly eaten foods have been created. The respondent is asked to estimate how frequently each of the foods is eaten. Food frequency lists have been developed that can be analyzed for all major nutrients, while shorter, nutrient-specific lists have also been developed. An example of selected pages of a food frequency instrument developed by the National Cancer Institute appears in Exhibit 16-6. Software to calculate nutrient content of the food frequency is available for use with this questionnaire, making it a convenient package. This questionnaire can be used in face-to-face, telephone, or mailed surveys to get information on dietary intake. Those interested in using this food frequency questionnaire should obtain

Exhibit 16-6 Quantified Food Frequency Questionnaire

	Medium Serving	Your Serving Size S M L	Day	Week	Month	Year	Rarely/ Never	OFFICE USE
FRUITS & JUICES								
EXAMPLE								
Apples, applesauce, pears	(1) or 1/2 cup							11 ----
Bananas	1 medium							15 ----
Peaches, apricots (canned, frozen, or dried, whole year)	(1) or 1/2 cup							19 ----
Peaches, apricots, nectarines (fresh, in season)	1 medium							23 ----
Cantaloupe (in season)	1/4 medium							27 ----
Watermelon (in season)	1 slice							31 ----
Strawberries (fresh, in season)	1/2 cup							35 ----
Oranges	1 medium							39 ----
Orange juice or grapefruit juice	6 oz. glass							43 ----
Grapefruit	(1/2)							47 ----
Tang, Start breakfast drinks	6 oz. glass							51 ----
Other fruit juices, fortified fruit drinks	6 oz. glass							55 ----
Any other fruit, including berries, fruit cocktail	1/2 cup	S M L	Da	Wk	Mo	Yr	Nv	59 ----
VEGETABLES								
String beans, green beans	1/2 cup							63 ----
Peas	1/2 cup							67 ----
Chili with beans	3/4 cup							71 ----
Other beans such as baked beans, pintos, kidney beans, limas	3/4 cup							75 ---- D
Corn	1/2 cup							11 ---- 79̄80
Winter squash, baked squash	1/2 cup							15 ----
Tomatoes, tomato juice	(1) or 6 oz.							19 ----
Red chili sauce, taco sauce, salsa picante	2 Tblsp. sauce							23 ----
Broccoli	1/2 cup							27 ----
Cauliflower or brussel sprouts	1/2 cup							31 ----

Exhibit 16-6 continued

	Medium Serving	Your Serving Size (S M L)	Day	Week	Month	Year	Rarely/ Never	OFFICE USE
Spinach (raw)	3/4 cup							35
Spinach (cooked)	1/2 cup							39
Mustard greens, turnip greens, collards	1/2 cup							43
Cole slaw, cabbage, sauerkraut	1/2 cup							47
Carrots or mixed vegetables containing carrots	1/2 cup							51
Green salad	1 med. bowl							55
Salad dressing, mayonnaise (including on sandwiches)	2 Tblsp.							59
French fries and fried potatoes	3/4 cup							63
Sweet potatoes, yams	1/2 cup							67
Other potatoes, including boiled, baked, potato salad	(1) or 1/2 cup							71
Rice	3/4 cup							E 75
Any other vegetable including cooked onions, summer squash	1/2 cup		Da Wk Mo Yr Nv					79 80 / 11
Butter, margarine, or other fat on vegetables, potatoes, etc.	2 pats							15
MEAT, FISH, POULTRY & MIXED DISHES		S M L						
Hamburgers, cheeseburgers, meat loaf	1 medium							19
Beef—steaks, roasts	4 oz.							23
Beef stew or pot pie with carrots, other vegetables	1 cup							27
Liver, including chicken livers	4 oz.							31
Pork, including chops, roasts	2 chops or 4 oz.							35
Fried chicken	2 sm. or 1 lg. piece							39
Chicken or turkey, roasted, stewed, or broiled	2 sm. or 1 lg. piece							43
Fried fish or fish sandwich	4 oz. or 1 sand.							47
Tuna fish, tuna salad, tuna casserole	1/2 cup							51
Shellfish (shrimp, lobster, crab, oysters, etc.)	(5) 1/4 cup or 3 oz							55
Other fish, broiled, baked	4 oz.							59
Spaghetti, lasagna, other pasta with tomato sauce	1 cup							63
Pizza	2 slices							67
Mixed dishes with cheese (such as macaroni and cheese)	1 cup							71

Food Item	Portion	S	M	L	Da	Wk	Mo	Yr	Nv
LUNCH ITEMS									
Liverwurst	2 slices								
Hot dogs	2 dogs								
Ham, lunch meats	2 slices								
Vegetable soup, vegetable beef, minestrone, tomato soup	1 med. bowl								
Other soups	1 med. bowl								
BREADS/SALTY SNACKS/SPREADS									
Biscuits, muffins, burger rolls (incl. fast foods)	1 med. piece								
White bread (including sandwiches), bagels, etc., crackers	2 slices, 3 cracks								
Dark bread, including whole wheat, rye, pumpernickel	2 slices								
Corn bread, corn muffins, corn tortillas	1 med. piece								
Salty snacks (such as chips, popcorn)	2 handfuls								
Peanuts, peanut butter	2 Tblsp.								
Butter on bread or rolls	2 pats								
Margarine on bread or rolls	2 pats								
Gravies made with meat drippings, or white sauce	2 Tblsp.								
BREAKFAST FOODS									
High fiber, bran or granola cereals, shredded wheat	1 med. bowl								
Highly fortified cereals, such as Product 19, Total, or Most	1 med. bowl								
Other cold cereals, such as Corn Flakes, Rice Krispies	1 med. bowl								
Cooked cereals	1 med. bowl								
Sugar added to cereal	2 teaspn.								
Eggs 1 egg = small, 2 eggs = medium									
Bacon	2 slices								
Sausage	2 patties or links								
SWEETS									
Ice cream	1 scoop								
Doughnuts, cookies, cakes, pastry	1 pc. or 3 cookies								
Pumpkin pie, sweet potato pie	1 med. slice								
Other pies	1 med. slice								
Chocolate candy	small bar, 1 oz.								
Other candy, jelly, honey, brown sugar	3 pc. or 1 Tblsp.								

Exhibit 16-6 continued

	Medium Serving	Your Serving Size (S M L)	How often? (Day / Week / Month / Year / Rarely/Never)	OFFICE USE
DAIRY PRODUCTS				
Cottage cheese	1/2 cup			51-
Other cheeses and cheese spreads	2 slices or 2 oz.			55-
Flavored yogurt	1 cup			59-
Whole milk and bevs. with whole milk (not incl. on cereal)	8 oz. glass			63-
2% milk and bevs. with 2% milk (not incl. on cereal)	8 oz. glass			67-
Skim milk, 1% milk or buttermilk (not incl. on cereal)	8 oz. glass			71-
BEVERAGES		(S M L)	(Da Wk Mo Yr Nv)	
Regular soft drinks	12 oz. can/bottle			75-
Diet soft drinks	12 oz. can/bottle			11-
Beer	12 oz. can/bottle			15-
Wine	1 med. glass			19-
Liquor	1 shot			23-
Decaffeinated coffee	1 med. cup			27-
Coffee, not decaffeinated	1 med. cup			31-
Tea (hot or iced)	1 med. cup			35-
Lemon in tea	1 teaspn.			39-
Non-dairy creamer in coffee or tea	1 Tblsp.			43-
Milk in coffee or tea	1 Tblsp.			47-
Cream (real) or Half-and-Half in coffee or tea	1 Tblsp.			51-
Sugar in coffee or tea	2 teaspn.			55-
Artificial sweetener in coffee or tea	1 packet			59-
Glasses of water, not counting in coffee or tea	8 oz. glass			63-

H
79 80

I
79 80

67 0 2 2 0 6 9 . . .

Source: Reprinted from *The Health Habits & History Questionnaire: Diet, History, and Other Risk Factors Personal Computer System Packet*, National Cancer Institute, Division of Cancer Prevention & Control, January 1988.

The Health Habits and History Questionnaire: Diet History and Other Risk Factors Personal Computer System Packet from the Division of Cancer Prevention and Control, National Cancer Institute, Bethesda, Maryland 20892. In addition to Exhibit 16-6, Quantified Food Frequency Questionnaire, the packet contains a restaurant questionnaire and a fat use questionnaire that are standard parts of this questionnaire and used in the nutrient calculations. There is also a vitamin supplement questionnaire. In using these materials, it is necessary to note the age and gender of the respondent. Computer-assisted interview programs and scannable versions are also available.

Computer-assisted food intake methods based on 24-hour intakes or quantified food frequencies have potential for gathering dietary data at less expense. A user-friendly computer program that includes useful visual prompts can be validated. It can immediately feed back a printed nutrient analysis to the respondent while aggregating and analyzing the demographic profile of the respondents and the nutrient content of their diets for researchers. These computers can be installed in clinics, stores, schools, work sites, malls, or other places where people gather. Unless carefully managed, the sample would be self-selected.

Questionnaire Development

Whether a manual or computer-based method is used to collect data, a form or format for recording must be developed. With a chart or record review, a simple tally sheet may suffice; with other methods, a questionnaire must be developed. Each question must be clearly phrased and unambiguous. Closed-ended questions that can be answered by only a few responses are easier to quantify and tabulate than are open-ended questions for which there are an infinite number of possible responses. Open-ended questions may be used in a pretest to generate the most likely responses, which then can be listed as choices in the closed-ended version. Closed-ended questions usually allow for an "other" category for responses that do not fit into the given list. In phrasing a question, it is very important that the wording be as objective as possible. It is helpful when reviewing wording to brainstorm and pretest all of the possible responses to the question.

When questions are agreed on, then the questionnaire needs to be laid out on paper. This is especially important for a form that the respondent will see, as in a mail survey or a self-assessment. The appearance of the questionnaire can make a significant difference in the response rate. For telephone and face-to-face questionnaires, the form should be easy for the interviewer to use. Often the response to one question determines whether the next series of questions is also asked or whether the interviewer skips to some later question. Dillman makes concrete suggestions for laying out questionnaires.[7]

Questionnaires must be pretested and validated on a group of people who are similar to the respondents. The pretest validates not only the content and wording of the questionnaire, but also the whole data collection process, including coding of the questionnaire and data entry. Ambiguities in the wording of the questionnaire, if not corrected, could invalidate the whole survey.

Sample Selection

It is important to decide whether to gather information from a convenience sample or from a broader segment of the population (population based). A convenience sample consists of people who are relatively easy to reach through some existing group. For example, people on food stamps are a convenience sample of low-income people. Children in public day care centers are a convenience sample of children in all forms of day care (including family day care). Collecting data from a convenience sample is easier and less expensive than conducting a representative population-based survey. It is appropriate if the convenience sample contains a large proportion of the population of interest. Otherwise, the people in the convenience sample may be very different from those not in the sample. If a convenience sample must be used, the results must be interpreted recognizing that the conclusions can be drawn only for the population sampled.

Collecting information on every single member of the population group of interest is not usually feasible. A sample of the population is considered representative if it truly parallels the larger population. The sample should contain the same proportion of men and women and of the ethnic, age, and socioeconomic groups in the population. Information from a nonrepresentative sample—for example, one with a higher proportion of elderly women than in the population as a whole—may lead to incorrect conclusions about the nutritional and health status of the whole population. Therefore, sample selection becomes an important consideration in the design of the data collection.

To assure a representative sample, members of the population should be randomly selected. For a mail survey, for instance, one could select every other name on a mailing list (or every fifth, tenth, hundredth, etc., depending on how large a sample is needed). A telephone survey could be conducted by selecting telephone numbers at random. It is more difficult to maintain a truly random sample selection with face-to-face interviews because interviewers tend to select people who appear willing to respond or are easily accessible. Interviewers must be trained in advance on how to select a substitute if the person chosen refuses to participate.

The size of the sample is critical in designing the survey. Generally, the larger the sample, the more accurate the predictions about the population as a whole. But a sample size that is larger than necessary for an acceptable level of accuracy wastes time and money. Several reference books suggested in the Public Health Nutrition Library (see Appendix N) discuss sample selection. To understand and apply the formulas requires a working knowledge of statistics.

Data Entry

Prior to data entry and analysis, all questionnaire forms must be carefully checked. To make sure that all responses have been answered clearly and completely, the interviewer should check each form after completing the interview. A second person should check to assure that all interviewers have completed the forms in the same way. Mail-back surveys should be checked for completeness and consistency.

Simple survey data can be tallied by hand, but it is more economical and accurate to use microcomputers to analyze data. When using a computer, questionnaire responses must be put into a form that the computer can read and manipulate. Numbers or codes are assigned to each possible response. If forms are precoded, responses numbered on the form are entered directly from the interview form into the computer. An example of a precoded form appears in Exhibit 16-7. If the respondent actually sees the form (e.g., in a mail survey), it is sometimes preferable not to precode it to keep it from looking cluttered and complicated. In this case, coding is done after the forms have been completed. Sometimes coding spaces are printed on the form (usually in the righthand margin) under such instructions as "For Office Use Only." Alternatively, the information from the questionnaire may be coded onto a separate sheet of paper.

Regardless of the method, code numbers must be assigned to all possible responses. Attention should also be given to distinguishing between different kinds of nonresponses. Different codes are used for "Don't know," "Refused," and "Missing information" because each response has a different meaning. Systems are also available for entering data from telephone or face-to-face interviews directly into the microcomputer, with checks built directly into the computer program to detect errors.

Once data are entered into the computer, and before analysis, the computer data must be checked for accuracy. For instance, if the only possible

Exhibit 16-7 Example of a Precoded Survey Instrument

SECTION D: WEIGHT CONTROL PRACTICES

"Now I would like to ask you about some of the things you may be currently doing to try to lose weight or keep from gaining weight."

17. Are you now trying to lose weight?   (61)

   a. Yes 1
   b. No *GO TO Q 21 (p. 9)* 2
   c. No, trying to gain weight *GO TO Q 28 (p. 11)* 3
      Don't know/Not sure *GO TO Q 21 (p. 9)* 7
      Refused *GO TO Q 21 (p. 9)* 9

18. About how long ago did you begin your current attempt to lose weight?   (62-64)

   a. Days .... 1 _ _
   b. Weeks .... 2 _ _
   c. Months .... 3 _ _
   d. Years .... 4 _ _
   e. Always trying to lose weight 5 5 5
      Don't know/Not sure 7 7 7
      Refused 9 9 9

19. About how much did you weigh when you began your current
    attempt to lose weight?   (65-67)
   a. Weight .... _ _ _
                                                       Pounds
      Don't know/Not sure 7 7 7
      Refused 9 9 9

Source: Behavioral Risk Factor Survey, Centers for Disease Control, Atlanta, Georgia.

---

responses to a question are "1" and "2," then any other numbers for that question are errors and should be corrected. Similarly, values that are not reasonable (either too large or too small) should also be identified. When collecting data on the heights of children, for instance, a value of seven feet is suspect.

Data Analysis

Data analysis for program planning usually involves fairly simple descriptive statistics. A key issue is usually what percentage of the target population has a particular nutrition-related condition or is at risk of developing a nutrition-related problem. Such questions can be answered by simple statistical determinations such as percentages and averages (means).

More sophisticated statistical analyses are used when comparing two different groups of people. For instance, one may be interested in whether there is a greater frequency of high fat intake among women or men at work sites. This information would be useful in determining which group to target for an intervention. For example, information collected from a sample of both men and women might reveal that 50 percent of men and 35 percent of women consumed a high-fat diet. Since data have been collected only from a sample and not the total population, it is important to determine if this difference is true of the larger population of working men and women or if it is only a chance occurrence due to the sample selected. Tests of significance can be used to answer that question. The statistician can assist in choosing the proper test and performing the calculations.

There are a variety of software packages available for analyzing dietary data for selected nutrients. These computer packages simplify the task of analyzing nutrient content of individual diets. However, each software package has different features that affect its usefulness. Thus, care must be taken in selecting appropriate dietary software. Gail Frank and Suzanne Pelican have reviewed some of the factors to consider in choosing such software packages.[8]

Reporting

The reason for conducting the survey is to report the data and any conclusions. Data are often presented to gain support for specific nutrition interventions. Whether presentations are written or oral, it is important to consider the audience in deciding what data to present and how to present them. The most pertinent data should be presented in an easily understood format and then interpreted for the audience.

A variety of easy-to-use computer software graphics packages help in preparing various types of visual presentations, such as bar charts, pie charts, trend lines, etc. Computer packages produce very professional-looking graphics. Graphic artists in the agency or in local schools, technical schools, and universities may be able to assist in preparing polished posters, flip charts, transparencies, or slides using the charts and graphs.

Data and reports generated are a vital part of program planning. Although there is a paucity of local-level data specifically on nutritional status, other local-level data can indicate populations at high risk of having nutrition problems. National and state data can be used to estimate the prevalence of nutrition-related problems and risk at the local level. With the increasing availability of microcomputers and improvements in survey techniques such as telephone interviewing, it is more feasible to collect and analyze data specific to local needs. However, before embarking on data gathering, it is necessary to consult a statistician to help define what information is needed, how much it will cost to collect it, and how it will be presented. Being clear on the issues throughout the data collection process helps to avoid spending valuable time and money on collecting unnecessary or useless data. Several state health agency nutrition units now employ nutritionists skilled in data collection and analysis; they have proved to be valuable consultants, as have consultants from the federal agencies and faculty from universities.

ISSUES TO DEBATE

- What are the minimum core data needed for public health nutrition program management?
- What resources should be allocated to collecting, analyzing, and reporting data for program planning and evaluation?
- How should the nutritionist decide between collecting data on a sample of convenience and using a randomly selected population-based sample?
- In selecting or designing a dietary assessment method, what are the tradeoffs in terms of simplicity, time, cost, interviewer skills, validity, and reliability?

NOTES

1. U.S. Department of Health and Human Services and U.S. Department of Agriculture, *Nutrition Monitoring in the United States: The Directory of Federal Nutrition Monitoring Activities* (Washington, D.C.: Government Printing Office, 1989).

2. U.S. Department of Health and Human Services and U.S. Department of Agriculture, *Nutrition Monitoring in the United States: A Progress Report from the Joint Nutrition Monitoring Evaluation Committee*, DHHS (PHS) Publication no. 86-1255 (Washington, D.C.: Public Health Service, 1986). Life Sciences Research Office, Federation of American Societies of Experimental Biology, *Nutrition Monitoring in the United States: An Update Report on Nutrition Monitoring* (Washington, D.C.: Government Printing Office, 1989).

3. Public Health Foundation, *Public Health Agencies 1989: An Inventory of Programs and Block Grant Expenditures* (Washington, D.C.: Public Health Foundation, 1989), 1, 7, 114–15.

4. Ibid.

5. Ibid.

6. Don A. Dillman, *Mail and Telephone Surveys: The Total Design Method* (New York: John Wiley & Sons, Inc., 1978).

7. Ibid.

8. Gail C. Frank and Suzanne Pelican, "Guidelines for Selecting a Dietary Analysis System," *Journal of The American Dietetic Association* 86, no. 1 (January 1986): 72.

BIBLIOGRAPHY

Burr, Michael L. "Epidemiology for Nutritionists: Some General Principles." *Human Nutrition: Applied Nutrition* 37A (1983): 259–64, 339–47.

Elwood, P.C. "Epidemiology for Nutritionists: 2—Sampling Methods." *Human Nutrition: Applied Nutrition* 38A (1983): 265–69.

Medlin, C., and Skinner, J.D. "Individual Dietary Intake Methodology: A 50-Year Review of Progress." *Journal of the American Dietetic Association* 88 (1988): 1250–57.

Sweetman, P.M. "Epidemiology for Nutritionists: 5—Some Statistical Aspects." *Human Nutrition: Applied Nutrition* 38A (1984): 215–22.

Yetley, Elizabeth, and Johnson, Clifford. "Nutritional Applications of the Health and Nutrition Examination Surveys (HANES)." *Annual Review of Nutrition* 7 (1987): 441–63.

chapter **17**

Managing Money

Katherine Cairns

READER OBJECTIVES

- Discuss the nutritionist's responsibilities for managing money.
- Identify collaborators in the agency budgeting process.
- Discuss justifications for each budgeted proposal.
- Describe the major sources for funding public health nutrition services.
- List and describe major categories for a nutrition program budget.
- Specify major items in a grant application.

FINANCING PUBLIC HEALTH NUTRITION PROGRAMS AND SERVICES

Providing the community with the nutrition program the people need and want requires that the agency allocate dollars to pay personnel salaries, reimburse their travel, buy equipment and supplies, provide for continuing education of nutrition personnel, and purchase other goods needed to deliver services. Every nutritionist who manages a program, service, or project must take responsibility for requesting, justifying, and negotiating a budget and controlling expenditures within the funds allocated. Fiscal management means understanding the financing and budgeting process and working closely with the

- *administrator and board members* who set the agency's fiscal policy and determine how the agency budget will be distributed to programs and overhead
- *finance or fiscal officer or business manager* who maintains accounts,

342

controls expenditures, and can provide advice on the organization's written and unwritten fiscal policies and procedures

- *other program directors* who request and manage budgets for programs that should utilize nutrition services. These directors can often be convinced to collaborate in funding nutrition services through their internal funding sources or by collaborating in writing grants for external funding.

Tighter federal, state, and local public agency budgets require nutritionists to compete for the money they need if they want to turn plans for comprehensive nutrition services into action. To convince a governmental unit or foundation to invest money in nutrition services, the value of each proposal must be justified.

- Is there really a need for the service? See Chapters 3, 4, and 14 on needs assessment and program planning and Chapters 8, 9, 10, 11, 12, and 13 on program areas.
- What are the competing options for the available and new money? The plan, budget, service, product, and their evaluation must stand out from the competition.
- What stakeholder support and contributions are there for the proposal? What support does the competition have?
- What potential does the proposed service have to generate income for the agency?
- Are there federal or foundation grants available to establish and maintain the service into the future?

Competitive proposals for spending new or ongoing money must show evidence of support from individuals and organizations in the community who will benefit from the product or service. They can demonstrate their support by paying fees for services; making in-kind contributions of staff or volunteer time or of space in offices or clinics; writing letters of support; presenting testimony; lobbying proactively; donating equipment, materials, or cash contributions.

Interdisciplinary teamwork and networking to increase the number of stakeholders in nutrition programs are discussed in Chapters 21 and 22. Financers prefer to fund a service that responds to a demonstrated need that can be met at a reasonable cost. A well-conceived budget for a new service or product details the cost per unit. Services with costly start-up should show a reasonable cost per unit after the implementation period. Fiscal managers will ask these questions:

- Will the proposed service or product have a reasonable cost-to-benefit ratio? Funders compare the costs and outcomes of varying types of service delivery options. (See Chapter 14, Cost Benefit Analysis.)
- Will the service be carried out with the most cost-effective intervention? For example, will reducing anemia in 80 percent of a population group within six months of diagnosis be less costly if nutrition counseling is provided by a trained and supervised paraprofessional rather than by a nutritionist? Whereas the outcome may be the same, the costs of different intervention models may vary. (See Chapter 14, Cost Effectiveness Analysis.)

These and additional questions can be used as a checklist in preparing to request the funds needed to initiate the service. Funds for nutrition services may be secured from a variety of sources. The more diversified the funding base, the more stable the program. The more funding sources used to maintain a public health nutrition program, the less dependent the program is on any one.

General Revenue

State governments generate funds through state income taxes, sales taxes, various types of business taxes, and taxes on such products as alcoholic beverages and cigarettes. In recent years, several states have begun to use lotteries to generate revenue for public services. Local governmental units have the authority to tax property owners for municipal services such as police and fire departments, schools, recreation, and public health. Tax levies are set annually based on the services needed, the priorities of policymakers, the demands of the taxpayers, and outside interests.

Most city, county, or state public health departments derive a portion of income from general revenue. Public health agencies generally seek their fair share of general revenue as a cornerstone of their base income. Usually there is keen competition for these funds in a health agency because they generally offer programs funding stability. If there is no general revenue in the budget for nutrition services, nutritionists need to discuss this funding source with agency administrators and business managers to prepare to submit their request for the next budget cycle. They may need to be persistent and assertive over several years to succeed. Some funding that is not restricted to a specific target population provides flexibility to plan more comprehensive and community-responsive programs.

Federal Grants

In FY 1987, grant funds administered by several federal agencies provided for 29 percent of the state and local health agency expenditures.[1] The U.S. Department of Agriculture's Special Supplemental Food Program for Women, Infants, and Children (WIC) provided for 20 percent of state health agency expenditures in FY 1987, the states' largest single federal grant source.[2] In 1989, the WIC funds paid the salaries of 61% percent of the public health nutrition personnel in state and local health agencies.[3] However, as described in Chapter 8, the WIC funds must be used specifically for services to eligible low-income women, infants, and children. When WIC is the sole funding source for nutrition services, it precludes comprehensive planning based on the community assessment.

The next largest federal grant to the states is the Department of Health and Human Services, Office of Maternal and Child Health, Maternal and Child Health (MCH) Block Grant, which in FY 1987 provided for 5 percent of state health agency expenditures.[4] In 1989 the MCH Block Grant paid for 8 percent of salaries of the nutritionists in state and local health agencies.[5] The Department of Health and Human Services Centers for Disease Control administers the Preventive Health Services Block Grant, which provided for 1 percent of state health agency expenditures in FY 1987[6] and 1 percent of public health nutrition personnel salaries that year.[7] Other federal grant funds for health services are available from the Drug and Alcohol Abuse Block Grant.

In addition to the Block Grants which are distributed to the states based on a preestablished formula based on the state's population, economy, and other characteristics, there are special federal grants which are awarded on a competitive basis and are announced in public documents. Personal contacts within each of the major federal or state agencies are useful to obtain advance notice of Requests for Proposals (RFPs) and special project funding. Publications discussing available grants are listed in Appendix N (the Management section of the Public Health Nutrition Library) and Appendix I (Prospecting for Grants).

State Grants

State departments of health, health and human services, and education usually provide some funds for nutrition services. The state funds may support selected statewide and/or local services. In many states a per capita or preestablished formula is used for allocating state and federal funds to local health agencies. State agencies may have special legislated funding for nutrition or project funding for nutrition programs. State agencies also serve as the conduits for federal funds earmarked for local program implementation. Specific federal project funds that state governmental agencies administer through a grants process include

- Special Supplemental Food Program for Women, Infants, and Children (WIC)
- Commodity Supplemental Food Program (CSFP)
- Nutrition Education and Training (NET) Projects
- Maternal and Child Health Block Grant and special projects of regional and national significance (SPRANS)
- Health promotion special projects
- Chronic disease intervention and reduction special projects

Each state's grant application procedure has special requirements that need to be determined through the local agency administrator or state health agency regional or central office nutrition consultants. Appendix D lists addresses and telephone numbers for state and territorial public health nutrition directors.

Local Grants or Contracts

Local human or social service agencies, home health agencies, area agencies on aging, mental health agencies, developmental disabilities councils, school districts, jails, community colleges, and other governmental units frequently need nutrition services or have special initiatives or ongoing projects that require nutrition expertise. When agencies do not employ a full-time nutritionist on their own staff, they will often contract for these services as the most efficient method for getting the short-term or long-term services they need. Those local agencies that need part-time nutrition services frequently maintain lists or files of available contractors and their specialists. It is important to cultivate contacts within the local agencies who can advise on their needs, availability of funding, and interest in developing contracts.

Local voluntary health agencies such as the heart association, diabetes association, cancer society, cystic fibrosis association, or March of Dimes chapter or affiliate offices also may need and contract for nutrition services or offer small competitive project grants. For short-term community projects, funds may be obtained from local businesses, banks, civic organizations, or churches.

Foundation Grants

Millions of dollars of private foundation projects are funded annually for foundation-specific priorities. The local public library is the most valuable resource for identifying these foundation funders. Foundation and grant information centers in public libraries maintain information on

- names and contact persons for local, state, regional, or national foundations
- information on past funding priorities and projects funded
- dollar amount of awards for foundation projects
- criteria and format for submitting funding requests
- timeline for review of grant requests

Priorities of foundations may change annually. Thus, putting a new twist on an old idea or need may be required for the foundation to consider the proposal. Some foundations prefer that proposals be submitted on behalf of a nongovernmental, nonprofit agency. Nutritionists working in a governmental agency who seek a foundation grant might collaborate with a nonprofit agency that will submit the proposal and subcontract the nutrition work to the public health agency. (See Appendix I, Prospecting for Grants.)

Fees for Services (First Party Reimbursement)

A fee-for-service adjusted for each target population is a useful method for recovering program costs. A basic market analysis (see Chapter 15) is required to determine the range of fees appropriate to charge the various target populations. Fees must be based on actual costs, not guesswork. Making a fee-for-service more acceptable to clients of a public health service is a second task, after calculating actual costs. In presenting a plan to establish fees to administrators, government officials, the public, and co-workers, three alternatives might be offered.

1. *sliding scale fee-for-service*: the fee is based on the client's ability to pay, with the maximum fee being the actual cost of the service; this can be used for all basic public health services.
2. *actual cost fee-for-service*: the actual cost of providing a service is calculated and is revised annually. It is charged for public health services where there are other private and nonprofit providers of the

services within a community; these service charges are not put on a sliding scale because of the potential legal issues of unfair competition by a governmental provider; a public agency will by design have few of these services because of need-based planning.

3. *cost-plus fee-for-service*: this pricing model permits a nonprofit agency to recover the actual cost of a service in addition to a profit which is then used to subsidize another service within the agency; these "cash cows" may include innovative services or products (healthy cooking demonstrations, diet and fitness classes) or long-standing, fully capitalized services (laboratory tests).

These pricing versus costing strategies are dependent on an accurate cost determination (discussed later in this chapter). Nutrition services that can generate fees include community classes for pregnant women or breast-feeding mothers, classes in child nutrition for young parents, weight management and fitness programs and classes, and support groups for adults requiring various types of diets to manage chronic diseases such as diabetes or hyperlipidemias. Many public health agencies are contracting with businesses or industries to conduct health promotion, wellness, or fitness programs for their employees (see Chapter 18).

Third Party Reimbursement

This is income derived by billing insurance carriers such as governmental health care programs (Medicaid, Medicare), Workers' Compensation, health maintenance organizations (HMOs), and/or other special health insurance pools (catastrophic health, state-sponsored alternative care pools, prenatal care pools). Each health carrier has its own billing procedures that the agency accounting office must determine and continuously keep updated. It is most cost-effective for the agency accounting department to select the third party reimbursement sources that cover the majority of the agency clients and to bill these carriers. Clients not covered by those carriers would be treated as fee-for-service clients and advised on the procedure to use to collect from their own carrier. Some organizations contract with health care reimbursement firms that require an assignment of benefits from all clients and handle all agency billing for a predetermined fee. Emerging opportunities for income generation are developing in this area of third party reimbursement. Private practice registered dietitians and public health nutritionists have convinced private health insurance carriers of the need for their services and the costs. States recognizing the need for prenatal and pediatric care for all women and children are developing

Medicaid waivers. As discussed in Chapter 8, nutrition services are increasingly being reimbursed within these provisions.

PREPARING BUDGETS AND DETERMINING PROGRAM COSTS

Generating the funds to cover the cost of delivering a nutrition service is an important part of fiscal management. Determining the real cost of a product or service is crucial to setting fees, collecting reimbursements, and writing grants. Preparing a budget for a program of services and then breaking it down into the actual cost of each product/service is the next step.

Budgets are the convergence of plans with the income-generating reality—what services can be implemented with the funds that can be made available to pay for them. An annotated budget, as shown in Exhibit 17-1, is the best way to walk through the process.

The Budget Summary

Controlling the budget requires a monthly comparison of projected income to actual expenses and encumbrances (items purchased but not yet paid for). Table 17-1 is an example of such a comparison. The agency's accounting section should provide a monthly financial summary listing the current status of expenditures compared to the amounts budgeted. The program manager must monitor this carefully so that all budgeted resources are spent to advantage, especially if allocated funds must be used before the end of a fiscal year. The monthly financial summary also enables the manager to determine when the income flow is inadequate compared to projections.

The monthly budget summary should be used to determine when there is a need to

- communicate with staff about the program's financial position
- trim discretionary costs (supplies, printing, etc.) or increase spending on consumable supplies
- increase or decrease staffing (overtime or voluntary reduction of hours)
- generate more income (find out why some health carriers are slower to pay or slow down agency billing process)

A computer spreadsheet for the personal computer is a clear, time-saving tool for preparing the budget summary.

Exhibit 17-1 The Annotated Program Budget

Income

Diversified income base is critical to a strong program. The only "fudge factors" are client fees and reimbursements.

Grant A	$X X X	
Grant B	X X X	
Client fees	X X X	
Third party reimbursement	X X X	
General revenue (tax levy support)	<u>X X X</u>	
Total income:		<u>$X X X</u>
		(This should equal or exceed total expenses)

Expenses

Salaries		$X X X	
Full-time	$X X X		
Part-time[1]	X X X		
Fringe benefits[2]		$X X X	
Full-time	$X X X		
Part-time	X X X		
Mileage for local travel		$X X X	
Telephone, local/long distance		X X X	
Postage		X X X	
Duplicating		X X X	
Film/video reproduction		$X X X	
Printing		X X X	
Supplies		X X X	
Office	$X X X		
Food	X X X		
Books			(Important to maintain
Subscriptions	$X X X		separate accounting for
Educational materials	X X X		all of these)
Software	X X X		
Office rental			$XXX (if applicable)
Equipment, rental			X X X
Copy machine	$X X X		
Computer	X X X		(Carefully evaluate the rent
Telephones	X X X		vs. buy option on all equipment)
Video	X X X		
Equipment, purchase			$X X X
Desks, chairs	$X X X		
Computer	X X X		(Important to plan for life
Office equipment	X X X		cycle replacement of equipment
Video	X X X		in each annual budget)
Auto, van	X X X		

Exhibit 17-1 continued

Utilities, electricity		$XXX
Staff Training and Continuing Education		XXX
Out-of-town travel	$XXX	
Lodging	XXX	(Usually need to provide detail
Registration fees	XXX	on all out-of-town trips, i.e.,
Registration, local	XXX	where, why, who, when?)
Memberships	XXX	
Other		$XXX
Indirect costs[3]		$XXX
Central service charge[4]		XXX
Consultant fees[5]		XXX
Student stipends[6]		XXX
Contingent reserve[7]		XXX
Contract consultants or staff[8]	$XXX	
Equipment maintenance contracts[9]		$XXX
TOTAL EXPENSES		$XXX
Income over expenses		XXX
Income under expenses		(XXX)
		(This is
		trouble!)

FOOTNOTES:

1. Part-time employees may be useful to provide staffing flexibility to cover peak service periods. This would permit scheduling two part-time (.5 FTE) employees to work at busier clinics rather than having one staff person working full-time.
2. Fringe benefit rates may be different for full- and part-time staff.
3. There may be an administrative overhead charge included as percent of each budget.
4. Overhead may be charged for a portion of the services of attorneys, accountants, executive directors, central purchasing, etc.
5. Include graphic consultants, contract nutrition consultants, external evaluation specialists, auditors.
6. Try to build in student stipends for student internships if quality supervision can be provided for the students.
7. Can build in a fund for carryover each year for new projects or emergencies.
8. May be useful to have contract physicians available for grant proposals or some direct service, especially if third party reimbursement will help cover their expense.
9. Fees are generally charged on a per copy or per month rate for major equipment maintenance; only use if there is a good payback for frequently broken equipment that cannot be replaced.

Table 17-1 Monthly Budget Summary

Month_____ Year_____

Income	Received This Period	Projected This Period	Year to Date Received	Year to Date Projected	Year to Date Last Year Received
All	$ X X	$ X X	$ X X	$ X X	$ X X
Sources	X X	X X	X X	X X	X X
Listed	X X	X X	X X	X X	X X
Total income	$ X X	$ X X	$ X X	$ X X	$ X X

Expenses	Spent/ Encumbered This Period	Projected This Period	Year to Date Spent	Year to Date Projected	Year to Date Last Year Spent
All	$ X X	$ X X	$ X X	$ X X	$ X X
Categories	X X	X X	X X	X X	X X
Listed	X X	X X	X X	X X	X X
Total expenses	$ X X	$ X X	$ X X	$ X X	$ X X

Variances from projections:

Comments from the accounting staff for action and planning.

Determining Costs for Each Service

Determining the costs for each specific service or product requires a slightly different adaptation of the program budget. The program manager must know the approximate utilization of staff and resources directed to each service. Staff time is the largest expense in any service. Time studies are frequently used to assess the amount of staff time each product or service requires. The reference listing in the Management section of the Public Health Nutrition Library (Appendix N) cites several useful references for conducting time studies. If a time study is not feasible for a variety of reasons (lack of time, staff issues, etc.), a quick, less precise method can be used to approximate the amount of staff time spent in each specific service area. This method is displayed in Table 17-2. Note that administrative time is factored into each service category.

Table 17-2 Staff Allocation by Service for Cost Determination

Staff Member Name	Total FTE	WIC	Diabetes Clinic	Home Visits	Education Presentations Group	Writing Newspaper Column	Weight Reduction Class
Clerical							
Amy Jones	1.0	0.9	0.0	0.0	0.0	0.0	0.1
Jean Brown	0.8	0.1	0.1	0.3	0.2	0.1	0.0
Paraprofessionals							
Tom Smith	1.0	1.0	0.0	0.0	0.0	0.0	0.0
Betty White	0.8	0.8	0.0	0.0	0.0	0.0	0.0
Pam Johnson	0.7	0.7	0.0	0.0	0.0	0.0	0.0
Terry Jones	1.0	0.5	0.0	0.5	0.0	0.0	0.0
Professionals							
Mary Stokes	0.8	0.8	0.0	0.0	0.0	0.0	0.0
Sue Austin	1.0	0.0	0.0	0.1	0.3	0.1	0.5
Steve Doe	1.0	0.0	0.0	0.1	0.3	0.1	0.5
Kate Conner	1.0	0.2	0.1	0.1	0.4	0.1	0.1
Total	9.1	5.0	0.2	1.1	1.2	0.4	1.2

Exhibit 17-2 Cost Determination for a Service

Service: Nutrition counseling in home visits Date of cost determination: Staff salary and fringe		
Salaries		
Jan Black, .3 FTE	$ X X X	Full-time equivalent
Sue Smith, .4 FTE	X X X	(FTE) multiplied by
Barbara Bates, .1 FTE	X X X	annual salary plus
Joe Down, .1 FTE	X X X	fringe
Jill White, .1 FTE	X X X	
Mileage for home visits	X X X	
Telephone	X X X	These should be all
Postage	X X X	allocated at a pre-
Duplicating	X X X	determined rate based
Supplies	X X X	on actual usage or
Office space, __ sq. ft .@ $____/ft.	X X X	estimated use
Equipment, %	X X X	
Training and education, %	X X X	
Other	X X X	
Subtotal	$ X X X	The agency has an
		overhead cost for
Indirect cost rate @ % of subtotal	X X X	administration
		that should be
Total cost	$ X X X	reflected here if not
		in "other" expenses

Divide total cost by number of clients or client visits (or relative value units used by some programs) expected to be served this year. This gives a cost per contact or encounter which is the actual cost to the program to provide each unit of this service.

The next step is to cost out staff, supplies, equipment, and other resources for each service area (Exhibit 17-2), then divide the total cost by the number of clients or client visits (or relative value units, a productivity measuring unit used by some programs) expected to be served during the year. This gives a cost per contact which is the actual cost to the program to provide each unit of service.

Starting from the program budget, this cost determination analysis takes approximately two hours to calculate for each service. A program manager could devote about two hours per month to identifying the actual costs of one program per month and make needed adjustments in charges. More complicated systems of cost determination exist, especially for federally funded programs. These can be developed with the guidance of the agency's business manager or accountant. Public health programs have

Exhibit 17-3 Service Productivity Analysis

Service: Nutrition Counseling in Home Visits

1. How long should it take to provide one unit (visit) of this service?

   2 hours   *(includes direct service time, travel time, charting, chart handling, case conference, administration, vacation and sick time).*

2. How long does it take to provide each unit (visit) of this service?

   The response to this question would be determined:

   Total FTEs: *1.5 X 2080 hours = 3120 hours*
   Total units: *650 visits*

   3120 ÷ 650 = 4.8 hours per home visit

3. Explain difference between answers to 1 and 2.

   - *4.8 hours per visit (actual) compared to 2.0 hours per visit (estimate) is significant. Thus, staff take twice as long to complete service as what they estimated or too much staff are assigned to this activity.*
   - *Adjust expectation to 3.0 hours per visit and expect 1040 home visits this year or reduce staff to 0.94 FTEs to provide 650 visits. In order to break even financially for this service, must increase staff productivity or reassign/reduce staff.*
   - *The budget for home visit service is based on an actual cost of $65.00 per home visit. If the number of home visits can be increased from 650 to 1040 with the existing staff, the program will generate an additional $25,350 this year. Reimbursers will not pay more than $65.00 per visit this year.*

---

dramatically increased their operating income after doing this type of analysis. Examples include immunization and health screening programs which are totally supported by fees and reimbursements.

Service Productivity Analysis

A second stage of analysis for program managers concerned about the high cost of a given service is a service productivity analysis. The resource list in the Management section of the Public Health Nutrition Library (Appendix N) includes several references on how to conduct a detailed productivity analysis of program services. A simple analysis of service productivity levels involves multiplying the total FTEs allocated to each service by 2,080 (paid hours for each full-time equivalent position) and dividing by the number of clients or contact visits (Exhibit 17-3).

Cost-Effectiveness and Cost-Benefit Analysis of Services

The third and final challenge of fiscal management is to evaluate the service/product once the costs and providers have been identified. Two types of analyses used are cost-benefit analysis and cost-effectiveness analysis.

A cost-benefit analysis is used in the planning process to decide if a program/service should be undertaken. A cost-effectiveness analysis is undertaken in planning to determine the least costly way to provide the service or program. Cost benefit and cost effectiveness are discussed in more detail in Chapter 14, and several pertinent references are listed in the Public Health Nutrition Library (Appendix N).

For the public health practitioner, the variety of analysis methods used in fiscal management are sometimes confusing. It may be useful for the practitioner to clarify the problem or question that is to be studied and then consider the appropriate analysis tools (Exhibit 17-4).

Through the application of these analysis tools, the nutritionist can make services generate income and become increasingly self-supporting. There is

---

Exhibit 17-4   Selecting Analysis Tools

Question	Analysis Tools
• How much can I spend on the program?	• Budget—income sources • Cost determination for services in program X
• Is the fee for service set at the right amount?	• Cost determination • Income projections based on service levels
• Can the budget be increased by providing a new service?	• Income projections based on projected service levels
• Why is money lost by offering this service?	• Actual income from service • Cost determination • Service productivity levels • Cost effectiveness analysis • Pricing strategy (sliding fee, cost, cost-plus)
• Why should this service be reimbursed?	• Cost effective • Cost benefit • Cost determination
• Why should this service be offered?	• Cost benefit

great risk in taking an innovative service idea, guessing at a charge for the service, providing the service, and later questioning why the staff time commitment is so excessive in relation to the financial return. An analysis of the project, including the documented need, the population to be served, favorable pricing, and realistic income expectation could turn the innovation into a source of income.

DEVELOPING SKILLS IN GRANTWRITING

Most nutritionists need to become grant writers so that they can obtain outside income to support innovative services, reach new populations, develop and test interventions, and initiate special projects; any or all of these may then turn into long-term, income-producing services. Several hints for grantwriting are as follows:

- Maintain a grant idea folder to file innovative ideas that would require external funding. These can be ideas with a one-paragraph description as contributed by staff members. The community needs assessment will help produce some ideas for needed community services.
- Foster staff development by conducting an internal seed grant program within the section or agency. Allocate a small amount of money each year to this research and development (R&D) fund.
- Find several grant writers and reviewers within the agency with whom to brainstorm ideas and advise on writing grant proposals.
- Reduce all grant proposals to a one-page worksheet as an initial step. A sample worksheet is shown in Exhibit 17-5.
- Maintain a large network of project collaborators to work with on grant proposals of mutual interest.
- Identify reliable people and organizations that can be counted on to write support letters—even on short notice. Some of these individuals/ agencies may prefer that the support letter be written for their signature.
- Plan on writing grants that will generate four times the dollar amount from the grant as the program is committing.
- Practice writing concisely. If the idea cannot be conveyed in two double-spaced pages, including needs statement, methods, objectives, budget, and collaborators, grantwriting will be too time-consuming.
- Maintain a file of agency information that can be pulled for grant attachments. Items such as Agency Internal Revenue Tax Exemption

Exhibit 17-5   Sample Grant Application Worksheet

Project Title: _____
                                    (5-7 words)

Amount Requested: $ Total Project Cost: $

Project Collaborators:

Project Summary:

Statement of Specific Problem or Need (brief literature review):

Target Population:

Objectives (measurable and time-specific):

Methods (program description, timeline):

Evaluation (tied to measurable objectives):

Budget, including in-kind contributions:

Letters of support to be sought:

(Cover letter)

501C-3 statements, audited budgets, lists of board members, agency descriptions, federal identification numbers for the agency, and personnel curriculum vitae should be in this file.

* Maintain a file of copies of grants submitted previously.
* When available use a word processor to write the narrative and a spreadsheet to calculate the budget. This makes it easier to revise the proposal without introducing errors.
* Get on the mailing lists of every agency and foundation that announces related grant/contract Requests for Proposals (RFPs) that can be identified.

These hints for grantwriting will undoubtedly be added to and shared with other people. Sharing the work and the glory when a new grant comes to the agency is the mark of a true professional. Researching grant funds and writing proposals take time. Alas, well-written proposals are not always funded. Even experienced grant writers receive rejections. It takes persistence. If a proposal is rejected, ask why and try again, and again.

ISSUES TO DEBATE

* Is the nutrition program using the best mix of staff and allocation of staff time to result in the desired outcomes?
* Is time balanced among financial management and responsibilities for networking, staff development, and service delivery?
* What new resources for funding nutrition services need to be generated? Which innovative ideas should be pursued for a well-rounded program?
* How should fees for services be established and how should this income be most effectively allocated?

NOTES

1. *1989 Public Health Chartbook* (Washington, D.C.: Public Health Foundation, May 1989), Figure 5.

2. Ibid., Figure 6.

3. Mildred Kaufman, Preliminary Report, *Nutrition Services in State and Public Health Agencies, 1989*, Report of Bienniel Survey of State Activities (Chapel Hill, N.C.: Unpublished, May 1989), Table 2-4.

4. *1989 Public Health Chartbook*, Figure 6.

5. Kaufman, *Nutrition Services*, Table 2-4.

6. *1989 Public Health Chartbook*, Figure 6.

7. Kaufman, *Nutrition Services*, Table 2-4.

BIBLIOGRAPHY

Berngen, Charles. *Introduction to Management Accounting.* 6th ed. Englewood Cliffs, N.J.: Prentice-Hall, 1984.

Conklin, M.T., and M.D. Simko. "Cost-Benefit and Cost-Effectiveness Analyses of Nutrition Programs." *Quality Review Bulletin* 9 (1983):166-168.

Disbrow, Doris. "The Costs and Benefits of Nutrition Services: A Literature Review." *Journal of The American Dietetic Association* Suppl. 89 (4): S4-S63.

Mali, Paul. *Improving Total Productivity—MBO Statistics for Business, Government and Not For Profit Organizations.* New York: John Wiley and Sons, 1978.

Schramm, W.F., "WIC Prenatal Participation and Its Relationship to Newborn Medicaid Costs in Missouri: A Cost/Benefit Analysis." *American Journal of Public Health* 75, no. 8 (1985):851-857.

Shepard, D.S., and M.S. Thompson. "First Principles of Cost-Effectiveness Analysis in Health." *Public Health Reports* 94 (Nov-Dec 1979):535–543.

Splett, Patricia, and Mariel Caldwell. *Costing Nutrition Services: A Workbook.* Minneapolis: University of Minnesota, 1985.

chapter **18**

Intervening To Change the Public's Eating Behavior

Alice R. Thomson and MaryAnn C. Farthing

READER OBJECTIVES

- Describe the complex interacting factors that influence people's eating behavior.
- Discuss intervention strategies that promote dietary behavior change.
- Compare and contrast population-based interventions with client interventions.
- Compare and contrast the sites and media that can be used to reach various populations in the community with nutrition and health messages.

CHANGING EATING BEHAVIOR

Every day most Americans are offered a smorgasbord of food choices in supermarkets, restaurants, cafeterias, delis, fast food outlets, and vending machines. It has been estimated that the average person eats more than 25 distinct foods during a typical three-day period.[1] National food consumption studies and observation of people checking out at their supermarkets or choosing from restaurant menus, as well as recording diet histories of health agency clients, confirm that the prevailing diet in the United States today is too high in calories, saturated fats, cholesterol, alcohol, sugar, and salt. At the same time it is too low in fiber, calcium, iron, and possibly other vitamins and minerals recommended for optimal reproduction, growth of children and health of people at all ages.

The nutritionist strives to guide and motivate people to choose and prepare foods to promote growth and health and prevent disease. Some people may be more receptive than others. As the dietary change agent for

361

a population, the nutritionist must understand that many complex interacting factors influence people to choose the foods they eat.

How Food Preferences Are Formed

Food preferences begin with the infant's first taste of milk and are molded by the child's experiences with feeding and at mealtimes. The child's attitudes toward food and eating develop as new foods are introduced. Taste preferences are very individual, as seen when siblings raised in the same home have different food likes and dislikes. People's food choices are influenced by their parents' tastes and education; their family's religious practices or ethnic heritage; the family's food budget; the family's usual methods of preparing food; and the time that family members can spend on shopping, cooking, and eating. How convenient the grocery store is, how well it is stocked, and whether they have the transportation to get there also influences what food is in the family meals. Food the family has on their table is what they can afford to buy at their local market or grow in their garden. Food habits are affected when parents, grandparents, spouses, or caretakers use food as a reward or the withdrawal of food as a punishment. Families or communities place values on foods they consider either high or low status. Some foods are "special" when they become traditions and are served at celebrations or holidays. Every family has favorite meals they enjoy serving to guests. Knowledge and concern about the effect of diet on health competes as just one more influence. Among the many conflicting emotional, social, cultural, religious, and economic factors that influence people when they choose their food, health and disease risk reduction may not be their highest priority.

Changing Food Choices

Taking medications every day or giving up smoking requires changing behavior, but changing food choices is even more overwhelming. The many food decisions people must make in the course of each day and the many factors which influence these choices explain why many people find it difficult to follow dietary guidelines or comply with prescribed dietary treatments even when health professionals clearly explain the benefits.

People are more likely to change food choices permanently if they proceed in gradual, incremental steps. Fad weight reduction diets that require dieters to make drastic changes in lifelong habits seldom contribute to long-term weight loss and changes that they can sustain. Fad diets provide no opportunity for the dieter to adopt the eating behaviors necessary for lifelong weight management. Dieters who return to their former eating patterns often gain back all of the body weight they worked so hard to lose. The nutritionist guiding health-promoting eating habits must present people with options and encourage them to take small steps toward achieving their long-term goals. People introduced to dietary changes must understand that continuing commitment is required for long-term benefits.

The steps in changing dietary behavior are shown in Figure 18-1. Progress through these steps may occur in different sequences. The more complete each step, the more likely the behavior change will be sustained.

Attitudes. People must have confidence that they can "take charge" of their own health and the emotions that surround eating. They must be convinced that they can control what they eat and enjoy a variety of health-promoting foods. They must be ready to try unfamiliar foods and new ways of preparing them.

Awareness. People need to understand the role of diet in promoting good health and lowering the risk of chronic diseases. Awareness also means that individuals know their own health status, health risks, and unique dietary needs. They must recognize that a health-promoting diet is "a way of life." A strategy to build community awareness is the "reach and repeat" technique that uses short, repeated commercials in the mass media.

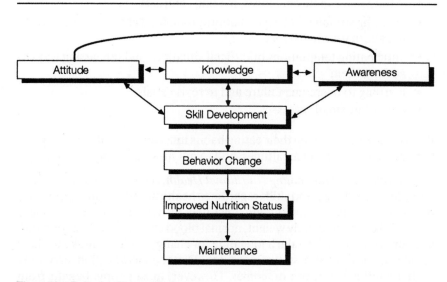

Figure 18-1 Behavior Change Chain

Knowledge. The public needs scientifically sound information explained to them so that they understand the reasons for the changes recommended. The scientific bases for the changes must be translated into everyday language. For some people, knowing what to do and why they should do it encourages them to make changes. For others, knowledge alone may not change behavior.

Skill Development. Competencies necessary to make and sustain new eating habits include selecting appropriate foods at the market; budgeting for the healthful foods to purchase; obtaining food stamps if needed to increase food buying power; growing fruits and vegetables and preparing foods with less fat, sugar, and salt. Behaviors that contribute to more controlled eating include eating more slowly, only eating when sitting down at a set place at the table, preparing health-promoting food to look and taste good, and eating with congenial companions. Helping people develop their skills starts by examining the factors that determine their eating behaviors and identifying which factors are most important to them. For example, persons who frequently travel for their work require more guidance on choosing and ordering from restaurant menus than in selecting foods in the supermarket and preparing them in their home kitchen.

Behavior Change. This step can be achieved by

- monitoring food intake and eating habits to identify problems
- setting reasonable objectives, making contracts
- avoiding stimuli that trigger inappropriate food choices and substituting alternative behaviors
- anticipating temptations or difficult situations and rehearsing ways to address them
- learning to overcome failure and to revise goals
- rewarding small successes

People who are changing their eating habits must learn to take one day at a time, to enjoy food and mealtimes, and to not make a fetish out of eating.

Promoting and Maintaining Nutritional Health. Attaining new awareness, attitudes, knowledge, and skills regarding "healthy eating" can improve nutrition and health. Successful outcomes may be measured by achievement of desired changes in body weight, normal blood chemistry values, or blood pressure control. It can take a long time for changes in food intake to show results in these health status measures. Dietary modification may only partially influence health outcomes. However, most people benefit from following the Dietary Guidelines for Americans.[2]

Once changes in food habits have occurred and improved health outcomes have been demonstrated, the new behaviors must become routine. Improvements that continue to benefit the individual will help to maintain change. Conversely, barriers contributing to relapse should be acknowledged and handled.

LEVELS OF INTERVENTION

Community-based intervention strategies provide the most "bang for the buck." When people in a community change food habits together they will be more likely to sustain the changes than when individuals try to act alone. Community-based interventions should work on some of the powerful cultural and social influences that are difficult for individuals to overcome on their own. When an office or factory replaces candy, potato chips, and soft drinks in vending machines with fresh fruits, dry roasted nuts, and low fat milk, workers will choose from these items. When fruit juice punch, raw vegetables with yogurt dip, or oatmeal cookies replace pie and ice cream at church socials, the guests will enjoy refreshments while controlling their fat intake. Since disease may occur in those who have no risk factors, a program targeted only at individuals identified with risk factors will miss many people who could benefit.[3]

The public health approach emphasizes population-based rather than clinical strategies. Interventions must be designed to be sufficiently aggressive and intense to achieve the objective. The action plan is driven by the objectives, the boldness and creativity of the planners, the available or anticipated resources, the support of the stakeholders, and the results of cost-effectiveness analysis.

POPULATION-BASED INTERVENTIONS

Systems Interventions

Systems interventions are environmental, food system, or institutional changes that alter the quality of people's nutrient intake while minimizing their need for individual action. Systems interventions demonstrate the health-related values of the community that support recommended dietary changes. Public health nutritionists can influence the system by using the following methods:

Policy Development. Chapters 5 and 6 discuss the processes through which nutrition policy is established. Policies made at the national, state, and local levels in the private and public sectors influence people's eating habits. Food processors, food advertisers, food distributors, and restaurateurs influence the ingredients, quality, and price of foods in the market through the formulation of products and their promotion. Federal and state laws and regulations on food labeling influence food quality and the nutrition and ingredient information available to the public. State regulations governing the licensing of group care facilities influence the food they serve and the nutritional care they give their residents. At worksites, personnel policies and schedules influence how much time employees have to eat and the food available in their cafeteria and vending machines.

Advocacy. This influences the quality of the community food supply by convincing food manufacturers, food marketers, food service establishments, policymakers, or legislators of their responsibilities. Advocacy groups also provide them with the technical expertise they need to ensure that food products are formulated, distributed, and labeled to promote and protect the health of the public.

Community Organization. The health and nutrition promotion efforts of community agencies, health professionals or organizations, the media, and concerned consumer groups should be mobilized and coordinated around strong, consistent health and nutrition messages to eliminate conflicting or duplicating efforts. Few agencies acting alone have the resources to impact on the eating habits of the whole community. To respond to the nutrition problems identified in the community assessment, the nutritionist should network with as many groups as possible. (See Chapter 22.)

Agencies that might be conducting relevant programs include local health departments, cooperative extension, area agencies on aging, schools, community colleges and universities, adult education, hospitals, health professional organizations, voluntary health agencies, civic and service organizations, libraries, and departments of parks and recreation. A community nutrition council or health promotion coalition can provide a forum to exchange information and coordinate planning. Publishing a community nutrition resource directory may be a first effort at community organization. Agencies can join together to coordinate their planning, service delivery, and staff training.

Modification of the Food Supply. Advocacy and policy development can lead to modification of the food supply. The food supply can be modified through the fortification or enrichment of commonly used foods, changes in the formulation of processed food products to reduce their calorie, fat, and sodium content, and production of leaner meat products through changes in animal husbandry practices. The food industry has responded to consumer interests by producing leaner meats, reducing sugar and sodium in baby foods, changing the kind and amount of fat in crackers and fast foods, increasing the fiber in breakfast cereals, offering calorie-controlled convenience meals, and voluntarily including more nutrition information on food labels.

Media Interventions

The media reach large numbers of people at one time to guide them in making individual changes. While the change each individual undertakes may be small, the aggregate change of many individuals can be significant.

Radio, Television, and Print Media

The mass media reach into almost every home in the nation. Mass media promote health by publicizing programs and services and broadcasting single-concept health and nutrition messages. National voluntary and federal health agencies air public service campaigns on a variety of subjects related to health promotion and nutrition. Local agencies can use media campaigns to promote their programs and services, as well as health messages. Planned campaigns coordinate television, radio, print media (newspapers and magazines), public transit ads and billboards, booklets, posters, and community events to focus attention on one significant health message. As nutritionists become experts in dealing with local media, they can continuously generate coverage for nutrition topics that have wide appeal.[4]

Nutritionists develop their expertise in working with the media by beginning with simple efforts. They might write a letter to the local newspaper editor or call a special feature reporter with a human interest story. They might distribute news releases or public service announcements (PSAs) produced by a national voluntary health agency or federal government agencies. Local television or radio stations using these messages may localize them by adding tag lines referring viewers to the agency or expert in their community for more information. Logging the numbers of calls or requests for pamphlets can quantify the reach of the PSAs. Seeking opportunities to be on a local radio or television talk or call-in show or writing articles or question-and-answer columns for the newspaper provides visibility for the nutritionist and more in-depth information for the public. Media efforts can be linked with the national health observances or special theme months, weeks, and days (Exhibit 18-1). Each of these nutrition and health-related celebrations generates media interest simultaneously throughout the country. To add to local publicity, the mayor or governor can be requested to issue a proclamation for the observance.

Exhibit 18-1 Calendar of National Health Observances

FEBRUARY	National Children's Dental Health Month
	American Heart Month
MARCH	National Nutrition Month
	Women in History Month
	National Kidney Month
APRIL	Cancer Control Month
	Health Fair Month
	National Consumer Protection Week (3rd week)
	World Health Day (1st Friday)
MAY	National Physical Fitness and Sports Month
	National High Blood Pressure Month
	Older Americans' Month
	National Osteroporosis Prevention Week (week following Mother's Day)
	Digestive Disease Awareness Week (2nd week)
	Hospital, Nursing Home, and Senior Centers Week (2nd week)
	National Employee Health and Fitness Day (May 18, 1990)
JUNE	National Dairy Month
AUGUST	Family Day (2nd Friday)
SEPTEMBER	National Adult Day Care Week (3rd week)
	National Cholesterol Education Month
	American Heart Association Food Festival
OCTOBER	Running and Fitness Week (3rd Monday)
	World Food Day (3rd Monday)
	World Vegetarian Day (1st Sunday)
	World Community Day (1st Monday)
	Child Health Day (1st Thursday)
	Family Health Month
	Breast Cancer Awareness Week
NOVEMBER	National Diabetes Month
	National Family Caregiver's Week (4th week)
	Great American Smokeout

A complete listing of celebrations and their sponsoring organizations is available from the National Health Information Clearinghouse at (301) 565-4167.

To increase the effectiveness of media campaigns, a specific audience should be targeted. The concerns and interests of this audience should be investigated through surveys and focus groups. Radio stations or newspapers that are known to speak directly to the specific targeted audience (i.e., Hispanics, teenagers, etc.) should be selected. Several forms of media used together can reinforce messages and impact on different points of the behavior change chain of knowledge, awareness, and attitude. Awareness is raised by brief, repeated messages. A brief message can be reinforced and more in-depth knowledge can be provided by a pamphlet mailed to those who call or write for more information. A public forum or series of classes can expand on the nutrition information in the media. Community festivals or health and food fairs in malls, parks, recreation centers, and schools stimulate excitement, involvement, visibility, and interaction, increasing the appeal and creating favorable attitudes for health-promoting foods.

Hotlines

Telephone hotlines or recorded telephone nutrition messages offer the public a convenient, credible, inexpensive access to answers to their questions about general nutrition, food composition, food preparation, or food safety. Nutritionists may answer the telephone line during scheduled hours. The telephone number and hours of operation can be publicized on radio or television or printed in the newspaper or on an insert to be sent with telephone, gas, electric, or water bills. When the calls cannot be answered personally, an answering machine can record the inquiry and the call can be returned as soon as possible with the requested information. The nutritionist who answers the hotline must maintain an extensive resource file and library to research the more complex or unusual questions. A written record of all questions and answers can document the popularity of the service and the questions asked most often. This record can be used to monitor the quality of the service. Callers who ask for counseling on an individual prescribed diet must be referred to a registered dietitian in a health agency, community hospital, or private practice. The nutritionist who answers the calls must be alert to cues that indicate that the caller might need more specific individualized diet counseling.

Recorded nutrition messages are a less personal but still useful telephone answering service. Brief recorded messages can provide information on a variety of popular topics on nutrition, diet, food safety, and health. To maintain interest, a fairly large repertory of tapes must be offered on a rotating basis with additions, revisions, and deletions made frequently. Each tape should conclude with a brief statement indicating the source of the tape, the speaker, the sponsoring agency, and additional nutrition services available in the community. Nutrition hotlines and resource centers are visible services that official health agencies or community nutrition councils can offer to the public. Agencies that cannot staff a nutrition hotline might refer interested callers to the Nutrition Resources Department of The American Dietetic Association, 312 899-0040 or 800 877-1600.

Nutrition Education at the Point of Food Choice

Supermarkets

The neighborhood supermarket may carry as many as 15,000 items with thousands of new products introduced each year.[5] Shoppers wishing to make dietary changes must know how to identify those foods that best meet their needs. Three-fourths of the consumers surveyed consider nutritional qualities before price and ease of preparation when they decide which food products to purchase.[6] More and more stores are providing nutrition information to meet customers' needs and maintain their loyalty.[7] Health agencies may find supermarkets willing to collaborate in community-based nutrition education. More and more stores have consumer information centers or kiosks to distribute nutrition pamphlets or recipes featuring healthful foods or preparation techniques. In-store public service announcements, videos, or interactive user-friendly computer programs can feature nutrition topics. These topics can also be featured in the weekly food ads in the newspaper. Bag stuffers or messages printed on bags transmit short, simple messages to every purchaser. Also, healthful foods can be featured in food demonstrations and tastings.

Several large supermarket chains have demonstrated that shoppers' food choices can be influenced by shelf labels displaying information about sodium, fat, and fiber content of food products. Informative shelf labels are becoming available for supermarkets to purchase. Labeling a large number of items carried in the supermarket is very labor-intensive both for the store personnel and the nutritionist. Criteria must be developed, labels designed, and long-term agreements negotiated to define responsibilities of participating stores and consulting nutritionists. Store staff must be trained, and the shelf-labeling installed and monitored. A shopping list featuring one category of food such as meat or dairy foods or a limited number of key foods from different categories can be distributed. The foods on the list can be identified on the store shelf with colorful tags.

In-store shopping tours can be offered and publicized to highlight healthful food choices to shoppers.[8] Small groups of participants can be led aisle-by-aisle through the supermarket. Using a wide variety of examples, participants can be taught to interpret the information on food labels. These tours can be designed for specific groups with a shared need such as pregnant women, parents of young children, senior citizens, or persons on a sodium-restricted or fat-controlled diet.

The American Heart Association (AHA) sponsors an annual Food Festival and the American Cancer Society sponsors the Eat Smart project implemented by volunteers in local grocery stores. The AHA is launching a nationwide program called HeartGuide. HeartGuide is a consumer health information program designed to teach Americans how to select foods in the marketplace to help them reduce the fat, cholesterol, and sodium in their diets. The program identifies processed food products that meet AHA criteria for total fat, saturated fat, cholesterol, and sodium by placing a seal on qualifying foods. The criteria are based on the AHA's "Dietary Guidelines for Healthy American Adults." HeartGuide also provides brochures in the supermarket listing the products bearing the seal and explaining the program, the scientific rationale linking diet to cardiovascular disease, other cardiovascular disease risk factors, and how to plan a healthful overall diet. Consumers have access to additional AHA nutrition information from a telephone hotline. Reinforcing messages also will appear in print and in electronic media advertising campaigns. HeartGuide is an example of a program with a secondary benefit of influencing the food industry to modify products and offer healthful alternatives in various product lines.[9]

Elements identified as key to the effectiveness of supermarket nutrition programs are

- messages relevant to consumer interests and concerns
- point-of-purchase shelf labels that direct consumers to healthful foods
- practical nutrition information from credible sources
- highly visible and appealing programs to help shoppers distinguish nutrition education from commercial advertising
- broad public awareness generated through mass media advertising and public service announcements
- programs maintained over an extended time period
- effective work with store personnel[10]

Other Food Sources

As ubiquitous as the modern supermarket has become, this is not the only place where people buy their food. Persons trying to make dietary changes may like to learn about alternate food sources, which include pick-your-own farms, food co-ops, farmer's markets, and buying clubs. They also might grow some of their own food. Some innovative nutrition education programs for elderly persons and school children promote home gardening. Participants attend a series of classes on nutrition and vegetable gardening. They receive assistance in building and planting a vegetable garden. Many participants improve their dietary intake by including more vegetables in their diet. Some WIC programs and nutrition programs for the elderly are testing distribution of special coupons for partipants to purchase locally grown fruits and vegetables at farmer's markets.

Eating Out

Americans eat about one-third to one-half of their meals in restaurants, cafeterias, and fast food outlets, and they are spending larger proportions of their food dollar to do so.[11] Many of these establishments are observing a growing public demand to serve more fruits, vegetables, fish, low-fat dairy products, whole grains, and foods prepared with less fat, salt, and sugar. The format or symbols on the menu can guide patrons to select menu items consistent with the Dietary Guidelines for Americans. Food service establishments that offer menu items reduced in calories, fat, and sodium desire visibility and credit.

Offering patrons health-promoting foods and nutrition education can be consistent with operating a profitable business.[12] Local "dining out" guides or newspaper articles can feature the restaurants which serve healthful items. Specific menu items can be reviewed, endorsed, and labeled as meeting defined dietary guidelines. Restaurants must be monitored and encouraged to ensure that the information they print on their menus remains current. Chefs, cooks, and servers must be trained to fulfill their responsibilities in maintaining program quality, to guide diners' food choices, and to provide accurate information.

The American Heart Association's Eating Away from Home program is also encouraging changes in the food supply. This program is designed to facilitate the adoption and/or maintenance of AHA's dietary recommendations by identifying menu items that comply with AHA's criteria for total fat, saturated fat, cholesterol, and sodium. Potential enrollees include a broad spectrum of establishments such as airlines, hotels, cruise ships, fast food chains, contract feeding corporations and concessionaires, as well as family and fine dining restaurants. The expansion of this program has placed a demand on food processors to manufacture more products that meet AHA's criteria.[13]

Worksites

Workers spend a large portion of their days at their factory, shop, or office and usually eat at least one meal there. Friendships formed at work can support healthy eating practices. Offices and factories are convenient places to offer nutrition and health promotion programs at less cost than comparable programs offered at other locations in the community.

Many employers consider health promotion programs a fringe benefit that they can offer to their employees to promote a positive company image in the community and among prospective employees. Worksite health promotion programs reduce the use of health services and cut health insurance costs and absenteeism.

At worksites, nutritionists can reach large numbers of people who do not usually use public health services. Worksites provide a convenient setting for screening programs since workers are a captive audience that can be followed at the same location over time. Education, referral, and follow-up can be linked to screening. Classes, pamphlets, newsletters, payroll stuffers, and posters raise employee awareness of risk factors. Small group meetings or individual counseling sessions build workers' skills and motivate them to make dietary changes to reduce weight, lower blood cholesterol, or control hypertension or diabetes.

Incentives can reinforce successful dietary changes. Exercise programs and healthful food choices in vending machines and cafeterias can educate employees about nutrition and fitness and support dietary changes while requiring minimal individual effort. Healthful foods, recipes, and informative handouts can be distributed whenever food is served at seminars, meetings, breaks, or parties.

Churches or Other Places of Worship

These are found in both rural areas and inner-city ghetto communities where the people may have the least access to health care.[14] Houses of worship have small meeting rooms and large social halls which can be used to conduct many types of group activities. Members include families and individuals of all ages. Religious commitment to community service provides a sound foundation on which to recruit and train volunteers and peer counselors for nutrition and health-promotion projects. Clergy and lay leaders are strong opinion leaders in their congregations. Many religious group activities revolve around social activities where healthful food can be served. Programs on nutrition, health, and fitness; recipe contests; developing a health-promoting cookbook; and "good nutrition" potluck suppers may interest the congregation as a whole or the affiliated men's, women's, or youth groups.

Civic, Service, and Social Clubs, Ys, and Recreation Centers

The educational programs of many civic and social clubs, Ys, and recreation centers include health and nutrition topics. Some have special health-promotion projects such as weight management or physical fitness. By participating in or working with these programs, the nutritionist can reach key community leaders, informing them about the value of health and nutrition services. As time constraints limit the actual number of organizations served, a speakers' bureau of qualified professional nutritionists and dietitians can be organized and publicized to spread scientifically sound nutrition education programs throughout the community.

Public Libraries

Libraries carry a variety of books on food, nutrition, and health. Those from authoritative sources may be few in number compared to popular "diet" books written by authors without nutrition science credentials. Authoritative books and materials on a variety of nutrition and food-related topics can be recommended for readers of different ages, interests, and educational backgrounds. Free materials from professional and voluntary health organizations and official health agencies can be distributed through the library "take-one" racks. Announcements about scientifically sound readable food and nutrition books and materials can be published in the library's news bulletins and the local newspaper. Consultation with the librarian provides another means for the nutritionist to disseminate sound nutrition information to the community.

Schools

Schools provide an important conduit for nutrition information to families with school age children. Nutrition education research literature documents the positive impact of nutrition education activities in schools on the eating habits of children. The Nutrition Education and Training (NET) Program was authorized in 1977 as an amendment to the National School Lunch Act because Congress was convinced of the value of nutrition education in the schools. (See Chapter 8.) The NET Program sponsors nutrition education for teachers, students, school food service managers, and child day care providers. By speaking to Parent-Teacher Associations (PTAs) about nutrition in promoting health throughout life, the nutritionist can reach middle and upper income families who may not use health agency services. Community health-promotion programs and food and health fairs for families can be sponsored by schools. Parents can be reached through take-home nutrition and health assignments to students as well as by projects that require the parent to assess their child's growth, development, health, and food choices.

EXTENDING THE NUTRITION MESSAGE THROUGH HEALTH CARE PROFESSIONALS

Consultation to Health Professionals (See Chapter 21)

One of the year 2000 nutrition objectives is to increase to at least 50 percent the proportion of primary care providers who offer nutrition counseling or referral to qualified nutritionists and/or dietitians.[15] The nutritionist can work toward implementing this objective by providing continuing nutrition education and consultation to physicians, dentists, pharmacists, nurses, therapists, dental hygienists, social workers, and health educators. For many health professionals, little or no education in nutrition and diet is included in their preservice training. Nutritionists can offer continuing education courses, lecture series, or self-instructional materials through their health care institutions or community health agencies, health professional schools in colleges or universities, professional organizations, or area health education centers. The nutritionist also serves as a resource person offering case consultation to health professionals to demonstrate effective nutrition counseling and nutrition education methods.

The nutritionist can train paraprofessionals such as community nutrition aides, lay health advisors, and volunteer peer counselors. Supervising paraprofessionals and volunteers as they provide basic food and nutrition information to low-risk clients and groups extends the reach of the public health nutritionist.

DIRECT NUTRITION CARE SERVICES

Screening

Screening services identify individuals at risk and empower them to eliminate or reduce their risk factors. Nutrition education should be appropriately incorporated into screening services.

In planning screening programs, the accuracy and reliability of the measurements must be ensured. Policies and procedures that include a quality control system should be established. Persons performing the measurements must be trained and monitored in correct techniques. Their equipment must be routinely calibrated and any chemical reagents used must meet preestablished standards.

The objectives of each screening program should be specified as either screening for disease detection (SDD) or screening for risk factors (SRF).[16] An example of SDD is screening for diabetes to identify persons or cases of the disease as early as possible. In SDD, little may be done for those who have normal test values. The emphasis is on referral and follow-up for those identified as possible "cases." In contrast, SRF seeks to identify the risk factors of participants for developing the disease in question and to counsel them about behavior changes necessary to lower these risks. Here the purpose is to identify behaviors that put individuals at risk and to provide counseling and education. In SRF, all participants may receive similar services, i.e., education and counseling on behavior change. For nutrition services, the two models can be combined. Screening should be planned so that effective nutrition education for all participants begins at the first contact, continues according to the individual's needs, and is coordinated with any medical intervention.[17]

Each client with an abnormal test result should be advised about the significance of this result and how to obtain diagnosis and treatment. Prior to conducting community screening programs, plans should be made with local physicians so that they will accept referrals. They must concur with the levels that define risk and know how to prescribe and implement diet and drug treatment. Arrangements should be made with physicians to accept referrals of clients who have no physician and for those who do not have health insurance or money to pay for care.

Each patient who is referred should be followed by phone or letter to ensure adequate medical care as part of the screening program. Because follow-up activities are time-consuming and costly, some planners of screening programs omit follow-up, asserting that the client is responsible for following the recommendations given by the screening program. This philosophy defeats the aim of screening, which is to identify risk factors and empower and support individuals to remedy them.

Coordinating Nutrition Services with Medical Intervention

Nutritionists build collaborative working relationships with community physicians by demonstrating the value of their services. Local physicians should be shown the cost benefit of diet counseling in reducing risk factors and controlling chronic health conditions. Copies of current references from scientific literature can be mailed to physicians, and medical continuing education events on nutrition topics can be offered. Physicians must be convinced that recommended dietary modifications are manageable and palatable. A simple referral system to communicate diet prescriptions and report back to the physicians that patients have been provided with appropriate diet counseling or education should be established. Physicians need to receive feedback regarding the results of their referrals. If physicians are informed that their patients received and benefited from nutrition services, they will be more likely to continue to refer patients.

Nutrition Education and Counseling

Clients who have diet-related health problems require nutrition education and counseling. Before creating demands through a screening or referral program, an inventory should be made of services in the community staffed by registered dietitians or qualified nutritionists and those available should be assessed for quality. Additional services may need to be developed.

Nutrition Education and Counseling

Nutritionists counsel groups of clients in clinics, health centers, schools, and worksites. Group counseling brings together people who share a common need for nutrition information. It uses time efficiently and is cost effective because more people are reached than in one-on-one counseling. In groups clients exchange information and make personal decisions to solve problems. Under the direction of a nutritionist, they share their own solutions to diet-related problems and become a support system for each other. However, some time for individual counseling must be planned so that no one leaves with inappropriate or incomplete information.

Some target audiences for interactive group classes include pregnant women, parents of young children, women who are breast-feeding, or persons who have weight problems. Each person in the group needs information that links diet with the identified health problem and gives general recommendations for the dietary behavior changes that are appropriate for group discussion. Classes attract a wider audience when held in conveniently located community centers, schools, churches, libraries, malls, community colleges, or congregate meal sites.

Individual and Family Counseling

Families and individuals who have complex nutrition problems or unique dietary needs require one-on-one counseling. Diet counseling is an interactive dialogue between the counselor and the client. The interview begins with a careful assessment of the client's health problems, nutrition-related risk factors, knowledge and ability to cope with the problems. The nutrition care plan, developed with the client and family, lists the sequence of manageable steps to be taken.

Nutrition counseling should promote understanding and knowledge about the role of diet for the individual's health. It uses interactive demonstrations to build client and family skills in planning meals and in purchasing and preparing food for the required diet modifications. Scheduled follow-up appointments provide the client and family with continuing guidance, encouragement, and support. They may be contacted by telephone to monitor progress in achieving their objectives, to answer their questions, or to determine their needs for additional help. Clients' needs for certain standardized diet information on topics such as food exchange lists, food shopping, label reading, or food preparation methods can be supplemented by programmed instruction. Interactive printed or computer-assisted programmed instruction is being employed by diet counselors to present basic information in an appealing format while freeing personnel time. Take-home printed, self-instructional materials or audio or video cassettes also support individual counseling. Counseling services from the nutritionist in the public health agency should be planned to augment and not compete with those available from registered dietitians at the community hospital or in private practice.

ISSUES TO DEBATE

• Recognizing that the public health approach is population based rather than client focused, what proportion of the public health nutritionist's time should focus on community interventions versus client counseling?

• What consultative and education roles are appropriate for tax-supported nutritionists in working with for-profit food processors, food market chains, restaurants, worksite wellness programs, and private physicians?

• How does the nutritionist translate complex scientific findings into clear, simple messages which motivate individuals to change their food habits?

• How does the nutritionist balance the needs to serve high-risk target populations with those of populations likely to generate income and/or political support?

NOTES

1. Helen Smicklas-Wright, Susan M. Krebs-Smith, and James Krebs-Smith, "Variety in Foods," in *What Is America Eating?* (Washington, D.C.: National Academy Press, 1986), 132.

2. U.S. Department of Agriculture and U.S. Department of Health and Human Services, *Dietary Guidelines for Americans* (Washington, D.C.: U.S. Government Printing Office, 1985).

3. U.S. Department of Health and Human Services, *Integration of Risk Factor Interventions—Two Reports to the Office of Disease Prevention and Health Promotion* (Washington, D.C.: U.S. Government Printing Office, November 1986).

4. U.S. Department of Health and Human Services, *Making PSAs Work; TV, Radio; A Handbook for Health Communication Professionals* (Bethesda, Md.: NIH Pub. no. 84-2485, April 1964).

5. Smicklas-Wright, Krebs-Smith, and Krebs-Smith, "Variety in Foods," 127.

6. Food Marketing Institute, *Trends: Consumer Attitudes and the Supermarket, 1988 Update*

(Washington, D.C.: Food Marketing Institute, 1988).

7. Susan T. Borra, "Considerations for Implementing Dietary Guidelines in the Retail Food Industry" (Presentation to the National Academy of Sciences Food and Nutrition Board, Washington, D.C., August 4, 1988).

8. Leni Reed, "Nutrition Education: Out of the Classroom and into the Supermarket," *Nutrition News* 51 (Spring 1988): 1-4.

9. Rebecca Lankenau, personal communication, The American Heart Association National Center, Dallas, Tex., September 19, 1989.

10. Luise Light et al., "Nutrition Education in Supermarkets," *Family and Community Health* 12, no. 1 (1989):43-52.

11. Karen J. Morgan and Basile Goungetas, "Snacking and Eating Away from Home," in *What Is America Eating?* (Washington, D.C.: National Academy Press, 1986), 91.

12. Claire Regan, "Promoting Nutrition in Commercial Foodservice Establishments: A Realistic Approach," *Journal of the American Dietetic Association* 87 (April 1987): 486-488.

13. Lankenau, personal communication, September 19, 1989.

14. U.S. Department of Health and Human Services, *Churches As an Avenue to High Blood Pressure Control* (NIH Pub. no. 87-2725, November 1987).

15. U.S. Department of Health and Human Services, "Summary Table of Objectives To Improve Nutrition," Draft, *Promoting Health/Preventing Disease: Year 2000 Objectives for the Nation*, Washington, D.C.: 1-4, 1-5.

16. M.A. Safer, "A Comparison of Screening for Disease Detection and Screening for Risk Factors" *Health Education Research* 1, no. 2 (1986): 131-138.

17. Safer, "A Comparison of Screening for Disease Detection."

BIBLIOGRAPHY

American Dietetic Association, Society for Nutrition Education, and the Office of Disease Prevention and Health Promotion, U.S. Department of Health and Human Services. *Worksite Nutrition: A Decision-Maker's Guide*. Chicago: The American Dietetic Association, 1986.

American Heart Association. "The Culinary Hearts Kitchen Course." Dallas, Tex.: American Heart Association, 64-751-A.

Board on Agriculture, National Research Council. *Designing Foods, Animal Product Options in the Marketplace*. Washington, D.C.: National Academy Press, 1988.

Brownell, K.D., and M.R.J. Felix. "Competitions to Facilitate Health Promotion: Review and Conceptual Analysis." *American Journal of Health Promotion* 1 (1987):28-36.

Gift, Helen H., Marjorie B. Washbon, and Gail G. Harrison. *Nutrition, Behavior, and Change*. Englewood Cliffs, N.J.: Prentice-Hall, Inc., 1972, pp. 254-295.

Halpin, Thomas J. Regarding Cholesterol Screening—Guidance for Local Health Commissioners from the State Director of Health. Thomas J. Halpin, Dept. of Health, State of Ohio, Columbus, Ohio, February 25, 1987.

National Cholesterol Education Program. *Public Screening for Measuring Blood Cholesterol—Issues for Special Attention*. Bethesda, Md.: National Heart, Lung, and Blood Institute, 1988.

Owen, A.L. "President's Page: Health Promotion and Disease Prevention: New Markets for Dietitians." *Journal of The American Dietetic Association* 85, no. 12 (December 1985):1635-1637.

part VI

Mobilizing Personnel

chapter **19**

Staffing Public Health Nutrition Programs and Services

Mildred Kaufman

READER OBJECTIVES

* Compare and contrast the levels and types of public health nutrition personnel.
* List the knowledge and skills that distinguish the public health nutritionist from the direct care nutritionist.
* Discuss the recommended educational qualifications for public health nutritionists and how these might be obtained.
* Compare and contrast administrative structures that enable nutritionists to function effectively in a public health agency.
* Recommend staffing ratios of public health nutritionists and direct care nutritionists.
* Discuss factors to be considered in assigning salaries for public health nutrition personnel.

EMPLOYING PUBLIC HEALTH NUTRITION PERSONNEL

Public health nutrition personnel are employed in community official or voluntary agencies whose mission is to promote health, prevent disease, and provide primary health care. Such agencies include federal, state, city, or county public health departments; voluntary health agencies; neighborhood ambulatory health centers; home health agencies; health maintenance organizations; and comprehensive community hospitals. Exhibit 19-1 displays the several types of public health nutrition personnel that might be employed and differentiates the roles for which their education and experience should prepare them.

Exhibit 19-1 Roles of Public Health Nutrition Personnel

	Public Health Nutrition Director/ Administrator	Public Health Nutrition Supervisor	Public Health Nutrition Consultant	Public Health Nutritionist	Direct Care Nutritionist	Nutrition Technician	Nutrition Aide
Planner/ Evaluator	●	●	●	●			
Coordinator	●	●	●	●	•		
Educator	○	○	●	●	●		
Consultant	○	●	●	●			
Standard Setter	●	○	○	○	○		
Manager	●	○		○			
Manager (Fiscal)	○	○	○				
Counselor		■		○	●	●	
Advocate	○	○	○	○	•	•	
Supervisor	○	●				■	
Manager (Personnel)	○	○					
Researcher/ Investigator	■	■	■	■			
Teacher						●	○
Outreach Worker						●	●

KEY: ● Major role (limited to 4 per position)   • Minor role

○ Intermediate role   ■ Optional role

Source: Adapted with permission from *Personnel in Public Health Nutrition for the 1980s* by M. Kaufman (Ed.), ASTHO Foundation, © May 1982.

The self-assessment tool for public health nutritionists in Appendix A can also be useful to administrators, personnel analysts, as well as nutritionists. The administrators and personnel analysts can use the knowledge and skill statements as guides when they write job descriptions, prepare recruitment notices and advertisements, and interview and select public health nutrition personnel. It will help them secure nutrition personnel with the knowledge and skills to meet the agency's program and service needs. Nutritionists and students can use the self-assessment tool to measure their own level of competency and plan for their continuing education and career development.

Public health agencies employ nutrition personnel to staff a mix of community programs and clinical services. Federal, state, and large city or county agencies and voluntary health agencies may emphasize their community or population-based programs. Smaller local agencies, community health centers, and ambulatory or home health services may put more resources into primary care or clinical services. Administrators, personnel analysts, and public health nutrition administrators must clearly determine the various levels of knowledge and skills they need for their programs and then recruit nutrition personnel with the desired qualifications. Based on the knowledge and skill statements listed in the self-assessment tool

- public health nutritionists should be "competent" or "expert" in all of these five areas: nutrition and dietetic practice; communications; public health science and practice; management; legislation and advocacy
- direct care nutritionists should be "competent" or "expert" in two of the five areas: nutrition and dietetic practice, and communications
- nutrition or dietetic technicians should be "adequate" or "competent" in nutrition and dietetic practice but may be beginners in communications, to which they can be oriented on the job
- nutrition aides are paraprofessionals trained on the job in the specific and limited knowledge and skills they need to carry out their assigned work.

To employ staff who can perform according to expectations, it is important to understand the difference in the roles, responsibilities, competencies, and educational preparation of the various types of nutrition personnel. When an adequate pool of qualified candidates is not available for recruitment in the geographic area, it may be necessary to arrange for promising but less prepared candidates to complete the coursework necessary to meet the needed qualifications.

PUBLIC HEALTH NUTRITIONISTS

The title public health nutritionist is used for the professional who has completed academic public health coursework in biostatistics, epidemiology, environmental sciences, health program planning, evaluation and management, and advanced nutrition. Because public health nutritionists need to be experts in nutrition and dietetic practice, it is recommended that they meet the education and experience requirements for eligibility for dietetic registration and dietetic licensure in the states that have a dietetic licensure law.

With the public health training, the public health nutritionist is prepared to assess community nutrition needs; recommend nutrition policy to administrators and planners; advise the administrator and agency board; and plan, organize, manage, coordinate, and evaluate nutrition services as part of the organization's comprehensive health program. The public health nutritionist coordinates the health agency's nutrition services with the related food and nutrition education programs in the community, including those offered through cooperative extension; Head Start or out-of-home child care; schools, colleges, and universities; community hospitals; private practice dietitians; and area agencies on aging. Public health nutritionists also collaborate with food assistance programs offered through human service agencies, food stamp offices, food pantries, soup kitchens, and congregate and home-delivered meal programs. They often seek opportunities to develop community or applied nutrition research with colleagues in their agency and with university faculty.

Public health nutritionists are distinguished from nutritionists or dietitians who provide direct care by their community or population perspective, i.e., their ability to see the "big picture." As discussed in Chapters 3, 4, and 16, they apply principles of epidemiology and utilize statistical analysis to assess the community's needs. This needs assessment provides the data base for planning targeted cost-effective programs (discussed in Chapter 14). Public health nutritionists extend their sphere of influence by working with the media (discussed in Chapter 18) and with the interdisciplinary team (discussed in Chapter 21) and by developing community networks (discussed in Chapter 22).

Large city, county, state, or federal health agencies with a complex of programs and services that employ a staff of public health and direct care nutritionists require a director, administrator, or supervisor who has demonstrated leadership and managerial skills. Large, complex agencies need a director with the sophistication and self-confidence developed through several years in progressively responsible positions because at this level, the major responsibilities are developing policy; advising the agency director and senior program officials, policymakers, and legislators; strategic and operational planning and evaluating large-scale programs; and managing the personnel and the budget for a comprehensive program.

Agencies with a variety of service programs may also employ one or more public health nutritionists in positions titled "deputy nutrition director," "associate," "assistant director," or "supervisor." The individuals in these positions would be delegated responsibilities needed for efficient program management. In state or large city or county health departments, the responsibilities that might be delegated include directing the Special Supplemental Food Program for Women, Infants, and Children (WIC); managing nutrition personnel, including recruitment, orientation, career development, inservice training, and supervising student placements; nutrition monitoring, surveillance, epidemiology, and data management; program evaluation and applied research; or writing grants and developing new programs. Specialized public health nutrition consultants might be employed to work in maternal and child health programs, programs for children with special health care needs, adult health promotion, geriatric or aging programs, food service systems management, and consumer protection. More targeted programs in public health agencies will increasingly employ nutrition consultants with specialties and subspecialties.

Educational Requirements

The requirement for a graduate degree that prepares the nutritionist for public health responsibilities should be written into the training and education sections of the job specifications in one of the following ways:

- master's degree in public health (MPH or MSPH) with a major in nutrition
- master of science degree (MS) in applied human nutrition with a minor in public health or community health
- master of science degree (MS) in applied human nutrition supplemented by credit courses in biostatistics, epidemiology, health administration, and health planning and management. For the nutritionist who has a graduate degree in nutrition, the required public health coursework might be obtained by enrolling in on- or off-campus courses or in one of the summer institutes in biostatistics and epidemiology offered by several of the schools of public health. (See Appendix J.)

To work in the specialties and subspecialties in public health nutrition requires more in-depth training in the selected area. This can be obtained through advanced coursework; a fellowship such as those that are available in maternal nutrition, adolescent nutrition, or developmental disabilities; a specialized clinical experience; or intensive noncredit continuing education courses in the specialty area.

The public health nutrition administrator will be better prepared for management responsibilities with advanced graduate coursework in public health administration, health planning, public or business administration, policy analysis, and personnel management.

Position descriptions should stipulate the number of years of progressively responsible experience required for each type of position. The number of years of experience required in public health or community service should increase with the level of responsibility of the position and the size and complexity of the program.

Educational qualifications for public health nutritionists were first published jointly by the American Dietetic Association, the American Home Economics Association, and the American Public Health Association in 1946.[1] These educational requirements have been reaffirmed in publications since that time, and most recently have been restated in *Personnel in Public Health Nutrition for the 1980s*.[2] Academic institutions offering the recommended graduate curriculum to prepare public health nutritionists are listed in Appendix K. The current knowledge base in nutrition, dietetics, food science, and public health required for credibility as a nutrition expert in public health now far exceeds that envisioned in 1946. And yet, a national survey of the Association of State and Territorial Public Health Nutrition Directors conducted in 1989 found that only 14 state personnel systems required a master's degree with the recommended public health coursework.[3] Sixteen other state personnel systems required a master's degree in human nutrition, but not public health coursework. This is unfortunate because if nutritionists are to take leadership in developing cost-effective, population-based approaches, they must know how to apply the epidemiological approach.

The 1955 publication *Nutrition Practices: A Guide for Public Health Administrators* contains an idea that is pertinent 35 years later.

> The principle that only qualified personnel be employed is here strongly endorsed even though there will be found many able persons of superior personal endowment who have long been doing a good job and are now adequately filling important positions despite lack of specialized training. In every discipline the pioneers have had to find their way, using self-developed skills. Their known successes do not negate the rule that once a body of professional training has been established the work is done better when it is done by personnel who are specifically trained as well as otherwise qualified.[4]

DIRECT CARE NUTRITIONISTS

Public health agencies that deliver primary care need a competent staff of direct care nutritionists to work in the agency's various clinical and home health services. They assess clients' nutritional needs, certify clients for nutritional risk for the WIC program, and counsel clients with nutritional needs for growth and development and those who require diets and feedings prescribed by their physicians, including enteral and parenteral nutrition. Direct care nutritionists also refer clients who need food or financial assistance, housing, or social services to the appropriate human service agencies. They can provide continuing follow-up support and encouragement to maintain continuity of nutritional care. The direct care nutritionist has the competencies to organize and teach classes of clients who have similar dietary needs. This nutritionist may also train and supervise nutrition technicians and community nutrition aides.

The nutritionist who counsels and educates clients in public health clinics should be a registered dietitian meeting the current Standards of Education and Standards of Practice established by the Commission on Dietetic Registration.[5] The approved educational and preprofessional practice programs (AP4s) and accredited dietetic internships and coordinated programs in dietetics are published in the annual *Directory of Dietetic Programs*, updated annually by The American Dietetic Association.[6]

The direct care nutritionist should be supervised by an experienced public health nutritionist. A continuing education plan for career development should be offered so that these workers maintain their dietetic registration and have opportunities to pursue graduate work according to their interests and career goals.

NUTRITION TECHNICIANS

Public health agencies that provide large numbers of children and adults with nutrition education for health promotion and uncomplicated diet counseling can effectively employ nutrition or dietetic technicians. The technician assists with nutrition screening and assessment according to preestablished protocols, may assist in certifying WIC clients, and advises clients about their routine nutritional needs. They advise and demonstrate preparation of the WIC foods and health-promoting foods to meet the Dietary Guidelines for Americans. Technicians also teach clients about economical food buying, use of food stamps, and use of foods in the WIC package. They can conduct supermarket tours to help clients identify and choose economical and health-promoting foods. The technician may phone or visit clients who fail to return for appointments.

The educational requirement for the nutrition care technician is a two-year associate degree in a dietetic technician training program approved by the American Dietetic Association. The list of the approved programs is also published in the *Directory of Dietetic Programs* that can be obtained from The American Dietetic Association.[7]

The technician works under the close supervision of the public health nutritionist or direct care nutritionist. When technicians are employed, a career development and continuing education program should be maintained to encourage those with academic ability to pursue a bachelor's degree and prepare themselves for dietetic registration.

NUTRITION AIDES

Where there are concentrated populations of low-income families, particularly those with ethnic backgrounds and languages different than those of the nutrition professionals, community nutrition workers or nutrition aides can be trained to provide selected nutrition care under supervision. Nutrition aides are usually recruited from the community and represent the ethnic groups that are in greatest need of dietary guidance. The aide is selected as a person who knows the community, speaks the language, eats the same foods prepared in the same ways, lives in similar housing, and is under the same financial constraints. Thus the aide can serve as a communicator and an interpreter between the people in the community and the professional nutritionist. Community nutrition aides must be natural leaders who are liked and respected by their peers. They must be interested in trying new ideas and helping their neighbors.

Their most important role is to assist clients to use community food and nutrition services. They help the assigned families to collect the documents they need to apply for food stamps or financial assistance. They arrange transportation or child care and help families obtain emergency food or housing. The nutrition aide also assists the nutritionist in designing nutrition education programs tailored to the needs and interests of the community families and appropriate to their indigenous food habits. They assist the nutritionists who are developing and pretesting nutrition education materials. They help to translate educational materials into the community's language and ensure that the preferred foods and the food preparation methods that have the greatest appeal to the community people are discussed.

Nutrition aides are trained on the job frequently in cooperation with a local vocational or technical school. They learn basic information about foods that promote good health, economical food buying, and how to prepare WIC foods and the ethnic or regional foods with less fat, calories, or salt. They particularly need to learn about the availability, eligibility, and access to the community's food, health, and social services. Aides must be closely supervised by a nutritionist who is assigned aide training and supervision as a major responsibility.

SUPPORT STAFF

The work of the nutrition personnel is enhanced by employment of appropriate ancillary personnel. All nutritionists need clerical support to handle routine paper work. It has been suggested that there be one secretary or clerk for each two nutritionists.[8]

As nutrition programs develop into new areas, they will need expertise in areas outside of nutrition and dietetics. Nutrition directors will need to employ administrative assistants, business managers, accountants, or account clerks when they administer large WIC or other grants. Nutrition units may need epidemiologists, statisticians, and computer programmers as the units move into monitoring, surveillance, and applied research functions. When nutrition programs increase the size and scope of their nutrition education efforts, they may need the expertise of health educators, writers, and graphic artists. Whereas these specialists may not be needed full-time, they might be employed as consultants or on contract for the amount of time they are actually needed. It may first be useful to determine the expert resources available within the agency. The fiscal or business office may provide accounting support, and a research or statistical unit may collaborate and assist with data management. The health education unit may offer its services in training and preparation of materials.

ADMINISTRATIVE PLACEMENT OF NUTRITION PERSONNEL

The health agency that appoints a well-qualified, proactive public health nutritionist should place the position at an administrative level high enough to enable the nutritionist to participate in agency policy making and planning. This placement will ensure that needed nutrition services reach the public. The administrative structure should facilitate formal and informal channels of communication and interaction of the administrative public health nutritionist with directors of all of the programs addressed to populations who require nutrition services. Public health nutritionists with pertinent expertise should advise key health officials and legislators who set policy and allocate resources. Since nutrition and diet relate to almost every current public health issue, public health nutritionists can contribute actively in planning comprehensive community health programs. Agency administrators who know the value and the essential contribution of nutrition to health should select the organizational placement that will give nutritionists the opportunities they need. In determining the appropriate administrative placement for nutrition expertise, administrators should consider these important functions of the nutritionist:

- monitoring emerging trends in nutrition research to recommend applications to current and future public health programs and services and advising the health official, legislators, and policymakers on the contributions of nutrition to public health problems
- conducting continuing community nutrition needs assessments and using the data as the basis to develop, implement, and evaluate a plan for nutrition services within the agency's strategic health plan
- setting consistent standards for all nutrition services offered through public health programs
- applying for internal and external funding to develop nutrition services in emerging areas
- working with personnel analysts on job specifications, training and experience requirements, and pay grades to compete in the recruitment of the "best and brightest" public health and direct care nutritionists
- providing for career development and mobility of all public health nutrition personnel employed in the agency
- providing technical assistance, continuing education, and a support system for nutrition personnel to ensure their coordination and cost-effective deployment

The following are two organizational models for nutrition services that accommodate these functions:

1. *Nutrition Program Unit Headed by a Director or Administrator of Public Health Nutrition Services.* This director should be responsible for planning and monitoring nutrition services and accountable for a budget earmarked for nutrition services. In this model all public health nutrition personnel and related support personnel are placed in a nutrition program or service unit with a nutrition director. This director is responsible to the chief health official, deputy or assistant health official, or an administrator responsible for a generic program such as preventive health services, community or local health services,

or professional services. From the centralized nutrition unit, the various public health nutrition personnel are assigned to work with categorical programs such as maternal and child health, developmental disabilities, adult health promotion, dental health, home health, environmental health, or facility licensure. Generalist nutrition consultants are assigned to regional or district offices. This nutrition unit should be responsible for the Special Supplemental Food Program for Women, Infants, and Children (WIC), particularly the nutrition risk certification and nutrition education. This structure ensures the assignment of qualified nutrition personnel to work with all of the ongoing and emerging programs according to program needs for personnel and time. (See Figure 19-1.)

2. *Matrix Organization.* Here a public health nutrition coordinator or the lead public health nutrition consultant is appointed by the chief health official to serve as the nutrition advisor and spokesperson for agency administration. The lead nutritionist's major role is to coordinate and provide technical guidance to nutrition specialists who are administratively responsible to categorical program directors. As the nutrition expert for the agency and the community, the nutrition coordinator performs the generalized functions listed. Specialized nutrition consultants are employed in categorical programs where the program director decides to employ a full-time or part-time nutrition consultant for that specialty area. Those programs not choosing to employ their own nutritionist have access to limited nutrition consultation from the coordinator or what they might negotiate from another categorical program (Figure 19-2). In the model shown in Figure 19-2, there are budgeted funds for specialized public health nutrition positions in the categorical units, but nutrition may not be visible in the agency health plan since no specific budget is labeled for nutrition. Since "he who has the gold rules," nutritionists have found this type of organization less effective

STAFFING RECOMMENDATIONS FOR PUBLIC HEALTH NUTRITION PERSONNEL

The staffing pattern for the numbers and levels of public health nutrition personnel depend on the agency philosophy, mission, and tradition. Factors that influence the numbers and types of positions needed include

- size of the total population
- proportion of the population estimated in the community assessment

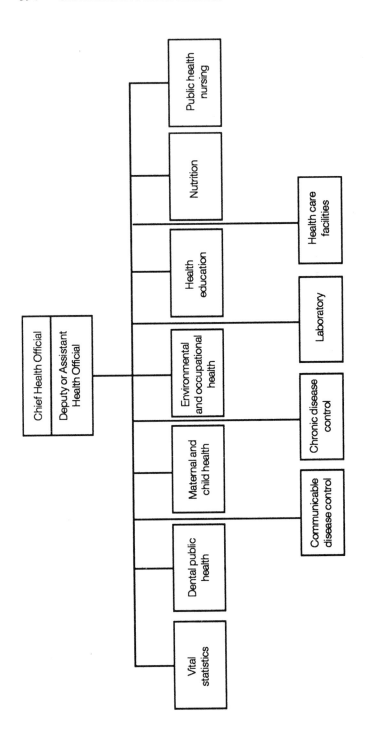

Figure 19-1 Organization Structure of a Public Health Agency with a Nutrition Unit. *Source:* Adapted from *Community Health,* 6th ed., by L. W. Green, p. 516, with permission of Times Mirror/Mosby College Publishing, St. Louis, © 1990.

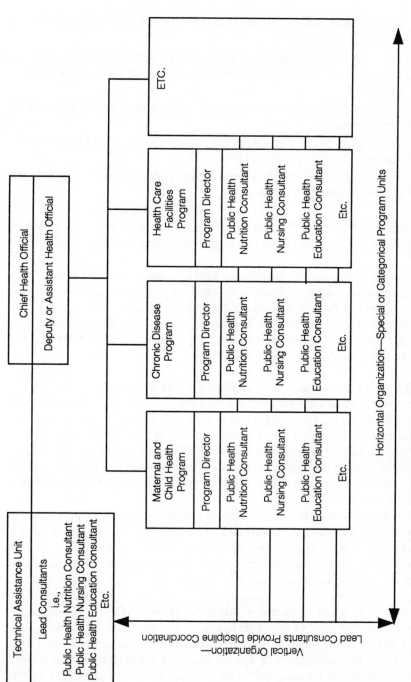

Figure 19-2 Matrix Organization Structure for Public Health Agency. *Source:* Adapted from *Management of Health Services* by A.D. Kaluzny et al., p. 91, with permission of Prentice-Hall, Inc., © 1982.

to have nutrition- or diet-related risk factors based on health status, income, or ethnicity
* agency's overall program of public health services and the existing nutrition services or potential for including nutrition services in these programs
* availability of nutrition services in other community agencies and institutions
* funding resources available or potentially available for nutrition personnel
* expectations and demand from other health professionals and the public for nutrition services

Staffing ratios for public health nutrition personnel in health agencies have been developed, empirically tested, and found to be useful guides.

For the public health nutritionist who provides leadership in planning, consultation, technical assistance, training, and supervision in a specified jurisdictional area the suggested ratio is one public health nutritionist per each 50,000 people in the community. This is the same ratio suggested for the local public health administrator, health educator, and social worker.[9]

The jurisdictional area of 50,000 people has been found to be a cost-effective planning base for public health services. This jurisdictional area might be a state service district or region, one county, a group of small counties joined together into a service district, or a service district within a densely populated city or county. This staffing ratio allows for one nutritionist to provide inservice education and case consultation to a group of 10 to 15 public health nurses, who can then advise clients on routine diet and nutrition needs.

Whenever more than one nutritionist is employed in the same agency, a supervising or a lead nutritionist should be appointed to be responsible to the administrator. A public health nutrition director or administrator is recommended for an agency employing five or more public health nutrition personnel. In addition, an assistant nutrition director or administrator is suggested for an agency employing ten or more public health nutrition personnel, or when there are multiple nutrition services or programs to oversee. As the number of public health nutrition personnel increase, it is desirable to employ supervising nutritionists as mid-managers. Where there are district or satellite health agency offices, a supervising public health nutritionist might be assigned to each of the larger offices that employ public health nutrition personnel.

Staffing of direct care nutritionists is determined by the needs for nutritional care of the populations receiving clinical services. The average amount of time required for each diet counseling encounter, the number of follow-up encounters, the mix of services provided, the efficiency of the clinic flow, the referral system, and travel time to clinic sites or homes visited must be studied to determine the number of direct care nutrition personnel needed. A method for estimating the number of direct care nutritionists based on these factors is shown in Exhibit 19-2. A rule of thumb recommended for staffing ambulatory nutrition care programs is one direct care nutritionist supervising two nutrition technicians for each 1,000 registrants.[10] Other recommendations suggest one nutritionist for each 500 to 800 clients who require nutritional counseling.

Some factors that affect the efficiency of direct care nutritionists and paraprofessionals, thereby influencing the staffing ratio positively or negatively, are shown in Table 19-1.

SALARIES FOR PUBLIC HEALTH NUTRITION PERSONNEL

Pay ranges established for public health nutrition personnel should be comparable to those for other health professionals who are assigned equivalent responsibility and who have equivalent years of education and experience to prepare them to perform their duties. The public health nutritionist with graduate training and dietetic registration should expect the salary assigned to other public health program managers such as nurses, health educators, environmental health specialists, and social workers. Salaries for entry-level direct care nutritionists with bachelor's degrees should be equivalent to those for staff public health nurses or health educators with bachelor's degrees.

Positions for nutrition or dietetic technicians with an associate degree should be assigned the pay range used for associate degree registered nurses. Nutrition aides should be assigned the same pay grade as other community health workers trained on the job.

Many public agencies have merit pay plans based on performance of specified competencies. The Self-Assessment Tool in Appendix A can be used as a basis for stating principle functions of positions with expected levels of performance.

Salaries for public health nutrition personnel should also be competitive with those of nutritionists employed in cooperative extension services and with those of registered dietitians with advanced degrees who are employed in major medical centers and community hospitals. Periodic salary surveys can be used to collect salary data in the geographical area. Noncompetitive salaries are the cause of many of the problems encountered in recruiting

Exhibit 19-2   A Method for Estimating Direct Care Nutritionist Staffing

1. Establish the priority target populations.
   A. Clients with special nutritional needs because of physiological stress, because of identified nutrition-related disorders, and/or because of chronic diseases requiring nutrition intervention and remedial services, such as pregnant or lactating women, women in childbearing years, infants and children with identified nutrition problems, persons requiring diets prescribed for chronic diseases (e.g., diabetes, heart disease, children with inborn metabolic errors).
   B. Persons identified as being at high nutritional risk through nutritional screening and assessment, i.e., evaluation of anthropometric, biochemical, clinical, dietary, and socioeconomic data.
   C. Health care providers, educators, social workers, child care staff providing nutrition care and food services to high-risk populations.
   D. School children and the general public involved in health promotion and disease prevention programs.

2. Specify the recommended service modality for each priority population.
   A. Type of encounter (e.g., individual vs. group vs. use of mass media).
   B. Frequency of encounter with client/group/media.
   C. Distribution of time for each type of encounter, such as home visit, clinic, school, community group, mass media.

3. Estimate the effective hours per worker per year or total hours available for service (total hours on duty less annual leave, holidays, sick leave, travel time, continuing education, personal time).

4. Based on experience, observation, and/or time studies, estimate the average effective hours or fraction of hours required per client or activity.

5. Estimate the effective hours or fraction of hours needed for adjunct activities including planning and preparation, recording and reporting, quality assurance, record audits, consultation, school/community/mass media programs, personal time.

6. Compute formula based on program plan as follows:

   Let n^1, n^2, n^3, etc. = average number of hours for each client or group activity in each priority group 1, 2, 3, etc.

   Let x^1, x^2, x^3, etc. = number of expected encounters per year in priority groups, 1, 2, 3, etc.

   Let h = the number of hours needed for adjunct activities per year

   Let k = effective hours per nutrition care provider per year, then

   $\dfrac{n^1x^1 + n^2x^2 + n^3x^3 + h}{k}$ = number of direct service nutrition care provider staff

Source: Adapted from *Administration of Public Health Services* by R.B. Freeman and E.M. Holmes, p. 189, with permission of W.B. Saunders Company. © 1960.

Table 19-1 Factors Influencing Direct Care Nutritionist to Client Staffing Needs Ratio

Require More Nutritionist Time	*Require Less Nutritionist Time*
CLIENT-RELATED	
Complex nutrition/diet/health problems (more high risk)	Less complex nutrition/diet/health problems (lower risk)
Clients with low literacy or language barriers; no interpreters available	Most clients able to read at least at 8th grade level and most clients speak and read English; nutritionists speak language of clients or use interpreters
Clients need many referrals for SES needs	Social worker or public health nurse available to facilitate referrals
Clients distracted by small children	Child care provided—Use of volunteers
SYSTEMS-RELATED	
WIC and MCH services not integrated requiring dual systems of screening, counseling, and recordkeeping	WIC and MCH services integrated and share nutrition services, personnel.
Program emphasis on one-to-one counseling	Program utilizes:
	• group counseling
	• peer counseling
	• computer-assisted instruction to reinforce counseling
	• media
Inexperienced or inadequately prepared nutrition personnel who lack needed knowledge/skills	Experienced, well-prepared, efficient nutrition personnel
Frequent staff turnover, poor morale	Stable nutrition staff, good morale
Lack of privacy for counseling or inconvenient location, inadequate space	Convenient location for nutrition staff with adequate space and privacy
Excessive travel time for nutrition personnel, long distance between clinics or home visits	One-stop center
Insufficient or inappropriate educational materials	Adequate supply of quality educational materials and audiovisual aids
Nutritionist required to handle clerical tasks	Clerical staff handle paper work
Excessive paper work	Computer available for diet analyses and recordkeeping
Medical/health records inaccessible, incomplete, and difficult to use	Medical/health records are easily accessible or computerized, well-organized, succinct, easy to read and to write notes on
No appointment system or protocol for referral; clients either come all at once or there are long periods between clients	Appointment system and protocols followed for referral; smooth clinic flow

qualified public health nutrition personnel.[11] As more positions for personnel requiring the competencies of public health nutritionists become available in the food industry, food services, the media, and private sector health promotion programs, their more appealing salaries will attract the more competent public health nutritionists away from agencies. A 1989 salary study of public health nutrition personnel in official state and local health agencies showed wide national variations in the averages and ranges of salaries for the several levels of public health nutrition personnel (Table 19-2).

ISSUES TO DEBATE

- What strategies can be used to educate administrators as well as personnel directors and analysts about the unique competencies needed by public health nutrition personnel?
- How can public health nutritionists recommend an organizational structure that will facilitate their influence and effectiveness in agency policy making?
- How can currently employed nutritionists in public health agencies meet the recommended public health coursework while remaining on the job?

Table 19-2 Mean Annual Salaries for Public Health Nutrition Personnel as Established by State Personnel Systems, Spring 1989 (from Survey of 55 State/Territorial Health Agencies)

Position	Minimum $	Midpoint $	Maximum $
Director/Administrator	13,309	35,780	69,651
Assistant Director/Administrator			
Senior Nutrition Consultant	12,732	32,778	57,200
Public Health Nutrition Consultants	12,180	29,211	48,997
Public Health Nutritionist—Sole	10,704	26,186	44,337
Direct Nutrition Care Providers:			
Dietitian/Nutritionist	8,688	23,373	38,800
Diet/Nutrition Technicians	11,196*	19,085	29,099

*State with lowest minimum salaries in above classifications does not use this level of personnel.

- What are some ways to recruit and retain qualified public health nutrition personnel in remote rural areas?
- What approaches can qualified public health nutritionists in official agencies use to advocate for competitive salaries?

NOTES

1. Committee on Professional Education, The American Public Health Association, "The Educational Qualifications of Nutritionists in Health Agencies," *Journal of the American Dietetic Association* 22, no. 1 (1946): 41–44.

2. Mildred Kaufman, ed., *Personnel in Public Health Nutrition for the 1980's* (McLean, Va.: ASTHO Foundation, May 1982), 39–43.

3. Mildred Kaufman, Preliminary Report, *Nutrition Services in State and Local Public Health Agencies, 1989*, Report of Bienniel Survey of State Health Agencies (Chapel Hill, N.C.: Unpublished, May 1989).

4. American Public Health Association, *Nutrition Practices: A Guide for Public Health Administrators* (New York: American Public Health Association, 1955), 30.

5. American Dietetic Association, *ADA Standard of Education Accreditation/Approval Manual for Dietetic Education Programs* (Chicago: The American Dietetic Association, 1988), 17–30.

6. American Dietetic Association, *ADA Directory of Dietetic Programs 1988* (Chicago: The American Dietetic Association, 1988), 2, 16–19.

7. Ibid.

8. Eileen Peck, ed., *Leadership and Quality Assurance in Ambulatory Health Care: What Is the Role of the Public Health Nutritionist?* (Berkeley: University of California, 1978), 132–33.

9. Kaufman, *Personnel in Public Health*, 39–43. Peck, *Leadership and Quality Assurance*, 132–133.

10. Peck, *Leadership and Quality Assurance*, 132–33.

11. Kaufman, *Nutrition Services*.

BIBLIOGRAPHY

Baird, S.C., and J. Sylvester. *Role Delineation and Verification for Entry Level Positions in Community Dietetics*. Chicago: The American Dietetic Association, 1983.

Kaufman, Mildred. *Personnel in Public Health Nutrition for the 1980's*. McLean, Va.: ASTHO Foundation, 1982.

Kaufman, Mildred. "Preparing Public Health Nutritionists to Meet the Future." *Journal of the American Dietetic Association* 86, no. 4 (1986):511–514.

chapter **20**

Managing Public Health Nutrition Personnel

Nancy L. Johnson

READER OBJECTIVES

- List responsibilities of the nutritionist who is in a supervisory role.
- Describe basic components of compensation systems.
- Discuss the values of writing complete job descriptions.
- List steps involved in employing personnel and considerations in conducting the process fairly.
- Discuss characteristics of effective performance evaluation.
- Describe strategies to increase and reward staff productivity.
- List the essential steps in the employee disciplinary process.

RESPONSIBILITIES OF THE PROGRAM MANAGER

The program manager's position is established to get work done through other people.[1] The effective manager delegates power and authority so that all employees can carry out their assigned responsibilities. Supervisors must train and nurture their staff so that they grow in their knowledge, skills, competence, and self-confidence. Clear instructions, watchful oversight, and constructive guidance save time, build self-esteem, and prevent frustration for both supervisors and staff. Techniques of effective supervision can be learned. They are largely based on common sense,[2] caring, and respect for the subordinate's point of view.

Skills in personnel management that the nutritionist in an administrative or supervisory role needs to master include

- selecting or participating in selecting staff and orienting them to their positions and the overall agency program

- delegating program responsibilities, making staff assignments, and ensuring staff accountability for performance
- developing and periodically reviewing standards of performance for nutrition personnel
- evaluating performance of nutrition and support personnel
- assessing staff training needs and planning for their career development and continuing education
- interpreting agency and nutrition program policies and procedures and monitoring compliance
- hearing and resolving personnel complaints and grievances[3]

Employment of appropriate numbers and kinds of professional and support personnel determines the outcome of the program plan. The nature of positions established depends upon competencies required. Roles, responsibilities, and competencies of the various levels of public health nutrition personnel, organization of public health services/personnel, and the hierarchy of public health nutrition personnel are discussed in Chapter 19.

The number of supervisors, consultants, professionals and paraprofessionals, nutrition care providers, and support positions needed will be influenced by the planned intervention strategies, characteristics of the target population, distances between sites, and number of hours available for services.

The nutritionist in an administrative or supervisory role must work closely with the agency's personnel director and staff. This nutritionist should develop an understanding of the agency's personnel policies and the interpretation and the day-to-day application of these policies. This includes understanding the compensation system, writing job descriptions, recruiting to find the right person for the job, understanding fair employment practices legislation, interviewing applicants, orienting new employees, assigning work and scheduling staff, motivating staff, appraising staff performance, developing a career ladder, and, when necessary, taking disciplinary action.

Understanding Compensation Systems

Wage or salary systems vary from agency to agency and in the public and private sector. The flexibilities and limitations in the compensation system in the agency must be clearly understood since it must be used skillfully to procure the most promising staff.

In official public health agencies the most commonly used compensation system is based on position classification. Pay grades are established and positions of equal complexity are grouped. Established class specifications (descriptions) for each type of position are used as benchmarks in assigning pay grades.

Where a ranking system is used, all positions (jobs) in the organization are ranked from the most complex to the simplest. Salaries are then determined by arranging the positions along a salary scale developed for the agency. Using a point system, factors for compensation are determined and points assigned to each factor. Factors generally used are skill (job knowledge, experience, education, training); effort (physical, mental concentration); responsibility (for equipment, money, safety, public relations, supervision of employees); and job conditions (working conditions, hazards, annoyances).[4] Positions are ranked according to total points and the pay grade is assigned accordingly.

In a contract system, an individual who may or may not receive a base salary is paid for specific services. For example, a nutritionist might be paid for hours worked, by the number of client encounters, for each class conducted, or the number of home visits made.

Writing Job Descriptions

Job descriptions serve as the basis for establishing positions, recruitment, selection, orientation, work planning, inservice education, and performance appraisal. Once the type and number of staff have been determined, job descriptions are written for each position based on the needs established in the program plan. The responsibilities and duties for each position must be described precisely to be sure that all personnel have the knowledge, skills, and experience needed to achieve the goals and objectives established in the program plan. Writing complete and informative job descriptions ensures that positions are classified at the appropriate level. The procedures for the final review and approval of the position description and assignment to a salary level depend upon the type of organization and its personnel system and policies.

Before writing any position descriptions, the administrator or supervisor must determine if the agency has an established system for classifying positions and approving class job specifications. If there are no class specifications for a nutritionist series, specifications written for other professionals working at a comparable level of training and experience can be used as a guide. Roles, duties/responsibilities, and knowledge/skills required for public health nutrition personnel are discussed in Chapter 19.

Public agencies generally have a personnel office with staff who provide a standard format or forms and guidelines to use in preparing job descriptions. Regardless of the format there are components common to all job descriptions. Position descriptions should include

- identifying information (job title, name and position of supervisor, and location of position)
- statement of the primary purpose of the position
- principal responsibilities, functions, or activities and percentage of time usually required for each
- prerequisite knowledge, skills, training, and credentials
- responsibilities for budgets, personnel, program content
- number of employees supervised
- complexity of decisions
- working conditions, hazards, and problems that may be encountered
- required physical effort
- relationships with other agency employees, the general public, or organizations or individuals outside the agency
- guidelines to be used, including reference materials, state and federal regulations, program manuals, and textbooks

Position descriptions are too important to prepare in haste. Care needs to be taken to accurately describe the scope of work, degree of difficulty, relative complexity of tasks, and estimated percentage of time spent at each task. Action verbs that graphically depict the work to be done and the complexity of the task should be used to describe roles and responsibilities. Key words reflecting complexity might include *policy making, planning and evaluation, data management, directing, coordinating, expert consultation to high level officials, training of professionals*, and *supervision of several staff*. For direct care nutritionists key words to use might be *counseling, assessing, interviewing*, or *educating*. Key words used must reflect the professional level of the work and the competency of the workers.

Consulting professional personnel analysts within the organization to learn their perspectives and their recommended key words saves time and prevents disappointment in position classification. Analysts have objective criteria that they use to classify positions fairly and differentiate levels of responsibility. Personnel analysts usually base classifications on job complexity, required expertise, and number and type of subordinate personnel supervised. They are expected to classify positions at parallel levels for comparable worth in the agency and community. In public agencies it is the personnel analysts' responsibility to get the work of the agencies done at least cost to the taxpayers and to ensure that there are no artificial barriers on the career ladder. It is useful to study position descriptions for other professionals in the organization to identify their key words. Personnel analysts frequently conduct desk audits in which they interview field staff regarding their job responsibilities. All nutrition personnel should be advised of the key words to use when their positions are audited.

The draft of the position description must be submitted to the agency personnel director. In large state, country, or city agencies the personnel office may be in a department of administration where all official agency positions are classified and established. Recruitment cannot be initiated until positions are officially established.

Finding the Right Person for the Job

For each position vacancy, a recruitment plan should be developed with the agency personnel or employment office and cleared with the agency administrator. Agency policies which must be strictly followed influence the recruitment plan and the search process. Recruitment plans should be tailored to the uniqueness of the position, qualifications required, and competitiveness of the job market. The recruitment plan should ensure an adequate pool of applicants for any opening. Finding the "best and brightest" applicants requires advertising widely and informing a large number of knowledgeable people about the position. This includes writing to potential applicants identified by staff or colleagues, persons who might refer potential applicants (such as college and university faculty), and peers in related agencies. Recruitment also includes advertising in the newspapers, newsletters, and professional journals read by potential applicants and contacting the job placement services of universities or professional organizations. Making contacts at professional meetings that job seekers frequently attend can be done both through the professional organization's job placement service and informal networking with colleagues.

Advertisements, position announcements, and letters should clearly describe the job responsibilities, location, training and experience required, and anything about the position responsibilities or location that might make it particularly appealing. The description should be clearly written to encourage qualified applicants while discouraging the unqualified.

Immediately after the closing date, a procedure should be in place for one person to screen the applications and inform those applicants that clearly do not meet the job requirements. Rejection letters should be friendly and state the objective criteria used to screen applications. The supervisor with a small search or recruitment committee should select and rank the qualified applicants. If any applications are incomplete, additional information should be requested. Each committee member should write an assessment of the strengths and limitations identified in each application. Having ranked the completed applications, the three to five most promising applicants should be invited by telephone or letter to come for an interview. Agency policy regarding paying applicant travel expenses for interviews should be clearly stated in these invitations.

In preparing to interview candidates, managers must carefully study and understand agency policies. The nutrition program manager should read the employment policy and procedure manual and discuss it with the personnel director or employment clerk. Each office's responsibilities and authority for offering the position, setting and offering the salary, discussing fringe benefits, paying moving expenses, and responding to personnel questions asked by applicants should be clearly defined.

All persons who are to participate in any aspect of the interview process should meet to agree upon the most important requirements for the position and the qualities the successful candidate should possess. Together this group should develop a list of interview questions to be asked of each candidate. Each question should have a specific purpose and be open-ended. Describing a situation that might be encountered in the job and asking how the applicant would handle it can be very revealing. The applicant might be asked to respond to a question that is frequently asked by clients or co-workers. It can also be informative to ask what the applicant liked best or least about previous positions and what strengths the candidates would bring to the position.

Fair Employment Practices

To conduct a proper interview, the interviewer(s) must understand pertinent equal employment opportunity legislation. Questions that relate to the candidate's age, race, marital status, physical handicaps, plans for pregnancy or child care, religious or political preference, ethnicity, or financial status are taboo. All candidates should be evaluated equally on their ability to perform the required work.

The current federal and state laws and the agency's policies and procedures must be reviewed and understood before interviewing. Major federal laws are explained below:

- The Equal Pay Act of 1963, as amended by the Educational Amendments of 1972 (Section 6(d) of the Fair Labor Standards Act), requires that employees of either sex receive equal pay for jobs performed under similar circumstances requiring equal skill, responsibility, and effort.

• Title VII of the Civil Rights Act of 1964, as amended by the Equal Employment Opportunity Act of 1972, prohibits discrimination on the basis of race, color, religion, sex, or national origin in recruiting, hiring, compensation, training, promotion, and discharge.

• The Age Discrimination and Employment Act of 1967, as amended in 1978, prohibits discrimination against individuals between the ages of 40 and 70.

• The Rehabilitation Act of 1973, as amended in 1974, prohibits discrimination against physically and mentally handicapped individuals.

Interviewing Applicants

The interview is used to select the most qualified person for the position. It gives applicants sufficient information about the position and the organization to make an informed decision. An interview is a two-way process.

The lead interviewer should introduce the persons who are participating in the interview and identify their positions in the organization. The organization and the position should be concisely and clearly described indicating where the position fits in the organization. In a conversational, nonintimidating manner the same predetermined questions should be asked of each candidate. Interviewers should listen carefully to the responses to their questions and to any information the applicant volunteers. Probing questions should be used for amplification and clarification. The candidate should be given ample time to ask questions. Interviewers should respect the candidate even when it becomes apparent that that person will not be selected.

The interviewer should trust hunches during the interview. If at any point there are questions or concerns about the candidate, these should be followed up and resolved. If it is not possible to verify a concern and there are doubts about hiring the applicant, it is wise not to do so.

All candidates should leave with a positive feeling since they may influence another applicant or may be appropriate for a future position. The interview should close by stating when the applicant can expect to hear about the decision and that the applicant will be notified regardless of the decision.

Immediately after each interview, key points of the conversation should be recorded, including both positive and negative responses to questions and overall impressions. This record prepares interviewers to state the reasons why one candidate was selected over another. In some organizations this must be documented for the files.

When the preferred candidates are selected, their past employers, professional colleagues, or teachers should be phoned for information. Questions to references should elicit information about the candidate's professional competencies and potential suitability for the position. References will seldom volunteer information. Past employers are often cautious about offering negative information, fearing libel if the applicant is not hired. Some references will want to have written permission from the applicant. Letters of reference that the applicant hand delivers should be considered biased.

Personnel decisions have long-lasting effects and should be based on complete and deliberately analyzed data. It is easier to hire than fire, promote than demote. Hiring mistakes are costly. If no suitable candidates apply, the search should be continued.

Orienting the New Employee

A well-planned orientation helps the newly selected employee assume the job responsibilities with confidence, and it assures management that the employee understands what is expected. Time spent in developing an orientation plan to ensure that all pertinent areas and policies are discussed will be cost-effective. Some organizations periodically offer formal orientation programs for all new employees. Others use a uniform orientation checklist that may need modifications or additions to make it applicable to specific positions. All orientation plans should include an explanation of the agency's mission and organization, materials to read on pertinent policies and procedures, and introductions to key administrators, program directors, and co-workers. It also should include thorough indoctrination in the basic job responsibilities.

The length of the orientation period depends on the experience and education of the employee and the requirements of the position. An experienced individual who has held a similar position in the same type of agency only needs to be oriented to the organization. The employee who has not worked in such a position previously may need several weeks of in-depth training and should be given time to develop confidence under the guidance of the supervisor or a capable co-worker.

Personnel policies generally establish a probationary period. This period allows the new employee to demonstrate competencies and skills and the ability to fit into the organization and to perform the assigned duties. During the probationary period, the supervisor has the unappealable right to terminate an employee. It is not wise to shorten a probationary period since the new worker is often demonstrating best behavior during the "honeymoon" period. If serious questions regarding the employee's ability to function in the position occur during the preestablished probationary period, it should be extended. Expectations should be made clear in writing.

Assigning Work and Scheduling Staff

The program plan with its objectives and action plan sets priorities for deployment of staff and allocation of their time. This time allocation should be displayed on a posted schedule. All regularly scheduled activities for each professional and paraprofessional should be displayed on a weekly or monthly calendar. The calendar shows all routine activities and the nutrition workers assigned to clinic counseling, teaching classes, attending scheduled meetings, speaking to community groups, appearing on the media, or coordinating activities with other agencies. Each worker should have blocks of time reserved for administrative activities that include program planning, writing records and reports, analyzing data, preparing for group or media presentations, making telephone calls, and preparing correspondence. Some flexible or discretionary time should be built into each schedule to respond to unanticipated requests or to cover emergencies.

In addition to the routine schedule of activities on the monthly calendar, a yearly time line chart should display deadlines and completion dates for long-term creative projects such as audio-visual material or curriculum development, computer applications, grant-writing, or applied research and writing for professional publication. Over the year, time must be scheduled for each professional to have personal leave and planned continuing education.

From the master schedule, each nutritionist should develop a personal work plan and maintain a professional calendar. The supervisor can review the individual schedules and calendars to monitor staff activities in relation to achieving the individual and program plan process objectives. Achievement of the program plan's objectives depends on the time management skills of both the supervisor and staff. Since personnel costs comprise the largest expenditure in the service agency's budget, time is a precious commodity and its use must be carefully controlled to achieve the program objectives. A balance must be maintained between routine, immediate time commitments, and longer range activities which may appear to be deferrable and discretionary. It is the long-term projects which may be more creative, cost-effective, visible, and satisfying. The effective supervisor constantly monitors time-wasting busy work activities and procrastination.

POLICIES AND PROCEDURES

Programs need written policies and procedures. As discussed in Chapter 5, a policy is a statement of principle that sets the direction of action based on demonstrated "best practices." A policy states the priorities for action, the reason for the action, and when the action will take place. A procedure states how each policy will be carried out, including step-by-step instructions. Policies and procedures establish criteria for program excellence based on currently accepted research and practice. They serve to

- standardize program activities
- facilitate training of new employees
- inform employees of expectations
- serve as a reference standard against which performance can be monitored
- provide uniform instructions for performing each task
- facilitate continuity of action when staff changes

Policies and procedures are derived from the program plan and are needed for each area in which nutritionists are providing services, e.g., prenatal care, well child care, adult health promotion, or home health services. Policies and procedures must be written clearly and logically. They must be continuously reviewed to be kept current with scientific findings and changes in practice. They need to be maintained on a computer or in a looseleaf binder where new or updated policies can be added. Policy and procedure manuals must be a readily available reference for all employees.

The policy and procedure manual should begin with a description of the nature and scope of nutrition services and the system for communicating and coordinating with professionals in related disciplines in the agency such as physicians, nurses, health educators, and social workers as well as with those in related services in the community. Polices and procedures for nutrition services should address

- standards for nutritional care
- nutrition screening and assessment procedures
- eligibility criteria for referral to food, nutrition, and health and social services within the agency and to outside agencies
- records and methods for documenting and retrieving nutrition and health data
- kinds and format of reports (monthly/quarterly/annual)
- the quality assurance system
- staff development and continuing education[5]

STAFF MEETINGS

Stimulating, productive staff meetings provide personnel employed in an agency with a forum for solving problems of mutual concern, exchanging ideas, learning new scientific and program information, debating controversial issues, and planning new initiatives to enrich the program. Periodic meetings should inspire, energize, and create a sense of shared mission. Meetings can be used by staff to try out creative ideas and to practice their skills in group presentation in a critical but supportive peer group. At these meetings, the nutrition staff can meet agency administrators, program directors, and policymakers; peers in other disciplines; representatives of other community agencies or the media; and local officials. Such introductions provide a two-way exchange, introduce the nutritionists to the thinking of their agency and community leaders, and build visibility and respect for public health nutrition expertise.

Agendas for staff meetings should be planned and distributed in advance. There should be a purpose for each staff meeting that is clear to each participant. To prepare participants for active discussion, assignments such as timely readings, review of a draft proposal, observation of a program, or responding to a questionnaire may be distributed with the agenda. Each agenda item should show a time limit for presentation, discussion, decision making, and closure. The chairperson, who may be the supervisor (or staff members on a rotating basis), should control the agenda, making sure that the meeting begins and ends at the scheduled time and that minutes summarizing decisions are prepared and disseminated within the week after the meeting.

These meetings should contribute to staff development. It is important that an atmosphere conducive to free idea exchange, open discussion, and constructive debate be established. If the group experiences problems with personality conflicts or reaching consensus, a structured group discussion method such as brainstorming or nominal group process can be used. A health educator or an outside group process facilitator might be invited to help guide the group toward more productive interaction.

Major grantwriting, long-range planning, development of audio-visual materials or curricula, or other time-consuming projects require appointment of special task forces or small working committees to meet over a period of several months. Staff meetings should not be devoted to these projects. To establish working groups, staff can be invited to volunteer their interests. Periodic progress reports can then be given at scheduled staff meetings to share information among work groups and to receive input from those not part of the work group and to accept the final product.

When staff complain that their meetings are not stimulating, productive, collegial, or interactive, a meeting agenda should be devoted to examining the process and content of meetings. Staff meetings can be valuable for communication, but since they represent a large investment of time and therefore money, meetings considered time-wasters should not be tolerated.

PERFORMANCE APPRAISAL

Performance appraisal is one of the nutrition program manager's most important responsibilities. Both newly employed and long-term employees learn from constructive feedback. It can motivate the "high achiever" to continually strive for innovation and excellence, and it can let less experienced or less productive staff members know that their performance is being monitored. It also provides staff with the counseling they need to assess their own productivity and work quality. Performance evaluation is needed as the basis for merit salary increments, promotion, lateral transfer, career development, and termination decisions. Some agencies have performance appraisal systems in place that may be tied to merit pay plans to serve as an incentive.

The nutrition program manager should discuss agency policies for performance appraisal with the administrator and personnel director and learn how to use the agency system to best advantage. Once the agency system is fully understood, it can be used as it is designed or supplemented to work more effectively for the individual program manager. If the agency does not have a formal procedure, then the nutrition program manager should develop one. An effective performance appraisal system

- is an on-going process rather than a once- or twice-a-year review
- is participative, with the employee setting objectives and assessing self-performance
- involves two-way communication between employee and supervisor rather than one-way communication from the supervisor
- depends on face-to-face interaction rather than written communication and forms
- is based on job performance criteria and job-relevant behaviors, not personality traits
- is based on the employee's own job performance, not comparison with other employees

- balances positive and negative feedback
- generates constructive and specific recommendations for overcoming weaknesses
- keeps the appraisal of current job performance separate from potential for future jobs[6]

Using program plan objectives, the employee and supervisor together must agree on position-specific objectives to use for the performance review. The manager must be sure that objectives are reasonable for the employee and the organization and that by meeting the objectives the employee will be performing satisfactorily. Substandard kinds and amounts of work should never be accepted as appropriate in setting objectives for a work plan. Additional training objectives to assist the employee to perform at a satisfactory level should be developed. Performance appraisal interviews should be conducted in private, free from interruptions, and sufficient time for meaningful discussion should be scheduled.

Regularly scheduled, frequent conferences with individual staff members are valuable supervisory tools for monitoring program performance as well as appraising staff. At these sessions, the staff member can describe program achievements, receive guidance and encouragement in problem solving, and identify opportunities for program growth and professional development. If regularly scheduled, such conferences are nonthreatening and allow the staff member and the supervisor to assess performance and provide guidance when it is most effective.

RECOGNIZING AND REWARDING STAFF

Staff need to be recognized and rewarded for productivity, creativity, and accomplishing individual and program objectives. This stimulates them to achieve at their highest potential. Monetary recognition of performance is through merit salary increases; however, "psychic paychecks" are also valued. Frequent "strokes" and "thank you's" for a job well done evoke loyalty and productivity. Recognition can be given with awards like the "nutritionist of the month" and by recommending accomplished staff for agency awards or awards of professional organizations. Individual and group achievements can be honored through news releases of program accomplishments or by special recognition at a staff meeting. Recognizing years of service with the agency or celebrating birthdays, anniversaries, and holidays together improves "esprit de corps" and demonstrates thoughtfulness and caring.

Undertaking activities that contribute to the professional development of the staff member and the enhancement of the nutrition program increases job satisfaction. The nutritionist with special interests might periodically be encouraged to consult with knowledgeable state or federal agency nutrition specialists or university faculty to increase visibility and develop competencies. More accomplished public health nutritionists might be encouraged to write grant applications, conduct applied research, write for publication, and make presentations at local, state, and national meetings.

BUILDING CAREERS

Open discussion with staff about their ultimate career goals should be encouraged. They should be advised of their options to reach their goals within the agency, the community, the public health or educational system, and the private sector. The supervisor who mentors and guides career advancement will influence greater productivity among energetic staff.

Each professional and paraprofessional should be encouraged to write an individual career development plan in addition to the individual work plan. The career development plan should include time lines for continuing education through credit and noncredit courses, attendance and presentations at professional meetings, and directed reading. Specific competency areas where additional knowledge or skills are needed can be identified using the Self-Assessment Tool for Public Health Nutritionists in Appendix A.

Recognizing that career-minded nutrition professionals seek achievement through progressively responsible experiences, it is desirable to develop a career ladder or career lattice of positions within the agency. Where this is not feasible, opportunities should be sought to expand the variety and scope of responsibilities within the existing positions.

The supervisor should know the progressively responsible position classifications in the agency and identify how functions would need to be expanded in order for positions to be reclassified. Positions with an incumbent are reclassified on the basis of functions expanding or added responsibilities actually assumed.

Staff members should be encouraged to volunteer for special agency projects or to participate in quality circles. This involvement should be discussed and made part of the career development or nutrition unit work plan. An important component of career development is participating in programs, working on committees, and holding appointed or elected offices in nutrition/dietetics, public health professional organizations, and community service clubs.

MENTORING IN PUBLIC HEALTH NUTRITION

Most successful business and professional leaders attribute their advancement to the guidance of a more experienced, well-established person who helped guide their careers and "opened doors" for them. Competent, ambitious nutritionists should seek mentors to coach and counsel them on achievement of their career goals. The mentor/protégé relationship usually begins during graduate school or early in a career. Mentors are influential and successful teachers, administrators, supervisors, officers in professional organizations, or more experienced colleagues who can identify talent and leadership potential. The mentor is a guide, counselor, teacher, and friend—a successful professional who gains satisfaction and pride through guiding a younger colleague to achieve some of the same success. Mentors are role models for leadership style, professional demeanor, and dress. The mentor must be available to coach and provide constructive feedback on career expectations, advancement, and performance. The protégé must respect and trust the mentor and be able to accept and use the continuing critique.

Some of the leadership activities that the mentor might encourage and help the career-minded nutritionist protégé achieve are

- serving in appointed and elected positions in professional, civic, and service organizations at the local, state, and national level
- accepting increasing levels of job responsibility
- writing for publication
- designing and conducting applied research
- working with the media
- applying for grants to develop innovative programs
- volunteering to work with community groups developing needed public services

The mentor uses position and power to recommend and introduce the aspiring young professional to move into more progressively responsible positions and to gain visibility in the community and in the profession. The protégé benefits from the wise counsel, experience, and status of the mentor, and the mentor gains pride and satisfaction from the achievements of the protégé. The relationship is based on mutual competence and trust. It moves through stages of guidance, development, and support toward professional maturity and independence as the protégé gains skills and self-confidence and achieves stature.[7]

TAKING DISCIPLINARY ACTION

Regardless of how careful selection, orientation, and supervision of employees has been, some employees do not meet the organization's performance standards. Then the decision must be made to take formal corrective action which may lead to termination of employment. Before formal disciplinary action is initiated with the employee, the situation needs to be thoroughly discussed with the personnel officer and administrator. Federal laws apply to the corrective action or termination process. Documentation must be maintained of actions taken and the reasons for the actions. The employee who has achieved permanent status generally has the right to appeal an adverse personnel action. The burden of proof is with the party who initiates the action.

The Oral Warning

An oral warning informs the employee of unsatisfactory behavior or productivity. The warning must be delivered in private, with time scheduled to discuss the issues and to mutually agree on a plan for corrective action. It is desirable to have a carefully selected objective observer participate in the conference. After the counseling session where the problems are cited, the plan of action and timeframe for improvement must be written. One copy must be given to the employee and another placed in the employee's personnel file.

The Written Notice

If unacceptable performance continues, the next step is a written warning that objectively states the reason for the warning and clearly lists and describes the areas of deficiency. This action must be based on well-documented, job-related behavior. The warning must state times or incidents of inappropriate or insufficient activity and state the actions that will be taken if behavior or performance is not improved.

The notice should be given to the employee in private and the employee must acknowledge receipt of the written notice. If the employee refuses to acknowledge receipt in writing or by signing a copy of the warning, arrangements must be made for reading the written warning to the employee in the presence of another supervisor or person designated by the personnel officer or administrator. Whether or not agency policy requires written warnings to be given in the presence of another person, it is advisable.

Agency policy must be strictly followed throughout the disciplinary process. Most agencies require two written notices of unsatisfactory performance prior to the notice of termination. When confronted with unacceptable behavior or work output, many individuals will voluntarily decide to seek other employment. If they do not leave and their performance remains unsatisfactory, the employee must be terminated.

Appeals

Most agencies have a formal employee grievance policy. Upon appeal an outside third party reviews the documentation supporting the decision to terminate the employee. In some cases a hearing is held with testimony from both sides. Some grievance policies grant the right for an employee to file a grievance upon the receipt of a written notice.

To be upheld, disciplinary actions must be consistent for all employees; for example, if dismissal is due to excessive tardiness, records for all staff must be maintained, and disciplinary action must be consistent. Action should be based on timely and accurate records. It must be progressive, with an oral warning after which the employee understands the problem and changes required or expected. Adequate time to demonstrate change needs to be given and all disciplinary actions must be documented.

ISSUES TO DEBATE

- What descriptive terms can be used in writing job descriptions that will ensure classification at a level to justify allocation to competitive pay grades?
- What is an appropriate response to a request for a reference for a former employee when the agency has a policy that only dates of employment should be provided to potential employers?
- How can program direction and accountability for staff performance be maintained when the supervisor's responsibilities also include extensive time in the field?
- How can the supervisor fairly assess an employee's rationale for less than satisfactory performance?

NOTES

1. Norman Metzger, *The Health Care Supervisor's Handbook*, 2d ed. (Rockville, Md.: Aspen Publishers, Inc., 1982), 1.

2. Ibid., 3.

3. Mildred Kaufman, ed., *Personnel in Public Health Nutrition for the 1980's* (McLean, Va.: Association of State and Territorial Health Officials Foundation, 1982), 27.

4. Wilbert E. Scheer, *The Dartnell Personnel Administration Handbook* (Chicago: Dartnell Press, 1979), 651.

5. U.S. Department of Health, Education, and Welfare, *Guide for Developing Nutrition Services in Community Health Programs* (Rockville, Md.: U.S. Department of Health, Education, and Welfare, Public Health Service, Health Services Administration, Bureau of Community Services, 1987), DHEW Publ. no. (ASA) 78-5103, 8-9.

6. Stephen L. Cohen and Cabot L. Jafee, "Managing Human Performance Effectively through Performance Appraisal: Introduction and Background," in *Supervisory Handbook: A Management Guide to Principles and Applications*, ed. Martin M. Broadwell (New York: John Wiley & Sons, Inc., 1985), 17.8-17.9.

7. Malinda Bunyes and Deborah D. Canter, "Mentoring Implications for Career Development," *Journal of the American Dietetic Association* 88, no. 6 (1988): 705.

BIBLIOGRAPHY

Beach, Dale S. *Personnel: The Management of People at Work*. 3rd ed. New York: Macmillan Publishing Co., Inc., 1975.

Benton, Lewis R. *Supervision and Management*. New York: McGraw-Hill Book Co., 1972.

Embey, Alice H. *The New Supervisor*. 3rd ed. Reading, Mass.: Addison-Wesley Publishing Co., Inc., 1984.

chapter **21**

Leveraging Nutrition Education through the Public Health Team

Gaye Joyner and Mildred Kaufman

READER OBJECTIVES

- Discuss roles of various health care providers in nutrition counseling and education.
- Describe some strategies to prepare health care professionals to provide nutrition education and diet counseling.
- List types of teams that might function in a health agency.
- Define teamwork.
- List and discuss stages of team development.
- Compare and contrast the values for a nutritionist in being a member of an effective team.

NUTRITION CARE THROUGH THE PUBLIC HEALTH TEAM

Compelling evidence summarized in *The Surgeon General's Report on Nutrition and Health*[1] and the National Academy of Science's *Diet and Health Implications for Reducing Chronic Disease Risk*[2] highlights the essential roles of nutrition and diet in promoting and protecting the public's health throughout their lifespan. Clearly the current cadre of less than 5,000 public health nutrition personnel[3] must extend their efforts by building up the nutrition knowledge and skills of their co-workers on the health team.

One of the year 2000 health promotion/disease prevention objectives is to increase to at least 50 percent the proportion of primary health care providers who provide nutrition counseling and/or referral to qualified nutritionists and/or dietitians.[4] Ensuring the scientific validity of their nutrition education and counseling requires all health professionals to have sound knowledge of current concepts in nutrition and diet. They must cultivate their skills in nutrition assessment, dietary counseling, nutrition education, and referral so that their clients will benefit from credible, practical dietary advice.

In the health agency's primary care services, nutritionists should be on the teams that staff family planning, prenatal, well-child, and children's special health services clinics and adult ambulatory care, geriatric, or home health services. To touch the lives of as many clients as possible, the nutritionist on these teams always functions as a consultant and inservice educator even while providing direct care. The nutritionist actively participates during client case conferences or primary care team meetings by exchanging information and observing intervention strategies. The result of teamwork is that the client experiences the "united front" of consistent health and nutrition education messages along with on-going support and encouragement. The health professionals in the various disciplines must get to know each other's respective roles in screening, diagnosis, treatment, patient education, and referral. It may be desirable for workers in each discipline to "shadow" a client through the clinic so that each can observe every other discipline's content and process when providing nutrition advice. Observation of these interactions reveals the strengths as well as the duplications, gaps, and contradictions as the client encounters them.

Each health professional brings the unique competencies of the individual discipline to client care. They each build on these roles and competencies as they contribute to nutrition care. Each member of the public health team has a unique role in nutritional care.

Physicians. Physicians recommend diet as part of health promotion and anticipatory guidance. They assess health and nutritional status, diagnose diet-related conditions, and prescribe dietary treatment and nutrient supplements. The physician can inform clients of the reasons why dietary change is important to them and give them some overall guidance. Because of their busy schedules, physicians may provide clients with general information but they usually need to refer high-risk clients for the more detailed dietary information needed to plan, purchase, and prepare appropriate daily meals and snacks. The degree of interest and conviction the physician displays will be reflected in the client's attitude toward dietary change.

Nurses. Nurses frequently function as case managers and care coordinators. They screen clients and provide basic health promotion nutrition information to those at low risk. Protocols used in the clinic for the various health conditions can outline dietary guidance and suggest suitable educational materials for nurses to use. Protocols can also specify when clients with more complex dietary requirements or feeding problems should be referred to the nutritionist. Friendly words of encouragement from the nurse to the clients in the clinic or during the home visit can motivate them to work harder to incorporate dietary recommendations into their daily routines.

Because of the rapport nurses often develop with clients and families, they can provide the nutritionist with valuable insights into any family or home situations that may interfere with dietary behavior change, e.g., lack of money to purchase the foods required, a home with a kitchen where the oven or refrigerator is out of order, the client who is unable to read the nutrition educational materials, or if families are unable or unwilling to comply with dietary instructions. Nurses and nutritionists should exchange information about nutritional care to help clients meet their dietary goals.

Social Workers. The social worker can assess emotional barriers that interfere with family and client abilities to cope with health care and dietary recommendations. Social workers can also help clients handle some of their family, social, emotional, and financial stresses and assist them in obtaining needed food, financial, educational, or housing assistance. They may offer practical guidance on normal family food selection or budgeting and can reinforce and support nutrition education.

Physical, Occupational, and Speech Therapists. These professionals work with clients to overcome physical handicaps and improve function. While therapists work with clients and families on how to feed, eat, or swallow, they must collaborate with the nutritionist on the appropriate kinds and amounts of nutritious foods to recommend and the appropriate textures and forms for these foods. They must understand the goals for the client's food and nutrient intake and how these are to be achieved. The nutritionist must understand the therapist's goals for the client and be acquainted with the use of adaptive equipment for self-feeding or food preparation.

Dentists and Dental Hygienists. Dentists, like nutritionists, are concerned with chewing, oral hygiene, and reduction in intake of simple sugars. They are usually interested in promoting nutrients that contribute to proper tooth development and dental hygiene.

Health Educators. These professionals participate in clinical or community health promotion and group education. Nutritionists can provide them with references and materials to use in their programs and jointly plan group education for various populations seen in clinics, schools, worksites, or the community.

CONSULTING ON CLIENT CARE

The nutritionist who understands the overall goals of patient care planning uses every teachable moment to educate co-workers regarding the contributions of nutrition to growth and development in children, health promotion at each stage of life, and prescribed dietary treatments. Colleagues might be invited to observe the nutritionist counsel or co-teach group nutrition education classes. Dialogue can be initiated by reading client records and asking for additional information about the client's appetite, weight loss or gain, and results of biochemical tests.

Information can be shared by flagging or attaching notes to client records. Physicians welcome information to use with specific clients. They particularly respect articles from prestigious scientific journals. Nurses, therapists, and social workers may prefer articles offering practical nutrition tips for their personal use as well as materials they can use with clients.

As contributing team members, nutritionists should work on the overall goals of care and recognize that there are situations when other care must take priority over nutrition.

Case consultation is an interactive process of problem solving. Professional consultation involves

> a process of planned change by which expert knowledge and skills are utilized in a relationship between consultant and consultee (individual, group or organization) for the purpose of enabling the consultee to increase, develop, free or modify knowledge, skills and attitudes and/or behaviors toward the solution of a current or anticipated work problem, and secondarily for enabling them to be more effective in preventing or solving similar problems in the future. . . .The consultant is responsible for assessing the areas in which he is competent to give consultation and for engaging in the relationship and guiding the process in a way which is functional for achievement of the consultation objectives. The consultee is responsible for making use of the consultation experience.[5]

Consulting on individual cases provides the nutritionist with the opportunity to sit down with a colleague at a scheduled conference and review the client and family record, obtain additional information, and discuss alternative approaches to plan the individual's nutritional care. Consultation sessions are used to provide factual information and teaching materials, recommend references, and negotiate on practical strategies for changing dietary behavior. Follow-up sessions are used to assess the client's progress, answer questions, and plan future directions. While case consultation may appear time-consuming, it is a means of providing staff inservice education, which helps health professionals acquire the nutrition information they need to work with individual clients they select. It enables them to build their knowledge, skills, and self-confidence in nutrition counseling and education, while responding to the needs of the people they are currently helping.

Consultation to home health nurses is particularly cost-effective. Existing Medicare home health policies pay the nutritionist under administrative overhead. However, the nurse can be reimbursed for the home visit when the nutrition counseling is part of the nursing care.

EDUCATING HEALTH CARE PROFESSIONALS

Nutritionists must continuously stimulate the interest and cultivate the nutrition knowledge and practice of their co-workers on the health care team. The new summary reports cited earlier in the chapter, the tenth edition of the National Academy of Sciences' *Recommended Dietary Allowances*, and the nutrition chapter of the U.S. Department of Health and Human Services' *Promoting Health/Preventing Disease, Year 2000 Objectives for the Nation* are some current publications that can be used to entice health professionals to participate in continuing education offerings. Continuing education for health professionals can be co-sponsored by health agencies with educational institutions, professional societies, and/or voluntary health agencies. The promotion and implementation of the March of Dimes-sponsored teaching package *Maternal Nutrition: Contemporary Approaches to Interdisciplinary Care*[6] demonstrate a model for training maternal health care providers to integrate nutrition counseling into all of their contacts with pregnant women.

Continuing and Inservice Education Programs

Continuing education programs can be designed to include health professionals who work in private practices, health care facilities, health maintenance organizations, community health centers, and educational institutions as well as those in the public health agency. Many states have area health education centers (AHECs) that co-sponsor, organize, and publicize continuing education events for practicing health professionals. Continuing education offices or centers in the health professional schools of universities also provide these services. A planning committee with representatives of the health professional audience for whom the training is being planned will be sure to provide an agenda that meets their interests, expectations, and time schedules. Offering continuing education credits approved by the accrediting agencies for physicians, nurses, nurse midwives, or dietitians motivates them to participate.

Inservice education programs for the staff of the health agency reach public health professionals on the job. Surveying or interviewing physicians, nurses, health educators, and other colleagues can determine their needs and interests. A small planning committee can help in developing meaningful programs on new and provocative scientific findings. Sufficient time for questions and interactive discussion, effective audio-visual aids, and group work on case studies liven up the presentation. Handouts provide take-home reading. Refreshments such as fruit punch, fresh fruit, flavored nonfat milk, and whole grain crackers demonstrate tasty, nutrient-dense, or health-promoting foods and make the nutrition topic come alive. Recipes for the "healthy foods" that are served promote their use. Every inservice education program should be evaluated with a user-friendly pre- and post-test to determine whether the program met its learning objectives. A satisfaction survey can solicit suggestions for future programs.

As a follow-up to planned programs, carefully selected journal articles, newsletters, and professional and client nutrition educational materials can be routed to co-workers according to their interests. Since desks are already piled high with reading material and reading time is precious, flagging and highlighting content specific to professional and personal interests and needs will make it more likely to be read. Notices of meetings or eye-catching materials can be posted on staff bulletin boards. Inhouse newsletters can summarize new research findings or highlight changes in community food assistance programs.

Friendly persuasion, more structured consultation, and continuing education in the agency and in the community are all designed to capture interest and enhance the nutrition knowledge and competencies of health professionals. The underlying purpose is to ensure standards of nutritional care to which all health professionals subscribe. Within the agency the interdisciplinary team should collaborate and agree on policies, procedures, and protocols for nutritional care to establish

- definitions and standards of nutrition education and care for health promotion for low-, medium-, and high-risk clients
- roles and responsibilities of the various health care providers for nutritional care
- criteria for referral to agency nutrition personnel, as well as WIC, community food assistance, and nutrition education programs
- criteria for selection and use of nutrient or dietary supplements, infant proprietary formulas, and products for enteral and parenteral feedings
- criteria for selection and use of nutrition education materials
- a quality assurance system for nutrition care incorporated in the overall agency quality assurance system

TEAMS FUNCTIONING IN THE HEALTH AGENCY

Membership on the various teams, work groups, or task forces functioning at various levels in the health agency can be used to extend the nutritionist's influence. Each member of the group can become invested in advancing the role of nutrition in public health, just as the nutritionist can learn and become an advocate for the many other aspects of public health and health care.

Primary Health Care Team

In delivering primary health care, the professionals of the several disciplines serving clients enhance their efficiency and improve care to clients if they take the time to improve their interactive group processes—to build their team they must learn to respect and trust each other. At its simplest level, teamwork is demonstrated by exchanging and sharing information. The various health care providers must understand enough about each other's contributions first to make appropriate referrals and then to reinforce each other's counseling. On a more sophisticated level, the team is organized with a leader or coordinator and meets on a regular schedule to discuss client cases, solve problems, and improve the quality of services. A team is functioning at maximum efficiency when it integrates service delivery; establishes working policies, procedures, and protocols; unifies its data collection system; implements an interdisciplinary quality assurance system; and collaborates in continuing education. The ultimate evidence is improved client health and nutritional health status and excellence in quality of care, as well as client satisfaction and cost-effective service delivery.

Quality Assurance Team

The interdisciplinary quality assurance team includes peer members of the several disciplines whose care is under review. The team writes and ratifies a single set of process and outcome criteria for care of those clients who have the same diagnoses or problems. These criteria are used to audit medical records from which the key data elements are collected. The team collaborates on selecting the key indicators, analyzing the data, identifying discrepancies or deficits, and recommending remedial actions. An interdisciplinary quality assurance team has been demonstrated to be the most cost-effective and least duplicative, since most disciplines base their assess-

Exhibit 21-1   Nominal Group Technique

Nominal Group Technique: Involves all group members, even those who are not leaders, in development of problem solutions.

Here's How:

1. Make sure all group members know the problem.
2. Working individually, each person writes possible solutions to the problem, and ranks them in order of importance.
3. Have a round robin reporting of the individual solutions. A pre-selected recorder writes them on a chart or board.
4. Clarify all ideas without judgement.
5. From the group's list, each individual ranks in writing his or her five priority items.
6. Tally the results.
7. Discuss the results of the rankings.
8. If necessary, vote and rank again.
9. The final tally combines individual judgements into a group decision and closure.

Advantages	Disadvantages
1. It involves all group members in the deliberations, regardless of status or shyness, and pools their judgement.	1. Group interaction diminishes.
2. Alternating discussion with individual work decreases group conflict and tension.	2. The tallying process can be time-consuming.
3. People may work more diligently on an individual assignment than on a group one.	3. Technique works best in small groups (5–9).
4. It ensures closure.	

Source: Adapted from *Manual for Session Leaders, Maternal Nutrition: Contemporary Approaches to Interdisciplinary Care*, p. 19, with permission of March of Dimes Birth Defects Foundation.

---

ments on many of the same biochemical, clinical, and anthropometric measures. An interdisciplinary quality assurance team, with its varied insights, uses a decision-making technique such as nominal group process to reach consensus on priorities (Exhibit 21-1). The team must prioritize the number and type of key criteria to use in an interdisciplinary audit, recognizing that time and cost are limiting factors.

Training Team

The interdisciplinary training team collaborates on problem-oriented inservice education for the professionals of the several disciplines who work together and relates it to any additional discipline-specific, in-depth training which might be needed. Mid-level supervisors who direct the day-to-day work of the client care staff monitor their scientific credibility and practice. A team approach to inservice education can expand the breadth and depth of scientific knowledge and practical application of nutrition for all of the professionals who work together. For example, interdisciplinary inservice training for the physicians, nurses, nutritionists, health educators, and medical technologists who are designing and implementing a cholesterol education program might keep everyone up to date on the epidemiology of cardiovascular disease, the public health aspects, the patho-physiology, current treatment philosophies, and the available intervention strategies.

All professionals in each discipline need to understand the current concepts of diet in prevention and treatment in context with exercise and medication. A case study method could demonstrate the client-centered team approach to lipid-lowering diets and the interaction of these diets with drugs prescribed.

Management Team

The management team advises the agency director and participates in developing policy and strategic planning. Meeting on a scheduled basis with the agency director, key program directors, and budget and personnel managers, the nutrition administrator can advise on the contributions of nutrition and diet in addressing emerging community health problems. Rationale of the cost benefits of preventive nutrition programs should be considered in agency planning and budgeting. Options for staffing and financing nutrition services should be discussed as plans for new programs are in their formative stages. Administrators and members of the management team can be shown that there are income-generating nutrition services for which there is popular demand.

TEAMWORK

A team is a group of persons of different competencies who are interdependent, have a common future, and work together to achieve a shared goal. On the ideal team each of the several associates plays a distinct part.

Teamwork is synergistic—the total effect exceeds the sum of the individual efforts. Team building has been found to be cost-effective in delivering health and human services. Participation on a team broadens each player's perspectives, helps the representatives of the several disciplines to learn about how their various contributions fit together, and enlists their commitment.

In public health, teamwork is crucial because the multifaceted nature of client and community problems requires the perspectives and skills of the many different disciplines. For example, a comprehensive community approach to reducing low birth weight requires input of nutritionists, health educators, nurses, physicians, and social workers. In nutritional care, the team can address the interrelated family, social, economic, cultural, and personal issues that the client, family, and community face along with their health problems.

Not all groups that convene to accomplish agency or community tasks meet the definition of a team. Together, the team plans and conducts an assessment, develops and implements interventions, and develops and implements a monitoring system to measure their progress. When this group strives to achieve a common goal and interacts to share their skills and resources, they are a team.

Team Building

To function effectively, each team member must understand and respect the group process. As the team works together and develops, one of its most important tasks is to learn about other disciplines' roles and contributions to the "big picture." This knowledge is required to build respect, trust, and cohesiveness essential for productive team functioning. Each member must listen and be attentive to others. All must be committed to accomplishing the goals and tasks assigned to the team above and beyond meeting personal objectives.

The mix of thinking styles is as important as professional expertise when putting together a team. Some individuals look at the big picture when approaching a problem and others think of the important details. Some individuals are skilled at reaching closure on issues and some look at all of the alternatives. Some focus more on people, others on ideas. Some people have a strong critical thinking ability and others are concerned with human values and interactions. All views are important when a group is working to achieve a common goal.

Teams work best when all members choose to belong. In a large agency, a skills and resources inventory could assist in the selection of team members for particular assignments. For example, an agency-wide inventory or computer database could identify agency members by discipline, knowledge, skills, training, and interests. As projects are initiated, the suitable disciplines and individuals can be quickly identified and assembled.

Teams are often formed across work unit lines. These efforts may not work if there is turfism, competition for scarce resources, and lack of understanding about the goals of the organization and of each unit. For cross-discipline and cross-unit teams to function effectively, there must be support from the administrators and supervisors, a clear indication of where the agency is headed, and why this effort is valued. There also must be a system that rewards team effort through the performance appraisal system and recognizes the amount of time required for project effort. The team must have the authority to accomplish its mission. It also must have the resources it needs.

Four functions to build the team are given below:

1. Set goals or priorities.
2. Analyze or allocate the way work is performed according to each member's roles and responsibilities.
3. Examine the way the team is working—its processes such as norms, decision making, and communications.
4. Examine relationships among members.[7]

It is suggested that team building can succeed under four conditions:

1. Interdependence. The team is working on important problems in which each person has a stake, teamwork is central to future success, not an expression of ideology or some misplaced "ought to."
2. Leadership. The "boss" will take risks to improve group performance.
3. Joint decision. All members agree to participate.
4. Equal influence. Each person has a chance to influence the agenda.[8]

Credible, effective team building is hard work and a continual process that focuses on both the task and the process work of the team. No organization or group should expect to conduct a serious team effort quickly.

Team Leadership

The team leader should be selected not only for professional expertise, but for understanding the team's assignment and skills in managing effective group process. The leader is responsible for maintaining productivity and enthusiasm. The leader also should participate in selecting and orienting team members, clarify their charge, and set the direction and tone. Leaders must manage conflict and facilitate participatory decision making within the organizational framework. When teams are formed (and routinely during their period of activity), it may be desirable for leaders and team members to engage in inservice education on the various types of group processes that they can use to arrive at their decisions. Periodically, they should discuss how they are functioning as a team, how to resolve their conflicts, how to reach consensus in making decisions, and how to be more productive. While initially the leader takes the responsibility for setting the direction and the norms, as trust, openness, and a mutual support system develop, the members maintain team functioning while the leader monitors the process.

Stages in Group Development

As a group evolves from its early formation to more mature phases, it faces certain interpersonal, group behavior, and leadership issues. Understanding the phases of group development can help the leader guide the growth of the group as it accomplishes its tasks. Stages in team development (Table 21-1) are

1. orientation to the group and task (forming)
2. conflict over control among the group members and the leader (storming)
3. group formation and solidarity (norming)
4. differentiation and productivity[9] (performing)

Membership Skills

Most groups working together in organizations can benefit from a dual focus on task functions (how to get the job done) and maintenance functions (how to meet and continue to satisfy the psychosocial needs of the group members). (See Exhibit 21-2.)

For effective and efficient work in groups, both task and maintenance behaviors need to be part of the repertoire of group members. Members also need to have adequate technical knowledge and skills to accomplish their task.

Table 21-1 Stages in Team Development

	Member Behaviors	Member Concerns	Leader Behaviors
Stage I: Orientation to group and task (Forming)	Direct comments to the leader Seek direction and clarification Accord status to group members based on their roles outside the group Fail to listen, resulting in non sequitur statements Discuss issues superficially	Who am I in this group? Who are the others? Will I be accepted? What is my role? What tasks will I have? Will I be capable? Who is the leader? Will he or she value me? Is the leader competent?	Provide structure by holding regular meetings and assisting in task and role clarification Encourage participation by all, domination by none Facilitate learning about one another's areas of expertise and preferred working modes Share all relevant information Encourage members to ask questions of leader and one another
Stage II: Conflict over control among the group's members and leader (Storming)	Attempts to gain influence by individual members Form subgroups and coalitions with possible conflict among them Test and challenge leader Judge and evaluate one another and the leader, resulting in ideas being shot down Avoid task	How much autonomy will I have? Will I have influence over others? What is my place in the pecking order? Whom do I like? Who likes me? Do I have some support in here?	Engage in joint problem solving; have members give reasons why idea is useful and how to improve it Support the expression of different viewpoints Discuss the group's decision-making process and share decision-making responsibility Encourage members to state how they feel and what they think when they obviously have feelings about an issue Provide members with the resources they need to do their jobs (when this is not possible, explain why)
Stage III: Group formation and solidarity (Norming)	Support one another, can disagree with the leader Laugh together; have fun; joke sometimes at the leader's expense Develop "we-ness" and group norms Feel superior to other groups in the organization Do not challenge one another as much as the leader would like	How close should I be to the group members? Can we accomplish our tasks successfully? How do we compare to other groups? What is my relationship to the leader?	Talk openly about issues and concerns Have group members manage agenda items Give and request both positive and constructive negative feedback in the group Assign challenging problems for consensus decisions Delegate as much as the members are capable of handling; help them as necessary

| Stage IV: Differentiation and productivity (Performing) | Understand roles and each person's contribution
Take the initiative and accept one another's initiatives
Discuss and accept differences among members' backgrounds and modes of operation
Challenge one another for creative problem solving
Seek feedback from one another and from the leader to improve performance | (Concerns of earlier stages have been resolved) | Jointly set challenging goals
Look for new opportunities to increase the group's scope
Question assumptions and traditional ways of behaving
Develop mechanisms for ongoing self-assessment
Appreciate each member's contribution
Develop members to their fullest potential through task assignments and feedback |

Source: Adapted with permission from NTL Institute, "Developing a Productivity Team: Making Groups at Work Work" by Jane Moosbruker, pp. 91-92, *Team Building: Blueprints for Productivity and Satisfaction*, edited by W. Brendon Reddy and Kaleel Jamison, © 1988.

Exhibit 21-2 Process in Groups

Task	Maintenance
• generating ideas	• participation
• making decisions	• inclusion
• setting the agenda	• support/encouragement
• working within	• dealing with dysfunctional
time frames	behaviors
• testing agreement/reality	• checking

Making Decisions

A team should be used for consensual decision making when it is not known who has the most expertise regarding the decision to be made and when implementation of the decision will require participation of most, if not all, members of the team. The team works well on issues when facts are few and judgments and opinions are required.[10]

Resolving Conflict

Conflict in groups is inevitable. It has been observed that the more that groups uncover and address their differences, the higher the quality of their decisions. As shown in Table 21-1, conflict, especially with the group leader, is the characteristic stage of group development referred to as "storming." Groups that do not "storm" have been found to remain passive and disjointed and are significantly less creative.[11]

Managing conflict in groups may require some skills in training to assist members to deal with their differences and unspoken expectations of each other. It is useful to set a norm to critique and evaluate ideas. Feedback to team members should be based on specific behaviors, not on personal evaluations.

Developing Openness, Feedback, and Trust

Groups must talk about what needs to be done and what uncertainties exist. Individuals need feedback on their skills and behaviors in a trusting and caring environment. Trust, needed for group commitment, is built with great difficulty and easily destroyed. It is often based more on perceptions of others' intent than on reality. Team-building sessions are useful to help groups build trust.[12]

BENEFITS OF TEAMWORK

The benefits of working on an effective public health team include

- broader perspectives on the community, the agency, and the clients
- learning how the care modalities of several disciplines interact
- communicating about problems and issues in a way that can ultimately lead to more efficient and effective health promotion and treatment
- avoiding duplication of effort

Teamwork encourages a more comprehensive view of community health problems and is more likely to move an agency toward forward-looking health promotion and disease prevention strategies. For nutritionists, membership on teams extends their influence in the agency and the community since each member of the team becomes vested in the contributions of nutrition in public health and in supporting the nutrition message.

Observing both effective and ineffective teams working on projects throughout the agency is helpful to learn from others' successes and mistakes. Even with limited resources, some teams are always on the cutting edge. These teams have learned how to extend themselves through others. They have transcended turfism that, if allowed to develop, can ruin the best team efforts. They realize that sharing roles does not negate any discipline's importance but enhances it. There is more than enough work for everyone.

ISSUES TO DEBATE

- What criteria should be used to determine which health care providers can provide safe, credible nutrition education and counseling?
- What are the tradeoffs in terms of time commitment for the nutritionists who participate on the various agency teams?
- How do teams handle competing needs and the various disciplines' limited resources?
- When does the nutritionist consider nutrition to be the priority for the team agenda and when should the nutritionist propose that other priorities prevail?
- How can nutritionists demonstrate their generic skills as planners, managers, educators, and leaders to be recognized for broader leadership responsibilities in their agency?

NOTES

1. U.S. Department of Health and Human Services, *The Surgeon General's Report on Nutrition and Health* (Washington, DC: U.S. Government Printing Office, 1988), 18, 19.

2. National Research Council, *Diet and Health Implications for Reducing Chronic Disease Risk* (Washington, DC: National Academy Press, 1989), 702-3.

3. Mildred Kaufman, *Preliminary Report: Nutrition Services in State and Local Public Health Agencies* (Chapel Hill, N.C.: University of North Carolina, unpublished), Table 2-1.

4. U.S. Department of Health and Human Services, *Promoting Health/Preventing Disease, Year 2000 Objectives for the Nation* (Draft) (Washington, DC: Public Health Service, 1989), 1-18–1-20.

5. Joanna Gorman, "Some Characteristics of Consultation," in *Consultation in Social Work*, ed. Lydia Rapoport (New York: National Assocation of Social Workers, 1963), 28.

6. Mildred Kaufman, Jonathan Kotch, William Herbert, Barbara Rumer, Carolyn Sharbaugh, and Cynthia France, *Maternal Nutrition: Contemporary Approaches to Interdisciplinary Care* (White Plains, NY: March of Dimes Birth Defects Foundation, 1988).

7. R. Beckhard, "Optimizing Team Building Efforts," *Journal of Contemporary Business* 1, no. 3 (1972): 22-32.

8. Marvin Weisbord, *Productive Workplaces: Organizing and Managing for Dignity, Meaning and Community* (San Francisco: Jossey-Bass Inc., Pubs., 1987), 299.

9. Jane Moosbruker, "Developing a Productivity Team: Making Groups at Work Work," in *Team Building: Blueprints for Productivity and Satisfaction*, ed. W. Brendon Reddy and Kaleel Jamison (Alexandria, VA, and San Diego, CA: NTL Institute for Applied Behavioral Science and University Associates, Inc., 1988), 91-92.

10. W. Warner Burke, "Team Building," in *Team Building: Blueprints for Productivity and Satisfaction*, 11.

11. Judith D. Palmer, "For the Manager Who Must Build a Team," in *Team Building: Blueprints for Productivity and Satisfaction*, 139.

12. Burke, "Team Building."

BIBLIOGRAPHY

Alexander, M. "The Team Effectiveness Critique." In *The 1985 Annual: Developing Human Resources*, edited by Leonard D. Goodstein and J. William Pfeiffer, 101-105. San Diego: University Associates Publishers, Inc., 1985.

Beckhard, R. "Optimizing Team Building Efforts." *Journal of Contemporary Business* 1, no. 3 (1972): 22-32.

Burke, W. Warner, "Team Building." In *Team Building: Blueprints for Productivity and Satisfaction*, edited by W. Brendon Reddy and Kaleel Jamison. Alexandria, VA and San Diego, CA: NTL Institute for Applied Behavioral Science and University Associates, Inc., 1988.

Dyer, William G. *Team Building: Issues and Alternatives.* 2d ed. Reading, PA: Addison-Wesley Publishing Co., Inc., 1987.

Moore, C.H. and Kovack, K.M. "Task Force: A Management Technique That Produces Quality Decisions and Employee Commitment." *Journal of the American Dietetic Association* 88 (1988): 1, 52.

chapter 22

Networking for Nutrition

Mildred Kaufman

READER OBJECTIVES

- Define networking.
- Name community nutrition issues that might be addressed by networking.
- List the steps to utilizing a network.
- Discuss a community coordinating council and how it would be useful to the nutritionist.
- List some allies that might be mobilized around key food and nutrition issues.
- State some tips for successful networking.

DEFINING NETWORKING

Networking is defined as an interconnected or interrelated chain, group, or system. John Naisbitt, who popularized this age-old process, says that "simply stated networks are people talking to each other, sharing ideas, information and resources."[1] He points out that "networking is a verb, not a noun,"[2] and that

> the network is the communication that creates the linkage between people and clusters of people.... Networks exist to foster self-help, to exchange information, to change society, to improve productivity and work life and share resources. They are structured to transmit information in a way that is quicker, more high touch, and more energy efficient than any other process. . . . Networks cut

437

diagonally across institutions that house information and put people in direct contact with the resource they seek.[3]

Naisbitt lists networking as one of his ten new directions for the future.[4]

NETWORKING TO PROMOTE AND PROTECT THE PUBLIC'S HEALTH

The American Public Health Association's *Model Standards: A Guide for Community Preventive Health Services* charges state and local governments with the responsibility for ensuring that standards for health services (including nutrition services) are met. It suggests that implementation "involves agencies in addition to the public health agency at any particular level."[5] It further states that

prevention is a shared responsibility of the public and private sectors. Thus, there is need for public and private cooperation and partnership. . . . In addition to the governmental public health agencies, the support for and delivery of community preventive health services will typically involve private providers and professional societies; the broadcast and print media; voluntary organizations, religious, civic, and social groups; and human service systems (e.g., schools, public assistance and day care). . . . Business, industry, and organized labor are also important prevention resources at the community level.[6]

The U.S. Department of Health and Human Services' *Promoting Health/ Preventing Disease, Public Health Service Implementation Plans for Attaining the Objectives for the Nation* lists a large number of federal and nonfederal agencies and organizations that must cooperate to achieve the objectives.[7] The report suggests

achievement of the objectives will require the development of activities which supplement and complement those of the Federal government. . . . State, local and private organizations will supplement this effort through activities that are compatible with their organization's mandate and available resources.[8]

These publications recommend networking to achieve national health promotion objectives.

CASTING A LONGER SHADOW

When nutritionists serve only those who are referred for one-on-one diet counseling, they probably make an impact on a few individuals and their families. Nutritionists employed in any one agency cannot address all the food-, diet-, and nutrition-related health issues in their communities. They must reach out to influence much larger numbers in the population. Networking involves individuals connecting and exchanging with others to solve community problems and achieve common goals. Those who work with and through others can create community awareness, educate the public, change the food system, and advocate for unserved or underserved vulnerable populations. By capturing the attention of the community, nutritionists can impact community values and norms. This process of exchanging and sharing information and services for mutual benefit involves initiating, cultivating, and maintaining multiple interactions.

The benefits of this networking are that it

- makes maximum use of limited resources when people pool their knowledge, skills, and insights
- reduces duplication of effort and unintentional intrusion on "turf"
- expands understanding of the various viewpoints on an issue
- overcomes political and bureaucratic barriers
- generates fresh, innovative approaches and interventions
- builds synergistic relationships
- speaks out with the unified, strong, powerful voice of many

Types of Networks

There are informal and formal ways to identify those key individuals, families, committees, agencies, and organizations within the community who have or should have a stake in food, nutrition, and health whether it be for personal, family, or public benefit. A number of different types of networks can be mobilized to improve access to nutritious food and promote optimal nutrition and health in the local community, state, region, and across the nation.

Every community has a multitude of natural, informal clusters of families (kin), friends, neighbors, social cliques, co-workers, or schoolmates. More readily identified are structured alliances, coalitions, clubs, societies, associations, fraternities or sororities, where people group together around their shared religion, ethnic identity, political affiliation, social status, educational attainment, interests, profession, philanthropy, or community cause. There are an increasing number of support groups being organized by individuals and families who share a mutual need or problem such as single parenthood, a disease diagnosis, or children with handicapping conditions.

In completing the community assessment both the informal and structured networks and their leaders should be sought out. Those with apparent interests in such issues as hunger, poverty, food safety, health and food fraud, fitness, health care costs, out-of-home child care, infant mortality, teenage pregnancy, and needs of the elderly can be investigated in depth.

Informal, appointed, or elected leaders should be interviewed as key informants to determine their perception of community needs. From them it is possible to learn their notion of community values, life styles, practices, as well as their frustrations in obtaining and using food, nutrition, and health services. Knowing their opinions on factors that influence local people's access to food and health care, available food choices, preferred eating patterns, and health practices is of particular value.

To get an insight into the spontaneous community networks, nutritionists can tap into informal networks of high-risk groups such as homeless families, parents of young children, new immigrants, persons with hypertension or diabetes, or senior citizens. Tapping into the natural networks makes it possible to learn by listening and observing characteristic life styles, food patterns, and social norms. It is useful to determine which factors constrain and which facilitate health-promoting diets. Opinion makers and leaders can recommend goals, objectives, and implementation plans to resolve problems and build community commitment toward necessary changes in eating behavior. Empowering the leaders in these communities to participate in the design of nutrition services builds their self-reliance and self-responsibility in the community and will have the most enduring effects.

Participating in Community Organizations

Joining and volunteering time to work with organized citizen, service, or health professional alliances, coalitions, or associations that are concerned with the human survival issues in the community will open new avenues for nutritionists to educate the public, develop policy, and advocate for change. Organized service groups welcome those who share their cause. These groups may provide valuable statistical and descriptive data for the community assessment. Professional nutrition expertise and data from the community assessment can help document the positions service groups may be taking. Also, professional nutrition expertise may add credibility to the coalition's stand.

Coalitions are most effective in confronting the "gutsy" community-wide food and nutrition issues. There is grassroots power when a number of informed and influential organizations join forces to

- ensure emergency food assistance for the hungry
- advocate for legislation for a safer food supply
- combat health and food fraud
- monitor nutrition status of the population and report findings to legislators, health professionals, and the public
- build social support for changing eating behavior toward meeting the national health promotion/disease prevention objectives
- ensure that credible nutrition counseling and education services are available and accessible as part of all health care and health promotion programs
- establish standards for food quality, nutritional care, and professional education and practice
- generate public and private funding for health and nutrition education and applied and basic nutrition research

IMPROVING THE NUTRITION OF THE PUBLIC

Utilizing the community assessment process described in Chapters 3 and 4, nutritionists can develop a blueprint for working with existing and newly developed networks. It can be used to describe and focus attention on the food and nutrition issues that most concern the whole community. Figure 22-1 illustrates the complex web of organizations within the community's health, social, educational, and business sector that might deal with food and nutrition issues. The combined resources of all of these systems can be brought to bear on the identified problems.

Specific planning steps for working with new and existing networks to improve community nutrition problems are:

1. Analyze the objective data and perceived needs identified in the community assessment:
   - rank important community food and nutrition issues in priority order
   - identify gaps

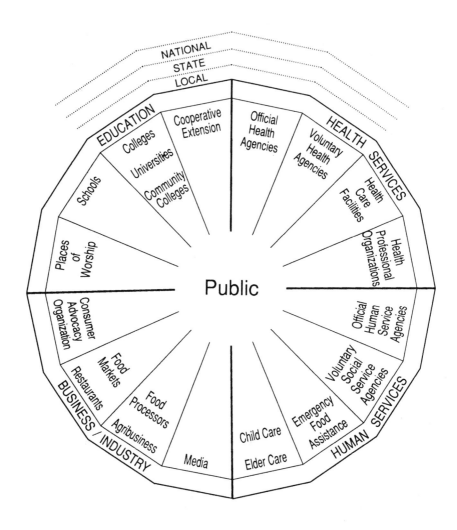

Figure 22-1 Building Community Networks To Address Nutrition Needs of the Population

2. Inventory the community opinion leaders as well as the agencies, organizations, programs, businesses, consumer groups, and elected and appointed officials who might have a stake in each issue:
   • need or demand for services
   • concern and potential for advocacy
   • legal or assumed responsibility
   • economic interest

- ability to get things done in their neighborhood, group, or community
3. Use every appropriate personal, family, professional, and organizational connection to involve the various powerful, indigenous, and concerned groups in the community and their selected, elected, or appointed leaders.
4. Determine the level of interest and concern about the various issues and the degree to which each group is willing to commit time, energy, and resources.
5. Investigate and discuss past community efforts that focused on the issue:
   - determine the lead actors and what they have done
   - assess the successful or unsuccessful elements
   - analyze factors that contributed to success or failure
6. Join with any existing organizations or groups that have knowledge, experience, and power to focus community action on one or more of the selected issues.
7. Work on a broad-based plan using the planning principles discussed in Chapter 14.

Community Coordinating Councils

In many communities health and social services are formally structured through a health and welfare council, an interagency community coordinating council, or a coordinating office of the state or local official human service agency. A coordinating council often sponsors an information and referral system; the council also brings together representatives of the official (tax-supported) and nonprofit voluntary agencies providing community-based health and mental health services, family counseling services, aging services, children's services, food and financial assistance, housing assistance, vocational rehabilitation, adult education, and other community support systems. It usually includes religious or interfaith groups, educational institutions, service leagues, and the area's united giving organization. All individuals and families in the community may seek services through a community coordinating unit or health and welfare council. However, the council usually brings together resources that particularly help those who are dependent because of age, illness, social isolation, substance abuse, or inadequate income or education. Such a council aims to ensure that services are available, coordinated, and publicized. It helps people find the services they need and tries to reduce the eligibility barriers and "red tape."

When this council or coordinating unit is funded by the community and employs staff, it can structure and coordinate health and human services to meet community needs. Nutritionists should be active participants in council activities. A food and nutrition committee sponsored by the community council can work on some of the issues, gaps, and deficiencies in nutrition services identified in the community assessment. Members on the nutrition committee should contribute a variety of interests and talents to give the committee power, visibility, and "clout" in the community. The committee should be made up not only of nutrition, health and human service professionals, but respected and influential community and consumer leaders, and representatives of religious groups, neighborhood ethnic groups, and the media.

Some communities have an informal or voluntary structure for coordinating community services. Nutritionists should investigate any groups of agency representatives, activated citizens, service clubs, interfaith or religious councils, or coalitions that meet periodically to talk about their concerns and plan to solve mutually agreed upon problems. They will work together on food and nutrition issues that capture their interest. Many communities started food pantries, soup kitchens, or home-delivered meal programs for the homebound through voluntary coalitions of professionals with religious groups or interfaith councils.

Publicizing Nutrition Services

Many community councils publish human service directories that publicize detailed information on the variety of community health and social services. The nutrition committee may be responsible for keeping information on the nutrition services in the directory up-to-date. A helpful directory lists and describes credible food assistance and nutrition services, including the name, address, telephone number, contact person, geographic coverage, eligibility criteria, fees, and staff credentials. The printed directory should be widely distributed at all the locations where people who need services might find it: health and human service agencies, health centers, hospitals, libraries, day care centers, senior centers, schools, community colleges, universities, churches, food markets, restaurants, soup kitchens, and bus stations. Also, it may be distributed by the local newspaper and radio and television stations. Information from the printed directory should be entered into the computer data base of the information and referral services, health and social services agencies, schools, hospital discharge planners, public health coordinators, and public libraries.

Inviting community leaders and consumers to an open house introduces them to nutrition services and offers them an opportunity to suggest services that they would like to have in the community. Inservice education or consultation with the staff of the information and referral agency can orient them to services, as can inviting them to visit and observe nutritionists in action.

The "nutrition hotline" discussed in Chapter 18 can be headquartered in a multiservice agency. Whereas the "hotline" answers questions about normal nutrition, food safety, and food preparation, it also provides information about available food assistance nutrition education and diet counseling services in the community.

Issues and Allies

Allies may be those with similar knowledge and skills, such as other nutritionists and dietitians who work in a variety of settings or nutrition educators in schools, colleges, and universities. Allies may be other health professionals, including physicians, dentists, nurses, pharmacists, social workers, and therapists. Those who have knowledge and skills that are different and complementary such as experts in education, media, marketing, public relations, community organization, fund raising, or public policy and legislation can also be allies. They may be influential community leaders such as clergy and congregational leaders; school superintendents, principals, and teachers; leaders in civic service and social clubs; and elected officials. They may be parents, consumers, or clients who have first-hand knowledge and experience with the issue. They are people who share concerns, dedication, and a commitment to constructive action for one or more causes.

Nutritionists have professional knowledge about food and nutrition needs in the community. Key allies have a long-standing interest from different perspectives, usually humanitarian, family, or personal. They bring dedication, experience, and enthusiasm. They may need to understand the scientific base of nutrition and to distinguish fact from fad, but survival and quality of life issues are what compel coalitions and public attention. Some examples of major nutrition issues and potential allies are shown in Table 22-1.

CREATING A STATE NETWORK

New York State's Five-Year Food and Nutrition Plan

Recognizing that despite the existence of many state and federal initiatives to improve people's access to an adequate diet and promote public

Table 22-1 Compelling Food and Nutrition Issues and Potential Allies

Issues	Allies (Examples)
Homelessness and hunger	Human service agencies Social/family agencies Dietetic association Health agencies Housing authorities Churches/interfaith councils Ministerial associations Bread for the World Food banks Soup kitchens/food pantries Junior Service League Civic and service clubs Chamber of Commerce Local government officials College and university students
Infant mortality, birth defects, and low birth weight infants, teen pregnancy	State and local health departments (WIC programs) Maternal and child health professionals (i.e., neonatal nurses, nurse midwives, obstetricians, neonatologists, pediatricians) School of public health, medical school Medical auxiliary Churches Schools, PTAs, teachers, principals Teen pregnancy programs March of Dimes/Birth Defects Foundation Planned Parenthood Healthy Mothers/Healthy Babies Coalition National Organization of Women Women's health centers Cooperative extension Women's clubs
Access to health care for the elderly and chronically ill	State and local health agencies Home Health Agency Meals on Wheels Area Agency on Aging Council on Aging Community action groups A.A.R.P. Hospital Association Health insurance carriers Long-term care facility administrators Hospice Social Security office

Table 22-1 continued

Issues	Allies (Examples)
Safety and quality of the food supply	State and local health agencies Chamber of Commerce Grocery store chains Cooperative extension Merchants Association Environmental health specialists Associations of public officials Restaurateurs and restaurant association Farmers Food processors
Food fads and fraudulent dietary claims, misleading advertising	Better Business Bureaus Legal Aid Community action groups A.A.R.P. Senior citizen groups
Heart disease, hypertension, stroke, cancer, and other leading causes of death attributed to life style factors	Health professionals and organizations Physicians Health agencies, health centers, hospitals Schools of public health Schools of medicine Industry wellness programs Cooperative extension HMOs Medical society, medical auxiliary, hospital association Dietetic association American Cancer Society American Heart Association American Diabetes Association Churches "Ys," fitness groups, diet and fitness centers, spas A.A.R.P. Private health insurance companies (Blue Cross/Blue Shield) Professional groups Schools

understanding of what constitutes good nutrition, a substantial number of New York State's citizens were neither adequately fed nor nourished, the governor established the New York State Council on Food and Nutrition Policy.[9] This council consists of the heads of seven state agencies involved in food and nutrition programs:

1. Department of Health
2. Office of Aging
3. Education Department
4. Department of Agriculture and Markets
5. Office of General Services
6. Department of Social Services
7. Council on Children and Families

The council has a 22-member advisory committee representing agriculture, nutrition, food production, and consumer interests and including the clergy, educators, health planners advocates, administrators, a local health official, a farmer, private citizens, and a legislator. The council was directed to develop a five-year plan for the period 1988 to 1992.

The plan the council developed recommends goals, measurable objectives, and action plans to achieve nutritional adequacy for New York State residents. Recommendations call for a task force of state directors of food and nutrition programs and a legislative interagency task force. Coordination and advocacy are essential roles of this network. The council specifies that implementing its recommendations requires networking by state agency programs with private and voluntary groups, agencies, and academic institutions. Areas of focus of this plan include

- food and nutrition programs/access to food
- health and nutrition
- public awareness
- planning for and monitoring state needs
- food production
- food processing, markets, and distribution

Staff work for this ambitious and statewide food and nutrition network was led by the chief nutritionist in the state department of health.[10]

PROFESSIONAL NETWORKING

The American Dietetic Association

Professional organizations provide a support system for nutrition and public health workers. The American Dietetic Association (ADA), with its

57,000 members nationwide, has established educational standards for the practice of nutrition and dietetics. Through its annual meeting, journal, publications, educational materials, and diverse workshops, it provides for extensive continuing education. It also conducts an active legislative program maintaining a Washington office and staff. The Ambassador program of selected trained media representatives provides a positive image on the national media. As the practice of nutrition and dietetics grows into new areas, national, state, and district dietetic association meetings; professional leadership activities; and community service projects provide opportunities for nutritionists to network with peers who work in health care facilities, community agencies, schools, colleges and universities, business and industry, the media, and private practice. The peer professional network is extended through the several practice groups within the national, state, and district associations. Within the ADA structure there is a Division of Community Dietetics and within it a Public Health Nutrition Practice Group which provides a designated "home" for nutrition workers interested in public health. Related organizational entities are the Commission on Dietetic Registration, the Council on Education, and The American Dietetic Association Foundation's National Center for Nutrition and Dietetics. This center is developing a resource center for the public as well as professionals.

The American Public Health Association

The American Public Health Association (APHA) provides a forum for workers who share interests in the broad practice of public health. It is made up of sections representing areas of professional expertise and caucuses that bring together members that share an active cause. APHA carries out an active legislative program as well as continuing education through its journal, publications, and annual meeting. APHA has affiliate state organizations that conduct annual meetings and sponsor legislative forums. At national and state levels, APHA has a food and nutrition section where nutritionists from agencies, educational institutions, and industry cluster around interests in issues such as public health nutrition programming, nutrition monitoring, food safety, and nutrition education. Working actively in APHA, however, offers nutritionists the opportunity to interact and cultivate leadership not just with nutrition professionals, but with the wider public health community of physicians, nurses, health educators, social workers, environmentalists, biostatisticians, epidemiologists, and others.

The Society for Nutrition Education

The Society for Nutrition Education (SNE) brings together a different mix of members with interests in nutrition education for both professionals and the public. This is a national organization that offers its members a journal, an annual meeting for discussion of provocative issues in nutrition education, excellent educational materials, and a legislative program. SNE is active mainly at the national level and includes a Division of Public Health. This organization provides a peer network of nutrition educators and those interested in nutrition education.

Other Professional Organizations

Related professional organizations include medical, dental, and nursing associations. The nutritionist can identify individuals within these organizations who may be willing to advocate for nutrition. Some organizations have established nutrition committees that welcome the opportunity to work with nutritionists as individuals or in collaborating with the professional nutrition or public health organizations.

Contact with the various professional groups can be developed by including them on mailing lists for newsletters about various current topics. Offering a speakers bureau for professional meetings of other disciplines or contributing articles to their journals or newsletters are ways to initiate contacts. Inviting related organizations to co-sponsor sessions at national, state, or local meetings around a topic of mutual interest can place nutrition issues on their agenda. Presently, coalitions of health professional organizations are working together on national legislation for nutrition monitoring, hunger relief, child nutrition, food programs, and out-of-home child care.

NETWORKING TIPS

Networking is used to extend an idea or product, such as food choices, service delivery, or legislation, into a larger arena. At the same time it can help a nutritionist achieve professional recognition and opportunities to serve in leadership roles in the community, state, or nation. Developing a large and solid network requires deliberate cultivation of casual contacts into helpful friends. Some tips that enhance the process are as follows:

- List community, professional, and personal goals and specify the contacts required to achieve them.

- Communicate interests and needs to a large number of professional, social, personal, and family contacts.
- Attend a wide variety of political, community, and professional meetings, conferences, and social events attended by influential leaders. Mix in the group and engage others in friendly but purposeful conversation; always behave as a host rather than as a guest. Introduce yourself clearly to others and get to know them. Listen for common links to spark a friendship such as mutual friends, the same hometown or attending the same college, similar hobbies, or interests.
- Exchange business cards with people who are key contacts. File these cards noting when and why these individuals should be contacted.
- Follow-up key contacts with a diplomatic note or phone call. To maintain a continuing dialogue, always provide any information that is promised or references of interest.
- Volunteer to work on community projects and always do a good job.
- Be sincere in interpersonal interactions, always offering to help others as well as receive help.

Networking is an active technique that involves skill and knowledge of one's own professional field, interpersonal skills, political astuteness, and integrity. If practiced and nurtured, it will yield far-reaching results to benefit the community and, as a by-product, the professional's career. Networking is a commitment to trading information and building trust and reciprocity; it is a two-way process of sharing! It is built on the premise that the cause is vital and the need is great; those in the network feel empowered, competent, and self-confident. Whereas professional credibility is based on "what you know," networking demonstrates the importance of "who you know."

ISSUES TO DEBATE

- How are the informal networks that will be most useful and effective selected?
- How is networking that is for community benefit distinguished from that which is for power and personal advancement?
- Are the values of networking worth the personal investment of time and energy?
- How should a person handle a networking relationship that proves to be manipulative or unproductive?

NOTES

1. John Naisbitt, *Megatrends: Ten New Directions Transforming Our Lives* (New York: Warner Books, 1982), 192.

2. Ibid., 192.

3. Ibid.

4. Ibid., 192–193.

5. American Public Health Association, et al., *Model Standards: A Guide for Community Preventive Health Services*, 2d ed. (Washington, DC: American Public Health Association, 1985), 4.

6. Ibid.

7. U.S. Department of Health and Human Services, Office of Disease Prevention and Health Promotion, "Promoting Health/Preventing Disease, Public Health Service Implementation Plans for Attaining the Objectives for the Nation," *Public Health Reports*, Supplement, Sept.-Oct. 1983, 134.

8. Ibid.

9. New York State Council on Food and Nutrition Policy, *5-Year Food and Nutrition Plan, 1988-1992* (Albany, NY: New York State Department of Health, 1988), 71.

10. Ibid.

BIBLIOGRAPHY

Eng, Eugenia, John Hatch, and Anne Callen. "Institutionalizing Social Support through the Church and into the Community." *Health Education Quarterly* 12, no. 1 (Spring 1982):81–92.

Guide for Developing Nutrition Services in Community Health Programs. Washington, DC: Department of Health and Human Services, 1978: 9, 11, 17.

Institute of Medicine. *The Future of Public Health.* Washington, DC: National Academy Press, 1988.

Lofquist, William A. *Discovering the Meaning of Prevention, A Practical Approach to Positive Change.* Tucson, AZ: AYD Publications (Associates for Youth Development), 1983.

Michaelson, Gerald. "It's a Small World If You've Got a Big Network." Sales and Marketing Management 140 (August 1988):10,74.

Miyasaka, Tadas, and Chieko Kawata. "The Neighborhood Organization: An Important Factor in Organizing for Community Health Education." *International Journal of Health Education* 22, no. 2 (1979):73–91.

Puetz, Belinda E. *Networking for Nurses.* Rockville, MD: Aspen Publishers, Inc., 1983. 1–79.

Welch, Mary Scott. *Networking.* New York: Harcourt Brace Jovanovich, 1980.

Wellman, Barry, and Barry Leighton. "Networks, Neighborhoods, and Communities. Approaches to Study of the Community Question." *Urban Affairs Quarterly* 14, no. 3 (March 1979):363–390.

part VII

Surviving in a
Competitive World

chapter 23

Earning Administrative Support

Elaine B. Culberson

READER OBJECTIVES

- Describe the ways the nutritionist can learn about the "big picture" of the agency.
- Compare and contrast alternative communication channels appropriate for interacting with the administrator.
- List some advice for developing assertiveness.
- Specify strategies for working with the agency board.
- Discuss ways to gain support for a proposal to expand nutrition programs and services.

WHERE IS THE ADMINISTRATOR COMING FROM?

The nutritionist employed by an organization or agency should keep in mind that the position was envisioned, created, and justified by an administrator to meet a documented or perceived need. The position's existence indicates some degree of administrative support. Administrators may establish positions for public health nutrition personnel because of

- commitment to the expanding body of knowledge linking diet to health promotion and disease prevention and applications to community health
- mandates of federal or state agencies that require nutrition personnel to be appointed to obtain categorical program funding
- tradition of a long-established, recognized nutrition program in the agency

• requests from program directors or staff who desire nutrition expertise in the agency to enhance their work

The kind and amount of administrative support may vary depending on
the administrator's level of interest in nutrition, past experiences with
nutrition personnel and the rationale for their employment. The administrator who understands the cost benefits of nutrition in promoting health
through the various agency and community programs will provide much
more enthusiastic support than the administrator who employs nutrition
personnel to conform to funding requirements. The administrator who has
worked with an energetic, creative nutritionist with a broad public health
perspective will be more supportive than the one who has observed the
nutritionist with "tunnel vision" functioning as a technical expert.

LOOKING AT THE "BIG PICTURE"

To earn administrative support it is essential that the nutritionist understand and respect the "big picture"—the broad perspective of public health
and the agency's mission, goals, constraints, problems, and challenges.
Viewing the "big picture" comes from studying the public health sciences,
participating in the public health organizations, and interacting with the
public health workers who understand the agency's internal and external
environments.

The Structure of the Agency

Understanding the agency's internal structure begins by studying its most
recent table of organization. It is useful to draw in the informal connections
between the organized units and individuals in the organization. It is important to note where nutritionists are placed in the structure and to whom
they report in relation to other disciplines and services.

It is informative to carefully study copies of the agency's official documents, including its goal or mission statement, strategic and operational
plans, and annual reports. The more evidence there is that the written
statements of the agency are used, the more important these official statements are to the agency director and policy board. An indicator of the
importance and acceptance of these official documents is their availability
and use by the various organizational levels. If the search for such documents ends with the director's secretary retrieving a plan of work from a
dead file or commenting that the plan is only prepared because the "feds"

or state funding agencies require it, the document is not a vital, integral part of the agency's life.

Even if the official agency documents are readily available and obviously utilized throughout the organization, developing the "big picture" also requires an assessment of the day-to-day operations of the agency. Sources of information to assess the agency's priorities and direction include the following:

- *Staff conference agendas.* Review the issues discussed most frequently over the past year and the decisions recorded.
- *Personnel reports.* Identify the units that are adding personnel and those that are losing personnel, and their disciplines.
- *Agency budgets/financial reports.* Compare the current year reports to last year and previous years to observe revenue shifts between federal, state, and local sources and between general revenue and third party reimbursement, fees for services, or external grants.
- *Annual reports.* Observe the report style, format, and organization, as well as those programs highlighted and accomplishments cited with pride and those programs that are given little or no mention.
- *Informal conversations with colleagues.* Discuss their plans, problems, hopes, dreams, morale, and frustrations.
- *Press releases.* Review the releases issued by the director and articles written about agency activities by staff.
- *Policy board meeting agendas and minutes.*

Understanding how the agency develops its policies is essential. This is learned by reading written agency policies and procedures and noting how and when each policy was adopted. Through conversations with peers, it is useful to find out if policies are known, respected, consistently administered, and how often they are changed.

A compilation of all of this information is useful in developing an overview of the agency. This agency composite can be used as a "road map" to structure a strategy for earning administrative support.

SHARING THE AGENCY VISION

Basic to gaining the administrator's support is a shared vision of the agency, the anticipated contributions of nutrition to fulfilling the agency's mission, and its leadership role in the community. Developing a shared vision requires careful study of the agency's operational plans and review of the lead nutritionist's job description to determine its breadth and involvement in agency policy and decision making. Does this nutritionist serve as an advisor to the agency administrator and board? Does the nutritionist attend and contribute to senior staff or agency management meetings where policy and budget are discussed?

In studying the responsibilities, duties, and time allocations on all of the nutritionists' job descriptions, it is useful to look also at whether supervision is general or close. At the time of employment the scope of the job descriptions of all nutritionists should be discussed with the administrator, noting the degree of flexibility which might be anticipated and the opportunities for expanding nutrition services. Responses to questions should reveal the administrator's interest and long-term expectations for the nutrition services and the potential for adding nutrition personnel.

Communicating with the Administrator

Some administrators welcome informal chats and frequent communication. Others encourage periodic structured appointments. Others prefer written memos or electronic mail messages, with face-to-face conferences reserved for crises or urgent issues. The administrator's approach to handling key issues, concerns, and conflict should be discussed.

Periodic conferences of the lead public health nutritionist with the administrator maintain dialogue and keep the administrator informed of current activities and accomplishments. Such conferences provide the opportunity to share successes and progress, convey information, and explore future program possibilities. Support is more readily obtained from an administrator with whom the groundwork is laid and who has input into the developmental stages of programs or projects. The administrator may know of related activities and plans of others in the agency or community and may promote collaboration. Administrators enjoy positive interactions and usually encourage innovative plans that will contribute to the agency's public image.

Regularly scheduled dialogues that are positive in tone smooth the relationship for the occasions when it may be necessary to seek administrative advice on a crisis. The continuing dialogue that keeps the administrator informed forestalls surprises which might put the administrator "on the spot" and cause embarrassment. Most administrators deplore surprises. When seeking advice or guidance on a crisis or conflict, the well-prepared manager will present several thoughtful alternative solutions. Most administrators prefer to guide the decision making rather than to be the decision maker.

Maintaining continuing, positive, mutually satisfying communication with the administrator earns support and respect. No matter how busy the administrator may appear, it should be remembered that the nutritionist's position was established because of administrative interest. This interest must be nurtured.

While maintaining open communication with the administrator, it is also useful to find out who has the "boss's ear." Cultivating the key people in the informal organization channels helps gain access to vital information useful in developing strategies. The administrator's secretary or administrative assistant can be a key ally in finding out about the administrator's calendar and staff meeting agendas. A friend in the "front office" can provide advice as to when to make a timely request for a new program and how to avoid a costly miscalculated strategy.

DEVELOPING ASSERTIVENESS

An effective "change agent" anticipates future directions, assesses the climate for change, gains support, proposes an action plan, and tests and evaluates the plan throughout the process. Input from others is sought to get them invested in the change and more willing to "buy into it." In working for change, the nutritionist should recognize the inherent resistance to it. Moving in slow, deliberate steps, monitoring feedback, negotiating, using suggestions, maintaining open communications, and sharing credit are strategies to overcome resistance. It sometimes means quietly planting and nurturing an idea and letting "the boss" claim credit for it.

Nutritionists must diplomatically request the information and the resources they need to carry out their managerial responsibilities. They may need information on the agency plan and budget. As agencies move to automated data systems, nutritionists should participate in the planning, implementing, and evaluating of management and client information systems.

Nutritionists, like others, are sometimes reluctant to speak out, fearing that they will be considered aggressive or self-serving. Learning to be assertive as a person and as a professional is an essential characteristic of leadership. To be assertive requires self-respect, self-worth, and self-confidence. The nutritionist must feel secure in an up-to-date knowledge base and be convinced that nutrition is a key factor in promoting health and preventing disease and that nutrition services have a significant place in public health programs. Viewpoints must be expressed with statements of conviction such as "I believe," "I am convinced," or "I feel strongly." Making forceful statements means taking risks. Others may not agree and

may need to be won over with documented justifications and persuasive arguments.
Guidelines for becoming more assertive include these:

- Start with a situation that will result in success.
- Be persistent; don't take no for a final answer.
- Control emotions and always be courteous.
- Be forceful; speak with conviction.
- Maintain a sense of humor.

Many nutritionists are afraid to say no to requests for services that are more than they or their staffs can handle well. This may result in "burnout." Saying no diplomatically can be an appropriate approach to demonstrate need for additional funding or staff in order to provide services to new or expanded programs.

WINNING WITH THE POLICY BOARD

In most health agencies the administrator is responsible to a board of health or board of directors. In tax-supported agencies this board is usually appointed by elected officials, and under statutes the membership must include designated numbers and kinds of health professionals, representatives of the public, and consumers. The board usually approves policies, programs, key personnel appointments, budgets, and legislative initiatives. The board members may have special interests that put pressures on the administrator and the agency. These pressures may place constraints on the administrator and on the availability of funds for some types of programs. To work successfully in the agency, it is useful to study backgrounds and interests and to observe the group dynamics of the board members as they interact at their meetings.

Strategies for the lead nutritionist to work with the agency board include the following:

- Attend board meetings routinely, or whenever permissible, whether or not a nutrition issue is on the agenda. Attendance demonstrates the nutritionist's interest in the "big picture" and will be recognized by the board members.
- Observe the interests and group dynamics in the meeting, the educational background of the members, and their values, sophistication, interests, concerns, and biases.

- Engage individual board members in conversation to learn about their views and priorities. When a board member expresses an interest in nutrition or asks for information, the appropriate materials or services should be offered. Prompt, helpful follow-up to these individual interests earns respect for the agency as well as its nutrition personnel.

- As appropriate, request the administrator to arrange a place on the agenda to report and orient board members to services and accomplishments in public health nutrition, using graphics, pictures, and human interest case studies to stimulate interest. Presentations should be brief, factual, lively, and to the point. Questions should be answered clearly, succinctly, and honestly.

- Justify requests for budget and new or expanded programs with graphics or visual aids that appeal to board members' logic and "hearts."

- Respect the judgment of the board members and treat them with the courtesy that goes with their office. If a request is not approved, reframe it and try again at one or more later meetings. Study the resistance, learn ways to overcome it, and be persistent .

In dealing with individual board members, a good "rule of thumb" is to do more listening than talking. Maintaining just the right balance of being personable with board members without being too informal requires preparing for each situation in advance.

MOBILIZING COLLEAGUES

Colleagues and staff in other disciplines and programs are primary allies in creating a successful strategy. Developing mutual trust and respect of agency peers is the foundation of good working relationships. Being honest and dependable in dealing with colleagues is basic. Winners usually have all groups "in their corner."

Usually a proposal for a new program prepared jointly by several program or service units or disciplines has broader impact than a proposal from a single unit. It may be useful to let a colleague take the lead in developing the joint project. Those who insist on always being in the lead risk getting a reputation as an "empire builder."

It is important to observe which projects and proposals gain support and which are not considered, and then try to figure out why. A collection of "whys" specific to the agency is valuable for developing future strategies.

PERSUASION, PERSISTENCE, NEGOTIATION

Defining the Need/Planning a Strategy

It is important to spend some time determining what agency support is needed today, tomorrow, next year, and in five years. Support takes many forms: more visibility and inclusion in agency policy making, invitations to participate on key committees, additional clerical support, additional nutritionist positions, more space, a computer system, more adequate training, and travel budget. Once the needed support is defined, it is time to plan strategy. A successful strategy begins by asking these questions:

1. Why is this request necessary?
2. How does the community or the public benefit? How does the agency benefit? How do other disciplines benefit? How does nutrition staff benefit?
3. What information is available that supports the request?
4. What will the request cost? Will revenues be generated with the proposed plan? If not, what is the funding source? Are funds known to be available?
5. Who has the authority to approve this request?

Answers to each question should be written. By answering the questions a decision can be made about the real need. If there is uncertainty about it, the request should be set aside and given more thought. The needs and benefits must be clear before trying to convince the administrator.

If the need is affirmed, the arguments to be used to present the request should be prepared in writing. Someone, preferably not employed in the agency, should be asked to listen to the presentation of what is needed and why it is important. The listener should be encouraged to question any aspect of the proposal that is not completely clear. Those questions can be used to sharpen the written proposal, the justification, and the oral presentation.

The next step is to consider the background and management style of the administrator who is to approve the plan. In presenting a request to a budget-minded director, using a cost-benefit or cost-effectiveness analysis is a wise approach. For the director concerned with human values or public image, the presenter should stress how the plan would benefit people in the community.

The proposal and supporting documentation should be prepared in writing. It is important to decide whether to precede a discussion by sending the written request first or to discuss it first and follow up with the written proposal. The answer depends in part on what method has been successful in the past. The analysis of the agency's mode of operation should provide guidance when experience is limited. The oral presentation should be rehearsed with a listener who is primed to "play the devil's advocate" and challenge every aspect of the plan. The extra time required to rehearse, revise, and rehearse again is critical to a well-developed presentation.

The nutritionist should always be prepared to negotiate. This means deciding what parts of the proposal are critical and what can be conceded. It is important to negotiate slowly—not to give up too much too soon.

Despite the careful preparation, research, analysis, strategy development, persuasion, and negotiating, the request may be rejected. It is important to determine why by asking thoughtful, unemotional questions, expressing genuine interest in understanding why the answer is no. It is important to determine whether the negative response is due to a real budget deficit, lack of agency priority, poor timing, opposition in the organization, the quality of the presentation, or other reasons.

Persistence

If the initial "game plan" or strategy failed, it is time to develop "Plan B," an alternative strategy. If the proposal represents a valid need, the development of alternative strategies should continue until the need has been fulfilled. Persistence or the "drip technique" pays off. For example, if a nutrition department needs to develop its computer capacity, a strategy is developed to gain agency approval. First, the need is documented via a utilization study. Second, the cost effectiveness of investing in personal computers is calculated. Third, the proposal is written and presented to the agency director. The needs and benefits are recognized but no funds are committed to the project. Twice a year for the next several years the computers are requested and finally the necessary support is won. After a year of utilization the benefits become very apparent. The persistence accomplished two things: first, the need was met, and second, the success of this proposal will lend credibility to the next one.

EMPOWERMENT

The enthusiastic support of the administrator and the board is vital in maintaining and expanding public health nutrition services. The desirable stance for the nutritionist is fair treatment both during periods of expansion and in periods of cutbacks. Some administrators make a sincere effort to be "even handed." Others tend to give the "goodies" to those whose programs they understand the best, to those who curry their favor, to those whose services provide the greatest agency visibility, to those who make the "best case," or to those who demonstrate that they can generate income. Public health nutritionists can learn lessons from those who are usually successful.

To maintain or expand services, nutritionists must demonstrate their managerial skills. Program development means moving toward more comprehensive nutrition services. Since the availability of federal funds for the Special Supplemental Food Program for Women, Infants, and Children (WIC), in 1974, many public health agencies that had previously allocated multiple funding sources to support nutrition personnel transferred nutrition staff to WIC funds during budget crunches. Such budgetary maneuvers have limited nutrition services to low-income, high-risk pregnant or lactating women and infants and children. Current interest is in the more broadly based adult health promotion/disease prevention objectives. It is now timely to educate administrators and policy boards about their obligation to provide nutrition services as part of health programming directed to the general public and across the age and income populations in the community. Services to middle- and upper-income populations can generate income and visibility for the agency. However, these services require some start-up funding. Nutritionists will earn the respect of administrators by proposing funding strategies to initiate new programs, as discussed in Chapter 17.

Expanding program scope without adding nutrition personnel requires testing more population-based and less labor-intensive interventions. When administrators demand "more with less" or "cutting out the fat," nutritionists should study their operations, effect all possible economies, and enhance productivity. The economies that are implemented should be documented to the administrator. When more severe cuts in the budget will sacrifice quality or quantity of services or hours of operation, the administrator should be presented with the options, which might include reducing services, using auxiliary personnel, training volunteers, or developing income generators. Loading more work on already overburdened staff only leads to "burnout," low morale, and costly staff turnover.

Interpreting nutrition service needs to the administrator is a responsibility of the lead public health nutritionist. Power is required to accomplish goals. Official power is attached to the placement of the leadership nutritionist position within an agency. Personal power rests on knowledge, skills, and the ability to develop successful strategies. Nutritionists are empowered by their competencies in health promotion and disease prevention. In the agency the nutritionist must build "position power" through persuasiveness, persistence, personality, and politics.

ISSUES TO DEBATE

- What is the balance between understanding the "big picture" and "fighting for" the role of nutrition? Is there conflict in one's priorities as a public health worker and as a nutritionist?
- How does a nutritionist differentiate between strategies that are ethical and appropriate from those that may be manipulative?
- What is the difference between being aggressive and assertive?
- What are the tradeoffs between advancing interdisciplinary and monodisciplinary projects or grant proposals?

BIBLIOGRAPHY

Puetz, Belinda. *Networking for Nurses* (Rockville, MD: Aspen Publishers, Inc., 1983), 165-200.

chapter *24*

Striving for Excellence

Harriet H. Cloud

READER OBJECTIVES

- Define excellence in public health nutrition practice.
- List some characteristics of excellence.
- Discuss legal obligations in implementing tax-supported nutrition services.
- Identify the components of an agency quality assurance system.
- Compare and contrast dietetic registration with state-legislated dietetic licensure.
- Suggest rationale for public health nutritionists to carry professional liability insurance.
- Discuss ethical issues in public health and nutrition practice.

MOTIVATION FOR EXCELLENCE

Excellence is defined as performance at the ultimate level of quality, caring, and proficiency. While perfection is rare in human endeavors, its pursuit is a worthy aspiration, as long as it does not become a fetish. The nutritionist must pursue excellence as a leader, motivator, and role model for the community, agency, staff, and peers.

Some characteristics of excellence derived from America's best run companies apply to public health agencies and nutrition programs:

- well-defined values
- commitment to quality
- dedication to service
- responsiveness to the consumer, client, and public

- stimulating, nurturing work environment
- pride in organization
- attention to detail
- creativity and innovation
- open lines of communication and sharing of information.[1]

As a standard setter, the nutritionist seeks excellence as a matter of personal satisfaction and professional pride. The pursuit of excellence is a continuing effort with legal as well as ethical obligations to the public, the agency, and the profession.

Personal Pride

Each professional should be dedicated to serve the community and clients with credibility, integrity, compassion, and a genuine concern to promote and protect the health, safety, and welfare of the public. Self-responsibility requires a commitment to planning and providing services that are ingenious and creative. These services must be sensitive to changing client, community, and societal values and needs and be cost-effective. Professionals have been found to be better motivated by self-generated quality control than by external requirements or regulations. Excellence in performance ensures the continuation of nutrition services.

Professionals must be responsible for continuous self-assessment and self-improvement. Each nutritionist should pursue a continuing education program based on a planned, periodic, written self-assessment. The individual's plan for professional knowledge and skill improvement might include a variety of approaches: study of self-instructional materials, reading current journals, or participating in workshops, lectures, journal clubs, or graduate courses. Each individual's self-directed continuing education contributes to the strength of the profession and practice.

Each nutritionist must participate in continuing education programs to keep pace with new knowledge and overcome deficiencies in preservice training. For example, the nutritionist who wishes to develop new programs for children with special health care needs may need advanced course work in child growth and development and behavioral management principles to be knowledgeable and effective.

AGENCY AND LEGAL OBLIGATIONS

Most positions in official public health agencies are established through federal, state, or local legislation that enables nutrition services. The law is further defined through regulations and guidelines from the funding agency which spell out the details about the services to be offered and the training and experience required of those who provide the services. The nutritionist employed with tax dollars must study the enabling legislation and regulations carefully and thoughtfully to ensure that funds are used as described in the law, that services are provided at the appropriate level, and that personnel are utilized as mandated. The nutritionist must be committed to planning, implementing, and evaluating services that conform with legal requirements and agency policy. It is imperative for nutritionists to understand and respect the intent as well as the letter of the law.

Legislation, regulations, and guidance materials from administering agencies define program purposes and expectations. These documents describe program content, plan requirements, appropriate use of funds, allowable budget items, staffing patterns, evaluation methods, and any requirements for periodic written reports and nondiscrimination in employment of staff and service to clients. Within the requirements of the law, there is usually opportunity to develop programs that can meet the mandate and at the same time be creative, cost-effective, and tailored to the community. When creative program implementation is frustrated by limitations in law and regulations, consultation should be sought from staff of the administering agency. If the law or regulations continue to be obstacles to implementing an effective program, it is appropriate to bring this to the attention of the local, state, or federal legislators who passed the legislation and suggest changes using the legislative process discussed in Chapter 7.

Federal Legislation

The federal legislation that most often enables and funds public health nutrition services in state and local health agencies includes

- Social Security Act (Department of Health and Human Services)
  —Title V Maternal and Child Health Block Grant
  —Title XVIII Medicare
  —Title XIX Medicaid
  —Title XX Social Services
- Public Health Service Act (Department of Health and Human Services)
  —Title X Family Planning
  —Preventive Health Services Block Grant

—Alcohol and Drug Abuse Block Grant
—Community Health Services
—Migrant Health Services
—Indian Health Services
—Public Health Training
• Older Americans Act (Department of Health and Human Services)
—Title III Meal Programs for the Elderly
• Child Nutrition Act (Department of Agriculture)
—Special Supplemental Food Program for Women, Infants, and Children (WIC)
—Child Day Care Feeding
—National School Lunch Act (breakfast, lunch, summer feeding)
—Nutrition Education and Training (NET)
• Food Stamp Act (Department of Agriculture)
• Education for the Handicapped (Department of Education)
—P.L. 94-142
—P.L. 99-457

State Legislation

State legislation as documented in the public health statutes or codes uses the general language, "... to promote and protect the health of the public." Within this language public health nutrition services can be implied and thereby funded. Several state legislatures have included legislative language in their public health code that specifically names nutrition services. Some states have enacted specific legislation to provide additional state funding to expand WIC services for perinatal care, for health promotion, for congregate meals for the elderly or to conduct nutrition monitoring and surveillance. State and local codes vary by jurisdiction, but often include specific nutrition and food service requirements for licensure of child day care, residential facilities for children, nursing homes, adult congregate living facilities, halfway houses for substance abusers, camps, and correctional facilities. Such requirements usually mandate that nutritionists or dietitians participate in writing the regulations and guidance materials, serve on the agency inspection teams, and provide or arrange continuing education or technical assistance to group care facility staff. Food service sanitation codes are of particular importance in group care facilities, so nutritionists working with these facilities must maintain close contact with environmental health staff who inspect and certify these programs, as discussed in Chapters 12 and 13.

Legislation Change and Review

Laws, regulations, and guidance materials are usually under periodic review and amendment in the legislatures and the federal, state, and local agencies responsible for their enforcement. The nutritionist is responsible for monitoring the laws and regulations that affect public health and nutrition practice. It is important to determine how the agency reviews the *Federal Register* as well as announcements of changes in state and local regulations. Procedures vary among agencies and may require some research to locate the information. Maintaining dialogue with the administrator's office and with consultants from the appropriate state and federal agencies is one way to "stay on top" of constantly changing legislation and regulations. See Appendixes D and G for listings of public health nutrition directors and federal resources and consultants. Reading legislative pages in the public health and dietetic newsletters and journals and the publications listed in Appendix N of this book can help.

QUALITY ASSURANCE

Quality assurance is defined as the guarantee or warranty of the degree of excellence and cost effectiveness of health care provided by health practitioners within the ambulatory or institutional setting. It involves the continuous assessment and improvement of health care outcomes.[2] A quality assurance program should be an integral part of program planning and evaluation and deserves both agency and individual attention. Terms utilized in the quality assurance process which must be understood are *criteria, indicators, outcome criteria, process criteria,* and *patient care audit* (Exhibit 24-1).

The process of quality assessment compares existing structures, processes, and outcomes of care with predetermined standards in order to determine any discrepancies that may exist. Quality assurance results when programs are developed and implemented to resolve the problems that led to the discrepancy.[3] The three basic elements of quality assurance are (1) standards (criteria) and measures (performance levels), (2) monitoring and evaluation, and (3) control and remedial action.

Standards for nutritional care in public health settings should be developed for each of the services offered by the agency. In these standards, criteria are developed to use to measure the elements of care. Model

Exhibit 24-1 Terms Used in Quality Assurance

Criteria:	Predetermined elements of health care services used for quality assessment; professionally developed statements of desirable health care processes or outcomes. Flexibility in such criteria allows for variations in methods and practices at different health care sites. Explicit criteria spell out specifics, implicit criteria allow flexibility.
Indicators:	Predetermined elements of health care services that may or may not specify the exact method to be used for verification.
Outcome criteria:	Predetermined elements demonstrating measurable and observable results of change in the health status of the patient or client.
Process criteria:	Predetermined elements of care selected from key activities or procedures in the delivery of patient care used by health professionals in management of a specified health condition.
Patient care audit:	Process of surveillance of the quality of patient care using predetermined criteria by the team of health care professionals as recorded in the medical record.

standards of care with appropriate criteria have been developed by state health agencies and professional organizations. Guidelines for clinical care have been published by several of the practice groups of The American Dietetic Association. These are based on current scientific knowledge and clinical practice. These models and guidelines can be individualized for specific care settings.[4]

The following components must be in place in the agency quality assurance system:

- *Staff Commitment to a Quality Assurance System.* Staff should understand that data collected can demonstrate the benefits of sound nutrition services. Where deficiencies are found, data can be used to justify additional facilities or staff positions. The quality assurance process can generate enthusiasm and creativity among the staff—both strong motivators.
- *Quality Assurance Chapter in the Nutritionists' Policy and Procedure Manual.* The policy statements should state that monitoring will occur, who is responsible for monitoring, and commitment to remedial action. The procedure section includes the monitoring plan, the fre-

quency of data collection, and the criteria used for each type of care (e.g., women's health; prenatal care; infant, well-child, or school child health; children's special health care; adult health promotion; geriatric services; group care facility consultation; home health services; community programs).

- *Information Systems to Collect Objective Statistics for the Assessment Process.* Data collection systems should preferably be computer assisted. If a manual system is required, easy-to-use forms must be designed to meet the unique needs of the agency.
- *Feedback or Reporting System to Communicate the Results of Data Collection.* Results should be compiled and disseminated quickly, usually once a month, so that remedial steps can be taken to maintain the quality of care. Since data are collected internally, corrections that can occur within the care unit can be initiated immediately.
- *Written Plan for Remedial Action That Includes Summaries of the Data Collected, Findings, and Remedial Steps.* This plan should be submitted to the authorized quality assurance coordinator in the agency and maintained in the unit's quality assurance file.

Remedial steps could include inservice education, budgeting for staff to attend continuing education courses, or seeking consultation on program planning, staffing, and service delivery. Periodic review and discussion of findings with the administrator maintains agency support and budget needed for additional staff, space, and equipment.

PROFESSIONAL STATURE

Professional organizations striving to maintain excellence and respect for their discipline take responsibility for establishing a code of ethics, setting standards of practice, providing for peer review, and maintaining continuing education opportunities. The basic academic preparation recommended for dietetic registration meets the Standards of Education established by The American Dietetic Association, whose mission is setting standards for nutrition practitioners. Their code of ethics, shown in Exhibit 24-2, includes standards of professional responsibility and principles reflective of health professional credentialing agencies, professional associations, and state dietetic licensure laws.[5] It applies to credentialed dietetic practitioners, including registered dietitians and dietetic technicians. It provides ethical guidelines; assists in protecting the nutritional health, safety, and welfare of the public; and enhances the profession's image.

Exhibit 24-2   Ethics Code of The American Dietetic Association

---

The ethics code of The American Dietetic Association states standards of professional responsibility that include the following principles:

"The dietetic practitioner:

- provides professional services with objectivity and respect for the unique needs and values of individuals
- avoids discrimination against other individuals on basis of race, creed, religion, sex, age, and national origin
- fulfills professional commitments in good faith
- conducts him/herself with honesty, integrity and fairness
- remains free of conflict of interest while fulfilling objectives and maintaining the integrity of the dietetic profession
- maintains confidentiality of information
- practices dietetics based on scientific principles and current information
- assumes responsibility and accountability for personal competence in practice
- recognizes and exercises professional judgment within the limits of his/her qualifications and seeks counseling to make referrals as appropriate
- provides sufficient information to enable clients to make informed decisions
- informs the public and/or colleagues of his/her services by using factual information and does not advertise in a false or misleading manner
- promotes or endorses products in a manner neither false nor misleading
- permits use of his/her name for the purpose of certifying that dietetic services have been rendered only if he/she has provided or supervised the provision of those services
- accurately presents professional qualifications and credentials
- presents substantiated information and interprets controversial information without personal bias, recognizing that legitimate differences of opinion exist
- makes all reasonable effort to avoid bias in any kind of professional evaluation
- voluntarily withdraws from professional practice if engaging in or has engaged in substance abuse which affects his/her practice, has been adjudged by a court to be mentally incompetent or has an emotional or mental disability that affects his/her practice
- complies with all applicable laws and regulations concerning the profession
- accepts the obligation to protect society and the profession by upholding the code of ethics for the profession of dietetics and reporting alleged violations of the code."

Source: Reprinted from *Journal of The American Dietetic Association,* Vol. 88, No. 5, pp. 1592-1593, with permission of The American Dietetic Association, © December 1988.

Along with the code of ethics and the standards of professional responsibility, The American Dietetic Association has an established review process for alleged violations.[6] This process uses an organizational ethics committee, legal counsel, and an administrator of policy administration. The process includes investigation of a complaint, then hearings, followed by a decision for either acquittal of the respondent, censure, suspension, or expulsion. There is an appeals process that the complainant can initiate. The code of ethics and the published standards function as a peer review process with an educational tool and a review mechanism for alleged violations.

Standards of practice for dietitians were published in 1986.[7] These standards outline the expectations that each professional and paraprofessional will perform an annual self-assessment, set personal career goals, and prepare an action plan based on the assessed needs and goals. The standards for the profession of dietetics set the following goals:

1. Establish performance criteria, compare actual performance with expected performance, document results, and take appropriate action.
2. Develop, implement, and evaluate an individual plan for practice based on assessment of consumer needs, current knowledge, and clinical experience.
3. Collaborate with other professionals, personnel, and/or consumers in integrating, interpreting, and communicating nutrition care principles.
4. Engage in lifelong self-development to improve knowledge and skills.
5. Generate, interpret, and use research to enhance dietetic practice.
6. Identify, monitor, analyze, and justify the use of resources.[8]

REGISTRATION AND LICENSURE

The ethics code and standards of responsibility establish the criteria for educational programs and professional practice. The assumption follows that nutrition care provided by the credentialed practitioner protects the consumer from receiving inadequate care, misinformation, and inappropriate counseling. Two credentialing mechanisms to ensure client protection include registration through the Commission on Dietetic Registration and licensure, now legislated in about half of the states.

Registration by the Commission on Dietetic Registration requires educational and experiential preparation for dietetics as established by The American Dietetic Association in published standards of education and standards of practice. It also requires successfully passing a standardized examination. Maintaining dietetic registration requires completing 75 clock hours of documented continuing education in each five-year period.

Licensure requires passage by each state legislature and sets up the criteria that a dietitian/nutritionist must meet to be licensed for practice in that state. The criteria for licensure are generally based on those for dietetic registration. The national dietetic registration examination may be accepted as the state's licensure examination. Most state licensing laws provide waivers for nutrition practice by persons with other specified credentials.

MALPRACTICE AND LIABILITY

Protection of the client is germane to the provision of quality nutrition care. By utilizing self-assessment, standards of practice, continuing education, quality assurance programs, and adherence to a code of ethics, the nutritionist protects the client and strives for personal protection against any liability for malpractice.

However, liability issues can arise inadvertently in any professional practice. It is advisable in today's litigious health care environment to make sure that the agency insurance policies cover the nutritionist's practice or that the nutritionist carries a professional liability insurance policy. Whereas the possibility of law suits may seem remote, nutritionists have been named. Liability insurance coverage for nutritionists is available. The American Dietetic Association can provide information on insurance carriers and costs.

ETHICAL ISSUES IN PUBLIC HEALTH NUTRITION

Ethics is defined as that branch of philosophy concerned with what is morally good and bad, right and wrong. Beyond the professional code of ethics included earlier in this chapter, many health care practitioners face current ethical issues that were never anticipated in the past. Many of these arise from the apparent conflicts in prevailing individual, family, professional, and societal values, obligations, responsibilities, and rights in making critical decisions about the health and welfare of individuals, family members, special interest groups, and society as a whole. These ethical dilemmas reflect very different perspectives and values. These issues require serious soul-searching by thoughtful professionals who make policies and decisions intended to provide for the greatest public good.

Ethical behavior always requires the objective study of the issues, careful weighing of the alternatives, consultation with administrators and other members of the health team, seeking advice of outside experts, and searching for a negotiation strategy that will achieve the greatest good for the greatest number. Respecting rights and preserving confidentiality are essential elements in resolving ethical issues.

ISSUES TO DEBATE

- What factors must be considered and who should be involved in deciding whether or not to deny or withdraw food and fluid from individuals who are severely handicapped or terminally ill, whose quality of personal and family life is totally impaired, and for whom costs for care are overburdening for family and society?
- What are the considerations in deciding to legally charge a parent or caretaker with neglect or abuse when they do not comply with diet counseling recommendations required to control or manage a health condition which if untreated can contribute to mental deficiency (e.g., inborn metabolic errors), disability (e.g., gross obesity), life-threatening conditions (e.g., renal disease) or costly medical care (e.g., diabetes)?
- How should eligibility criteria for food assistance and nutritional care programs be established when serving a selected target population discriminates against others in the community who view themselves as equally needy?
- How should the professional decide about accepting hospitality, program sponsorship, grants, or honorariums from organizations that may appear to cause a conflict of interest in program policies or practices?

NOTES

1. Thomas J. Peters and Robert H. Waterman, *In Search of Excellence: Lessons from America's Best-Run Companies* (New York: Harper & Row, 1982), 13-16.

2. Mildred Kaufman, ed., *Quality Assurance in Ambulatory Nutritional Care* (Chicago: The American Dietetic Association, 1983), 1.

3. Valerie I. Bradley, *Assessing and Enhancing the Quality of Services: A Guide for the Human Services Field* (Boston: Human Services Research Institute, 1984), 16-20.

4. Ibid.

5. The American Dietetic Association, *Standards of Professional Responsibility and Review Process for Alleged Violations* (Chicago: The American Dietetic Association, 1988).

6. Ibid.

7. The American Dietetic Association, Council on Practice, Quality Assurance Committee, *Standards of Practice: A Practitioner's Guide to Implementation* (Chicago: The American Dietetic Association, 1986), 14-26.

8. The American Dietetic Association, *Professional Standards Review Procedure Manual* (Chicago: The American Dietetic Association, 1976), 2-4.

BIBLIOGRAPHY

Welch, Larry. "The Emergence of an Interdisciplinary Approach to Patient Care Review." *Hospitals* 52, no. 10 (1978): 64.

chapter **25**

Envisioning the Future

Meg Binney Molloy

READER OBJECTIVES

- List emerging roles for the public health nutritionist.
- Suggest some ways that nutritionists can reorder priorities to reach a wider audience in the community.
- Discuss societal changes that will create new demands for nutrition services.
- Propose new technologies that can be used to provide more cost-effective nutrition education to people in the community.

WHAT IS? WHAT MIGHT BE?

Many factors in the community and workplace interfere with the practice of public health nutrition in the "textbook" sense. These factors challenge the nutritionist to be realistic and creative at the same time, always trying to weave nutrition into the fabric of health services of the agency and the community. This handbook assists public health nutritionists in developing the skills they need to keep "their eyes on the stars and their feet on the ground."

This stance requires the nutritionist to have a clear vision of the food and nutrition needs of the people living in the community. It may be difficult to maintain clear vision when agency and community health priorities shift quickly and the vital role of food in health is often forgotten. When this happens does frustration and professional burnout inevitably occur? Not for the nutritionist who accepts the fickleness of public interests and the reality of the political climate. The nutrition program must be continually fine-tuned to lead the way and to respond to the changing needs and demands of the people in the community.

478

It is necessary to continually assess current and emerging food, diet, and health-related issues and ask, "What are we doing about this? What should we be doing about it?" There are many opportunities to take a proactive role and move nutrition forward on the public health agenda.

It may feel comfortable to continue with the same old nutrition services to clients, but this only creates an illusion of stability. The program is strengthened when the leader continuously asks for input and feedback from the stakeholders, who include program participants, representatives from the target population, agency co-workers, administrators, legislators, and others in the community. Their concerns and recommendations suggest opportunities to enrich the nutrition program. By marshalling the energy and ideas of stakeholders, allies and proponents of nutrition programs are nurtured.

Continuing program development and enrichment prepares for the future of public health nutrition. It is essential to build self-confidence to interpret nutrition research to the public. Nutrition questions must be investigated within one's scope of practice. Use of new technologies, educational approaches, vehicles, partnerships, and networks must be explored. The ultimate goal is to provide all of the people in the community with access to a safe, adequate food supply and encourage them to make healthy food choices that will promote their optimal health and result in improved quality of personal, family, and community life.

TAKING A PROACTIVE STAND

Keeping Abreast of Research and Information

Researchers continue to pursue many unanswered questions in the young science of nutrition. The nutrition practitioner must continuously clarify contradictory and ever-changing scientific reports, government recommendations and standards, and popular nutrition misconceptions. New information is introduced continuously via the scientific and popular press. A pragmatic message must be conveyed to guide the public to understand these issues. This means drawing upon information from recent studies and continuously testing existing nutrition guidelines to be sure that they still apply. Chapter 2 reviews the nutritionist's primary tools in incorporating accurate nutrition research into beneficial applied nutrition programs.

Does this mean that the nutritionist must zealously read all of the current research literature? This is not humanly possible with the typical pace of a busy nutrition program! A more realistic approach is to tap the many available publications that review current nutrition research and legislation and interpret them in context with credible nutrition practice. Books, journals, and newsletters that summarize and report contemporary issues in nutrition research are listed in the Public Health Nutrition Library (Appendix N) in the back of this handbook.

Interpreting and Relaying Scientific Information

Nutritionists who have studied the potential for error and controversies in human nutrition research and dietary data collection methods often feel insecure in interpreting nutrition science to other health professionals or to the public. They fear that conclusions may change and that they will be embarrassed by citing flawed studies. It is critical, however, to respond to popular issues in a timely manner to reduce the sensationalism surrounding each newly promoted "miracle diet," weight loss gimmick, or nutrient supplement. Nutritionists should feel comfortable in challenging unfounded nutrition-related concepts held by colleagues or health professionals who may have little training in nutrition. It is more likely that a physician, nurse, or pharmacist will continue to seek the nutritionist's opinion on nutrition questions if they have learned to respect the expert position and rationale.

It is appropriate to explain the consensus of existing nutrition research, even when a highly publicized new study indicates different results. In presenting the consensus it is important to be positive about the information presented, not apologizing for the methodology or the potential for error. The message will not be valued or heard at all if there are too many caveats in the presentation. The explanation should begin with what is known, fitting new information into this framework and explaining that nutrition research is never static. The theories held to be fact today may be changed tomorrow. Rather than speaking of absolutes, colleagues and the public should be kept informed of the state-of-the-art nutrition guidelines.

To feel more confident about the unknowns of an emerging nutrition issue, the nutritionist should find out what peers and mentors have to say about it. This includes weighing the scientific reports in the literature, studying writings of advocacy groups, reading statements of food companies marketing products, and reviewing publications of government agencies and then drawing one's own conclusions. All viewpoints in an issue should be considered so that when a client, reporter, or health professional asks a question, the response is framed in their particular language and from their perspective. After investigating the various stands on an issue, it is useful to reflect on experiences in dealing with similar issues in the past. Do experiences and observations confirm the recommendations from the scientific literature? Critical thinking and evaluation of contemporary nutrition issues are necessary to take a confident stand on the many "gray areas."

THE PUBLIC HEALTH NUTRITIONIST AS AN INVESTIGATOR

Applied research and publication support practice and offer new experiences and professional recognition for the practitioner.[1] Researching an innovative or alternative approach to nutrition intervention for a perplexing problem may be useful when performed in the "real world" of clients and working professionals. An applied nutrition research project can be an evaluation of a nutrition intervention used with selected individuals or groups. A study can investigate trends observed in eating patterns of local population groups or assess the benefits of a community program enabled by nutrition legislation. Surveys and focus groups are used to obtain client and staff input on nutrition program components. Chart audits and state and local reporting systems can provide data on process and outcome objectives as a measure of nutrition program quality assurance. Applied research projects can involve observing, recording, comparing, and reporting the most cost-effective mode of bringing nutrition services to targeted populations or presenting nutrition information to the public. Publication of findings in refereed journals or speaking or presenting poster sessions at professional meetings disseminates information, brings visibility to the program, develops new networks, and generates ideas for further study.

Some applied nutrition research questions observed every day in practice include the following:

- Can computer-assisted programmed instruction deliver basic nutrition information to clients as effectively as live teaching by a professional or paraprofessional?
- What are the most effective components of a weight loss intervention—diet counseling, exercise, behavior modification, or are they synergistic?
- How do television or radio spot announcements compare with newspaper articles in publicizing nutrition services and eliciting requests for information?
- Will more participants be reached with nutrition classes if held at a worksite, school, church, community center, library, grocery store, or health department clinic?

A question raised by asking "What if?" may be easily modelled into a research question. Once the research question and hypothesis are formulated these can be developed into the study design, data collection and analysis, and presentation. Exhibit 25-1 lists the steps in conducting an applied research project.

There are many ways to develop a research proposal. From the service agency's perspective, the most realistic way may be to raise the question and then seek collaboration with faculty at a nearby university. A faculty member may provide expertise in research methodology and possibly help write a grant. One or more graduate students may be interested in collecting and analyzing the data with guidance from the faculty member and the practitioner. This meets the needs of the agency, the students and faculty, and demonstrates partnership in problem solving.

Attending a short course on applied research methods and reading publications on research methodologies are useful for the nutritionist who chooses to pursue a research question. The nutritionist should consult with researchers in developing the study so that the design is appropriate. Statisticians within the local or state agency or in a university can assist with the study design and development of survey instruments as well as data analysis. The expertise of the statistician should be sought early in the design stage to be sure that only needed data are collected in a useful, reliable, and valid form. Chapter 16 provides more information on data management in this context.

Exhibit 25-1 Steps in Conducting an Applied Research Project

1. Formulate research question and hypothesis.
2. Review the literature.
3. Select the study design.
   —Survey
   —Case Series
   —Experimental or Quasi-Experimental
4. Develop the protocol or methodology.
5. Determine resources needed and sources, e.g., funding, personnel, space, equipment.
6. Prepare grant application if needed.
7. Implement project and collect data.
8. Analyze, report results and conclusions.
9. Disseminate findings by reporting at professional meetings and publishing a summary article.

NEW APPROACHES FOR SPREADING THE NUTRITION MESSAGE

Getting Other Professionals Involved

As public dollars are stretched, even today's limited monies for public health nutrition programs can be threatened. Cost-effective program approaches disseminate nutrition by networks through every possible agency and community contact. As discussed in Chapter 21, power is generated by educating the whole health team to "talk nutrition." In the clinic this includes the clerk, community health assistant, nurse, therapist, social worker, dental hygienist, dentist, and physician. The nutritionist must train them all to participate in appropriate nutrition screening, monitoring, referral, and basic education. Receptionists can routinely instruct clients to complete a computer-read dietary assessment questionnaire in the waiting room. Community health assistants can be trained to take careful anthropometric measurements and ask screening questions to identify those who should be referred for food and financial assistance (WIC, EFNEP, food stamps, etc.). Nurses and dental hygienists can review the computerized nutrient analysis from the diet questionnaires to note high-risk eating practices and provide immediate nutrition information feedback. Dentists and physicians can explain the significance of identified nutrition problems, reinforce nutrition education, and refer high-risk clients to nutritionists. For high priority nutritional problems, the nutritionist's specialized knowledge and educational techniques may be utilized more appropriately in interactive skill-building classes or group counseling sessions. The team approach (Chapter 21) to nutrition programming has a much greater impact than the traditional one-on-one, often one-shot, nutrition counseling.

Clients As Educators

Using activated clients as educators has also proved effective. Peers speak the same language and feel an immediate bond with those who share their problem.[2] A client with diabetes who has successfully changed eating and exercise practices speaking to a group of newly diagnosed diabetics becomes a role model. Pregnant women believe a nursing "mom" who speaks about how she has handled intrusive remarks about breast-feeding; they can formulate their own response and feelings in a similar situation. Sharing and exchanging personal concerns has a far greater impact on mothers' infant feeding decisions than a scientific discussion about the benefits of breast milk to the infant. Peer counselors must be trained with sound information to convey, but client-educators should be encouraged to share personal experiences and talk about how they managed to change their food habits.

Community Groups and Programs

Community development programs around the world utilize approaches that build independence and self-sufficiency in communities and individuals.[3] Public health agencies recognize the effectiveness of community-based programs, particularly for training and empowering community people to take charge in solving their own problems. Nutritionists who move from the offices and agency clinics out into worksites, food markets, restaurants, schools, places of worship, senior citizen centers, day care programs, women's clubs, civic groups, soup kitchens, and other targeted sites make contact with people where they are most likely to make their food choices. By consulting with these groups, the nutritionist can raise their awareness of the importance of food to health and quality of life, provide nutrition programs to community groups in their natural setting (with built-in supports), and implement nutrition standards to be carried out by others. By training club members, volunteers, students, teachers, coaches, and parents to provide credible nutrition information using carefully selected films, videos, audiotapes, computer-assisted learning, and printed materials tailored to each particular group, the same seed can be planted and flourish throughout the community.

The Media

Nutritionists can capitalize on public awareness and provide information to the public via television, radio, magazines, and newspapers.[4] Since competitive marketing techniques are used by businesses that do not always convey accurate information, nutritionists will always need to speak out more persuasively to overcome the barrage of nutrition misinformation. Television reaches a cross-section of the population including all socioeconomic groups. Cable television is more targeted to specific audiences. Radio programs have a listening audience with defined characteristics, so in working with radio one must look at the demographic profile of listeners of a particular program to design messages to effectively reach that audience. Newspaper columns are widely read, but usually catch the attention of literate and motivated consumers. In working with any of the media, the straightforward, simple message is the most readily understood. Distilling the nutrition topic down to an easily understood "sound-byte" or using a question and answer format will capture the attention of more people.

Influencing the System

A systems approach makes healthy foods available and appealing to the public.[5] It is possible to influence the quality and safety of foods that people eat by consulting with food production, processing, and packaging companies; grocery stores; restaurants; school and worksite cafeterias; and vending machine companies. Creating the food environment that makes lower fat, nutrient-dense foods appealing and easily accessible creates a cultural norm linking healthy eating to the enjoyment of good food. Most food establishments welcome help and promote it aggressively since in today's marketplace healthy foods increase their competitive position.

PARTNERSHIPS AND NETWORKS

As discussed in Chapter 22, because the demands upon nutritionists are many and their numbers few, they seek partners to support and extend their outreach. Partners found within the same agency and throughout the community share common goals. Nutrition councils bring together professionals from a variety of agencies who share related goals and serve the same populations. Working together, nutritionists define a continuum of nutrition services. Gaps in the continuum can be identified for program development; programs that provide similar services can collaborate to reduce duplication. Interagency referrals work together when the individuals who provide various programs know and respect each other. Public health nutritionists should assume leadership in establishing and supporting a community nutrition consortium. A directory of community nutrition resources developed by members of the local council will assist all nutrition practitioners to develop comprehensive care plans for clients. The directory can be mailed to physicians, pharmacists, dentists, psychologists, as well as to hospitals to increase referrals, and to newspapers, radio, and television stations to increase utilization and support of existing services.

District dietetic associations mobilize volunteer efforts of registered dietitians for nutrition projects that will promote public relations. Nutritionists who are active in their district and state dietetic associations can suggest useful voluntary community nutrition projects such as nutrition screening at a health fair, advising legislators or business leaders, promoting food for fitness on the media, or sponsoring meals at the local soup kitchen.

Several community agencies provide nutrition information. Collaborating with such public agencies as Cooperative Extension and schools reaches a wide audience with a more effective message than anyone can do alone. Powerful volunteer groups that promote nutrition messages are the American Heart Association, the American Cancer Society, the American Diabetes Association, and the March of Dimes. Other agencies that can carry food and nutrition messages to their clients include county departments of social services, housing and community development, area agencies on aging, recreation and parks, mental health services, and the public library. Partnerships in addressing the priority needs of a community stretch limited resources.

Involving legislators in nutrition issues in a community leads to nutrition-related policy development. Political networks promote support for funding to continue and expand nutrition services to meet the needs of the population.

HARNESSING NEW TECHNOLOGIES

The nutritionist may lead the way in testing new technologies to promote nutrition knowledge and access to a healthier food supply. Technologies that the rising generation depends upon and uses with ease include computers, electronic mail, videos, facsimile machines, cable television, microwaves, and telephone answering machines. All of these will become more efficient and diversified, and ultimately may be replaced by new, undreamed of technological developments in the future.[6] The imagination can conceive limitless possibilities for spreading the nutrition messages as the information age makes personnel and facts accessible by pushing a button. Nutritionists can take advantage of technological resources more readily than other health professionals because nutrition assessment, education, and counseling rely on information exchange in contrast to the "hands-on" clinical examination and treatment procedures of physicians, dentists, nurses, and therapists. Utilizing new, hi-tech media, nutrition professionals can become more visible to consumers and broadcast nutrition information widely and competitively.

It boggles the mind to think of the impact of nutrition education spread by video displays in health centers and grocery stores; interactive computers in shopping malls and subway stations; participant-active classes on cable TV with telephone hookups; hotlines via FAX machines; and ordering groceries and meals to meet special dietary needs on the home computer. There can be nutrition services that computer-generate health-prescribed home menus and recipes for families; home and office robots programmed to prepare nutritious meals; and nutritionists assisting people to choose healthy foods under the sea or on the moon. If these sound impossible within a foreseeable lifetime, so did television, microwaves, and computers just 40 years ago.

Nutritionists earn their place in a changing society by providing services that meet the perceived food and nutrition needs of consumers. As farmers, food producers, and packagers modify their products, consumers must become more nutrition literate. Concerns about the environmental hazards of nonbiodegradable food packages and food toxicology due to pesticides concern the public. This will affect how future crops are grown and marketed. As the food supply changes, the public will seek nutrition and health information about new foods. A synthetic fat substitute is being tested. Who knows what the next 100 years will bring to grocery store shelves? By the year 2090, the food supply will no doubt be unrecognizable to the people of 1990, but the public will need to know how to choose, prepare, and purchase foods to meet their health needs. Advocating for legislation to ensure the provision of a nutritious and ecologically sound food supply will remain a role for nutritionists even as technologies change.

One vision of the future is of an aging population, where women are active in the work force throughout their childbearing years, and where humans are fast becoming a sedentary race with robots and automobiles doing their physical work.[7] Leading causes of morbidity and mortality will include more mental health and developmental problems, substance abuse, cancer, and obesity-related conditions.[8] As the health of the elderly becomes a top national priority, nutrition intervention can maintain the quality of life that these consumers demand. Nutritionists may expect to consult with worksite child and adult day care programs; set standards for infant, toddler, and elder food services programs; and advocate for needs of nursing mothers in corporation workforces. Social changes will demand innovative programs to address emerging nutrition and health concerns.

CHALLENGING AND CHANGING THE CULTURAL NORM

Exploring new areas will keep nutritionists excited about their profession; developing new skills will make them a valuable asset in their organization and in the health care field. Nutritionists are recognized as leaders when they develop cost-effective and innovative programs that have desired and measurable benefits.

Program changes in the community come as slowly as dietary change for program consumers. Gradual, forward steps can move the nutrition programs to a higher level on the public health agenda. Mobilizing existing resources in the community can help in planning and collaborating for this initiative.

Nutritionists must examine their daily schedules critically to weed out "busy work" that can be delegated to clerks, volunteers, and computers. Individual nutrition counseling can be shifted into small groups or to trained peer counselors so that nutritionists can have the time to implement programs with greater impacts. Students can help deliver needed educational programs or conduct applied nutrition research projects. With guidance and leadership, the local professional and volunteer service organizations might provide some person-power for more community-based nutrition programs. The local media might support a regularly scheduled nutrition feature.

Unlimited opportunities exist for the nutritionist who makes time for activities that challenge the cultural norm. With a positive attitude and a clear vision of the health needs and interests of the community, the nutritionist can successfully steer nutrition programs into the future.

ISSUES TO DEBATE

- Is it possible for nutritionists to provide ongoing nutrition services and incorporate applied research? Test new technologies? Maintain a dialogue with the media? Be involved with legislative advocacy? Be active in professional organization activities?
- How can public health nutritionists extend their influence into the future in time and space?
- Where should public health nutrition "be" in the year 2000? In the year 2020? 2050?

NOTES

1. Elaine R. Monson and C.L. Cheney, "Research Methods in Nutrition and Dietetics: Design, Data Analysis, and Presentation," *Journal of the American Dietetic Association* 88, no. 9 (September 1988): 1047-65.

2. Richard K. Manoff, "Nutrition Education: Lessons Learned," *Mothers and Children: A Bulletin on Infant Feeding and Maternal Nutrition* 2, no. 3 (September 1982): 2-4.

3. John O. Field, "Development at the Grass Roots: The Organizational Imperative," *Fletcher Forum Journal* 4, no. 2 (Summer 1980): 145-64.

4. Kristen W. McNutt, "Toward a More Rational Approach to Informing the Public about Nutrition," *Food and Nutrition News* 57, no. 2 (March/April 1985).

5. F. James Levinson, "Toward Success in Combating Malnutrition: An Assessment of What Works," *Food and Nutrition Bulletin* 4, no. 3 (July 1982): 23-44.

6. John Naisbitt, *Megatrends: Ten New Directions Transforming Our Lives* (New York: Warner Books, 1982), 39-53, 249-252.

7. John Naisbitt and Patricia Aburdene. *Reinventing the Corporation: Transforming Your Job and Your Company for the New Information Society* (New York: Warner Books, 1986), 251-56.

8. U.S. Department of Health and Human Services, Office of Disease Prevention and Health Promotion, Draft, *Promoting Health/Preventing Disease: Year 2000 Objectives for the Nation* (Washington, D.C.: Public Health Service, 1989). Children's Defense Fund, *A Children's Defense Budget by 1988* (Washington, D.C.: Children's Defense Fund, 1987).

BIBLIOGRAPHY

Adams, E.A., and A.M. Messersmith. "Robots in Food Systems: A Review and Assessment of Potential Uses." *Journal of the American Dietetic Association* 86, no. 4 (April 1986): 476-90.

Austin, James E., et al. *Nutrition Intervention in Developing Countries: An Overview.* Boston: Oelgeschlager, Gunn, and Hain, 1980.

Barker, Randolph. "A Summary of Proceedings." In *Workshop on Village Level Studies*, IRRI. Los Banos, Phillipines: March 1978.

FAO/WHO Joint Expert Committee on Nutrition. *Food and Nutrition Strategies in National Development.* Rome: FAOUN, 1976.

Short, Sarah H., and R. William. "The Nutrition Message and the Medium." *Food and Nutrition News* 58, no. 5 (November/December 1986).

Sims, Laura, and Helen Smicklas-Wright. "An Ecologic Systems Perspective: Its Application to Nutrition Policy, Program Design and Evaluation." In *Community Nutrition, People, Policies and Programs.* California: Wadsworth Health Sciences Division, 1981.

U.S. Department of Health and Human Services, Office of Disease Prevention and Health Promotion. *Promoting Health/Preventing Disease: Objectives for the Nation.* Washington, D.C.: Public Health Service, 1980.

Self-Assessment Tool for Public Health Nutritionists

"The public health nutritionist is that member of the public health agency staff who is responsible for assessing community nutrition needs and planning, organizing, managing, directing, coordinating and evaluating the nutrition component of the health agency's services. The public health nutritionist establishes linkages with community nutrition programs, nutrition education, food assistance, social or welfare services, child care, services to the elderly, other human services, and community based research."

From Kaufman, M. Ed. et al. Personnel in Public Health Nutrition for the 1980's, Washington, DC; ASTHO Foundation, 1982

This tool is designed to help me implement the ADA Standards of Practice (#4) and objectively assess my expertise in the five general areas of public health nutrition and then use the assessment to develop a career development plan. It is important to complete each item even though the particular skill or knowledge may not be required in my present job.

For the purpose of this self-assessment, the following definitions are used for guidance:

1. Expert—possess this knowledge/skill as a result of training and/or experience and feel able to speak and act with authority in this area.
2. Competent—feel knowledge/skill exceeds the average but is less than the level of "expert."
3. Adequate—consider knowledge/skill is satisfactory or average.
4. Beginner—feel knowledge/skill is characterized by uncertainty and lack of confidence.
5. Unqualified—assess knowledge/skill as inadequate and performance in area would be difficult without technical assistance; assistance would be needed if required to apply this knowledge/skill.

Source: Public Health Nutrition Practice Group of The American Dietetic Association, © 1988. Reprinted with permission.

I. Nutrition and Dietetics Practice

	Expert ⟷ Unqualified				
• Knowledge of the principles and practice of nutrition throughout the life cycle					
– normal nutrition	1	2	3	4	5
– therapeutic nutrition	1	2	3	4	5
– meal planning, food selection, preparation, processing and service for individuals and groups	1	2	3	4	5
• Knowledge of human behavior, particularly health and diet-related behaviors	1	2	3	4	5
• Knowledge of techniques for effecting behavior change	1	2	3	4	5
• Skill in process of interviewing and counseling	1	2	3	4	5
• Knowledge of the cultures and life styles of ethnic and socioeconomic groups represented in the community	1	2	3	4	5
• Knowledge and skill in nutrition assessment techniques:					
– anthropometric	1	2	3	4	5
– biochemical	1	2	3	4	5
– clinical	1	2	3	4	5
– dietary	1	2	3	4	5
– socioeconomic	1	2	3	4	5
• Skill in the interpretation and use of data from nutrition assessment for:					
– individuals	1	2	3	4	5
– populations	1	2	3	4	5

II. Communications

	Expert ⟷ Unqualified				

- Skill in communicating scientific information at levels appropriate for different audiences, both orally and in writing:
  - consumers/public   1   2   3   4   5
  - health professionals   1   2   3   4   5
  - the media   1   2   3   4   5

- Skill in using various communication channels and working with the media:
  - printed media (newspapers, magazines, newsletters)   1   2   3   4   5
  - radio   1   2   3   4   5
  - films/videos   1   2   3   4   5
  - television   1   2   3   4   5

- Knowledge of methods to outreach to prospective clients to enhance their participation in health and nutrition programs   1   2   3   4   5

- Knowledge of the principles of social marketing for use in health and nutrition programs   1   2   3   4   5

- Skill in negotiation and use of group process techniques (brainstorming, focus groups, nominal group process) to achieve goals and objectives   1   2   3   4   5

- Skill in participating effectively as a member of agency and/or community boards, committees, and task forces   1   2   3   4   5

- Skill in using the consultation process   1   2   3   4   5

III. Public Health Science and Practice

	Expert ⟷ Unqualified				
• Knowledge and understanding of the epidemiologic approach to measure and describe health and nutrition problems in the community	1	2	3	4	5
• Knowledge of biostatistics, including principles of:					
– data collection and management	1	2	3	4	5
– statistical analysis and inferences	1	2	3	4	5
– computer applications for data compilation and analyses	1	2	3	4	5
• Knowledge of research design and methodology	1	2	3	4	5
• Skill in interpreting research and its implications for the practice of public health and nutrition	1	2	3	4	5
• Skill in conducting a community health and nutrition needs assessment, including:					
– knowledge of local community including community networks and power structures	1	2	3	4	5
– knowledge of available data sources and their use	1	2	3	4	5
– skill in soliciting input on perceived needs from clients, community leaders, and health professionals	1	2	3	4	5
– knowledge of community health and human service programs and of appropriate resources for client referral	1	2	3	4	5

IV. Management

	Expert ⟷ Unqualified				
• Skill in community organization	1	2	3	4	5
• Skill in translating community assessment data into agency program plan for nutrition services, including:					
– prioritizing goals	1	2	3	4	5
– development of measurable objectives	1	2	3	4	5
– development of achievable action plans	1	2	3	4	5
– use of quality control measures	1	2	3	4	5
– development of evaluation systems	1	2	3	4	5
• Skill in integrating plan for nutrition services into overall mission and plan of the health agency	1	2	3	4	5
• Skill in organizing and prioritizing work	1	2	3	4	5
• Knowledge of quality assurance methodology, including the writing of measurable health outcomes and nutrition care standards	1	2	3	4	5
• Skill in applying the principles of personnel management, including:					
– recruiting	1	2	3	4	5
– staffing	1	2	3	4	5
– supervising	1	2	3	4	5
– performance appraisal	1	2	3	4	5
– staff development	1	2	3	4	5
• Skill in applying principles of financial management of health services, including:					
– forecasting of fiscal needs	1	2	3	4	5
– budget preparation and justification	1	2	3	4	5
– reimbursement systems	1	2	3	4	5
– control of revenues and expenditures	1	2	3	4	5
• Knowledge of available funding sources for public health and public health nutrition programs	1	2	3	4	5
• Skill in grant and contract management, including:					
– preparation	1	2	3	4	5
– negotiation	1	2	3	4	5
– monitoring	1	2	3	4	5
• Skill in applying principles of cost/benefit and cost/effectiveness analysis	1	2	3	4	5

V. Legislation and Advocacy

	Expert ⟷ Unqualified				
• Knowledge of current and emerging public health and nutrition problems	1	2	3	4	5
• Skill in identifying economic and societal trends which have implications for the health and nutritional status of the population	1	2	3	4	5
• Knowledge of the political considerations involved in agency planning and decision making	1	2	3	4	5
• Knowledge of the legislative base for public health and public health nutrition programs	1	2	3	4	5
• Knowledge of federal, state, and local governmental structures and the processes involved in the development of public policy, legislation, and regulations that influence nutrition and health services	1	2	3	4	5
• Knowledge of the purposes, function, and politics of organizations in the community which influence nutrition and health	1	2	3	4	5
• Skill in participating in organized advocacy efforts for health and nutrition programs	1	2	3	4	5

REFERENCES

Association of State and Territorial Public Health Nutrition Directors. *Model State Nutrition Objectives.* 1988, unpublished.

ASTHO Foundation Nutrition Services Project Committee. "Nutrition Services in State and Local Health Agencies." *Public Health Rep.* 98:1, 9–20, 1983.

Baird, S.C., and J. Sylvester. *Role Delineation and Verification for Entry-level Positions in Community Dietetics.* Chicago: The American Dietetic Association, 1983.

Committee on Professional Education, The American Public Health Association. "The Educational Qualifications of Nutritionists in Health Agencies." *J. Amer. Diet. Assoc.* 22:1, 41–44, 1946.

Curriculum and Membership Committee, Association of Faculties of Graduate Programs in Public Health Nutrition. *A Description of Graduate Programs in Public Health Nutrition.* 1980, unpublished.

Egan, M.C. "Public Health Nutrition Services: Issues Today and Tomorrow." *J. Amer. Diet. Assoc.* 77:4, 423–27, 1980.

Kaufman, M., ed, et al. *Personnel in Public Health Nutrition for the 1980's,* Washington, DC: ASTHO Foundation (Association of State and Territorial Health Officials Foundation), 1982.

Kaufman, M. "Preparing Public Health Nutritionists to Meet the Future." *J. Amer. Diet. Asso.* 86:4, 511–14, 1986.

Peck, E.B. "The Public Health Nutritionist-Dietitian: An Historical Perspective." *J. Amer. Diet. Assoc.* 64:6, 642–47, 1974.

The American Dietetic Association. *Standards of Practice: A Practitioner's Guide to Implementation.* Chicago: The American Dietetic Association, 1986.

My Career Development Plan

To help me implement The American Dietetic Association Standards of Practice this outline for a career development plan will aid me in planning to strengthen the areas I identified as needing improvement. The relative priority to work on any item will be determined by my individual needs and career goals. Setting a target time frame for each area will be based on my priorities. Establishing a time frame will enhance the usefulness of this tool for my professional growth and development as a public health nutritionist.

1. My personal career goal is: _____

2   As I review my responses on the self-assessment tool, I identify three items that are most critical to my career goals.

   My first priority is: _____

My plan will include the following courses, activities, consultations.	My time frame(s)
1.	
2.	
3.	
Notes:	

My second priority is: _____

My plan will include the following courses, activities, consultations.	My time frame(s)
1.	
2.	
3.	
Notes:	

My third priority is: _____

My plan will include the following courses, activities, consultations.	My time frame(s)
1.	
2.	
3.	
Notes:	

Adequate Food for All

—ASTPHND Position Statement—March 1988

Issue Statement:

Nationwide, there is a recognition that hunger and homelessness are increasing. Although there is much debate about the actual numbers, current estimates are that over two million people are homeless nationwide, with many more families on the brink of homelessness. Many families must choose between buying food and paying the rent.

Increases in the use of emergency food relief nationwide clearly indicate a problem with access to food. At the same time, when inflation is taken into account, spending for most nutrition programs has decreased, more restrictive eligibility criteria have been imposed, and administrative procedures have been increased. All of this has resulted in declining participation. It is estimated that only half of all people eligible for food stamp benefits participate and only forty-four percent of eligible women, infants and children participate in the Special Supplemental Food Program for Women, Infants and Children (WIC) (Children's Defense Budget - FY 1989: Children's Defense Fund, Washington, DC, p. 132).

Background and Justification:

"The availability and accessibility of safe food is fundamental to the public health" (Public Health Reports 98: 7-20, 1983 ASTHO/ASTPHND Position Statement 1981). State public health agencies and their local counterparts are mandated to oversee food safety. However, the problem of inadequate food is usually left to public or private social services agencies without acknowledgement of the resulting nutrition and health implications.

Source: Reprinted with permission from The Association of State and Territorial Public Health Nutrition Directors.

In many states, health departments carry out and coordinate planning, develop policies and services aimed at reduction of low birthweight and infant mortality and specifically target nutrition programs and services to high-risk populations including the poor and minorities, pregnant women, infants, children, adolescents, adults with chronic disease, and the elderly. State health departments carry out numerous activities related to ensuring a safe food supply. Yet activities ensuring an adequate food supply ("adequate" being in relation to quantity and quality) often receive limited attention even in the face of increasing numbers of people who do not have access to a nutritionally wholesome and adequate food supply.

Position To Be Adopted:

State Health Agencies should provide leadership in ensuring that adequate, safe, affordable, and nutritious food is available to all citizens regardless of income. Public Health Agencies are uniquely qualified for this leadership role and should participate with other agencies in any or all of the following activities:

1. Development of recommendations for practical policies that facilitate participation in food and nutrition programs.

2. Establishing a data system to monitor access to and availability of adequate food as well as participation in food and nutrition programs.

3. Providing training and technical assistance with regard to data collection to local county, public and/or private groups, including food banks, who are distributing food to people.

4. Maintaining surveillance activities to monitor status of nutritional health in all segments of the population with a focus on high-risk groups.

5. Coordination of appropriate agencies and activities to address problems of food adequacy and access.

6. Development of recommendations for appropriate nutrition training regarding healthful dietary patterns including food choices at pantries.

7. Development of recommendations for appropriate nutrition components in health care programs, both public and private.

8. Promoting of adequate state and federal funding for food and nutrition programs and services.

Coordination:

Addressing the broad spectrum of nutrition needs of the population requires a combined effort of public organizations and the private sector working cooperatively to provide appropriate services. State health departments can be the catalysts for improving the nutritional status of residents of the state. In addition, copies of this statement will be distributed to state social service and education agencies and advocacy groups concerned with improving access to adequate food to foster coordination.

The Association of State and Territorial Public Health Nutrition Directors (ASTPHND) is an affiliate of the Association of State and Territorial Health Officials (ASTHO), whose executive committee has endorsed this statement. ASTPHND's members, nutrition directors from each state and territory, are dedicated to the achievement of optimal nutritional status for all sectors of the United States population. For further information regarding this statement, contact Ruth Palombo, MS, RD, Director, Office of Nutrition, Division of Family Health Services, Massachusetts Department of Public Health, 150 Tremont Street, Boston, MA 02111, 617-727-9283.

Model State Nutrition Objectives

Association of State and Territorial Public Health Nutrition Directors
Ratified June 1988

Improved Health Status

1. By 19___, the prevalence of nutrition-related growth and developmental anomalies and/or risk factor(s) namely ____*____ among (target group) will be reduced from _____ to _____.
   * Low birth weight, delayed growth, underweight, iron deficiency, fetal alcohol syndrome, inappropriate infant feeding practices, inadequate pregnancy weight gain, dental caries, eating disorders, inborn errors of metabolism (specific conditions), and "children with special needs" conditions (specify).
2. By 19___, the incidence/prevalence/morbidity/mortality associated with nutrition-related chronic disease namely ____*____ among (target group) will be reduced from _____ to _____.
   * Cardiovascular disease (abnormal exercise stress test, angina, coronary bypass surgery), cancers, hypertension, strokes, diabetes, osteoporosis, dental problems, malnutrition.

Reduced Risk Factors

3. By 19___, _____ percent of pregnant women will avoid the harmful substance ___*___ during pregnancy.
   * Tobacco, alcohol, drugs and caffeine.
4. By 19___, _____ percent of women will breastfeed upon hospital discharge and _____ percent will continue breastfeeding for _____ months.
5. By 19___, _____ percent of * will consume a nutritionally adequate and prudent diet consistent with established state or federal recommendations.
   * Pregnant women, lactating women, infants, preschool children, school-age children, adolescents, school-age children in day care, women of child-bearing age, adults, and elderly.
6. By 19___, the chronic disease risk factor ____*____ among (target population) will be reduced from _____ percent to _____ percent.

Source: Reprinted with permission from The Association of State and Territorial Public Health Nutrition Directors.

  * Obesity; hypertension; elevated serum cholesterol; poor physical fitness; excess intake of dietary fat, cholesterol, sodium, alcohol and sugar; inadequate intake of dietary fiber, fruits and vegetables, and calcium.

7. By 19___, the following contaminants will not be present in the state food supply above toxic/hazardous levels as defined by state or federal agencies.

  Agricultural: pesticides, fertilizers, growth regulators

  Drugs: antibiotics, steroids/hormones, growth regulators

  Environmental: organics, inorganics/heavy metals

  Food additives: preservatives, colors, flavors, sweeteners, stabilizers

  Industrial: organics, inorganics/heavy metals, radioactives

  Microbial: bacteria, molds, fungi, virus, protozoa, and related toxins

  Naturally occurring toxins: carcinogens, mutagens, neurotoxins

Increased Public/Professional Awareness

8. By 19___, there will be an on-going interdisciplinary information program for public health and food industry professionals on food safety, labeling, health claims, nutrition fraud, and the reporting of foodborne illness.

Improved Services/Protection

9. By 19___, the State Health Agency (in cooperation with other official, professional, voluntary agencies and organizations and industry) will establish dietary guidance recommendations for the general public and (target population), and promote the availability, accessibility, and consumption of a nutritionally adequate and prudent diet in ___*___ .

  * Restaurants, food markets, schools, media, worksites, and institutions.

10. By 19___, _____ percent of restaurants, _____ percent of secondary school districts will provide/include nutrition education as part of required comprehensive school health education; and _____ percent of school food service programs will comply with established state or federal recommendations for implementation of the Dietary Guidelines.

11. By 19___, _____ percent of restaurants, _____ percent worksite cafeterias, and _____ percent of food markets exceeding _____ size will participate in point of purchase nutrition education and promotion programs.

12. By 19___, the state will be protected by an operational system of inspection, surveillance, reporting, investigation, intervention, enforcement, and follow-up and training for protection against hazardous chemical or biological contamination of food.

13. By 19___, the state will have a ___*___ program to educate the public on the issues of normal nutrition, diet and disease, food safety, and nutrition fraud.

  * Mass media, training, professional seminar.

14. By 19___, _____ percent of ___*___ contacts should include some element of nutrition screening, assessment, counseling or education provided by the health professional in ** (settings).

  * Well-child care; prenatal visits; screenings for CVD or cancer risk factors; medical management of diabetes, hypertension, elevated cholesterol; preventive care of the elderly.

  ** Publicly funded programs, private medical care, health fairs, etc.

Improved Surveillance and Evaluation

15. By 19___, the State Health Agency will have a nutrition monitoring system which would assess and report on any or all of the following:
    a. Nutritional status of various population groups
    b. Food intake patterns
    c. Quantity, quality, and distribution of the food supply including the adequacy of public and private food assistance efforts
    d. Availability and quality of nutrition services and staff
    e. Nutrition education needs
16. By 19___, the State Health Agency will establish and implement a quality assurance mechanism for monitoring, evaluating, and auditing current activities to measure progress; identify factors that interfere with program effectiveness; and determine the need for continuation or modification of operations and compliance with nutrition standards.
17. By 19___, the State Health Agency will have a systematic comprehensive nutrition program plan.
18. By 19___, the State Health Agency will establish standards for the following:
    a. Nutritional status of the population
    b. Dietary intake of the population
    c. Public and professional nutrition education
    d. Delivery of nutrition services, e.g., nutrition screening, assessment, referral, intervention, and follow-up
    e. Nutrition personnel qualifications and performance
19. By 19___, mechanisms will be established to finance and/or recover costs for public health nutrition program/services utilizing ___*___ .
    *   Federal funds, state and local funds, fee-for-service, third-party reimbursements, grants, contracts, donations, and in-kind contributions.

appendix *D*

State and Territorial Public Health Nutrition Directors

ALABAMA, Director WIC/Nutrition Services, Division of Family Health Services, 434 Monroe Street, Montgomery, AL 36130; 205/261-5561.

ALASKA, Nutrition Services Manager, Department of Health and Social Service, P. O. Box H-06B, Juneau, AK 99811; 907/465-3103 or 465- 3105.

AMERICAN SAMOA, Director, Public Health Nutrition, Department of Health Services, Public Health Division, Pago Pago, American Samoa 96799.

ARIZONA, Chief, Office of Nutrition Services, Department of Health Services, 1740 W. Adams, Room 208, Phoenix, AZ 85007; 602/542-1886 or 542-1890.

ARKANSAS, Director, Nutrition Services, Department of Health, 4815 W. Markham Street, Little Rock, AR 72205; 501/661-2253 or 661-2186.

CALIFORNIA, Chief, Nutrition and Cancer Prevention Program, Department of Health Services, 714 P Street, P. O. Box 942732, Sacramento, CA 94234; 916/322-1520 or 322-4787.

COLORADO, Director, Nutrition Services, Department of Health, 4210 E. 11th Avenue, Denver, CO 80220; 303/331-8380.

CONNECTICUT, Chief, Nutrition Section, State Department of Health Services, 150 Washington Street, Hartford, CT 06106; 203/566-2520.

DELAWARE, Director, Office of Nutrition/WIC, Division of Public Health, Department of Health and Social Services, Robbins Building, Silver Lake Plaza, Dover, DE 19901; 302/736-3671.

DISTRICT OF COLUMBIA, Nutrition Coordinator, Department of Human Services, 1660 L Street, NW, Washington, DC 20026; 202/673-6707.

FLORIDA, Program Supervisor, WIC and Nutrition Services, Department of Health and Rehabilitative Services, 1317 Winewood Boulevard, Tallahassee, FL 32301; 904/488-8985.

GEORGIA, Director, Office of Nutrition, Division of Public Health, Department of Human Resources, 878 Peachtree Street, NE, Room 218, Atlanta, GA 30309; 404/894-7600.

GUAM, WIC Coordinator, Department of Public Health and Social Services, P. O. Box 2816, Agana, GU 96910; 671/734-3343.

HAWAII, Chief, Nutrition Branch, State Department of Health, 1250 Punchbowl Street, Honolulu, HI 96813; 808/548-6552.

IDAHO, Maternal and Child Health Nutrition Consultant, Bureau of Child Health, Department of Health and Welfare, 450 West State Street, State House Mail, Boise, ID 83720; 208/334-5950.

ILLINOIS, Department of Public Health, 535 West Jefferson Street, Springfield, IL 62761; 217/782-4977.

INDIANA, Director, Nutrition Division, State Board of Health, 1330 W. Michigan Street, Indianapolis, IN 46206; 317/633-0206.

IOWA, Director, Public Health Nutrition, Department of Public Health, Lucas Building, Des Moines, IA 50319; 515/281-7501.

KANSAS, Director, Office of Nutrition, Bureau of Family Health, Department of Health and Environment, Forbes Field, Building 740, Topeka, KS 66620; 913/296-1320.

KENTUCKY, Manager, Nutrition Branch, Bureau of Health Services, Division of Maternal and Child Health, Department of Human Resources, 275 East Main Street, Frankfort, KY 40621; 502/564-3827.

LOUISIANA, Administrator, Nutrition Section, Department of Health and Human Resources, Office of Preventive and Public Health Services, P. O. Box 60630, New Orleans, LA 70160; 504/568-5065.

MAINE, Nutritionist, Division of Maternal and Child Health, Department of Human Services, 157 Capitol Street (Station 11), Augusta, ME 04333; 207/289-3311.

MARYLAND, Nutrition Coordinator, Family Health Administration, Department of Health and Mental Hygiene, 201 W. Preston Street, Baltimore, MD 21201; 301/225-6748.

MASSACHUSETTS, Director, Office of Nutrition, Division of Family Health Services, Department of Public Health, 150 Tremont Street, Boston, MA 02111; 617/727-9283.

MICHIGAN, Chief Nutritionist, Bureau of Community Services, Department of Public Health, 3423 N. Logan, P. O. Box 30035, Lansing, MI 48909; 517/335-8913.

MINNESOTA, Nutrition Director, Division of Disease Prevention and Control, Department of Health, 717 Delaware Street, SW, Minneapolis, MN 55440; 612/623-5437.

MISSISSIPPI, Director, Nutrition Services, Bureau of Personal Health, Department of Health, 2423 N. State Street, P. O. Box 1700, Jackson, MS 39215; 601/960-7476.

MISSOURI, Nutrition Specialist, Department of Health, 1730 Elm Street, P.O. Box 570, Jefferson City, MO 65102; 314/751-6250.

MONTANA, Health Services Division, Department of Health and Environmental Sciences, Cogswell Building, Helena, MT 59620; 406/449-4740.

NEBRASKA, Director, Nutrition Division, Department of Health, P. O. Box 95007, Lincoln, NE 68509; 402/471-2781.

NEVADA, WIC Program Coordinator, State Health Division, 505 East King Street, Room 204, Carson City, NV 89710; 702/885-4797.

NEW HAMPSHIRE, Nutrition Consultant, Bureau of Maternal and Child Health, Division of Public Health Services, Health and Welfare Building, 6 Hazen Drive, Concord, NH 03301; 603/271-4541.

NEW JERSEY, Nutrition Consultant, Department of Health, 120 S. Stockton Street, Trenton, NJ 08926; 609/292-4076.

NEW MEXICO, Chief, Nutrition Bureau, Health and Environment Department, Runnels Building N-3064, 1190 St. Francis Drive, Santa Fe, NM 87503; 505/827-0020.

NEW YORK, Director, Bureau of Nutrition, Department of Health, Corning Tower Building, Room 859, Albany, NY 12237; 518/474-1912.

NORTH CAROLINA, Director, WIC Program, Maternal and Child Health Section, Division of Maternal and Child Health Services, Department of Health, Environment and Natural Resources, P. O. Box 27687, Raleigh, NC 27611-7687; 919/733-2351.

NORTH DAKOTA, Maternal and Child Health Nutritionist/WIC Director, Department of Health, Judicial Wing, State Capitol Building, Bismark, ND 58505; 701/224-2496.

NORTHERN MARIANA ISLANDS, Nutrition Services Coordinator, Division of Public Health, Chalan Kanoa Village, Saipan, CM 96950.

OHIO, Chief, Nutrition Division, Department of Health, 131 N. High Street, 4th Floor, Columbus, OH 43266; 614/466-0666.

OKLAHOMA, Director of Nutrition Services, Department of Health, 1000 NE 10th Street, P. O. Box 53551, Oklahoma City, OK 73139; 405/271-4676.

OREGON, Nutrition Consultant, State Health Division, P. O. Box 231, Portland, OR 97207; 503/229-5691.

PENNSYLVANIA, Chief of Public Health Nutrition, Department of Health, Division of Health Promotion, Room 912-A, Health-Welfare Building, P. O. Box 90, Harrisburg, PA 17108; 717/787-6967.

PUERTO RICO, Director, Nutrition and Dietetics Division, Department of Health, BPO Box 70184, San Juan, PR 00936; 809/764-2521.

RHODE ISLAND, Chief, Office of Nutrition Services, Division of Family Health, Department of Health, 75 Davis Street, Room 302, Providence, RI 02908; 401/277-2309.

SOUTH CAROLINA, Director, Office of Public Health Nutrition, Department of Health and Environmental Control, 2600 Bull Street, Columbia, SC 29201; 803/734-4890.

SOUTH DAKOTA, Director, WIC/Nutrition Services, Department of Health, 523 E. Capitol, Pierre, SD 57501; 605/773-3737.

TENNESSEE, Director, Nutrition and Supplemental Food Programs, Department of Health and Environment, 100 9th Avenue, N, Nashville, TN 37219; 615/741-7218 or 741-0268.

TEXAS, Director, Nutrition Services, Department of Health, 1100 W. 49th Street, Austin, TX 78756; 512/458-7785.

U.S. VIRGIN ISLANDS, Nutrition Services, Department of Health, P.O. Box 7309, St. Thomas, VI 00801; 809/776-1770.

UTAH, Nutrition Coordinator, Family Health Services, Department of Health, 44 Medical Drive, Salt Lake City, UT 84113; 801/533-4084.

VERMONT, Public Health Nutrition Chief, Department of Health, 1193 North Avenue, P. O. Box 70, Burlington, VT 05402; 802/863-7606.

VIRGINIA, Public Health Nutrition Supervisor, Department of Health, James Madison Building, 6th Floor, 109 Governor Street, Richmond, VA 23219; 804/786-6776.

WASHINGTON, Nutrition Consultant, Division of Health, Department of Social and Health Services, 1112 S. Quince, MS ET-12, Olympia, WA 98504; 206/753-7254.

WEST VIRGINIA, Director, Nutrition Services, Department of Health, 1800 Washington Street, E, Charleston, WV 25305; 304/348-8870.

WISCONSIN, Public Health Nutrition Consultant, Division of Health, 718 W. Clairemont Avenue, Eau Claire, WI 54701; 715/836-3826.

WYOMING, Nutrition Services Manager, Hathaway Building, Room 456, Cheyenne, WY 82002; 307/777-7494.

Congressional Committees and Government Agencies Responsible for Nutrition Education, Labeling Activities, Food Assistance Activities, Food Safety and Quality Activities, and Nutrition Research and Monitoring Activities and Issues

Appendix E-1 Congressional Committees and Government Agencies Responsible for Nutrition Education and Labeling Activities and Issues.[*]

Education	House	Senate	Executive Branch
Nutrition Education & Training (NET)	Appropriations Committee Education & Labor Committee	Agric, Nutrition & Forestry Com. Appropriations Committee	Food & Nutrition Service, USDA Training-
Dietary Guidance for the Public (Dietary Guidelines)	Appropriations Committee Agriculture Committee Energy & Commerce Committee	Agric, Nutrition & Forestry Com. Appropriations Committee Labor & Human Resources Com.	Human Nutrition Information Service, USDA, Office of Disease Prevention & Health Promotion, DHHS
Nutrition Education Resources	Appropriations Committee Agriculture Committee	Appropriations Committee Agric, Nutrition & Forestry Com.	Food and Nutrition Information Center, Nat. Agric. Library, USDA
Expanded Food & Nutrition Education Program (EFNEP)	Agriculture Committee Appropriations Committee	Agric, Nutrition & Forestry Com. Appropriations Committee	Extension Service, USDA
Sodium Reduction Campaign	Energy & Commerce Committee	Labor & Human Resources Com.	Food & Drug Admin., DHHS
Cancer Communication Program	Appropriations Committee Energy & Commerce Committee	Appropriations Committee Labor & Human Resources Com.	National Cancer Institute, DHHS
National Cholesterol Education Project	Appropriations Committee Energy & Commerce Committee	Appropriations Committee Labor & Human Resources	National Heart, Lung, and Blood Institute, DHHS
Nutrition Labeling	Energy & Commerce Committee	Labor & Human Resources Com.	Food & Drug Admin., DHHS
Meat & Poultry Labeling	Agriculture Committee	Agric, Nutrition & Forestry Com.	Marketing & Inspect. Ser, USDA
Health Claims	Energy & Commerce Committee	Labor & Human Resources Commerce, Science & Transportation Committee	Food & Drug Admin., DHHS Federal Trade Commission

[*]This chart does not represent an exhaustive list of nutrition education activities conducted by the federal government.

Appendix E-2 Congressional Committees and Government Agencies Responsible for Food Assistance Activities and Issues

Food Asssistance	House	Senate	Executive Branch
Food Stamp Program	Agriculture Committee Appropriations Committee	Agric., Nutrition & Forestry Com. Appropriations Committee	Food & Nutrition Service, USDA
National School Lunch and Breakfast Programs	Appropriations Committee Education & Labor Committee	Agric., Nutrition & Forestry Com. Appropriations Committee	Food & Nutrition Service, USDA
Women, Infants & Children Supplemental Food Program (WIC)	Appropriations Committee Education & Labor Committee	Appropriations Committee Agric., Nutrition & Forestry Com.	Food & Nutrition Service, USDA
Other Child Nutrition Programs	Appropriations Committee Education & Labor Committee	Agric., Nutrition & Forestry Com. Appropriations Committee	Food & Nutrition Service, USDA
Temporary Emergency Food Assistance Program (TEFAP)	Agriculture Committee Appropriations Committee	Agric., Nutrition & Forestry Com. Appropriations Committee	Food & Nutrition Service, USDA
Elderly Feeding Program	Appropriations Committee Education & Labor Committee	Appropriations Committee Labor & Human Resources Com.	Administration on Aging, DHHS

Appendix E-3 Congressional Committees and Government Agencies Responsible for Food Safety and Quality Activities and Issues. [*]

Food Safety & Quality	House	Senate	Executive Branch
Meat & Poultry Safety and Inspection	Agriculture Committee Appropriations Committee	Agric., Nutrition & Forestry Com. Appropriations Committee	Food Safety & Inspection Service, USDA
Food Safety	Agriculture Committee Appropriations Committee Energy & Commerce Committee	Agric., Nutrition & Forestry Com. Appropriations Committee Labor & Human Resources Committee	Food Safety & Inspection Service, USDA Food & Drug Administration, DHHS Office of Pesticides, EPA
Food Fortification	Appropriations Committee Energy & Commerce Committee Science & Technology Committee	Appropriations Committee Labor & Human Resources Committee	Food & Drug Administration, DHHS

[*]This chart does not represent an exhaustive list of food safety and quality activities conducted by the federal government.

Appendix E-4 Congressional Committees and Government Agencies Responsible for Nutrition Research and Monitoring Activities and Issues.[1]

Research	House	Senate	Executive Branch
USDA Human Nutrition	Agriculture Committee Appropriations Committee Science, Space, & Technology Committee	Agriculture, Nutrition & Forestry Committee Appropriations Committee Governmental Affairs Committee	Agriculture Research Service, USDA
DHHS Diet-Related Diseases	Appropriations Committee Energy & Commerce Committee Science, Space, & Technology Committee	Appropriations Committee Governmental Affairs Committee Labor & Human Resources Committee	National Institutes of Health, DHHS
Health and Nutrition Examination Survey	Appropriations Committee Energy & Commerce Committee Science, Space, & Technology Committee	Appropriations Committee Labor & Human Resources Committee	National Center for Health Statistics, DHHS
USDA Food Consumption Surveys	Agriculture Committee Appropriations Committee Science, Space, & Technology Committee	Agric, Nutrition & Forestry Com. Appropriations Committee Governmental Affairs Committee	Human Nutrition Information Service, USDA

*This chart does not include nutrition-related research and monitoring activities conducted by the Centers for Disease Control, the Food and Drug Administration, Agency for International Development, the Department of Defense, National Science Foundation, and the Veteran's Administration.

Sources of Information on Federal Legislation and Regulations

Congressional Handbook, directory of members of Congress and Senate (annual). U.S. Chamber of Commerce, Legislative Action Department, 1615 H Street, NW, Washington, DC 20062.

Congressional Quarterly, Inc. (documents related to legislative, executive, and judicial branch activities). Congressional Quarterly, Inc., 1414 22nd Street, NW, Washington, DC 20037.

Congressional Yellow Book, comprehensive directories of Congress and federal agencies. Washington Monitor, Inc., 1301 Pennsylvania Avenue, NW, #1100, Washington, DC 20004.

Federal Register, Congressional Register, Congressional and agency reports. Superintendent of Documents, Government Printing Office, Washington, DC 20402.

House and Senate Bills—from offices of members of Congress or Senate, or from

House Document Room	Senate Document Room
H-226, U.S. Capitol	SH B-04
Washington, DC 20515	Hart Senate Office Building
	Washington, DC 20515

National Health Directory, John T. Grupenhoff, Editor, Aspen Publishers, Inc., P.O. Box 990, Frederick, MD 21701-9782.

National Journal: The Weekly on Politics and Government, The Almanac of American Politics (annual). National Journal, Inc., 1730 M Street, NW, Washington, DC 20036.

Reports of Congressional Audits of Federal Programs. General Accounting Office, Information Handling and Support Facility, Document Handling and Information Service Component, P.O. Box 6015, Gaithersburg, MD 20877.

Federal Resources and Consultants

U.S. DEPARTMENT OF HEALTH AND HUMAN SERVICES

Information Centers and Clearinghouses

Cancer Information Service, National Cancer Institute, Building 31, 9000 Rockville Pike, Bethesda, MD 20892; 800/4-CANCER (Alaska, 800/638-6070).

Centers for Disease Control, Center for Chronic Disease Prevention and Health Education, 1600 Clifton Road, NE, Atlanta, GA 30333; 404/639-3534.

Food and Drug Administration, Office of Consumer Affairs, 5600 Fishers Lane, Rockville, MD 20857; 301/443-3170. (For offices around the U.S. see Exhibit 13-2, Chapter 13).

High Blood Pressure Information Center, Information Specialist, National Institutes of Health, Bethesda, MD 20892; 301/496-1809.

National Center for Education in Maternal and Child Health, Georgetown University, 38th and R Streets, NW, Washington, DC, 20057; 202/625-8400. National Maternal and Child Health Clearinghouse; 202/625-8410.

National Clearinghouse for Alcohol Information, P.O. Box 2345, Rockville, MD 20852; 301/468-2600.

National Diabetes Information Clearinghouse, Information Specialist, Box NDIC, Bethesda, MD 20892; 301/468-2162.

National Digestive Diseases and Education Information Clearinghouse, 1255 23rd Street, NW, #275, Washington, DC 20037; 202/296-1138.

NHLBI Education Programs Information Center, 4733 Bethesda Avenue, #530, Bethesda, MD 20814-4820; 301/951-3260.

Office of Disease Prevention and Health Promotion, Health Information Clearinghouse, ODPHP/NHIC, P.O. Box 1133, Washington, DC 20013-1133; 800/336-4797; Washington, 202/429-9091; Maryland, 301/565-4167; Virginia, 703/552-2590.

Public Affairs Office, National Institute on Aging, Building 31, 9000 Rockville Pike, Bethesda, MD 20892; 301/496-1752.

Public Inquiries and Reports Branch, Technical Information Specialist, National Heart, Lung, and Blood Institute, Building 31, 9000 Rockville Pike, Bethesda, MD 20892; 301/496-4236.

Scientific and Technical Information Branch, National Center for Health Statistics, Federal Center Building, 3700 East-West Highway, Hyattsville, MD 20782; 301/436-7080.

Nutrition Consultants

Bureau of Maternal and Child Health and Resources Development, Chief Nutritionist, 301/ 443-2370; Clinical Nutrition Specialist, 301/443-5720; Nutrition Specialist, 301/443-4026; Parklawn Building, 5600 Fishers Lane, Rockville, MD 20857.

Centers for Disease Control, Division of Nutrition, Public Health Nutritionists, 1600 Clifton Road, NE, Mail Stop A42, Atlanta, GA 30333; 404/639-3075.

Federal Bureau of Prisons, Nutrition Consultant, 320 1st Street, NW, Room 1008, Washington, DC 20534; 202/724-6887.

Food and Drug Administration, Clinical Nutrition Branch, Division of Nutrition, 200 C Street, SW, Washington, DC 20204; 202/245-1561.

National Cancer Institute, Diet and Cancer Branch, Blair Building, Bethesda, MD 20892; 301/ 427-8753.

National Heart, Lung, and Blood Institute, Office of Preventive Education and Control, Nutrition Coordinator, Federal Building, Bethesda, MD 20892; 301/476-2533.

Office of Disease Prevention and Health Promotion, Nutrition Advisor, Switzer Building, Room 2132, 330 C Street, SW, Washington, DC 20201; 202/245-7611.

Regional Nutrition Consultants

Region I: (Connecticut, Maine, Massachusetts, New Hampshire, Rhode Island, Vermont) Regional Nutrition Consultant, Division of Health Resources Development, USDHHS/ PHS, JFK Federal Building, Room 1401, Boston, MA 02203; 617/565-1459.

Region II: (New Jersey, New York, Puerto Rico, Virgin Islands) Nutrition Consultants, Health Care Financing Administration, Federal Building, Room 3821, 26 Federal Plaza, New York, NY 10278; 212/264-2223.

Region III: (Delaware, Maryland, Pennsylvania, Virginia, West Virginia, District of Columbia) Regional Nutrition Consultant, Maternal and Child Health, USDHHS/PHS, Gateway Building, 4th Floor, 3535 Market Street, Philadelphia, PA 19101; 215/596-6686.

Region IV: (Alabama, Florida, Georgia, Kentucky, Mississippi, North Carolina, South Carolina, Tennessee) Regional Nutrition Consultant, USDHHS/PHS, Family Health Branch, Room 1202, 101 Marietta Towers, Atlanta, GA 30323; 404/331-5394. Nutritionists, Health Care Financing Administration, 101 Marietta Towers, Room 700, Atlanta, GA 30323; 404/ 331-2370.

Region V: (Illinois, Indiana, Michigan, Minnesota, Ohio, Wisconsin) Regional Nutrition Consultant, Maternal and Child Health, USDHHS/PHS, 300 South Wacker Drive, 34th Floor, Chicago, IL 60606; 312/353-1656. Nutrition Consultant, Health Care Financing Administration, 175 W. Jackson Street, 9th Floor, Chicago, IL 60604; 312/353-3255.

Region VI: (Arkansas, Louisiana, Texas, New Mexico, Oklahoma) Regional Nutrition Consultant, Division of Health Services Delivery, USDHHS/PHS, 1200 Main Tower Building, Room 1850, Dallas, TX 75202; 214/767-3072. Nutrition Consultants, Health Care Financing Administration, 1200 Main Tower Building, 19th Floor, Dallas, TX 75202; 214/ 767-6301.

Region VII: (Iowa, Kansas, Missouri, Nebraska) Regional Nutrition Consultant, USDHHS/ PHS, 601 East 12th Street, 5th Floor West, Kansas City, MO 64106; 816/426-2924.

Region VIII: (Colorado, Montana, North Dakota, South Dakota, Utah, Wyoming) Regional Nutrition Consultant, Maternal and Child Health, USDHHS/PHS, Federal Building, Room

1194, 1961 Stout Street, Denver, CO 80294; 303/844-5955. Nutrition Consultants, Health Care Financing Administration, Federal Building, 1961 Stout Street, Denver, CO 80294; 303/844-4726.

Region IX: (American Samoa, Arizona, California, Guam, Hawaii, Nevada, Trust Territory of Pacific Islands) Regional Nutrition Consultant, Child and Family Health, USDHHS/PHS, 50 United Nations Plaza, Room 347, San Francisco, CA 94102; 415/556-8623. Nutrition Consultant, Health Care Financing Administration, 100 VanNess Avenue, San Francisco, CA 94103.

Region X: (Alaska, Idaho, Oregon, Washington) Regional Nutrition Consultant, Clinical Services Branch, USDHHS/PHS, 2201 6th Avenue, Mail Stop RX27, Seattle, WA 98121; 206/442-0215. Nutrition Consultant, Health Care Financing Administration, Mail Stop 409, Third and Broad Building, 2901 Third Avenue, Seattle, WA 98121; 206/442-7222.

Indian Health Service

Nutrition and Dietetics

Chief, Nutrition and Dietetics Section, Indian Health Service, Parklawn Building, Mail Delivery Station 6A-38, 5600 Fishers Lane, Rockville, MD 20857; 301/443-1114.

Chief, Nutrition and Dietetics Training Program, P.O. Box 5558, Santa Fe, NM 87502-5558; 505/988-6470, 505/988-6518.

Nutrition Specialist, Indian Health Service, Diabetes Program, 2401 12th Street NW, Room 211, North Albuquerque, NM 87102; 505/766-3980.

Chief, Nutrition and Dietetics Branch, ABERDEEN AREA Indian Health Service, Federal Building, 115 4th Avenue SE, Aberdeen, SD 57401; 605/226-7456.

Chief, Area Dietetics Section; Chief, Area Nutrition Section, ALASKA AREA Native Health Service, 250 Gambell Street, Anchorage, AK 99501; 907/257-1315, 907/257-1316.

Dietetics Officer, Public Health Nutrition Officer, ALBUQUERQUE AREA Indian Health Service, 505 Marquette NW, #1502, Albuquerque, NM 87102-0097; 505/766-2162.

Chief, Nutrition and Dietetics Branch, BEMIDJI AREA Indian Health Service, 203 Federal Building, Bemidji, MN 56601-3060; 218/751-7701.

Area Nutrition and Dietetics Consultant, BILLINGS AREA Indian Health Service, P.O. Box 2143, Billings, MT 59103; 406/657-6177.

Nutrition Program Liaison, CALIFORNIA AREA Indian Health Service, 29999 Fulton Avenue, Sacramento, CA 95821; 916/978-4191.

Director, Nutrition Services, NASHVILLE AREA Indian Health Services, 1101 Kermit Drive, #810, Nashville, TN 37219-2191; 615/736-5104.

Chief, Nutrition and Dietetics Branch, NAVAJO AREA Indian Health Service, P.O. Box G, Window Rock, AZ 86515; 602/871-5867.

Chief, Area Dietetics Branch, Chief, Area Nutrition Branch, OKLAHOMA CITY AREA Indian Health Service, 215 Dean M. McGee Street NW, Oklahoma City, OK 73102-3477; 405/231-5181.

Chief, Nutrition and Dietetics Branch, PHOENIX AREA Indian Health Service, 3738 N 16th Street, Suite A, Phoenix, AZ 85016-5981; 602/241-2173.

Chief, Nutrition and Dietetics Branch, PORTLAND AREA Indian Health Service, Federal Building, Room 476, 1220 SW Third Avenue, Portland, OR 97204; 503/221-2027.

U.S. DEPARTMENT OF AGRICULTURE

Information Centers and Services

Extension Service, National Program Leader, Department of Agriculture, Room 3443, Washington, DC 20250; 202/447-2908.

Food and Nutrition Service, Public Information Service, Park Office Center, 3101 Park Center Drive, Alexandria, VA 22302; 703/756-3276.

Food Safety and Inspection Service, Information Specialist, Office of Public Awareness, Department of Agriculture, Room 1163-S, Washington, DC 20250; 202/472-4485; Meat and Poultry Hotline, 800/535-4555 (10:00 A.M. to 4:00 P.M., E.S.T.).

Human Nutrition Information Service, Public Affairs Staff, 6505 Belcrest Road, Hyattsville, MD 20782; 301/436-8617; Office of Administrator, 301/436-7725.

National Agricultural Library, Food and Nutrition Information Center, Food Irradiation Information Center, Family Information Center, 10301 Baltimore Boulevard, Beltsville, MD 20705; 301/344-3719. Offer Pathfinders (short bibliographies in selected food and nutrition topics for three user levels: consumer, educator, or professional). Topics currently available include

- Anorexia Nervosa and Bulimia
- Children's Literature on Food and Nutrition
- Common Sense Nutrition
- Diet and Cancer
- Diet and Dental Health
- Diet and Hypertension
- Dietary Fat and Heart Disease
- Fad Weight Loss Diets
- Food Allergy, Sensitivity, Intolerance
- Food Composition
- Food Irradiation
- Food Safety
- Irradiated Fruits
- Nutrition and Alcohol
- Nutrition and Cardiovascular Disease
- Nutrition and Diabetes
- Nutrition and the Elderly
- Nutrition and Pregnancy
- Nutrition and the Handicapped
- Nutrition during Adolescence
- Nutrition, Fitness, and Well-being
- Nutrition for Infants/Toddlers
- Nutrition, Learning, and Behavior
- Osteoporosis
- Safety and Wholesomeness of Irradiated Foods

- Sports Nutrition
- Teenage Pregnancy and Nutrition
- Vegetarianism
- Vitamin/Mineral Supplements
- Weight Control

Quick Bibliography Series

Adult Nutrition Education Materials, 1/82 to 10/88, 149 citations, March 1989.

Audiovisuals in Personnel Supervision 1970-1986, 186 citations, January 1988.

Diet, Race, and Ethnicity in the U.S.: Research and Reference Materials, 1979-1987, 178 citations, February 1988.

Food Irradiation Overview, 1989, 119 citations.

Food Safety and Sanitation Audiovisuals, 1979-1988, 63 citations.

Infant Nutrition: Research and Reference Materials, 1984-1987, 182 citations, February 1988.

Iron and Human Nutrition: Research and Reference Materials, 1983-1987, 138 citations, February 1988.

Maternal and Infant Nutrition Education Materials, 1981-1988, 152 citations.

Nutrition Education Materials: Grades Preschool through 6, 1979-March 1987, 306 citations, May 1987.

Nutrition Education Materials: Grades 7 through 12, 1979-March 1987, 223 citations, May 1987.

Personnel Supervision (Books), 1979-1986, 231 citations, January 1988.

Special Reference Briefs

Childhood Antecedents to Adult Coronary Artery Disease, 56 citations, April 1988, Myron Winick, MD.

Childhood Obesity, 83 citations, April 1988, Myron Winick, MD.

Food and Nutrition Services Consultants

Nutritional and Technical Services Division, Food and Nutrition Service, 3101 Park Center Drive, Room 607, Alexandria, VA 22302; 703/756-3554.

Regional Offices

Northeast Region (Connecticut, Maine, Massachusetts, New Hampshire, New York, Rhode Island, Vermont), Regional Nutrition Coordinator, FNS/USDA, 10 Causeway Street, Boston, MA 02222; 617/565-6370.

Mid-Atlantic Region (Delaware, District of Columbia, Maryland, New Jersey, Pennsylvania, Puerto Rico, Virginia), Regional WIC Nutritionist, FNS/USDA, Mercer Corporate Park, Corporate Boulevard, Trenton, NJ 08691; 609/259-5025.

Southeast Region (Alabama, Florida, Georgia, Kentucky, Mississippi, North Carolina, South Carolina, Tennessee), Regional WIC Nutritionist, FNS/USDA, 1100 Spring Street, NW, Atlanta, GA 30367; 404/347-4131.

Midwest Region (Illinois, Indiana, Michigan, Minnesota, Ohio, Wisconsin), Regional WIC Nutritionist, FNS/USDA, 50 East Washington Street, Chicago, IL 60602; 312/353-6664.

Southwest Region (Arkansas, Louisiana, New Mexico, Oklahoma, Texas), Regional WIC Nutritionist, FNS/USDA, 1100 Commerce Street, Dallas, TX 75242; 214/767-0222.

Mountain Plains Region (Colorado, Iowa, Kansas, Missouri, Montana, Nebraska, North Dakota, South Dakota, Utah, Wyoming), Regional Nutrition Coordinator, Program Specialist, Nutrition Liaison, FNS/USDA, 1224 Speer Boulevard, #903, Denver, CO 80204; 303/844-0300.

Western Region (Alaska, Arizona, California, Guam, Hawaii, Idaho, Nevada, Oregon, Washington), Regional WIC Nutritionist, FNS/USDA, 550 Kearney Street, Room 400, San Francisco, CA 94108; 415/705-1310.

appendix *H*

Sources for National Data

SURVEILLANCE SYSTEMS—CENTERS FOR DISEASE CONTROL

Pediatric and Pregnancy Surveillance Systems

Division of Nutrition, Center for Chronic Disease Prevention and Health Promotion, Centers for Disease Control, Mail Stop A-42, 1600 Clifton Road, NE, Atlanta, GA 30333; 404/639-3075.

Behavioral Risk Factor Surveillance Systems

Office of Surveillance and Analysis, Center for Chronic Disease Prevention and Health Promotion, Centers for Disease Control, Mail Stop A-42, 1600 Clifton Road, NE, Atlanta, GA 30333; 404/639-1557.

HEALTH AND NUTRITION EXAMINATION SURVEYS— NHANES AND HHANES AND NATIONAL HEALTH INTERVIEW SURVEY

Scientific and Technical Information Branch, National Center for Health Statistics, 3700 East-West Highway, Hyattsville, MD 20782; 301/436-8500.

FOOD CONSUMPTION DATA

National Food Consumption Survey and Continuing Survey of Intake of Individuals

Human Nutrition Information Service, Room 365, Federal Building, Hyattsville, MD 20782; 301/436-7725.

INCOME DATA

Consumer Expenditure Survey

Division of Consumer Expenditure Survey, Bureau of Labor Statistics, 600 E Street, NW, Room 4216, Washington, DC 20212; 202/272-5156.

Survey of Income and Program Participation, Room 2025, FOB 3, Office of Director, Census Bureau, Washington, DC 20233; 301/763-5784.

DIETARY METHODOLOGY

Food Frequency Questionnaire

National Institutes of Health, National Cancer Institute, Division of Cancer Prevention and Control, Executive Plaza North, Room 313, 9000 Rockville Pike, Bethesda, MD 20892; 301/496-8500.

PUBLIC HEALTH PROGRAM AND EXPENDITURE DATA

Public Health Foundation, 1220 L Street, NW, Suite 350, Washington, DC 20005; 202/

appendix *I*

Prospecting for Grants

Maintaining open communication with colleagues in state and federal agencies and the regional offices will provide clues to potential funding sources for contracts, Requests for Proposals (RFPs), and grants. Federal regional and central offices are listed in Appendix G.

The Foundation Center maintains libraries in each of the states, Puerto Rico, and the Virgin Islands. Call 800/424-9836 to locate their most convenient library. Main offices of the Foundation Center are 79 Fifth Avenue, New York, NY 10003; 212/620-4230; 1001 Connecticut Avenue, NW, Washington, DC 20036; 202/331-1400; 1422 Euclid Avenue, Cleveland, OH 44115; 216/861-1933; and 312 Sutter Street, San Francisco, CA 94108, 415/397-0902.

The following major references on grant sources are available in public or university libraries:

Catalog of Federal Domestic Assistance, Washington, DC, U.S. Government Printing Office, 20402; 202/783-3238. Complete current listing of federal agency grants and contracts.

Directory of Biomedical and Health Care Grants, 3rd ed., Phoenix, AZ, Oryx Press, 1988, 602/ 254-6156. Concise information on grant programs of foundations, corporations, government agencies.

Federal Register, Washington, DC, U.S. Government Printing Office, 202/783-3238. Published daily. Announces available federal grants and contracts as they become available.

Foundation Directory, 12th ed., New York, Foundation Center, 800/424- 9836. Lists major foundations with their interest areas, application procedures and dates, addresses, and contact persons.

Foundation Fundamentals: A Guide for Grant Seekers, 3rd ed., New York, The Foundation Center, 1986, 800/424-9836. Step-by-step manual for identifying appropriate foundations related to state or local projects.

Health Grants and Contracts Weekly, Alexandria, VA, Capital Publications, 703/683-4100. Newsletter lists federal grants, RFPs, and RFAs.

Locating Funds for Health Promotion Projects, Office of Disease Prevention and Health Promotion, Washington, DC, U.S. Department of Health and Human Services, 1988; 800/ 336-4797.

522

Schools of Public Health and Graduate Public Health Programs Accredited for 1989 by the Council on Education for Public Health (CEPH)

University of Alabama at Birmingham, School of Public Health, University Station, Birmingham, AL 35294.

Boston University, School of Public Health, School of Medicine, 80 East Concord Street, Boston, MA 02118-2394.

University of California at Berkeley, School of Public Health, 19 Earl Warren Hall, Berkeley, CA 94720.

University of California at Los Angeles, School of Public Health, Center for Health Sciences, Los Angeles, CA 90024.

Columbia University, School of Public Health, 600 West 168th Street, New York, NY 10032.

Harvard University, School of Public Health, 677 Huntington Avenue, Boston, MA 02115.

University of Hawaii, School of Public Health, 1960 East West Road, Honolulu, HI 96822.

University of Illinois at Chicago, School of Public Health, Health Sciences Center, P.O. Box 6998, Chicago, IL 60680.

The Johns Hopkins University, School of Hygiene and Public Health, 615 North Wolfe Street, Baltimore, MD 21205-2179.

Loma Linda University, School of Public Health, Loma Linda, CA 92350.

University of Massachusetts, Division of Public Health, School of Health Sciences, 108 Arnold House, Amherst, MA 01003-0037.

University of Michigan, School of Public Health, 109 South Observatory Street, Ann Arbor, MI 48109-2029.

University of Minnesota, School of Public Health, 1360 Mayo Memorial Building, 420 Delaware Street SE, Minneapolis, MN 55455-0318.

University of North Carolina, School of Public Health, CB 7400, Rosenau Hall, Chapel Hill, NC 27599-7400.

University of Oklahoma, College of Public Health, Health Sciences Center, P.O. Box 26901, Oklahoma City, OK 73190.

University of Pittsburgh, Graduate School of Public Health, 111 Parran Hall, Pittsburgh, PA 15261.

University of Puerto Rico, School of Public Health, Medical Sciences Campus, G.P.O. Box 5067, San Juan, Puerto Rico 00936.

San Diego State University, Graduate School of Public Health, College of Human Services, San Diego, CA 92182-0405.

University of South Carolina, School of Public Health, College of Health, Columbia, SC 29208.

University of South Florida, College of Public Health, MHH-104, 13301 Bruce B. Downs Boulevard, Tampa FL 33612-3899.

University of Texas, School of Public Health, Health Science Center at Houston, P.O. Box 20186, Houston, TX 77025.

Tulane University, School of Public Health and Tropical Medicine, 1430 Tulane Avenue, New Orleans, LA 70112.

University of Washington, School of Public Health and Community Medicine, F356d Health Sciences Building, Mail Drop SC-30, Seattle, WA 98195.

Yale University, Department of Epidemiology and Public Health, School of Medicine, P.O. Box 3333, 60 College Street, New Haven, CT 06510.

appendix **K**

Graduate Programs in Public Health Nutrition

The following programs meet the criteria of the Association of Faculties of Graduate Programs in Public Health Nutrition.

Case Western Reserve University, Department of Nutrition, 2121 Abington Road, Room 318A, Cleveland, OH 44106; 215/368-2440.

Cornell University, Division of Nutritional Sciences, Savage Hall, Ithaca, NY 14853; 607/256-5436.

Eastern Kentucky University, Community Nutrition Program, Department of Home Economics, Richmond, KY 40475; 606/622-1175.

Loma Linda University, Department of Nutrition, School of Public Health, Loma Linda, CA 92354; 714/796-9402.

New York Medical College, Nutrition Program, Department of Community and Preventive Medicine, Munger Pavillion, Valhalla, NY 10595; 914/993-4257.

Pennsylvania State University, Nutrition in Public Health, College of Human Development, 216 Henderson Human Development Building, University Park, PA 16802; 814/863-0772.

Southern Illinois University, Food and Nutrition, Department of Animal Science, School of Agriculture, Carbondale, IL 62901; 618/453-5193.

Teachers College, Columbia University, Department of Nutrition Education, Box 137, New York, NY 10027; 212/678-3951.

Tulane University, Nutrition Program, School of Public Health and Tropical Medicine, 1430 Tulane Avenue, New Orleans, LA 70112; 504/588-5371.

University of California at Berkeley, Program of Public Health Nutrition, School of Public Health, Earl Warren Hall, Berkeley, CA 94720; 415/642-4216.

University of California at Los Angeles, Environmental Sciences Division, School of Public Health, Center for Health Sciences, Los Angeles, CA 90024; 213/825-5157.

University of Hawaii, Public Health Nutrition Program, Department of Public Health Sciences, School of Public Health, 1960 East West Road, D104F, Honolulu, HI 96822; 808/948-8491.

University of Michigan, Program in Public Health Nutrition, School of Public Health, 1420 Washington Heights, Ann Arbor, MI 48109; 313/764-5425.

University of Minnesota, Public Health Nutrition, School of Public Health, Box 197 Mayo,

D355 Mayo Memorial Building, 420 Delaware Street, SE, Minneapolis, MN 55455; 612/625-4100.

University of North Carolina, Department of Nutrition, School of Public Health, McGavran-Greenberg Building, C.B. Box 7400, Chapel Hill, NC 27599-7400, 919/966-7215.

University of Puerto Rico, Public Health Nutrition Section, School of Public Health, Medical Sciences Campus, GPO Box 5067, San Juan, PR 00936; 809/758-2525.

University of Tennessee, Department of Nutrition and Food Sciences, 229 Jessie Harris Building, 1215 Cumberland Avenue, Knoxville, TN 37996-1900; 615/974-6241.

University of Toronto, Department of Nutrition and Food Sciences, Faculty of Medicine, Fitzgerald Building, Toronto, Ontario, Canada M5S 1A8.

appendix *L*

Organizations for Networking for Nutrition and Health

Professional Organizations

American Academy of Family Physicians, 1740 West 92nd Street, Kansas City, MO 64114, 800/274-2237, 816/333-9700; 600 Maryland Avenue, SW, Washington, DC 20024; 202/488-7448.

American Academy of Pediatrics, 114 Northwest Point Boulevard, P.O. Box 927, Elk Grove Village, IL 60007; 312/228-5005. Office of Government Liaison, 1331 Pennsylvania Avenue, NW, Washington, DC 20004-1703; 800/336-5475; 202/662-7460.

American Association for Continuity of Care, 1101 Connecticut Avenue, #700, NW, Washington, DC 20036; 202/857-1194.

American Association of Diabetes Educators, 500 N. Michigan Avenue, #1400, Chicago, IL 60611; 312/661-1700.

American Association of Health Care Consultants, 1235 Jefferson Davis Highway, #602, Arlington, VA 22202; 703/979-3180.

American Association of Mental Deficiency, 1719 Kalorama Road, NW, Washington, DC 20009; 202/387-1968.

American Association of Occupational Health Nurses, 50 Lenox Pointe, Atlanta, GA 30324; 404/262-1162.

American Association of University Affiliated Programs, 8695 Cameron Street, #406, Silver Spring, MD 20910; 301/588-8252.

American College of Allergists and Immunologists, 800 E. Northwest Highway, #101, Mt. Prospect, IL 60056; 312/255-0380.

American College of Cardiology, 9111 Old Georgetown Road, Bethesda, MD 20814; 301/897-5400.

American College Health Association, 15879 Crabbs Branch Way, Rockville, MD 20855; 301/963-1100.

American College of Health Care Administrators, 8120 Woodmont Avenue, #200, Bethesda, MD 20814; 301/652-8384.

American College of Nurse Midwives, 1522 K Street, NW, #1120, Washington, DC 20005; 202/347-5445.

American College of Nutrition, P.O. Box 831, White Plains, NY 10602; 914/948-4848.

527

American College of Obstetricians and Gynecologists, 409 12th Street, SW, Washington, DC 20024-2188; 202/638-5577.

American College of Physicians, 4200 Pine Street, Philadelphia, PA 19104; 215/351-2400.

American College of Preventive Medicine, 1015 15th Street, NW, #903, Washington, DC 20005; 202/789-0003.

American Dental Association, 211 East Chicago Avenue, Chicago, IL 60611; 312/440-2500; 1111 14th Street, NW, Washington, DC 20005; 202/898-2400.

American Dental Hygienists Association, 444 North Michigan Avenue, #3400, Chicago, IL 60611; 312/440-8900.

American Dietetic Association, 216 West Jackson Boulevard, Chicago, IL 60606-6995; 800/877-1600, 312/899-0040; Division of Government Affairs, 1667 K Street, NW, #430, Washington, DC 20006; 202/296-3956, 800/877-0877.

American Geriatrics Society, 770 Lexington Avenue, #400, New York, NY 10021; 212/308-1414.

American Health Care Association, 1200 15th Street, NW, Washington, DC 20005; 202/842-4444.

American Home Economics Association, 1555 King Street, Alexandria, VA 22314; 703/706-4600.

American Hospital Association, 840 North Lake Shore Drive, Chicago, IL 60611; 800/621-6712; 312/280-6000; 50 F Street, NW, #100, Washington, DC 20001; 202/638-1100.

American Institute of Nutrition, 9650 Rockville Pike, Bethesda, MD 20814; 301/530-7050.

American Medical Association, 535 North Dearborn Street, Chicago, IL 60610; 312/645-4547, 312/645-4663; Washington Office, 1101 Vermont Avenue, NW, Washington, DC 20036; 202/789-7400.

American Medical Association Auxiliary, 535 N. Dearborn Street, Chicago, Il 60610; 312/645-4470.

American Nurses' Association, 2420 Pershing Road, Kansas City, MO 64108; 816/474-5720; 1101 14th Street, NW, Washington, DC 20036; 202/789-1800.

American Occupational Therapy Association, 1383 Piccard Drive, #301, Rockville, MD 20850; 301/948-9626.

American Osteopathic Association, 212 E. Ohio Street, Chicago, IL 60611; 800/621-1773, 312/280-5800.

American Pharmaceutical Association, 2215 Constitution Avenue, NW, Washington, DC 20037; 202/628-4410.

American Physical Therapy Association, 1111 North Fairfax Street, Alexandria, VA 22314; 703/684-2782.

American Psychological Association, 1200 17th Street, NW, Washington, DC 20036; 202/955-7618.

American Public Health Association, 1015 15th Street, NW, Washington, DC 20005; 202/789-5600.

American School Food Service Association, 1600 Duke Street, 7th Floor, Alexandria, VA 22314; 703/739-3900; 800/877-8822.

American School Health Association, P.O. Box 708, 1521 S. Water Street, Kent, OH 44240; 216/678-1601.

American Society for Allied Health Professionals, 1101 Connecticut Avenue, NW, Washington, DC 20036; 202/857-1100.

American Society for Clinical Nutrition, 9650 Rockville Pike, Bethesda, MD 20814; 301/530-7110.

American Society for Parenteral and Enteral Nutrition, 8605 Cameron Street, Suite 500, Silver Spring, MD 20910; 301/587-6315.

American Society of Internal Medicine, 1101 Vermont Avenue, NW, #500, Washington, DC 20005; 202/289-1700.

Association of Maternal and Child Health Programs, 2001 L Street, NW, #300, Washington, DC 20036; 202/466-8960.

Association of Schools of Public Health, 1015 15th Street, NW, Washington, DC 20005; 202/842-4668.

Association of State and Territorial Health Officials, Association of State and Territorial Public Health Nutrition Directors, 6728 Old McLean Village Drive, McLean, VA 22101; 703/556-9222.

Institute of Food Technologists, 221 N. LaSalle Street, Chicago, IL 60601; 312/782-8424.

International Association of Milk, Food and Environmental Sanitarians, P.O. Box 701, Ames, IA 50010; 515/232-6699.

NAACOG: The Organization for Obstetric, Gynecologic and Neonatal Nurses, 409 12th Street, SW, Washington, DC 20024-2191; 800/533-8822, 202/638-0026.

National Academy of Sciences, Institute of Medicine, 2101 Constitution Avenue, NW, Washington, DC 20418; 202/334-2357.

National Association of County Health Officials, 440 First Street, NW, Washington, DC 20001; 202/783-5550.

National Association of Pediatric Nurse Associates and Practitioners, 1101 Kings Highway, #206, Cherry Hill, NJ 08034; 609/667-1773.

National Association of School Nurses, Inc., Lamplighter Lane, P.O. Box 1300, Scarborough, ME 04074; 207/883-2117.

National Association of Social Workers, 7981 Eastern Avenue, Silver Spring, MD 20910; 301/565-0333.

National Association of WIC Directors, 1516 W. Mount Royal Avenue, Baltimore, MD 21217; 301/383-2766.

National Education Association, 1201 16th Street, NW, Washington, DC 20036; 202/822-7200.

National League for Nursing, 10 Columbus Circle, New York, NY 10019; 212/582-1022.

National Medical Association, 1012 10th Street, NW, Washington, DC 20001; 202/347-1895.

Public Health Foundation, 1220 L Street, NW, #350, Washington, DC 20005; 202/898-5600.

Society for Adolescent Medicine, 10727 White Oak Avenue, #101, Granada Hills, CA 91344; 818/368-5996.

Society for Public Health Education, Inc., 2001 Addison Street, #220, Berkeley, CA 94704, 415/644-9242.

Society for Nutrition Education, 1700 Broadway, Suite 300, Oakland, CA 94612; 415/444-7133.

United States Conference of Local Health Officers, 620 Eye Street, NW Washington, DC 20006; 202/293-7330.

Voluntary Health and Education Associations

Alan Guttmacher Institute, 2010 Massachusetts Avenue, NW, Washington, DC 20036; 202/296-4012.

American Anorexia/Bulimia Association, Inc., 133 Cedar Lane, Teaneck, NJ 07666; 201/836-1800.

American Association for Maternal and Child Health, 233 Prospect, P-204, La Jolla, CA 92037; 619/459-9308.

American Association on Mental Retardation, 1719 Kalorama Road, NW, Washington, DC 20009-2684; 800/424-3688, 202/387-1968.

American Cancer Society, 3340 Peachtree Road, NE, Atlanta, GA 30026; 404/320-3333; Government Relations, 224 E. Capitol Street, NE, Washington, DC 20002; 202/546-4011.

American Council on Science and Health, 1995 Broadway, 18th Floor, New York, NY 10023; 212/362-7044.

American Diabetes Association, 1660 Duke Street, Alexandria, VA 22314; 800/ADA-DISC, 703/549-1500.

American Digestive Diseases Society, 7720 Wisconsin Avenue, Bethesda, MD 20814; 301/652-9293.

American Health Foundation, 320 E. 43rd Street, New York, NY 10017; 212/953-1900.

American Heart Association National Center, 7320 Greenville Avenue, Dallas, TX 75231; 214/373-6300; Office of Public Affairs, 1250 Connecticut Avenue, NW, Washington, DC 20036; 202/822-9380.

American Industrial Health Council, 1330 Connecticut Avenue, NW, Washington, DC 20036; 202/659-0060.

American Liver Foundation, 998 Pompton Avenue, Cedar Grove, NJ 07009; 201/857-2626.

American Lung Association, 1740 Broadway, New York, NY 10019-4374; 212/315-8700.

Arthritis Foundation, American Juvenile Arthritis Organization, 1314 Spring Street, NW, Atlanta, GA 30309; 404/872-7100.

Association for the Advancement of Health Education, 1900 Association Drive, Reston, VA 22091; 703/476-3440.

Association for the Care of Children's Health, 3615 Wisconsin Avenue, NW, Washington, DC 20016; 202/244-1801.

Association for Retarded Citizens, 10801 Rockville Pike, Rockville, MD 20852; 301/897-5700.

Asthma and Allergy Foundation of America, 1717 Massachusetts Avenue, NW, #305, Washington, DC 20036; 202/265-0265.

Cystic Fibrosis Foundation, 6931 Arlington Road, Bethesda, MD 20814; 800/FIGHTCF, 301/951-4422.

Future Homemakers of America, 1910 Association Drive, Reston VA 22091; 703/476-4900.

International Life Sciences Institute, Nutrition Foundation, 1126 16th Street, NW, #300, Washington, DC 20036; 202/659-0074.

Juvenile Diabetes Foundation International, 432 Park Avenue South, 16th Floor, New York, NY 10016; 212/889-7575.

La Leche League International, Inc., 9816 Minneapolis Avenue, P.O. Box 1209, Franklin Park, IL 60131; 312/455-7730.

March of Dimes Birth Defects Foundation, 1275 Mamaroneck Avenue, White Plains, NY 10605; 914/428-7100; 1725 K Street, NW, #814, Washington, DC 20006; 202/659-1800.

Maternity Center Association, 48 East 92nd Street, New York, NY 10128; 212/369-7300.

National Association for Home Care, 519 C Street, NE, Stanton Park, Washington, DC 20002; 202/547-7424.

National Association for Public Health Policy, 208 Meadowood Drive, South Burlington, VT 05403; 802/658-0136.

National Association for the Education of Young Children, 1834 Connecticut Avenue, NW, Washington, DC 20009; 800/424-2460, 202/232-8777.

National Association of Community Health Centers, 1330 New Hampshire Avenue, NW, #122, Washington, DC 20036; 202/659-8008.

National Association of Developmental Disabilities Councils, 1234 Massachusetts Avenue, NW, #103, Washington, DC 20005; 202/347-1234.

National Center for Clinical Infant Programs, 733 15th Street, NW, #912, Washington, DC 20005; 202/347-0308.

National Center for Health Education, 30 East 29th Street, New York, NY 10016; 212/689-1886.

National Congress of Parents and Teachers, 700 North Rush Street, Chicago, IL 60611; 312/787-0977.

National Council on Patient Information and Education, 666 11th Street, NW, #810, Washington, DC 20001; 202/347-6711.

National Council on the Aging, 600 Maryland Avenue, SW, Washington, DC 20024; 202/479-1200.

National Easter Seal Society, 2023 West Ogden Avenue, Chicago, IL 60612; 312/243-8400; 1350 New York Avenue, NW, Washington, DC 20005; 202/347-3066.

National Headstart Association, 1220 King Street, #200, Alexandria, VA 22314, 703/739-0875.

National Health Council, 622 Third Avenue, 34th Floor, New York, NY 10017; 800/622-9010, 212/972-2700.

National Kidney Foundation, 2 Park Avenue, #908, New York, NY 10016; 212/889-2210.

National Maternal and Child Health Resource Center, College of Law Building, The University of Iowa, Iowa City, IA 52242; 319/355-9067.

National Migrant Referral Project, Inc., 2512 South, IH-35, #220, Austin, TX 78704; 512/447-0770.

National Perinatal Association, 101-1/2 Union Street, Alexandria, VA 22314-3323; 703/549-5523.

National Rehabilitation Association, 633 South Washington Street, Alexandria, VA 22313; 703/836-0850.

National Rural Health Care Association, 301 East Armour Boulevard, #420, Kansas City, MO 64111; 816/756-3140.

National Sanitation Foundation, P.O. Box 1468, 3475 Plymouth Road, Ann Arbor, MI 48106; 313/769-8010.

National Wellness Association, University of Wisconsin-Stevens Point, South Hall, Stevens Point, WI, 54481; 715/346-2172.

Planned Parenthood Federation of America, 810 Seventh Avenue, New York, NY 10019; 212/541-7800.

Public Policy/Public Interest Organizations

Action for Children's Television, 20 University Road, Cambridge, MA 02138; 617/876-6620.

American Association of Retired Persons, 1909 K Street, NW, Washington, DC 20049; 202/872-4700.

Association of Junior Leagues, 825 Third Avenue, New York, NY 10022; 212/355-4380.

Bread for the World, 802 Rhode Island Avenue, NE, Washington, DC 20018; 202/269-0200.

Center for Science in the Public Interest, 1501 16th Street, NW, Washington, DC 20036; 202/332-9110.

Center on Budget and Policy Priorities, 236 Massachusetts Avenue, NE, Suite 305, Washington, DC 20002; 202/544-0591.

Children's Defense Fund, 122 C Street, NW, #400, Washington, DC 20001; 202/628-8787.

Children's Foundation, 815 15th Street, NW, Washington, DC 20005; 202/347-3300.

Child Welfare League of America, 440 First Street, NW, #310, Washington, DC 20001; 202/638-2952.

Community Nutrition Institute, 2001 S Street, NW, Washington, DC 20009; 202/462-4700.

Congressional Caucus for Women's Issues, 2471 Rayburn Building, Washington, DC 20515; 202/225-6740.

Food Research and Action Center, 1319 F Street, NW, Suite 500, Washington, DC 20004; 202/393-5060.

Healthy Mothers, Healthy Babies Coalition, 409 12th Street, SW, 3rd Floor, Washington, DC 20024-2188; 202/863-2458.

National Association for Family Day Care, P.O. Box 71268, Murray, UT 84107; 801/268-9148.

National Black Women's Health Project, 1237 Gorden Street, NW, Atlanta, GA 30310; 404/753-0916.

National Center for Food and Agricultural Policy, Resources for the Future, 1616 P Street, NW, Washington, DC; 202/328-5082.

National Child Nutrition Project, 1501 Cherry Street, Philadelphia, PA 19102; 215/662-1024.

National Citizens' Coalition for Nursing Home Reform, 1424 16th Street, Suite L2, Washington, DC 20036; 202/797-0657.

National Coalition of Hispanic Health and Human Services Organizations (COSSMO), 1030 15th Street, NW, Washington, DC 20005; 202/327-2100.

National Commission to Prevent Infant Mortality, 330 C Street, SW, #20006, Washington, DC 20201; 202/472-1364.

National Conference of State Legislatures, 1050 17th Street, #2100, Denver, CO 80265; 303/623-7800.

National Governors' Association, 444 North Capital Street, #250, Washington, DC 20001; 202/624-5300.

National Organization, Adolescent Pregnancy and Parenting, P.O. Box 2365, Reston, VA 22090; 703/435-3948.

National Resource Center for Children in Poverty, 154 Haven Avenue, 3rd Floor, New York, NY 10032; 212/927-8793.

National Urban League, 500 East 62nd Street, New York, NY 10021; 212/310-9000.

National Women's Health Network, 1325 G Street, NW, Lower Level, Washington, DC 20005; 202/347-1140.

Public Voice for Food and Health Policy, 1001 Connecticut Avenue, NW, Suite 522, Washington, DC 20036; 202/659-5930.

Southern Governors' Association, Hall of States #240, 444 N. Capitol Street, NW, Washington, DC 20001; 202/624-5897.

The Urban Institute, 2100 M Street, NW, Washington, DC 20037; 202/833-7200.

Food/Commodity/Industry/Trade Organizations

American Meat Institute, 1700 N. Moore Street, Arlington, VA 22209; 703/841-2400.

Food and Drug Law Institute, 1000 Vermont Avenue, NW, Washington, DC 20005; 202/371-1420.

Food Marketing Institute, 1750 K Street, NW, Washington, DC 20006; 202/452-8444.

Grocery Manufacturers of America, 1010 Wisconsin Avenue, Washington, DC 20007; 202/337-9400.

National Cattlemen's Association, 1301 Pennsylvania Avenue, NW, Suite 111, Washington, DC 20004; 202/347-0228.

National Dairy Council, 6300 N. River Road, Rosemont, IL 60018-4233; 312/696-1020.

National Dairy Promotion and Research Board, 2111 Wilson Boulevard, Suite 600, Arlington, VA 22201; 703/528-4800.

National Livestock and Meat Board, 444 N. Michigan Avenue, Chicago, IL 60611; 312/467-5520.

National Milk Producers Federation, 1840 Wilson Boulevard, Arlington, VA 22209; 703/243-6111.

National Restaurant Association, 1200 17th Street, NW, Washington, DC 20001; 202/331-5900.

United Fresh Fruit and Vegetable Association, 727 N. Washington Street, Alexandria, VA 22314; 703/836-3410.

appendix **M**

Nutrition and Public Health Information Resources

Consumer Information Catalog, Consumer Information Center, Pueblo, CO 81009; 202/566-1794.

Health and Safety Education Division, Metropolitan Life Insurance Company, One Madison Avenue, New York, NY 10010.

Health Promotion Program, Kaiser Family Foundation, 2400 Sand Hill Road, Menlo Park, CA 94025; 415/854-9400.

Health Promotion Resource Center, Stanford Center for Research in Disease Prevention, 1000 Welch Road, Palo Alto, CA 94304-1885; 415/723-1000.

National Resource Center on Health Promotion and Aging, AARP, 1909 K Street, NW, 5th Floor, Washington, DC 20049; 202/728-4476.

Nutrition Resources Department, The American Dietetic Association, 216 West Jackson Boulevard, Chicago, IL 60606-6995, 800/877-1600 or 312/899-0040.

Pawtucket Heart Health Program, Memorial Hospital, Prospect Street, Pawtucket, RI 02860; 401/722-6000.

Penn State Nutrition Center, Pennsylvania State University, Benedict House, University Park, PA 16802; 814/865-6323.

President's Council on Physical Fitness and Sports, #7103, 450 5th Street, NW, Washington, DC 20001; 202/272-3421.

Publications Center, WHO (World Health Organization), 49 Sheridan Avenue, Albany, NY 12210.

The Public Health Nutrition Library

The following is a selected list of books recommended by contributing authors. Readers should be guided by their needs and interests in selecting references from this list and the many other excellent references available.

I. NUTRITION SCIENCE AND DIETETIC PRACTICE

General

Bennett, Anne. *Dietitian's Desk Reference.* Englewood, CO: Tri-County Health Department, 1989.

Braunwald, Eugene, Kurt J. Isselbacher, Robert G. Petersdort, Jean D. Wilson, Joseph B. Martin, and Anthony S. Fauci, eds. *Harrison's Principles of Internal Medicine,* 11th ed. New York: McGraw-Hill, 1987.

Department of Family Medicine. *Nutrition and Health Promotion in Primary Care, 26 Modules.* Columbus, OH: The Ohio State University, 1989.

Food and Nutrition Board. *Recommended Dietary Allowances,* 10th ed. Washington, DC: National Academy of Sciences, 1989.

Guthrie, Helen A. *Introductory Nutrition.* St. Louis: Times Mirror/Mosby College Publishing, 1989.

Guyton, Arthur C. *Textbook of Medical Physiology,* 7th ed. Philadelphia: W. B. Saunders Co., 1986.

Hunt, Sara, and James L. Gross. *Human Nutrition and Metabolism.* St. Paul, MN: West Publishing Co., 1990.

Manual of Clinical Dietetics, 3d ed. Chicago: The American Dietetic Association, 1988.

Murray, Robert K., ed. *Harper's Review of Biochemistry,* 21st ed. Norwalk, CT: Appleton & Lange, 1988.

National Restaurant Association. *A Nutrition Guide for the Restaurateur.* Washington, DC: 1986.

Nutritive Value of Convenience and Processed Foods. Chicago: The American Dietetic Association, 1986.

Pennington, Jean A.T. *Bowes and Church's Food Values of Portions Commonly Used*, 15th ed. Philadelphia: J.B. Lippincott Company, 1989.

Rodwell-Williams, Sue, and Bonnie S. Worthington-Roberts. *Nutrition throughout the Life Cycle*. St. Louis: Times Mirror/Mosby College Publishing, 1988.

Roe, Daphne. *Diet and Drug Interactions*. New York: Van Nostrand Reinhold Publishers, 1989.

Roe, Daphne. *Handbook on Drug and Nutrient Interactions: A Problem Oriented Reference Guide*, 4th ed. Chicago: The American Dietetic Association, 1989.

Shils, Maurice E., and Vernon R. Young, eds. *Modern Nutrition in Health and Disease*, 7th ed. Philadelphia: Lea and Febiger, 1988.

Simko, M.D., C. Cowell, and J.A. Gilbride. *Nutrition Assessment: A Comprehensive Guide for Planning Intervention*. Rockville, MD: Aspen Publishers, Inc., 1984.

Simko, M.D., C. Cowell, and M.S. Hreha. *Practical Nutrition: A Quick Reference for the Health Care Practitioner*. Rockville, MD: Aspen Publishers, Inc., 1989.

Sports Nutrition. Chicago: The American Dietetic Association, 1986.

U.S. Department of Agriculture and U.S. Department of Health and Human Services. *Nutrition and Your Health: Dietary Guidelines for Americans*, 2nd ed. Washington, DC: U.S. Government Printing Office, 1985.

U.S. Department of Health and Human Services. *The Surgeon General's Report on Nutrition and Health*. Washington, DC: U.S. Government Printing Office, 1988.

Weinsler, Roland L., Douglas C. Heimburger, and Charles E. Butterworth, Jr. *Handbook of Clinical Nutrition*, 2d ed. St. Louis: C.V. Mosby Co., 1989.

Whitney, Eleanor Noss, Corinne Balog Cataldo, and Sharon Rady Rolfes. *Understanding Normal and Clinical Nutrition*, 2d ed. St. Paul, MN: West Publishing Co., 1987.

Williams, Sue Rodwell. *Nutrition and Diet Therapy*, 6th ed. St. Louis: Times Mirror/Mosby College Publishing, 1989.

Maternal and Child Nutrition

American Academy of Pediatrics. *Pediatric Nutrition Handbook*, 2d ed. Elk Grove Village, IL: American Academy of Pediatrics, 1985.

Bureau of Maternal and Child Health and Resources Development. *Nutrition Issues in Adolescent Health*. Rockville, MD: U.S. Department of Health and Human Services, 1988.

Institute of Medicine. *Nutrition during Pregnancy, Weight Gain and Nutrient Supplements*. Washington, DC: National Academy Press, 1990.

Kaufman, Mildred, Jonathan Kotch, William N.P. Herbert, Barbara B. Rumer, Carolyn Sharbaugh, and Cynthia France. *Maternal Nutrition: Contemporary Approaches to Interdisciplinary Care*. White Plains, NY: March of Dimes Birth Defects Foundation, 1988, 10 modules.

Mahan, L. Kathleen, and Jane M. Rees. *Nutrition in Adolescence*. St. Louis: Times Mirror/Mosby College Publishing, 1984.

Parker, Lynn. *The Relationship between Nutrition and Learning: A School Employees' Guide to Information and Action*. Washington, DC: National Education Association, 1989.

Pipes, Peggy L. *Nutrition in Infancy and Childhood*, 4th ed. St. Louis: Times Mirror/Mosby College Publishing, 1989.

U.S. Department of Agriculture, Food and Nutrition Services. *Promoting Breastfeeding in WIC: A Compendium of Practical Approaches*. FNS-256. Washington, DC: 1988.

Worthington-Roberts, Bonnie S., and Sue Rodwell Williams. *Nutrition in Pregnancy and Lactation*, 4th ed. St Louis: Times Mirror/Mosby College Publishing, 1989.

Chronic Disease Nutrition

A Clinical Guide to Nutrition Care in End-Stage Renal Disease. Chicago: The American Dietetic Association, 1987.

Berkowitz, Sarah A., ed. *National Weight Control Resource Directory*. Oakland, CA: Society for Nutrition Education, 1988.

Committee on Diet, Nutrition, and Cancer, National Research Council. *Diet, Nutrition, and Cancer*. Washington, DC: National Academy Press, 1982.

Dietary Treatment of Hypercholesteremia: A Handbook for Counselors. Dallas, TX: American Heart Association, 1988.

Frankle, Reva T., and Mei-Uih Yang, eds. *Obesity and Weight Control*. Rockville, MD: Aspen Publishers, Inc., 1988.

Gallagher-Allred, Charlotte R. *Nutritional Care of the Terminally Ill*. Rockville, MD: Aspen Publishers, Inc., 1989.

Hermann-Zaidins, Mindy, and Reva Touger-Decker. *Nutrition Support in Home Health*. Rockville, MD: Aspen Publishers, Inc., 1989.

Home Enteral/Parenteral Nutrition Therapy. Chicago: The American Dietetic Association, 1986.

Home Tube Feeding Instruction Packet. Chicago: The American Dietetic Association, 1986.

Kris-Etherton, Penny M. *Cardiovascular Disease Prevention and Treatment*. Chicago: The American Dietetic Association, 1990.

Meal Planning Approaches in the Nutrition Management of the Person with Diabetes. Chicago: The American Dietetic Association, 1987.

National Research Council. *Diet and Health: Implications for Reducing Chronic Disease Risk*. Washington, DC: National Academy Press, 1989.

Nutrition Committee. *Dietary Guidelines for Healthy American Adults*. Dallas, TX: American Heart Association, 1988.

Powers, Margaret A., ed. *Handbook of Diabetes Nutritional Management*. Rockville, MD: Aspen Publishers, Inc., 1987.

Powers, Margaret A., ed. *Nutrition Guide for Professionals: Diabetes Education and Meal Planning*. Chicago: The American Dietetic Association, 1988.

Skipper, Anna Lynn. *Dietitian's Handbook of Enteral and Parenteral Nutrition*. Rockville, MD: Aspen Publishers, Inc., 1989.

Elderly Nutrition

Hegsted, D. Mark, William S. Cain, and Claire Murphy. *Nutrition and the Chemical Senses in Aging*. New York: New York Academy of Sciences, 1989.

McCool, A.C., and B.M. Posner. *Nutrition Services for Older Americans: Food Service Systems and Technologies*. Chicago: The American Dietetic Association, 1982.

Natow, Annette B., and JoAnn Heslin. *Nutritional Care of the Older Adult*. New York: Macmillan Publishing Co., Inc., 1986.

Roe, Daphne. *Geriatric Nutrition*, 2d ed. Englewood Cliffs, NJ: Prentice-Hall, Inc., 1987.

Schlenker, Eleanor D. *Nutrition in Aging*. St. Louis: Times Mirror/Mosby College Publishing, 1984.

Food Habits

Bryant, Carol A., et al. *The Cultural Feast—Introduction to Food and Society*. St. Paul, MN: West Publishing Company, 1985.

Food and Nutrition Board, Commission on Life Sciences, National Research Council. *What Is America Eating?* Washington, DC: National Academy Press, 1986.

Gift, Helen H., Marjorie B. Washbon, and Gail G. Harrison. *Nutrition, Behavior, and Change*. Englewood Cliffs, NJ: Prentice-Hall, 1972.

National Research Council. *Assessing Changing Food Consumption Patterns*. Washington, DC: National Academy Press, 1981.

U.S. Department of Agriculture, Food and Nutrition Service. *Nutrition Education Resource Guide for American Indians and Alaska Natives*. Washington, DC: U.S. Government Printing Office, 1988.

Cookbooks (Quantity)

The American Dietetic Association. *Dietitians' Food Favorites*. Des Plaines, IL: Cahners Publishing Co., 1985.

Arnowitz, Vivienne, and Stephanie Turner. *The Healthwise Quantity Cookbook*, Nutrition Program. Washington, DC: Center for Science and the Public Interest, 1989.

Cavaiani, Mabel, and Muriel Urbashich. *Simplified Quantity Recipes for Nursing/Convalescent Homes and Hospitals*. Washington, DC: National Restaurant Association, 1986.

McCormack, Nell J. *Creative Quantity Cooking*. Rockville, MD: Aspen Publishers, Inc., 1989.

Shugart, Grace, and Mary Molt. *Food for Fifty*, 8th ed. New York: Macmillan Publishing Co., Inc., 1989.

U.S. Department of Agriculture, Food and Nutrition Service and Technical Services Division. *Quantity Recipes for School Food Service*, Program Aid No. 1371. Washington, DC: Superintendent of Documents, U.S. Government Printing Office, 1988.

Cookbooks (Family)

Brody, Jane E. *Jane Brody's Good Food Book*. New York: W.W. Norton, 1985.

Cooking Light. Birmingham, AL: Oxmoor House, 1988.

Grundy, Scott. *American Heart Association Low Fat, Low Cholesterol Cookbook*. Dallas, TX: American Heart Association, 1989.

Roth, Harriet. *Deliciously Simple*. New York: New American Library, 1986.

Scribner, Peggy Rhodes. *Adventures in Healthful Cooking*. Stone Mountain, GA: Dogwood Press, Inc., 1985.

II. COMMUNICATIONS

The American Dietetic Association. *The Competitive Edge: Marketing Strategies for the Registered Dietitian*. Chicago: The American Dietetic Association, 1986.

Britt, Steuart H., and Norman F. Guess, eds. *The Dartnell Marketing Manager's Handbook*, 2d ed. Chicago, IL: Dartnell Press, 1983.

Chernoff, Ronni. *Communicating as Professionals*. Chicago: The American Dietetic Association, 1986.

Cuming, Pamela. *The Power Handbook*. Boston: CBI Publishing Co., 1981.

Delbecq, Andre L., Andrew H. Van de Ven, and David H. Gustafson. *Group Techniques for Program Planning: A Guide to Nominal Group and Delphi Processes*. Glenview, IL: Scott Foresman and Co., 1975.

Doak, Cecilia, Leonard G. Doak, and Jane H. Root. *Teaching Patients with Low Literacy Skills*. Philadelphia: J.B. Lippincott Co., 1985.

Dyer, William G. *Team Building: Issues and Alternatives*, 2d ed. Reading, PA: Addison-Wesley Publishing Co., 1987.

Epstein, R.S., and N. Liebman. *Biz Speak*. New York, Toronto: Franklin Watts, 1986.

Frank, Milo O. *How to Get Your Point Across in 30 Seconds or Less*. New York: Simon and Schuster, 1986.

Gehlbach, Stephen H. *Interpreting the Medical Literature: A Clinician's Guide*. Lexington, MA: The Collamore Press, 1982.

Guidelines for Providing Facts to Foodservice Patrons: Ingredient Nutrition Information. Washington, DC: National Restaurant Association, 1987.

Holli, Betsy B., and Richard J. Calabrese. *Communication and Education Skills: The Dietitian's Guide*. Philadelphia: Lea and Febiger, 1986.

Israel, Ronald C. *Operational Guidelines for Social Marketing Projects in Public Health and Nutrition*. Paris, France: United Nations Educational, Scientific and Cultural Organization, 1987.

Kugler, Eileen G., and Ellen Haas. *Reducing Dietary Fat: Strategies for State and Local Community Leaders*. Washington, DC: Public Voice for Food and Health Policy, 1989.

Manoff, Richard K. *Social Marketing: New Imperative for Public Health*. New York: Praeger Publishers, 1985.

Naisbitt, John. *Megatrends: Ten New Directions Transforming Our Lives*. New York: Warner Books, 1982.

Nutrition Service and Office of Information. *Guidelines: Writing for Adults with Limited Reading Skills*. Alexandria, VA: U.S. Department of Agriculture, 1988.

Puetz, Belinda E. *Networking for Nurses*. Rockville, MD: Aspen Publishers, Inc., 1983.

Randall, David E. *Strategies for Working with Culturally Diverse Communities and Clients*. Washington, DC: Association for the Care of Children's Health, 1989.

Reddy, Brendan W., and Kaleel Jamison. *Team Building: Blueprints for Productivity and Satisfaction*. San Diego, CA: University Associates, 1988.

Rubricht, Robert, and Dan MacDonald. *Marketing Health and Human Services*. Rockville, MD: Aspen Publishers, Inc., 1981.

Schilling, Brenda, and Elizabeth Brannon. *Cross Cultural Counseling: A Guide for Nutrition and Health Counselors*. Washington, DC: U.S. Government Printing Office, 1987.

Schindler-Rainman, Eva, Ron Lippitt, and Jack Core. *Taking Your Meeting Out of the Doldrums*. San Diego, CA: University Associates, 1975.

Snetselaar, Linda G. *Nutrition Counseling Skills: Assessment, Treatment, and Evaluation*, 2d ed. Rockville, MD: Aspen Publishers, Inc., 1988.

U.S. Department of Health and Human Services. *Churches as an Avenue to High Blood Pressure Control*. NIH Pub. No. 87-2725, 1987.

Warschaw, T.A. *Winning by Negotiation*. New York: McGraw-Hill Book Company, 1980.

Weisbord, Marvin. *Productive Workplaces: Organizing and Managing for Dignity, Meaning, and Community*. San Francisco: Jossey-Bass Inc., Pubs., 1987.

Whitener, Carole B., and Masie H. Keeling. *Nutrition Education for Young Children— Strategies and Activities*. Englewood Cliffs, NJ: Prentice-Hall, Inc., 1984.

Wileman, Ralph E. *Exercises in Visual Thinking*. New York: Hastings House Publishers, 1980.

III. PUBLIC HEALTH PRACTICE

American Public Health Association et al. *Model Standards: Guidelines for Community Attainment of the Year 2000 Objectives*. Washington, DC: American Public Health Association, 1990.

ASTHO Foundation Nutrition Services Project Committee. "Nutrition Services in State and Local Public Health Agencies Special Supplement." *Public Health Reports* 98, no. 1 (1983:9-20).

Bouchard, Carla, and Martha Bureau. *Guidelines for Nutrition Services in Local Health Jurisdictions*. San Bernadino, CA: Conference for Local Health Department Nutritionists. San Bernadino County, Department of Public Health, 1987.

Community-Oriented Primary Care: New Directions for Health Services Delivery. Washington, DC: National Academy Press, 1983.

Future Directions, Meeting on Nutrition and Chronic Disease. Atlanta, GA: Centers for Disease Control, 1989.

Institute of Medicine. *The Future of Public Health*. Washington, DC: National Academy Press, 1988.

National Research Council. *Health in an Older Society*. Washington, DC: National Academy Press, 1985.

1989 Public Health Chartbook. Washington, DC: Public Health Foundation, 1989. (Updated annually.)

Owen, Anita Yanochek, and Reva T. Frankle. *Nutrition in the Community: The Art of Delivering Services*, 2d ed. St. Louis: Times Mirror/Mosby College Publishing, 1986.

Pickett, George E., ed. *Public Health Administration and Practice*. St. Louis: Times Mirror/Mosby College Publishing, 1989.

Public Health Agencies. *An Inventory of Programs and Expenditures, 1989*. Washington, DC: Public Health Foundation, 1989. (Updated annually.)

U.S. Department of Health and Human Services. *Promoting Health/Preventing Disease. Public Health Service Implementation Plans for Attaining the Objectives for the Nation.* Washington, DC: Government Printing Office, Public Health Reports, Supplement to September-October 1983 issue.

U.S. Department of Health and Human Services. *Promoting Health/Preventing Disease: Year 2000 Objectives for the Nation.* Washington, DC: Public Health Service, 1990.

U.S. Department of Health, Education, and Welfare. *Healthy People: The Surgeon General's Report on Health Promotion and Disease Prevention.* Washington, DC: Government Printing Office, 1979.

Maternal and Child Health

American Academy of Pediatrics. *Guidelines for Health Supervision II.* Elk Grove Village, IL: American Academy of Pediatrics, 1988.

American Academy of Pediatrics and American College of Obstetricians and Gynecologists. *Guidelines for Perinatal Care,* 2d ed. Elk Grove Village, IL: American Academy of Pediatrics, 1988.

Baer, M.T. *Nutrition Services for Children with Handicaps: A Manual for State Title V Programs,* University Affiliated Training Program, Center for Child Development and Developmental Disorders. Los Angeles, CA: Children's Hospital of Los Angeles, 1982.

Cefalo, R.C., and M-K Moos. *Preconceptional Health Promotion: A Practical Guide.* Rockville, MD: Aspen Publishers, Inc., 1988.

Committee on Nutrition of the Mother and Preschool Child, Food and Nutrition Board, National Research Council. *Nutrition Services in Perinatal Care.* Washington, DC: National Academy Press, 1981.

Dwyer, J., and Mary C. Egan, eds. *The Right to Grow: Putting Nutrition Services for Children with Special Long-Term Developmental and Health Needs into Action.* Boston: Frances Stern Nutrition Center, New England Medical Center Hospital, 1986.

Egan, M., and A. Fernandez. *Title V in Review: Two Decades of Analysis of Selected Aspects of the Title V Program.* Washington, DC: Association of Maternal and Child Health Programs and National Center for Education in Maternal and Child Health, 1989.

Miller, C. Arden, Amy Fine, Sharon Adams-Taylor, and Lisbeth B. Schorr. *Monitoring Children's Health: Key Indicators.* Washington, DC: The American Public Health Association, 1986.

National Center for Education in Maternal and Child Health. *Starting Early: A Guide to Federal Resources in Maternal and Child Health,* 2d ed. Washington, DC: National Center for Education in Maternal and Child Health, 1988.

Prenatal Care: Reaching Mothers, Reaching Infants. Washington, DC: National Academy Press, 1988.

Preventing Low Birthweight. Washington, DC: National Academy Press, 1985.

Public Health Service Expert Panel on the Content of Prenatal Care. *Caring for Our Future: The Content of Prenatal Care.* Washington, DC: Department of Health and Human Services, 1989.

U.S. Department of Health and Human Services. *Healthy Mothers, Healthy Babies: A Compendium of Program Ideas for Serving Low-Income Women.* Washington, DC: U.S. Government Printing Office, 1986.

U.S. Department of Health and Human Services, Public Health Service. *Surgeon General's Report: Children with Special Health Care Needs.* DHHS Publication No. HRS/D/MC87-2. Rockville, MD: 1987.

Wallace, Helen M., George M. Ryan, and Alan C. Oglesby. *Maternal and Child Health Practices,* 3d ed. Oakland, CA: Third Party Publishing Co., 1988.

Adult Health Promotion

American Diabetes Association. *Meeting the Standards: A Manual for Completing the American Diabetes Association Application for Recognition.* Alexandria, VA: 1988.

American Dietetic Association, Society for Nutrition Education, and the Office of Disease Prevention and Health Promotion, U.S. Department of Health and Human Services. *Worksite Nutrition: A Decision-Maker's Guide.* Chicago, IL: The American Dietetic Association, 1986.

Greenwald, Peter, and Edward J. Sondik. *Cancer Control Objectives for the Nation: 1985-2000.* Bethesda, MD: National Cancer Institute, 1986.

Health Implications of Obesity. NIH Consensus Development Conference Statement 5, no. 9. Bethesda, MD: National Institutes of Health, February 1985.

National Diabetes Advisory Board. *The National Long-Range Plan to Combat Diabetes.* NIH Publication No. 87-1587. Washington, DC: U.S. Department of Health and Human Services, 1987.

National Heart, Lung, and Blood Institute. *NHLBI Kit '90: Health at a Glance in 1990. The Right Moves.* Bethesda, MD: NHLBI Kit Information Center, 1990.

National Heart, Lung, and Blood Institute. *The 1988 Report of the Joint National Committee on Detection, Evaluation and Treatment of High Blood Pressure.* Bethesda, MD: National High Blood Pressure Education Program, 1988.

National Heart, Lung, and Blood Institute. *The National Cholesterol Education Program, Report of the Expert Panel on Detection, Evaluation, and Treatment of High Blood Cholesterol in Adults,* NIH Publication No. 88-2925. Bethesda, MD: U.S. Department of Health and Human Services, 1988.

National Heart, Lung, and Blood Institute. *With Every Beat of Your Heart.* Bethesda, MD: U.S. Department of Health and Human Services, 1987.

Older Adults

A National Survey of Nutritional Risk among the Elderly. Washington, DC: Food Research and Action Center, 1987.

Improving the Quality of Care in Nursing Homes. Washington, DC: National Academy Press, 1986.

Nutrition Programs for Senior Americans: An Action Guide. Washington, DC: Food Research and Action Center, 1984.

Phillips, Harry T., and Susan A. Gaylord. *Aging and Public Health.* New York: Springer Publishing Company, 1985.

The Aging Population in the Twenty-First Century: Statistics for Health Policy. Washington, DC: National Academy Press, 1988.

Epidemiology/Biostatistics

Abramson, J.H. *Survey Methods in Community Medicine*. New York: Churchill Livingstone, 1984.

Kahn, Harold A., and Christopher T. Sempos. *Statistical Methods in Epidemiology. An Introduction to Epidemiologic Methods*. New York: Oxford University Press, 1989.

Last, John. *A Dictionary of Epidemiology*, 2d ed. New York: Oxford University Press, 1988.

Levy, Paul S., and Stanley Lemeshow. *Sampling for Health Professionals*. Belmont, CA: Lifetime Learning Publications, 1980.

Mausner, Judith S., and Shira Kramer. *Epidemiology—An Introductory Text*. Philadelphia: W.B. Saunders Co., 1985.

Remington, Richard D., and M. Anthony Schork. *Statistics with Applications to the Biological and Health Sciences*, 2d ed. Englewood Cliffs, NJ: Prentice-Hall, Inc., 1985.

Rosner, Bernard. *Fundamentals of Biostatistics*. Boston: Duxbury Press, 1982.

Schlesselman, J.J. *Case-Control Studies: Design, Conduct and Analysis*. New York: Oxford University Press, 1982.

Willett, Walter. *Nutritional Epidemiology*. New York: Oxford University Press, 1989.

Food Safety

Bacteria Associated with Foodborne Disease: A Scientific Status Summary by the Institute of Food Technologists' Expert Panel on Food Safety and Nutrition. Chicago: Institute of Food Technologists, April 1988.

Bryan, F.L. *Diseases Transmitted by Foods: A Classification and Summary*, 2d ed. Atlanta: U.S. Department of Health and Human Services, Public Health Services, Centers for Disease Control, Center for Professional Development and Training, 1984.

Doyle, Michael P. *Foodborne Bacterial Pathogens*. New York: Marcel Decker, Inc., 1989.

Food and Drug Administration. *Safety First: Protecting America's Food Supply*. Rockville, MD: Food and Drug Administration, HF-40, 5600 Fishers Lane 20857, 1988.

Gravani, R.B. *Professional Perspectives*. Division of Nutritional Sciences, Cornell University, Department of Food Science, November/December 1985 to 1986. November/December 1985 issue: *The Causes and Costs of Foodborne Disease*. 1986, no. 4 issue: *Chemical Foodborne Diseases*. 1986, no. 5 issue: *Parasitic and Viral Foodborne Diseases*.

Guthrie, Rufus K. *Food Sanitation*, 3d ed. New York: Van Nostrand Reinhold Co., 1988.

The Safe Food Book—Your Kitchen Guide. Pueblo, CO: Consumer Information Center, 1985.

IV. MANAGEMENT

General

Blanchard, K., and S. Johnson. *The One-Minute Manager*. New York: Berkeley Books, 1982.

Block, Peter. *The Empowered Manager: Positive Political Skills at Work*. San Francisco: Jossey-Bass, Inc., Publishers, 1988.

Bryson, J.M. *Strategic Planning for Public and Nonprofit Organizations: A Guide to Strengthening and Sustaining Organizational Achievement.* San Francisco: Jossey-Bass, Inc., Publishers, 1988.

Chase, Gordon, and Elizabeth Reveal. *How to Manage in the Public Sector.* New York: Random House, Inc., 1983.

Dignan, Mark B., and Patricia A. Carr. *Program Planning for Health Education and Health Promotion.* Philadelphia: Lea and Febiger, 1987.

McNeil, C., and J. Borstel. "Using Health Objectives to Make a Difference." In *Management by Objectives in Public Health.* Washington, DC: Office of Disease Prevention, Health Information Center, Department of Health and Human Services, 1988.

Program Evaluation Handbook for Health Promotion and Health Education, Nutrition Education. Los Angeles: IOX Assessment Associates, 1988.

Walker, S., and P. Choate. *Thinking Strategically: A Primer for Public Leaders.* Washington, DC: Council of State Planning Agencies, 1984.

Quality Assurance

American Dietetic Association, Council on Practice, Quality Assurance Committee. *Standards of Practice: A Practitioner's Guide to Implementation.* Chicago: The American Dietetic Association, 1986.

Kaufman, Mildred, ed. *Quality Assurance in Ambulatory Nutritional Care.* Chicago: The American Dietetic Association, 1983.

Quality Assurance Criteria Sets for Pediatric Nutrition Conditions: A Model. Chicago: The American Dietetic Association, 1988.

Financial Management

Berngren, Charles. *Introduction to Management Accounting*, 6th ed. Englewood Cliffs, NJ: Prentice-Hall, Inc., 1984.

Costs and Benefits of Nutritional Care: Phase I. Chicago: The American Dietetic Association, 1979.

Coverage and Reimbursement Policies for Nutrition Care Services. Chicago: The American Dietetic Association, 1986.

Disbrow, Doris. "The Costs and Benefits of Nutrition Services: A Literature Review." *Journal of the American Dietetic Association* 89 4 (supplement), April 1989: S4-S63.

Disbrow, Doris, and Karen Bertram. *Cost-Benefit, Cost-Effectiveness Analysis: A Practical Step-by-Step Guide for Nutrition Professionals.* Modesto, CA: Bertram Nutrition Associates, 1984.

Dowling, P., and A. Smith. *Benefits of Nutrition Services: A Costing and Marketing Approach. Report of the Seventh Ross Roundtable on Medical Issues.* Columbus, OH: Ross Laboratories, 1987.

Mali, Paul. *Improving Total Productivity—MBO Statistics for Business, Government and Not-for-Profit Organizations.* New York: John Wiley & Sons, Inc., 1978.

Nutrition Services Payment System: Guidelines for Implementation. Chicago: The American Dietetic Association, 1985.

Splett, Patricia, and Mariel Caldwell. *Costing Nutrition Services: A Workbook.* Minneapolis, MN: University of Minnesota, 1985.

Task Force on Financing Quality Health Care for Persons with Diabetes. *Third Party Reimbursement for Diabetes Outpatient Education: A Manual for Health Care Professionals.* Alexandria, VA: American Diabetes Association, 1986.

Grantsmanship

Haughton, Betsy, Gina Smith, Marion Peyton, and Mark McGrath. *The Grant Game: Strategic Planning, Playing and Winning! A Computer-Aided Instruction Operating Manual and Workbook for Public Health Nutritionists,* IBM-PC or PC compatible. Knoxville, TN: University of Tennessee, Department of Nutrition and Food Sciences, 1988.

Office of Disease Prevention and Health Promotion. *Locating Funds for Health Promotion Projects.* Washington, DC: ODPHP National Health Information Center, 1988.

White, Virginia P. *Grants: How to Find out about Them and What to Do Next.* New York: Plenum Press, 1975.

Personal Management

Broadwell, Martin M. *The New Supervisor,* 3d ed. Reading, MA: Addison-Wesley Publishing Co., Inc., 1984.

Kaufman, Mildred. *Personnel in Public Health for the 1980s.* McLean, VA: ASTHO Foundation, 1982.

Lakein, Alan. *How to Get Control of Your Time and Your Life.* New York: New American Library, Inc., 1973.

McKenzie, Alec R. *The Time Trap.* New York: McGraw-Hill Book Co., 1972.

Metzger, Norman. *The Health Care Supervisor's Handbook,* 3d ed. Rockville, MD: Aspen Publishers, Inc., 1988.

Role Delineation for Entry Level Positions in Community Dietetics. Chicago: The American Dietetic Association, 1983.

Strategies for Success: Curriculum Guide, Didactic and Experiential Learning. Graduate Programs in Public Health Nutrition, Association of Faculties of Graduate Programs in Public Health Nutrition, 1989.

Food Service Systems

Consultant Dietitians in Health Care Facilities. The *Consultant Dietitian, How to Consult Manual.* Chicago: The American Dietetic Association, 1981.

Jernigan, Anne Katherine. *Nutrition in Long-Term Care Facilities: A Handbook for Dietitians.* Chicago: The American Dietetic Association, 1987.

Puckett, Ruby P., and Bonnie B. Miller. *Food Service Manual for Health Care Institutions*. Chicago: The American Dietetic Association, 1988.

Rinke, Wolf J. *The Winning Foodservice Manager: Strategies for Doing More with Less*. Rockville, MD: Aspen Publishers, Inc., 1989.

West, Bessie B., and LeVelle Wood, revised by Virginia F. Harger, Grace S. Shugart, and June Payne-Palacio. *Food Service in Institutions*, 6th ed. New York: MacMillan Publishing Co., Inc., 1988.

V. POLICY, ADVOCACY, AND LEGISLATION

Children's Defense Fund. *A Child's Defense Budget, FY 1989—An Analysis of Our Nation's Investment in Children*. Washington, DC: Children's Defense Fund, 1988.

Clancy, Katherine, ed. *Consumer Demands in the Marketplace: Public Policies Related to Food Safety, Quality and Human Health*. Washington, DC: National Center for Food and Agricultural Policy, 1988.

Community Nutrition Institute. *Programs to Help Older People Eat Better*. Washington, DC: 1987.

Edelman, Marion Wright. *Families in Peril—An Agenda for Social Change*. Cambridge, MA: Harvard University Press, 1987.

Food Research and Action Center. *Hunger in the Eighties*. Washington, DC: FRAC, 1984.

Food Research and Action Center. *Miles to Go: Barriers to Participation by the Rural Poor in the Federal Food Assistance Programs*. Washington, DC: FRAC, 1987.

Food Research and Action Center. *A Guide to the Food Stamp Program*, 8th ed. Washington, DC: FRAC, 1988.

Food Research and Action Center. *WIC Foods*. Washington, DC: FRAC, 1988.

Institute of Medicine. *Homelessness, Health, and Human Needs*. Washington, DC: National Academy Press, 1988.

Life Sciences Research Office, Federation of American Societies for Experimental Biology. *Nutrition Monitoring in the United States: An Update Report from the Expert Panel on Nutrition Monitoring*. Washington, DC: U.S. Government Printing Office, 1989.

Sidel, Ruth. *Women and Children Last—The Plight of Poor Women in Affluent America*. New York: Viking Penguin, Inc., 1986.

U.S. Department of Health and Human Services and U.S. Department of Agriculture. *Nutrition Monitoring in the United States: A Progress Report from the Joint Nutrition Monitoring Evaluation Committee*. Washington, DC: U.S. Government Printing Office, 1986.

Legislation

Heart in Government: A Guide to Lobbying. Washington, DC: American Heart Association, 1987.

"How Our Government Works." *U.S. News and World Report*, January 28, 1985.

League of Women Voters Education Fund. *Facts on PACs: Political Action Committees and American Campaign Finance*. Washington, DC: League of Women Voters Education Fund, 1984.

National Research Council. *Regulating Pesticides in Food—The Delaney Paradox*. Washington, DC: National Academy Press, 1987.

Scott, S., and J. Acquaviva. *Lobbying for Health Care*. Rockville, MD: American Occupational Therapy Association, 1985.

Society for Nutrition Education. *Influencing Food and Nutrition Policy: A Public Policy Handbook*. Oakland, CA: Society for Nutrition Education, 1987.

PERIODICALS

Journals

Aging, Administration on Aging, Government Printing Office, Washington, DC 20402, Ed.: Priscilla James Jones.

American Journal of Clinical Nutrition, American Society for Clinical Nutrition, Inc., 9650 Rockville Pike, Bethesda, MD 20814; 301/530-7027, Ed.: Albert I. Mendeloff, MD.

American Journal of Health Promotion, 746 Purdy St., Birmingham, MI 48009; 312/258-3754.

American Journal of Public Health, American Public Health Association, 10015 15th Street, NW, Washington, DC 20005; 202/789-5600, Ed.: Alfred Yankauer, MD, PhD.

Annual Review of Nutrition, Annual Reviews, Inc., 4139 El Camino Way, Box 10139, Palo Alto, CA 94306-0897; 415/493-4400, Ed.: Robert E. Olson, PhD.

Caring, National Association for Home Care, 205 C Street, NE, Washington, DC 20002; 202/547-7424, Ed.: Val J. Halamandaris.

Clinical Nutrition, C.V. Mosby Co., 11830 Westline Industrial Drive, St. Louis, MO 63146; 314/872-8370, Ed.: David M. Paige, MD.

Diabetes Care, American Diabetes Association, 1660 Duke Street, Alexandria, VA 22314; 703/549-1500, Ed.: David C. Robbins, MD.

Ecology of Food and Nutrition, Gordon and Breach Science Publishers, P.O. Box 786, Cooper Station, New York, NY 10276; 212/243-4411, Ed.: John J.K. Robson.

Family Economics Review, Superintendent of Documents, U.S. Government Printing Office, Washington, DC 20402; 301/436-8461, Ed: Joan C. Courtless.

FDA Consumer, Superintendent of Documents, U.S. Government Printing Office, Washington, DC 20402, Ed.: William M. Rados.

Food and Nutrition, Food and Nutrition Service, USDA, Government Printing Office, Washington, DC 20402, Ed.: Jan Kern.

Food News for Consumers, U.S. Department of Agriculture, Food Safety and Inspection Service, U.S. Government Printing Office, Washington, DC 20402; 202/447-9351, Ed.: Mary Ann Parmley.

Food Technology, Institute of Food Technologists, 221 N. LaSalle Street, Chicago, IL 60601; 312/782-8424, Ed.: John B. Klis.

Foundation News, Council on Foundations, Inc., 1828 L Street, NW, Washington, DC 20036; 202/466-6512, Ed.: Arlie W. Schardt.

Journal of the American College of Nutrition, John Wiley and Sons, 605 Third Avenue, New York, NY 10158; 212/850-6645, Ed.: Mildred S. Selig.

Journal of The American Dietetic Association, 216 W. Jackson Boulevard, Chicago, IL 60606-6995; 312/899-0400, Ed.: Elaine Monsen, PhD, RD, Managing Ed.: Delores Henning.

Journal of the American Home Economics Association, 1555 King Street, Alexandria, VA 22314; 703-706-4600.

Journal of Community Health, Human Sciences Press, Inc., 233 Spring Street, New York, NY 10013; 212/620-8000.

Journal of Dietetic Software, P.O. Box 5853, Austin, TX 78763.

Journal of Nutrition Education, Williams and Wilkins, P.O. Box 23291, Baltimore, MD 21203-9990; 800/638-6423, Ed.: Audrey Maretzky, PhD.

Journal of Nutrition for the Elderly, Hayworth Press, Inc., 10 Alice Street, Binghamton, NY 13904-1580; 800/342-9678, Eds.: Annette B. Natow and Jo-Ann Heslin.

Journal of Obesity and Weight Regulation, Human Sciences Press, Inc., 233 Spring Street, New York, NY 10013; 800/221-9369, 212/620-8000, Ed.: Jonathan K. Wise.

Journal of Parenteral and Enteral Nutrition, Williams and Wilkins, 428 E. Preston Street, Baltimore, MD 21202, Ed.: H.M. Shizgal.

Journal of Pediatric and Perinatal Nutrition, Haworth Press, 10 Alice Street, Binghamton, NY 13904-1580; 800/342-9678, Ed.: Lynn Jacobson-White.

National Food Review, USDA, Economics Research Service, Commodity Economics Division, P.O. Box 1608, Rockville, MD 20850; 800/999-6799, Managing Eds.: Wendy Pinchas, Juliana King.

New England Journal of Medicine, Massachusetts Medical Society, 1440 Main Street, Waltham, MA 02254; 617/893-3800, Ed.: Arnold S. Relman.

Nutrition Reviews, Springer-Verlag New York, Publishers, Journal Fulfillment Service, P.O. Box 2485, Secaucus, NJ 07094; 212/460-1500, Editor-in-Chief: Irvin H. Rosenberg, MD.

Nutrition Today, Williams and Wilkins, 428 E. Preston Street, Baltimore, MD 21202; 301/528-4000, Editor: Helen A. Guthrie, PhD.

Public Health Reports, Superintendent of Documents, U.S. Government Printing Office, Washington, DC 20402; 301/443-0762. Ed.: Marion Priest Tebben.

QRB, Quality Review Bulletin, Journal of Quality Assurance, 875 N. Michigan Avenue, Chicago, IL 60611; 312/642-6061, Ed.: Karen Gardner.

The Diabetes Educator, American Association of Diabetes Educators, 500 N. Michigan Avenue, Chicago, IL 60611; 312/661-1700, Ed.: James W. Pichert, PhD.

The Journal of Compliance in Health Care, Springer Publishing Co., 536 Broadway, New York, NY 10012, Ed.: Raymond A. Ulmer.

Topics in Clinical Nutrition, Aspen Publishers, Inc., 1600 Research Boulevard, Rockville, MD 20850, 301/251-5491, Ed.: JoAnne Cassell.

Newsletters

Berkeley Wellness Newsletter, University of California, Berkeley, P.O. Box 359162, Palm Coast, FL 32035; 212/515-2255.

Contemporary Nutrition, General Mills, Inc., P.O. Box 5588, Stacy, MN 55079.

Columbia University Nutrition and Health, Institute of Human Nutrition, College of Physicians and Surgeons, 701 W. 168th Street, New York, NY 10032.

Dairy Council Digest and Nutrition News, National Dairy Council, 6300 N. River Road, Rosemont, IL 60018-4233; 312/696-1020.

Dietetic Currents, Ross Laboratories, 625 Cleveland Avenue, Columbus, OH 43215.

Environmental Nutrition, 2112 Broadway, Suite 200, New York, NY 10023; 212/362-0424.

Food Facts for Dietitians, Nutrition Service Department, Riverside Methodist Hospital, 3535 Olentangy River Road, Columbus, OH 43214; 614/261-5355.

Food Insight, Current Topics in Food Safety and Nutrition, International Food Information Council, 1100 Connecticut Avenue, NW, Washington, DC 20036; 202/662-1280.

Food and Nutrition News, National Livestock and Meat Board, 444 N. Michigan Avenue, Chicago, IL 60611; 312/467-5520.

Foodlines, Food Research and Action Center, 1319 F Street, NW, Suite 500, Washington, DC 20004; 202/393-5060.

Government Relations Highlights, American Public Health Association, 1015 Fifteenth Street, NW, Washington, DC 20005; 202/789-5600.

Health Facts, Center for Medical Consumers and Health Care Information, 237 Thompson Street, New York, NY 10012.

Health Legislation and Regulations, Weekly Newsletter, McGraw-Hill Health Care Information Center, 1120 Vermont Avenue, NW, Suite 1200, Washington, DC 20005; 202/463-1600.

Healthline, 11830 Westline Industrial Drive, St. Louis, MO 63146; 800/325-4177, ext. 351.

Hot Off the Press, The American Dietetic Association, Division of Marketing and Communications, 216 W. Jackson Boulevard, Chicago, IL 60606-6995; 800/877-1600, ext. 4806.

Legislative Newsletter, The American Dietetic Association, Division of Government Affairs (for members only), 1667 K Street, NW, #430, Washington, DC 20006; 202/296-3956.

Mayo Clinic Nutrition Letter, Mayo Foundation for Medical Education and Research, 200 First Street, SW, Rochester, MN 55905; 507/284-4777.

Monthly Vital Statistics Report, Provisional Data from the National Center for Health Statistics, National Center for Health Statistics, 3700 East-West Highway, Hyattsville, MD 20782; 301/436-8500.

Morbidity and Mortality Weekly Report, MMWR (Centers for Disease Control), Publishing Division of Massachusetts Medical Society, P.O. Box 9120, Waltham, MA 02254-9120; 617/893-3800.

Nutrition Action Newsletter, Center for Science and the Public Interest, 1501 16th Street, NW, Washington, DC 20036; 202/332-9110.

Nutrition and the M.D., P.M. Inc., P.O. Box 2468, Van Nuys, CA 91404; 800/365-2468.

Nutrition Clinics, J.B. Lippincott Company, East Washington Square, Philadelphia, PA 19105; 215/238-4200, 800/635-3030.

Nutrition Focus for Children with Special Health Care Needs, CDMRC-WJ-10, University of Washington, Seattle, WA 98195; 206/545-1297.

Nutrition Forum, J.B. Lippincott Co., East Washington Square, Philadelphia, PA 19105; 215/238-4200.

Nutrition Funding Report, P.O. Box 75035, Washington, DC 20013.

Nutrition Research Newsletter, Lydia Associates, Box 700, Palisades, NY 10964; 914/359-8282.

Nutrition Week, Community Nutrition Institute, 2001 S Street, NW, Washington, DC 20009; 202/462-4700, Ed.: Rodney E. Leonard.

Professional Perspectives, Division of Nutritional Sciences, Martha Van Rensselaer Hall, Cornell University, Ithaca, NY 14853.

Public Health Currents, Ross Laboratories, 625 Cleveland Avenue, Columbus, OH 43215.

Public Health Macroview, Public Health Foundation, 1220 L Street, NW, Washington, DC 20005; 202/898-5600.

The Lean Letter, Project LEAN, 1001 30th Street, NW, 2nd Floor, Washington, DC 20007.

The Nation's Health, The American Public Health Association, 1015 15th Street, NW, Washington, DC 20005; 202/789-5600.

Tufts University Diet and Nutrition Letter, P.O. Box 57857, Boulder, CO 80322-7857; 800/525-0643.

WIC Currents, Ross Laboratories, 625 Cleveland Avenue, Columbus, OH 43215.

WIC Newsletter, Center for Budget and Policy Priorities, 236 Massachusetts Avenue, NE, #305, Washington, DC 20002; 202/544- 0591.

THE AMERICAN DIETETIC ASSOCIATION BIBLIOGRAPHY OF POSITION PAPERS AND POLICY STATEMENTS

Position Papers

1. "The Position of the ADA on a National Nutrition Policy." *J. Am. Diet. Assoc.* 76: 596, 1980. (Reaffirmed)
2. "Diet and Criminal Behavior." *J. Am. Diet. Assoc.* 85: 361, 1985. (Expired in 1989)
3. "Promotion of Breastfeeding." *J. Am. Diet. Assoc.* 86: 1580, 1986. (Expires in 1991)
4. "Issues in Feeding the Terminally Ill Adult." *J. Am. Diet. Assoc.* 87: 78, 1987. Legal considerations updated 1989. (Expires in 1991)
5. "Child Nutrition Services." *J. Am. Diet. Assoc.* 87: 217, 1987. (Expires in 1991)
6. "Nutrition, Aging, and the Continuum of Health Care." *J. Am. Diet. Assoc.* 87: 344, 1987. (Expires 1991)
7. "Nutrition Standards in Day Care Programs for Children." *J. Am. Diet. Assoc.* 87: 503, 1987. (Expires in 1991)
8. "Nutrition: Essential Component of Medical Education." *J. Am. Diet. Assoc.* 87: 643, 1987. (Expires in 1991)
9. "Nutrition for Physical Fitness and Athletic Performance for Adults." *J. Am. Diet. Assoc.* 87: 933, 1987. (Expires in 1991)
10. "Nutrition in Comprehensive Program Planning for Persons with Developmental Disabilities." *J. Am. Diet. Assoc.* 87: 1068, 1987. (Expires in 1991)
11. "Nutrition Services in Health Maintenance Organizations and Alternative Health Care Delivery Systems." *J. Am. Diet. Assoc.* 87: 1391, 1987. (Expires in 1992)
12. "Appropriate Use of Nutritive and Non-nutritive Sweeteners." *J. Am. Diet. Assoc.* 87: 1689, 1987. (Expires in 1992)
13. "Nutrition Intervention in the Treatment of Anorexia Nervosa and Bulimia." *J. Am. Diet. Assoc.* 88: 68, 1988. (Expires in 1992)
14. "Health Implications of Dietary Fiber." *J. Am. Diet. Assoc.* 88: 216, 1988. (Expires in 1992)
15. "Vegetarian Diet." *J. Am. Diet. Assoc.* 88: 351, 1988. (Expires in 1992)

16. "Identifying Food and Nutrition Misinformation." *J. Am. Diet. Assoc.* 88: 1589, 1988. (Expires in 1993)
17. "Nutrition Management of Adolescent Pregnancy." *J. Am. Diet. Assoc.* 89: 104, 1989. (Expires in 1993)
18. "Nutritional Monitoring of the Home Parenteral and Enteral Patient." *J. Am. Diet. Assoc.* 89: 263, 1989. (Expires in 1993)
19. "Nutrition Intervention in the Treatment of Human Immunodeficiency Virus Infections." *J. Am. Diet. Assoc.* 89: 839, 1989. (Expires in 1994)
20. "The Impact of Fluoride on Dental Health." *J. Am. Diet. Assoc.* 89: 971, 1989. (Expires in 1994)
21. "Children with Special Health Care Needs." *J. Am. Diet. Assoc.* 89: August 1989. (Expires in 1994)

ADA Support of Other Groups' Positions

1. "American Diabetes Association: Nutritional Recommendations and Principles for Individuals with Diabetes Mellitus: 1986." *J. Am. Diet. Assoc.* 88: 432, 1988.
2. "New York Academy of Medicine: Statement and Resolution on Cytotoxic Testing for Food Allergy (Bryan's Test)." *J. Am. Diet. Assoc.* 88: 1026, 1988.
3. "ADA Supports National Cholesterol Education Project Adult Treatment Panel Guidelines." *J. Am. Diet. Assoc.* 89: 174, 1989.

Policy Statements

1. "Policy Statement on Nutrition Education for the Public." *J. Am. Diet. Assoc.* 85: 980, 1985. (Expires in 1990)
2. "Policy Statement on Licensure for Dietitians/ Nutritionists." *ADA Courier* 25:2, Oct. 1986. (Expires in 1990)
3. "Board of Directors Statement on Nutrition and Your Health: Dietary Guidelines for Americans." *J. Am. Diet. Assoc.* 86: 107, 1986.
4. "Policy Statement on Continuing Education." *ADA Courier* 26:1, Jan. 1987.
5. "Statement of the Task Force on the Safe Use of Vitamin and Mineral Supplements." J. *Am. Diet. Assoc.* 87: 1342, 1987.

Index

A

Accreditation, group care facilities, 244-246
Acesulfame, 262
Actual cost fee-for-service, 347-348
Administration on Aging, 128
Administration for Children, Youth, and Families, 128
Administrative duties. *See* Management role
Adolescent health care
nutrition guidance, 157-158
pregnant teens, 158
Adult day care, for elderly, 216
Adult health
death, causes of, 172-173
nutrition guidance
for disease prevention, 177-179
to manage risk factors, 179-194
nutritionists, role of, 194-195
prevention levels
implications of, 176-177
primary prevention, 174-175
secondary prevention, 175
tertiary prevention, 176
Adult Treatment Panel, 185

Adverse Reaction Monitoring System, 269
Advertising, in marketing, 306-308
Aflatoxins, food contamination, 258-259
Agency policy, 89
See also Public health agency.
Aging
demographic data, 200-201
diseases of, 201
problems of, 201-202
See also Older Americans.
Aid to Families with Dependent Children, 166, 233
AIDS
nutrition counseling, 194
risk factors, 194
Alar, 265
American Association of Diabetes Educators, 191
American Association of Retired Persons, 207
American Dietetic Association, 191
activities of, 448-449
American Public Health Association, activities of, 449
Animal drug residues, in food, 265
Animal studies, nutrition research, 18

553

Antibiotics, in food, 265
Applied research project, 481-482
Arthritis
    nutritional guidance and, 192
    risk factors, 191-192
    types of, 192
Aspartane, 262
Aspergillus flavus, food contamination,
    258-259
Association of State and Territorial
    Public Health Nutrition Directors,
    position statement, 500-502

B

Behavioral Risk Factor Surveillance
    System, scope of, 326-327
Behavioral Risk Factor Survey, 127
Better Eating for Better Health Program,
    212
Block grants, 195, 345
Breast-feeding, infants, 147-148
Budget, federal
    congressional action on, 121-123
    development of, 120-121
    executive development/control of,
        123-124
    timetable for, 121
Budget Reconciliation Act, 227
Budgets, 349-352
    annotated program budget, 350-351
    monthly budget summary, 349, 352
Bureau of Alcohol, Tobacco, and
    Firearms, 129, 267
Bureau of Consumer Protection of the
    Federal Trade Commission, 267
Business marketing, 298
Butylated hydroxyanisole/
    hydroxytoluene, food additive, 263

C

Cachexia, 188-189
Calcium, osteoporosis and, 193
Cancer
    cachexia, 188-189

incidence of, 187
    nutrition support during treatment,
        188-189
    risk factors, 188
Cardiovascular disease
    lack of exercise and, 187
    mortality trends, 187
    prevention of, 184, 186, 187
    risk factors, 184, 186, 187
    smoking and, 186
Career building, supervisor's role,
    415-416
Case consultation, public health team,
    422-424
Case-control study, nutrition research,
    17-18
Center for Chronic Disease Prevention
    and Health Promotion, 127
Centers for Disease Control, 58, 112,
    127, 267
    surveillance systems
        Behavioral Risk Factor
            Surveillance System, 326-327
        Pediatric Nutrition Surveillance
            System, 326
        Pregnancy Nutrition Surveillance
            System, 326
        Public Health Reporting system,
            327
Changing eating behavior
    changing food choices, steps in,
        362-365
    church involvement, 373
    clubs/recreation centers, 373
    eating out intervention, 372
    health professionals, role of, 374-375
    hotlines, 369
    library materials, 374
    media intervention, 367-369
    nutrition counseling, 376-378
    schools, 374
    screening programs and, 375-376
    supermarket programs, 370-371
    systems intervention, 365-367
    worksite intervention, 372-373
Child Care Food Program, 129, 153

Child health
  adolescent health, 157-159
  Aid to Families with Dependent
    Children, 166
  dental health, 159
  Early Periodic Screening, diagnosis
    and Treatment Program, 166
  infants, 147-149
  issues in, 139-140
  preschooler health, 149-154
  school child health, 154-157
  special needs children, 159-164
  Special Supplemental Food Program
    for Women, Infants, and Children
    (WIC), 164-165
Child Nutrition Amendments, 156
Children's Year Campaign, 107
Cholesterol, elevated levels
  prevention of, 185-186
  risk indicators, 184-185
  treatment approaches, 185
Chore service, for elderly, 214
Chronic disease, dietary guidance, 31-36
Church involvement, changing eating
  behavior, 373
Clients, role as educators, 483-484
Clubs/recreation centers, changing eating
  behavior, 373
Coalition building, nutritionists, 135-136
Colors, food additive, 261
Commission on Accreditation for
  Correctional Institutions, 245
Committees
  congressional committees, 510-513
  planning group, 281-282
Commodity Supplemental Food
  Program, 129
Community, definition of, 46
Community health centers
  for elderly, 205-207
  federally funded, 227-229
    nutrition services, 229
    sources of funds, 227-228
    staffing, 228
Community networks
  activities of, 441

allies for nutrition, 445, 446-447
coordinating councils, 443-445
improving nutrition, steps in, 441-443
issues for nutrition, 446-447
publicizing nutrition services,
  444-445
Community nutrition assessment
  assessment data
    Consumer Expenditure Survey, 319
    Continuing Survey of Food Intakes
      by Individuals, 318
    demographic data, 314
    health indicators, 314-315
    Hispanic HANES, 316-317
    local program reports, 320-321
    national food consumption surveys,
      318
    National Health Interview Survey,
      318-319
    National Health and Nutrition
      Examination Survey, 315-317
    Survey of Income and Program
      Participation, 320
  community resources, 58-59
  individuals, assessment of, 58
  interviews with professionals, 49-51
  objective data, 53-58
  problem list, development of, 59-61
  SOAP plan, 47
  subjective assessment, 47-53
  systems approach, 47
Compensation systems
  salaries of public health personnel,
    397, 400
  types of, 403-404
Comprehensive Health Amendments,
  227
Computer programs
  data analysis, 339
  data reports, 339
  dietary data collection, 330, 335
Congregate meal programs, 211-212
Congressional committees, nutrition
  related, listing of, 510-513
Consolidated Omnibus Budget
  Reconciliation Act, 227

Consumer Affairs Offices, of FSA, 270
Consumer Expenditure Survey, scope of,
    319
Consumer satisfaction, evaluation of
    nutrition service, 293
Continuing education programs, public
    health team, 424
Continuing Survey of Food Intakes by
    Individuals, 17, 112, 128
    scope of, 318
Contract system, salaries, 404
Cooperative Extension agent, 210
Cooperative Extension Service, 128
Coordinating councils, community,
    443-445
Cost-benefit analysis, for nutrition
    services, 284-286_ 356-357
Cost effectiveness analysis, for nutrition
    services, 287-288
Cost-plus fee-for-service, 348
Costs for services, determination of,
    352-355
Credentialing, for professional practice,
    474-475
Cultural barriers, as vulnerability factor,
    67-68

D

Data collection
    data analysis, 338-339
    data entry, 337
    data reporting, 339-340
    dietary data collection, 330-335
        computer programs, 330, 335
        food frequency questionnaire,
            331-334
    questionnaire development, 335-336
    sample selection, 336-337
    sources for national data, 521-522
    survey planning, 328-330
Data management
    community assessment data,
        314-321
    data collection, 328-340
    data needs, 312-313

program management data, 321-327
    See also specific topics.
Death, leading causes of, 172-173
Delaney Clause, 113, 260
Demographic data, in community
    assessment, 53-56
Dental health, children, 159
Dentists, role in public health team, 422
Department of Agriculture,
    agencies/activities of, 128-129
Department of Education,
    agencies/activities of, 129
Department of Health and Human
    Services, 111, 226
    agencies/activities of, 126-128
Department of Justice, 267
Department of Treasury,
    agencies/activities of, 129
Designing Foods, 101
Diabetes
    complications of, 190
    educational programs for, 191
    nutrition support and, 190-191
    risk factors, 190
Diabetes Care and Education Practice
    Group, 191
Dietary data collection, 330-335
    computer programs, 330, 335
    food frequency questionnaire,
        331-334
Dietary Goals for the United States, 31,
    108
Dietary Guidelines Advisory Committee,
    32, 36
Dietary Guidelines for Americans, 175,
    179, 245, 372
Diet counseling services, for elderly,
    209-210
*Diet and Health: Implications for
    Reducing Chronic Disease Risk*, 36,
    37, 38, 101, 108, 179, 420
Dieticians, role of, group care facilities, 251
Diet, Nutrition and Cancer, 23, 101
Dining out
    health promotion for, 372
    programs for elderly, 212-213

Direct care nutritionists, 389
staffing of, 397
Discipline
grievance policy, 418
oral warning, 417
written notice, 417-418
Disease, risk factors associated with, 174
Disease prevention
dietary guidelines for, 177-179
prevention levels
implications of, 176-177
primary prevention, 174-175
secondary prevention, 175
tertiary prevention, 176
preventive health services (ages
19-39), 180-181
Distribution, marketing aspects, 304-305
Division of Maternal and Child Health
Resources Development, 127
Drug and Alcohol Abuse Block Grant,
345

E

Early Periodic Screening, Diagnosis, and
Treatment Program, 128, 166
Eating Away from Home, 194, 372
Eating behavior. *See* Changing eating
behavior
Eat Smart project, 370
Economic Opportunity Act, 227
Education, accredited public health
programs, listing of, 525-528
Education of the Handicapped
Amendments of 1986, 129, 162
Emulsifiers, food additive, 261
Enrichment, food additive, 260
Environmental Protection Agency,
267
Epidemiological research, nutrition
research, 16-17
Ethics
definition of, 475
ethical behavior, components of,
475-476
and marketing, 310

professional organizations, code of
ethics, 472-474
Evaluation of nutrition service
algorithms for, 289-291
measures used, 292-293
consumer satisfaction, 293
inputs, 293
outcomes, 292-293
outputs, 293
program evaluation, 292-294
reporting program success, 294
report/recommendations for program,
294
Excellence, definition of, 466-467
Exercise, cardiovascular disease and,
187
Expanding services, agency level, 464
Experimental designs, nutrition research,
17
Expert Panel on Detection, Evaluation,
and Treatment of High Blood
Cholesterol in Adults, 185

F

*Factors Personal Computer System
Packet*, 335
Fair employment practices, 407-408
Family Food Distribution Program, 239
Fat substitutes, food additive, 264
Federal agencies. *See* specific agencies
Federal government
block grants, 195
budget
congressional action on, 121-123
development of, 120-121
executive development/control of,
123-124
timetable for, 121
dietary guidance, chronic disease
prevention, 31-36
dietary recommendations to public,
33-35
executive responsibilities, 124-125
Federal Register, 125-126
food assistance programs, 70-78

judicial branch, 129-130
legislature
    House of Representatives, 119
    legislative process, 119-120
    Senate, 118-119
national nutritional objectives, 36-38
public health and, 7-8
See also National nutrition policy.
Federal grants
    administration of, 345
    types of, 345
Federal information centers, listing of,
    515-520
Federal legislation, 468-469
    information sources on, 514
Federally funded programs for primary
    care
    community health centers, 227-229
    homeless health care, 232-237
    Indian Health Service, 237-240
    migrant health centers, 229-232
Federal Register, 125-126, 130-131
Federal Trade Commission,
    agencies/activities of, 129
Fee-for-services, types of arrangements,
    347-348
Financial management
    activities of, 342-343
    budgets, 349-352
    cost benefit analysis, 356-357
    costs for services, determination of,
        352-355
    federal grants, 345
    fee-for-services, 347-348
    foundation grants, 347
    general revenue, 344
    grantwriting, 357-359
    local contracts, 346
    service productivity analysis, 355
    state grants, 345-346
    third party reimbursement, 348-349
Fish contamination, 265-266
    red tide, 259
Flavors, food additive, 261
Food Additives Amendment, 259-260
Food and Agriculture Act (1977), 111

Food assistance programs, 70-78
    history of, 107, 110-111
Food/commodity/industry/trade
    organizations, listing of, 533
Food and Drug Administration, 127,
    255, 264, 267, 269
    Consumer Affairs Offices, 270
Food, Drug, and Cosmetic Act, 259
Food Festival, 194, 370
Food frequency questionnaire, 331-334
Food group guides, 27-30
    federal dietary recommendations, 29-30
Food labels, consumer use of, 272
Food and Nutrition Service, 128, 129
Food preferences, formation of, 362
Food preparation, group care facilities,
    248
Food safety
    consumer education and, 269-274
    federal agencies for, 267
    food handling rules, 273
    national nutrition policy, 112-113
    organic/natural foods, 266
    as public health issue, 254-255
    state actions, 267-269
Food Safety and Inspection Service, 128,
    129, 267
Food safety issues
    animal drug residues, 265
    chemical additives, 259-264
        colors, 261
        emulsifiers, 261
        enrichment, 260
        fat substitutes, 264
        flavors, 261
        fortification, 260
        preservatives, 262-263
        sodium, 264
        sweeteners, 261-262
    fish contamination, 265-266
    microbial contamination, 255-258
    naturally occurring food toxicants,
        258-259
    pesticides, 265
Food services regulation, group care
    facilities, 245-246

Food shopping assistance, for elderly, 213-214
Food Stamp Allowances, basis for, 70
Food Stamp Program, 110, 210
   for elderly, 210-211
Food supply, modification of, 366-367
Formula-feeding, infants, 148-149
Fortification, food additive, 260
Foundation grants, 347
Fry Graph Reading Level, 67

G

Generally Recognized as Safe, 260
Gerontology Research Center, 203
Gillet, Lucy, 107
Government agencies, nutrition related, listing of, 510-513
Grants, references on grant sources, 523-524
Grantwriting, 357-359
   grant application worksheet, 358
   guidelines for, 357
Grievance policy, 418
Group care facilities
   dieticians, role of, 251
   food preparation, 248
   food services regulation, 245-246
   licensure/regulation/certification/ accreditation, 244-246
   meal service, 248-249
   menu planning, 247-248
   nutritional care, 249-250
   nutritional counseling services, 250-251
   nutritionists, role of, 251
   training for administrator/personnel, 246-247
   types of facilities, 243-244
Group development, stages in, 431-434
Growth charts, infants, 149
Guidelines for Nutrition Services in Local Health Jurisdictions, 226

H

Handbook of Diabetes Nutritional Management, 191

Hatch Act, 131
Head Start Program, 108, 128, 153
Health Care Financing Administration, 110, 128, 245
Health Care for the Homeless project, 233-234
Health educators, role in public health team, 422
Health Habits and History Questionnaire: Diet History and Other Risk, 330-331
Health professionals, changing eating behavior, 374-375
Health promotion services, for elderly, 207-209
Health Promotion and Wellness National Resource Center, 207
Health Resources and Services Administration, 127
Health services information systems, 322
Health United States, 1988, 221
Healthy Older People, 207
Healthy People, 36, 109
Heart guide, 194, 370-371
Hepatitis A virus, food contamination, 258
High risk factors
   cultural barriers, 67-68
   homelessness, 68-69
   hunger, 69-71, 78
   illiteracy, 66-67
   improvements to services and, 80, 83
   non-access to health care, 80
   poverty, 64-65
   social isolation, 79-80
   unemployment, 66
Hiring personnel
   fair employment practices, 407-408
   interviews, 408-409
   orientation, 409-410
   recruitment, 406-407
Hispanic HANES, scope of, 316-317
Home-delivered meals, for elderly, 214-215
Home health care, for elderly, 216-217
Homeless
   definition of, 232

health care services for, 233-234
health services barriers and, 233
homelessness, as vulnerability factor,
   68-69
nutrition services for, 235-237
primary care for, 234-235
profile of homeless, 232-233
Homeless Assistance Act, 234
Homemaker services, for elderly, 214
Hormones, in food, 265
Hospice, for elderly, 217
Hotlines, changing eating behavior, 369
House of Representatives, role of, 119
Human Nutrition Information Service,
   128
Human Nutrition Research: Federal
Five-Year Plan, 111
Hunger
   definition of, 69
   food assistance programs, 70-78
   as vulnerability factor, 69-71, 78
Hunger Watch, 98
Hypertension
   prevention of, 184
   risk factors, 184

I

Illiteracy, as vulnerability factor, 66-67
Index of Nutritional Quality, 26-27
Indian Health Care Improvement Act
   (Public Law 94-437), 238
Indian Health Service, 237-240
Infants
   growth, monitoring of, 149
   infant mortality rates, 143
   nutrition guidance, 147-149, 151
Inputs, evaluation of nutrition service,
   293
Inservice education programs, public
   health team, 424-425
Institute of Medicine Committee, 222
Institutional care, for elderly, 218
Interviews
   with professionals for community
     nutrition assessment, 49-51

prospective employees, 408-409
Irritation of food, 263

J

Job descriptions
   development of, 404-406
   keywords in, 405
Joint Commission on Accreditation of
   Healthcare Organizations, 245

K

Kaiser Family Foundation, 194

L

Leadership, team leadership, 430-431
Legislature
   House of Representatives, 119
   legislative process, 119-120
   Senate, 118-119
Liability, for professional practice, 475
Library materials, changing eating
   behavior, 374
Listeria monocytogenes, food
   contamination, 255, 258
Lobbying, nutritionists, 132-134
Local contracts, administration of, 346
Local policy, 89-90
Local program reports, scope of,
   320-321
Low birthweight infants, risks associated
   with, 143-144
Low Cost Food Plan, 64
Low-density lipoprotein (LDL)
   cholesterol levels, 185

M

Malpractice, for professional practice,
   475
Management role, 402-418
   career-building role, 415
   compensation system management,
     403-404

disciplinary actions, 417-418
hiring function, 406-410
job descriptions, 404-406
mentoring role, 416
performance appraisal, 413-414
policy/procedure development, 411
scheduling function, 410
skills required, 402-403
staff meetings, 412-413
staff recognition activities, 414-415
Management team, role of, 428
Market disincentives, 306
Market incentives, 305
Marketing, definition of, 297
Marketing nutrition services
business marketing, 298
ethical issues, 310
marketing mix
distribution in, 304-305
price in, 305-306
product in, 302, 304
promotion in, 306-310
market research
market segmentation, 300-302
primary data, 299
secondary data, 300
social marketing, 298-299
Maternal and Child Health Block Grant,
139, 345
Maternity and Infancy Act, 139
Meal programs, for elderly, 211-212
Meal service, group care facilities,
248-249
Meals on Wheels, 214-215
Media
changing eating behavior, role of,
367-369
effectiveness for nutrition message,
484-485
policymaking and, 95-96
Medicaid, 128, 166, 214, 218, 227
Medicare, 128, 214, 216, 218, 227
Meetings, staff meetings, 412-413
Mentor/protege relationship, 416
Menu planning, group care facilities,
247-248

Metabolic diet studies, nutrition
research, 18
Migrant Health Act, 230
Migrant health services, federally funded
nutrition care, 231-232
sources of funds, 230
Migrant workers, profile of, 229-230
Mission statement, for nutrition services,
283-284
*Model Standards: A Guide for
Community Preventive Health
Services,* 438
*Model Standards, Guidelines for
Community Attainment of the Year
2000 Objectives,* 90, 91, 194

N

National Agricultural Library, 128
National Cancer Institute, 127, 194
National Center for Health Statistics,
127, 318
National Cholesterol Education Program,
127, 185, 194
National Diabetes Advisory Board,
191
National Food Consumption Survey, 17,
112
scope of, 318
National Health Interview Survey, scope
of, 318-319
National Health and Nutrition
Examination Survey, 17, 20, 56, 112,
127
scope of, 315-317
National Health Observances, calendar
of, 368
National Heart, Lung, and Blood
Institute, 127
National High Blood Pressure Education
Program, 127, 194
National Institute on Aging, 203
National Institutes of Health, 127
National Marine Fisheries Service, 267
National Nutrition Monitoring and
Related Research Act, 112

National nutrition policy, 102-114
  congressional committees/executive
    agencies, 102
  domestic policy initiatives (1862-
    1988), 105-106
  food assistance, 110-111
  food safety/quality, 112-113
  future directions, 113-114
  historical view, 104, 107-108
  nutrition monitoring, 111-112
  nutrition research, 111
  nutrition services/education, 108-110
National policy, policymaking steps,
  103-104
National Research Council, 245
National School Breakfast Program, 110,
  129
National School Lunch Act, 156, 374
National School Lunch Program, 107,
  110, 129
National Standards for Diabetes Patient
  Education Programs, 191
Nationwide Food Consumption Survey,
  128
Native Americans
  demographic data, 237
  Indian Health Service, 237-240
  laws related to, 237-238
  nutrition services, 239-240
Networking
  benefits of, 439
  community coordinating councils,
    443-445
  community participation and, 440-441
  definition of, 437-438
  food/commodity/industry/trade
    organizations, listing of, 533
  professional network, 448-450
  professional organizations, listing of,
    527-529
  publications used for, 438
  public policy/public interest
    organizations, listing of, 531-532
  state network, 445-448
  tips for, 450-451
  types of networks, 439-440

voluntary health/education
  associations, listing of, 529-531
Newborn feeding
  breast-feeding, 147-148
  formula-feeding, 148-149
New York State Council on Food and
  Nutrition Policy, 447-448
1988 Report of the Joint National
  Committee on Detection, Evaluation,
  and Treatment of High Blood
  Pressure, The, 184
Nitrates, food additive, 262
Nominal group technique, 427
Northern California Anti-Hunger
  Coalition, 97-98
Norwalk viruses, food contamination,
  258
Nurses, role in public health team,
  421-422
Nutrition
  community SOAP plan, 9, 10
  health conditions related to, 8-9
Nutrition aides, 390-391
Nutritional Assessment: A
  Comprehensive Guide to Planning
  Intervention, 56
Nutritional care, group care facilities,
  249-250
Nutritional information, public health
  information resources, listing of, 536
Nutrition counseling and guidance,
  376-378
  adolescents, 157-158
  disease prevention, 177-179
  family counseling, 377
  group care facilities, 250-251
  group counseling, 377
  preschoolers, 151-152
  target audiences, 377
  topics for, 377-378
  women
    preconception care, 140-141
    pregnant women, 145-147
Nutrition density, 26-27
Nutrition Education and Training
  Program, 129, 156-157, 374

Nutrition and Health: Dietary Guidelines for Americans, 32, 108
Nutrition information
  clients, role in, 483-484
  community groups, 484, 486
  media and, 484-485
  technology and information distribution, 486-487
  volunteers, use of, 485-486
  See also Networking.
Nutritionists
  advocacy for elderly, 218-219
  direct care nutritionists, 389, 397
  keeping abreast of developments, 479-481
  knowledge requirements, 14-16
  leadership role, 96-97
    coalition building, 135-136
    commenting on proposals, 126
    legislative activities, 131-132
    lobbying, 132-134
    political action committee membership, 135
    testifying at hearings, 134-135
  management role, 402-418
  proactive stand of, 479-480
  promotion activities, telephone tree, 130-131
  role in disease prevention, 194-195
  role of, 9-12
  See also Public health nutritionists.
Nutrition monitoring, national nutrition policy, 111-112
Nutrition Monitoring Act, 97-98
Nutrition Monitoring in the United States: The Directory of Federal Nutrition Monitoring Activities, 315
Nutrition policy, versus nutrition science, 23-24
Nutrition Practices: A Guide to Administrators, 388
Nutrition research, 16-19
  animal studies, 18
  case-control study, 17-18
  epidemiological research, 16-17
  experimental designs, 17

metabolic diet studies, 18
  monitoring research, 38
  national nutrition policy, 111
  randomized clinical studies, 18-19
  surveys, 17-18
Nutrition services
  data management, 312-340
  evaluation of, 292-294
  financial management, 342-359
  implementation of, 291-292
  marketing of, 297-311
  organizational models, 392-393
  planning of, 279-281
Nutrition Support in Home Health, 164
Nutrition technicians, 389-390

O

Obesity
  definition of, 151
  weight-management programs, 182-183
Objective data, community nutrition assessment, 53-58
Objectives, for nutrition services, 284, 286-287
Office of Disease Prevention and Health Promotion, 127
Older Americans
  adult day care, 216
  chore service, 214
  community nutrition programs, 205-207
  diet counseling services, 209-210
  dining out programs, 212-213
  drug use and, 205
  food shopping assistance, 213-214
  food stamp program, 210-211
  health promotion services, 207-209
  home-delivered meals, 214-215
  home health care, 216-217
  homemaker services, 214
  hospice, 217
  institutional care, 218
  meal programs, 211-212
  nutritional assessment, 202-203

nutritional recommendations for, 203, 205
nutrition education goals for, 206
nutritionists as advocates of, 218-219
preventive health services, 204
research on aging, 203
respite services for care providers, 217-218
Older Americans Act, 128, 211
Olestra, 264
Omnibus Budget Reconciliation Act, 109, 167
Omnibus Health Care Access Act (1984), 224
Oral warning, discipline, 417
Organic food, definition of, 266
Organic Foods Production Association, 266
Organizational models
director headed model, 392-393
matrix organization, 393
Orientation, new employees, 409-410
Osteoporosis
incidence of, 192
nutrition support, 193
risk factors, 193
Outcomes, evaluation of nutrition service, 292-293
Outputs, evaluation of nutrition service, 293

P

Pediatric Nutrition Surveillance System, 58, 112
scope of, 326
Performance appraisal, 413-414
guidelines for, 413-414
Personal Health Program Inventory and Expenditure Summary, 327
Personal selling, in marketing, 308
Personnel in Public Health Nutrition for the 1980s, 388
Pesticides, in food, 265
Physical therapists, role in public health team, 422

Physicians, role in public health team, 421
Planning nutrition services
format for plan, 295
implementation of plan, 291-292
planning
characteristics of plan, 280-281
definition of, 279-280
planning group, role of, 281-282
planning process
action plan, 287-291
data analysis, 282-283
goal setting, 284-287
mission statement, 283-284
Point system, salaries, 404
Policy
activities related to, 88
agency policy, 89
definition of, 87-88
importance of, 88
initiation/change of policy, 88
local policy, 89-90
national nutrition policy, 102-114
policy/procedure development, 411
private sector versus public sector, 100-102
state policy, 90-91
Policy making strategies
adoption of proven strategies, 95
alternative approaches and, 95
analysis of opposition, 94
message to media, 95-96
political aspects, 92, 94
resources/time estimation, 95
scientific base in, 93-94
steps in policy development, 92
support factors, 94
winning policy, elements of, 93
Political action committee membership, nutritionists, 135
Political aspects, policy making strategies, 92, 94
Poverty
income guidelines
formulation of, 64
1989 figures, 65
as vulnerability factor, 64-65

Pregnancy Nutrition Surveillance
System, 58, 112
scope of, 326
Pregnant adolescents, 158
Pregnant women
guidelines for, 144-145
newborn feeding, 147-149
nutrition guidance, 145-147
prenatal care, 143-147
risk assessment, 144
Prenatal care
nutritional care, 145-147
reference works for, 144-145
risk assessment schedule, 144
Preschool child health care, 149-154
Child Care Food Program, 153
Head Start Program, 153
nutrition guidance, 151-152
out-of-home child care, 152-154
Preservatives, food additive, 262-263
President, executive responsibilities,
124-125
Pretesting, products, 304
Prevention levels
implications of, 176-177
primary prevention, 174-175
secondary prevention, 175
tertiary prevention, 176
Preventive Health Services Block Grant,
196, 345
Price, marketing aspects, 305-306
Primary care
definition of, 222
federally funded programs
community health centers,
227-229
homeless health care, 232-237
Indian Health Service, 237-240
migrant health centers, 229-232
needs for, 221-222
nutrition services, 223-224
state programs, 224-226
Primary Care Block Grant, 227
Primary health care team, role of, 426
Primary prevention, 174-175
Product, marketing aspects, 302, 304

Professional organizations
American Dietetic Association,
448-449
American Public Health Association,
449
code of ethics, 472-474
listing of, 527-529
Society for Nutrition Education, 450
Program management data
Behavioral Risk Factor Surveillance
System, 326-327
client information systems from state
health services, 322-325
display of, 321-322
Pediatric Nutrition Surveillance
System, 326
Pregnancy Nutrition Surveillance
System, 326
Public Health Reporting System, 327
Program manager. *See* Management role
Project LEAN, 177, 194
*Promoting Health/Preventing Disease:
Year 2000 Objectives for the Nation,*
37, 109
*Promoting Health/Preventing Disease,
Public Health Service Implementation
Plans for Attaining the Objectives for
the Nation,* 438
Promotion
advertising, 306-308
marketing aspects, 306-310
personal selling, 308
promotional tools, 309
public relations, 308-309
Public health
advocacy of personnel, 117-118
definition of, 3
dynamics of, 6-7
early community nutrition pioneers,
107
governmental responsibilities for,
7-8
issues related to, 12-13
nutrition in, 8-11
nutritionists, role of, 9-12
scope of approach, 4-6

Public Health Agencies 19XX: An Inventory of Programs and Block Grant Expenditures, 327
Public health agency
expanding services, 464
legal aspects
federal legislation, 468-469
state legislation, 469-470
needs definition, 462
nutritionist and
assertiveness and, 459-460
nutritionist/administrator relationship, 458-459
working with colleges, 461
working with policy board, 460-461
planning strategies, 462-463
quality assurance, 470-472
sources of information about, 457
structure of, 456-457
Public health nutrition directors, listing of, 506-508
Public health nutritionists, 385-389
activities of, 386
applied research project, 481-482
educational requirements, 387-388
role of, 386
self-assessment tool, 491-500
staffing of, 396
titles associated with, 387
Public health nutrition library, listing of works, 535-551
Public health personnel
direct care nutritionists, 389
nutrition aides, 390-391
nutrition technicians, 389-390
placement of personnel, 391-393
public health nutritionists, 385-389
qualifications, 385
roles of, 384
salaries, 397, 400
sources for positions, 455-456
staffing pattern, 393-397
Public health problems, types of, 45-46
Public Health Reporting system, scope of, 327

Public Health Service, 226, 227
Public Health Service Act, 230
Public health team
benefits of teamwork, 435
case consultation, 422-424
group development, stages in, 431, 434
management team, 428
members of
dentists, 422
health educators, 422
nurses, 421-422
physical therapists, 422
physicians, 421
social workers, 422
speech therapists, 422
primary health care team, 426
quality assurance team, 426-427
team building, 429-430
team leadership, 430-431
training/education of, 428
continuing education programs, 424
inservice education programs, 424-425
publications used, 424
Public Law 87-692, 230
Public Law 95-166, 156
Public Law 96-537, 238
Public Law 99-280, 227
Public Law 99-457, 129, 162
Public Law 99-509, 167
Public Law 100-203, 167
Public policy/public interest organizations, listing of, 533-535
Public relations, in marketing, 308-309
Public service announcements, 309

Q

Quality assurance
public health agency, 470-472
role of team in, 426-427
Quantified Food Frequency Questionnaire, 335
Questionnaires
computers programs for, 330, 335

data analysis, 338-339
data entry, 337-338
data reporting, 339-340
development of, 335-336
sample selection, 336-337

R

Randomized clinical studies, nutrition
research, 18-19
Ranking system, salaries, 404
Recommended dietary allowances
evolution of, 19-20, 27
limitations on use of, 20-22
rejection of 1985 revision, 23-24
risk/benefit analysis and nutritional
program, 24-26
Recruitment, activities of, 406-407
Requests for Proposals (RFPs), 345
Research, applied research project,
481-482
See also Nutrition research.
Respite services for care providers, for
elderly, 217-218
Restaurant dining, health promotion
methods, 372
Risk factors
for AIDS, 194
for arthritis, 191-192
for cancer, 188
for cardiovascular disease, 184, 186,
187
criteria in selection of, 179
for diabetes, 190
for elevated blood cholesterol,
184-185
for hypertension, 184
major diseases/risk factors, 174
for obesity, 182
for osteoporosis, 193

S

Saccharin, 261-262
Salaries, public health personnel, 397,
400

Salmonella, food contamination, 255,
258
Scheduling staff, scope of, 411
School child health care, 154-157
nutrition guidance, 156-157
School lunch program, 107
Schools, changing eating behavior, 374
Screening
counseling and abnormal results, 376
for disease detection, 375
for risk factors, 375
Secondary prevention, 175
Self-assessment tool
public health nutritionists, 384-385,
491-499
Senate, role of, 118-119
Service productivity analysis, 355
Shepherd Towner Maternity and Infancy
Act, 107
Simplesse, 264
Sliding scale fee-for-service, 347
SMOG Readability Formula, 67
Smoking
cardiovascular disease and, 186
smoking cessation programs, 186
SOAP plan, 9, 10
Social isolation, as vulnerability factor,
79-80
Social marketing, 298-299
Social Security Act, 107, 139, 166
Social workers, role in public health
team, 422
Society for Nutrition Education,
activities of, 450
Sodium, food additive, 264
Special Milk Program, 107
Special needs children, 159-164
definition of, 159
home-based care, 162-164
parental guidance for, 161
prevalence of handicapping
conditions, 160
Public Law 99-457, 162
services, scope of, 160-161
technology-dependent child, 163
university-affiliated programs, 162

Special Projects of Regional and
    National Significance, 127
Special Revenue Sharing Act, 227
Special Supplemental Food Program for
    Women, Infants, and Children, 108,
    110, 111, 129, 228, 327, 345
    scope of program, 164-165
Speech therapists, role in public health
    team, 422
Staffing
    estimation method for, 398
    influencing factors, 399
    patterns for nutrition personnel,
        393-397
Staff meetings, 412-413
Staff recognition activities, 414-415
State grants
    administration of, 345-346
    types of, 346
State health services
    client information systems, 322-325
    for primary care, 224-226
State legislation, 469-470
State network, New York State Council
    on Food and Nutrition Policy,
    447-448
State nutrition objectives, model,
    503-506
State policy, 90-91
    documents for development of, 91
    examples of
        Hunger Watch, 98
        nutrition-monitoring program, 97-98
    health and nutrition policy, 91
    state executive branch in, 91
    state legislature in, 90
Step One Diet, 185-186
Step Two Diet, 185-186
Stern, Frances, 107
Subjective assessment, community
    nutrition assessment, 47-53
Sulfites, food additive, 263
Summer Feeding Program, 129
Sunette, 262
Supermarket programs, changing eating
    behavior, 370-371

Supplemental Nutrition Assistance
    Program, 98
Supplemental Security Income, 233
*Surgeon General's Report on Nutrition
    and Health*, 36, 37, 38, 79, 108, 111,
    420
Survey of Income and Program
    Participation, scope of, 320
Surveys, nutrition research, 17-18
Sweeteners, food additive, 261-262
Systems intervention, changing eating
    behavior, 365-367

T

Team approach
    nominal group technique, 427
    See also Public health team.
Technology-dependent child, 163
Telephone tree, 130-131
Temporary Emergency Food Assistance
    Program, 110
Ten-State Nutrition Survey, 112
Tertiary prevention, 176
Testifying at hearings, nutritionists,
    134-135
Third party reimbursement, 348-349
Thrifty Food Plan, 64, 210
Total Diet Study, 264
Toward Healthful Diets, 32, 36
Training of public health team, 428
    continuing education programs, 424
    inservice education programs,
        424-425
    publications used, 424

U

Unemployment, as vulnerability factor, 66
University-affiliated programs, special
    needs children, 162

V

Veterans Administration (VA) health
    care, 233

Vital and Health Statistics, Series 11, 316
Vitamin A
    RDA standards and, 23
    toxicity of, 26
Vitamin C
    biochemical functions, 24-26
    RDA standards and, 23
Voluntary health/education associations,
    listing of, 529-531

W

Weight-management programs
    characteristics of, 182-183
    diabetes and, 190

Women's health
    issues in, 140
    legislation related to, 139-140
    nutrition services, types of,
        142-143
    preconception care, 140-141
    prenatal care, 143-147
    Special Supplemental Food Program
        for Women, Infants, and Children
        (WIC), 164-165
    unmet needs in, 167
Worksite intervention, changing eating
    behavior, 372-373
Written notice, discipline,
    417-418

About the Editor

Mildred Kaufman, M.S., R.D., is Professor and Chair, Department of Nutrition, School of Public Health, University of North Carolina at Chapel Hill. Since 1978 she has prepared graduate students for careers as public health nutritionists in local, state, federal, and international official and voluntary health agencies. Her areas of interest are public health nutrition policy, planning, evaluation, and program management with emphasis on maternal and child health.

Prior to her academic career, she was Nutrition Program Supervisor and WIC Director for the Florida Department of Health and Rehabilitative Services and a Nutrition Consultant with the U.S. Public Health Service and the Visiting Nurse Society of Philadelphia. She has held elected and appointed offices in The American Dietetic Association, American Public Health Association, Association of State and Territorial Public Health Nutrition Directors, and Association of Faculties of Graduate Programs in Public Health Nutrition. She has served as a consultant; a member of several federal, national, and state expert panels and committees; and a delegate to the White House Conference on Food, Nutrition, and Health.

In 1988 she received The American Dietetic Association Foundation Award for Excellence in Community Dietetics Practice and in 1989 the President's Award of the Alumni Association of the School of Public Health, University of North Carolina. She holds degrees from Teacher's College, Columbia University (M.S.), and Simmons College (B.S.) and completed a dietetic internship at Indiana University Medical Center.